Cooking With Taste

CONTENTS

OVER 1200 FAMILY–PROVEN RECIPES!

EXCLUSIVELY DISTRIBUTED BY:

P.S.I. & ASSOCIATES, INC.

13322 SW 128TH ST.
MIAMI, FL 33186
(305) 255-7959
ISBN# 1-55993-220-1
28667

Address all correspondence to the address above.

© MAGAZINE PRINTERS, INC., 169 S. JEFFERSON, BERNE, IN 46711
ALL RIGHTS RESERVED   PRINTED IN THE USA

Appetizers

APPEALING

DOUBLE SHRIMP MOLD

1 can cream of shrimp soup
1 envelope unflavored gelatin
2 (8-ounce) packages cream cheese, softened
1 cup mayonnaise
1½ tablespoons green onion, chopped
¾ cup celery, finely chopped
2 (6-ounce) cans small deveined shrimp
Dash salt and pepper, to taste

Heat undiluted soup to boiling point. Add gelatin to ½ cup cold water. Add to soup; mix well. Add cream cheese; blend well. Cool slightly. Add remaining ingredients; mix well. Spoon into mold or molds. Refrigerate for several hours. Unmold and serve with assorted crackers. May be frozen.

MUSHROOM TARTS
Makes 60

⅔ cup butter
2½ cups flour
½ teaspoon salt
⅓ cup sour cream
1 egg, slightly beaten

Cut butter into flour and salt. Add sour cream and egg. Cut with pastry blender until well-blended. Using 1 teaspoon dough, press into bottom and side of tart muffin pans. Bake at 400 degrees for 12–15 minutes, or until golden. Remove from tart pan and cool.

Filling:
2 tablespoons chopped green onions
½ pound chopped mushrooms
¼ cup butter
¼ cup flour
½ teaspoon salt
1 cup heavy cream

Sauté mushrooms and onions in butter. Stir in flour and salt. Add cream; stir until thick and smooth. Fill shells; garnish with parsley and serve. Can be frozen. To serve, heat 10 minutes at 400 degrees.

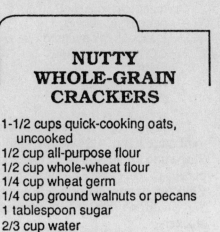

NUTTY WHOLE-GRAIN CRACKERS

1-1/2 cups quick-cooking oats, uncooked
1/2 cup all-purpose flour
1/2 cup whole-wheat flour
1/4 cup wheat germ
1/4 cup ground walnuts or pecans
1 tablespoon sugar
2/3 cup water
1/4 cup vegetable oil
2 teaspoons water, divided
1/4 teaspoon salt, divided

Combine first 6 ingredients in a large bowl; stir well. Add 2/3 cup water and oil, stirring just until dry ingredients are moistened. Divide dough in half. Roll half of dough to a 12x12-inch square on an ungreased baking sheet. Cut into 2-inch squares. Brush dough with 1 teaspoon water; sprinkle evenly with 1/8 teaspoon salt. Repeat procedure with remaining half of dough. Bake at 350 degrees for 25 minutes or until crisp and lightly browned.

Separate crackers; remove from baking sheets and cool on wire racks. Store in an airtight container.

HOT HAMBURGER DIP

1 pound ground beef
½ cup chopped onion
1 (8-ounce) can tomato sauce
¼ cup ketchup
1 (8-ounce) package cream cheese
1 cup grated Parmesan cheese
1 clove garlic, mashed
1 teaspoon oregano
1 tablespoon parsley
1 tablespoon sugar
1 (4-ounce) can mushrooms, chopped
Salt to taste
Pepper to taste

Sauté beef until brown. Add onion and garlic; cook until tender. Add all other ingredients and stir over low heat until cream cheese melts. Pour into Crockpot and keep warm. Serve with corn chips or taco chips.

SPICY STUFFED EGGS
Makes 8

- 6 large eggs, hard-cooked
- 1 green onion, including top, finely chopped
- 1 tablespoon reduced-calorie mayonnaise
- 1 tablespoon minced parsley
- 2 sweet gherkin pickles, finely chopped
- ½ teaspoon prepared mustard
- ⅛ teaspoon salt
- ⅛ teaspoon black pepper
- 8 sprigs parsley (optional)

Cook eggs; peel and halve lengthwise. Place 1 yolk in small bowl; discard remaining yolks. Mash the yolk with a fork, then add 4 of the white halves and mash. Mix in onion, mayonnaise, parsley, pickles, mustard, salt and pepper. Mound the mixture into remaining white halves, dividing it equally. Garnish each half, if desired, with a sprig of parsley. Cover loosely and refrigerate until ready to serve.

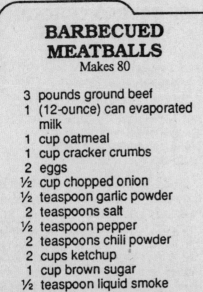

BARBECUED MEATBALLS
Makes 80

- 3 pounds ground beef
- 1 (12-ounce) can evaporated milk
- 1 cup oatmeal
- 1 cup cracker crumbs
- 2 eggs
- ½ cup chopped onion
- ½ teaspoon garlic powder
- 2 teaspoons salt
- ½ teaspoon pepper
- 2 teaspoons chili powder
- 2 cups ketchup
- 1 cup brown sugar
- ½ teaspoon liquid smoke
- ½ teaspoon garlic powder

- ¼ cup chopped onion

Combine beef, milk, oatmeal, crumbs, eggs, ½ cup onion, ½ teaspoon garlic powder, salt, pepper and chili powder (mixture will be soft). Shape into walnut-size balls. Place meatballs in a 13 x 9 x 2-inch baking pan.

To make sauce, combine ketchup, brown sugar, liquid smoke, garlic powder and ¼ cup onion. Pour this over the pan of meatballs. Bake in a 350-degree oven for 40–45 minutes.

To freeze for later use: Line cookie sheets with waxed paper; place meatballs in single layer; freeze until solid. Store frozen meatballs in freezer bags until ready to cook. Place frozen meatballs in baking pan; pour on sauce. Bake at 350 degrees for 1 hour.

PEANUT DEVILED-HAM BALL

- 1 (8-ounce) package cream cheese, softened
- 1 (4½-ounce) can deviled ham
- 2 tablespoons grated onion
- 1 teaspoon horseradish
- ¼ teaspoon liquid hot pepper seasoning
- ¼ teaspoon dry mustard
- ¼ cup chopped, salted peanuts
- 1 tablespoon dried parsley

Combine first 6 ingredients; beat until smooth and well-blended. Chill. Shape into a ball. Roll in peanuts and parsley to coat outside of cheese ball. Chill for 30 minutes before serving. Serve with party rye bread or assorted crackers.

OLD-FASHIONED SODA CRACKERS
Makes 8 dozen

4-1/2 cups all-purpose flour

- 1/2 teaspoon baking soda
- 1/2 teaspoon salt
- 1/2 cup margarine
- 1-1/2 cups water
- Salt

Heat oven to 350 degrees. In large bowl combine flour, baking soda, and salt. Cut in margarine until crumbly. Add water; stir just until mixed. Turn dough onto lightly floured surface; knead until thoroughly mixed (about 3 minutes). Roll out dough, 1/4 at a time, on well-floured surface to 1/8-inch thickness. Cut into 2-inch squares; place 1 inch apart on ungreased cookie sheets. Prick two or three times with fork; sprinkle with salt. Bake for 20-25 minutes or until lightly browned.

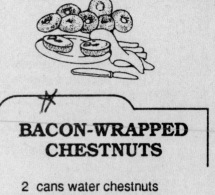

BACON-WRAPPED CHESTNUTS

- 2 cans water chestnuts
- ½ cup soy sauce
- 18 slices bacon, cut in half

Marinate water chestnuts in soy sauce for 1 hour. Wrap each chestnut with bacon. Secure with toothpick. Place in pan and bake at 400 degrees for 30 minutes. Drain on paper toweling. Serve.

CHILI POPCORN

- 1 tablespoon margarine, melted
- ⅓ teaspoon chili powder
- ⅛ teaspoon salt
- ⅛ teaspoon garlic powder
- ⅛ teaspoon paprika
- 6 cups popped corn

Combine margarine, chili powder, salt, garlic powder and paprika; drizzle over warm popcorn. (41 calories per 1-cup serving)

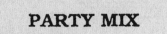

PARTY MIX

2 cups Cheerios
2 cups Corn Chex
2 cups Rice Chex
2 cups thin pretzels
1-1/2 cups pecans
1 stick margarine
1 teaspoon salt
1 tablespoon Worcestershire sauce
3/4 teaspoon garlic powder

Heat oven to 250 degrees. Melt margarine; stir in salt, worcestershire, and garlic powder. Mix in cereals and nuts; mix well. Heat in 300-degree oven on cookie sheet about 45 minutes, stirring often, until nuts are brown.

CHOCOLATE PEANUT-BUTTER APPLES
Makes 6-8

6-8 medium-size apples
6-8 wooden skewers
1 cup semisweet chocolate mini
  chips
1 cup peanut-butter-flavored chips
1 tablespoon vegetable oil

Wash apples and dry thoroughly. Insert wooden skewer into each apple. Set aside. Melt mini chips and peanut-butter chips with oil in top of double boiler or in a heavy 1-1/2-quart saucepan over low heat; stir constantly until smooth. Remove from heat; dip apples in mixture (tilting pan as needed). Twirl to remove excess coating; place apples on waxed-paper-covered cookie sheet. Refrigerate until firm.

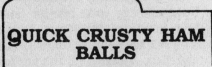

QUICK CRUSTY HAM BALLS
Makes 16

1 cup cooked ham, chopped
3/4 cup grated Cheddar cheese
2 tablespoons onion, grated

1 egg
1/4 cup dry cracker crumbs
1/2 cup sweet milk
1 cup cornflakes, crushed
Vegetable oil

Combine first 5 ingredients; mix well. Shape into 1-1/2-inch balls. Dip ham balls into milk; coat with cornflakes. Fry in vegetable oil until crusty and golden.

BUBBLING HOT CRAB WITH BEAN SPROUTS

1 (8-ounce) package cream cheese
6 ounces crab
1 tablespoon milk
2 tablespoons minced onion
2 tablespoons mayonnaise
1 teaspoon salt
Dash pepper
1/3 can bean sprouts, drained
2 tablespoons chopped chives
1/2 cup grat d Parmesan cheese
1/3 cup sliced almonds

Mix all together, except cheese and almonds. Bake at 350 degrees for 20-25 minutes. Top with cheese and almonds. Serve with crackers.

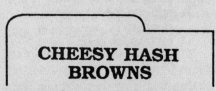

CHEESY HASH BROWNS

1 (2-pound) package frozen hash
  browns, thawed
1 stick butter, melted
2 cups sour cream
2 cups Cheddar cheese, grated
1 can cream of chicken soup
1 cup chopped onions
1 teaspoon salt
1/2 teaspoon pepper
2 cups crushed corn flakes
1/2 stick margarine

Mix and combine all ingredients. Pour into a 13x9-inch dish. Top with 2 cups crushed corn flakes, mixed with 1/2 stick melted margarine. Bake in 350 degree oven 30-40 minutes.

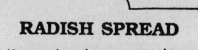

VEGETABLE DIP

1 cup mayonnaise
1/2 teaspoon lemon juice
1/4 teaspoon salt
1/4 teaspoon paprika
1 teaspoon chopped onions
1 teaspoon salad herbs
1 teaspoon garlic salt
1 teaspoon dried chives
1/8 teaspoon curry powder
1/2 teaspoon Worcestershire sauce
1/2 cup sour cream

Mix ingredients together and serve with raw celery, carrots, cauliflower, and broccoli.

RADISH SPREAD

1 (8-ounce) package cream cheese,
  softened
1/2 cup butter, softened
1/2 teaspoon celery salt
1/8 teaspoon paprika
1/2 teaspoon Worcestershire sauce
1 cup finely chopped radishes
1/4 cup finely chopped green onions

Combine cheese and butter, and mix until thoroughly creamed. Add remaining ingredients and mix. Serve on party rye bread or crackers.

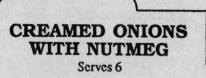

CREAMED ONIONS WITH NUTMEG
Serves 6

24 small white onions
3 tablespoons butter
3 tablespoons flour
1-1/2 cups milk
Salt and pepper to taste
1/4 teaspoon nutmeg
1/4 teaspoon garlic powder
Paprika

Peel onions and steam for about 20 minutes or until tender. Heat butter in saucepan; add flour; stir in milk. Stir constantly until mixture is smooth and thick. Add salt, pepper, nutmeg, and garlic powder. Blend well. Drain onions and pour cream sauce over them. Sprinkle with paprika. Keep in warm oven until ready to serve.

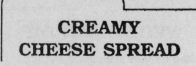

CREAMY CHEESE SPREAD

1/2 cup sour cream
6 ounces processed American cheese, cut in cubes
1 (3 ounce) package cream cheese, cut in cubes
2 tablespoons chopped onion
2 teaspoons Worcestershire sauce
2 teaspoons chopped dried chives
2 teaspoons parsley flakes
1/4 teaspoon dried minced garlic
1/4 teaspoon cracked black pepper

Put all ingredients in food processor or blender and process until smooth. Chill and serve with pretzels, crackers, chips, and/or raw vegetables.

SAUSAGE-CHEESE BALLS

Makes 75 appetizers

1-1/2 cups biscuit mix
1 pound grated Cheddar cheese
1 pound lean ground pork sausage or "hot" ground sausage

Preheat oven to 350 degrees. Combine ingredients until dough sticks together. Roll into 1-1/2 inch balls. Bake about 25 minutes. Drain on paper towels. Serve warm on toothpicks.

Note: Spray baking sheet with no stick coating before putting sausage balls on sheet.

HAM 'N CHEESE SNACKS

1-1/2 cups finely chopped, cooked ham
1 (8 ounce) carton plain yogurt
1/4 cup shredded Swiss cheese
1/4 cup finely chopped crackers
2 tablespoons butter or margarine
2 teaspoons caraway seed
6 eggs

Combine first six ingredients. Beat eggs until thick lemon-color.. Fold eggs into yogurt mixture; blend well. Pour evenly into 8-inch square pan. Bake in preheated 375 degree oven for 15-17 minutes, until nicely browned. Cut into squares and serve hot.

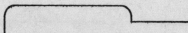

FRIED CHEESE

4 slices Swiss cheese, cut 3/4 inch thick
Salt to taste
1/2 cup flour
1 egg, beaten
2/3 cup bread crumbs
1 cup shortening

Sprinkle cheese with salt. Dip slices first in flour, then in beaten egg, fry quickly in hot shortening until golden brown.

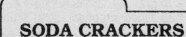

SODA CRACKERS

4 cups flour
3 tablespoons lard or shortening
1/2 teaspoon baking soda
1/8 cake yeast
1 teaspoon sugar
Pinch of salt
1/2 teaspoon malt extract
Water sufficient to make stiff dough

Roll out 1/4 inch thick on lightly floured board. Cut into desired shapes. Brush lightly with milk. Bake on ungreased baking sheet at 425 degrees for 15 to 18 minutes, or until lightly browned.

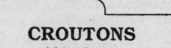

CROUTONS

Makes 2 cups

4 slices firm bread (stack slices and trim off crusts)
Cut bread into 1/2 inch cubes
1-1/2 ounces unsalted butter
1 teaspoon vegetable oil

Melt butter with oil in a heavy pan. Add bread cubes. Although white bread is most traditional for croutons, any good-quality bread will do. Experiment with whole wheat, rye, pumpernickel. Sauté bread cubes, about 2 minutes, turning to brown cubes evenly. Remove croutons with slotted spoon; drain on paper towels. Serve or keep warm in low oven until ready to serve.

CHICKEN HORS D'OEUVRES

Makes 38

1 (3 ounce) package cream cheese, softened
1 (5 ounce) can chicken spread
1/3 cup chopped apples
1/4 cup chopped walnuts
5 tablespoons chopped parsley
1/2 teaspoon Worcestershire sauce
Dash of cayenne pepper
Toasted wheat germ

Stir cream cheese in bowl until smooth; blend in remaining ingredients except wheat germ. Chill. Shape into thirty-eight (38) balls; roll in wheat germ. Place on serving platter.

PRETZELS

2 eggs, separated
1/4 cup butter, softened
2 cups flour
Salt & pepper
Milk
Coarse salt

Beat egg whites until stiff, but not dry. Beat egg yolks until lemony. Work (with hands or a spoon) the butter and egg yolks into the flour. Fold in beaten egg whites. Season with salt and pepper. Roll out; slice and shape as desired. Brush pretzels with milk and sprinkle with coarse salt. Bake on cookie sheets in preheated 350 degree oven for about 10 minutes, turning once.

CHEESE DIP
Makes 3-1/2 cups

2 cups sour cream
1-1/2 cups shredded Cheddar
  cheese
1/4 cup sliced pimiento-stuffed
  olives
1/2 teaspoon salt
1/4 teaspoon sage

Blend sour cream with remaining ingredients. Serve chilled. Especially good with saltine crackers!

DIPPETY DOO DIP

1 squeeze tube of hickory smoked
  cheese
1 cup sour cream
1 can bean with bacon soup (undiluted)
2 or 3 minced green onions (use all)

Combine all ingredients and warm over double boiler or in Microwave. Mix well. Serve with tortilla chips.

You can't eat just one!

BLUE CHEESE DIP

3 ounces blue cheese, crumbled
1/2 cup sour cream
1/2 cup mayonnaise
Dash of paprika
Dash of garlic powder
Assorted vegetables, cut in strips

Mix together all ingredients except vegetables and chill 2 hours to blend flavors. Serve with vegetables.

FRUIT DIP
Make 3 cups

2 cups sour cream
1/4 cup drained crushed pineapple
2/3 cup chopped red apples
1/2 teaspoon curry powder
1/2 teaspoon garlic salt
Apple slices for garnish

Blend sour cream with apple, pineapple, curry powder, and garlic salt. Place in bowl and chill. Garnish with sliced apples around outer edge of bowl.

Good with corn chips or shredded wheat wafers.

SNACKIN DIPS FOR CHIPS
Serves 4

1 can (6 1/2 ounce) chunk tuna
1 envelope instant onion soup mix
1 cup dairy sour cream
1 tablespoon prepared horseradish
Parsley for garnish
Potato chips - celery sticks - cherry
  tomatoes

Drain tuna. Combine tuna with soup mix, sour cream, and horseradish. Garnish with parsley. Arrange potato chips, celery sticks, and tomatoes on platter.

RAW VEGETABLE DIP
Yield - 2-1/2 cups

2 cups applesauce
1/2 pint dairy sour cream
2 tablespoons minced onion
1 teaspoon Worcestershire sauce
1/2 teaspoon salt

Slowly cook applesauce abut 5 minutes to evaporate some of the liquid; chill. Combine the applesauce, sour cream, onion, Worcestershire sauce and salt. Mix well. Use as a dip for fresh, raw vegetables of your choice.

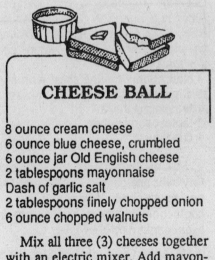

FRESH MUSHROOM DIP

1-8 ounce package cream cheese,
  softened
2 tablespoons snipped ripe olives
2 tablespoons snipped parsley
3/4 teaspoon seasoned salt
4 drops bottled hot pepper sauce
1/2 cup sour cream
1/2 pound fresh mushrooms, finely
  chopped

Combine cream cheese and seasonings; fold in sour cream and chill. Stir in mushrooms just before serving.

LOW CAL CLAM DIP
Makes 2 cups

1-8 ounce can minced clams
1-1/2 cups cottage cheese
1/2 teaspoon seasoned salt
2 teaspoons lemon juice
1 teaspoon Worcestershire sauce
1 tablespoon minced green onions
Assorted crisp vegetable dippers

In blender container, combine clams with liquid, cottage cheese seasoned salt, lemon juice, and Worcestershire sauce. Cover and whirl around until smooth. Stir in green onions. Cover and chill at least two hours to blend flavors. Serve with cauliflower, broccoli, and strips of carrots, zucchini, and cucumbers.

CHEESE BALL

8 ounce cream cheese
6 ounce blue cheese, crumbled
6 ounce jar Old English cheese
2 tablespoons mayonnaise
Dash of garlic salt
2 tablespoons finely chopped onion
6 ounce chopped walnuts

Mix all three (3) cheeses together with an electric mixer. Add mayonnaise, garlic salt, onion, and walnuts to cheese mixture. Shape into a ball and wrap with plastic wrap. Refrigerate twenty-four (24) hours before serving. When ready to serve, sprinkle paprika.

RYE CRACKERS

2 cups rye flour
2 cups wheat flour
Salt to taste
1/4 teaspoon baking soda
1/2 cup vegetable oil
1 cup (or more) water
1 tablespoon caraway seeds

Mix together. Roll out thinly on floured surface. Cut into desired shapes. Bake on cookie sheets at 275 degrees for about 30 minutes.

DILL CRACKERS

2/3 cup Wesson oil
1 envelope ranch-style dry salad dressing
1 teaspoon dill
1/2 teaspoon lemon pepper
1/4 teaspoon garlic salt
10 ounce package oyster crackers

Mix all together, except crackers. Coat crackers with mixture, tossing until well coated, about 5 or 6 minutes.

NUT BALLS

1 stick butter
1 cup pecans
1 teaspoon vanilla
2 tablespoons sugar
1 cup flour

Mix all ingredients and roll into tiny balls and bake at 250 degrees for one hour. Cool slightly and roll in confectioners' sugar. Roll in sugar again about half-hour later.

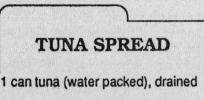

TUNA SPREAD

1 can tuna (water packed), drained

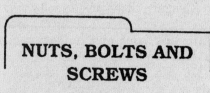

1 (8-ounce) package cream cheese, softened
1 small onion, finely chopped
Salt and pepper to taste

Blend all ingredients until smooth. Serve with crackers. This can be rolled into a log and used for all types of festive entertaining.

NUTS, BOLTS AND SCREWS

1 pound pecans
1 large box Cherrios
1 medium box stick pretzels
1 tablespoon Worcestershire sauce
1 box Wheat Chex
2 tablespoons salt
1 tablespoon garlic salt
1 pound oleo or butter
8 8

Melt butter in large roaster. Pour in all cereals, nuts and pretzels and seasonings. set oven at 200 degrees. Stir every 15 minutes for 1 hour.

WHEAT GERM CRUNCHIES
Makes 3-1/2 dozen

1/2 cup all-purpose flour
1/2 teaspoon soda
2 teaspoons baking powder
1/4 teaspoon salt
1 cup brown sugar, firmly packed
1/2 cup shortening
1 egg, beaten
1/2 teaspoon vanilla
1/2 cup coconut
1/2 cup uncooked oatmeal
1 cup wheat germ
1-1/2 cups corn or wheat flakes

Sift flour, soda, baking powder and salt. Cream shortening and sugar. Add egg and vanilla. Add dry ingredients and wheat germ. Mix well. Stir in coconut, oatmeal and cornflakes just enough to mix. Drop by teaspoons on greased cookie sheet or roll into walnut-sized balls with fingers and place on greased cookie

sheet. Bake 15 minutes at 350 degrees.

TAFFY APPLES

1 large can crushed pineapple (save drained juice)
2-1/2 cups miniature marshmallows
1 egg
1 tablespoon flour
12 ounces Cool Whip
3/4 cup cocktail or Spanish peanuts
1-1/2 tablespoons vinegar
1/2 cup sugar
4-6 apples, unpeeled and chopped

Combine drained pineapple and marshmallows; refrigerate overnight. Beat pineapple juice, egg, flour, vinegar and sugar; heat until thick, stirring constantly. Cool and refrigerate overnight, separate from pineapple.

Next day: Mix sauce and Cool Whip; add peanuts, marshmallow mixture and apples; stir. Refrigerate at least 2 hours before serving.

CELERY PINWHEELS

1 medium stalk celery
1 (3-ounce) package cream cheese
2 tablespoons crumbled Roquefort cheese
Mayonnaise
Worcestershire sauce

Clean celery and separate branches. Blend together the softened cream cheese with the Roquefort cheese. Add mayonnaise to make the mixture of spreading consistency and season with a dash of Worcestershire sauce. Fill the branches of celery with cheese mixture. Press branches back into the original form of the stalk. Roll in waxed paper and chill overnight in refrigerator. Just before serving, slice celery crosswise forming pinwheels. Arrange pinwheels on crisp lettuce for serving.

FAVORITE SPOON BREAD
Serves 8

1 1/3 teaspoons sugar
1 1/2 teaspoons salt
1 cup cornmeal, sifted
1 1/3 cups water, boiling (cool 5 minutes)
1/4 cup butter *or* margarine
3 eggs, lightly beaten
1 1/4 cups milk
1 teaspoon baking powder

Preheat oven to 350 degrees. Mix together sugar, salt and cornmeal. Pour water over meal mixture, stirring constantly. Mix in butter; let stand until cooled; add eggs, milk and baking powder, blending well.

Pour into buttered pan (2-quart). Place in shallow pan of hot water. Bake in a 350-degree oven for 35 minutes, or until crusty. Spoon out; serve.

This spoon bread has a light texture, soft center, and crusty top. Most delicious!

NO–KNEAD ROLLS
Makes 2 dozen

1/2 cup scalded milk
3 tablespoons shortening
3 tablespoons sugar
2 teaspoons salt
1/2 cup water
1 cake yeast *or* 1 package active dry yeast
1 egg
3 cups all-purpose flour
Melted shortening

Blend together milk, 3 tablespoons shortening, sugar, and salt. Cool to lukewarm by adding water. Add yeast, and mix well. Add egg. Add flour, gradually, mixing until dough is well-blended. Place in greased bowl. Brush top with melted shortening and allow to rise until light. Knead dough a few times to make smooth ball. Form into desired shapes and bake in 400-degree oven for 15-25 minutes or until golden brown. Easy and very tasty.

POPPY SEED BREAD

1 package Duncan Hines Yellow Cake Mix
1 package toasted coconut instant pudding (Royal brand)
1/4 cup (scant) poppy seeds
4 eggs
1 cup hot water
1/2 cup Crisco oil

Mix well; pour into 2 well-greased loaf pans 9x5-1/2x2 1/2-inches. Bake at 350 degrees for 40-50 minutes. This is a very moist bread!

This is very delicious spread with Philadelphia Cream Cheese, plus makes a nice bread to serve along with fruit salad!

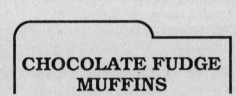

CHOCOLATE FUDGE MUFFINS

1 cup butter or margarine
4 squares semisweet chocolate
1-1/2 cups white sugar
1 cup flour
1/4 teaspoon salt
4 eggs, beaten
1 teaspoon vanilla

In a saucepan over low heat, combine margarine and chocolate. Melt, stirring frequently, so the chocolate does not burn or stick.

In a bowl, combine sugar, flour and salt. Stir in chocolate mixture. Beat eggs, then add them to batter with the vanilla. Stir until eggs are well-blended, but do not beat the mixture. Line muffin tins with paper liners. Fill each one about two-thirds full. Bake at 300 degrees for 30–40 minutes. Check to see if muffins are done by inserting a toothpick in one near the center of the muffin. If the toothpick does not come out clean, bake for another 5 minutes. Let muffins cool 5 minutes before removing them from the pan. These taste much like brownies. Keep any leftovers in a covered container, then rewarm them.

CRANBERRY BANANA NUT BREAD

2 cups flour
3 teaspoons baking powder
1/2 teaspoon salt
1/2 teaspoon cinnamon
1 cup fresh cranberries, ground
1 teaspoon grated orange rind
1 cup mashed very ripe bananas (3 large)
1/2 cup milk
4 tablespoons butter
1 cup sugar
1 egg
1 cup chopped pecans

Sift together flour, baking powder, salt and cinnamon. Blend orange rind with ground cranberries. In 2-quart bowl, blend bananas and milk. Cream butter and sugar together; blend in egg. Sift dry ingredients alternately with banana mixture, stirring until just blended. Stir in cranberry mixture and pecans. Bake in 9x5x3-inch pan at 350 degrees for 1 hour and 15 minutes. Store at least 24 hours before slicing.

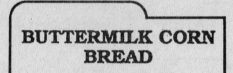

BUTTERMILK CORN BREAD

3/4 cup Lysine cornmeal
1 cup white flour
3 tablespoons sugar
1 teaspoon soda
3/4 teaspoon salt
1 cup buttermilk
1 egg, beaten
2 tablespoons melted margarine

Preheat oven to 400 degrees. Stir together cornmeal, flour, sugar and salt. Set aside.

Dissolve soda in buttermilk. Add beaten egg and melted margarine; stir until mixed, then add to dry ingredients and mix well. Turn into greased 9x9-inch pan, or into greased muffin pan. Bake 20 minutes, or until golden and done.

These are delicious and healthful eating.

BRAUNSCHWEIGER BALL

1 (8-ounce) package cream cheese, softened
1 pound braunschweiger, at room temperature
1/4 cup mayonnaise
1/4 teaspoon garlic salt
2 tablespoons dill pickle juice
1/2-3/4 cup chopped dill pickle
1/4 cup (or more) chopped onion
3 drops Tabasco sauce
1 tablespoon Worcestershire sauce
1/2 cup salted peanuts, chopped

Combine half the cream cheese with the remaining ingredients, except peanuts; mix well. Spread in a mold. Chill for several hours. Unmold. Frost with remaining cream cheese. Garnish with chopped peanuts. Snack with assorted crackers or slices of party loaf bread.

SAVORY CHEESE BITES
Makes 7 dozen

1 cup water
1/8 teaspoon salt
4 eggs
1/2 cup butter
1 cup flour
1 cup shredded Swiss cheese

Combine water, butter, and salt in a pan; bring to a boil. Stir until butter melts. Add flour; stir vigorously until mixture leaves sides of pan to form a smooth ball. Remove from heat. Add eggs, one at a time; stir until well-blended. Return to heat and beat mixture until smooth. Remove from heat; stir in cheese. Drop batter by heaping teaspoonfuls onto a greased baking sheet. Bake 400 degrees for 20 minutes, or until puffed and golden brown.

SALMON LOG

1 (1-pound) can salmon
1 (8-ounce) package cream cheese, softened
1 tablespoon lemon juice
2 tablespoons grated onion
1 teaspoon prepared horseradish
1/4 teaspoon salt
1 teaspoon liquid smoke seasoning
1/2 cup chopped walnuts
3 tablespoons snipped parsley

Drain and flake salmon, removing skin and bones. Combine salmon with the next 6 ingredients; mix well. Chill several hours. Combine walnuts and parsley. Shape salmon mixture into 8x2-inch log, or use a fish mold. Roll in nut mixture. Chill well. Serve with crisp crackers.

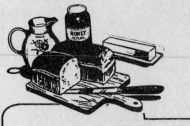

CRAB PUFFS

1 cup water
1 stick margarine
1 cup flour
4 eggs

Bring water to boil and add margarine, return to boil. Add flour all at once. Remove from heat and beat in 1 egg at a time. Then add all the following ingredients:

3 scallions, chopped
1 teaspoon dry mustard
1 (6½-ounce) can crabmeat
1 teaspoon Worcestershire sauce
½ cup sharp cheddar cheese, grated

Drop on cookie sheet by spoonfuls. Bake at 400 degrees for 15 minutes. Turn oven down to 350 degrees and bake 10 additional minutes.

These can also be frozen.

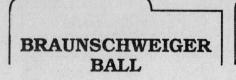

DILL WEED DIP

2/3 cup real mayonnaise
2/3 cup sour cream
1 tablespoon dried onion
1 tablespoon dried parsley
2 teaspoons dill weed
1 teaspoon Lawry's seasoning salt
Dash pepper
2 drops Tabasco sauce
1/2 teaspoon Worcestershire sauce
1/2 teaspoon Accent

Mix together and let set at least 2 hours before serving. Fresh vegetables and bread cubes are great to serve with the dip.

SAUSAGE TEMPTERS IN APPLESAUCE
Makes 4 dozen

1 pound pork sausage
2 cups applesauce
1 ounce cinnamon red candies
2 drops red food coloring

Form sausage in ¾-inch balls. Brown and cook meatballs in a skillet. Turn them so they brown evenly. Place a toothpick in each ball. Heat applesauce, candies and food coloring until candies dissolve. Place sausage balls in sauce, toothpick side up. Serve hot.

Note: A chafing dish would be ideal in which to keep sausages hot while serving.

HAM BALLS

Makes approximately 48 appetizers

4 cups ground lean ham
1/2 cup finely chopped onion
1/4 teaspoon pepper
2 eggs
1 cup plain bread crumbs

Combine and mix all ingredients. Shape into 1-inch balls. Place in a shallow pan and bake at 400 degrees for 25 minutes.

Sour Cream Gravy:
2 tablespoons shortening
2 tablespoons flour
1/4 teaspoon dill seed
1/4 teaspoon marjoram
1/2 cup water
1 1/2 cups sour cream

Melt shortening; add flour and seasonings. Cook until it bubbles. Add water and sour cream, stirring constantly. Cook until thick. Makes 2 cups sauce.

Serve *Ham Balls* with *Sour Cream Gravy;* provide toothpicks for dipping.

DEVILED TURKEY BONBONS

1 cup cooked, finely chopped turkey
1 cup finely chopped nuts
1 tablespoon chopped onion
2 tablespoons chopped pimiento
1/4 teaspoon salt
Hot pepper sauce to taste
1/4 cup cream of mushroom soup.

Combine turkey and 1/2 cup nuts. Add remaining ingredients except remaining nuts; mix well. Shape into small balls and roll in remaining chopped nuts. Chill until serving time.

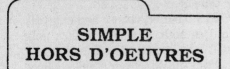

SIMPLE HORS D'OEUVRES

It's true that these tempting tidbits have a French name, may be very elaborate, and are usually met in hotels, but that's no reason for not serving them simply, in the home, for a little variety.

Try a bit of pink, moist salmon on a piece of rye toast . . . some ripe olives . . . celery, stuffed with cream cheese flavored with mayonnaise, salt and paprika, or filled with a mixture of equal parts cream cheese and Roquefort cheese which has been seasoned with Worcestershire sauce . . . slices of salami. . . . All these are as truly and delightfully "hors d'oeuvres" as the most elaborate arrangement of caviar and egg.

CHEESE SURPRISE APPETIZERS

2 cups grated sharp cheddar cheese
1/2 cup softened butter
1 cup flour
1 small jar green, pimiento-stuffed olives

Mix cheese, butter and flour to form dough. Shape into small balls about 1 inch in diameter. Flatten ball with hands; place one olive in center, wrap dough around it, sealing edges completely. Freeze until just before ready to serve. (These *must* be frozen.)

When ready to serve, place frozen appetizers on baking sheet and immediately place in 375-degree oven. Bake about 10 minutes, or until golden. Cheese will puff up and melt.

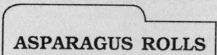

ASPARAGUS ROLLS

Makes 20 appetizers

20 slices bread
1 package frozen asparagus
1 5-ounce jar processed pimiento cheese spread

Trim crusts from bread slices; spread each with cheese. Cook asparagus until just tender. Chill. Lay one piece asparagus diagonally across slice of bread. Turn opposite corners over asparagus, overlapping. Press firmly to seal. Wrap several sandwiches together in waxed paper. Place in covered container and chill for several hours.

MEATBALL APPETIZERS

Makes about 8 dozen tiny meatballs and 2 cups sauce

1 1/2 pounds ground beef
2 eggs
1/4 cup milk
1 cup plain bread crumbs
1/4 cup chopped onion
1 1/2 teaspoons chopped parsley
1 1/2 teaspoons salt
1/8 teaspoon pepper
3 tablespoons oil
10-ounce bottle chili sauce
1/2 cup grape jelly
1 tablespoon instant coffee

Combine meat, eggs, milk, crumbs, onion, parsley, salt and pepper and mix well. Shape into tiny meatballs and brown well on all sides in skillet in hot oil. Remove meatballs from pan. Drain excess drippings, leaving just 2-3 tablespoons. Add chili sauce, jelly and instant coffee to pan drippings and simmer, stirring occasionally, until jelly melts (about 4 minutes). Add meatballs and simmer 10 more minutes. Serve on toothpicks.

Meatballs can be browned, refrigerated, then cooked with sauce just before serving.

ANTIPASTO

2 cans tuna fish, undrained
1 can anchovies, undrained
1 small jar stuffed olives, drained
1 small bottle cocktail onions, drained
1 medium can mushrooms, cut up and drained
1 jar sweet pickled cauliflower, drained and cut in small pieces
1 small jar tiny sweet pickles, drained and cut in small pieces
1 No. 2 can green beans, drained
1 cup carrots, cooked crisp, cut in small rings
1 bottle chili sauce
1 bottle catsup

Mix all ingredients. Add a little salad oil if not moist enough. Marinate in refrigerator for at least one day. Eat with crackers. Makes a delicious hors d'oeuvre.

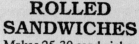

CHEESE-COCONUT BALLS
Makes about 30

2 packages (3 ounces each) Roquefort cheese
1 package (4 ounces) shredded cheddar cheese
1 package (8 ounces) cream cheese, softened
1 package (3 1/2 ounces) flaked coconut

Mash cheeses and combine them thoroughly with electric mixer. Chill for at least one hour. Shape into 1-inch balls and roll in coconut. Serve with fresh apple slices.

PINEAPPLE CHICKEN WINGS
Serves 4

12 chicken wings
3 tablespoons butter
1 small onion, sliced
8 1/2-ounce can pineapple chunks, drained, juice reserved
Orange juice
1/4 cup soy sauce
2 tablespoons brown sugar
1 tablespoon vinegar
1 teaspoon ground ginger
1/2 teaspoon salt
1/2 teaspoon ground mace
1/2 teaspoon hot pepper sauce
1/4 teaspoon dry mustard
1 1/2 tablespoons cornstarch

Fold chicken wing tips under to form triangles. Melt butter in large skillet; add wings and onion. Cook until wings are brown on both sides, about 10 minutes. Measure reserved pineapple syrup and add enough orange juice to make 1 1/4 cups liquid. Blend in soy sauce, sugar, vinegar, ginger, salt, mace, hot pepper sauce and mustard. Pour over chicken.

Cover and simmer 30 minutes, or until chicken is tender, basting top pieces once or twice. Remove chicken to hot plate. Add a small amount of water to cornstarch, blending to dissolve. Add slowly to the hot liquid in pan, stirring, and bring to boil to thicken. Return chicken to skillet, along with pineapple chunks.

Serve chicken wings and sauce with steamed rice.

BROILED CHICKEN LIVER ROLL-UPS

2 cans water chestnuts
1 pound chicken livers
1/2 pound bacon (cut each slice into thirds)
1 bottle soy sauce
1/2 cup brown sugar

Drain water chestnuts and slice each into 3 pieces. Wrap each water chestnut with a small piece of chicken liver and bacon piece. Secure with a toothpick and marinate in soy sauce for at least 4 hours.

Just before serving, remove roll-ups from soy sauce and roll each in brown sugar. Place on broiler rack and broil for about 10 minutes, or until crisp. Serve at once.

TASTY CHICKEN BASKETS
Makes 40-50 baskets

Baskets (directions follow)
Filling:
2 cups chopped cooked chicken meat
5 slices bacon, fried and crumbled
3 tablespoons diced, pared apple
1/2 teaspoon salt
1/8 teaspoon pepper
1/4 cup mayonnaise
1/4 cup finely chopped pecans
4-ounce can mushrooms, chopped

Combine and mix all filling ingredients. Cover and refrigerate for 2 hours. Makes 2 1/2 cups filling, enough for 40-50 baskets.

To make Baskets:
Cut 90-100 rounds from regular sliced bread using a 1 1/2-inch round cookie cutter. Spread half the rounds with softened butter.

Cut a small hole from the centers of remaining bread rounds, "doughnut" fashion. Place each "doughnut" atop a buttered round, and fill center with chicken filling, mounding high. Garnish with sprigs of parsley.

ROLLED SANDWICHES
Makes 25-30 sandwiches

1 loaf of bread, sliced into lengthwise slices
Filling:
1/4 pound (1 stick) butter, softened
4 ounces cream cheese
1/4 teaspoon paprika
1/4 teaspoon salt
1 tablespoon mayonnaise
3/4 cup minced nuts, raisins, dates and/or figs

Slice crusts from long pieces of bread. Combine *Filling* ingredients well. Spread on bread slices. Roll up from narrow ends. (Before rolling, strips of sweet pickles or olives may be placed over filling for colorful variations.) Press end of roll firmly and wrap each roll tightly in plastic wrap. Store in refrigerator overnight.

Before serving, slice each roll into 1/4-inch slices. Arrange on serving plate.

Note: Instead of the nuts-and-dried-fruit filling, you can use one of the following: 1 1/2 cups tuna salad, crab, shrimp, salmon, finely chopped raw vegetables, grated cheddar cheese, chicken, turkey or ham filling.

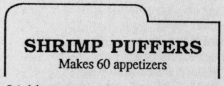

SHRIMP PUFFERS
Makes 60 appetizers

8 tablespoons softened butter or margarine
2 eggs, separated
3 cups shredded sharp cheddar cheese
15 slices white bread (thin-sliced)
60 cooked shrimp, shelled and deveined

Blend butter, cheese and egg yolk until smooth. Beat egg whites until stiff; fold into cheese mixture.

Trim crusts from thinly sliced bread; cut each piece in quarters diagonally. Top each slice with a shrimp and 1 teaspoon of the cheese mixture. Bake in a preheated 350-degree oven on lightly greased cookie sheets for about 15 minutes, or until puffy and golden.

CANAPE PUFFS
Makes about 25 puffs

1/2 cup water
1/4 cup (1/2 stick) butter
1/2 cup flour
2 eggs

Heat water and butter to boiling; reduce heat and stir in flour all at once. Stir about 1 minute until mixture forms ball around spoon. Remove from heat and beat in eggs, one at a time, until mixture is smooth.

Place by rounded teaspoonsful onto ungreased cookie sheets. Bake in a preheated 400-degree oven for about 25 minutes or until golden. Remove and cool on racks.

Slice off tops; remove any doughy insides. Fill with any sandwich filling; chill until serving time.

EGG & HAM HORS D'OEUVRES
Makes 20 appetizers

5 hard-cooked eggs
1 teaspoon minced chives
Salt and paprika
1-2 drops hot pepper sauce
Mayonnaise
1/2 pound boiled ham

Separate yolks and whites of eggs. Force yolks through a sieve; add chives, seasonings and mayonnaise to moisten. Beat to a smooth paste. Chop egg whites and ham together and mix with yolks. Form into 1-inch balls and garnish with additional mayonnaise.

BLUE CHEESE MUSHROOMS

1 pound mushrooms (1-1 1/2 inches in diameter)
1/4 cup green onion slices
2 tablespoons butter or margarine
1 cup (4 ounces) crumbled blue cheese
1 small package (3 ounces) cream cheese, softened
Remove stems from mushrooms;

chop stems. Saute stems and green onion in margarine until soft. Combine with cheeses, mixing well. Stuff mixture into mushroom caps. Place on a broiler pan rack and broil for 2-3 minutes or until golden brown. Serve hot.

SWEET AND SOUR MEATBALLS

1 pound lean ground beef
1 envelope dry onion-soup mix
1 egg
Combine beef, soup mix and egg and form into tiny meatballs. Brown in skillet; discard all but 1 tablespoon fat.
Sauce:
8-ounce can tomato sauce
16-ounce can whole-berry cranberry sauce

Combine ingredients for sauce with reserved tablespoon of fat from meat in saucepan. Heat; add meatballs. Cover and simmer for about an hour. Serve with toothpicks.

PEPPERONI BALLS

1 package hot roll mix
1/4 pound mozzarella cheese, cut in cubes
1/4-1/2 lb. pepperoni, thinly sliced

Prepare roll mix according to package directions, but *omitting egg* and using *1 cup water*. Dough does *not* need to rise. Place one cheese cube on one pepperoni slice. Pinch off a piece of dough and shape carefully around cheese and pepperoni, forming a ball. Repeat until all ingredients are used.

Fry in deep hot oil for about 5 minutes, or until golden brown, turning once. Drain on paper towels and serve warm.

BLUE CHEESE BITES
Makes 40 appetizers

1 package (10-count) refrigerated biscuits

1/4 cup margarine
3 tablespoons crumbled blue cheese or grated Parmesan cheese

Cut each biscuit into four pieces. Arrange pieces on two greased 8x1 1/2-inch round baking pans. Melt margarine; add cheese and stir to blend. Drizzle cheese mixture over biscuits. Bake in 400-degree oven for 12-15 minutes.

CHICKEN WINGS

1 pound chicken wings
1/4 pound (1 stick) butter
1/4 teaspoon garlic powder
2 tablespoons parsley
1 cup fine, dry bread crumbs
1/2 cup Parmesan cheese
1 teaspoon salt
1/4 teaspoon pepper

Cut off tips from chicken wings and discard; split remaining portion of wing at joint to form two pieces. Melt butter, mixing in garlic powder. Combine bread crumbs, Parmesan cheese and seasonings. Dip chicken wing portions in seasoned butter, then roll in crumbs. Bake on a greased baking sheet (use one with edges) in a preheated 325-degree oven for about 50 minutes.

These can be frozen and baked later.

DEVILED EGGS

4 hard-cooked eggs
1/3 cup grated Parmesan cheese
1 teaspoon prepared mustard
Pepper
Skim milk
Paprika

Halve the eggs lengthwise; remove yolks and mash. Add the cheese, mustard, few grains pepper, and enough milk to moisten well. Beat until fluffy and refill the egg whites. May want to garnish with paprika for added color. (65 calories per egg half)

Beverages
REFRESHING

FRUIT-FLAVORED MILK
Makes 2 quarts

1 envelope powdered fruit drink (any flavor)
1 cup sugar
1 cup water
7 cups milk

Combine powdered drink mix, sugar and water. Stir until dissolved. Add mixture to milk and pour into pitcher to serve.

ORANGE APPLE CIDER

Mix the following ingredients together:
1 gallon apple cider
1 cup sugar
1 small can frozen orange juice, diluted
1 small can frozen lemonade, undiluted

Take out 2 or 3 cups and add:
2 teaspoons whole cloves
2 sticks cinnamon

Bring to a boil for a few seconds; then turn off heat and let sit for a little while. Strain and return to other liquid.

Keep in refrigerator until needed and heat up as desired.

FIRECRACKER PUNCH
Serves 30

4 cups cranberry juice
1½ cups sugar
4 cups pineapple juice
1 tablespoon almond extract
2 quarts ginger ale

Combine first 4 ingredients; stir until sugar is dissolved. Chill. Add ginger ale just before serving.

WEDDING PUNCH
Makes 1 gallon

3 cups sugar
6 cups boiling water
¼ cup green tea leaves
3 cups fresh *or* prepared orange juice
1 cup fresh *or* frozen lemon juice
3 cups pineapple juice
Food coloring (optional)
1½ quarts ginger ale

Combine sugar and 3 cups of boiling water; stir until sugar is dissolved. Boil about 7 minutes; do not stir. Pour remaining boiling water over tea leaves; cover and let steep about 5 minutes. Strain and cool. Combine fruit juices, sugar mixture, tea and food coloring. Add ginger ale and enough ice cubes to keep chilled.

SPICED PEACH PUNCH
Serves 12 (Hot drink)

1 (46 ounce) can peach nectar
1 (20 ounce) can orange juice
1/2 cup brown sugar, firmly packed
3 (3 inch) pieces stick cinnamon, broken
1/2 teaspoon whole cloves
2 tablespoons lime juice

Combine peach nectar, orange juice, and brown sugar in a large saucepan. Tie cinnamon sticks and cloves in a cheesecloth bag and drop into saucepan.

Heat slowly, stirring constantly, until sugar dissolves; simmer 10 minutes. Stir in lime juice; ladle into mugs. You may garnish with cinnamon sticks. Serve warm.

HIGH-CALCIUM BANANA SHAKE
Serves 6

2 cups non-fat milk
1/4 cup non-fat dry milk
1 tablespoon vanilla extract
2 tablespoons fructose
1 banana
1 cup ice cubes

Place all ingredients in a blender and blend until smooth. Serve immediately, preferably in a chilled glass. (90 calories per shake)

CRANBERRY COCKTAIL PUNCH
Serves 30

2 (32 ounce) bottles cranberry juice cocktail, chilled
2 cups orange juice, chilled
1 cup pineapple juice, chilled
1/2 cup sugar
1/2 cup lemon juice, chilled
1 (28 ounce) bottle ginger ale, chilled
1 tray ice cubes
Lemon slices for garnish

In large punch bowl, stir first 5 ingredients until sugar is dissolved. Add remaining ingredients, except lemon slices, which should be added just before serving.

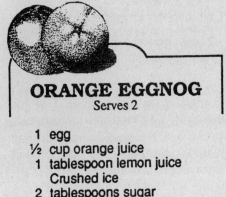

ORANGE EGGNOG
Serves 2

1 egg
1/2 cup orange juice
1 tablespoon lemon juice
Crushed ice
2 tablespoons sugar
Dash nutmeg

Dissolve sugar in the fruit juices. Add egg and crushed ice. Shake until egg is thoroughly beaten and foamy. Strain and serve over crushed ice. Put a few grains of nutmeg on top.

HONEY-SPICED TEA
Makes 1 quart

1 quart boiling water
2 large tea bags
1/2 cup honey
2 tablespoons lemon juice
1/4 teaspoon ground allspice
1/8 teaspoon ground nutmeg
Lemon slices, halved

Pour boiling water over tea bags; cover and let stand 4 minutes. Remove tea bags. Add next 4 ingredients, stirring until honey dissolves. Stir over low heat until thoroughly heated. Serve with lemon slices.

HOT MULLED CIDER

1 quart apple juice
1 quart pineapple juice
2 cinnamon sticks
12 whole cloves

Combine all ingredients and simmer gently for about 5 minutes. Save time by mixing the day before and then heating when ready to serve on the day of the breakfast.

CAFE SWISS MOCHA

1/4 cup powdered non-fat dairy creamer or non-fat dry milk
1/4 cup instant coffee
1/3 cup sugar
2 tablespoons cocoa

Shake in jar to mix. Use 1 level tablespoon, to 6 ounces boiling water. Put 1 heaping teaspoon into 1 cup cold water; heat in microwave for 1 minute, 15 seconds; let sit a moment; stir.

PEANUT BUTTER SHAKE
Makes 4 cups

2 cups milk
1 pint vanilla ice cream
1/4 cup creamy peanut butter

Combine all ingredients in container of electric blender; process until smooth. Serve at once.

HOT TEA PUNCH

1/2 cup sugar
1/2 cup water
1 (2-inch) stick cinnamon
1 teaspoon grated lemon rind
1 1/2 teaspoons grated orange rind
1/4 cup orange juice
2 tablespoons lemon juice
1/4 cup canned pineapple juice
3 cups boiling water
3 tablespoons tea leaves *or* 9 tea bags

In saucepan combine sugar, water, cinnamon, lemon and orange rinds; boil 5 minutes. Remove cinnamon stick. Add orange, lemon and pineapple juice; keep hot. Pour boiling water over tea; steep 5 minutes; strain. Combine with juice. Serve hot, float orange slices with cloves on top.

ICED TEA A LA MODE
Serves 3

2 cups double-strength cold tea
1 pint vanilla ice cream

Blend tea and ice cream until smooth and pour into a tall glass.

SWEET CHERRY SODA
Serves 2

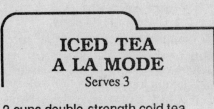

1/3 cup ruby-red cherry sauce
2 scoops vanilla ice cream
Club soda
2 whole sweet cherries

In a blender container, combine cherry sauce and ice cream. Cover and process until smooth. Pour half of mixture into each of 2 tall glasses. Fill glasses with club soda. Garnish each serving with a whole cherry.

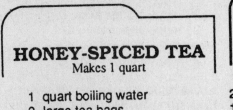

CITRUS ICED TEA A LA MODE
Serves 5

3 cups double-strength cold tea
1/2 cup chilled orange juice
1 pint vanilla ice cream

Blend ingredients until smooth and pour into a tall glass.

PINEAPPLE-ORANGE PUNCH
Makes 5 quarts

½ gallon orange sherbet
1 (46-ounce) can pineapple juice, chilled
1 (33½-ounce) bottle ginger ale, chilled
3 cups orange-flavored drink, chilled
3 cups lemon-lime carbonated beverage, chilled

Place sherbet in a large punch bowl; add remaining ingredients and stir well. Chunks of orange sherbet will remain in punch.

PACIFIC FRUIT PUNCH

1 large can orange juice
1 large can apriocot nectar
1 large can pineapple juice
1 quart ginger ale
1 cup fresh strawberries
1 quart orange sherbet, soften in refrigerator

Combine juices and ginger ale in punchbowl. Add sherbet, strawberries, and ice. Garnish individual glasses with pineapple spears and small umbrellas.

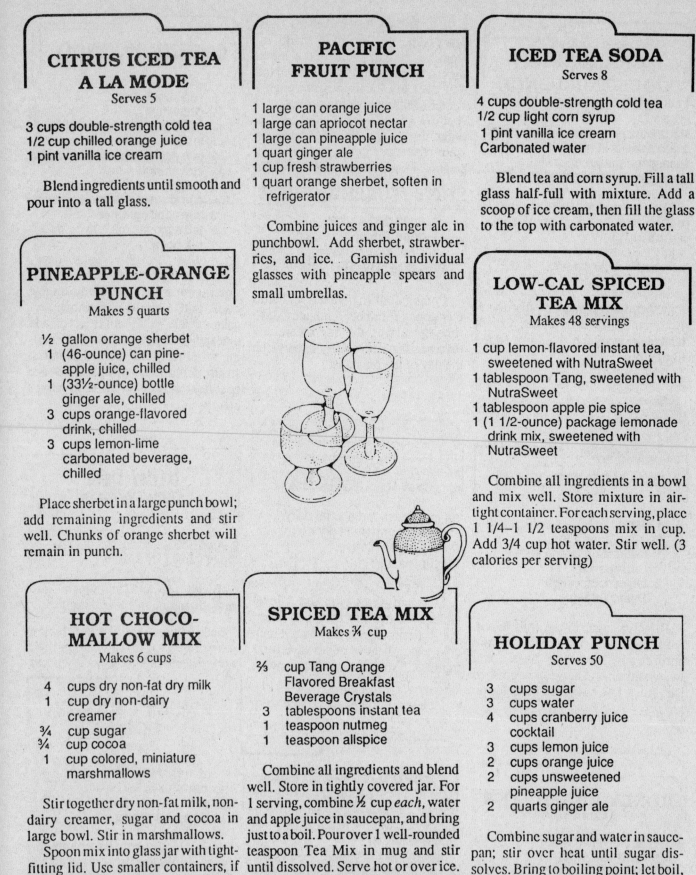

ICED TEA SODA
Serves 8

4 cups double-strength cold tea
1/2 cup light corn syrup
1 pint vanilla ice cream
Carbonated water

Blend tea and corn syrup. Fill a tall glass half-full with mixture. Add a scoop of ice cream, then fill the glass to the top with carbonated water.

LOW-CAL SPICED TEA MIX
Makes 48 servings

1 cup lemon-flavored instant tea, sweetened with NutraSweet
1 tablespoon Tang, sweetened with NutraSweet
1 tablespoon apple pie spice
1 (1 1/2-ounce) package lemonade drink mix, sweetened with NutraSweet

Combine all ingredients in a bowl and mix well. Store mixture in air-tight container. For each serving, place 1 1/4–1 1/2 teaspoons mix in cup. Add 3/4 cup hot water. Stir well. (3 calories per serving)

HOT CHOCO-MALLOW MIX
Makes 6 cups

4 cups dry non-fat dry milk
1 cup dry non-dairy creamer
¾ cup sugar
¾ cup cocoa
1 cup colored, miniature marshmallows

Stir together dry non-fat milk, non-dairy creamer, sugar and cocoa in large bowl. Stir in marshmallows.

Spoon mix into glass jar with tight-fitting lid. Use smaller containers, if desired. Attach instruction label: For each serving combine ¼ cup mix and 6 ounces boiling water in mug. Stir and serve.

SPICED TEA MIX
Makes ¾ cup

⅔ cup Tang Orange Flavored Breakfast Beverage Crystals
3 tablespoons instant tea
1 teaspoon nutmeg
1 teaspoon allspice

Combine all ingredients and blend well. Store in tightly covered jar. For 1 serving, combine ½ cup *each*, water and apple juice in saucepan, and bring just to a boil. Pour over 1 well-rounded teaspoon Tea Mix in mug and stir until dissolved. Serve hot or over ice. For 1 quart, combine 2 cups each water and apple juice, and bring just to a boil. Add ⅓ cup mix; stir until dissolved. Serve hot or over ice.

HOLIDAY PUNCH
Serves 50

3 cups sugar
3 cups water
4 cups cranberry juice cocktail
3 cups lemon juice
2 cups orange juice
2 cups unsweetened pineapple juice
2 quarts ginger ale

Combine sugar and water in saucepan; stir over heat until sugar dissolves. Bring to boiling point; let boil, without stirring, for about 7 minutes. Cool; add fruit juices. When ready to serve pour over ice; add ginger ale. Garnish with sprigs of mint.

SPICED TEA

1 cup instant tea
2 cups Tang
1/3 cup lemonade mix (crystals)
2 tablespoons sugar
1 teaspoon cinnamon
1 teaspoon ground cloves

Mix thoroughly. Keep in airtight container. Use 1 rounded teaspoonful per cup hot water.

CINNAMON TEA
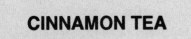

1-1/2 cups instant tea
1 cup Tang
1 (3-ounce) package lemonade mix
2-1/2 cups sugar
1 teaspoon cloves
2 teaspoons cinnamon

Mix all ingredients. Use 2 teaspoonfuls to one cup hot water.

NEW ENGLAND SWEET CIDER PUNCH

3 oranges
1 lemon
1/4 cup maraschino cherries
1 quart cider

Extract juices from oranges and lemon; add to cider together with cherries. Chill thoroughly before serving.

FRUIT SMASH PUNCH

Makes 1 gallon

2 cups hot water
1 package raspberry gelatin
1 package cherry gelatin
6 cups cold water
1-1/2 cups lime or lemon juice
5 cups fresh or frozen orange juice
1/2 to 1 cup sugar
5 or 6 ripe bananas
1 quart chilled ginger ale

Make gelatin in usual manner; add cold water and fruit juices; stir in sugar. Just before serving, mash or whip bananas until smooth and creamy. Beat into mixture. Add ginger ale, the last minute.

PEACH PICK ME UP

Makes 3-1/2 cups

2 containers (8-ounce each) peach yogurt
6 ounces frozen apple juice concentrate
1/2 teaspoon almond extract
3 ice cubes

Place all ingredients in blender container; cover. Blend on high speed until ice is reduced to small pieces and mixture is well combined. Serve immediately in tall chilled glasses.

CHOCOLATE TOFU NUTRITIONAL SHAKE

Serves 4

3 cups milk
1 cup Silken Tofu, drained
2 bananas, broken into chunks
4 tablespoons instant cocoa mix powder
2 tablespoon honey
1 tablespoon wheat germ

Combine ingredients in blender, 1/2 at a time; whirl until smooth and creamy. Serve cold. Wonderful as a complete protein breakfast drink or for snack any time.

Any fresh fruit in season such as berries, cantaloupe or papaya can be substituted for the chocolate flavor.

Pour into tall glasses, sprinkle with nutmeg.

COFFEE EGGNOG

2 eggs, separated
1/3 cup sugar
1/3 cup instant coffee
Dash salt
1 teaspoon vanilla extract
2 cups milk, chilled
3/4 cup water
1 cup heavy cream, whipped
Shaved unsweetened chocolate

In small bowl, beat egg whites at high speed until soft peaks form. Gradually, beat in sugar until stiff peaks form. In large bowl, beat egg yolks until lemon colored. Gradually beat in coffee, salt, vanilla, milk, and 3/4 cup water. Stir in egg-white mixture and whipped cream; mix well. Serve well chilled, with chocolate shavings sprinkled over each serving.

EGGNOG

Makes 6 large glasses

4 eggs
4 cups milk
4 tablespoons lemon juice
1/2 cup cream
1/8 teaspoon nutmeg
1/8 teaspoon salt
1/3 cup sugar

Beat eggs until thick and lemon colored. Add sugar, salt, nutmeg, and lemon juice; add ice cold milk and cream. Beat with mixer until frothy.

FRIENDSHIP TEA
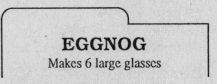

1 pound 2 ounce jar Tang
3/4 to 1 cup instant tea
2 tablespoons cinnamon
1 pound package dry lemonade
2-1/2 cups sugar

Mix together; store in closed container. To use: add 2 spoonfuls of mixture to one cup of hot water.

ZESTY FRUIT REFRESHER

1 cup cranberry cocktail juice
1 cup prune juice (Welch's)
2 cups apple juice

Mix all the above juices and place in refrigerator. When ready to serve, place 1/2 cup fruit juice mixture into glass tumbler and fill rest of glass with ginger ale.

FRUIT LOW-BALL

Serves 6

1 (10-ounce) package frozen peaches
1/4 cup firmly-packed light brown sugar
1/4 teaspoon cinnamon
1 quart buttermilk
1 medium orange

Thaw peaches. Combine peaches, sugar, and cinnamon in blender. Whirl at medium speed until smooth. Add buttermilk; whirl again.

To serve, pour into six 8-ounce glasses. Slice orange very thin; garnish each glass edge with an orange wheel. Top with dash of cinnamon. Very zesty and refreshing with the buttermilk!

ORANGE-TOMATO COCKTAIL

Serves 6

1-1/2 cups chilled tomato juice
1 cup chilled orange juice
1 tablespoon lemon juice
1/2 teaspoon salt
1 slice onion

Blend all ingredients in blender about 30 seconds or until thoroughly mixed. Add 4 ice cubes, one at a time, and blend until mixed.

PINEAPPLE SLUSH

Makes 3 cups

1 (5-1/4 ounce) can pineapple tidbits, undrained
1 medium banana, chilled
1/4 cup milk
2 cups pineapple sherbet

Combine all ingredients in container of electric blender; process until smooth.

MOCHA

Serves 8-10

2/3 cup instant cocoa mix
1/2 cup instant coffee
8 cups boiling water
Sweetened whipped cream or Cool Whip

Mix cocoa and coffee in pot or pitcher. Pour in boiling water and stir. Serve hot and topped with Cool Whip or whipped cream.

CHOCOLATE-PEANUT-BUTTER MILK SHAKE

Makes 2 cups

2 tablespoons powdered chocolate drink mix
3 tablespoons crunchy peanut butter
1 cup milk, chilled
1 teaspoon honey
Dash cinnamon
Dash nutmeg
8 ice cubes

Place all ingredients in blender. Cover and process until frothy. Pour into vacuum containers.

MELON SHAKE

1 serving

1/2 cup watermelon, cantaloupe or honeydew melon balls
2 large scoops vanilla ice cream (about 1 cup)
1/4 cup milk

Place melon balls in blender. Add ice cream and milk. Cover and blend until smooth. Serve immediately.

LO-CALORIE BANANA MILK SHAKE

6 ounces skimmed milk
1/2 teaspoon vanilla
1 banana, sliced frozen
1/2 teaspoon Sprinkle Sweet or sweetener

Put milk in blender. Add vanilla and frozen banana, a little at a time. If a thicker shake is desired, add ice cubes until desired thickness.

SPICY MILK TEA

Serves 4

6 whole cloves
4 thin slices fresh ginger or 1/2 teaspoon ground ginger
2 cinnamon sticks
4 cups water
4 teaspoons jasmine tea
1 cup milk or half-and-half
Honey
Cardamom, optional
Mint sprigs for garnish

Bring water to boil. Add cinnamon, cloves, and ginger. Cover; simmer 10 minutes. Add tea and steep for a few minutes. Add milk. Bring to boil again. Remove from heat. Strain into a teapot. Serve with a sprinkle of cardamom and a bit of honey. Garnish with mint.

For 1 serving:

Boil 1 cup water. Add 1/2 cinnamon stick, 3 cloves, 2 slices fresh ginger, and 1 teaspoon tea.

EASY PARTY PUNCH

3-ounce package raspberry gelatin
3-ounce package cherry gelatin
3 cups boiling water
5 cups cold water
3 cups pineapple juice
12 ounces frozen orange juice
2 pints pineapple or lemon sherbet

Dissolve gelatins in boiling water; add next 3 ingredients. Stir in one tray ice cubes until melted. Spoon in sherbet. Serve immediately or let stand at room temperature.

GOOD LUCK PUNCH
Makes 1 gallon

1 quart fresh rhubarb
Water to cover
3 cups sugar
2 cups water
Juice of 6 lemons
1 cup pineapple juice
1 quart gingerale

Cut rhubarb into 1-inch pieces; cover with water and cook until soft, about 12-15 minutes. Drain through cheesecloth. Should be about 3 quarts of juice. Dissolve sugar in the 2 cups water and cook 10 minutes to make a syrup.

Combine all juices, except ginger ale, pouring over chunk of ice in punch bowl. Just before serving, add ginger ale.

PARTY PINK PUNCH

1 (46-ounce) can pineapple juice
1 large bottle lemon lime pop
1 small can pink lemonade, frozen
1 can water
2 large bottles strawberry pop
Sugar, if desired
Raspberry sherbet

Mix first six ingredients. Drop spoonfuls of sherbet on top before serving. Delicious!

AUTUMN PUNCH
Makes 7-1/2 quarts

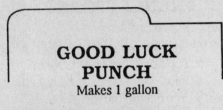

1-1/2 cups honey
3/4 cup lemon juice
6 whole cardamom seeds
3 (3-inch) sticks cinnamon
1 teaspoon whole allspice
2 teaspoons whole cloves
1-1/2 quarts cranberry juice
5 cups apple juice
5 cups apricot nectar
3 quarts ginger ale
Crushed ice

Combine first 6 ingredients in a saucepan; bring to a boil; reduce heat; simmer 10 minutes. Strain and discard spices. Chill. Combine chilled mixture with remaining juices and ginger ale. Serve over ice.

HOT SPICED CIDER

1 gallon apple cider
½ cup brown sugar
2 lemons, sliced
2 oranges, sliced
8 whole cloves, studded into orange/lemon slices (1 clove to a slice)
4 cinnamon sticks

Combine all ingredients in a saucepan. Bring to a boil over medium heat; reduce and simmer for about 10 minutes.

PINK PUNCH
Makes 8 cups

2 (6-ounce) cans frozen pink lemonade
1 (46-ounce) can pineapple juice
1 (46-ounce) can Hawaiian Punch
4 cups ginger ale

Add water to lemonade to make 8 cups. Add other ingredients and mix well. Chill.

SPICY CALIFORNIA PUNCH

4 cups unsweetened grapefruit juice
4 cups orange juice
2 cups honey
1/4 cup lime juice
1 teaspoon allspice
1 teaspoon nutmeg

In a 3-quart container, combine 4 cups each of both grapefruit juice and orange juice, then add honey, lime juice, and spices. Let stand at room temperature for 1 hour to allow flavors to blend. Chill. To serve, pour over ice in a punch bowl or several pitchers.

TROPICAL FRUIT SMOOTHIE
Makes 5 cups

1 (15-ounce) can cream of coconut
1 medium banana
1 (8-ounce) can juice packed crushed pineapple
1 cup orange—juice
1 tablespoon bottled lemon juice
2 cups ice cubes

In blender, combine all ingredients, except ice; blend well. Gradually add ice; blend until smooth. Serve immediately; refrigerate leftovers.

COFFEE COOLER

4 quarts strong coffee, cold
1 cup sugar
2 quarts vanilla ice cream
1 tablespoon vanilla
1 quart whole milk

Combine coffee, milk, and vanilla. Add sugar and stir until dissolved. Chill thoroughly and pour over ice cream that has been spooned into a punch bowl. Serves about 50 small punch cups.

Brunch
BUFFET

BASIC WAFFLE RECIPE

2 cups flour
2 teaspoons baking powder
1½ teaspoons baking soda
⅛ teaspoon salt
3 eggs, separated
1 tablespoon melted margarine
2 cups cold milk

Sift flour, baking powder, baking soda and salt together. Set aside. Separate eggs and beat yolks. Gradually add milk and melted margarine, stirring well. Stir in flour mixture. Beat egg whites until stiff and fold into mixture.

Blueberry Waffles:
1 cup blueberries, washed and dried
Basic Waffle Recipe

Fold blueberries into Basic Waffle Recipe and cook in waffle iron.

Strawberry Waffles:
1 cup strawberries, washed and uniformly sliced
Basic Waffle Recipe

Fold sliced strawberries into Basic Waffle Recipe. Cook.

Hint: Both of these recipes taste extra-special when served with a small amount of whipped cream topping!

Cheese Waffles:
1 cup grated cheddar cheese
Basic Waffle Recipe

Fold the grated cheddar cheese into the Basic Waffle Recipe and cook.
Hint: These enticing waffles can be served with creamed tuna fish, ham, chicken or vegetables!

Corn Waffles:
2 cups canned corn, drained
Basic Waffle Recipe

After preparing the Basic Waffle Recipe, mix in the corn and cook in waffle iron.
Hint: These waffles taste great at a barbecue with butter served beside fried chicken or barbecued beef.

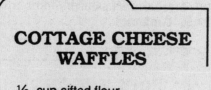

COTTAGE CHEESE WAFFLES

½ cup sifted flour
½ teaspoon salt
4 eggs
½ cup milk
⅓ cup vegetable oil
1 teaspoon vanilla
1 cup cottage cheese

Sift flour and salt together. Set aside. Beat eggs, milk, vegetable oil and vanilla together. Add cottage cheese and beat until smooth. Combine with flour. Cook as usual.

GET-UP-AND-GO FRENCH TOAST
Serves 4

½ cup creamy peanut butter
¼ cup apple butter *or* favorite jelly
8 slices white bread
1 egg, beaten
½ cup milk
2 teaspoons sugar
Dash salt
Margarine

Make 4 peanut butter and jelly sandwiches. Mix egg, milk, sugar and salt. Melt enough margarine over medium heat to cover bottom of skillet. Dip both sides of sandwiches in egg mixture. Fry until brown on both sides.

CHEDDAR EGG BAKE

6 eggs, slightly beaten
1 cup shredded cheddar cheese (4 ounces)
½ cup milk
2 tablespoons margarine, softened
1 teaspoon prepared mustard
½ teaspoon salt
¼ teaspoon pepper

Heat oven to 325 degrees. Mix all ingredients. Pour into an ungreased 8 x 8 x 2-inch pan. Bake 25–30 minutes, or until eggs are set. A simple and delicious way to make eggs!

TOPPINGS

PINEAPPLE SAUCE

2 tablespoons margarine
1½ cups canned crushed pineapple
1 tablespoon brown sugar

Combine all ingredients in a saucepan and cook until heated through. This can be served hot or cold over waffles along with vanilla ice cream.

CREAM CHEESE TOPPING

1 (8-ounce) package cream cheese
¼ cup milk (or less)
1 cup chopped dates

Beat cream cheese and add milk gradually until desired consistency.

BLUEBERRY TOPPING

1½ cups blueberries, washed and drained
¼ cup sugar
1 tablespoon cornstarch
⅓ cup hot water

Combine blueberries and sugar together. Heat water and cornstarch in a saucepan. Add blueberries and heat slightly. Again, this can be served hot or cold.

HAM PANCAKE PIE
Serves 6

2 medium sweet potatoes, peeled and thinly sliced

3 cups diced, cooked ham
3 medium apples, peeled, cored and sliced
½ teaspoon salt
¼ teaspoon pepper
3 tablespoons brown sugar
¼ teaspoon curry powder
⅓ cup apple juice *or* water
1 cup pancake mix
1 cup milk
½ teaspoon dry mustard
2 tablespoons butter, melted

In a 2-quart greased casserole dish, layer half the potatoes, half the ham and half the apples. Combine salt, pepper, brown sugar and curry powder; sprinkle half the mixture over layers in dish. Repeat this process with remaining potatoes, ham, apples and brown sugar mixture. Pour apple juice or water over all. Cover dish and bake at 375 degrees until potatoes are tender, about 40 minutes. Beat together pancake mix, milk, mustard and butter. Remove casserole from oven when potatoes are done; pour pancake batter over top. Bake 20 minutes more, uncovered, or until pancake is puffed and golden.

NIGHT-BEFORE FRENCH TOAST
Serves 4–6

1 loaf French bread, cut into ¾-inch slices
4 tablespoons butter
⅔ cup brown sugar
4 eggs, beaten
2 cups milk
½ teaspoon cinnamon

The night before serving, melt butter and brown sugar in a small pan, stirring. Pour into a 9 x 13-inch baking dish. Lay bread slices on top of brown sugar mix. Combine eggs with milk and cinnamon. Pour over the bread. Cover with plastic wrap and refrigerate overnight. In the morning preheat oven to 350 degrees and uncover baking dish. Bake for 30 minutes. Serve with syrup, honey or chopped blueberries mixed with 2 tablespoons orange juice.

PIMIENTO-CHEESE SOUFFLE

6 tablespoons butter
6 tablespoons flour
⅛ teaspoon dry mustard
Dash cayenne pepper
1½ cups milk
6 large eggs, separated
1½ cups shredded Swiss cheese
1 (4-ounce) jar pimientos, drained and chopped

Heat oven to 350 degrees. Lightly grease a quart soufflé dish. Melt butter in a medium saucepan. Stir in flour, mustard and cayenne. Gradually stir in milk over medium heat until mixture thickens and begins to boil, about 5 minutes. Stir in cheese and pimientos. When cheese is melted, set aside. Beat yolks in a large bowl until light and lemon colored. Stir cheese mixture into beaten yolks. Beat egg whites in a large bowl until soft peaks form.
Gently fold beaten whites into cheese-yolk mixture. Pour mixture into soufflé dish. Bake until golden, puffy and a knife inserted comes out clean, approximately 45 minutes.

PEACH AND COTTAGE CHEESE SALAD
Single serving

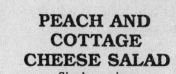

2/3 cup cottage cheese
1/8 teaspoon cinnamon
Artificial sweetener to equal 2 teaspoons sugar
1/2 cup cooked, enriched rice
1 medium peach, sliced
1/4 cup skim milk

Combine cottage cheese, cinnamon, and sweetener; mix well. Add rice and peach. Toss lightly until well-mixed. Chill. Just before serving, pour skim milk over mixture.

BREAKFAST BAKED FRENCH TOAST
Serves 4

- 3 eggs
- 1 tablespoon all-purpose flour
- ¼ cup sugar
- ½ teaspoon cinnamon
- ¼ teaspoon allspice
- ¼ teaspoon salt
- ½ teaspoon baking powder
- ½ teaspoon vanilla extract
- 1 cup milk
- 8 (1-inch) slices French bread
- 2 tablespoons butter *or* margarine, melted

Beat eggs; add flour, sugar, cinnamon, allspice, salt, baking powder and vanilla; mix until smooth. Beat in milk; pour into baking dish. Dip bread into mixture; turn over; cover; refrigerate overnight. Before baking turn slices over; melt butter; drizzle over top. Bake at 400 degrees for 10 minutes; turn bread; bake an additional 5 minutes until golden brown. To serve, sprinkle with confectioners' sugar, maple syrup, honey, sour cream, jelly or preserves of your choice. Can be sprinkled with cinnamon-sugar or topped with fruit.

BAKED DOUGHNUTS

- ⅓ cup sugar
- 2 teaspoons nutmeg
- 2 teaspoons salt
- ⅓ cup shortening
- 2 eggs
- 2 cakes yeast
- ¼ cup lukewarm water
- 3¾ cups flour
- ¾ cup milk

In saucepan add sugar, nutmeg salt and shortening to milk. Stir until shortening is melted over low heat. Cool to lukewarm; add well-beaten eggs and yeast dissolved in ¼ cup lukewarm water. Add flour and beat briskly. Let rise until double in bulk, or about an hour. Roll to ½-inch thickness and cut with floured cutter;

place on greased pan and brush with melted butter. A cookie sheet is good for this. Let rise about ½ hour, or until about double. Bake at 450 degrees for about 10 minutes. Brush with butter when done, then dust with confectioners' sugar. These are also great with a brown-sugar frosting.

QUICK & EASY PUFFY OMELET

- 2 tablespoons bread crumbs
- 3 eggs
- ⅛ teaspoon pepper
- 4 tablespoons milk
- ½ teaspoon salt
- 3 tablespoons butter

Soak bread crumbs in milk. Separate eggs. Beat yolks until thick and lemon colored. Add crumbs and milk, salt and pepper. Beat egg whites until stiff. Gradually, fold the egg yolk mixture into the whites. Melt butter in the omelet pan or frying pan and allow it to run around the sides of the pan. Pour mixture into the pan and cook slowly for 10 minutes, or until lightly brown underneath. Put pan in a moderate 350-degree oven for 5–10 minutes until it is dry on top. Fold and turn onto a hot platter. Serve at once.

CINNAMON RAISIN BATTER BREAD

- 1 package active dry yeast
- 1-1/2 cups warm water (105-115 degrees)
- 2 tablespoons honey
- 2 tablespoons butter
- 1 teaspoon salt
- 3 cups flour, divided
- 1 tablespoon cinnamon
- 1 cup raisins

In a large bowl, dissolve yeast in warm water. Stir in honey. Add butter, salt, and 2 cups of the flour. Beat with electric mixer on low speed until blended. Beat 1 minute on high speed.

Stir in remaining flour with a wooden spoon. Cover and let rise in a warm place until doubled in size. Punch down by stirring with a heavy spoon. Add cinnamon and raisins. Spoon batter into a loaf pan. Let rise again until batter reaches the top of the pan (not over!). Bake in preheated 350-degree oven for about 40 minutes or until loaf sounds hollow when lightly tapped. Cool on wire rack.

This batter bread is a wonderful treat for breakfast or in the "munchkin's" lunch sack as a peanut-butter-and-jelly sandwich.

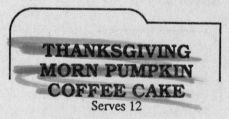

THANKSGIVING MORN PUMPKIN COFFEE CAKE
Serves 12

- ½ cup butter
- ¾ cup sugar
- 1¼ teaspoons vanilla extract
- 3 eggs
- 2 cups all-purpose flour
- 1 teaspoon baking powder
- 1 teaspoon baking soda
- ½ cup sour cream
- 1¾ cups solid-pack pumpkin
- 1 egg, lightly beaten
- ⅓ cup sugar
- 1½ teaspoons pumpkin pie spice
  Streusel (recipe follows)

Cream butter, ¾ cup sugar and vanilla; add eggs; beat well. Combine dry ingredients; add to butter mixture alternatly with sour cream. Combine pumpkin, beaten egg, ⅓ cup sugar and pie spice. Spoon half of batter into 13 x 9 x 2-inch baking pan; sprinkle half of streusel mixture over batter; spread remaining pumpkin mixture over streusel; sprinkle remaining streusel over top. Bake at 325 degrees for 50–60 minutes, or until tested done in middle.

Streusel:
- 1 cup brown sugar
- ⅓ cup butter
- 2 teaspoons cinnamon
- 1 cup chopped nuts

SAUSAGE WEDGES

½ pound bulk pork sausage
1 cup (4 ounces) shredded cheddar cheese *or* American
2 tablespoons diced onion
¾ cup milk
4 eggs, beaten
1 teaspoon dried parsley
2 tablespoons butter

Crumble sausage in a 9-inch pie plate. Cover with paper towel and microwave for 3–4 minutes on HIGH. Drain off fat; sprinkle cheese over sausage; stir in onion. In a medium bowl combine milk and eggs; add parsley and butter. Pour over sausage; cover with plastic wrap and microwave 4 minutes on HIGH. Stir; cover and microwave for 6–8 minutes on MEDIUM (50 percent) Let stand, covered, 5 minutes.

FRUIT DELIGHT

Prepare this ahead of time to allow flavors to develop.

1 (20-ounce) can pineapple chunks, juice pack
2 (11-ounce) cans mandarin orange sections, drained
½ to 1 cup seedless grapes, halved
2 kiwis, halved lengthwise and sliced
½ cup orange juice
¼ cup honey
1 tablespoon lemon juice

Drain pineapple; reserve juice. In a large bowl combine pineapple, mandarin oranges, grapes and kiwi. Combine pineapple liquid, orange juice, honey and lemon juice. Pour over fruit. Cover and chill until ready to serve.

BAKED WESTERN OMELET
Serves 4

4 large eggs
1/4 cup water
4 ounces cooked ham, cut into thin strips
1 cup sliced mushrooms
1/2 cup chopped tomato
1/4 cup sliced scallions
1/4 cup chopped green bell pepper
1/8 teaspoon freshly ground pepper

Preheat oven to 375 degrees. Lightly spray a 10-inch glass pie pan with non-stick cooking spray. In medium bowl, with wire whisk, beat eggs with 1/4 cup water until well-blended. Stir in remaining ingredients. With rubber spatula, scrape into prepared pie pan. Bake 20-30 minutes until omelet is set, slightly puffed, and browned. Cut into four servings and serve at once. (141 calories per serving)

HAM GRIDDLE CAKES
Makes 11

1 cup milk
1 cup quick-cooking oats, uncooked
2 tablespoons vegetable oil
2 eggs, beaten
½ cup all-purpose flour
2 tablespoons sugar
2 teaspoons baking powder
1 cup diced, cooked ham
Maple syrup

Combine milk and oats in a large bowl; let stand 5 minutes. Add oil and eggs, stirring well. Combine flour, sugar and baking powder; add to oat mixture, stirring just until moistened. Stir in ham.

For each pancake, pour about ¼ cup batter onto a hot, lightly greased griddle. Turn pancakes when tops are covered with bubbles and edges look cooked. Serve with maple syrup.

BREAKFAST HONEY MUFFINS
Makes 9

1 cup sifted all-purpose flour
2 teaspoons baking powder
½ teaspoon salt
½ cup unsifted whole-wheat flour
½ cup milk
1 egg, well-beaten
½ cup honey
½ cup coarsely chopped, cooked prunes
1 teaspoon grated orange peel
¼ cup salad oil *or* melted shortening

Preheat oven to 400 degrees, and lightly grease 9 (2½-inch) muffin pan cups. In large bowl, sift the all-purpose flour with the baking powder and salt. Stir in whole-wheat flour. Combine milk and rest of ingredients in medium bowl. Add, all at once, to flour mixture, stirring only until mixture is moistened. Spoon into cups; bake 20–25 minutes, or until nicely browned. Serve warm.

SCRAMBLED EGGS AND SAUSAGE

¼ pound bulk sausage
6 eggs
3 tablespoons milk
½ cup herb-seasoned croutons

Put sausage in a 9-inch pie plate and microwave on HIGH for 2–3 minutes; drain and crumble meat. Beat eggs and milk together. Stir in sausage and microwave on HIGH for 3 minutes; stir twice. Fold croutons into eggs and microwave on HIGH for 1–2 minutes, or until eggs are soft and moist. Do not overcook.

OMELET SUPREME
Serves 3

3 slices bacon, cut into small pieces
2 small potatoes, peeled and sliced
8 fresh spinach leaves, stems removed, sliced into 1/4 inch slices
6 eggs, lightly beaten with fork
1/2 cup yogurt
Salt and pepper to taste

In skillet, heat bacon; add potatoes; fry until bacon is crisp, and potatoes lightly browned. Add spinach; remove mixture to bowl. In shallow bowl, mix eggs, yogurt, salt, and pepper; pour into skillet. Distribute potato mixture evenly over eggs; cook over low heat without stirring. As eggs set on bottom, lift edges; let uncooked mixture run underneath. When omelet is set, fold with fork. Serve immediately.

BROCCOLI OVEN OMELET
Serves 6

9 eggs
1 (10 ounce) package frozen chopped broccoli, thawed and drained
1/3 cup finely chopped onion
1/4 cup grated Parmesan cheese
2 tablespoons milk
1/2 teaspoon salt
1/2 teaspoon dried basil
1/4 teaspoon garlic powder
1 medium tomato, cut into 6 slices
1/4 cup grated Parmesan cheese

Beat eggs with whisk in bowl until light and fluffy. Stir in broccoli, onion, 1/4 cup Parmesan cheese, milk, salt, basil, and garlic powder. Pour into ungreased 11x7x2 inch baking dish. Arrange tomato slices on top. Sprinkle with 1/4 cup Parmesan cheese. Bake uncovered in 325 degree oven until set, 25-30 minutes.

Great for holiday brunch, also as vegetable side dish.

GARDEN MEDLEY
Serves 6

1/4 cup butter or margarine
2 cups cauliflower
1/4 cup chopped onion
2 cups sliced zucchini
1/2 cup halved cherry tomatoes
1/4 teaspoon salt
1/4 teaspoon thyme leaves, crushed
2 tablespoons grated Parmesan cheese, if desired

In large skillet, melt butter. Add cauliflower and onion; sauté 2-3 minutes. Add zucchini; cover and cook over medium heat, stirring occasionally, 3-5 minutes, or until vegetables are crisp-tender. Stir in tomatoes, salt, and thyme; cook 1-2 minutes until thoroughly heated. Spoon into serving dish; sprinkle with Parmesan cheese. (100 calories per serving)

OLD FASHIONED BREAD OMELET

Combine and soak for 10 minutes:
2 cups bread cubes
1 cup milk

Preheat oven to 325 degrees.
Combine in bowl:
5 eggs, beaten
1/2 cup grated cheese
1 cup alfalfa sprouts, chopped
1 small onion, finely chopped
1 tablespoon parsley flakes
1 teaspoon garlic powder
Salt and pepper to taste
Bread and milk mixture

Heat in skillet:
1/4-1/2 cup bacon pieces until done

Pour in egg mixture and cook over medium heat without stirring, about 5 minutes. When browned underneath, place pan in oven for 10 minutes to finish cooking the top. Turn out onto hot platter. Omelet can be folded in half.

QUICHE LORRAINE

1 (9-inch) pie crust
1 tablespoon soft butter
12 bacon slices
4 eggs
2 cups whipping cream
3/4 teaspoon salt
1/8 teaspoon nutmeg
1/4 pound natural Swiss cheese, shredded (1 cup)

Spread crust with soft butter; beat eggs, cream, salt, and nutmeg with wire whisk; stir in cheese and pour egg mixture into crust. Fry bacon until crisp and brown. Drain on paper towels and crumble; sprinkle in pie crust. Bake 15 minutes at 400 degrees; turn oven to 325 degrees and bake 35 minutes. Quiche is done when knife inserted in center comes out clean. Let stand 10 minutes before serving.

QUICK AND EASY BUCKWHEAT PANCAKES

1/2 cup bread crumbs
2-1/2 cups scalded milk
2 cups buckwheat flour
1/2 teaspoon salt
1/2 yeast cake
2 tablespoons molasses
1/4 teaspoon baking soda

Add bread crumbs and salt to scalded milk. Cool. When lukewarm add yeast and stir until yeast is dissolved. Add buckwheat flour and stir until smooth. Put in warm place overnight. In the morning add molasses and soda mixed with a little lukewarm water. Beat smooth. Bake on hot griddle.

These pancakes are delicious and more healthful than the regular kind. Your family will love them!

LUNCHEON TUNA IN TOAST CUPS

2 ribs celery, thinly sliced
1 medium onion, chopped
1 small green pepper, chopped
1 tablespoon vegetable oil
1 package white sauce mix
1 cup American cheese, cut into small cubes
1 (7-ounce) can tuna, drained and flaked
3 tablespoons pimiento, chopped
Toast cups (recipe follows)

In a skillet, cook celery, onion, and green pepper, in vegetable oil until tender. Prepare white sauce as instructed on package. Into the white sauce, stir the celery, onion, green pepper, cheese, tuna, and pimiento; heat until cheese melts and is hot and bubbly. Serve in warm toast cups.

Toast Cups:
Trim crusts from fresh wheat or white bread; spread lightly with soft butter. Press buttered side down into muffin cups. Bake 10-12 minutes in a 350 degree oven or until lightly toasted.

ELEGANT QUICHE LORRAINE

3 eggs, slightly beaten
1 cup light cream
5 slices bacon, crisply cooked and crumbled
3 tablespoons Dijon type mustard
1/4 cup finely minced onion
1 cup grated Swiss cheese
1/4 teaspoon salt
1/8 teaspoon pepper
1 unbaked 9-inch pie shell

Combine all ingredients, except pie shell. Pour into pie shell and bake in a pre-heated 375 degree oven for 35-40 minutes, or until knife inserted in filling comes out clean.

BACON ROLL-UPS
Makes 6 dozen

1/2 cup margarine
3 cups herb-seasoned stuffing mix
2 eggs, beaten
1/4 pound ground beef
1/4 pound hot sausage, crumbled
1 pound sliced bacon, cut slice into thirds

Melt margarine in 1 cup water in saucepan. Remove from heat. Combine with stuffing. Mix in large bowl, mixing well; chill. Add remaining ingredients except bacon, mixing well.

Shape into pecan-shaped balls. Wrap with bacon; secure with toothpicks. In baking dish, bake at 375 degrees for 35 minutes or until bacon is crisp.

CHEESE, HAM 'N OLIVE SWIRLS
Makes 45

1-one pound loaf frozen ready-dough
6 thin slices cooked ham (4 x 7 inches)
4 ounces softened cream cheese
6 tablespoons chopped olives (black or green)

Let frozen dough thaw until pliable. (To thaw dough in the microwave, wrap in plastic wrap and cook on lowest setting for six minutes, rotating occasionally.) On a lightly floured board, roll thawed dough out to a 14-inch square. Cut in half. Cover each half with three slices of meat. Spread each half with two ounces softened cream cheese and sprinkle with 3 tablespoons chopped olives.

Beginning with 14-inch sides, roll each half in jelly-roll fashion. Pinch long edge to seal. Cut rolls into 1/2 inch slices. Place slices on greased baking sheets. Let rise for 30 minutes. Bake in 350 degree oven for 15 minutes or until golden brown. Remove from pan immediately.

ZUCCHINI QUICHE
Serves 8

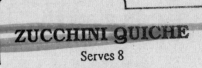

2 cups zucchini, sliced thin
1 cup onion, sliced
3 tablespoons oil
1 clove garlic, minced
1-1/2 teaspoons salt
4 eggs, beaten
1 cup milk
1 cup heavy cream
1/2 cup mozzarella cheese, grated
10-inch pie crust

Saute zucchini, onion, and garlic in oil. Season with salt. Cover pie crust with this mixture. Combine remaining ingredients and pour into pie shell. Bake in preheated 375 degree oven 30-35 minutes until custard is set. Serve hot.

COCONUT CRUNCH CEREAL
Yields 8 cups

3 cups rolled oats
1-1/2 cups shredded coconut
1/3 cup wheat germ
1 cup toasted, unsalted sunflower kernels
1/3 cup sesame seeds
1/4 cup soy flour
2 teaspoons cinnamon
1/4 cup honey
1/4 cup vegetable oil
1/2 cup water
1 cup almonds, chopped

Mix first seven ingredients. Heat honey and water; pour slowly over cereal. Pour oil over cereal and mix until crumbly. Pour mixture into a heavy, shallow baking pan that has been oiled. Bake in a 325 degree oven for 1-1/2 hours; stirring every 15 minutes. Add chopped almonds and bake for 30 additional minutes. Cereal should be crisp. Turn off the oven; cool. Store cereal mixture in a tightly covered container. Serve plain with fresh fruit or milk.

BACON PUFFED PANCAKES

Makes about 15

2 eggs
3/4 cup sweet milk
2-1/3 cups baking mix (I use Bisquick)
2 tablespoons sugar
1/4 cup oil
8 slices bacon, fried and crumbled

Beat eggs with mixer on high speed for about 5 minutes or until thick and lemon colored. Add remaining ingredients. Pour about 1/4 cup batter onto hot, ungreased griddle or use skillet. Cook as usual, turning once.

Kids love these because they are so light and have the bacon right inside. Awfully good on a cold day or any day!

OATMEAL PANCAKES

2 cups milk
1-1/2 cups quick rolled oats (uncooked)
1 cup sifted flour
2-1/2 teaspoons baking powder
1 teaspoon salt
2 tablespoons sugar
2 eggs, beaten
1/3 cup melted butter or margarine

Pour milk over oats and let stand 5 minutes. Sift together flour, baking powder, salt, and sugar. Add beaten eggs to rolled oats mixture. Add butter. Add sifted dry ingredients; mix quickly and lightly. If not used right away, store in refrigerator and mix again just before using. Keeps for several days in refrigerator.

POTATO PANCAKES

Serves 6

4 large potatoes
1 small onion
1/2 cup milk
1 teaspoon salt

1 egg, beaten
2 tablespoons flour
Fat for frying

Peel and grate potatoes; mix with onion and milk. Mix with salt, egg, and flour. Drop by tablespoonsful into hot fat in skillet. Brown on both sides and serve immediately.

POTATO PANCAKES WITH CHEDDAR

Serves 4

1 egg
1/3 cup milk
1/2 teaspoon salt
3 tablespoons flour
1 small onion, grated or chopped fine
1/2 cup grated Cheddar cheese
4 medium potatoes
Shortening or salad oil for frying
Applesauce

In bowl, beat egg; beat in milk, salt and flour. Add grated or chopped onion and grated cheese. Wash and peel potatoes. Grate directly into egg mixture, working rapidly as grated potatoes tend to darken.

In heavy skillet, heat shortening or salad oil, using enough to coat surface generously. Add potato mixture by tablespoons; cook until brown and crisp on both sides. Serve hot with applesauce.

SOUFFLE PANCAKES

Serves 6

6 egg yolks
1/3 cup pancake mix
1/3 cup sour cream
1/2 teaspoon salt
6 egg whites

Beat egg yolks until thick and lemon colored; fold in pancake mix, sour cream and salt, until well blended. Beat egg whites until stiff but not dry. Carefully fold into yolk mixture. Drop by tablespoonsful onto

hot, well greased griddle. Cook until golden brown on both sides.

Serve hot with butter, maple syrup, honey or favorite fruit sauce.

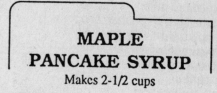

MAPLE PANCAKE SYRUP

Makes 2-1/2 cups

2 cups sugar
2 cups water
1 teaspoon maple flavoring

Combine sugar, water, and maple flavoring in small saucepan. Bring to boil; cook for 5 minutes. Bottle and refrigerate.

CORN FRITTERS

1 to 2 cups corn
1 egg, well beaten
1 teaspoon sugar
1/2 teaspoon salt
1 tablespoon butter, melted
2 teaspoons baking powder
1 cup flour
2/3 cup milk

Mix thoroughly. Drop spoonfuls of batter into fat in hot frying pan. Brown both sides.

BUFFET RYE SLICES

1 cup Swiss cheese, grated
1/4 cup bacon, cooked and crumbled
1/4 cup mayonnaise
1 teaspoon Worcestershire sauce
1/4 cup green onions, chopped
1/2 cup chopped ripe olives

Mix all ingredients and spread on party rye slices. Bake in 375 degree oven for 8-10 minutes; serve warm.

BREAKFAST EGG DISH

Serves 6

8 slices bread
1/2 cup melted butter
1 cup grated Cheddar cheese
Bacon or ham bits
Chopped green pepper
Sliced mushrooms, optional
2 cups milk
1/4 teaspoon salt
1/8 teaspoon pepper

Cut crust off the slices of bread and cube bread. Put in a 9x13 inch buttered pan. Pour the melted butter over the bread cubes; sprinkle on bacon bits, green pepper, and mushrooms.

Separate the eggs. Beat the yolks with the milk, salt, and pepper; pour over ingredients in the pan. Beat egg whites until stiff. Seal above mixture with egg whites. Cover and keep in the refrigerator overnight.

Bake at 325 degrees for 40-45 minutes.

EGG 'N' CHIPS

Serves 6

6 hard-boiled eggs, chopped
2 tablespoons chopped green pepper
1/2 teaspoon salt
2/3 cup mayonnaise or salad dressing
1-1/2 cups diced celery
3/4 cup coarsely chopped walnuts
1 teaspoon minced onion
1/4 teaspoon pepper
1 cup grated Cheddar cheese
1 cup crushed potato chips

Combine eggs, celery, walnuts, green pepper, onion, salt, pepper and salad dressing or mayonnaise. Toss lightly, but thoroughly, so ingredients are evenly moistened. Use additional salad dressing if needed. Place in a greased 1-1/2 - quart baking dish. Sprinkle with cheese and top with crushed chips. Bake at 375 degrees for about 25 minutes or until thoroughly heated and cheese has melted.

FOOLPROOF SCRAMBLED EGGS

Serves 3-4

6 eggs
1/3 cup light cream
3/4 teaspoon salt
1/8 teaspoon pepper
1/2 teaspoon Worcestershire sauce

Beat eggs; beat in cream and seasonings. Cook in upper part of double boiler, over hot water, until just set, stirring often. Serve at once with toast.

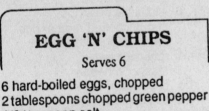

SCRAMBLED BAGEL ROYALE

Serves 2

2 bagels
1-1/2 tablespoons butter
  or margarine
4 eggs
2 tablespoons milk
3 tablespoons chopped onion
1/4 cup lox pieces or smoked salmon
2 ounces cream cheese
2 slices tomato garnish

Slice bagels in half horizontally. Lightly spread with one tablespoon of butter or margarine; toast lightly. Over medium high heat, saute chopped onion in remaining half tablespoon of butter or margarine until translucent. Beat eggs with milk; add to onions. Stir eggs. When eggs are almost set, add lox pieces and cream cheese that has been cut into small chunks; scramble in pan until cheese begins to melt.

Spoon mixture over bagels. Garnish with tomato slices.

TOLEDO HAM AND EGGS

Serves 6

1 cup chopped, cooked ham
1 tablespoon olive oil
2 cups cooked peas
2 canned pimentos, chopped
1/4 cup chopped green olives
Salt and pepper, if desired
6 eggs
2 tablespoons olive oil

Saute ham in olive oil for 2-3 minutes. Combine with peas, pimento, and olives. Heat well; add salt and pepper if desired. Put in the middle of a hot platter and surround with the eggs, which have been slowly cooked in the 2 tablespoons of olive oil.

TUNA STUFFED EGGS

Makes 24 halves

12 eggs
6 slices bacon
1 - 3-1/4 to 3-1/2 - ounce can tuna, drained and finely flaked
3/4 cup mayonnaise
1 tablespoon lemon juice
1/2 teaspoon hot pepper sauce
1/2 teaspoon salt

In 4-quart saucepan, place eggs and enough water to come one inch above tops of eggs over high heat; heat to boiling. Remove saucepan from heat; cover tightly and let eggs stand in hot water 15 minutes; drain.

Meanwhile, in 10-inch skillet, cook bacon until browned, remove to paper towel to drain. Crumble bacon, set aside.

Peel and slice eggs lengthwise in half. Remove yolks and place in medium bowl. With fork, finely mash yolks. Stir in tuna, mayonnaise, lemon juice, hot pepper sauce and salt until smooth. Pile egg yolk mixture into egg whites center. Sprinkle with bacon. Cover and refrigerate.

Casseroles
CREATIVE

AMISH-STYLE YUM-A-SETTA
Serves 6–8

2 pounds hamburger
  Salt and pepper to taste
2 tablespoons brown sugar
¼ cup chopped onion
1 (10¾-ounce) can tomato soup, undiluted
1 (10¾-ounce) can chicken soup, undiluted
1 (16-ounce) package egg noodles
1 (8-ounce) package processed cheese, such as Kraft or Velveeta

Brown hamburger with salt, pepper, brown sugar and onion. Add tomato soup. Cook egg noodles according to package; drain. Add cream of chicken soup. Layer hamburger mixture and noodle mixture in 9 x 12-inch casserole with processed cheese between layers. Bake at 350 degrees for 30 minutes.

TUNA BAKE
Serves 6–8

1 (1-pound, 1-ounce) can green peas
1½ cups diced potatoes
1 cup diced carrots
½ cup chopped onion
4 tablespoons butter
4 tablespoons flour
  Milk

1 teaspoon salt
⅛ teaspoon pepper
2 teaspoons soy sauce
2 (7-ounce) cans tuna, drained

Drain peas; reserve liquid. Cook potatoes, carrots and onions in reserved liquid for 8–10 minutes. Drain; save liquid. Melt butter in saucepan; stir in flour to make a smooth paste. Add milk to vegetable liquid to make 2 cups. Add to butter mixture. Cook over low heat; stir until mixture thickens. Add seasonings. Combine vegetables and tuna in buttered 2-quart casserole. Pour sauce over all (may be refrigerated overnight). To serve, bake covered in 325-degree oven for 1 hour.

HAM & RICE CASSEROLE
Serves 6

2 cups Spam, cut up in small squares
3 cups cooked rice *or* 2 cups uncooked rice
1 cup peas, drained
1 teaspoon salt
1 teaspoon prepared mustard
¼ teaspoon pepper
1 cup grated cheddar cheese
1 (10-ounce) can cheddar cheese soup, undiluted
¼ cup milk

Preheat oven to 350 degrees. Grease a 3-quart casserole. Combine ham, rice, peas, salt, mustard, pepper, ½ cup cheddar cheese, cheddar cheese soup and milk. Turn into casserole. Top with remaining ½ cup cheese. Bake 30 minutes, until bubbly. If chilled before baking, bake 1 hour.

ROMAN RICE

1 (2¼-ounce) can sliced black olives, drained
1 (11-ounce) can Green Giant Delicorn, drained
1 (15-ounce) can red kidney beans, drained
6 slices bacon strips
1 cup uncooked regular rice
1 small onion, chopped
1 teaspoon salt
⅛ teaspoon pepper
1½ cups water
½ cup chicken broth
¼ cup ketchup
  Dash minced garlic
1 (16-ounce) can tomatoes, undrained and cut up
½ cup mozzarella cheese, shredded
½ cup Monterey Jack cheese, shredded
¼ cup mixture Parmesan and Romano cheese, grated
1 tablespoon sugar

Fry bacon, saving 2 tablespoons of drippings. Cook rice and onion in it until onion is tender. Add drained Delicorn, beans, olives, seasonings and tomatoes. Stir well. Add grated cheese mixture, ketchup, water and broth. Cover and simmer for 30–45 minutes. Sprinkle shredded cheeses on top.

RANCHO SAUSAGE SUPPER
Serves 6

1 pound pork sausage
1 cup chopped onions
1 green pepper, chopped
2 cups stewed tomatoes
2 cups dairy sour cream
1 cup uncooked elbow macaroni
1 teaspoon chili powder
1 teaspoon salt
1 tablespoon sugar

In a large skillet fry sausage until pink color disappears. Drain. Add onions and green pepper; cook slowly for 5 minutes. Stir in tomatoes, sour cream, macaroni, chili powder, salt and sugar. Cover. Simmer 30 minutes, stirring frequently, until macaroni is done. Serve hot.

Serve with a green salad and hard rolls.

FAMILY GOULASH
Serves 4

4 ounces noodles
1 pound ground beef
1 medium onion, chopped
2 cups sliced celery
½ cup ketchup
1 (2½-ounce) jar sliced mushrooms
1 (14½-ounce) can tomatoes
1 teaspoon salt

Cook noodles as directed on package. While noodles cook, cook and stir ground beef and onion in large skillet until meat is brown and onion tender. Drain off fat. Stir in drained noodles, celery, ketchup, mushrooms (with liquid), tomatoes and salt. Cover; simmer 30–45 minutes.

MARDI GRAS MAGIC
Serves 6

1 pound red beans
1 pound smoked sausage, cut into bite-size pieces (kielbasa is fine)
1-2 stalks celery, chopped
1 onion, chopped
1 garlic clove, crushed
1 teaspoon sugar
1 teaspoon salt
1 bay leaf
8-10 cups water
1-1/2 cups uncooked rice (white, wild, or brown rice)

Rinse beans. In a large pot combine beans, sausage, celery, onion, garlic, sugar, salt, bay leaf, and 8-10 cups water. Bring to boil and stir frequently so mixture does not stick.

Reduce heat to low and cook, covered, until beans are tender, 1-1/2-2 hours. Add uncooked rice and cook until tender, about 15-20 minutes.

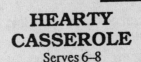

HEARTY CASSEROLE
Serves 6–8

1 (11-ounce) can cheddar cheese soup
1 (1-pound) can julienne carrots, drained (reserve 1/3 cup liquid)
3/4 teaspoon crushed rosemary
1/4 teaspoon pepper
1 (9-1/4-ounce) can tuna, drained and flaked
1 (15-ounce) can macaroni and cheese
1/4 cup minced parsley
1 (3-1/2-ounce) can french-fried onion rings

Heat oven to 375 degrees. Mix soup with reserved liquid from carrots. Stir in rosemary and pepper. Spread tuna in oblong baking dish, 11-1/2 x 7-1/2 x 1-1/2-inch. Layer with macaroni and cheese, carrots and parsley. Pour cheese soup mixture over layers. Bake, uncovered, for 30–35 minutes, or until bubbly. Top with onion rings and bake 5 minutes longer.

DRIED BEEF CASSEROLE
Serves 4–6

1 cup uncooked elbow macaroni
1 (10½-ounce) can condensed cream of mushroom soup
½ cup milk
1 cup shredded cheddar cheese
3 tablespoons finely chopped onion
¼ pound dried beef, cut into bite-size pieces
2 hard-cooked eggs, sliced

Heat oven to 350 degrees. Cook macaroni according to package directions. Blend soup and milk. Stir in cheese, onion, drained macaroni and dried beef; fold in eggs. Pour into an ungreased 1½-quart casserole. Cover; bake 30 minutes, or until heated through.

MEXICAN DINNER PRONTO
Serves 4

2 tablespoons vegetable oil
1 onion, chopped
1 (15-ounce) can tamales in chili gravy
1 (15-ounce) can chili without beans
1 (15-ounce) can chili with beans
¼ teaspoon oregano
½ cup Monterey Jack cheese, shredded

In a skillet heat oil; sauté onion until tender; transfer to ovenproof baking dish. Unwrap tamales; arrange ½ over onions. Add the 2 cans of chili; sprinkle with oregano; top with remaining tamales. Bake at 350 degrees for 30 minutes, or until bubbling hot. Remove from oven; sprinkle with cheese; bake 15 minutes longer, or until cheese has melted.

PORK CHOW MEIN
Serves 6

- 1 pound pork steak
- 3 tablespoons cooking oil
- 1 cup sliced onion
- 1 cup sliced celery
- 1 (8-ounce) can mushrooms
- 1 (8-ounce) can water chestnuts, drained and sliced
- 1 (13¾-ounce) can chicken broth
- ¼ cup soy sauce
- 1 (16-ounce) can chop suey vegetables, undrained
- 5–6 tablespoons cornstarch
- 1 chicken bouillon cube
  Hot cooked rice

Boil celery and onion in ½ cup water. Add 1 chicken bouillon cube. Cook until tender. Set aside. Slice partially frozen pork in thin, bite-size slices, across the grain. Preheat a large skillet or wok. Add cooking oil. Stir-fry pork for 2–3 minutes. Add bouillon mixture, mushrooms, water chestnuts, chicken broth, soy sauce and chop suey vegetables. Cook to a boil. Add cornstarch. Stir after each tablespoon of cornstarch. Serve over rice. Enjoy!! It is my favorite!.

ONION LOVERS' CASSEROLE
Serves 4–6

- 1 pound ground beef
- 3 large onions, sliced
- 1 large green pepper, chopped
- 1 (1-pound) can tomatoes
- ½ cup uncooked regular rice
- 1 teaspoon chili powder
- 1 teaspoon salt

Heat oven to 350 degrees. In large skillet, cook and stir ground beef until light brown; drain off fat. Add onions and green pepper; cook and stir until onion is tender. Stir in tomatoes, rice, chili powder and salt. Pour into an ungreased 2-quart casserole. Cover; bake 1 hour.

MACARONI HOT DISH
Serves 6

- 2 cups warm, cooked macaroni
- 1-1/2 cups grated cheese
- 1-1/2 cups bread crumbs
- 1 green pepper, diced
- 3 eggs, beaten
- 1 onion, diced
- 2 tablespoons margarine, melted
  Pepper and salt to taste
- 1-1/2 cups milk
- 1 can mushroom soup

Mix all ingredients, except mushroom soup, and place in pan set in hot water. Bake at 350 degrees for 45 minutes. Cut in squares and then pour over undiluted mushroom soup which has been heated.

NO-FUSS SHORTCUT PAELLA
Serves 6

- 2 cups cooked chicken, cut into 1-inch pieces
- 1-1/2 cups chicken broth
- 10 ounces shrimp, shelled
- 1 (8-1/2-ounce) can peas, drained
- 2 cups rice
- 1 (3-ounce) can mushrooms, sliced and drained
- 1 envelope onion soup mix
- 1 teaspoon paprika

Combine chicken, chicken broth, shrimp, peas, rice, mushrooms, onion soup mix and paprika. Pour into 3-quart casserole; bake at 350 degrees, covered, for 1-1/4 hours until rice is tender.

CHICKEN-IN-A-SHELL
Serves 6

- 6 baking potatoes
- 2 tablespoons butter or margarine
- 1 (10-3/4 ounce) can cream of chicken soup
- 1 cup Parmesan cheese, grated
- 3 tablespoons fresh parsley, chopped
- 1-1/2 cups cooked chicken, cubed

Bake potatoes until done; cut potatoes in half lengthwise; scoop out insides and reserve, leaving a thin shell. Mash potatoes with butter; add 1/2 cup cheese and remaining ingredients. Spoon into potato shells; sprinkle with remaining cheese. Arrange potatoes in shallow 3-quart baking dish. Bake 375 degrees for 15 minutes.

CHEESEBURGER PIE

- 1 package crescent rolls
- 1 pound hamburger
- 1/2 small onion, chopped
- 1/2 teaspoon oregano
- 1/4 teaspoon basil
  Salt and pepper to taste
- 1 (6-ounce) can tomato paste
- 1 (8-ounce) package Mozzarella cheese

Press crescent rolls into pie crust for 9-inch pan. Brown hamburger, onion, oregano, basil, salt, and pepper to taste. Drain. Add tomato paste; pour into pie shell. Top with cheese. Bake at 425 degrees for 15-20 minutes.

BAKED CHICKEN WITH ORANGE SOY SAUCE
Serves 4

- 1 (2-1/2 pound) chicken, cut up (skin removed)
- 2 tablespoons soy sauce
- 1/4 teaspoon salt
- 1/2 teaspoon celery seed
- 1/2 teaspoon garlic powder
- 1/4 teaspoon ground ginger
- 2/3 cup orange juice

Preheat oven to 400 degrees. Place chicken in 13x9-inch baking pan in a single layer. Top with soy sauce, salt, celery seed, garlic powder, and ginger. Pour orange juice over chicken. Bake 40-45 minutes, until juices run clear when chicken is pierced with a fork. (220 calories per serving)

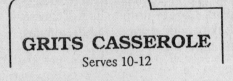

GRITS CASSEROLE
Serves 10-12

1 pound sausage
1/2 cup chopped green peppers
1 cup chopped onion
1 cup chopped celery
1 cup grits, uncooked
4 cups water
1 teaspoon salt
1 can cream of chicken soup
1 cup grated cheese

Preheat oven to 375 degrees. Brown sausage. Add peppers, onion, celery, and sauté. Cook grits in 4 cups water with 1 teaspoon salt. Combine cooked grits with sausage, peppers, onion, and celery. Pour mixture into 2-quart buttered casserole. Spread soup on top and sprinkle with cheese. Bake 30 minutes.

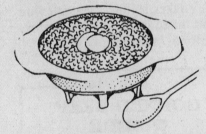

BEEF-ONION RING CASSEROLE
Serves 4–6

1-1/2–2 pounds ground chuck
Salt and pepper
1 can condensed cheddar cheese soup
1 can condensed cream of mushroom soup
1 package frozen Tater Tots
1 package frozen onion rings

Press raw meat into bottom of casserole; season with salt and pep-per. Combine the 2 soups and spread half over meat. Add Tater Tots. Pour rest of soup over Tater Tots. Top with onion rings. If canned onion rings are used, stir them into last half of soup mixture. Bake at 350 degrees for 1–1-1/2 hours.

JIFFY MINESTRONE
Serves 8

4   cups coarsely chopped cabbage (½ medium-size head)
1   medium onion, coarsely chopped
¼   cup parsley, chopped
1   clove garlic, chopped
1   teaspoon salt
1   teaspoon oregano
¼   teaspoon pepper
3   tablespoons oil
5   cups beef broth
1   (16-ounce) can toma-toes *or* 2 cups chopped fresh
¼   pound spaghetti, broken up
1   medium zucchini, sliced
1   (16-ounce) can red kidney beans

In Dutch oven, over medium heat, sauté cabbage, onion, parsley, garlic ,salt, oregano and pepper in oil, stir-ring often, 5 minutes, or until cabbage is crisp-tender. Add broth and toma-toes; bring to boil. Stir in spaghetti, zucchini and beans. Cook, stirring oc-casionally, for 10 minutes, or until spaghetti is of desired doneness. (200 calories per serving)

ZUCCHINI AND CHICKEN SKILLET

2 medium zucchini, sliced
2 tablespoons shortening
½ cup tomatoes, drained
2 pounds chicken
1 can cream of celery soup
1 teaspoon paprika
1 teaspoon basil
Salt and pepper to taste

In skillet brown chicken in shorten-ing. Pour off excess fat. Add soup, tomatoes and seasonings. Cover. Cook on low heat for 30 minutes. Add zuc-chini. Cook about 15 minutes longer.

SMOKED SAUSAGE AND SAUERKRAUT
Serves 4

1 pound smoked sausage
1 can sauerkraut
1 tablespoon cooking oil
1/2 pint water
1 potato, grated
1 carrot, grated
Pinch salt
1/3 cup sugar
2 onions, chopped

Heat oil in skillet and fry chopped onions; add sauerkraut and simmer for 2 minutes. Add water and sau-sage; cook until done. Add grated potato, salt, sugar, and grated carrot. Cook 4-5 additional minutes.

PIZZA RICE PIE
Serves 4-5

2-2/3 cups cooked rice
1/3 cup minced onion
2 eggs, beaten
2 tablespoons melted butter or
   margarine
1 (8-ounce) can tomato sauce with
   cheese
1/4 teaspoon oregano
1/4 teaspoon basil
1 cup shredded mozzarella cheese
1 (4-1/2-ounce) package sliced
   pepperoni or salami
1/2 cup sliced stuffed olives

Mix together rice, onion, eggs, and melted butter. Line a 12-inch pizza pan with rice mixture and bake 12 minutes at 350 degrees, or until set. Spread tomato sauce with cheese over rice crust. Sprinkle with spices and cheese. Top with pepperoni and olives. Bake at 350 degrees for 20-25 minutes. After removing from oven, allow to stand a few minutes before serving.

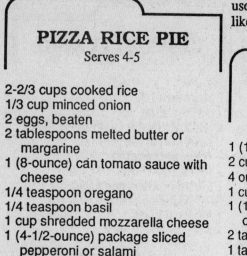

SAUCY PIZZA SURPRISE
Serves 6

3 cups cooked rice
2 cups (8 ounces)
   cheese, shredded
½ teaspoon basil
2 eggs, beaten
2 (8-ounce) cans tomato
   sauce
½ teaspoon oregano
½ teaspoon garlic powder

Combine rice, eggs and 1 cup cheese. Press firmly into 2 (9-inch) pans. Spread evenly. Bake at 450 degrees for 20 minutes. Combine tomato sauce and seasonings. Spread evenly over rice crust. Top with remaining cheese. Bake 10 minutes longer. *Note:* Other ingredients, such as cooked sausage, green pepper, mushrooms, etc., may be added before baking.

This pizza is great. A good way to use leftover rice, which makes a crust like deep-dish.

CHICKEN-BROCCOLI BAKE
Serves 4–5

1 (10-ounce) package broccoli cuts
2 cups chopped, cooked chicken
4 ounces medium noodles
1 cup sour cream
1 (10 3/4-ounce) can cream of
   chicken soup
2 tablespoons chopped pimiento
1 tablespoon minced onion
1 teaspoon salt
1/2 teaspoon Worcestershire sauce
1 tablespoon melted butter
1/2 cup soft bread crumbs
1 cup grated Swiss cheese

Prepare broccoli as directed on package; drain. Cook noodles and drain. Combine chicken, sour cream, soup, pimiento, onion, salt and Worcestershire sauce. Add butter to bread crumbs and mix well. Place noodles in greased, shallow 2-quart baking dish. Sprinkle with 1/3 of the cheese. Add broccoli. Sprinkle with 1/2 of the remaining cheese. Pour on the chicken mixture. Sprinkle with rest of cheese, and then with bread crumbs. Bake at 350 degrees for 1 hour.

BEEFY CASSEROLE
Serves 4

1 large eggplant
1 medium onion, chopped
2 tablespoons butter
1 pound ground beef
Salt and pepper to taste
1 bay leaf

Peel eggplant and cut into slices 1 or 1 1/2 inches thick. Cook in boiling, salted water for 10–15 minutes, or just until tender. Drain. Sauté onion in butter until soft; add beef and seasonings. Cook until meat is nicely browned. Place slices of eggplant in a greased baking dish. Remove bay leaf and add meat/onion mixture to eggplant. Cover with thin slices of cheese. Bake at 400 degrees for 20 minutes, or until cheese is melted.

TOWN AND COUNTRY CASSEROLE

1 package French's Real Cheese
   Scalloped Potatoes
1 pound smoked kielbasa or Polish
   sausage, cut in 1/4-inch slices
1 cup thinly sliced carrots
1 tablespoon freeze-dried chives
1 cup soft bread crumbs
1 tablespoon butter or margarine
1 tablespoon parsley flakes

Follow microwave method on package, except *increase* water to 3 cups and add carrots; microwave, covered, for 15 minutes. Add seasoning mix, milk, sausage, and chives. Microwave, covered, for 3-5 minutes. Combine crumbs, butter and parsley flakes; sprinkle casserole with crumb mixture; microwave, uncovered, for 5-7 minutes.

CORNED BEEF QUICHE

1 (9-inch) pie shell, unbaked
1 (15-ounce) can corned beef hash
1 small onion, finely shredded
1 cup Swiss cheese, shredded
2 teaspoons flour
1/4 teaspoon salt
Dash allspice
2 eggs, slightly beaten
1-1/4 cups milk

Pre-bake pie shell at 375 degrees for 7 minutes; remove from oven; set aside. Reduce oven temperature to 325 degrees. Crumble corned beef hash into pie shell; sprinkle onion over meat; top with Swiss cheese. Combine remaining ingredients; pour over hash and cheese. Bake 35-40 minutes, or until set. Cool 20 minutes before serving.

VEGETABLE CASSEROLE

1 can French-style green beans, drained
1/2 cup chopped celery
1/2 cup chopped green pepper
1/2 cup sour cream
1 can white shoepeg corn, drained
1/2 cup chopped onion
1/4 cup grated sharp cheese
1-1/2 cups crushed cheese crackers
1 can cream of mushroom soup
1/4 cup margarine
1/2 cup sliced almonds

Mix drained beans, corn, celery, green pepper, and onion. Alternate one layer vegetables with a layer of soup, grated cheese, then sour cream. Bake 25 minutes at 350 degrees.

Melt margarine and stir in crackers and almonds. Spread this on top of casserole and cook for 10 more minutes.

CORN AND SAUSAGE CASSEROLE

1 pound sausage
1/4 cup bell pepper, chopped
1 can whole kernel corn, drained
1 large can evaporated milk
2 tablespoons flour
1/4 teaspoons salt
1-1/2 cups grated cheese

Brown sausage and pepper until sausage is cooked. Drain and save 2 tablespoons sausage drippings. Add sausage to casserole dish with corn. Blend sausage drippings with flour in skillet over medium heat. Add milk and salt; simmer 2-3 minutes until thickened, stirring constantly. Pour over sausage and corn mixture; stir together. Top with grated cheese. Bake in a 350 degree oven for 25-30 minutes until bubbly.

SPAGHETTI RING

1/2 pound spaghetti
2 cups hot milk
1/4 cup butter
2 cups shredded Cheddar cheese
2 cups soft bread crumbs
2 eggs, well beaten
2 tablespoons minced onions
2 tablespoons minced parsley
2 tablespoons minced pimento
1 teaspoon salt
1/4 teaspoon pepper

Cook and drain spaghetti. Combine remaining ingredients. Mix thoroughly. Pour into well-greased 10-inch ring mold. Set in pan of hot water 1-inch deep. Bake at 350 degrees until set, about 30 minutes. Unmold on hot platter. Fill center with choice of creamed chicken, creamed seafood or any combination of creamed vegetables.

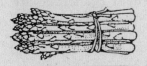

HASH BROWN POTATO CASSEROLE

1 (32-ounce) package frozen hash brown potatoes
1/2 cup melted margarine
8 ounces shredded Cheddar cheese
1 cup onions, chopped
1 pint sour cream
1 can cream of chicken soup
1 teaspoon salt
1/2 teaspoon garlic salt
1 cup corn flakes
1/4 cup melted margarine

Partially defrost hash browns. Mix potatoes, 1/2 cup margarine, cheese, onions, sour cream, soup, and spices. Put into greased 9 x 13-inch dish. Sprinkle corn flakes on top of potatoes; pour the 1/4 cup margarine over corn flakes. Bake uncovered in 350 degree oven for 1 hour and 15 minutes.

LAZY DAY LIMA BEAN CASSEROLE

2 cups grated American cheese
2/3 cup undiluted evaporated milk
1/2 teaspoon prepared mustard
2 cups cooked, large lima beans
2 medium tomatoes
Salt and pepper to taste

Combine cheese, milk and mustard. Cook and stir over hot water until cheese melts and sauce is smooth. Put lima beans into ovenproof casserole. Cover with 3/4 of sauce. Top casserole with tomato slices, salt and pepper and the remaining sauce. Bake in a 375 degree oven for 25 minutes or until lightly browned and bubbly on top.

SKILLET MACARONI AND CHEESE

Serves 6 to 8

1/4 cup butter or margarine
1 cup chopped onion
1 tablespoon all-purpose flour
1-1/2 teaspoons salt
1/4 teaspoon oregano
7 or 8 ounce package elbow macaroni
3-1/2 cups milk
2 cups shredded Cheddar cheese

Melt butter in skillet; add onion and saute until tender. Stir in flour, salt and oregano; add macaroni and milk. Cover and bring to boil; reduce heat and simmer 15 minutes or until macaroni is tender, stirring occasionally. Add cheese and stir until cheese is melted (do not boil).

CREAMY CHIPPED BEEF CASSEROLE

2 packages chipped beef
1/2 package (16-ounce) frozen hash brown's (thawed)
1 can cream of mushroom soup
1 cup evaporated milk
2 tablespoon Crisco
1 can Durkee French fried onion rings

Snip beef in bite size pieces. Brown in Crisco until edges curl; drain. Mix milk and soup. Add beef, hash brown's and 1/2 can onion rings. Place in 2-quart casserole dish; bake covered for 30 minutes in 350 degree oven. Remove lid; crumble remainder of onion rings over top. return to oven for 5 to 10 minutes. **NOTE:** Also good with hamburger or leftover ham.

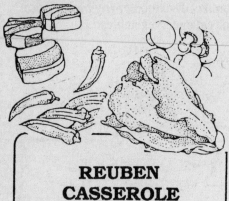

REUBEN CASSEROLE

5 cups herb seasoned croutons
1 cup hot water
1 (8-ounce) package Swiss cheese (sliced), set aside 2 slices
6-9 slices of canned corn beef
1/2 cup melted margarine
2 cups sauerkraut (drained)
1 teaspoon caraway seeds (if desired)

In a large bowl, put in croutons and margarine; toss gently. Add hot water, sauerkraut, and caraway seeds. Set aside 1 cup of mixture. Grease casserole dish. Layer crouton mixture, corn beef, and cheese slices. End up with the 1 cup of crouton mixture. Cover and bake in a 350 degree oven for 20 minutes. Top with the 2 cheese slices and bake uncovered 10 minutes until cheese melts.

DRESSING CASSEROLE

Serves 12

2 cups diced celery
1 clove garlic
12 cups toasted bread cubes
4 cups cubed corn bread
1/2 teaspoon pepper
4 cups turkey or chicken broth
1-1/2 cups chopped onion
1/2 cup butter
1 tablespoon sage
2 tablespoons salt
1 (13 ounce) can evaporated milk
2 eggs, slightly beaten

Cook celery, onion, and garlic in butter until light brown. Crumble bread cubes and corn bread in large bowl. Add sage, salt, and pepper. Stir celery mixture into bread cubes. Add evaporated milk, broth, and eggs. Mix well. Pour into greased 9 x 13" pan. Bake at 325 degrees for 35 to 40 minutes.

This is a good way to use up leftover corn bread. Recipe can easily be cut in half and baked in an 8 x 8" pan for smaller families. Bouillon may be substituted for the broth.

NIGHT BEFORE CASSEROLE

Serves 10

2 cups macaroni, cooked
2 cups chicken, turkey, *or* tuna (if using chicken or turkey, it should be cooked)
2 cans mushroom soup
1/2 pound American cheese, cut into fine pieces
3 eggs, hard-cooked, cut into small pieces
2 cups milk
Chopped pimiento and green pepper to taste

Mix all ingredients together and refrigerate overnight or for at least 6-12 hours. Remove from refrigerator and bake for 1 hour in 350 degree oven.

PENNYWISE CASSEROLE

1 pound lean stewing beef, cut into 1" cubes
(Lamb or pork can also be used for this recipe)
Salt and pepper
1/3 cup vegetable oil
2 medium onions, sliced
2 teaspoons honey
1/2 teaspoon ground cinnamon
1/2 teaspoon ground nutmeg
1/2 teaspoon parsley
1/2 teaspoon basil
8 ounce can tomatoes
4 slices wheat (or white) bread, buttered and quartered

Lightly salt and pepper beef. In skillet over moderate heat, fry beef cubes until browned. Transfer meat to ovenproof dish. In the same skillet, fry onions for 5 minutes until soft, but not browned. Stir in remaining ingredients (except bread); bring to a boil. Pour over meat; cover. Bake in a 350 degree oven for 1 hour. Taste and adjust seasonings, if necessary. Arrange bread slices neatly on top; return to oven for 30 minutes (or until the bread is golden and crisp).

MEXICAN COMBO

1 pound ground beef
1 medium onion, diced
1 medium green pepper, diced
2 tablespoons chili powder
1-1/2 cups hot water
1/2 pound sharp cheese, diced
1 can red kidney beans
Salt & pepper to taste

Brown ground beef, onion, and pepper in a large skillet, using fork to break up meat. Mix chili powder and hot water; pour over meat mixture. Simmer 5 to 10 minutes. Add cheese, beans with juice, salt, and pepper. Simmer until cheese melts. Be careful not to let it burn.

PORK CHOP CASSEROLE
Serves 4

6 pork chops
1 teaspoon salt
1/8 teaspoon pepper
4 medium apples, peeled and sliced
1 cup water
4 medium sweet potatoes, peeled and sliced
1 teaspoon Worcestershire sauce
1 medium onion, chopped

Wipe chops; brown them in a little fat in frying pan. Place chops in a large casserole; sprinkle with half the salt and pepper. Place apples and sweet potatoes in layers on chops and sprinkle with remaining salt and pepper. Sauté onion in the same frying pan where chops were browned. Add water and Worcestershire sauce. Mix and pour over chops, apples and potatoes. Cover and bake 1-1/2 hours in a moderate 375-degree oven.

LEMON DILLED BEEF

2 1/2 pounds stewing beef
1/2 cup butter
2 1/2 cups chopped celery
1 1/2 cups chopped onion
1 cup chopped green pepper
1/3 cup lemon juice
2 cups beef stock
3 cloves garlic, finely chopped
1 1/2 teaspoons dill weed
Salt to taste
1 1/2 cups sour cream
3 tablespoons butter, softened
3 tablespoons flour
1 medium package noodles

Lightly brown beef in butter. Add vegetables, liquid and seasoning. Cover and simmer on low for 2 hours. Add sour cream and simmer, uncovered, for 30 minutes. Combine flour and butter; add by spoonfuls to bubbling mixture. Simmer 10 minutes and serve on prepared noodles.

DELI REUBEN CASSEROLE
Serves 6.

3 cups sauerkraut, drained
1-1/2 cups tomatoes, drained
2 tablespoons Thousand Island dressing
2 tablespoons butter or margarine
3 packages corned beef, shredded
1 (10-ounce) can refrigerated flaky biscuits
3 rye crackers, crushed
1/4 teaspoon caraway seeds

Spread sauerkraut in a 13x9x2-inch baking dish; arrange tomatoes on top; spread with dressing; dot with butter. Place shredded corned beef and cheese over all. Separate each biscuit into halves; arrange over casserole. Sprinkle with the rye crackers and caraway seeds. Bake at 350 degrees, 12 minutes, or until biscuits are flaky and golden.

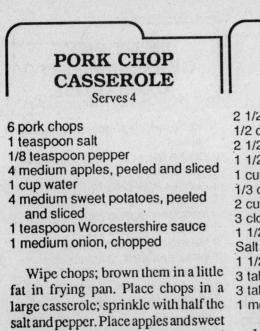

HAM & NOODLE BAKE

2 cups cooked ham, cubed
1/4 cup onion, chopped
1/8 teaspoon thyme leaves, crushed
2 tablespoons margarine
1 (10-3/4-ounce) can cream of chicken soup
3/4 cup water
2 cups cooked noodles (5 ounces)
1 cup canned, cut green beans, drained
1/2 cup shredded cheddar cheese

In saucepan, brown ham, cook onion with thyme in margarine until tender. Stir in remaining ingredients, except cheese. Pour into 2-quart casserole. Bake at 350 degrees for 30 minutes. Top with cheese; bake until cheese melts, 8 minutes longer. If refrigerated before cooking, bake 45 minutes longer.

This is made quickly and is nice for a company dinner.

CHICKEN AND BROCCOLI RICE CASSEROLE
Serves 6

1/2 cup chopped onions
1/2 cup sliced mushrooms
1 tablespoon butter
2 cups hot, cooked rice
2 cups cubed chicken breast
2 cups chopped, fresh broccoli (steamed) *or*
1 (10-ounce) package frozen broccoli, thawed
1 (10-3/4-ounce) can cream of mushroom soup, condensed
1/2 cup (2 ounces) shredded cheddar cheese

Simmer onions and mushrooms in large skillet with butter until tender. Stir in rice, chicken, broccoli, and soup. Pour into buttered 1-1/2-quart baking dish. Top with cheese. Bake at 350 degrees for 20-25 minutes.

My husband is fussy about casseroles, but he *loves* this one.

CHICKEN CASSEROLE SUPREME

3 cups cooked chicken, deboned
1 (6-ounce) package Uncle Ben's rice, cooked
1 can cream of celery soup, undiluted
1 can cream of chicken soup, undiluted
1 can French-style green beans, drained
1 medium jar pimientos, sliced
1 cup mayonnaise
1 small can water chestnuts. sliced
Salt and pepper to taste

Mix all ingredients together and pour into 3-quart casserole. Bake 25–30 minutes at 350 degrees.

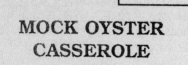

MOCK OYSTER CASSEROLE

Serves 6

1 large eggplant
1 cup cracker crumbs (approx. 25 soda crackers, crushed)
2 eggs
1/2 cup milk
3 tablespoons butter
1/4 cup chopped celery
1/4 cup chopped green pepper
1/4 cup chopped onion
1 (11 ounce) can mushroom soup
Tabasco sauce to taste

Peel eggplant and cut into cubes. Boil eggplant for 3 minutes in salt water; set aside. Place 1/3 of the crushed crumbs in a buttered 2 quart casserole dish; add 1/2 the eggplant. Repeat layering the cracker crumbs and eggplant. Beat eggs slightly, add 1/2 cup milk, mushroom soup, peppers, onions, celery and Tabasco sauce, mixing well. Pour slowly over eggplant mixture. Dot with butter. Cover and bake at 375 degrees for 30 minutes. Uncover and add more milk if needed. Bake 15 minutes more uncovered, until golden brown.

RICE OLE

Serves 3-4

2 slices bacon
1/3 cup chopped onion
1/4 cup finely chopped green pepper
1-1/2 cups water
2 envelopes Lipton Tomato Cup-a-Soup
1 cup uncooked instant rice
1/2 teaspoon garlic salt

In skillet cook bacon until crisp; drain, reserving 2 tablespoons drippings. Crumble bacon; set aside. Add onion and green pepper to skillet; cook until tender. Add water and bring to boil. Stir in Cup-a-Soup, uncooked rice, garlic salt, and crumbled bacon; cover and remove from heat. Let stand for 5 minutes.

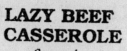

LAZY BEEF CASSEROLE

Serves 4

1 pound lean beef chuck, cut into 1-1/2-inch cubes
1/2 cup red wine
1 (10-1/2-ounce) can consomme, undiluted
1/4 cup all-purpose flour
Freshly ground black pepper, to taste
1 medium onion, chopped
1/4 cup fine dry bread crumbs
1/4 teaspoon rosemary

Put meat in a casserole with the wine, consomme, pepper, rosemary, and onion. Mix flour and bread crumbs and stir into the liquid. Cover and bake at 300 degrees, about 3 hours. Serve with rice or noodles. (206 calories per serving)

EASY BEEF GOULASH

Serves 4

1 to 2 tablespoons vegetable oil
1 pound ground beef (chuck)
3 cups uncooked medium egg noodles
2 cups water
1 (8-ounce) can tomato sauce
1 envelope dry onion soup mix

Heat oil in a medium-size skillet over medium heat. Add ground beef and cook until lightly browned, stirring occasionally with a fork to break up meat. Drain off any excess fat. Sprinkle uncooked noodles over meat. Combine water, tomato sauce, and onion soup mix. Pour over noodles in skillet. Do not stir. Cover and bring to a boil. Reduce heat to moderately low and simmer about 30 minutes, or until noodles are tender. Stir and serve.
Note: You may have to add a small amount of water if the noodles seem to be sticking. This is very easy and quick for those hectic days.

GERMAN POTATO CASSEROLE

6 medium-size potatoes, peeled and sliced
1 pound hot pork sausage, cooked and drained
8 ounces sour cream
2 teaspoons dry onion soup mix
2 teaspoons lemon juice
1 can cream of mushroom soup
2 teaspoons Dijon mustard
1 can sauerkraut, washed and drained
1 cup buttered bread crumbs
Salt and pepper to taste

Peel, wash, and slice potatoes. Boil in salted water until tender. Mix sour cream, dry onion soup mix, mushroom soup, lemon juice, and mustard. Heat sauerkraut in 2 tablespoons sausage drippings. Alternate layers of potatoes, cream mixture, and sauerkraut. Put bread crumbs on top and bake in 350-degree oven until hot and bubbly, about 20-25 minutes.

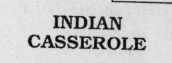

INDIAN CASSEROLE

1 can hominy, drained
1 pound ground beef
1/2 cup chopped onion
1/2 cup chopped green pepper
1-3/4 cups canned tomatoes
1/2 teaspoon salt
1/4 teaspoon pepper
1 cup grated cheese

Brown beef, salt, onions, and green pepper. Add tomatoes and hominy. Pour into buttered casserole and bake at 350 degrees for 40 minutes. Remove from oven and sprinkle cheese on top. Return to oven and bake 15 minutes.
Note: I tried this recipe and cooked it in an electric skillet. I cooked it on low until thick, then placed slices of cheese over the top and put lid of skillet on until cheese melted. I served it with French bread and a cottage cheese and peach salad.

YELLOW SQUASH CASSEROLE

6-8 Servings

2 pounds yellow squash, sliced (6 cups)
1/4 cup chopped onion
1 can cream of chicken soup
1 cup sour cream
1 cup shredded carrots
1 (8-ounce) package herb-seasoned stuffing mix
1/2 cup melted margarine

Cook squash and onion in boiling, salted water for 5 minutes; drain. Mix soup and sour cream. Stir in the carrots; fold in squash and onion. Combine stuffing mix and margarine. Spread half stuffing mixture in lightly buttered 12 x 7-1/2-inch baking dish; spoon vegetable mixture over stuffing. Sprinkle remaining stuffing mixture over vegetables. Bake in preheated 350 degree oven for 25-30 minutes, until heated thoroughly.

PINTO BEAN CASSEROLE

Serves 4-6

1 to 1-1/2 pounds ground beef
1/2 cup chopped onion
1/2 cup chopped green pepper
1 clove garlic, minced
1 (15-ounce) can tomato sauce
2 teaspoons chili powder
1 teaspoon salt
1 cup cooked rice
1 (15-ounce) can pinto beans
1-1/2 cups grated Cheddar cheese

Brown beef, onion, green pepper, and garlic. Blend in tomato sauce, chili powder, and salt. In greased 2-quart casserole, layer part of meat sauce, beans, half of cheese, and remainder of meat sauce. Top with other half cheese. Bake 350 degrees for 15-20 minutes. Let stand a few minutes before serving.

Rolls or garlic toast and salad with this casserole make a complete meal.

YAM AND CRANBERRY CASSEROLE

Serves 8

1 (40 ounce) can yams, drained
3 cups fresh, whole cranberries
1-1/2 cups sugar
1 small orange, sliced
1/2 cup pecan halves
1/4 cup orange juice or brandy
3/4 teaspoon cinnamon
1/4 teaspoon nutmeg
1/4 teaspoon mace

Combine cranberries, sugar, orange slices, pecans, orange juice, and spices in 2-quart casserole. Bake uncovered at 375 degrees for 30 minutes. Stir yams into cranberry mixture. Bake until heated through—about 15 minutes.

Nice to serve with your holiday turkey.

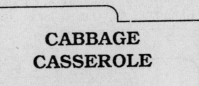

CABBAGE CASSEROLE

1 medium onion, chopped
3 tablespoons butter
1/2 pound ground beef
1 teaspoon salt
1/8 teaspoon pepper
6 cups chopped cabbage
1 can tomato soup

Sauté meat and onion. Place 3 cups cabbage in 2 quart casserole; cover with meat mixture; top with remaining cabbage. Pour soup over top. Bake 350 degrees for 1 hour.

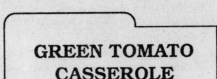

GREEN TOMATO CASSEROLE

4 large green tomatoes, sliced
Salt and pepper to taste
3/4 cup Cheddar cheese, grated
1 tablespoon butter

Preheat oven to 400 degrees. Butter casserole dish. Lay 1/3 of tomato slices on bottom. Sprinkle with salt and pepper and 1/4 cup of cheese. Repeat with remaining slices. Top with 1/2 cup of cheese and dot with butter. Bake covered 40 to 60 minutes. Brown under broiler if desired.

This is a simple way to use green tomatoes and it tastes great.

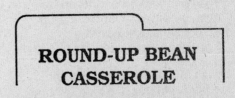

ROUND-UP BEAN CASSEROLE

1 pound ground beef
1 can red (kidney) beans
1 can butter beans
1 can pork and beans
1/2 cup catsup
3/4 cup brown sugar
1 teaspoon mustard
2 tablespoons vinegar
Chopped onion and bell pepper (optional)

Brown beef; season with salt and pepper. (Add onion and bell pepper at this time.) Combine with remaining ingredients. Put into casserole dish. Bake about 1 hour at 350 degrees.

This is also good cooked in a slow pot. It is simple to prepare, and with a salad makes a quick meal.

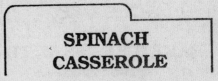

SPINACH CASSEROLE

1 package frozen spinach
1 (8 ounce) package cream cheese
1 can cream of mushroom soup
1 can French onion rings
6 tablespoons butter or margarine
Cracker crumbs

Cook spinach according to package directions. Heat soup and cream cheese to soften. Mix with spinach; add onion rings. Pour into casserole. Melt butter; add enough cracker crumbs to absorb butter. Spread buttered crumbs on top and bake at 350 degrees for 20 minutes.

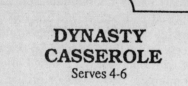

DYNASTY CASSEROLE
Serves 4-6

1 (8-ounce) can water chestnuts
  sliced
1 (3-ounce) can chow mein noodles
1 carrot sliced
1 can bean sprouts, drained
1 can cream of mushroom soup
1 cup half-and-half cream
1 cup chopped celery (cut on the diagonal)
Dash of hot—pepper sauce and
  black pepper
2 tablespoons soy sauce
1-1/2 cups cooked chicken chunks
  or strips
1/4 cup minced green onion
3/4 cup chopped cashew nuts
Hot cooked rice

Preheat oven to 350 degrees and
set aside 1/2 cup of crisp chow mein
noodles. Mix all other ingredients
(except rice) in a large buttered 2-
quart casserole or long baking dish.
Bake, uncovered, for about 30 minutes. Sprinkle remaining chow mein
noodles on top of casserole and bake
10 minutes longer. Serve casserole
over hot cooked rice. Pass the soy
sauce at the table.

CHILI RELLENOS CASSEROLE

16 ounces Ortega whole green.
  chilies
12 ounces Cheddar cheese, grated
12 ounces Monterey Jack cheese,
  grated
2 eggs, separated
2 egg whites
3 tablespoons flour
12 ounces evaporated milk
14 ounces Ortega green chili salsa

Remove seeds from chilies; flatten
and drain. In a greased 9x9-inch pan,
layer half the chilies and top with
Cheddar cheese. Cover with rest of
chilies and top with Monterey Jack
cheese. Mix egg yolks, flour, and
milk. Whip the 4 egg whites until
stiff, then fold into yolk mixture. Pour
the whole mixture over chilies and
cheese. Bake in a 325 degree oven for
45 minutes. Pour green chili salsa
over the top and return to oven for 30
minutes. After baking, allow to sit for
10 minutes. Cut into squares.

BACON MACARONI 'N CHEESE
Serves 4-6

3/4 pound bacon, diced
1 cup onions, chopped
1 quart milk
2 teaspoons celery salt
1/2 teaspoon pepper
1/4 teaspoon Tabasco sauce
2 cups elbow macaroni
1 cup cheese, grated
1/2 cup pimiento, chopped

In large skillet, cook bacon and
onion over low heat for 15 minutes.
Drain drippings. Add milk, celery salt,
pepper, and Tabasco. Heat to boiling;
gradually add macaroni, so that milk
continues to boil. Simmer, uncovered, for 20 minutes, stirring often.
Add cheese and pimiento; stir until
cheese melts. Serve hot.

BAKED BEANS WITH SAUSAGE
Serves 6

1/4 cup molasses
2 tablespoons prepared mustard
2 tablespoons vinegar
2 teaspoons Worcestershire sauce
1/4 teaspoon Tabasco sauce
2 (1-pound) cans baked beans
1 (20-ounce) can apple slices
1 pound pork sausage links, cooked

Mix all ingredients, except sausages, and place in a bean pot. Bake at
350 degrees for 40 minutes. Top with
hot sausages and serve.

This is a complete meal with French
or garlic bread and a crisp salad.

SHRIMP CASSEROLE
Serves 4-5

1 can condensed mushroom soup
1/2 cup milk
2 tablespoons minced parsley
1 tablespoon instant minced onion
1/2 teaspoon salt
2-3 dashes Tabasco sauce
2-1/2 cups cooked rice
2 cups cooked shrimp
1 cup corn flakes
2 tablespoons melted butter
2 tablespoons toasted slivered
  almonds (optional)

Combine soup, milk, parsley, onions and seasonings. Add rice and
shrimp; mix thoroughly. Pour into
greased 10x6x2-inch baking dish.
Slightly crush corn flakes; combine
with melted butter and almonds;
sprinkle over top of casserole. Bake at
375 degrees for about 20 minutes or
until bubbly.

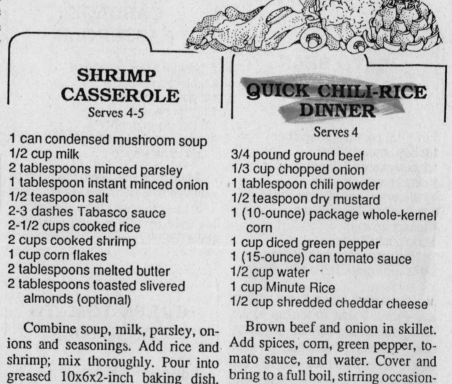

QUICK CHILI-RICE DINNER
Serves 4

3/4 pound ground beef
1/3 cup chopped onion
1 tablespoon chili powder
1/2 teaspoon dry mustard
1 (10-ounce) package whole-kernel
  corn
1 cup diced green pepper
1 (15-ounce) can tomato sauce
1/2 cup water
1 cup Minute Rice
1/2 cup shredded cheddar cheese

Brown beef and onion in skillet.
Add spices, corn, green pepper, tomato sauce, and water. Cover and
bring to a full boil, stirring occasionally. Stir in rice; reduce heat; cover
and simmer for 5 minutes. Sprinkle
with cheese.

Good for when time is limited;
takes only 20 minutes to prepare.

MACARONI LOAF

2 cups cooked macaroni
1/2 cup bread crumbs
1/2 cup grated cheese
3 tablespoons butter
1/2 tablespoon chopped parsley
1/2 tablespoon chopped onion
1/2 teaspoon salt
1/2 cup milk
1 egg, beaten

Place a layer of cooked macaroni into a greased baking dish. Sprinkle bread crumbs, grated cheese, parsley, onions, salt, and butter between each layer. Repeat until all ingredients are used. Pour egg and milk over mixture. Bake in 350 degree oven for 30 minutes or until it is set.

ORIENTAL RICE CASSEROLE

6-8 servings

1 pound ground beef
1 cup chopped celery
1 cup chopped onions
4 ounce can mushrooms
8 ounce can water chestnuts, sliced
.8 ounce can bamboo shoots, drained
1/3 cup soy sauce
1 can cream of mushroom soup
2 beef bouillon cubes
2 cups hot water
3/4 cup rice

Brown beef, celery and onions. Drain off excess fat. Mix in mushrooms, water chestnuts, bamboo shoots and soy sauce. Dissolve bouillon cubes in hot water, stir in mushroom soup. Add to beef mixture. Stir in rice, place in 13 x 9 inch baking pan. Bake uncovered for 1 hour in a 350 degree oven. Delicious!

TOSTADO CASSEROLE

Serves 6

1 pound ground beef
15-ounce can (2 cups) tomato sauce
1 envelope taco seasoning mix
2-1/2 cups corn chips
15-1/2 - ounce can refried beans
2 ounces (1/2 cup) shredded Cheddar cheese

In skillet, brown ground beef. Add 1-1/2 cups of tomato sauce and seasoning mix, stirring to mix well. Line bottom of 11 x 8 x 2-inch baking dish with 2 cups corn chips. Crush remaining corn chips; set aside. Spoon meat mixture over corn chips in baking dish. Combine remaining tomato sauce and refried beans; spread over ground beef mixture. Bake at 375 degrees for 25 minutes. Sprinkle with shredded cheese and crushed corn chips. Bake 5 minutes more.

POT LUCK CASSEROLE

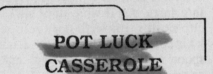

8 ounces noodles
1-1/2 pounds hamburger
1 onion, chopped
1 teaspoon salt
Pepper
2 (8 ounce) packages cream cheese
1 cup cottage cheese
1/4 cup sour cream
1/3 cup chopped green pepper
1/3 cup chopped green onion

Cook noodles. Simmer hamburger, onion, salt, pepper and tomato sauce. Cream in blender the cottage cheese, cream cheese and sour cream. Add chopped peppers and green onions. Layer noodles, meat and cheese sauce. Top with grated cheese and bake at 350 degrees for 30-40 minutes.

HAMBURGER CASSEROLE

Serves 4

1 pound lean ground beef
1 (26 1/4 ounce) can of Franco-American Spaghetti
1 medium onion, chopped
1 medium green pepper, chopped

Saute onions and green pepper in 2 tablespoons margarine until nearly done, remove from pan and drain. Saute ground beef until brown; drain grease. Add spaghetti from can. Slightly chop while mixing. Add peppers and onions. Mix well. Pour into 1-1/2 quart casserole. Bake 375 degrees for 30-45 minutes.

Optional additions:
Mushrooms, sliced
Black and or green olives, sliced
1 small can green beans

Serve with Parmesan cheese, garlic bread and tossed salad.

HAMBURGER MACARONI CASSEROLE

2 cups macaroni
1 pound ground beef
1 can condensed tomato soup
1 can condensed mushroom soup
1 medium green pepper
1/4 cup colby cheese, cubed
1/4 cup chopped pimiento, optional
1 (3-ounce) can French fried (Durkee) onions

Cook macaroni; drain. Brown the ground beef; drain. Add soups, green pepper, pimiento, macaroni, and the ground beef. Place half the mixture in a greased 2-quart casserole. Sprinkle with half the cheese and onions. Top with remaining macaroni mixture and cheese. Bake at 350 degrees for 25 minutes. Sprinkle with remaining onions, bake 5 additional minutes.

Desserts
DELICIOUS

ICE CREAM GELATIN DESSERT
Serves 5

- 1 (3-ounce) package gelatin, any flavor
- 1 cup boiling water
- ½ cup cold water
- 1 cup vanilla ice cream (or your favorite flavor)
- 1 cup canned fruit, drained (fruit cocktail, sliced peaches or mandarin oranges)

Dissolve gelatin with boiling water in an 8-inch or 9-inch metal pan. (The pan helps the gelatin cool faster.) Then remove ½ cup and pour into a bowl. Add ½ cup cold water to the gelatin in the pan and place in the freezer until it thickens (10–15 minutes).

Meanwhile, add 1 cup ice cream to the gelatin in the bowl; stir until smooth. Remove thickened gelatin from the freezer and, if desired, stir in fruit, reserving a few pieces for garnish.

Spoon thickened gelatin and fruit into individual dessert glasses.

Top with ice cream/gelatin mixture. Chill 30 minutes. Garnish and serve.

CHERRY WHIP

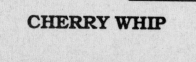

- 1 stick margarine
- 2 cups graham cracker crumbs

- 1 cup cold milk
- 2 envelopes whipped topping mix
- 1 teaspoon vanilla
- 1 cup sugar
- 1 (8-ounce) package cream cheese
- 1 large can cherry pie filling

Melt margarine over low heat. Mix with 2 cups graham cracker crumbs. Put into 9 x 13 x 2-inch pan. In a large bowl, whip until stiff, 1 cup cold milk with 2 envelopes whipped topping mix. Add 1 teaspoon vanilla, cup sugar and cream cheese (softened). Spread over crumb mixture. Spoon 1 large can cherry pie filling over whipped mixture. Set in refrigerator overnight. Slice and serve.

CANDY CANE DESSERT
Serves 9

- 1 graham cracker crust (your favorite recipe)
- 1 (8-ounce) container frozen whipped topping, thawed
- 1 small package miniature marshmallows
- 4 large candy canes, crushed (about ½ cup)

Place graham cracker crust in bottom of 11 x 7-inch pan. Combine whipped topping, marshmallows and ¾ of the candy. Spoon on crust. Spread remaining crushed candy cane over mixture. Chill thoroughly.

CHOCOLATE WAFER PUDDING
Serves 6–8

- 1 (3¼-ounce) package vanilla pudding and pie filling
- 2 cups milk
- 8 chocolate waters
- 1 cup whipped cream
- 2 tablespoons chocolate syrup (optional)

Prepare pudding with 2 cups milk according to package directions. Cover surface of pudding with waxed paper or plastic wrap; refrigerate until cool.

Alternate layers of chocolate wafers and pudding in a 1-quart casserole, ending with vanilla pudding. Garnish with whipped cream and drizzle with chocolate syrup, if desired.

PEANUT BUTTER INSTANT PUDDING
Serves 4

- ⅓ cup creamy peanut butter
- 2 cups cold milk
- 1 (3¾-ounce) package vanilla, 1 (4-ounce) package butterscotch or 1 (4½-ounce) package chocolate *instant* pudding

Stir peanut butter and milk together. Add pudding mix and beat slowly with rotary beater for 1–2 minutes, or until well-blended. Pudding will be soft. Let stand for 5 minutes and serve.

PISTACHIO TORTE

Crust:

1	cup flour
½	cup butter *or* margarine
½	cup chopped nuts
¼	cup confectioners' sugar

Filling:

1	(8-ounce) package cream cheese, softened
1	cup confectioners' sugar
1	cup whipped topping

Topping:

2	packages instant pistachio pudding
2½	cups milk

Garnishes:

Crushed nuts
Whipped topping

Combine ingredients for crust and press onto bottom of 9 x 13-inch pan. Bake at 350 degrees for about 15 minutes, or until golden brown. Cool.

Combine ingredients for filling and spread over cooled crust. For topping, combine pudding and milk. Spread over cream cheese mixture. Top with nuts and frost with whipped topping.
Variation:

Add 1 small can of crushed pineapple (drained) to filling ingredients.

HEAVENLY HASH CAKE
Serves 12–16

1	(12-ounce) package semisweet chocolate chips
4	eggs, separated
2	tablespoons sugar
1	teaspoon vanilla extract
½	teaspoon salt
1	pint whipping cream
1	cup pecans, broken
1	large angel food cake

Melt chocolate chips over low heat.

Beat egg yolks and add to chocolate. Beat egg whites and add 2 tablespoons sugar. Add egg whites to chocolate mixture. Stir and add pecans, vanilla and salt. Whip cream and fold in last.

Break angel food cake into chunks and cover bottom of tube pan or deep bowl. Cover with layer of chocolate mixture; add another layer of cake pieces and cover with chocolate mixture. Then add another layer of cake pieces and cover with remaining chocolate mixture.

Chill in refrigerator overnight. Turn onto cake plate and slice to serve.

CREAMY CHOCOMINT TORTE
Serves 12

2	envelopes unflavored gelatin
½	cup sugar
4	eggs, separated
1½	cups milk
½	cup creme de menthe
2½	cups chocolate sandwich cookie crumbs
¼	cup butter *or* margarine, melted
2	cups (1 pint) whipping *or* heavy cream, whipped

In medium saucepan, mix unflavored gelatin with ¼ cup sugar; blend in egg yolks beaten with milk. Let stand 1 minute. Stir over low heat until gelatin is completely dissolved, about 5 minutes; add liqueur. Pour into large bowl and chill, stirring occasionally, until mixture mounds slightly when dropped from spoon. Meanwhile, in small bowl, combine cookie crumbs and butter. Reserve 1½ cups mixture. Press remaining onto bottom of 9-inch springform pan; chill.

In medium bowl, beat egg whites until soft peaks form; gradually add remaining sugar and beat until stiff. Fold egg whites, then whipped cream into gelatin mixture. Turn ⅓ mixture into prepared pan and top with ¾ cup reserved cookie crumbs; repeat, ending with gelatin mixture. Chill until set. Garnish, if desired, with additional whipped cream and miniature chocolate-mint candy bars.

FESTIVE RASPBERRY FRAPPÉ
Serves 8

4	packages frozen whole red raspberries, plus syrup
¼	cup lemon juice
¼	cup sugar
1½	cups heavy cream, whipped
1	pint vanilla ice cream, softened

Purée thawed raspberries and syrup in blender or food processor; strain to remove seeds. Combine purée with lemon juice and sugar. Stir in whipped cream and ice cream; chill. Fill individual serving dessert bowls; serve ice-cold.

BRANDIED MINCEMEAT MOUSSE
Makes 1½ quarts

2	egg whites
2	cups whipping cream
1	cup sugar
⅛	teaspoon salt
1	teaspoon brandy *or* rum extract
1½	cups mincemeat

Place egg whites and cream in mixing bowl; beat until stiff. Add sugar gradually and continue beating until blended. Fold in salt, brandy (or rum) and mincemeat. Spoon into freezing tray or small paper cups. Place in freezing compartment of refrigerator and set control for coldest temperature. Freeze until firm; about 2–3 hours.

LINCOLN LOG
Serves 5

Cake:
- 5 eggs, separated
- 6 tablespoons sugar
- ½ cup all-purpose flour
- ½ teaspoon vanilla extract

Mocha Cream Filling and Frosting:
- 1 cup butter *or* margarine, softened
- 4½ tablespoons confectioners' sugar
- 2 tablespoons unsweetened cocoa
- 2 tablespoons strong, cooled coffee
- 2 cups whipping cream, whipped

Beat egg yolks with sugar; mix in flour and vanilla. Fold in stiffly beaten egg whites; spread mixture on a buttered waxed-paper–lined jelly roll pan. Bake at 350 degrees for 15 minutes; transfer to a dampened cloth dusted with confectioners' sugar. Roll cake in cloth; cool. Beat butter and confectioners' sugar; stir in cocoa and coffee. Unroll pastry; cover with a thin layer of mocha cream and whipped cream. Reroll cake (without cloth); cut off 2 ends diagonally; reserve. Cover cake and 2 slices with remaining mocha cream; place 1 slice on top of cake, the other slice on the side of cake (to resemble branches). With a fork, trace lines into the cream to simulate the bark.

PEACH BLUEBERRY COBBLER
Serves 8

- ½ cup sugar
- 1 tablespoon cornstarch
- ¾ cup orange juice
- 1½ cups fresh *or* frozen peach slices
- 1½ cups blueberries
- ½ cup all-purpose flour
- ½ cup whole-wheat flour
- 1½ teaspoon baking powder
- ⅓ cup milk
- 1 tablespoon vegetable oil
- 1 teaspoon sugar

In small saucepan, stir together ½ cup sugar, cornstarch and orange juice. Cook until bubbly; add peaches and blueberries; cook until hot. Keep warm. Stir together flours and baking powder; add milk and oil and stir until mixture forms a ball. On floured surface, pat into an 8-inch circle. Cut into wedges. Spoon hot berry mixture into 9-inch pie plate and top immediately with pastry wedges. Sprinkle with sugar. Bake in 425-degree oven for 20–30 minutes, or until pastry is browned. This cobbler has a grandmother flair!

CREAM CHEESE AND CHERRY DESSERT
Serves 18–20

Crust:
- 2 cups crushed pretzels
- 1 cup melted butter *or* margarine
- ¾ cup sugar

Filling:
- 1 (8-ounce) package cream cheese, softened
- 1 cup confectioners' sugar
- 1 (8-ounce) container whipped topping

Topping:
- 1 (30-ounce) can cherry pie filling

For crust: Combine ingredients and press into a 9 x 13-inch pan, reserving some for garnish.

For filling: Combine and beat cream cheese with confectioners' sugar. Add whipped topping to the cheese mixture, ½ cup at a time, mixing gently. Spread over crust.

Spread pie filling over top and sprinkle with reserved pretzel mixture. Refrigerate 2–3 hours.

PEACHES AND CREAM DESSERT

- 3/4 cup all-purpose flour
- 4 serving size package regular vanilla pudding mix
- 1 teaspoon baking powder
- 1 beaten egg
- 1/2 cup milk
- 3 tablespoons margarine, melted
- 16-ounce can peach slices
- 8-ounce package cream cheese, softened
- 1/2 cup sugar
- 1 teaspoon sugar
- 1/2 teaspoon ground cinnamon

Stir together flour, pudding mix and baking powder. Combine egg, milk and melted margarine; add to dry ingredients. Mix well; spread in greased 8-inch square baking pan. Drain peaches, reserving 1/3 cup liquid. Chop peaches; sprinkle on top of batter. Beat together cream cheese 1/2 cup sugar and reserved peach liquid; pour on top of peaches in pan. Combine 1 tablespoon sugar and cinnamon; sprinkle over all. Bake at 350 degrees for 45 minutes. Cool in refrigerator.

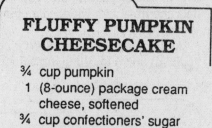

FLUFFY PUMPKIN CHEESECAKE

- ¾ cup pumpkin
- 1 (8-ounce) package cream cheese, softened
- ¾ cup confectioners' sugar
- 2 tablespoons milk
- 1 teaspoon ground cinnamon
- ¼ teaspoon ground cloves
- ½ teaspoon ground ginger
- ½ teaspoon nutmeg
- 1 (8-ounce) container frozen whipped topping, thawed
- 1 graham cracker pie crust

In small bowl beat cream cheese and sugar together until fluffy. Add pumpkin, milk and spices, beating until creamy. Fold whipped topping into pumpkin mixture. Turn into graham cracker pie crust. Chill 5 hours. (May be frozen for later use.)

FUDGE RICE

2 cups milk
1 cup cooked rice
1/4 cup sugar
2 tablespoons flour
1/4 teaspoon salt
2 eggs, beaten
1/2 teaspoon vanilla
1/4 cup chopped walnuts

Scald milk in heavy saucepan. Stir in rice. Mix sugar, flour and salt. Whisk into scalded milk. Cook, stirring over medium heat, for 5 minutes. Stir small amount of hot mixture into eggs. Then stir back into saucepan. Cook stirring for 1 minute. Add vanilla. Pour into shallow, 1-1/2 - quart buttered baking dish. Bake at 300 degrees for 30 minutes until knife inserted comes out clean. Cool slightly. Spread with fudge topping. Sprinkle with nuts. Let stand until firm.

Fudge Topping:
1 cup powdered sugar
Dash of salt
1-1/2 tablespoons milk
1 tablespoon softened butter
1-1/2 squares unsweetened chocolate, melted
1/4 teaspoon vanilla

Beat powdered sugar, salt and milk together; stir in butter, chocolate and vanilla. Beat until blended and of spreading consistency.

IRISH COFFEE PUDDING

Use this for your centerpiece.

6 eggs
1/3 cup Irish whiskey
3/4 cup sugar
1 1/4 cups heavy cream
1 cup strong, black espresso
2 tablespoons finely crushed walnuts
3 tablespoons gelatin
1 cup whipped cream
2 tablespoons chopped walnuts

Separate eggs and beat yolks with sugar. Heat coffee and dissolve gelatin in it. Add to egg-sugar mixture. Heat over double boiler until thickened; add whiskey or extract; beat until creamy. Place bowl over cracked ice and stir until it begins to set. Whip cream and fold in; then whip egg whites and fold in.

Pour into mold or waxed-paper–lined bowl; press an oiled jar into center to form a well. Chill to set. Fold nuts into whipped cream; fill center.

BAKED BLUEBERRY PUDDING

1/2 cup plus 1 tablespoon margarine
1/2 cup brown sugar
2 cups blueberries
1/2 cup sugar
1 egg, lightly beaten
1/2 cup milk
1 cup flour
1 teaspoon baking powder
Whipped cream

Preheat oven to 350 degrees. In saucepan, combine 1 tablespoon margarine and brown sugar. Cook over medium heat until sugar melts. Stir in blueberries and pour into greased baking dish. Beat together the remaining margarine and 1/2 cup white sugar; beat in egg and milk. Sift together flour and baking powder. Combine with mixture and cover blueberry mixture with the batter and bake for 30 minutes. Serve with whipped cream.

LIME CHEESECAKE
Serves 10–12

1 cup shredded coconut
2 tablespoons flour
2 tablespoons margarine, melted

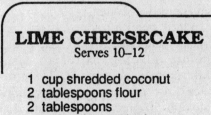

1 envelope unflavored gelatin
2 (8-ounce) packages cream cheese
3 eggs, separated
3/4 cup sugar
1/4 cup lime juice
Grated lime rind
Green food coloring (optional)
1 cup whipping cream, whipped

Combine coconut, flour and margarine; press into a 9-inch springform pan. Bake at 350 degrees for 12–15 minutes. Soften gelatin in 1/4 cup cold water. Soften cream cheese. Combine egg yolks, 3/4 cup water and sugar in saucepan; cook, stirring constantly, over medium heat for 5 minutes. Stir in gelatin until dissolved. Add gelatin mixture gradually to cream cheese; mix until blended. Stir in lime juice, 1 teaspoon lime rind and several drops of green food coloring, if desired. Fold in whipped cream and stiffly beaten egg whites; pour over crust. Chill until firm. Garnish with lime rind. A dreamy, delightful dessert!

CRESCENT APPLE PASTRIES
Makes 16

2 cups (2 large) apples, peeled and finely chopped
1/3 cup sugar
2 tablespoons flour
1/4 teaspoon cinnamon
2 (8 ounce) cans Pillsbury Quick Crescent Dinner Rolls

Glaze:
1/2 cup powdered sugar
2-3 teaspoons water

Heat oven to 350 degrees. Combine first 4 ingredients. Stir until apples are well coated. Separate crescent dough into 16 triangles. Spoon about 1 rounded tablespoon apple mixture onto center of each triangle. Fold 3 points of dough over filling, overlapping like an envelope. Place 1 inch apart on ungreased cookie sheet. Bake at 350 degrees for 20-25 minutes until golden brown. Remove and cool on rack. Blend glaze; drizzle over warm rolls.

EASY CHERRY COBBLER

2 cans tart cherries, undrained
1 package white cake mix
1 stick margarine, melted
1 cup nuts

Pour cherries in bottom of 9 x 13-inch pan, then sprinkle dry cake mix over cherries and *do not stir*. Pour melted margarine over cake mix; sprinkle nuts on top. *Do not mix.* Bake at 400 degrees for 30 minutes, or until set. Delicious topped with ice cream.

HAPPY DAY CAKE
Serves 8–10

1 (3¾-ounce) package chocolate fudge pudding and pie filling
2 cups milk
1 (11¼-ounce) frozen pound cake
⅓ cup coconut
½ gallon vanilla ice cream (optional)

Prepare pudding with 2 cups milk according to package directions. Cover surface of pudding with waxed paper or plastic wrap; refrigerate until cool.

Slice pound cake lengthwise into 3 layers. Spread pudding between each layer and frost top with pudding. Sprinkle with coconut. Serve with a scoop of vanilla ice cream, if desired.

PEANUT BUTTER PARFAIT
Serves 4

1 cup brown sugar
⅓ cup milk
¼ cup white corn syrup
1 tablespoon butter
¼ cup peanut butter
Vanilla ice cream
Peanuts

Combine first 4 ingredients in medium saucepan. Cook over medium heat until sugar dissolves and butter melts, stirring constantly. Remove from heat; add peanut butter. Beat with rotary beater or mixer until smooth; cool. Alternate layers of peanut sauce and ice cream in parfait glasses, beginning and ending with ice cream. Top with peanuts.

MILK DUD DESSERT

6 egg yolks
1 cup sugar
1 cup rusk crumbs
½ cup chopped walnuts
1 teaspoon vanilla
1 teaspoon baking powder
6 egg whites
4 small packages Milk Duds
¹/₂ cup milk
1 cup confectioners' sugar
2 tablespoons butter
½ pint whipping cream

Beat egg yolks; add sugar and beat again.

Mix together rusk crumbs, nuts, vanilla and baking powder. Add to egg mixture. Fold in stiffly beaten egg whites. Bake in 9 x 13-inch greased pan at 350 degrees for 30 minutes. Cool. Melt Milk Duds, milk, confectioners' sugar and butter until smooth, stirring constantly. Let stand until cool and creamy. Whip the cream; spread over baked portion. Pour sauce on top and refrigerate overnight.

FRUIT COCKTAIL DESSERT

The topping melts as it cooks and makes a tasty dessert.

1 (16-ounce) can fruit cocktail, drained
1 egg, beaten
1 cup sugar
1 teaspoon soda
1 cup flour
⅛ teaspoon salt
½ cup chopped nuts
½ cup brown sugar

Add egg to fruit and then fold in dry ingredients. Pour the batter into a 9-inch round or square microwave-safe baking dish.

Combine nuts and brown sugar and pour over batter.

Place small glass or custard cup, open end up, in center of baking dish before placing batter in dish. Microwave, uncovered, 7–8 minutes. For varying power, use 5 minutes on 50 percent power and 4–5 minutes on HIGH.

CARAMEL CHRISTMAS CUSTARD
Serves 5

¾ cup sugar
3 eggs
⅛ teaspoon salt
2 cups milk, scalded
1 teaspoon vanilla extract

Heat ½ cup sugar slowly in a small heavy skillet, stirring constantly, until sugar melts and turns a light caramel color. Pour into 5 (6-ounce) custard cups. Let stand until slightly cooled. Lightly beat eggs with remaining ¼ cup sugar, salt, milk and vanilla. Pour mixture into the cups, being careful not to disturb the caramel. Place cups in pan of hot water (water should be almost level with top of cups) and bake at 350 degrees for 40 minutes, or until a knife inserted in center comes out clean. Remove immediately from water. Chill if desired. To serve, loosen edges with knife and turn out onto serving dishes.

PRETTY PUMPKIN CUSTARD

2 cups canned pumpkin
1 cup soft bread crumbs
2 eggs, separated
1½ cups sweet milk
1 cup sugar
3 tablespoons butter, melted
¼ teaspoon salt
1¼ teaspoons orange extract

Combine all ingredients 1 at a time, except egg whites; mix well after each addition. Pour into ovenproof dish or individual custard cups. Bake at 325 degrees until mixture thickens and browns. Beat egg whites until stiff; add 2 tablespoons sugar. Spread on top of custard; place under broiler until golden brown.

CRANBERRY PUDDING

1 cup flour
½ cup sugar
1½ teaspoons baking powder
Salt
1 cup halved cranberries
1½ tablespoons melted butter
½ cup milk

Mix the dry ingredients. Blend in butter and milk. Add cranberries. Bake in greased 9 x 9-inch pan at 375 degrees for 30 minutes.

Sauce:
½ cup butter
1 cup brown sugar
¾ cup cream (evaporated milk is fine)

Place ingredients in saucepan on medium heat until well-blended. Serve pudding in squares with warm sauce.

HOLIDAY MINCEMEAT-STUFFED APPLES
Serves 8

8 medium-size Granny Smith apples
4 tablespoons butter *or* margarine
1 tablespoon rum extract
8 tablespoons mincemeat

Wash and core apples; do not peel. Place apples in an ovenproof dish. Fill cavities with butter, rum extract and mincemeat. Bake at 350 degrees for 25 minutes, or until apples are tender. Serve with baked pork loin, lamb or baked ham.

BLUEBERRY SALAD
Serves 12

1 (3-ounce) package blackberry gelatin
2 cups boiling water
1 (15-ounce) can blueberries with juice (*or* 1 pound of your own, frozen)
1 (8-ounce) can crushed pineapple, drained

Topping:
1 (8-ounce) package cream cheese, softened
¼ cup sugar
¼ pint sour cream
½ teaspoon vanilla
½ cup nuts

Dissolve gelatin in boiling water. Add blueberries and pineapple; pour into 9 x 12-inch glass baking dish. Refrigerate until set.

Blend cream cheese and sugar. Add sour cream slowly and then vanilla. Spread over gelatin salad and sprinkle with nuts. Refrigerate until serving time.

This salad may be varied with the use of black raspberry gelatin.

BAKED BANANAS

2 bananas
Lemon juice
Brown sugar *or* granulated sugar with cinnamon
Butter

Peel bananas and slice in half lengthwise. Place in a buttered pie plate or casserole. Sprinkle with lemon juice and sugar. Dot with butter. Bake at 350 degrees for 15 minutes. This is also a delicious way to make a dessert using pears or apples.

FRUIT PARFAITS

2 tablespoons frozen orange juice concentrate
1 tablespoon sugar
½ cup whipped topping
1 orange, peeled, sectioned and cut up
1 banana, sliced
½ cup pineapple chunks
⅓ cup marshmallows

Combine orange juice and sugar; mix well. Fold in whipped topping. In another bowl, combine fruit pieces. In 2 parfait glasses, alternately layer fruit, marshmallows and then whipped topping; repeat. Chill. May be topped with a maraschino cherry.

QUICK BAKED ALASKA
Serves 4

4 packaged dessert shells
Jam *or* jelly
4 scoops of favorite ice cream
Whipped cream

Turn oven temperature to 475 degrees. Spread dessert shells with jam or jelly. Place on baking sheet. Bake dessert shells with jam or jelly for 5 minutes. Place a scoop of ice cream in center; top with whipped cream; serve.

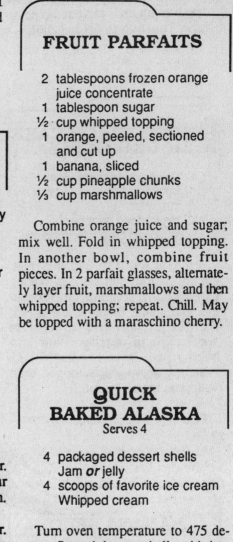

MOCHA FLUFF
Serves 4

1 envelope gelatin
¼ cup water
¼ cup sugar
¼ teaspoon salt
1½ cups hot, strong coffee
2 tablespoons lemon juice
2 egg whites, stiffly beaten

Soften gelatin in cold water. Add sugar, salt and hot coffee, stirring thoroughly to dissolve. Add lemon juice and cool. When nearly set, beat until stiff. Add egg whites and continue beating until mixture holds its shape. Turn into molds and chill.

GINGER PEACH CAKE
Serves 6–8

2 tablespoons margarine
1 package ginger bread mix
½ cup water
2 cups sliced peaches
Whipped cream for topping

Preheat oven to 375 degrees. Grease bottom and sides of baking pan. In bowl, combine gingerbread mix and water. Blend at low speed; then beat 2 minutes at medium speed. Stir in peaches. Pour into baking pan. Bake in oven for 35 minutes. Serve warm topped with whipped cream.

BANANA SPLIT
Serves 4

1 (3⅝-ounce) package chocolate pudding and pie filling
2 cups milk
4 bananas, sliced lengthwise
½ gallon vanilla ice cream

1 (8½-ounce) can pineapple tidbits, drained
½ cup chopped pecans
1 cup whipped cream
4 maraschino cherries, drained

Prepare pudding with 2 cups milk according to package directions. Cover surface of pudding with waxed paper or plastic wrap; refrigerate until cool.

Put 1 sliced banana in each of 4 serving dishes. Top with 3 scoops of ice cream; cover with ¼ of pudding; sprinkle with pineapple tidbits and pecans. Garnish with whipped cream and a cherry.

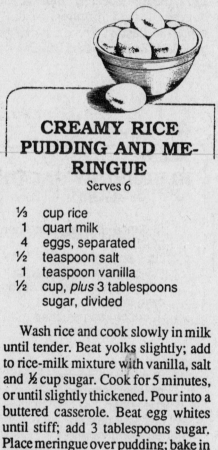

CREAMY RICE PUDDING AND MERINGUE
Serves 6

⅓ cup rice
1 quart milk
4 eggs, separated
½ teaspoon salt
1 teaspoon vanilla
½ cup, *plus* 3 tablespoons sugar, divided

Wash rice and cook slowly in milk until tender. Beat yolks slightly; add to rice-milk mixture with vanilla, salt and ½ cup sugar. Cook for 5 minutes, or until slightly thickened. Pour into a buttered casserole. Beat egg whites until stiff; add 3 tablespoons sugar. Place meringue over pudding; bake in a 350-degree oven for 15 minutes, or until meringue is golden brown.

AMBROSIA PARFAITS

1 (8-ounce) can mandarin orange segments, drained
¼ cup chopped, toasted blanched almonds

2 cups prepared whipped topping
1 package *instant* toasted coconut pudding
2 cups cold milk
Mint sprigs

Reserve 5 orange segments for garnish. Fold oranges and almonds into topping. Combine pudding with milk; beating slowly for 2 minutes. Alternate topping and pudding in parfait glasses. Garnish with oranges and mint.

MAGIC MALTED PARFAIT
Serves 2

4 scoops-vanilla ice cream
1 cup caramel topping
½ cup crushed malted milk balls
2 whole malted milk balls
Whipped cream

Put a scoop of ice cream into each parfait glass. Pour a tablespoon of caramel topping over ice cream, followed with a layer of crushed malted milk balls.

Repeat these steps by adding another scoop of ice cream, a layer of caramel topping and a sprinkling of milk balls. Top off with whipped cream, and garnish with a malted milk ball.

CRANBERRY FLUFF
Serves 6

1 pound cranberries, chopped
1 cup sugar
½ cup seeded grapes, halved
½ cup small marshmallows
½ cup chopped pecans
½ cup maraschino cherries, halved
½ pint whipping cream, whipped

Combine fruits, marshmallows and nuts; fold in whipping cream. Transfer mixture to a serving bowl. Chill in refrigerator 1–2 hours.

APPLE ROLY POLY
Serves 6-8

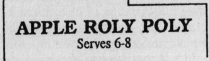

2 cups prepared baking mix
1/2 cup honey
3/4 teaspoon cinnamon
1/4 teaspoon nutmeg
1/4 teaspoon cloves
3 tablespoons sugar
5 large tart apples, peeled, cored, finely chopped
2 tablespoons butter or margarine

Prepare biscuit mix as directed on package. On lightly floured board, roll dough into 1/4 inch oblong (about 10x12 inches). Spread with honey to within 1 inch of the edges of dough. Combine spices and sugar. Toss with apples. Spread apples evenly over the honey, and dot apples with butter. Roll up like a jelly roll and seal well. Bake in greased pan with sides at 350 degrees for 40 minutes. Slice and serve hot with whipped cream, hot lemon, or vanilla sauce.

COLONIAL BAKED APPLES
Serves 8

3 medium sweet potatoes
1/2 teaspoon finely shredded orange peel
2 tablespoons orange juice
1 tablespoon brown sugar
1 tablespoon butter or margarine
1/4 teaspoon nutmeg, ground
1/4 teaspoon salt
1 beaten egg
2 tablespoons milk
8 large cooking apples, peeled and cored
1/2 cup corn syrup
2 tablespoons lemon juice

Cook sweet potatoes, covered in enough boiling salted water to cover, for 25 to 35 minutes or until tender. Drain, peel, dice and mash with electric mixer on low speed until smooth. Should have about 1-3/4 cups mashed potatoes. Add orange peel, orange juice, sugar butter, nutmeg and salt. Add egg and milk; set aside. Remove

a slice from top of each apple. Score apple by going around the outside surface with tines of a fork in circular pattern. Using pastry bag fitted with star tip, fill apples with sweet potato mixture. Place apples in 12 x 7-1/2 x 2-inch baking dish. Stir corn syrup and lemon juice together and pour over apples. Bake uncovered in 325 degree oven for 45 minutes or until tender, basting several times with the corn syrup mixture. Serve hot.

BOILED APPLE DUMPLINGS

3 cups flour
4 teaspoons baking powder
1/2 teaspoon salt
2 tablespoons sugar
2 tablespoons vegetable shortening
1/4 cup milk
3 large tart apples
6 teaspoons sugar
Milk
Sugar

Sift baking powder, salt, and sugar with flour into bowl. Cut in shortening until mixture is in crumbs the size of peas. Stir in 1/4 cup milk. On floured board, roll dough to 1-1/2 inch thickness. Cut into six squares. Pare and core apples and cut in half. Place a half on each square of dough and sprinkle with 1 teaspoon sugar.

Pull the four corners of the dough together, dampen slightly, and press edges to seal. Tie each dumpling in a clean piece of white muslin. Drop dumplings into a large kettle of boiling water. Cook 20-25 minutes depending on size of apple. Serve with milk, cinnamon, and sugar, if desired.

MAPLE APPLE BROWN BETTY
Serves 4

1-1/2 cups fine bread crumbs, toasted lightly
3/4 stick (6 tablespoons) unsalted butter
4 apples, peeled and diced
1/2 cup maple syrup
3/4 teaspoon cinnamon
Vanilla ice cream, as an accompaniment

Sprinkle bottom of well-buttered baking dish with one fourth of the crumbs; dot the crumbs with one fourth of the butter. Spread one third of apples over the crumbs. In a small bowl combine the syrup and cinnamon; drizzle one third of mixture over apples. Layer the remaining crumbs, butter, apples and syrup mixture, ending with a layer of crumbs and butter. Bake in a preheated 375 degree oven for 40 minutes or until apples are tender. Serve the dessert with ice cream, if desired.

MARSHMALLOW APPLE CRISP
Serves 6

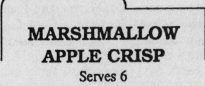

4 cups peeled, sliced apples
1/4 cup water
3/4 cup flour
1/2 cup sugar
1 teaspoon cinnamon
1/4 teaspoon salt
1/2 cup margarine
1/2 cup miniature marshmallows

Place apples and water in 8-inch square baking dish. Combine flour, sugar, cinnamon, and salt; cut in margarine until mixture is like coarse crumbs. Sprinkle over apples. Bake at 350 degrees for 35 to 40 minutes or until apples are tender. Sprinkle with marshmallows. Broil until lightly browned.

CARAMEL CORN
Serves 6-8

6 toffee bars, (1-1/8 ounce each)
1/4 cup light corn syrup
8 cups popped popcorn
1 cup unsalted roasted peanuts

In heavy saucepan, heat toffee bars and corn syrup over low heat until melted, stirring often. Pour popcorn into large, deep pan. Add warm toffee mixture and peanuts. Toss well until popcorn is coated. Cool; break into chunks.

Children and adults all enjoy caramel corn.

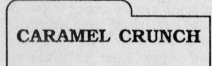

CARAMEL CRUNCH

1 cup light brown sugar, firmly
   packed
1/2 cup butter or margarine
1 (6 ounce) package chocolate
   chips
1 cup coarsely chopped nuts

Combine sugar and butter in saucepan; boil 7 minutes. Melt chocolate chips in saucepan over low heat. Spread nuts over bottom of buttered 8x8 inch pan. Pour butter and sugar mixture slowly over nuts. Pour melted chocolate over top. Cool. Cut into pieces.

DATE NUT BALLS

Cook together for 5 minutes:
1 stick margarine
1 cup sugar
1 egg, beaten
1 (8 ounce) package dates, cut up
Pinch of salt

Remove from heat and cool.
Add:
1 cup chopped nuts
2 cups Rice Krispies
1 teaspoon vanilla

Stir well and shape in small balls. Roll in flaked coconut.

EASTER EGG CANDY

1 cup hot mashed potatoes
2 tablespoons butter
1 cup shredded coconut
1 teaspoon vanilla
3 - 1 pound boxes confectioners'
   sugar
1 - 8 ounce package of chocolate
   chips
1/8 cake paraffin

Combine potatoes and butter; stir in coconut and vanilla. Add sugar gradually, mixing well after each addition. Form into egg shapes, using 1 tablespoon mixture for each egg; place on waxed paper. Let harden for 1-3 days. Melt chocolate over hot water; dip eggs into chocolate, using 2 spoons. Place on waxed paper to harden. Chopped nuts, candied fruits, or peanut butter may be used instead of coconut.

EASTER PEANUT BUTTER EGGS

2 eggs, well beaten
1/8 teaspoon salt
1-1/2 to 2 cups peanut butter
4-5 cups powdered sugar
1 teaspoon vanilla
1 Hershey chocolate bar
1 - 6 ounce package chocolate chips

Mix the eggs, salt, peanut butter, sugar, and vanilla in order listed. Form dough into egg shapes. Melt the chocolate bar and the chocolate chips in a double boiler. Dip egg shapes into chocolate mixture. Arrange on waxed paper until set.

ICE CREAM SANDWICHES
Makes 15

32 graham cracker squares
2 tablespoons milk
1 tablespoon cornstarch
1 tub Creamy Deluxe ready to spread
   frosting (any flavor)
1-1/2 cups chilled whipping cream.

Line 13x9x2 inch pan with aluminum foil. Arrange 16 graham crackers on foil, cutting about 6 of the squares to completely cover foil. Mix milk and cornstarch in large bowl; stir in frosting and whipping cream. Beat on medium speed, scraping bowl constantly, 2 minutes. Beat on high speed until thick and creamy; scrape bowl occasionally. Beat about 3 minutes. Spread over graham crackers in pan. Arrange remaining graham crackers over frosting mixture, cutting about 6 of the squares to completely cover mixture. Cover and freeze until firm, about 8 hours. Cut into 2-1/2 inch squares.

HOMEMADE MARSHMALLOWS

2 cups granulated sugar
3/4 cup water
2 tablespoons gelatin
1/2 cup cold water
1 teaspoon vanilla
1/2 teaspoon salt
Cornstarch
Confectioners' sugar

Mix granulated sugar with 3/4 cup water. Simmer to soft ball stage. Remove from fire. Soften gelatin in cold water. Place on large platter. Pour hot syrup over softened gelatin. Stir until dissolved. Let stand until partially cooled; whip until thick and white, and mixture will nearly hold its shape. Add vanilla and salt. Pour into straight sided pans lined with equal parts of cornstarch and confectioners' sugar, mixed together. Let stand in cool place until firm (not in ice box). Cut into squares with scissors and dust with confectioners' sugar.

CHOCOLATE DELIGHT

Crust:
1/2 cup chopped pecans
1-1/2 cups flour
1-1/4 sticks margarine

Melt margarine; add flour, nuts, and mix well. Pat into 9x13-inch pan. Bake 20-25 minutes at 350 degrees until slightly brown.

First layer:
1 cup powdered sugar
1 medium size Cool Whip
1 (8 ounce) cream cheese

Mix powdered sugar and cream cheese; blend well. Add 1 cup of Cool Whip; spread over crust.

Second layer:
2 (6 ounce) boxes instant chocolate
  pudding mix
3 cups milk

Combine pudding mix and milk. Pour mixture over first layer.

Third layer:
Spread remaining Cool Whip over top. Make dessert 24 hours before serving and refrigerate, but do not freeze.

LEMON DELIGHT

Serves 12-15

1-1/2 cups flour, sifted
1-1/2 sticks margarine
1/2 cup chopped pecans
1 - 8 ounce package cream cheese
1 cup sifted powdered sugar
1 - 9 ounce container frozen whipped
  topping
2 - 6 ounce packages instant lemon
  pudding mix
2 tablespoons lemon juice
3 cups milk
1/2 cup chopped pecans

Blend together flour, margarine and 1/2 cup pecans. Press into a 13 x 9 inch pan. Bake 20 minutes at 350 degrees. Cool.

Blend together cream cheese, powdered sugar, and 1/2 of 9 ounce carton of whipped topping. Spread over crust. Combine 2 packages instant lemon pudding mix with 2 tablespoons lemon juice and 3 cups milk. Pour over previous layer. When firm, top with remainder of whipped topping. Sprinkle with 1/2 cup pecans. Chill overnight and keep in refrigerator. A delightful tasting dessert.

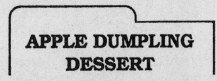

APPLE DUMPLING DESSERT

1 can (10) country-style refrigerator
  biscuits
2 cups thinly sliced peeled apples
1/2 cup packed brown sugar
1/2 cup evaporated milk
1/2 cup dark corn syrup
1/4 cup margarine

Preheat oven to 375 degrees.
Grease an 8-inch square baking dish. Separate biscuits into 10 individual ones. Place on bottom of buttered baking dish. Arrange apple slices over top.

In small saucepan combine all remaining ingredients and bring to a boil, stirring constantly. Pour hot syrup mixture over apples and biscuits. Bake at 375 degrees for 25-35 minutes or until golden brown and biscuits are done in the center. Serve warm.

For extra goodness, top with whipped cream.

APPLE DESSERT

1 box yellow cake mix
1/2 cup margarine
1/2 cup coconut
2-1/2 cups sliced apples
1/2 cup sugar
1 teaspoon cinnamon
1 cup sour cream
1 egg

Put yellow cake mix, margarine and coconut in bowl and mix like you would for pie crust. Pat into ungreased 13 x 9 inch pan. Bake 10 minutes at 350 degrees. Mix sugar, cinnamon, and apples and put over baked crust. Blend the sour cream and egg; drizzle over top. Bake at 350 degrees for 25 minutes. You can use any flavor cake mix or any kind of fruit. This is a really delicious dessert you will enjoy.

BANANA SPLIT DESSERT

First layer:
2 cups graham cracker crumbs
1/2 cup sugar
1 stick melted margarine
Mix and spread in bottom of 11 x 14-inch casserole.

Second layer:
2 egg whites, stiffly beaten
1 stick softened margarine
1 (1-pound) box powdered sugar

Beat with mixer for 10 minutes, spread over crumbs.

Third layer:
Slice 2-3 bananas over sugar mixture.

Fourth layer:
Spread 1 large can crushed pineapple, drained, over banana layer.

Fifth layer:
Spread 1 large or 2 small cartons Cool Whip over pineapple.

Sixth layer:
Sprinkle chopped pecans and maraschino cherries over all.

BUTTERSCOTCH-PEANUT FUDGE

Makes 4 dozen squares

1 (12 ounce) package butterscotch pieces
1 (14 ounce) can condensed sweetened milk
1-1/2 cups miniature marshmallows
2/3 cup chunk-style peanut butter
1 teaspoon vanilla
1 cup chopped peanuts
Dash of salt

In saucepan combine butterscotch pieces, milk, and marshmallows. Stir over medium heat until marshmallows melt. Remove from heat; beat in peanut butter, vanilla, and dash salt. Stir in nuts. Pour into buttered 9x9x2 inch pan. Chill. Cut in squares. Store in refrigerator.

CHUNKY MACADAMIA ORANGE FUDGE

3 cups sugar
3/4 butter
2/3 cup evaporated milk
12 ounce package semi-sweet chocolate morsels
7 ounce jar marshmallow cream
1 cup macadamia nuts
2 tablespoons orange flavored liquer

In heavy saucepan, combine sugar, butter and milk. Bring to full rolling boil over moderate heat, stirring constantly; boil 5 minutes, stirring constantly. Remove from heat. Add morsels; stir until morsels melt and mixture is smooth. Add marshmallow cream, nuts and liquer; beat until well blended. Pour into foil-lined 9" x 13" pan. Chill until firm.

HONEYPOT FUDGE

1/2 cup butter or margarine
2 tablespoons honey
1 pound confectioners' sugar
1/8 teaspoon cream of tartar

Mix all ingredients in 3-quart saucepan. Bring slowly to boil, stirring constantly. Bring to full rolling boil for about 8 minutes, stirring occasionally (a small amount dropped into cold water should form a soft ball at 235 degrees.) Remove pan from heat; cool slightly; beat mixture until thick. Pour into greased shallow pan. When nearly set, mark into squares. Separate pieces, when set, and leave to harden on plate.

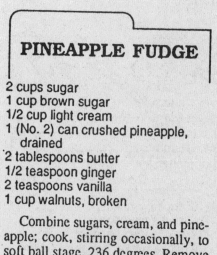

MAPLE SYRUP FUDGE

Makes about 25 - 1-1/2" pieces

2 cups maple syrup
1 tablespoon light corn syrup
3/4 cup half and half
1 teaspoon vanilla
3/4 cup coarsely chopped walnuts

Combine maple syrup, corn syrup and half and half in 1-1/2 - quart saucepan. Place pan over moderate heat; stir constantly until mixture starts to boil. Continue cooking mixture without stirring until it reaches 234 degrees on candy thermometer or until a small amount of syrup forms a soft ball in cold water. Remove pan from heat; do not stir. Let mixture stand until it cools to lukewarm, about 110 to 120 degrees. Beat mixture until it thickens and begins to lose its gloss. Add vanilla and walnuts; pour immediately into a buttered 8 x 8 x 2-inch pan. When cool, cut into squares.

NOEL FUDGE

2 cups sugar
3/4 cup milk
1 teaspoon Karo syrup
1 teaspoon vanilla
2 tablespoons butter
1 cup diced red or green candied cherries
1/2 cup chopped nuts

Mix together sugar, milk, and Karo in saucepan. Bring to boil; lower heat and simmer for 8 to 10 minutes, stirring occasionally. When a drop forms a firm ball in cold water, remove from heat; stir in butter and vanilla. Let cool. Beat well with large spoon until mixture loses gloss. Quickly stir in candied fruit and nuts; pour into buttered 8 or 9 inch square pan. When set, cut in squares.

Variations: For chocolate fudge, stir 4 tablespoons cocoa into sugar before adding milk. For peanut butter flavor, substitute 3 tablespoons peanut butter for the butter. Use chopped or diced dates, if desired, or coconut, instead of fruits and nuts. Wrap in foil to store.

This is an excellent fudge which keeps well.

PINEAPPLE FUDGE

2 cups sugar
1 cup brown sugar
1/2 cup light cream
1 (No. 2) can crushed pineapple, drained
2 tablespoons butter
1/2 teaspoon ginger
2 teaspoons vanilla
1 cup walnuts, broken

Combine sugars, cream, and pineapple; cook, stirring occasionally, to soft ball stage, 236 degrees. Remove from heat. Add butter, ginger, and vanilla. Cool to room temperature, stirring, until lukewarm. Beat until mixture loses its gloss. Add nuts. Pour into buttered 8x8x2 inch pan. Score candy in squares. Press walnut half on each. Finish cutting when firm.

Foreign & EXOTIC

SMOKED PORK PLATTER (AUSTRIA)
Serves 6–8

1 boneless smoked pork shoulder roll (approximately 2½ pounds)
  Water
4 medium potatoes, pared and halved
3 small onions, quartered
1 (27-ounce) can sauerkraut
1 teaspoon caraway seeds
¼ teaspoon pepper (optional)

Place pork shoulder roll in a Dutch oven and add enough water to cover meat. Cover and cook over low heat for 1½ hours. Remove meat from pan and pour off all but 2 cups of liquid. Add potatoes and onions to liquid in pan. Place meat on top. Cover and continue cooking for 30 minutes, or until meat and vegetables are done. During last 10 minutes of cooking time, add sauerkraut, caraway seeds and pepper. Remove meat and vegetables to hot platter.

STEAK ROLL (BRACIOLA)
Serves 8–10

3 eggs
1 center-cut round steak, ½ inch thick
6 slices salami
3 tablespoons Romano cheese
  Salt and pepper to taste

Beat eggs; cook in form of an omelet. Remove bone from steak and season meat. Place omelet on top of steak; then make a layer of salami slices on top of omelet. Sprinkle Romano cheese, salt and pepper over all and begin to roll steak, jelly roll fashion. The meat roll can be secured with heavy cord or rolled in aluminum foil. Bake at 350 degrees for 1 hour, depending on weight of meat. Slice and serve with a vegetable.

EGG FOO YONG (CHINESE)

6 eggs, beaten well
⅔ cup finely sliced onion
¼ cup finely chopped celery
1 cup bean sprouts, drained
1 to 1½ cups cooked chicken, turkey *or* pork roast*
  Salad oil

Combine eggs, onion, celery, bean sprouts and meat. Use a large griddle or skillet greased well with salad oil. For each patty, use about ¼ cup of egg mixture poured on hot griddle. Use a broad spatula to keep egg mixture from spreading too much. When the patties are set and brown, turn over to brown other side. Serve hot.

Hot Soy Sauce:
5 teaspoons soy sauce
2 teaspoons cornstarch
2 teaspoons sugar
2 teaspoons vinegar
¾ teaspoon salt
1 cup cold water

Serve with Egg Foo Yong.
*1–2 (6½-ounce) cans tuna may be substituted for chicken.

POTATOES ITALIANO
Serves 4 to 6

4 large baking potatoes
1 tablespoon olive or vegetable oil
1/4 cup grated Parmesan cheese
1 cup shredded Mozzarella cheese
3 medium tomatoes, sliced
1 large onion, peeled and thinly sliced
1/2 teaspoon oregano
1/2 teaspoon salt
1/8 teaspoon pepper
2 tablespoons butter

Peel and slice potatoes in 1/4-inch slices. Oil 9 x 13-inch casserole dish. Combine two cheeses, reserving some for topping. Arrange potatoes, tomatoes and onion slices in layers; sprinkle each layer with cheese and seasonings. Dot with butter and bake uncovered at 400 degrees for 30 minutes. Remove from oven and sprinkle with remaining cheese; bake for an additional 20 minutes.

INDONESIAN VEGETABLE SALAD (GADO-GADO)
Serves 6–8

- 4 cups shredded cabbage
- ½ cup flaked coconut
- 2 tablespoons peanut oil *or* vegetable oil
- ¼ cup thinly sliced green onions
- 2 cloves garlic, minced
- ½ cup peanut butter (smooth)
- 1 teaspoon light brown sugar
- 1 teaspoon salt
- ¼ teaspoon dried, ground chili peppers
- 2 teaspoons grated lemon rind
- ¾ cup light cream
- ¾ cup water
- 2 medium-size tomatoes, diced (Use ripe, but firm tomatoes; drain if overly juicy)
- 2 cucumbers, seeded and diced (small to medium size)
- 2 hard-cooked eggs, coarsely chopped

Cover cabbage with water; bring to a boil and cook only 2 minutes. Drain. Rinse coconut under cold water; drain and pat dry with paper towels. Heat oil in a skillet; sauté onions and garlic for 3 minutes. Stir in coconut, peanut butter, sugar, salt, chili peppers and lemon rind, and very gradually the cream mixed with water. Cook over low heat for 5 minutes, stirring frequently. Cool. In a bowl, toss together cabbage, tomatoes and cucumbers. Pour dressing over and mix lightly. Chill 1 hour before serving. Sprinkle with chopped egg just before serving.

SCANDINAVIAN PORK PATTIES (FRIKADELLER)
Serves 4

- 1 pound ground pork
- 1⅔ cups tart apples, peeled and coarsely shredded
- ⅓ cup bread crumbs, Italian style
- ½ teaspoon salt
- Freshly ground black pepper (to taste)
- 2 large eggs, beaten
- 2 tablespoons vegetable oil
- ½ cup currant jelly
- ½ cup port wine
- ½ cup heavy cream
- Chopped parsley

In medium bowl, combine pork, apples, bread crumbs, salt, pepper and beaten eggs. Mix well with hands and form into 8 (3-inch) patties. In large skillet, heat vegetable oil; add patties and cook over medium heat until browned on both sides and no longer pink in center, about 7 minutes a side. Remove patties to warm serving platter and keep warm. Drain off drippings in skillet and discard. Add jelly, wine and cream; cook and stir over medium heat until bubbly and reduced to the consistency of heavy cream, about 3–5 minutes. Pour sauce over patties and serve at once. Garnish with sprigs of chopped parsley.

CARROT SALAD (OMOK-HOURIA)
Serves 6 to 8

- 5 large carrots, scraped and washed, cut into 1/4" pieces
- 2 cloves garlic crushed
- 4 tablespoons very finely chopped fresh coriander leaves
- 4 tablespoons lemon juice
- 4 tablespoons olive oil
- 1-1/2 teaspoons salt
- 1/2 teaspoon pepper
- 1/8 teaspoon cayenne
- 2 hard-boiled eggs, sliced
- 12 black olives, pitted and cut in half
- 1 small tomato, thinly sliced

Place carrots in saucepan; cover with water; bring to boil; cook for 5 minutes over medium heat. Drain and allow to cool; place in food processor; process for a moment, until carrots are coarsely ground.

Transfer to mixing bowl; add garlic, coriander leaves, lemon juice, oil, salt, pepper and cayenne; mix. Place on flat serving plate. Decorate with eggs, olives and tomato.

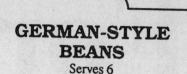

GERMAN-STYLE BEANS
Serves 6

- 4 slices bacon
- ½ cup onion, chopped
- 1½ tablespoons sugar
- 1½ tablespoons flour
- ¼ teaspoon celery seed
- ½ teaspoon salt
- 2 (15½-ounce) cans green and shelled beans
- ⅓ cup vinegar

Cook bacon until crisp; remove and drain bacon. Add onion to bacon drippings. Cook until tender. Add sugar, flour, celery seed and salt. Cook until bubbly. Drain beans; reserve ⅓ cup liquid. Add bean liquid and vinegar to flour mixture. Stir; add beans. Simmer about 10–15 minutes, or until slightly thickened and thoroughly heated. Crumble bacon and add to beans.

BOEUF BOURGUIGNON

- 1 tablespoon oil
- 1 pound lean beef cubes
- 1 onion, thinly sliced
- 1 cup beef bouillon
- 1 cup dry red wine
- 12 small onions
- 1/2 pound whole mushrooms
- Salt and pepper to taste
- 1 tablespoon cornstarch
- 1 tablespoon cold water

Heat oil in heavy saucepan and brown beef cubes until deeply colored. Remove from pan and brown sliced onions until golden brown. Return beef cubes to pan; add bouillon and dry red wine. Simmer until beef cubes are almost tender. Add onions and cook until tender. Add mushrooms and heat through; adjust seasoning. Mix cornstarch and water. Add to beef stock and boil for 1 minute, or until sauce is thickened and clear. Serve with noodles or rice.

EGG NOODLES WITH PORK SAUCE (CHINA)
Serves 4

- 1 large onion, finely chopped
- 4 garlic cloves, finely chopped
- 2 tablespoons peanut oil
- 1 pound ground pork
- ¼ teaspoon hamburger seasoning
- 2 tablespoons Worcestershire sauce
- 1 tablespoon soy sauce
- 1 teaspoon brown sugar
- 1 teaspoon hoisin sauce
- ½ cup chicken broth
- 4 cups cooked, buttered egg noodles
  Chives *or* parsley chow mein noodles *or* rice noodles

Brown onion and garlic in oil. Add pork. Cook; drain grease. Add remaining seasonings and broth. Cook 15–20 minutes. Spoon sauce over egg noodles. Garnish with chives or parsley; top with chow mein noodles or rice noodles.

This recipe originated from China. I love the flavors of their cooking and I also have developed new flavors by combining some of their choice ingredients with my favorites.

SEZCHUAN BEEF

- 1 pound round, flank *or* sirloin steak
- 1–2 tablespoons vegetable oil
- ¼ cup slivered orange peel (optional)
- 1 clove garlic, minced
- ½ teaspoon ginger*
- ¼ to ½ teaspoon crushed red pepper flakes
  Steamed broccoli
- 2 tablespoons cornstarch
- 1 cup beef broth

- 2 tablespoons soy sauce
- 2 tablespoons sherry
- ¼ cup orange marmalade**
  Hot cooked rice
- ⅛ teaspoon Kitchen Bouquet sauce

Can partially freeze meat to make it easier to thinly slice diagonally. Heat oil in large skillet or wok over medium heat. Add half the beef; stir-fry 3 minutes until browned. Remove browned meat and add rest of beef; brown. Return all beef to the wok; add orange peel, ginger, garlic and red pepper flakes; stir-fry 1 minute. Stir together cornstarch, beef broth, soy sauce, sherry and Kitchen Bouquet in a bowl; then mix in orange marmalade. Add to beef in wok. Stirring constantly, bring to a boil over medium heat and boil 1–2 minutes. Serve over hot, cooked rice with steamed broccoli on the side.

For Sezchuan Chicken:
- 1 pound boneless chicken breasts, thinly sliced
- 1 cup cool chicken broth—prepared as above

*Can use (I do) fresh minced ginger-root to taste, about 1 teaspoon.
**Can substitute ¼ cup honey for orange peel and marmalade for a different, delicious sauce.

PAKISTANI CURRIED PEAS (CURRY MATAR PAKISTANI—INDIA)
Serves 4

- 1 teaspoon butter
- 1 teaspoon vegetable oil
- ½ cup sliced green onions
- ¼ teaspoon turmeric
- ½ teaspoon ground coriander
- ⅛ teaspoon ground red pepper
- 1½ teaspoons curry powder
- ¼ teaspoon salt
- 1 tablespoon Garam Masala (recipe follows)
- 1 (10-ounce) package frozen peas

Garam Masala:
- 1 tablespoon cardamom seeds
- 1 (2-inch) stick cinnamon
- 1 teaspoon cumin seeds
- 1 teaspoon whole cloves
- 1 teaspoon black peppercorns
- ¼ teaspoon nutmeg

Put all ingredients of Garam Masala in grinder for 30–40 seconds.

In saucepan heat butter and oil; add green onions; cook, stirring, 2 minutes. Stir in turmeric, coriander, red pepper, curry powder, salt and Garam Masala. Cook, stirring occasionally, about 10 minutes. Add peas. Reduce heat; cook about 10 minutes. Serve with plain hot rice and Indian bread (chapati or poori).

PAPRIKAS POTATOES (HUNGARY)
Serves 6–8

- 3 pounds potatoes, peeled and sliced to ¼-inch thickness
- 2 tablespoons shortening *or* bacon drippings
- 1 small onion, minced
- 3 cloves garlic, pressed
- 1 tablespoon salt
- 2 tablespoons Hungarian paprika
- 2 cups chicken broth
- 2 cups water
- 1 cup sour cream

In medium-size Dutch oven, melt shortening and sauté onion and garlic until limp. Add paprika and salt. Stir and cook for about 1 minute. Add chicken broth and water. Bring to boil. Add potatoes; bring back to boil and reduce heat to simmer. Continue cooking until potatoes are tender. Stir with care occasionally. Stir in sour cream and bring back just to boil. Ready to serve.

The Hungarian love of sour cream, paprika and garlic is used to enhance the lowly potato into a tasty side dish. Brought from Hungary by grandparents.

MIDDLE EAST TABOULEH SALAD

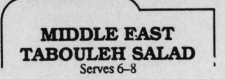

Serves 6–8

- 1 cup fine burghul (wheat pilaf)
- 2 cups chopped parsley
- ½ cup finely chopped green onions
- ¼ cup finely chopped mint
- ¼ cup olive oil
- ¼ cup lemon juice
- ½ teaspoon salt
- ½ teaspoon pepper, black
- 2 firm, ripe tomatoes, chopped
- 1 cucumber, sliced
- 1 green pepper, chopped

Wash burghul with cold water and drain at once, squeezing all water out, then add lemon juice, oil, salt and black pepper. Stir well. Let stand for a few minutes, or until burghul has absorbed the lemon and oil. Sliced and chopped vegetables must be pretty dry so that when you add the burghul, which has been mixed with oil and lemon juice, it will not be soggy but just hold together very nicely. Add your mint last. If you wish, you can also chop lettuce and add to your salad.

MEATBALLS WITH SAUERKRAUT (HUNGARY)

Serves 6

- ¾ pound ground beef chuck
- ¾ cup ground pork
- ¾ cup minced onion
- 3 cloves garlic, pressed
- 2 eggs, slightly beaten
- 1 tablespoon salt
- ½ teaspoon freshly ground pepper
- ¾ cup long-grain rice, partially cooked and cooled
- 2 tablespoons shortening (lard is best; next best, bacon drippings)
- 2 tablespoons flour
- 2 pounds sauerkraut
- Water

Additional salt to flavor, to personal taste
Pepper to taste

In large bowl mix thoroughly the first 8 ingredients. Set aside. In large Dutch oven, melt shortening and add flour. Under low heat cook flour until lightly browned. Add 1 cup water. Place sauerkraut in sieve and slightly wash under cold water. Remove pan from heat and place a layer of sauerkraut on bottom. With your hands, form the meat mixture into about 2½-inch balls. Place on top of sauerkraut. Cover with remaining kraut. Add water to cover by about 1 inch. Bring to boil, then reduce heat to simmer and cover. Cook for about 1½ hours, until meat is tender. Season the liquid with salt and pepper to taste. Serve in soup bowls with good rye bread.

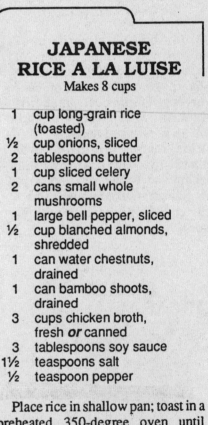

POTICA (YUGOSLAVIAN CHRISTMAS BREAD)

- 3½ cups flour
- 1 package yeast
- 1 cup milk
- 2 tablespoons sugar
- 2 tablespoons butter
- 1 teaspoon salt
- 1 egg

Filling:

- 2 cups finely ground walnuts
- 1 egg, beaten
- ¼ cup brown sugar
- 2 tablespoons honey
- 2 tablespoons milk
- 1 tablespoon melted butter
- 1 teaspoon cinnamon
- ½ teaspoon vanilla

Stir together 1½ cups flour and yeast. Heat milk, sugar, butter and salt until warm. Add to flour/yeast mixture. Add egg and beat with electric mixer at low speed. Scrape bowl. Beat for 3 minutes at high speed. Stir in remaining flour to make a moderately stiff dough. Turn out and knead until smooth and elastic. Place in greased bowl and let rise until doubled—about 1½ hours. Combine filling ingredients and set aside. Punch down dough and let sit for 10 minutes. Roll out until very thin and approximately 20 x 30 inches. Spread out nut filling and roll up along longer side. Pinch edge to seal. Place in U-shape on greased baking sheet. Let rise until doubled. Bake at 350 degrees for 30–35 minutes.

JAPANESE RICE A LA LUISE

Makes 8 cups

- 1 cup long-grain rice (toasted)
- ½ cup onions, sliced
- 2 tablespoons butter
- 1 cup sliced celery
- 2 cans small whole mushrooms
- 1 large bell pepper, sliced
- ½ cup blanched almonds, shredded
- 1 can water chestnuts, drained
- 1 can bamboo shoots, drained
- 3 cups chicken broth, fresh *or* canned
- 3 tablespoons soy sauce
- 1½ teaspoons salt
- ½ teaspoon pepper

Place rice in shallow pan; toast in a preheated 350-degree oven until lightly browned, stirring occasionally. Melt butter in large saucepan and sauté onions until translucent. Add all other ingredients and stir over medium heat until hot, but not boiling. Add salt to taste, if necessary. Place browned dry rice in a 3-quart casserole and pour contents of saucepan over it; stir. Cover and bake in 350-degree oven until liquid is absorbed, about 45 minutes.

BISCOUTI (ITALIAN BISCUIT COOKIES)
Makes 5–6 dozen

- 6 tablespoons Crisco shortening
- 1 cup sugar
- 3 eggs
- 1 teaspoon anise extract
- 5 teaspoons baking powder
- ¾ cup milk
- 6 cups flour, sifted

Cream together shortening and sugar. Add 1 egg at a time. Add anise extract. Add flour and baking powder alternately with milk. Grease pan. Bake at 400 degrees for 10–12 minutes. Cookies can be iced with confectioners' sugar and milk combination. (Add food coloring to icing for holiday flair, if desired.)

RED SNAPPER A LA VERACRUZANA (HUACHINANGO A LA VERACRUZANA)
Serves 4–6

- 1 (2½ pound) red snapper
- 2½ cups chopped tomatoes
- 2 onions, chopped
- 3 green peppers, chopped
- 3 cloves garlic, minced
- 1 bunch parsley, finely chopped
- 2 chili peppers, finely chopped (small elongated green chilies)
- ⅓ cup finely chopped green olives
- ⅓ cup capers
- 4 tablespoons vinegar
- 8 jalapeño peppers (cut in half, fried and cut in strips)
- 1 pint oil

- 1 teaspoon oregano
  Salt and pepper
- ¼ pint dry sherry

Cut red snapper into 6-ounce fillets. Sauté tomatoes in a skillet; add onions, then green peppers, garlic, parsley and chili peppers. Add chopped olives, capers, vinegar and jalapeño strips. Blend in oil. Season with oregano, salt and pepper. Simmer slowly until all is tender and thickened. Add sherry during last part of cooking. In a separate skillet, heat a little oil and add rinsed red snapper fillets. Cover fish with sauce. Cover and cook over low heat 20 minutes. Keep fish from sticking with wide spatula. Serve with rice.

SOUPE AUX LEGUMES DU QUEBEC (VEGETABLE SOUP, "QUEBEC STYLE")
Serves 8

- 1½ to 2 pounds brisket of beef *or* beef shoulder
- 1 meatless beef bone
- 2 cups diced carrots
- ½ cup diced parsnips
- 3 large onions, cut in very thin slices
- 1 cup of finely chopped celery
- 1 teaspoon savory
- ½ teaspoon marjoram
- ¼ teaspoon aniseed
- 1 teaspoon peppercorns
- 2 tablespoons coarse salt
- 1 tablespoon sugar
- 1 (20-ounce) can tomatoes
- 3 quarts water

Place all ingredients in a large heavy pan. Bring to a boil; cover and simmer for approximately 4 hours. Mix a few times during the first hour. The dish may be served at the table as a "pot au feu," or the meat may be carved before presenting at the table.

This recipe is from my mother's collection of Canadian recipes.

GOLDEN-CRUST BREAD, POLISH STYLE
Makes 2 loaves

- 1 cup sour cream
- ¼ teaspoon soda
- 1¼ cups hot water
- 1 cake yeast
- ¼ cup sugar
- ½ teaspoon salt
- 2 tablespoons shortening, melted
- 6½ cups flour

Combine sour cream and soda; add water, yeast, sugar, salt and melted shortening. Gradually add flour. Mix until well-blended. Knead 5–8 minutes. Put in greased bowl and allow to rise in a warm place until double. Shape into 2 loaves. Allow to rise again until double. Bake in a 375-degree oven for 45 minutes. Let stand 45 minutes before cutting.

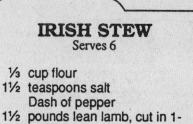

IRISH STEW
Serves 6

- ⅓ cup flour
- 1½ teaspoons salt
  Dash of pepper
- 1½ pounds lean lamb, cut in 1-inch cubes
- 2 tablespoons fat
- 3 cups water
- 3 medium onions, sliced
- 4 medium potatoes, cubed
- 1 turnip, diced
- 5 medium carrots, quartered
- 1½ cups frozen peas
- ¼ cup water

Combine flour, salt and pepper. Coat meat. Save remaining flour. Brown meat in hot fat in a 4-quart saucepan. Add water and cover. Simmer until meat is tender, about 1½ hours. Add onions, potatoes, turnip and carrots. Cover. Simmer 15 minutes. Add peas. Cover and simmer until vegetables are tender. Blend water with remaining flour. Add to stew. Stir. Cook until thick.

HUNGARIAN SHORT RIBS
Serves 6

- 4 pounds beef short ribs
- 2 tablespoons oil
- 2 large onions, sliced
- 1/4 cup brown sugar
- 1 small can tomato sauce
- 2 1/2 cups water
- 1/4 cup white vinegar
- 1 teaspoon salt
- 1 teaspoon dry mustard
- 1 teaspoon Worcestershire sauce
- 6 ounces medium-size noodles

In Dutch oven brown meat in the oil. Add onions. Blend tomato sauce with 1½ cups water, ¼ cup brown sugar, vinegar, salt, mustard and Worcestershire sauce. Pour over meat. Cover and simmer for 2–2½ hours, until meat is tender. Stir in noodles and remaining 1 cup water. Cover again and simmer for 15–20 minutes, or until noodles are tender.

REUBEN CROQUETTES (GERMAN)

- 1/2 cup raw rice, cooked
- 1 (1-pound) can kraut, well-drained
- 1 can corned beef
- 1/4 cup chopped onion
- 3 eggs
- 1 cup shredded Swiss cheese
- 1 teaspoon salt
- 1/4 teaspoon pepper
- 2 tablespoons water
- 1 1/2 cups fine bread crumbs

Chop the kraut and beef together very fine. Add onion, 2 eggs, cooked rice, cheese, salt and pepper. Mix well. Shape into 18 balls or patties. Use ¼ cup for each ball.

Mix the other egg and 2 tablespoons water together. Roll each croquette in bread crumbs, then in egg mixture and then in bread crumbs again. Let dry for 10 minutes.

If frying the croquettes, fry in shallow oil for 5–7 minutes; turn over once to brown on both sides.

If baking, bake at 400 degrees for 10 minutes in a pan; then turn and bake for another 10 minutes.

Serve with sauce (recipe follows).

Sauce for Croquettes:
- 1 cup mayonnaise
- 1/3 cup milk
- 1/4 cup prepared mustard
- 4 teaspoons lemon juice

Mix all together and serve over croquettes.

BEET BORSCHT (RUSSIAN SOUP)
Serves 6

- 4 cups beef broth
- 2 teaspoons salt
- 1/2 teaspoon pepper
- 4 cups raw beets, peeled and shredded
- 3 cups shredded cabbage
- 1 cup chopped onion
- 1/2 cup sour cream
- 2 tablespoons brown sugar
- 1 can beer (optional)

In Dutch oven or large pan bring beef broth to a boil; add prepared beets, cabbage, onions, salt and pepper (unless broth is already seasoned). Simmer for about 35–40 minutes. Add brown sugar and beer. Reheat; serve in bowls; top with teaspoonful of sour cream.

Great served with thick slices of dark rye bread and butter.

HAWAIIAN SWEET-SOUR PORK
Serves 7

- 1½ pounds lean pork, cut in 2 x 2½-inch strips
- 2½ cups pineapple chunks
- 1/4 cup brown sugar
- 2 tablespoons cornstarch
- 1/4 cup vinegar
- 2/3 tablespoon soy sauce
- 1/4 teaspoon salt
- 1 small green pepper, cut in strips
- 1/4 cup thinly sliced onion

Brown pork in small amount of vegetable oil. Add ½ cup water; cover and simmer (do not boil) until tender, about 1 hour or less. Drain pineapple and reserve syrup. Combine sugar and cornstarch. Add pineapple syrup, vinegar, soy sauce and salt. Add to pork. Cook and stir until mixture thickens. Add pineapple, green peppers and onion. Cook 2–3 minutes. Serve on hot steamed rice.

EUROPEAN TORTE SQUARES

- 1/2 pound butter (2 sticks)
- 1 cup sugar
- 6 egg yolks
- 2 cups flour
- 1 teaspoon salt
- 1 teaspoon baking powder
- Grape jelly

Cream butter and sugar. Add the 6 egg yolks and cream well. Sift flour, salt and baking powder; add to creamed mixture. Pat this mixture on a cookie sheet and spread top surface with grape jelly. Top this with icing (recipe follows).

Icing:
- 6 egg whites
- 1 cup ground nuts
- 1 cup sugar

Beat egg whites until they hold peaks. Add nuts and sugar; blend well. Use this on top of torte. Cut in squares and bake for 30 minutes at 375 degrees.

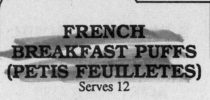

FRENCH BREAKFAST PUFFS (PETIS FEUILLETES)
Serves 12

⅓ cup shortening
1 cup granulated sugar
1 egg
1½ cups sifted flour
1½ teaspoons baking powder
½ teaspoon salt
¼ teaspoon nutmeg
½ cup milk
⅓ cup melted butter
1 teaspoon cinnamon

Heat oven to 350 degrees; grease muffin tins. Mix shortening, ½ cup sugar and egg thoroughly. Sift together flour, baking powder, salt and nutmeg; stir in alternately with milk. Fill muffin tins two-thirds full. Bake for 20–25 minutes. Immediately remove from tins and roll in melted butter; roll in mixture of ½ cup sugar and cinnamon. Serve hot.

HOT SALAD DRESSING (HEIS SALAT SAUCE)
Serves 6

3 slices bacon
3 tablespoons vinegar
1 tablespoon sugar
½ teaspoon salt
1 tablespoon flour
½ teaspoon pepper
1 tablespoon sour cream
1 egg, well-beaten
Lettuce, spinach *or* endive

Dice bacon and fry crisp; pour off some of the fat. Add vinegar, sugar, salt, flour and pepper; brown well. Stir in sour cream and egg; stir until thick and smooth. Pour over chopped lettuce, spinach greens or endive.

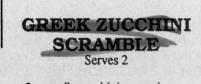

GREEK ZUCCHINI SCRAMBLE
Serves 2

2 small zucchini squash
3 tablespoons butter
2 large eggs
Salt and pepper

Wash and scrape zucchini. Slice across into thin slices and drop into melted butter in large 12-inch skillet. Cover; let cook over low heat until tender and browned lightly, stirring occasionally to prevent sticking. Beat eggs; pour over zucchini in pan. Add salt and pepper. Stir gently until eggs are cooked.

BRAMBORY NA KYSELO (SOUR POTATOES)
Serves 6

2½ pounds potatoes, peeled and sliced
½ teaspoon caraway seeds
¼ cup flour
¼ cup shortening
1 cup sour cream
1 tablespoon vinegar
½ teaspoon sugar
1 tablespoon chopped dill *or* chives
2 egg yolks

Boil potatoes in salted water with caraway seeds. Drain, and reserve liquid. Brown flour in shortening, stirring constantly; stir in 1–1½ cups of potato water. Simmer for 10–15 minutes. Add the remaining ingredients and potatoes. Serve as is, or add diced, boiled meat.

GREEK-STYLE BEEF STEW

2 pounds stew meat, cut in cubes
3 tablespoons oil
2 teaspoons parsley flakes
1 teaspoon salt
1 teaspoon pepper
4 whole cloves, broken up
¼ teaspoon each nutmeg and allspice
1 clove garlic, crushed
1 can whole tomatoes *or* stewed tomatoes
½ cup red wine
1 cup chopped onions
10 black olives

Brown meat in a Dutch oven. Combine flakes, salt, pepper, cloves, nutmeg and allspice. Add garlic. Add oil to meat mixture. Add remaining ingredients. Bring to a boil; cover. Bake at 350 degrees for 2 hours.

HUNGARIAN CHERRY EVEN-WEIGHT CAKE (EGYENSULY)

¾ pound (1½ cups) unsalted butter
¾ pound (1½ cups) sugar
6 large eggs
¾ pound (3 cups) sifted flour
Pinch of salt
Grated rind of 1 lemon
1 pound sweet *or* sour pitted cherries *or* sliced peaches

Preheat oven to 350 degrees. Grease and flour a 9-inch springform or loaf pan. Cream butter and sugar extremely well. Add each egg separately, beating after each addition. Sift flour with salt 4 times through a fine sifter held high in the air. Combine flour and lemon rind, then add gradually to batter. Mix well, scraping sides often. Fold in cherries or peaches. Bake for 1 hour, or until cake springs back when touched and pulls from sides of pan. Cool on a rack and turn out.

CARAWAY MEATBALLS (KUMMEL UND FLEISCH GERMAN)

Serves 4–6

- 1 tablespoon caraway seed
- 1 tablespoon diced onion
- 3 tablespoons red wine vinegar
- 1 pound ground beef
- ½ ground ground pork
- 1½ cups soft bread crumbs
- ¾ cup milk
- 1 egg
- 1½ teaspoons salt
  Pinch of pepper

Soak caraway seed, onion and vinegar for 10 minutes. Add remaining ingredients and mix well. Shape into meatballs; roll in flour. Brown in melted fat. Add 1 cup water. Cover. Simmer for 30 minutes.

BEEF MORTOUN (BOEUF MORTOUN-FRENCH)

Serves 6

- 2½ pounds cooked round roast
- 2 onions, finely chopped
- 2 tablespoons butter
- 2 tablespoons flour
- 1 cup beef stock
  Salt and pepper
  Bread crumbs

Slice beef thinly; trim away gristle and fat. Lay slices in a greased baking dish. Brown onions in butter. Add flour and cook to form paste. Add stock to make a thin gravy. Add salt and pepper; pour over beef. Sprinkle with bread crumbs. Heat in oven at 350 degrees for 30 minutes.

SWEET-AND-SOUR ITALIAN SALAD (INSALATA AGRO-DOLCE)

Serves 20

- 1 pint carrots, cooked, diced and drained
- 1 pint green peas, cooked, diced and drained
- 1 pint green beans, cooked, diced and drained
- 1 pint red beans, cooked, diced and drained
- 1 cup diced onion
- 1 cup chopped green pepper
- ¼ cup chopped pimiento
- ½ cup salad oil
- 1 teaspoon celery seed
- 1 cup sugar
- 1 cup white vinegar

Combine all ingredients in a large bowl; stir lightly. Marinate overnight in refrigerator.

BULKOKI

Serves 4–6

- 2 pounds sirloin, frozen and thinly sliced
- ¼ cup brown sugar
- 4–6 small cloves garlic, chopped *or* minced
- 2 tablespoons chopped onion
- ½ cup salad oil
- ¼ cup soy sauce
- ½ teaspoon pepper
  Fluffy cooked rice

Mix sugar, garlic, onion, salad oil, soy sauce and pepper for marinade. Marinate meat for 2–4 hours. Prepare rice. Remove meat from marinade and stir-fry in an ordinary skillet or wok for about 8 minutes, or until meat is done.

NORWEGIAN WAFERS

Makes 4 dozen

- ⅔ cup butter
- 4 hard-cooked egg yolks, sieved
- ½ cup honey
- 2 teaspoons vanilla
- 2¼ cups flour, sifted
- 1 cup miniature chocolate chips

Preheat oven to 400 degrees. Combine butter, egg yolks, honey and vanilla; blend well. Add flour and chocolate chips. Divide dough in half and roll between 2 sheets of waxed paper to ¼-inch thickness. Cut in 2-inch circles. Bake 8 minutes.

TAHINI DRESSING

Makes ¾ cup

- 3 tablespoons tahini (sesame seed paste)
- 6 tablespoons cold water
- 1 garlic clove
  Fresh lemon juice
- 2 teaspoons minced fresh parsley
  Paprika

Combine tahini and cold water; stir well until blended. Peel garlic and put through a press into the tahini mixture. Add lemon juice to taste and the minced parsley. Add a light sprinkling of paprika and mix again.

ITALIAN BEEF— MANZO AL ITALIANO

Serves 6

- 3 pounds beef roast, thinly sliced
- ½ pound suet
- 1 teaspoon oregano
- ½ teaspoon red pepper
- 1 teaspoon onion salt
- ½ teaspoon garlic salt
- 1 teaspoon black pepper
- 1 teaspoon salt

Place beef in Dutch oven; cover with water. Add suet and seasonings; cover. Simmer 2–3 hours until beef is tender. Serve on French bread.

KOREAN VEGETABLE DISH

2 cloves garlic
1/4 cup vegetable oil
1 quart stewed tomatoes
1 package frozen spinach
1 cup uncooked rice

Brown garlic in oil. Add tomatoes and simmer for 1/2 hour. Add spinach and rice. Cover tightly, cook until rice is tender, adding more water or tomato juice if needed. Add salt and pepper to taste.

This is unusual and very tasty.

ALMOND AND SESAME SEED PIES (MAQRUD)

Makes about 24 pies

2-1/2 cups semolina flour
3 eggs
1 cup butter
1 teaspoon baking powder
1 teaspoon vanilla
1/4 cup pulverized almonds
1/4 cup pulverized sesame seeds
1/4 cup sugar
1 cup honey
1/2 cup water
2 teaspoons rose water
Oil for frying
Icing sugar

Make dough by thoroughly mixing semolina, eggs, butter, baking powder and vanilla (add a few tablespoons of water if the dough is thick); form into 2" long rolls, about 3/4" in diameter; set aside.

Make filling by mixing almonds, sesame seeds and sugar. In your palm, flatten each roll to about 1/4" thicknesses; place 1 heaping teaspoon of filling in middle; pinch to close, in the process turning the ends in to form a rectangular pie. Allow *maqruds* to rest a few moments while preparing syrup.

Make a syrup by placing honey and water in pot, stirring constantly bring to a boil; reduce heat to low and stir in rose water. Keep on low heat.

In frying pan, pour oil 3/4" thick; heat. Then fry pies over medium heat until light brown, turning over once.

Place pies in syrup for at least 2 minutes, remove; allow to cool. Sprinkle heavily with icing sugar and serve.

NOTE: If fresh coriander is not available, a mixture of half chives-half parsley can be substituted. Also, vegetable oil may be used instead of olive oil.

SPAGHETTI WITH RICOTTA AND WALNUT SAUCE

2 cloves garlic
1 cup walnuts
1 tablespoon snipped parsley
1 tablespoon chopped fresh basil or mint
1 pound ricotta cheese
1 cup grated Parmesan cheese
1 teaspoon seasoned salt
1/4 teaspoon pepper
(optional) pinch or two of red pepper

Put garlic, walnuts and herbs in blender, whirl until creamy. Turn out into bowl with remaining ingredients, mix thoroughly. Set aside. Cook and drain 3/4 pound spaghetti, add while hot to bowl mixture. Toss until pasta is well coated with sauce. Garnish with snipped parsley and a few chopped walnuts.

CHICKEN CHOW MEIN (CHINESE DISH)

Serves 4

1 whole chicken
1 stalk celery, chopped
2 onions, chopped
1 tablespoon butter
1 tablespoon soya sauce
Salt and Pepper

1 tablespoon Worcestershire sauce
3 tablespoons cornstarch

Cook chicken until tender. Remove bones. Stir-fry chopped celery and onion in butter. Add to chicken and broth; cook celery until tender. Add soya sauce, Worcestershire sauce, salt, and pepper. Make thickening with cornstarch. Add to chow mein. Serve over chow mein noodles.

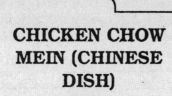

AUSTRIAN SALZBURG DUMPLINGS

Serves 3 to 6

6 eggs, separated
1/2 cup granulated sugar
1/4 teaspoon vanilla extract
1/3 cup all-purpose flour
3 tablespoons unsalted butter
Powdered sugar

Preheat oven to 425 degrees. In medium bowl, beat egg whites until soft peaks form. Gradually beat in granulated sugar until stiff, but not dry. In small bowl, beat egg yolks; stir in vanilla and 2 tablespoons beaten egg whites; do not stir. Sift flour over egg mixture. Fold egg yolk mixture and flour into egg whites, quickly but carefully. Place butter in shallow baking dish; place in oven until butter melts. Spoon egg mixture into hot dish. Using 2 tablespoons, shape egg mixture into 3 to 6 equal rolls or mounds.

Place dish in center of oven. Bake 8 to 10 minutes or until golden brown. Sprinkle top with powdered sugar while hot. Serve immediately.

NOTE: This is a Soufflé type of dessert. deep out of drafts to keep from collapsing.

HUNGARIAN NOODLES OR KLUSE
Serves 5

2 cups flour
2 eggs
1 cup water
1 teaspoon salt

Beat all the above ingredients with a wooden spoon until the dough is soft, and bubbles form. Make dough somewhat stiff. Cut with a spoon into boiling salted water. Let noodles boil until they rise to the top and boil for 5 minutes. Drain and serve with chicken.

This recipe was made by my mother-in-law. She used to cool the mixture and then fry them with a pound of side pork and onion, like fried potatoes. She did this to serve a family of 15 at one time. This recipe is about 50 years old. It takes about 20 minutes to prepare.

HONEY-HAM CHOW MEIN

1 medium green pepper
1 medium onion
2 ribs celery
1 small can mushrooms
2 tablespoons vegetable oil
2 cups cooked ham strips
1 cup chicken bouillon
2 tablespoons honey
1 tablespoon corn starch
1 tablespoon soy sauce
1/4 cup water

Cut green pepper in strips, onion in slices, celery in pieces (for Chinese effect, cut on the bias) and mushrooms in slices. Heat oil; add onions and ham; cook until ham is slightly browned. Add bouillon, pepper, celery and mushrooms; cover tightly; cook slowly for 6 minutes. Mix remaining ingredients; add and cook for 2 minutes, stirring constantly. Serve with crisp noodles, or over a bed of rice.

ITALIAN VEGETABLE SALAD

1 head cauliflower, cut into pieces
1 bunch broccoli, cut into pieces
3 zucchini, sliced
5 tomatoes, cut into chunks or 1 basket of cherry tomatoes
1 can black pitted olives, sliced
1 (16 ounce) bottle of Seven Seas Italian Dressing
1 teaspoon salt
1/2 teaspoon pepper

Mix all ingredients together and let stand overnight in refrigerator. This is a great recipe for picnics or potlucks.

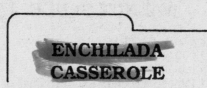

ENCHILADA CASSEROLE

12 corn tortillas
2 pounds hamburger
2 tablespoons chili powder
1/2 teaspoon garlic powder
1 medium onion, chopped
15 ounce can tomato sauce
Salt and pepper
1 cups grated Colby or Cheddar cheese
1 can cream of chicken soup
3/4 cup milk

Brown meat, garlic and onion. Add tomato sauce, chili powder, salt and pepper. Heat 9 x 13 inch pan. Line bottom with 6 tortillas. Add meat on top. Cover with 6 more tortillas. Spread chicken soup over these and then milk. Cover with cheese. Bake 25 minutes at 350 degrees. A very easy and tasty dish!

QUICK MEXICAN DISH
Serves 6-8

1 can cream of cheese soup
1 can cream of onion soup

16 ounce can tomatoes, chopped and drained
1 pound ground beef
1 package taco seasoning
8 ounce package Cheddar cheese, grated
11 ounce package Doritos, crushed
Onion, chopped
16 ounce can corn, drained
1 can green chilies, chopped

Brown meat and onion; drain. Add seasonings and corn. Mix together. Add soups and tomatoes. Grease an oblong baking dish. In bottom of dish crush Doritos to completely cover the bottom. Add meat mixture, then pour soup mixture over the meat. Top with cheese. Bake 350 degrees for 25 minutes.

Add sour cream on top of baked casserole, and sliced ripe olives. This is quick and easy!

ENCHILADA SQUARES

1 pound ground beef
1 cup chopped onion
4-ounce can diced green chilies, drained
4 eggs
8-ounce can tomato sauce
5-1/3-ounce can (2/3 cup) evaporated milk
1 (12-ounce) envelope enchilada sauce mix and 1 teaspoon chili powder
1 cup shredded Cheddar cheese
1/2 cup sliced black olives

Brown beef and onion, drain. Spread meat mixture in lightly buttered 10 x 6 x 2-inch baking dish. Sprinkle diced green chilies over meat mixtures. Beat eggs, tomato sauce, evaporated milk, enchilada sauce. Sprinkle sliced black olives over top.

If desired, sprinkle 2 cups corn chips over top.

Bake in a 350 degree oven for 25 minutes or until set. Sprinkle with cheese and bake 5 more minutes. Let set 10 minutes before cutting.

MEXICAN PIE

Crust:
2 cups beef broth
1 cup long-grain rice
1 tablespoon margarine
1 teaspoon salt
2 eggs, slightly beaten
2 tablespoons chopped pimiento

Filling:
1 pound ground beef
1 garlic clove, crushed
1 teaspoon cumin
1/2 teaspoon salt
1/2 cup mild taco sauce
1 egg, beaten

Guacamole:
1 large avocado, peeled and quartered
1 tablespoon chopped onion
1 tablespoon mild taco sauce
1/2 teaspoon salt
1/2 teaspoon lemon juice

1 cup sour cream

Crust: Grease a 10-inch pie pan. In medium saucepan, heat broth to boiling. Stir in rice, margarine and salt. Return to a boil. Cover reduce heat; simmer until rice is tender. Remove from heat; let cool slightly; stir in eggs and pimiento. Press against bottom and sides of pie plate.

Filling: Preheat oven to 350 degrees. In skillet, brown beef. Drain. Stir in garlic, cumin and salt; cook 2 more minutes. Remove from heat; stir in taco sauce and egg. Spoon filling into crust. Bake 25 minutes.

Guacamole: In small bowl, mash 3 avocado quarters (reserve 1 quarter for garnish). Stir in remaining ingredients. Cover and set aside.

Remove pie from oven. Spread guacamole over meat. Top with sour cream. Return to oven and bake 5 more minutes. Slice remaining avocado; sprinkle on pie.

CRAB MEAT PIES (BRIKS)
Makes 10 pies

4 tablespoons butter
2 medium sized onions, finely chopped
3 cloves garlic, crushed
1/4 cup finely chopped fresh coriander leaves
1 hot pepper, finely chopped
1 teaspoon salt
1/2 teaspoon pepper
4.5-ounce can crab meat, drained
1/2 cup Parmesan cheese
11 small eggs
10 sheets filo dough
Oil for frying

In frying pan, melt butter. Over medium heat, stir-fry onions, garlic, coriander leaves, hot pepper, salt and pepper for 10 minutes. Remove from heat. Make a filling by stirring in crab meat and cheese; set aside. Beat one of the eggs; set aside. Fold a sheet of filo dough over twice to make a square. Place 1/10 of the filling in center; form into a well. Keep dough soft by placing wet towel over sheets while making pies. Brush edges of square with beaten egg; break an egg into the well; fold over to form a triangle. Press edges together. Turn them in about 1/2"; brush again with egg to make sure they are well sealed. In frying pan, pour oil to 3/4" thickness; heat; gently slide in pies; fry over slightly higher than medium heat for about 2 minutes on each side, or until sides are golden brown. Remove and place on paper towels; drain. When all the pies are finished, serve immediately.

LUAU RIBS
Serves 6-8

1/2 cup brown sugar, firmly packed
2 teaspoons ginger
1/3 cup catsup
1/3 cup vinegar
2 cloves garlic, minced
2 (4-1/2-ounces each) cans apple and apricot baby food
2 tablespoons soy sauce or Worcestershire sauce
6 to 8 pounds meaty spareribs
1 teaspoon salt
Dash of pepper

Mix brown sugar and ginger. Combine with baby food, catsup, vinegar, soy sauce and garlic. Rub ribs with salt and pepper. Place ribs, meat side up, on rack in a shallow pan. Bake at 450 degrees for 15 minutes; pour off fat. Reduce oven temperature to 350 degrees. Baste ribs with sauce and continue baking for 1-1/2 hours (depending on your oven.) While baking, baste with sauce several times.

ITALIAN TURKEY LOAF

1-1/4 pounds ground turkey
1 cup egg plant, diced
1 onion, chopped
6-8 mushrooms, chopped
1 egg white, beaten
1/3 teaspoon sage
1/3 teaspoon tarragon
2 tablespoons low sodium tomato sauce
2 cups bran flakes cereal
1 medium pepper, chopped
2 medium tomatoes, peeled and chopped
1 whole egg, beaten
1/3 teaspoon oregano
1 clove garlic
1/4 teaspoon pepper

Place all ingredients, except tomato sauce, in large mixing bowl. Mix until well blended. Press mixture in loaf pan 8x5x3-inches. Spread tomato sauce evenly over top of loaf; bake at 350 degrees for 30 minutes. Remove from oven and drain off excess liquid. Return to oven for additional 45 minutes or until loaf is done. Allow to sit a few minutes before removing from pan and slicing.

FRENCH ONION SOUP
Serves 4

2 large onions, sliced thin and
    sautéed in butter until light brown
2 cups beef stock or beef bouillon
1/2 cup cream
1 teaspoon Worcestershire sauce
Salt and pepper to taste
Toast
Parmesan Cheese

Boil the sautéed onions in stock for
10 minutes. Add cream, salt and pepper to taste. Just before serving, add the Worcestershire sauce. Put a thin slice of toast covered with Parmesan cheese into each bowl.

SCOTTISH BANNOCKS

1 cup whole wheat flour
1 cup rolled oats
1 scant teaspoon baking soda
1-1/4 cups buttermilk
2 tablespoons vegetable oil
2 teaspoons honey

Mix flour, oats, and baking soda. In another bowl, mix remaining ingredients; then stir into dry ingredients until the combination is creamy smooth. Spoon batter into muffin tins and bake in preheated oven at 300-325 degrees for 20-25 minutes. The oatcakes will be golden brown with a top nicely textured from the rolled oats.

SCOTTISH BANANA COOKIES
Makes 5 dozen

2/3 cup butter
1 cup sugar
2 eggs
1 teaspoon almond flavoring
2-1/4 cups flour
2 tablespoons cornstarch
1 teaspoon baking powder
1/2 teaspoon baking soda
1/2 teaspoon salt
1-1/2 cups mashed bananas

Cream together butter and sugar until light and fluffy. Add eggs, one at a time, and beat well after each addition. Add almond flavoring. Sift together flour, cornstarch, baking powder, baking soda, and salt. Add alternately with mashed bananas.

Drop by teaspoonfuls onto greased cookie sheets. Bake in a 400 degree oven for 15 minutes.

POLISH BOWS

8 egg yolks
1 tablespoon vanilla
1 ounce whiskey
Sour cream (same amount as yolks)
1 teaspoon salt (level)
1 teaspoon baking powder
All the flour it will take

Put yolks into bowl; beat until yolks turn light yellow (about 5 minutes). Add sour cream; mix until well blended. Add vanilla; mix a little; add whiskey, salt and baking powder. Mix for short time until everything looks mixed. Start to add sifted flour until you can scoop it out of bowl. Scoop out onto more sifted flour on table. Knead until dough starts to make a popping noise; form loaf; wrap in plastic wrap; place in refrigerator overnight.

Next day, cut piece about 1-1/2-inches; roll out very thin. Cut into strips 2-inches wide and 6-inches long. Cut slit in center; put 1 end through slit.

When all dough is rolled out, slit and turned, you are ready to fry in shortening (about 4 at a time), until they look done.

ITALIAN BOW KNOT COOKES
Makes 6 dozen medium cookies

This recipe has made many a kaffe klatch more enjoyable. Keeps well, if they last that long.

4 cups flour
4 teaspoons baking powder
2 teaspoons salt
6 beaten eggs
1 cup sugar
1/2 cup oil
1-1/2 teaspoons lemon extract

Blend beaten eggs into dry ingredients, following with all other ingredients. Knead until smooth. Roll into pencil lengths and tie in bow knots. Bake on greased cookie sheets in a 400 degree oven for 15 minutes.

Lemon Icing:
1/4 cup butter
1 pound confectioners' sugar
Juice of 2 lemons

Cream butter; add remaining ingredients. Stir until well blended. If too thin, add more sugar. Too thick, add more lemon juice.

FUNNEL CAKES (DRECHTER KUCHE)

3 eggs
2 cups milk
1/4 cup sugar
3-4 cups flour
1/2 teaspoon salt
2 teaspoons baking powder

Beat eggs; add sugar and milk. Sift half the flour, salt, and baking powder together and add to milk and egg mixture. Beat the batter smooth and add only as much more flour as needed. Batter should be thin enough to run through a funnel. Drop from funnel into deep, hot fat (375 degrees). Spirals and endless intricate shapes can be made by swirling and criss-crossing while controlling the funnel spout with a finger. Serve hot with molasses, tart jelly, jam, or sprinkle with powdered sugar.

CHICKEN COUSCOUS
Serves 8 to 10

To prepare *couscous*, a couscoussiére which is a double boiler with the top part perforated is required.

NOTE: Cost is approximately $25 for a 6-quart pot.

2 cups couscous
5 tablespoons butter
4 tablespoons olive oil
1 pound chicken, cut into small serving pieces
2 medium sized onions, chopped
4 cloves garlic, crushed
1/4 cup finely chopped fresh coriander leaves
1 hot pepper, finely chopped
1 large carrot, scraped and sliced into 4 pieces lengthwise and cut into 1" pieces
4 small potatoes, quartered
2 zucchini about 6" long, sliced lengthwise and cut into 2" pieces
1 cup 1" cubes of turnips
2 cups chopped cabbage
4 medium sized tomatoes, chopped
19-ounce can chick peas, with water
2 teaspoons salt
1 teaspoon ground caraway
1 teaspoon cumin
1/2 teaspoon pepper
Pinch of saffron
1/2 cup slivered almonds, toasted

In mixing bowl, place *couscous* and butter; knead with fingers until *couscous* kernels are coated; set aside.

In bottom half of couscoussiére, heat oil; sauté chicken pieces over medium heat until they begin to brown. Stir in onions, garlic, fresh coriander and hot pepper; stir-fry for 8 more minutes. Add 4 cups of water and all remaining ingredients except almonds and *couscous*; bring to a boil. Fit top of couscoussiére with the *couscous* on the bottom part. Seal two parts together with piece of cloth impregnated with flour (the cloth should be about 4" wide and long enough to fit around the couscoussiére, then folded 4 times lengthwise and dipped in 1 cup of water in which 1/4 cup of flour has been dissolved); then cook over medium heat for 20 minutes. Sprinkle 1 cup water over *couscous*, stirring constantly to make sure lumps do not form; cook for 40 minutes, stirring *couscous* occasionally.

Mound *couscous* on large serving plate; make a well on top; decorate *couscous* with almonds. With slotted spoon, remove meat and vegetables; arrange in well on top of *couscous*. Place remaining juice in gravy boat, to be added as desired

MOSTACCIOLI

1 pound ground beef
1/2 cup chopped green pepper
2 cups tomatoes
6-ounce can tomato paste
1/2 cup water
1/2 pound Cheddar cheese
Shredded Parmesan cheese
1 onion, chopped
1 bay leaf
1/2 teaspoon salt
1/4 teaspoon pepper
8-ounce Mostaccioli noodles (4 cups)

Brown meat slowly, along with green pepper and onion. Cook until tender. Stir in water, tomatoes, tomato paste and seasonings. In a 2-quart casserole, mix together cooked noodles, meat sauce and Cheddar cheese. Sprinkle with Parmesan cheese. Bake at 350 degrees for 30 minutes. Delicious family favorite.

MEXICAN OVEN FRIED CHICKEN
Serves 6
178 calories per serving

3 pound broiler-fryer, skinned and cut into serving-size pieces
1-1/2 cups Bloody Mary mix
1/2 cup crushed corn flakes
1/2 teaspoon dried oregano leaves
1/2 teaspoon ground cumin
1/2 teaspoon chili powder
1/2 teaspoon paprika
1/4 teaspoon onion salt
1/8 teaspoon garlic powder

Vegetable cooking spray

Combine chicken and Bloody Mary mix in a large bowl; cover and refrigerate 6 hours or overnight.

Combine next 7 ingredients. Drain chicken and dredge in mixture. Arrange chicken in jellyroll pan coated with cooking spray. Bake at 350 degrees for 50 - 60 minutes.

GERMAN SAUERKRAUT ROLLS

1-1/2 large cans sauerkraut
4 eggs
3/4 cup shortening or oil
1/2 teaspoon salt
3 cups flour
1/4 cup water

Drain juice from kraut. In skillet, heat oil or shortening; stir in kraut; add salt and pepper to taste. Fry about 20 minutes, or until browned; cool. Mix flour and salt; add eggs and water. Knead until dough is smooth and elastic, like noodle dough. On floured board, roll to 1/4 inch thick. Spread cooled kraut on top; roll up like jelly roll. Slice cross-wise; place cut pieces in frying pan. Cover with small amount of water; add salt. Cook over medium heat for one hour. OPTIONAL: For added flavor, place hot dogs or Polish sausage around dough.

Meat DISHES

BREADED PORK CHOPS
Serves 6

6 pork chops
¾ cup fine bread crumbs
1 teaspoon salt
⅛ teaspoon pepper
1 egg, beaten
¼ cup milk
¼ cup boiling water

Add salt and pepper to bread crumbs. Beat egg and add milk. Dip chops in liquid and roll in crumbs. Put 3 tablespoons fat into skillet; brown chops. Place chops in a baking pan or dish and add boiling water. Cover and bake at 400 degrees for about 50 minutes. (I take the cover off for about the last 10 minutes.) These are delicious and so easy to prepare, too. The chops turn out very tender. This is one of my favorite pork chop recipes.

HERB-STUFFED HAM SLICES
Serves 6

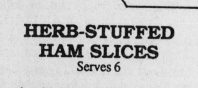

4 tablespoons butter
  or margarine
1 onion, finely chopped
10 mushrooms, finely chopped
1¼ teaspoons prepared mustard
2 tablespoons parsley, finely chopped
2 tablespoons chives, finely chopped
¼ teaspoon ground sage

¾ cup herb bread crumbs
½ to 1 cup chicken stock
  Salt and pepper to taste
6 large slices cold boiled *or* baked ham, ¼–½ inch thick

Heat half the butter in a skillet; add onion and mushrooms; sauté 5 minutes; remove to bowl.

Add rest of ingredients with enough chicken stock to moisten the mixture and hold it together. Spread the prepared mixture on ham slices; fold slices in half; arrange on shallow, buttered baking dish. Melt remaining butter; pour over ham slices. Cover; bake at 375 degrees for 20 minutes.

SASSY SAUSAGES
Serves 5–6

1 cup water
⅓ cup red cinnamon candies
  Red food coloring
3 red tart apples, cored and cut into ½-inch rings
1 pound pork sausage links
3 tablespoons water

In skillet, heat 1 cup water, the cinnamon candies and a few drops red food coloring until candies are melted. Place apple rings in syrup; cook slowly, turning occasionally, about 20 minutes, or until tender. Place links in another skillet; add 3 tablespoons water. Cover tightly; cook slowly for 8 minutes. Uncover; cook, turning sausages until well-browned. To serve, insert hot sausage link in center of each apple slice.

SOUPY PORK CHOPS

6 pork chops, ½ inch thick, fat removed
1 can tomato soup
1 package dry onion soup mix
1 medium onion, sliced
1 green pepper, sliced
1 cup mushrooms, sliced

Arrange chops in an oblong casserole. Mix remaining ingredients and pour over chops. Cover with waxed paper. Microwave at 70 percent for 30 minutes.

SPARERIBS "ALOHA"

3 pounds spareribs
½ cup finely chopped onion
¼ cup green pepper, chopped
1 (16-ounce) can tomato sauce
½ teaspoon dry mustard
1 tablespoon Worcestershire sauce
1 (2½-cup) can crushed pineapple
¼ cup brown sugar

Cut every third rib about halfway through the strip. Sprinkle with salt and pepper. Place in shallow pan. Bake 1¼ hours at 350 degrees. Pour off fat. Mix remaining ingredients and let stand to blend flavor. Pour over ribs. Bake 45–50 minutes, basting frequently to glaze ribs.

ROAST GOOSE
Serves 6

1 (6–8 pound) goose

Preheat oven to 400 degrees. Place goose, breast side up, on rack about 1 inch from bottom of roaster. After 30 minutes, turn down to 375 degrees and prick goose with fork around breast, back and drumsticks, letting excess fat escape. Let cook about 20 minutes per pound.

Apple Stuffing:
- 3 cups stale bread
- 1 egg
- ¼ cup chopped onion
- ½ cup melted butter
- ½ teaspoon salt
- ½ teaspoon poultry seasoning
- ¼ teaspoon sage
- ¼ teaspoon white pepper
- 1 cup chopped apples
- Chicken stock, enough to moisten

Sauté onions in butter until transparent. Cool. Add egg, bread, seasoning and apples; mix thoroughly, moistening with the stock until wet, but not soupy. Place in heavily buttered small baking dish and bake at 300 degrees for 1 hour 15 minutes.

Tangerine Sauce:
- 2 tablespoons sugar
- 1 lemon
- 1 orange
- ¾ cup red current jelly
- ¼ cup wine vinegar
- ½ cup orange juice concentrate
- 1 pint brown gravy
- 2 tangerines

Grate peel from orange and lemon; save. Place sugar in heavy-bottomed saucepan and caramelize with lemon and orange split in two. Add jelly, orange juice and vinegar. Bring to a boil; remove lemon and orange. Add brown gravy and simmer for 15 minutes. Strain. Add tangerine segments and peel as garnish.

CHICKEN-VEGETABLE-FRENCH-FRY CASSEROLE
Serves 8

This provides meat, potatoes and vegetables in 1 dish. Put together ahead of time, and it is ready to eat 35 minutes after popping in the oven.

- 2 fryer chickens, cut up
- ¼ cup (½ stick) butter
- ¼ cup flour
- 1 teaspoon salt
- 2 cups reserved chicken broth
- 1 (10½-ounce) can cream of celery soup
- 1 (10-ounce) package frozen peas and carrots
- ½ cup (1 stick) butter
- 1 (1-pound) box frozen french fries
- Parmesan cheese

Cook, cool and bone chicken. Save 2 cups of broth. In a buttered 9 x 13-inch pan, put good-sized pieces of chicken. Melt butter; add flour, salt, broth and soup. Cook until thick and smooth. Cook peas and carrots for 3 minutes. Drain. Mix with sauce and pour over chicken.

Melt stick of butter; stir frozen french fries in butter until coated. Place on top of other ingredients. Sprinkle generously with Parmesan cheese. Bake, uncovered, at 450 degrees for 20–25 minutes. If it has been put together earlier and refrigerated, bake for 35 minutes.

CHICKEN NOODLE MEDLEY
Serves 6

- 10 ounces green noodles
- 1 medium-size onion
- 1 bay leaf
- 2 tablespoons butter
- 1 teaspoon onion salt
- ⅛ teaspoon pepper

- 3 pounds broiler-fryer chicken, cut up
- 1 (10¾-ounce) can cream of mushroom soup
- ¾ cup milk
- ⅔ cup grated Parmesan cheese
- 2 tablespoons chopped chives
- ½ teaspoon sage
- Paprika
- 1 (1-pound) package frozen baby carrots, drained and cooked

Preheat oven to 350 degrees. Cook noodles according to package directions, adding onion and bay leaf to cooking water. Drain noodles; discard onion and bay leaf. Toss together noodles, butter, onion salt and pepper. Spoon into buttered 13 x 9-inch baking dish. Sprinkle chicken pieces with salt and pepper; place on noodles. Combine soup, milk, ⅓ cup cheese, chives and sage; pour over chicken. Sprinkle with remaining cheese and paprika. Bake 45 minutes; add carrots. Bake additional 20 minutes, or until chicken is tender.

CRUSTY BAKED CHICKEN
Serves 4

- 2 cups potato chips, finely crushed
- ¼ teaspoon salt
- ¼ teaspoon pepper
- ¼ teaspoon curry powder
- ⅛ teaspoon ginger
- 1 (3-pound) frying chicken, cut up
- 2 eggs, beaten
- ¼ cup milk
- ½ cup butter *or* margarine, melted

Mix potato chips, salt, pepper, curry powder and ginger. Combine eggs and milk; pour butter into shallow baking dish. Dip chicken in chips, then in egg mixture, then in chips again. Put pieces side by side in dish; bake at 375 degrees for 45 minutes.

BAKED CHICKEN

- 2 chicken breasts
- 1 tablespoon butter *or* margarine, melted
- ½ cup Parmesan cheese
- 2 tablespoons butter *or* margarine

Preheat oven to 400 degrees. Dip chicken in melted butter and coat with cheese. Melt remaining butter in a pie plate and place chicken in pie plate, skin-side up. Bake at 400 degrees for 50 minutes. Baste with juice during baking. Cover with foil if chicken browns too quickly.

CHICKEN AND BISCUITS
Serves 4

Filling:
- 2 tablespoons vegetable oil
- 1 small onion, peeled and chopped
- ½ green pepper, finely chopped
- ⅔ cup sliced mushrooms
- 2 tablespoons cornstarch
- 1½ cups milk
- 2 cups cooked chicken, cubed
  Salt and pepper

Biscuits:
- 2 cups flour
- 2½ teaspoons baking powder
- ⅓ cup margarine
- ⅔ cup milk

Heat oil in skillet. Add onion, green pepper and mushrooms. Sauté for a few minutes. Add cornstarch; cook 1 minute, stirring constantly. Add milk gradually; stir until boiling. Add chicken and seasoning. Turn into deep 9-inch pie plate. In bowl, sift flour and baking powder. Cut in margarine with pastry blender. Stir in milk with fork to make soft dough. Knead lightly on floured board; roll to about ½-inch thickness. With cookie, cut into 1½-inch rounds. Place rounds on top of chicken; brush with milk. Bake at 425 degrees for 10–15 minutes, or until biscuits are done.

PATRICIA NIXON'S HOT CHICKEN SALAD
Serves 8

- 4 cups cold chicken, cut up into chunks (cooked)
- 2 tablespoons lemon juice
- ⅔ cup finely chopped toasted almonds
- ¾ cup mayonnaise
- 1 teaspoon salt
- ½ teaspoon monosodium glutamate
- 1 cup grated cheese
- 2 cups chopped celery
- 4 hard-cooked eggs, sliced
- ¾ cup cream of chicken soup
- 1 teaspoon onion, finely minced
- 2 pimientos, finely cut
- 1½ cups crushed potato chips

Combine all ingredients, except cheese, potato chips and almonds. Place in a large rectangular dish. Top with cheese, potato chips and almonds. Let stand overnight in refrigerator. Bake in a 400-degree oven for 20–25 minutes.

GINGER AND RUM ROASTED CORNISH GAME HENS

- 4 Cornish game hens
  Salt and freshly ground pepper
- 1 large garlic clove, crushed
- ¼ cup honey
- ¼ cup chicken stock
- ¼ cup soy sauce
- ¼ cup rum
- 1 tablespoon peanut *or* vegetable oil
- 1 teaspoon ground ginger

Preheat oven to 375 degrees. Season Cornish hens well with salt and pepper, inside and out. Combine remaining ingredients in bowl. Spoon 2 tablespoons of the mixture into each hen cavity. Tie the legs together and fold the wings back. Place the hens in a roasting pan.

Brush each hen with the sauce. Roast for 55 minutes, or until tender. Baste the hens twice during the cooking time with the sauce.

CHICKEN CHOLUPAS

- 4 chicken breasts, cooked, deboned and diced
- 3 cans cream of chicken soup
- 1 large can green chilies, diced
- 1 onion, finely diced
- 16 ounces sour cream
- ¾ pound Monterey Jack cheese, grated
- ¾ pound mild cheddar cheese, grated
- 12 small flour tortillas

Mix all ingredients together, except tortillas and only half the cheeses. Put 3 tablespoons mixture in each tortilla. Roll up and place in a greased baking dish. Pour rest of mixture over tortillas. Sprinkle remaining cheeses over all. Bake at 350 degrees for 45 minutes.

FAVORITE CHICKEN LOAF
Serves 6

- 1 cup soft bread crumbs
- 2 cups milk
- 2 eggs, lightly beaten
- ½ teaspoon salt
- ¼ teaspoon paprika
- 3 cups cooked chicken, diced ¼ inch thick
- ½ cup cooked peas
- ¼ cup chopped pimiento
- 1 (10½-ounce) can condensed cream of mushroom soup for sauce

In a bowl blend bread crumbs, milk, eggs, salt and paprika. Stir in chicken, peas and pimiento. Turn into a well-greased loaf pan (9 x 5 x 3-inch). Bake in a moderate 325-degree oven until firm, about 40 minutes. Serve with mushroom sauce made from soup.

QUICK CHICKEN BAKE
Serves 6

2 cups cooked chicken, cubed
1 can cream of chicken soup
1 cup sour cream
½ cup celery, diced
½ cup onion, chopped
½ cup water chestnuts, thinly sliced
1 cup cooked rice
Bread crumbs

Mix together and place in a buttered 2-quart casserole. Sprinkle bread crumbs on top. Microwave on HIGH for 6–8 minutes.

If you prefer cream of mushroom soup or cheddar cheese soup—go for it. Do not be afraid to experiment.

CRISPY SESAME CHICKEN
Serves 6–8

10 pieces chicken
½ cup butter
½ cup bread crumbs
1 cup grated Parmesan cheese
6 tablespoons sesame seeds

Preheat oven to 350 degrees. Rinse chicken and pat dry with paper towels. Combine bread crumbs, cheese and sesame seeds. Melt butter. Dip chicken into the butter and then the seasoned crumbs. Place chicken in a shallow pan (lining with foil helps with cleanup). Bake at 350 degrees for 1 hour.

TUNA AND CHEESE CASSEROLE

⅓ cup chopped onion
1 teaspoon butter *or* margarine
7 tablespoons (⅓ of a 10¾-ounce can) condensed cream of celery soup

2 teaspoons lemon juice
⅔ cup tuna, drained and flaked
1 cup cooked rice
Salt to taste
Black pepper to taste
¼ cup grated cheddar cheese

Preheat oven to 350 degrees. Cook onion in butter until tender, but not brown. Stir in remaining ingredients, except cheese. Turn into a buttered, shallow 6-inch casserole for 20 minutes, or until heated through. Top with cheese and bake 5 minutes longer.

PATIO LICKIN' CHICKEN
Serves 4 to 6

1 frying chicken, cut up
1 envelope dry onion soup mix
3/4 cup uncooked rice
1 can cream of mushroom soup or cream of chicken soup
1 soup can water
1 small can mushrooms, drained
1/2 teaspoon salt
1/4 teaspoon pepper

Season chicken; brown slightly in frying pan. Mix remaining ingredients together; place in 9 x 13-inch baking dish. Arrange chicken on top. Cover with foil; bake one hour at 350 degrees. Remove foil and bake 20 minutes longer.

BARBECUED LEMON CHICKEN

3 roasting *or* broiling chickens
1 cup salad oil
¾ cup fresh lemon juice
1 tablespoon salt
2 teaspoons paprika
2 teaspoons onion powder

1 teaspoon garlic powder
2 teaspoons crushed sweet basil
2 teaspoons crushed thyme

Have butcher split chickens and remove wings, backbone and tail. Clean well; place in shallow pan. Combine remaining ingredients; pour into jar. Cover; shake well to blend. Pour over chicken; cover tightly. Marinate overnight in refrigerator, turning chicken occasionally. Remove to room temperature 1 hour before grilling. Barbecue chicken over hot coals for 15–20 minutes on each side, basting often with marinade.

PEPPER STEAK
Serves 6

1½ pounds round steak, ½ inch thick
1 cup sliced onion
1 cup beef broth
2 stalks celery, chopped
1 tablespoon salt
½ teaspoon garlic powder *or* 1 garlic clove, minced
½ teaspoon ginger
2 green peppers, cut in strips
1 cup sliced mushrooms
1 (1-pound) can tomatoes, chopped
3 tablespoons soy sauce
2 tablespoons cornstarch
1 cup water

Cut round steak into thin strips and brown in Dutch oven in small amount of oil and margarine. Add beef broth, onion, celery, salt, garlic and ginger; simmer, covered, for 35–40 minutes, or until tender. Add green peppers, mushrooms and tomatoes; cook an additional 10 minutes. Mix soy sauce and cornstarch in 1 cup water until smooth. Slowly stir into sauce and cook, stirring constantly, until thickened. Serve over rice. This can be made the day before serving and reheated in the microwave.

GREEN VEGETABLE MEAT LOAF
Serves 8

2 pounds lean ground meat
2 (10-ounce) boxes frozen chopped broccoli, thawed and drained
1 cup chopped onion
⅔ cup uncooked quick cooking oatmeal
2 large eggs
½ cup milk *or* water
1 (1.5-ounce) package meat loaf seasoning mix

Heat oven to 375 degrees. Lightly grease a 9 x 5 x 3-inch loaf pan. Put all ingredients into a large bowl. Mix with hands 3–4 minutes until well-blended. Press mixture into prepared pan. Bake 1 hour in the middle of oven. Remove from oven; cover loosely with foil and let stand 10–15 minutes. Drain off juice. This vegetable-laced meat loaf is delicious fresh from the oven, and even better the next day cold.

MEAT LOAF CHOW MEIN

1 pound ground beef
1 package Chow Mein Oriental Seasoning Mix
¾ teaspoon garlic powder
½ teaspoon salt
½ teaspoon pepper
2 eggs
1 can crispy Chinese noodles (optional)

Mix all ingredients together, except crispy Chinese noodles. Mold into 2 loaves. Bake at 350 degrees for 1 hour. Arrange Chinese noodles around loaves for garnish before serving.

MEXICAN MEAT LOAF

1½ pounds ground beef
1 medium onion, chopped
½ cup chopped mushrooms
¼ cup chopped green pepper
½ cup taco sauce
2 tablespoons barbecue sauce
1 egg, beaten
½ cup tortilla chips, finely crushed
½ teaspoon salt
Dash black pepper

Combine all ingredients; mix well. Pack into an oiled 8-inch loaf pan. Bake at 400 degrees for 1¼ hours, or until done.

LAYERED MEAT LOAF WITH MUSHROOM SAUCE

6 ounces herb-seasoned stuffing mix
1½ pounds lean ground beef
½ pound bulk pork sausage, with sage
1 egg, beaten
2 slices bread, crumbled
¼ cup milk
1 teaspoon garlic salt
2 teaspoons minced onion
1 teaspoon Worcestershire sauce
½ teaspoon pepper (No salt is needed as it is seasoned enough with other ingredients)
1 can mushroom soup
¼ cup water

Prepare the stuffing mix, using 1½ cups water and 3 tablespoons melted butter. Mix well and fluff lightly. Set aside.

Combine remaining ingredients, except soup and water, in a bowl; mix well. Spread half the meat mixture in bottom of a loaf pan. Spread stuffing over, patting it down evenly. Pat remaining meat mixture over stuffing. Preheat oven to 350 degrees. Bake loaf for 45 minutes, or until top is lightly browned. Combine mushroom soup with water and pour over meat loaf. Continue baking for 30 minutes longer.

TENDER MEATBALLS IN MUSHROOM GRAVY
Serves 4-6

1 pound hamburger
4 slices soft white bread
1 teaspoon salt
1/4 teaspoon pepper
1 tablespoon minced onion
1 can mushroom soup
1/3 cup water

Pull apart bread into small, dime-size pieces. Combine hamburger, bread, salt, pepper, and minced onion in large mixing bowl. Using a spoon, scoop out rounds of meat, or shape into several round, 2-inch balls by hand.

Brown meatballs in a hot skillet using a small amount of butter or oil. Turn them occasionally so all sides are browned. Place meat in cooker. Add soup and water. Cook on *low* for 6 to 12 hours, *high* for up to 6 hours.

SOUPER MEAT LOAF

2 pounds ground chuck
1 package dry onion soup mix
1 egg
½ cup ketchup
½ cup baked crumbs
4 slices American cheese

Mix all ingredients, except cheese; blend well. Divide mixture in half. Place half of meat in a ring mold. Place cheese strips over meat. Add remaining meat and seal well. Cover with waxed paper. Microwave on HIGH for 15 minutes. Rest 5 minutes or microwave at 50 percent for 25–30 minutes.

HAM LOAF

2 pounds ground beef
2 pounds ground ham
4 slices bread, cut up
¼ pound soda crackers, crushed
1 small onion
2 cans tomato soup
4 eggs
1 teaspoon salt
½ teaspoon pepper
4 tablespoons mustard
2 tablespoons Worcestershire sauce

Mix well and add just enough milk to give a soft consistency. Bake in preheated oven at 350 degrees for 2 hours.

MUSTARD-GLAZED HAM LOAF

Serves 8–10

1½ pounds ground ham
1 pound boneless pork shoulder, trimmed and ground
3 eggs, slightly beaten
½ cup finely crushed saltine crackers (14 crackers) or
½ cup finely crushed bread crumbs (3 or 4 slices)
½ cup tomato juice
2 tablespoons chopped onion
1 tablespoon prepared horseradish
½ teaspoon salt
⅛ teaspoon pepper
1–2 recipes Mustard Sauce (recipe follows)

Mix ingredients. Shape into a 9 x 5-inch loaf in shallow baking dish. Bake in a 350-degree oven for 1¼ hours.

Meanwhile prepare Ham Loaf Mustard Sauce. Drain fat from pan.

Pour Mustard Sauce over loaf. Bake 30 minutes more, basting with sauce occasionally.

Mustard Sauce:

½ cup brown sugar, firmly packed
2 tablespoons vinegar
½ teaspoon dry mustard

REAL BAKED HAM

5 pounds ham
Cider to cover
½ cup brown sugar
1 teaspoon mustard
20 whole cloves

Cover the ham with cold water and bring slowly to the boil. Throw out the water and replace with the cider to cover ham. Bring this to a boil; lower heat, keeping the liquid barely simmering for 20 minutes to the pound of ham; remove from heat and allow to stand in the liquid for 30 minutes. Take out ham; skin it and score fat with a sharp knife in a diamond pattern. Stud with whole cloves. Mix the sugar and mustard; rub well into ham. Bake in a preheated oven for an additional 10 minutes to the pound in a 400-degree oven. Carve; serve with sweet potatoes or a salad.

HAM CASSEROLE

½ pound egg noodles, cooked
2 cups ham, cubed
1 to 1½ cups cheddar cheese, shredded
1 can cream of mushroom soup
¾ cup milk
1 teaspoon dry mustard
1 box frozen peas

Pierce box of peas in several places. Microwave for 5 minutes; set aside. Combine ham, cheese, soup, milk and mustard in a 3-quart glass casserole. Add noodles and peas; stir to blend. Microwave on HIGH for 6–8 minutes, stirring one time.

HAM STEAK WITH PINEAPPLE GLAZE

1 ham steak (2 pounds)

Glaze:

1 (8-ounce) can crushed pineapple, drained, reserving juice
¾ cup brown sugar
3 teaspoons prepared mustard
1½ teaspoons dry mustard
1½ to 2 tablespoons reserved juice

Combine the ingredients to make a smooth paste. Place ham steak on a slotted bacon rack or oblong casse-

SWISS STEAK

Serves 6

2 pounds round steak
6 tablespoons flour
1 teaspoon salt
½ teaspoon pepper
4 onions
6 tablespoons shortening
½ cup chopped celery
¾ cup chili sauce
¾ cup water
1 green pepper

Combine flour, salt and pepper; rub into both sides of steak; cut into 6 portions. Peel and slice onions. Preheat skillet; add half of shortening, then onions; brown lightly; remove from skillet. Add remaining shortening; brown steak on both sides. Reduce heat. Add celery, chili sauce and water. Cover; simmer 1 hour. Cut green pepper into slices. Add pepper and onions to meat. Continue cooking for 30 minutes.

BURGUNDY STEAK
Serves 2

- 1 cup burgundy wine
- 1 tablespoon Worcestershire sauce
- ½ teaspoon dried leaf basil
- ½ teaspoon dried leaf thyme
- ¼ teaspoon dry mustard
- Dash garlic powder
- 2 (8-ounce) beef rib-eye steaks
- ¼ cup butter *or* margarine
- 4 frozen french-fried onion rings
- ½ cup fresh mushroom slices

In a small bowl, mix burgundy, Worcestershire sauce, basil, thyme, mustard and garlic powder. Place meat in a plastic bag; put in a shallow baking pan. Pour marinade into bag; seal bag. Marinate in refrigerator 8 hours or overnight, turning bag over occasionally. Melt butter or margarine in a large skillet. Add onion rings. Cook over medium-high heat until golden brown. Remove onion rings and keep warm; reserve butter or margarine in skillet; Drain steak; reserve ½ cup marinade. Cook steaks in butter or margarine in skillet until done as desired, turning several times. Place steaks on a platter; reserve drippings in skillet. Cook and stir mushrooms in drippings until barely tender. Stir in reserved marinade. Cook and stir until heated through. Pour over steaks. Top with cooked onion rings.

SOUR CREAM SWISS STEAK
Serves 4

- 2 pounds round steak, 1 inch thick
- ¹/₄ cup flour
- 1 teaspoon salt
- ¹/₄ teaspoon pepper
- 2 tablespoons vegetable oil
- 2 onions, sliced
- ¹/₂ cup water
- ¹/₄ tablespoon steak sauce
- ¹/₂ cup sour cream
- 2 tablespoons Swiss cheese, grated
- ¹/₈ teaspoon paprika

Dredge steak on both sides with flour seasoned with salt and pepper. Heat oil in skillet; brown steak on both sides. Add remaining ingredients, except cheese; cover skillet. Simmer 1 hour, or until meat is fork-tender; sprinkle Swiss cheese on steak while still hot.

BARBECUED FLANK STEAK

- ¼ cup soy sauce
- 3 tablespoons honey
- 2 tablespoons vinegar
- 1 green onion, chopped, *or* 2 teaspoons onion powder
- ½ to 1½ teaspoons garlic powder
- 1½ teaspoons powdered ginger
- ¾ cup salad oil
- Flank steaks

Mix first 7 ingredients in large bowl; add steaks. Marinate at room temperature for 3–6 hours. Broil over hot coals until medium-rare or rare; slice diagonally, cutting in ½–¾-inch strips. Marinade will keep indefinitely in refrigerator if green onion is removed.

ROLLED STEAK SKILLET SUPPER
Serves 4

- 1 onion, finely cut
- 1 green pepper, finely cut
- 1 clove garlic, minced
- 3 tablespoons butter *or* margarine
- 1 (7-ounce) can tomato paste
- 30 saltine crackers, crumbled
- ¼ teaspoon salt
- ¼ teaspoon pepper
- 4 cubed steaks
- ¾ cup beef bouillon

Sauté onion, green pepper and garlic in butter. Combine half tomato paste with cracker crumbs, salt and pepper; add to onion mixture. Spoon mixture onto steaks; roll each, fasten with toothpicks; brown in butter. Blend remaining tomato paste with beef bouillon. Pour over steaks; cover skillet. Simmer gently 40–50 minutes; remove toothpicks before serving.

SWISS STEAK
Serves 4

- ¼ cup flour
- ¾ teaspoon salt
- ¼ teaspoon black pepper
- 1½ pounds round steak
- 3 tablespoons fat
- 1 medium onion, chopped
- 1½ cups stewed tomatoes
- ½ cup sliced carrots
- ½ cup sliced celery

Mix flour, salt and pepper. Dredge steak with flour; pound the flour into both sides of steak. In a Dutch oven, heat the fat; brown the steak well on both sides. Add vegetables; cover and simmer gently for 1½ hours.

SALISBURY STEAK

- 2 pounds hamburger
- 1 can onion soup
- 1 cup bread crumbs
- 2 eggs, beaten
- 1 can tomato soup
- 1 can celery soup

Mix the hamburger, bread crumbs, onion soup and eggs as for meat loaf. Add salt to taste. Add more bread crumbs, if needed. Make into patties; dip in flour and brown on each side.

Arrange in a greased baking dish. Make a gravy of 1 can celery soup, 1 can tomato soup and 1 can water.

Pour over the patties and bake in a 350-degree oven for 1 hour.

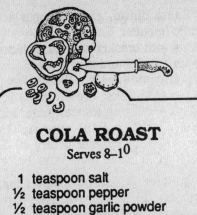

COLA ROAST
Serves 8–10

1 teaspoon salt
½ teaspoon pepper
½ teaspoon garlic powder
1 (4–5-pound) bottom-round roast
3 tablespoons vegetable oil
1½ cups cola-flavored soda
12 ounces chili sauce
2 tablespoons Worcestershire sauce
2 tablespoons hot sauce

Combine salt, pepper and garlic powder; rub over surface of roast. Brown roast on all sides in vegetable oil in Dutch oven. Drain off drippings. Combine remaining ingredients; pour over roast. Cover and bake at 325 degrees for 3 hours, or until tender.

BAKED PORK CHOPS & APPLES
Serves 4

4 pork chops
¼ teaspoon nutmeg
1 tablespoon shortening
1¼ cups apple juice
2 cups sliced raw potato
1 tablespoon cornstarch
1 cup sliced onion
1 teaspoon salt
2 apples, cored and cut into wedges

In skillet, brown chops on both sides in shortening. Remove chops from skillet; arrange in 2-quart casserole. Add potato and onion to pan drippings; heat thoroughly, stirring carefully. Sprinkle with salt and nutmeg; stir in apple wedges. Spoon mixture over chops. Add 1 cup apple juice to skillet; heat until simmering; pour over apple-potato mixture.

Cover casserole; bake at 350 degrees for 45 minutes, or until chops and vegetables are tender. Using slotted spoon, place apple-potato mixture on serving platter; arrange chops on top. Combine remaining apple juice and cornstarch, stirring until free of lumps; pour into pan juices; cook until thickened, stirring constantly. Serve sauce over chops, or separately, if desired.

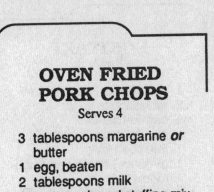

PORK CHOP 'N' POTATO BAKE

1 can cream of celery soup
½ cup milk
½ cup sour cream
1 package hash brown potatoes
1 cup shredded cheddar cheese
1 can French onion rings
6 medium pork chops
Seasoned salt
¼ teaspoon salt
¼ teaspoon pepper

Brown chops and sprinkle with seasoned salt. Mix soup, milk, sour cream, potatoes, salt, pepper, ½ cup of the cheese and ½ can of the onion rings. Spoon into a greased casserole or 9 x 13-inch pan, and arrange chops over top. Cover and bake at 350 degrees for 40 minutes. Top with remaining cheese and onion rings. Bake, uncovered, 5 minutes more.

OVEN FRIED PORK CHOPS
Serves 4

3 tablespoons margarine *or* butter
1 egg, beaten
2 tablespoons milk
1 cup corn bread stuffing mix

4 pork loin chops (about 1½ pounds), cut ½ inch thick

Set oven to 425 degrees. Place margarine or butter in a 13 x 9 x 2-inch baking pan. Place pan in the oven about 3 minutes, or until margarine melts. Stir together egg and milk. Dip pork chops in egg mixture. Coat with stuffing mix. Place chops on top of melted margarine in pan. Bake 20 minutes. Turn. Bake 10–15 minutes more, or until pork is no longer pink.

These are delicious and so tender!

CHERRY PORK CHOPS
Serves 6

6 pork chops, cut 3/4-inch thick
1/4 teaspoon salt
1/4 teaspoon pepper
1/2 can cherry pie filling (1 cup)
2 teaspoons lemon juice
1/2 teaspoon instant chicken bouillon granules
1/8 teaspoon ground mace

Trim excess fat from pork chops. Brown pork chops in hot skillet with butter or oil. Sprinkle each chop with salt and pepper. Combine cherry pie filling, lemon juice, chicken bouillon granules, and ground mace in cooker. Stir well. Place pork chops in Crock-pot. Cover. Cook on *low* for 4-5 hours. Place chops on platter. Pour cherry sauce over meat.

TROPICAL PORK CHOPS
Serves 4

4 thin pork chops
1 small can crushed pineapple
1 cup orange juice

Preheat oven to 325 degrees. Place chops in shallow baking dish. Top with pineapple and orange juice. Bake for 1 hour, uncovered.

SWEET SOUR PORK STEAKS
Serves 4

1 tablespoon cooking oil
2 pork steaks
¾ cup chicken broth
¼ cup finely chopped celery
1 tablespoon brown sugar
1 tablespoon vinegar
1 teaspoon prepared mustard
¼ teaspoon salt
Dash of pepper
2 tablespoons crushed gingersnaps (2 cookies)
Hot cooked noodles

Heat skillet over high heat. Add oil to skillet. Cook steaks in oil about 8 minutes, or until meat is no longer pink, turning once. Remove steaks and keep warm. Drain fat from skillet. In same skillet, stir together chicken broth, celery, brown sugar, vinegar, mustard, salt and pepper. Stir in gingersnaps. Cook and stir until mixture is thick and bubbly. Serve meat and sauce over hot cooked noodles.

SAUSAGE 'N' CHEESE TURNOVERS
Makes 10 sandwiches

1 (10-ounce) can refrigerated big flaky biscuits
½ pound Italian bulk sausage *or* ground beef, browned and drained
¼ teaspoon Italian seasoning
1 (4-ounce) can mushroom pieces and stems, drained
4 ounces (1 cup) shredded mozzarella or provolone cheese
1 egg, slightly beaten
1–2 tablespoons grated Parmesan cheese

Heat oven to 350 degrees. Grease a cookie sheet. Separate dough into 10 biscuits; press or roll each to a 5-inch circle. In a medium bowl, combine browned sausage, seasoning, mushrooms and mozzarella cheese. Spoon about 3 tablespoons meat mixture onto center of each flattened biscuit. Fold dough in half over filling; press edges with fork to seal. Brush tops with beaten egg; sprinkle with Parmesan cheese. Place on prepared cookie sheet. Bake for 10–15 minutes, or until deep golden brown.

Tip: To reheat, wrap loosely in foil. Heat at 375 degrees for 10–15 minutes.

SMOKED SAUSAGE CASSEROLE

2 pounds smoked sausage, cut into 4-inch lengths
1 teaspoon butter *or* margarine
1 medium onion, cut into wedges
2 (16-ounce) cans sauerkraut
1 cup apple juice
2 medium apples, cut into wedges
4 medium potatoes, cut in half
Salt and pepper

Brown sausage in butter in a 1½-quart Dutch oven or large casserole. Arrange onion, sauerkraut, apples and potatoes around sausage. Top with apple juice; salt and pepper to taste. Cover tightly and simmer over low heat for 30–40 minutes, or until potatoes test done with a fork. Stir once during cooking time.

SUKIYAKI
Serves 8

2 pounds lean ground beef
2 tablespoons sugar
⅓ cup soy sauce
¼ cup A-1 steak sauce
1 teaspoon salt
1 (6-ounce) can sliced mushrooms
2 medium onions, thinly sliced
1 green pepper, sliced in thin strips
6 scallions, cut in 1-inch pieces
1 cup thinly sliced celery
1 (8-ounce) can water chestnuts, thinly sliced
1 (8-ounce) can bamboo shoots
1 tablespoon cornstarch
Cooked rice

In large skillet, brown beef until crumbly. In small bowl, mix sugar, soy sauce, A-1 steak sauce and salt. Set aside. Drain mushrooms, reserving liquid. When meat is cooked, mix in vegetables. Add sauce. Simmer for 3 minutes, or until vegetables are just crisp-tender. Combine cornstarch and reserved mushroom liquid. Stir into sukiyaki. Cook just until thickened. Serve over rice.

BAKED BEEF CUBES CACCIATORE
Serves 4

3½ pounds lean beef, cut into 1-inch cubes
Flour for dredging
Vegetable oil
1 large onion, chopped
1 clove garlic, minced
¼ teaspoon salt
½ teaspoon oregano
½ teaspoon red pepper, crushed
1 (10½-ounce) can crushed tomatoes
1 (1-pound, 12-ounce) can crushed tomatoes
1 large green pepper, cut into strips
12 ounces thin noodles, cooked, drained

Dredge beef with flour; brown in skillet with vegetable oil. Remove from heat; place beef in a large ovenproof casserole; add next 8 ingredients; cover. Bake at 300 degrees for 2½ hours. Remove from oven; stir in cooked noodles.

BEEF RING WITH BARBECUE SAUCE

1½ pounds ground chuck
¾ cup quick-cooking oats
1 cup evaporated milk
3 tablespoons onion, finely chopped
2 tablespoons Worcestershire sauce
3 tablespoons vinegar
2 tablespoons sugar
1 cup ketchup
½ cup water
6 tablespoons onion, finely chopped

Mix together ground chuck, oats, evaporated milk and 3 tablespoons onion. Pack into an 8-inch ring mold and bake 10 minutes. Remove to a larger pan.

Combine remaining ingredients to form the sauce. Pour sauce over beef ring. Bake at 350 degrees for approximately 1½ hours. Baste frequently with sauce during baking time.

FILET MIGNON TETA-A-TETA
Valentine's Dinner for 2

4 tablespoons butter
2 tablespoons shallots, minced
1 clove garlic, whole
1 tablespoon Worcestershire sauce
1 teaspoon soy sauce
2 (6-ounce each) Filets Mignons
3 ounces brandy
1 tablespoon cashew nuts, coarsely chopped

Heat 2 tablespoons butter in skillet; add shallots and garlic; sauté over medium heat for 5 minutes. Remove and discard garlic. Increase heat to high, add Worcestershire sauce and soy sauce; place filets in pan. Let cook 3 minutes on each side, turning once for slightly rare. Transfer filets to warm dish. Deglaze pan with brandy and then ignite with a match (be careful of flames). Remove pan from heat, swirl in remaining butter to thicken sauce. Pour over filets and top with cashew nuts. Serve immediately.

FRUITED POT ROAST

4 pounds chuck roast or pot roast
2 tablespoons margarine
1-1/2 teaspoons salt
1/8 teaspoon pepper
1 cup apple juice
1 cup dried apricots
1 cup pitted prunes
1 cup tart apples, pared and sliced
2 cinnamon sticks, or 1/4 teaspoon ground cinnamon

Brown meat in margarine. Pour off the drippings. Season with salt and pepper. Cover and simmer in Dutch oven (or bake at 350 degrees) for 2-2-1/2 hours, or until tender.

Turn meat over and add fruit. Continue cooking for 30 minutes or until apples are tender. Serve on a warm platter, surrounded by the fruit.

MOCK STROGANOFF
Serves 6

1/4 cup onion, chopped
1 tablespoon margarine, melted
2 tablespoons oil, any kind (except olive oil)
Salt to taste
3 cups cubed, cooked beef
1 can (10-3/4 ounces) condensed tomato soup
1 can (3 or 4 ounces) chopped mushrooms
1 (8 ounce) can peas, drained
1 teaspoon sugar
1 cup dairy sour cream
Hot cooked and buttered noodles of your choice

Saute onion in oil and margarine in a large frying pan; add beef and brown lightly. Stir in tomato soup, mushrooms, peas, sugar, and salt. Cover mixture, simmer 20 minutes to blend flavors. Stir in sour cream; heat just to boiling point (Don't let sauce boil, as sour cream may curdle). Serve over buttered hot noodles.

BROILED SCALLOPS
Serves 3

1½ pounds scallops
6 tablespoons butter
½ teaspoon salt
⅛ teaspoon black pepper
⅛ teaspoon dry mustard

Wash; clean the scallops; pick them over for shells; season with the mixture of above seasonings. Place in drip-pan tray, with wire grill removed. Dot with butter. Broil at medium heat on 2nd shelf for 5 minutes. Turn the scallops with a broad spatula and broil for 2–3 minutes.

Melt additional butter to serve with the scallops.

SPANISH RICE STEAKS
Serves 4

4 cube steaks
1 cup all-purpose flour
1/2 cup vegetable oil
Salt and pepper to taste
1 onion, sliced
1 (5 ounce) can Spanish rice
1/4 teaspoon sugar
2 teaspoons parsley flakes

Coat steaks with flour. In skillet, brown steaks in oil. Transfer to lightly greased 9 inch square baking dish. Season with salt and pepper; set aside. Saute onions slices; add Spanish rice and sugar; mix well. Spoon rice mixture over steaks; sprinkle with parsley flakes.

HERBED SEAFOOD PIE

1 pound fish fillets (ocean perch,
   haddock or cod)
1 cup water
1/8 teaspoon salt
1 teaspoon dried tarragon
1 teaspoon dried chervil
4 tablespoons butter or margarine
2-1/2 tablespoons celery, minced
2-1/2 tablespoons onion, minced
4 tablespoons all-purpose flour
2 cups half-and-half cream
1/4 teaspoon dry mustard
1 tablespoon pimiento, chopped
Pastry for two-crust (9-inch) pie,
   unbaked

In a skillet, place fish fillets, water, salt, tarragon, and chervil. Bring water to a boil; reduce heat; cover and simmer 7 minutes. Remove fish gently; drain; cool and flake; set aside. Sauté celery and onion in butter; stir in flour; add half-and-half and dry mustard. Cook until thickened. Remove from heat; stir in flaked fish and pimiento. Spoon mixture into pastry-lined 9-inch pie pan; cover with top crust; seal and flute edges. Cut steam vent in top crust. Bake at 375 degrees for 35-40 minutes for a golden top. Before cutting, allow pie to rest for 15 minutes.

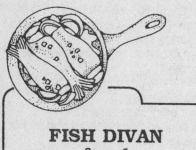

FISH DIVAN
Serves 5

1 (16-ounce) package frozen fish
   fillets
2 (10-ounce) packages frozen
   broccoli spears
1 teaspoon salt
1 (10-3/4 ounce) can condensed
   cream of chicken soup
1/2 cup milk
1 (3-ounce) can French fried onions

Cut frozen fish crosswise into five equal parts (let stand at room temperature 10 minutes before cutting). Rinse frozen broccoli under running cold water to separate; drain. (If broccoli stems are more than 1/2 inch in diameter, cut lengthwise into halves.) Place fish in center of ungreased 9x13x2-inch baking dish. Arrange broccoli around fish. Sprinkle fish and broccoli with salt. Mix soup and milk; pour over top. Bake uncovered in 350-degree oven until fish flakes easily with fork, about 30 minutes. Sprinkle with onions; bake 5 minutes longer.

STIR-FRIED TUNA
Serves 4

2 cans (6-1/2 ounce each) water-
   packed tuna
3 tablespoons salad oil
1 red or green pepper, seeded and
   cut into 1/2-inch cubes
8 green onions, cut into 1/2-inch
   slices
1 clove garlic, minced
1 cup celery, sliced 1/2-inch diagonally
2 cups snow peas
1 (8-ounce) can water chestnuts,
   drained and sliced
Seasoning Sauce (recipe follows)

Seasoning Sauce: (Mix together)

1 tablespoon salad oil
1 tablespoon cornstarch
3 tablespoons soy sauce
3 tablespoons water
3 tablespoons sugar
1 tablespoon white vinegar
1/4 teaspoon ground ginger

Drain tuna. Break into chunks; set aside. Heat oil in wide frying pan. Add pepper, onions, and garlic. Stir-fry for 15 seconds. Add celery, snow peas, and water chestnuts. Stir-fry for 1 minute or until vegetables are brightly colored.

Stir in Seasoning Sauce. Cook over high heat, tossing and stirring until sauce is slightly thickened. Add tuna, mixing well. Serve over hot rice.

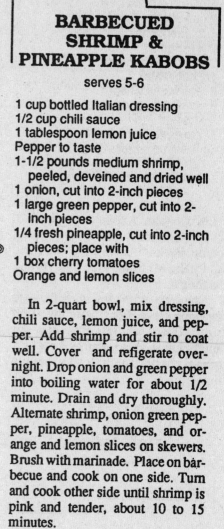

BARBECUED SHRIMP & PINEAPPLE KABOBS
serves 5-6

1 cup bottled Italian dressing
1/2 cup chili sauce
1 tablespoon lemon juice
Pepper to taste
1-1/2 pounds medium shrimp,
   peeled, deveined and dried well
1 onion, cut into 2-inch pieces
1 large green pepper, cut into 2-
   inch pieces
1/4 fresh pineapple, cut into 2-inch
   pieces; place with
1 box cherry tomatoes
Orange and lemon slices

In 2-quart bowl, mix dressing, chili sauce, lemon juice, and pepper. Add shrimp and stir to coat well. Cover and refrigerate overnight. Drop onion and green pepper into boiling water for about 1/2 minute. Drain and dry thoroughly. Alternate shrimp, onion green pepper, pineapple, tomatoes, and orange and lemon slices on skewers. Brush with marinade. Place on barbecue and cook on one side. Turn and cook other side until shrimp is pink and tender, about 10 to 15 minutes.

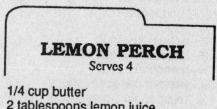

LEMON PERCH
Serves 4

1/4 cup butter
2 tablespoons lemon juice
1/2 teaspoon salt
1/4 teaspoon dill weed
1 pound perch fillets

Melt butter in skillet; stir in lemon juice and seasonings. Place fish in skillet, skin side down; cook 4-5 minutes over medium heat. Turn; continue cooking until fish flakes easily with fork. Serve butter mixture over fish.

LASAGNA
Serves 8

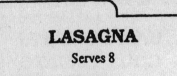

1 pound ground beef
1 cup chopped onion
1-2 teaspoons garlic powder
2 teaspoons oregano
2 cans tomato soup
1/2 cup water
2 teaspoons vinegar
9 lasagna noodles, cooked and drained
1 cup grated mozzarella cheese
5 slices mozzarella cheese
1 cup cream-style cottage cheese or grated Parmesan cheese

In skillet, brown beef, onion, garlic, oregano. Add soup, water, and vinegar. Cook over low heat 30 minutes.

Arrange alternate layers of cooked noodles, grated cheeses, and meat sauce in a 9 x 13" pan. Top with mozzarella slices.

Bake at 350 degrees for 35 minutes. Let set 15 minutes for easier cutting.

Serve with warm garlic French bread and tossed salad.

PARTY LIVER PLATE
Makes 1-1/2 cups

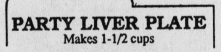

1 pound liver (chicken, calf, beef or pork)
1/2 pound lard (butter or chicken fat)
2 tablespoons minced onion
1/2 bay leaf
1/2 teaspoon thyme
1 teaspoon salt
1/4 teaspoon pepper

Put liver through grinder twice, using finest knife. Add lard and seasonings, mix well and put through grinder again. Pat firmly into small bowls. Cover with foil, fasten tightly, and steam over hot water for 1-1/2 hours. Remove foil, cool and chill. Serve with crackers, Melba toast or assorted chips, if desired.
NOTE: A small peeled clove of garlic may be ground with the liver.

BACON CHEESEBURGERS

2 pounds ground beef
8 slices crisp bacon, crumbled
1/2 cup Cheddar cheese, shredded
1 teaspoon seasoned salt
1/2 cup onion, chopped
1 teaspoon parsley flakes

Mix ground beef with remaining ingredients; shape into patties. Grill until done.

BEEF TURNOVERS
Makes 20

1/2 pound ground beef
1 small onion, finely chopped
1 teaspoon cornstarch
1/4 teaspoon salt
3 tablespoons ketchup
1 medium egg
1 tablespoon water
2 rolls, (7-1/2 ounce each) refrigerated biscuits, ten per roll
Sesame seeds

In skillet, cook ground beef and onion until beef is browned, drain off all fat. Stir cornstarch and salt into beef mixture. Stir in ketchup, cook until mixture is slightly thickened. Remove from heat and cool well. Heat oven to 400 degrees. Lightly grease two large baking sheets. In cup, beat together egg and water. To shape each turnover, press a biscuit into a 3-1/2 inch round. Brush with some egg mixture. Place a tablespoon of meat mixture in center. Fold in half, press biscuits around unfolded edge to seal. Place on baking sheet; brush turnovers with egg mixture. Pierce each one with fork on top of surface. Sprinkle each one with sesame seeds. Bake 10-12 minutes, or until golden brown. These are nice for children's school box lunches.

BEEF PINWHEELS ITALIANA

1-1/2 pounds ground chuck
1 teaspoon salt
1/8 teaspoon pepper
3/4 teaspoon oregano
1/4 cup evaporated milk
1 egg, beaten
1/2 cup green pepper, chopped
1/4 cup onion, chopped
2/3 cup soft bread crumbs
1/2 pound Mozzarella cheese, shredded

Combine all ingredients except cheese. Pat on wax paper into 12-inch squares; sprinkle with cheese, patting down a little. Roll meat into a roll. Seal edges. Refrigerate overnight. Cut into 12 slices. Broil 12 to 15 minutes 6 inches from heat source, turning once. Garnish with small mushrooms if desired.

This looks good and is a pleasant change from pizza meatloaf — even the kids like this.

INSIDE-OUT RAVIOLIS

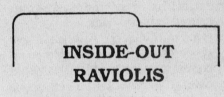

1 pound ground beef
1/2 cup chopped onion
Garlic salt to taste
10 ounce package frozen spinach
1 quart Ragu sauce or you own spaghetti sauce
1/2 teaspoon salt
2 cups shells (small), cooked and drained
1/2 cup Cheddar cheese, grated
1/2 cup Parmesan cheese, grated
1/2 cup bread crumbs
2 well beaten eggs
1/4 cup oil

Brown beef, onion and garlic salt. Add salt and simmer. Cook spinach, following package directions. Drain. Add salt to sauce. Combine spinach, shells, cheeses, bread crumbs, eggs and oil.

Spread in a 9 x 12 x 2" baking dish. Top with sauce. Bake at 350 degrees for 30 minutes. Let stand 10 minutes before serving.

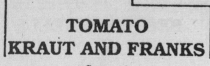

TOMATO KRAUT AND FRANKS
Serves 4

1 (16 ounce) can sauerkraut
1/2 teaspoon pepper
1 (4 ounce) can mushrooms
1 medium onion, thinly sliced
1 cup tomato juice
8 frankfurters, in 1-inch pieces

Drain sauerkraut; rinse with cold water, drain again. Grease or spray 1-1/2-quart casserole. Mix sauerkraut, mushrooms, onions, and frankfurters. Put in casserole, sprinkle with pepper and pour tomato juice over all. Cover and bake at 350 degrees 45 minutes. Then uncover and bake 15 minutes longer.

RAISIN SAUCE FOR HAM

This is wonderful sauce over canned or boned ham.

Mix 1/2 cup brown sugar, 1 teaspoon dry mustard, 2 tablespoons cornstarch. Slowly add 2 tablespoons vinegar. Then add 1/4 teaspoon grated lemon peel, 2 tablespoons lemon juice, and 1-1/2 cups water. Use medium saucepan. Cook over low heat, stirring constantly until thick. Add 1/2 cup raisins and 2 tablespoons butter. Serve hot over ham.

EASTER BAKED HAM

Heat oven to 325 degrees. Place whole ham, fat side up, on a rack in a shallow pan. Insert meat thermometer in center of thick part; making sure thermometer tip does not touch bone. Do not cover; roast ham to an internal temperature of 160 degrees. Picnic or shoulder hams should be baked to an internal temperature of 170 degrees.

Half an hour before ham is done,

Place a little piece of aluminum foil over ham so the top doesn't get tough. The sides are left open. Turn occasionally, once or twice during cooking time. Bake at 350 degrees for 3-5 hours depending on size of ham. I cook a 3 pound for 3-4 hours.

HAM ROLLS
Serves 4

2 tablespoons soft butter
1-1/2 teaspoons prepared mustard
1 cup ground ham
2 cups all-purpose flour
4 teaspoons baking powder
1/2 teaspoon salt
1/4 cup shortening or lard
3/4 cup milk

Combine butter and mustard with the ground ham; set aside. Sift together flour, baking powder, and salt. Cut in shortening until mixture resembles fine crumbs. Add the milk to make a soft dough. Roll out 1/4-inch thick and spread with the ham mixture. Roll up like a jelly roll and cut into 1-1/2 inch slices. Place cut side down in a greased baking pan. Bake in a 425 degree oven for 15-20 minutes.

FRANK-MACARONI SKILLET
Serves 4

2-1/2 cups water
8 ounce can tomato sauce
1 envelope spaghetti sauce mix
1 cup uncooked macaroni
4 or 5 franks, cut into 1-inch pieces
1-1/2 teaspoons Worcestershire sauce

In large saucepan, combine water, tomato sauce and spaghetti sauce mix. Bring to boiling; stir in macaroni; cover and cook over low heat until macaroni is tender, about 15 to 20 minutes, stirring frequently. Stir in franks and Worcestershire sauce; heat through.

HAM STRIPS IN CHILI-TOMATO SAUCE

1/2 cup vegetable oil
2 cups green pepper, chopped
2 cups celery, chopped
1 cup onion, chopped
1 clove garlic, minced
2-15 ounce cans tomato sauce
1/2 teaspoon chili powder
4 cups cooked ham, cut into strips
1/2 cup tomato juice
1-8 ounce jar Picante sauce

Heat oil in skillet. Add green peppers, celery, onion and garlic. Saute until tender, about 8 minutes (do not brown). Stir in tomato sauce and chili powder; cook until mixture comes to a boil, about 2 minutes. Reduce heat to low and simmer, uncovered, 20 minutes. Stir in ham, tomato juice and Picante sauce. Cover; simmer 5 minutes or until heated thoroughly. Serve over rice, noodles or spaghetti.

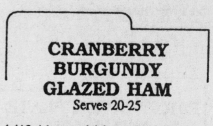

CRANBERRY BURGUNDY GLAZED HAM
Serves 20-25

1 (10-14 pounds) bone-in, fully-cooked ham
Whole cloves
1 (16 ounce) can whole cranberry sauce
1 cup brown sugar
1/2 cup burgundy
2 teaspoons prepared mustard

Place ham, fat side up, in shallow roasting pan. Score fat in diamond pattern; stud with cloves. Insert meat thermometer. Bake in 325 degree oven for 2-1/2 to 3 hours, or until meat thermometer registers 130 degrees.

In saucepan, stir together cranberry sauce, brown sugar, burgundy, and mustard; simmer 5 minutes, uncovered. During last 30 minutes baking time for ham, spoon half of cranberry glaze over it. Pass remaining as a sauce. Makes 3 cups sauce.

JELLIED TURKEY OR CHICKEN LOAF

Serves 4

2 cups diced turkey or chicken
2-1/4 tablespoons powdered gelatin
3-1/2 cups turkey or chicken stock
1 cup mayonnaise
1 teaspoon onion juice
1/2 teaspoon lemon juice
2 cups diced celery or chopped cabbage
3 hard-cooked eggs, sliced
1 teaspoon salt
2 teaspoons pimiento
Parsley or watercress

Soften gelatin in little of the stock and dissolve in remainder that has been heated. Chill in refrigerator. When begins to thicken, stir in mayonnaise; add remaining ingredients, which have also been chilled. Place in loaf pan; return to refrigerator to chill and stiffen. Unmold; garnish with parsley or watercress.

HOLIDAY TURKEY-HAM ROLL-UPS

Serves 4

5 cups cabbage, cooked, chopped, and drained
1 cup Swiss cheese, shredded
8 slices cooked turkey ham
1/4 cup onion, minced
3 tablespoons butter or margarine
3 tablespoons flour
1-1/2 cups sweet milk
2 teaspoons Dijon mustard
1 tablespoon parsley, chopped
1/4 cup bread crumbs

Combine cabbage and 1/2 cup cheese; spoon 3 tablespoonfuls onto each ham slice; roll up; place seam side down in a greased baking dish. Sauté onions in 2 tablespoons butter; blend in flour; add milk and mustard; boil gently, stirring constantly. Add remaining 1/2 cup cheese and the parsley; pour over turkey ham rolls. Melt remaining 1 tablespoon butter; combine with bread crumbs; sprinkle over cheese sauce. Bake at 375 degrees, uncovered, for 25-30 minutes.

PHYLLO TURKEY PUFFS

Serves 6

2 tablespoons butter or margarine
2 tablespoons flour
2 cups chicken broth
3/4 cup milk
2 eggs, beaten lightly
1 tablespoon Parmesan cheese, grated
3 ounces cream cheese
1/4 teaspoon pepper
1/4 teaspoon nutmeg
2 cups turkey, cooked and cubed
1/2 cup butter, melted
12 sheets frozen phyllo dough, thawed

In saucepan melt butter; add flour gradually. Stir in broth and milk; cook over medium heat; stir until thickened. Remove from heat; beat mixture into eggs, then return egg mixture to pan. Add cheeses, pepper, nutmeg, and turkey. Brush inside of muffin cups with melted butter; set aside. Stack 12 sheets of phyllo dough together; brush each with butter; cut into 6 pieces. Line muffin cups with phyllo; fill with turkey filling. Fold corners of pastry over filling to cover; brush with melted butter. Bake at 375 degrees for 25-30 minutes or until puffed and golden. Let stand in pan 5 minutes before removing.

SEAFOOD LOAF

1 (1 pound) can salmon
1 (10-1/2 ounce) can cream of celery soup
1 cup fine dry bread crumbs
2 eggs, slightly beaten
1/2 cup chopped onion
1 tablespoon lemon juice

Drain salmon, reserving 1/4 cup liquid. Remove skin and bones from salmon; flake. Thoroughly mix salmon liquid and remaining ingredients. Pack into a well greased 9x5x3 inch loaf pan. Bake at 375 degrees for 1 hour or until browned. Cool loaf in pan for 10 minutes; loosen from sides of pan and turn out on serving platter. Garnish with parsley, lemon, and orange slices.

FRENCH-STYLE SALMON MEAL

Serves 6

1 can (7-3/4 ounces) salmon
2 hard-boiled eggs, diced
2 tablespoons finely chopped celery
2 green onions, chopped
2 tablespoons cocktail sauce
2 tablespoons mayonnaise
12 slices bread
3 eggs, slightly beaten
1/2 cup milk
1/4 teaspoon salt
1-1/4 cups crushed potato chips
Butter

Drain salmon, reserving liquid. Flake salmon and combine with hard-boiled eggs, celery, onion, cocktail sauce and mayonnaise. Spread filling on 6 slices of bread. Top with remaining slices. Combine eggs, reserved salmon liquid, milk and salt. Dip salmon sandwiches in egg mixture, then in crushed chips. Brown sandwiches on both sides in small amount of butter on hot griddle.

STUFFED CORNISH GAME HENS

Serves 8

4 Cornish game hens
1/2 cup chopped mushrooms
1/2 cup chopped onions
6 tablespoons minced parsley
3/4 pound hot Italian sausage meat
1 teaspoon minced garlic
1 egg, beaten
1/2 cup bread crumbs from fresh Italian bread
2 tablespoons butter

Saute onion, garlic, and mushrooms until soft. Add sausage meat and saute until no longer pink. Remove from heat; stir in parsley and bread crumbs; let cool. Add egg. Stuff each hen with 1/4 of the stuffing. Baste hens with a mixture of one stick unsalted, melted butter and 1 cup Sauterne wine. Bake in a preheated 350 degree oven for 1-1/2 to 2 hours, until brown, basting often.

HOT CHICKEN DISH

1 - 7 ounce box croutons
2 pounds chicken; skinned, boned, cut into chunks
1 onion, chopped
3 stalks celery, chopped
1 small green pepper, chopped
1/2 cup margarine
1 can cream of chicken soup
1 can cream of celery soup
1 can of water

Saute onion, celery, and green pepper in the margarine. Add the soups and water to pan; stir. Heat until hot. In a greased 9 x 13 inch pan, arrange chicken chunks. Then pour over the croutons, the mixture of sauted ingredients and soups. Cover with foil and bake in a 350 degree oven for 1 hour. Remove foil; bake an additional 30 minutes.

CHICKEN AND MUSHROOMS WITH MUENSTER CHEESE

4 whole chicken breasts, boned and skinned
3 eggs
1/2 cup Italian flavored bread crumbs
6 tablespoons butter
10-3/4-ounces chicken broth
2 teaspoons lemon juice
6 ounces sliced Muenster cheese
8 ounces fresh mushrooms

Cut chicken breasts into bite-size pieces. Soak several hours or overnight in 3 beaten eggs. Preheat oven to 350 degrees. Roll chicken pieces in bread crumbs; sauté with sliced mushrooms in margarine for 10 to 15 minutes. Place in casserole. Pour chicken broth over chicken and mushrooms. Sprinkle with lemon juice. Cover with sliced Muenster cheese. Bake uncovered for 30 to 40 minutes.

CHICK-A-DEE DIPPERS

1 large chicken breast, boneless and skinned
1-1/2 slices white bread
1 egg yolk
1 tablespoon minced parsley
1 tablespoon grated onion
1/2 teaspoon salt
1/4 teaspoon pepper
1/4 teaspoon ground cumin
1/8 teaspoon garlic powder
1/8 teaspoon ground tumeric
1/3 cup all-purpose flour
Vegetable oil

Cut chicken into 1-inch pieces and put chicken and bread slices into fine blade food grinder until finely ground. Place into bowl and mix with egg yolk, parsley, onion, salt, pepper, cumin, garlic powder and tumeric. Cover and refrigerate for 30 minutes. Shape mixture into balls (1 rounded teaspoon each) and roll in flour to coat. Pour 1 inch oil in a 2-quart saucepan. Heat to 350 degrees. Fry 6 balls at a time until golden (3-4 minutes). Drain on paper towel. Keep warm in 200 degree oven until ready to use.

Dipping Sauce:
1/2 cup mayonnaise
1/4 cup chili sauce
2 tablespoons peach jam
2 tablespoons dry onion soup mix

Cook all ingredients until hot, but not boiling.

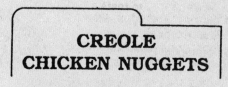

CREOLE CHICKEN NUGGETS

1 small onion, grated
1/2 cup plain dry bread crumbs
1-1/2 teaspoons chili powder
1 teaspoon ground cumin
2-4 drops hot pepper sauce
1 teaspoon dried thyme
1 teaspoon garlic powder
2 pounds boneless chicken breasts, cut into 1-inch pieces
Oil

Combine first 7 ingredients. Dip chicken in mixture, coating well. Heat oil in skillet. Cook chicken until tender and golden; drain on paper towels.

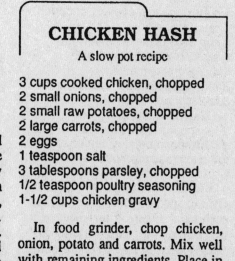

CHICKEN HASH

A slow pot recipe

3 cups cooked chicken, chopped
2 small onions, chopped
2 small raw potatoes, chopped
2 large carrots, chopped
2 eggs
1 teaspoon salt
3 tablespoons parsley, chopped
1/2 teaspoon poultry seasoning
1-1/2 cups chicken gravy

In food grinder, chop chicken, onion, potato and carrots. Mix well with remaining ingredients. Place in slow pot; cook on low for 8 to 10 hours.

CHICKEN AND NOODLES ROMANOFF

2 packages wide noodles
1 cup diced cooked chicken (large pieces)
1 pint white sauce made with chicken stock or broth
1 cup mushrooms
2 tablespoons butter
1/2 cup chopped pimiento (optional)
Salt and pepper to taste

While noodles are cooking according to package directions, sauté mushroom slices in butter; adding pimiento just before done. Combine sauce, mushrooms, pimiento, and chicken. Simmer together over low heat. Drain cooked noodles; butter them and mix with other ingredients; salt and pepper to taste. Pour into greased casserole. Place in 350 degree oven for 20 minutes. Serve hot.

1890 CHICKEN AND MACARONI SUPPER
Serves 4

8 ounces macaroni
Boiling salted water
4 cups cooked chicken, cut into bite-size pieces
1/4 cup butter or margarine
Salt and pepper to taste
1 cup chicken broth
1 cup half and half
Parsley sprigs as garnish

Cook macaroni in boiling salted water until almost tender, about 12 minutes; drain. Place 1/3 of macaroni on bottom of 2-quart lightly-greased casserole. Top with 1/2 the chicken pieces; dot chicken with 1/2 the butter or margarine, salt and pepper and 1/2 the chicken broth. Repeat layers, ending with remaining 1/3 of macaroni on top. Pour cream over all; bake at 350 degrees for 20-30 minutes, or until bubbly.

mixture; roll up as for jelly roll. Pinch ends of dough together; place on lightly greased jelly roll pan. Brush roll lightly with melted butter.

CHICKEN RICE PILAF
Serves 4-6

2/3 cup long grain rice
2/3 cup broken thin spaghetti
1/3 cup olive oil
3 cups chicken broth
1 cup fresh or frozen broccoli florets
1/4 teaspoon thyme, crushed
1 cup cooked chicken, (cut in julienne strips)
1/2 cup sliced green onion (scallions)
1/4 cup chopped walnuts
1/4 cup diced red pepper

In saucepan, sauté rice and spaghetti in oil until golden, stirring often. Add chicken broth and bring to boil. Add broccoli and thyme. Cover; simmer 15 minutes or until rice is tender, stirring occasionally. Add remaining ingredients and cook through.

CHICKEN 'N BISCUIT TRIANGLES
Makes 16 biscuits

1-1/2 cups all-purpose flour
1/4 teaspoon salt
4 teaspoons baking powder
1/4 teaspoon nutmeg
2 tablespoons shortening
1 cup cooked potatoes, mashed
3/4 cup cooked chicken, chopped finely
1 egg
1/4 cup sweet milk
Melted butter or margarine
1 tablespoon parsley, minced

Combine first 4 ingredients; cut in shortening; add mashed potatoes and chicken. Mix egg with milk; add to flour mixture; stir until just blended. Knead dough lightly; pat to 3/4 inch thickness. Cut into 3-inch squares, then into triangles. Place on a greased baking sheet; bake at 375 degrees for 10 minutes. Brush with melted butter; sprinkle with parsley; bake 5 additional minutes.

COUNTRY CHICKEN ROLL
Serves 6

Filling:
2 tablespoons shortening
2 tablespoons flour
1 cup chicken stock
1/4 teaspoon salt
1/8 teaspoon pepper
2 cups cooked chicken, chopped

Dough for roll:
3 cups buttermilk biscuit mix
2 tablespoons parsley, minced
2 tablespoons melted butter for brushing

Melt shortening; remove from heat. Add flour; stir to a smooth paste. Add chicken stock gradually, stirring constantly; cook until thick. Add salt, pepper, and cooked chicken. Set aside to cool. Prepare biscuit mix according to package directions. Roll dough to about 1/3 inch thick; add parsley; spread dough with chicken

CHICKEN DUMPLINGS
From 1904
Serves 6

3 cups flour
1 teaspoon baking powder
1/2 teaspoon salt
3 eggs, beaten
1/4 cup milk

Mix all ingredients well; pour out onto well-floured board. With rolling pin, roll out 1/2 batter at a time. Cut into 1" squares. Drop one at a time into 2 quarts boiling chicken broth in a 4-quart Dutch oven. Cook 20 minutes.

FLOUNDER FILLETS IN ROSE SAUCE
Serves 4

4 fillets of flounder
½ cup vegetable oil
1 large onion, sliced
2 small cloves garlic, minced
1 cup tomato juice
¼ cup dark, seedless raisins
2 teaspoons curry powder
1 teaspoon cumin
⅛ teaspoon cayenne pepper
1 cup plain yogurt
¼ cup sliced almonds, toasted

Pat fish dry; salt and pepper. Heat oil and brown fish on both sides; remove fish from pan; keep warm. Sauté onions and garlic; do not brown. Add tomato juice, raisins and seasonings; bring to a boil. Simmer 3 minutes on low heat; stir in yogurt; return fish to skillet. Simmer gently 3 minutes until fish is heated through. To serve, sprinkle fish with toasted almonds.

CREOLE FISH FILLETS
Serves 4–6

1 medium onion, chopped
½ cup chopped celery
1 tablespoon butter *or* margarine
1 (8-ounce) can tomato sauce
½ teaspoon salt
½ teaspoon curry powder
Dash freshly ground black pepper
1 cup chopped green pepper
2 pounds thick fish fillets

Sauté onion and celery in butter in large skillet. Add rest of ingredients, except fish. Bring to boil and add fish. Simmer about 15 minutes, or until fish is flaky.

SALMON PUFFS WITH TOMATO SAUCE
Serves 6

2 cups salmon, flaked
2 eggs, slightly beaten
1 cup milk
2 tablespoons parsley
1 tablespoon onion, chopped
2 tablespoons fresh lemon juice
¼ teaspoon salt
⅛ teaspoon pepper
Tomato Cream Sauce (recipe follows)

Mix all ingredients. Grease and flour 6 custard cups or an 8 x 8 x 2-inch baking dish. Pour salmon mixture into pan; bake at 350 degrees for 35 minutes, or until firm.

Tomato Cream Sauce:
1 tablespoon butter *or* margarine
2 tablespoons onion, finely chopped
1 (10½-ounce) can tomato soup
¼ teaspoon salt
⅛ teaspoon pepper
¾ cup milk

Melt butter in saucepan; add onion, cook 5 minutes. Add rest of ingredients; serve at once over hot salmon puffs.

SAUSAGE WEDGES

½ pound bulk pork sausage
1 cup (4 ounces) shredded cheddar cheese *or* American
2 tablespoons diced onion
¾ cup milk
4 eggs, beaten
1 teaspoon dried parsley
2 tablespoons butter

Crumble sausage in a 9-inch pie plate. Cover with paper towel and microwave for 3–4 minutes on HIGH. Drain off fat; sprinkle cheese over sausage; stir in onion. In a medium bowl combine milk and eggs; add parsley and butter. Pour over sausage; cover with plastic wrap and microwave 4 minutes on HIGH. Stir; cover and microwave for 6–8 minutes on MEDIUM (50 percent). Let stand, covered, 5 minutes.

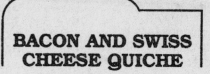

BACON AND SWISS CHEESE QUICHE

1 (9-inch) single crust pie shell
½ pound bacon (9–11 strips)
2 tablespoons flour
¼ teaspoon salt
½ teaspoon ground nutmeg
⅛ teaspoon cayenne pepper
¼ cup chopped onion
2 cups half-and-half
4 eggs
⅓ cup grated Swiss cheese
Paprika
Parsley flakes

Microwave pie shell in a glass pie plate on HIGH for 5–7 minutes; rotate ½ turn after 2½ minutes. Cool. Arrange bacon in single layer on microwave bacon rack; top with paper towels. Microwave on HIGH for 9 minutes, or until crisp. Cut into bite-sized pieces and sprinkle over bottom of crust.

In a 1½-quart casserole combine flour, salt, nutmeg, cayenne and onion; whisk in half-and-half to blend well. Microwave on HIGH for 4–6 minutes, whisking every minute until hot and thick. Meanwhile in small bowl beat eggs to blend; add about ¼ of half-and-half mixture to eggs and whisk well. Then add mixture back to warm half-and-half; microwave on MEDIUM HIGH (70 percent) for 3–5 minutes. Pour into pie shell. Distribute cheese evenly over top, then sprinkle with paprika and parsley; microwave at MEDIUM (50 percent) for 6–9 minutes. Let stand 15 minutes.

Micro-MAGIC

TUNA VEGETABLE CHOWDER

1½ cups water
1 medium potato, diced
2 tablespoons chopped onion
¼ cup diced carrot
¾ teaspoon salt
¼ teaspoon celery salt
Dash pepper
1 teaspoon chopped chives
1 teaspoon Worcestershire sauce
⅔ cup fresh or frozen corn
1 (6½-ounce) can tuna, drained
1 cup half-and-half

In 2-quart container combine water, potato, onion, carrot, salt, celery salt, pepper, chives and Worcestershire sauce. Cover and microwave on HIGH for 7–15 minutes, or until vegetables are just about tender. Add corn; cover and return to microwave; heat for 5–8 minutes on HIGH, or until corn is tender. Stir in tuna and cream; cover and microwave for 2–4 minutes until heated through

SHRIMP STIR-FRY

1 head bok choy, sliced (about 8 cups)
1 large red pepper, chopped
1 tablespoon cooking oil
2 cloves garlic, minced
8 drops hot pepper sauce
1 teaspoon sesame seed
12 ounces uncooked fresh shrimp, well-drained
1 tablespoon water
2 teaspoons cornstarch

Combine bok choy and red pepper in a 2-quart bowl; microwave on HIGH, uncovered, for 5–6 minutes; stir once or twice; set aside. Combine oil, garlic, hot pepper sauce and sesame seed in casserole; microwave on HIGH, uncovered, for 2–2½ minutes, stir in shrimp; microwave on HIGH, uncovered, for 2–2½ minutes until shrimp are pink; stir once. Combine water and cornstarch in a 1-cup glass measure; mix well. Drain juices from vegetables and from shrimp into measure; blend well. Microwave on HIGH, uncovered, for 1–1½ minutes, or until mixture boils and thickens. Add to shrimp along with vegetables; toss lightly to coat. Microwave on HIGH, uncovered, for 1–2 minutes, or until heated through.

FISH CREOLE

1 pound sole or orange roughy fillets
1 (8-ounce) can tomato sauce
1 (2.5-ounce) jar sliced mushrooms
½ green pepper, diced
¼ teaspoon garlic powder
¼ teaspoon oregano
3 green onions, sliced
1 stalk celery, diagonally sliced
3 tablespoons water
1 teaspoon instant chicken bouillon

Rinse fish and pat dry. Arrange in 3-quart oblong baking dish with thicker portions toward outside of dish. Combine remaining ingredients in a 4-cup glass measure; pour evenly over fish. Cover with plastic wrap; microwave on HIGH for 8–10 minutes, or until fish flakes easily. Let stand 5 minutes.

SALMON STEAKS

2 (8-ounce) salmon steaks
1 tablespoon butter
½ tablespoon lime juice
1 green onion, chopped
⅛ teaspoon ground pepper
⅛ teaspoon dill weed

Place salmon steaks on microwave-safe plate; place a paper towel over top of steaks and microwave on HIGH for 3–3½ minutes. Set aside. Combine butter, lime juice, onion, dill weed and pepper in small dish; microwave on HIGH for 30–45 seconds until melted. Pour over salmon. Garnish with lime slices.

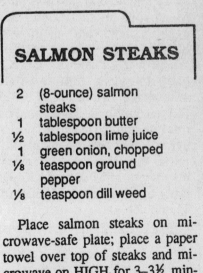

BACON AND SWISS CHEESE QUICHE

1 (9-inch) single crust pie shell
½ pound bacon (9–11 strips)
2 tablespoons flour
¼ teaspoon salt
½ teaspoon ground nutmeg
⅛ teaspoon cayenne pepper
¼ cup chopped onion
2 cups half-and-half
4 eggs
⅓ cup grated Swiss cheese
  Paprika
  Parsley flakes

Microwave pie shell in a glass pie plate on HIGH for 5–7 minutes; rotate ½ turn after 2½ minutes. Cool. Arrange bacon in single layer on microwave bacon rack; top with paper towels. Microwave on HIGH for 9 minutes, or until crisp. Cut into bite-sized pieces and sprinkle over bottom of crust.

In a 1½-quart casserole combine flour, salt, nutmeg, cayenne and onion; whisk in half-and-half to blend well. Microwave on HIGH for 4–6 minutes, whisking every minute until hot and thick. Meanwhile in small bowl beat eggs to blend; add about ¼ of half-and-half mixture to eggs and whisk well. Then add mixture back to warm half-and-half; microwave on MEDIUM HIGH (70 percent) for 3–5 minutes. Pour into pie shell. Distribute cheese evenly over top, then sprinkle with paprika and parsley; microwave at MEDIUM (50 percent) for 6–9 minutes. Let stand 15 minutes.

SAUSAGE WEDGES

½ pound bulk pork sausage
1 cup (4 ounces) shredded cheddar cheese

or American
2 tablespoons diced onion
¾ cup milk
4 eggs, beaten
1 teaspoon dried parsley
2 tablespoons butter

Crumble sausage in a 9-inch pie plate. Cover with paper towel and microwave for 3–4 minutes on HIGH. Drain off fat; sprinkle cheese over sausage; stir in onion. In a medium bowl combine milk and eggs; add parsley and butter. Pour over sausage; cover with plastic wrap and microwave 4 minutes on HIGH. Stir; cover and microwave for 6–8 minutes on MEDIUM (50 percent). Let stand, covered, 5 minutes.

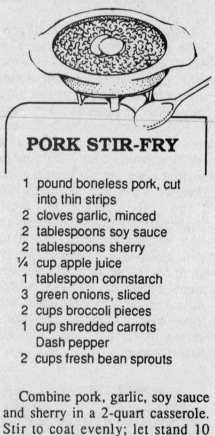

PORK STIR-FRY

1 pound boneless pork, cut into thin strips
2 cloves garlic, minced
2 tablespoons soy sauce
2 tablespoons sherry
¼ cup apple juice
1 tablespoon cornstarch
3 green onions, sliced
2 cups broccoli pieces
1 cup shredded carrots
  Dash pepper
2 cups fresh bean sprouts

Combine pork, garlic, soy sauce and sherry in a 2-quart casserole. Stir to coat evenly; let stand 10 minutes. Blend together apple juice and cornstarch; stir into pork mixture. Cover with casserole lid. Microwave on HIGH for 4–5 minutes; stir once. Add onion, broccoli, carrots and pepper; do not stir; cover, microwave for 3–4 minutes, or until vegetables are tender-crisp. Add sprouts; cover and microwave for 1½–2 minutes. Toss to mix.

HEARTY MINESTRONE
Serves 6–8

5 cups water
1 can condensed beef bouillon
5 teaspoons instant beef bouillon granules
1 clove garlic, finely minced
1 small onion, finely chopped
1 (16-ounce) can tomatoes, undrained
1 cup broken spaghetti pieces, uncooked
1 teaspoon salt
⅛ teaspoon pepper
¼ teaspoon oregano
¼ teaspoon basil
1 cup frozen peas
1 (16-ounce) can kidney beans, undrained
1–2 cups cooked beef, cubed

Combine water, bouillon, garlic, onion, tomatoes, spaghetti, beef, salt, pepper, oregano and basil in 3-quart casserole. Cover and microwave on HIGH for 22–30 minutes, or until spaghetti is tender. Add peas and beans; cover and return to microwave to cook for 8 more min-

RICE PILAF

1 cup regular rice, long grain
1 cup pearl barley
¼ cup butter
8 green onions, chopped
3 cubes beef bouillon
4 cups water
½ pound fresh mushrooms, sliced
2 large cloves garlic
1 teaspoon salt

Combine rice, barley and melted butter; microwave for 5 minutes on HIGH; stir twice. Add remaining ingredients; cover and microwave on HIGH for 6 minutes, then 16–18 minutes on 70 percent power.

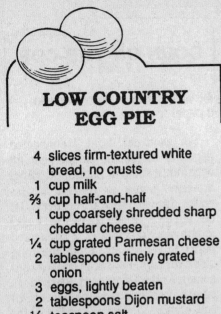

LOW COUNTRY EGG PIE

- 4 slices firm-textured white bread, no crusts
- 1 cup milk
- ⅔ cup half-and-half
- 1 cup coarsely shredded sharp cheddar cheese
- ¼ cup grated Parmesan cheese
- 2 tablespoons finely grated onion
- 3 eggs, lightly beaten
- 2 tablespoons Dijon mustard
- ½ teaspoon salt
- ¼ teaspoon ground hot red pepper
- ⅛ teaspoon white pepper
- 1 tablespoon *each* parsley flakes and paprika
- 2 hard-cooked eggs, peeled and coarsely chopped

Soak bread in milk and half-and-half for 5 minutes. Combine with cheeses, onion, eggs, mustard, salt, hot red pepper and white pepper; fold in hard-cooked eggs. Spoon into 9-inch round, 1½-quart casserole; sprinkle with paprika and parsley. Microwave, uncovered, on MEDIUM (50 percent) for 18–21 minutes. Rotate casserole every 4 minutes, or until set. Cover pie with foil and let stand 5–7 minutes; cut into wedges and serve warm.

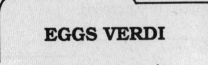

EGGS VERDI

- ½ cup butter *or* margarine
- 1 tablespoon lemon juice
- ⅛ teaspoon ground red pepper
- 3 large egg yolks, beaten
- 1 (12-ounce) package frozen spinach soufflé, thawed
- 4 large eggs
- 2 English muffins, split and toasted

In a 1-quart bowl combine butter, ¼ cup water, lemon juice and pepper; microwave, uncovered, on HIGH for 2½ minutes or until boiling. With a wire whisk beat in egg yolks a little at a time. Cook, uncovered, on HIGH for 15 seconds (will be thin). Let stand 5 minutes; stir twice.

Place soufflé in custard cups divided evenly; microwave on HIGH for 4 minutes; stir once. Crack an egg into each cup over soufflé mixture; with wooden pick puncture yolk. Cover the cups with waxed paper; microwave on HIGH for 3–4 minutes. Rearrange the cups in oven after 2 minutes. Let stand, covered, for 3 minutes. Reheat sauce on HIGH for 1 minute. Run spatula around edge of soufflé mix in each cup; turn out each onto a muffin half. Spoon sauce over. Serve immediately.

PLAN AHEAD BRUNCH

Serves 9

- 1 package (12 ounces) frozen hash brown potatoes
- 6 eggs
- 1/3 cup whipping or light cream
- 1 cup (4 ounces) shredded Cheddar cheese
- 2 tablespoons chopped chives
- 1/4 teaspoon salt
- Dash of pepper
- 1 cup (4 ounces) diced ham, or Canadian bacon

Place potatoes in 8-inch square baking dish; cover with plastic wrap and microwave on HIGH 6-7 minutes until steaming, stir once. Combine eggs, cream, chives, salt, pepper, cheese, and ham. Add mixture to potatoes, cover with waxed paper, and microwave 12 minutes at MEDIUM (50%) stirring twice. Then finish cooking for 3-4 minutes on HIGH or until set. Let stand 5 minutes, cut into squares.

FRUIT DELIGHT

Prepare this ahead of time to allow flavors to develop.

- 1 (20-ounce) can pineapple chunks, juice pack
- 2 (11-ounce) cans mandarin orange sections, drained
- ½ to 1 cup seedless grapes, halved
- 2 kiwis, halved lengthwise and sliced
- ½ cup orange juice
- ¼ cup honey
- 1 tablespoon lemon juice

Drain pineapple; reserve juice. In a large bowl combine pineapple, mandarin oranges, grapes and kiwi. Combine pineapple liquid, orange juice, honey and lemon juice. Pour over fruit. Cover and chill until ready to serve.

CARROTS WITH VINEGAR

- 1½ pounds carrots, peeled and cut into ½-inch cubes
- ¼ cup minced onion
- 3 tablespoons red wine vinegar
- 1 bay leaf
- ¼ teaspoon salt
- Dash pepper

Mix carrots and onion in 2-quart casserole. Add vinegar and bay leaf; cover with lid and microwave on HIGH for 10 minutes; stir at halftime. Stir and cover with paper towel; microwave on HIGH for 5 minutes, until almost all liquid evaporates and carrots are tender. Add salt and pepper to taste. Let stand covered for 3 minutes.

VEGETABLE STIR-FRY

1 tablespoon oil
1 clove garlic, minced
1 small onion, sliced
1 cup sliced mushrooms
2 cups sliced cauliflower pieces
¾ cup thinly sliced carrot
½ cup sliced green pepper pieces
3 tablespoons teriyaki sauce
½ tablespoon cornstarch
3 tablespoons cashews *or* peanuts

Combine oil, garlic, onion and mushrooms in a microwave casserole. Microwave on HIGH, uncovered, for 1½–2 minutes; stir in cauliflower, carrot and green pepper; cover with lid. Microwave for 3½–4 minutes. Stir once. Combine teriyaki sauce and cornstarch in 1-cup glass measure. Drain juices from vegetables into cup and mix well. Microwave on HIGH, uncovered, for 1–1½ minutes; stir once. Pour over vegetables; sprinkle with nuts; toss lightly.

ORANGE ASPARAGUS

1½ pounds fresh asparagus
1 tablespoon water
1 tablespoon honey
2 teaspoons cornstarch
¹/₂ cup orange juice
1 tablespoon margarine

Snap off tough ends of asparagus spears; place in a 10 x 6-inch pan; add water; cover with plastic wrap and vent. Microwave on HIGH for 5–6 minutes; drain and set aside. Combine honey, cornstarch and orange juice in a 1-cup measure; microwave on HIGH, uncovered, for 1–1½ minutes; stir once. Stir in margarine; spoon sauce over asparagus.

SHALIMAR SALAD

4 stalks broccoli
1 large head cauliflower
2 bell peppers, thinly sliced
1 can water chestnuts, drained and sliced
½ pound fresh mushrooms, cut in large pieces
1 (8-ounce) jar Indian chutney
3 tablespoons curry powder
1½ to 2 cups mayonnaise
1 cup chopped pecans

Break broccoli florets into bite-size pieces, discarding heavy stalks. Microwave fon HIGH or 2 minutes; rinse immediately in cold water; drain and repeat with cauliflower. Mix broccoli and cauliflower with peppers, water chestnuts and mushrooms. Cover and refrigerate.

To make dressing: Thoroughly mix chutney, mayonnaise and curry powder; refrigerate. One hour before serving, toss vegetables well with the dressing. Refrigerate until needed. Just before serving, sprinkle with nuts.

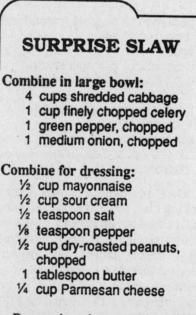

SURPRISE SLAW

Combine in large bowl:
4 cups shredded cabbage
1 cup finely chopped celery
1 green pepper, chopped
1 medium onion, chopped

Combine for dressing:
½ cup mayonnaise
½ cup sour cream
½ teaspoon salt
⅛ teaspoon pepper
½ cup dry-roasted peanuts, chopped
1 tablespoon butter
¼ cup Parmesan cheese

Brown in microwave on HIGH for 3–6 minutes; stir twice. Add ¼ cup grated Parmesan cheese; sprinkle on top of slaw mixture.

CORN-ON-THE-COB
Serves 4

4 medium ears of corn (in husk)
8 paper towel sheets

For each ear, hold 2 connected paper towel sheets under running water until soaked, but not dripping. Squeeze gently to remove excess water. Spread paper towel sheets flat on counter. Place corn (in husk) lengthwise in center of 2 connected paper towel sheets. Fold one long side over corn. Fold both ends toward center. Roll up over corn. Place loose edge of packet down on microwave-safe platter. Microwave on HIGH for 9 to 15 minutes, or until tender, rearranging ears once. Let stand for two minutes. Remove and discard paper towels. If desired, place corn in husks on edge of grill to keep warm, turning ears once or twice.

SUPREME RICE CASSEROLE

1 stick butter, cut into pieces
1⅓ cups uncooked instant rice
1 can onion soup
⅓ pound fresh mushrooms, sliced, *or* 1 (4-ounce) can
½ teaspoon pepper

Combine all ingredients in baking dish; cover tightly and microwave 5 minutes on HIGH. Stir and microwave 5 additional minutes on 50 percent power. Let stand several minutes before serving.

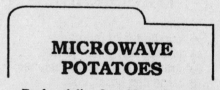

MICROWAVE POTATOES

Peel and dice 3 or 4 large potatoes. Place in microwave casserole dish; dot with 1/2 stick margarine. Return to microwave and cook 3-5 minutes more, or until potatoes are done. Season with salt, pepper, and parsley flakes.

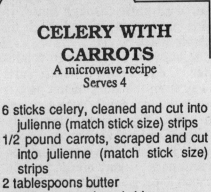

CELERY WITH CARROTS

A microwave recipe
Serves 4

6 sticks celery, cleaned and cut into julienne (match stick size) strips
1/2 pound carrots, scraped and cut into julienne (match stick size) strips
2 tablespoons butter
1 tablespoon snipped chives
1 teaspoon marjoram
Dash salt
Dash pepper
1 teaspoon chopped parsley

The total weight of the vegetables should be about 12 ounces. Arrange the celery and carrots in 3-3/4 cup oval or round casserole dish. Flake butter over vegetables. Sprinkle with chopped chives and marjoram; season well with salt and pepper. Spoon over 2 tablespoons water. Cover with plastic wrap and pierce. Microwave on HIGH for 10 minutes. Vegetables should be stirred half way through cooking, to make sure they cook evenly. Allow to stand 5 minutes, covered. Sprinkle with parsley before serving. Total Microwave cooking time: 10 minutes.

BAKED CUSTARD

2 cups milk
4 eggs, beaten
1/3 cup sugar
1 teaspoon vanilla
Dash of salt
Dash ground nutmeg

In a 4-cup glass measure, heat milk on HIGH for 4 minutes until very hot, but not boiling. Meanwhile, combine beaten eggs, sugar, vanilla and a dash of salt. Beat until well-blended; gradually add hot milk to beaten egg mixture; beat well. Divide egg mixture evenly between 6 (6-ounce) cups. Place in a 13 x 9 x 2-inch baking dish; sprinkle with nutmeg.

Pour about 1/2 cup boiling water around cups in dish; cover with waxed paper. Microwave on medium power (50 percent) for 8 1/2 minutes; rearrange cups every 3 minutes. Remove any that are soft-set. Rearrange the remaining custards in dish; microwave on medium power (50 percent) for 5 minutes. Let stand 10 minutes.

MOCHA CREAM PUDDING

2/3 cup sugar
2 tablespoons cornstarch
1/4 teaspoon salt
1 2/3 cups milk
1 1/2 (1-ounce) squares unsweetened chocolate
1 egg, beaten
2 tablespoons butter *or* margarine
1 teaspoon instant coffee crystals
1 teaspoon vanilla

In a 1 1/2-quart bowl combine sugar, cornstarch and salt. Stir in milk and chocolate; mix well; microwave on HIGH for 6 minutes, stirring after 3 minutes, then every minute.

Gradually stir small amount of the hot milk mixture into the beaten egg; return all to bowl and mix well; microwave on HIGH for 30 seconds; stir after 14 seconds; add butter, coffee crystals and vanilla. Stir until butter melts. Cover with waxed paper. Cool, then chill.

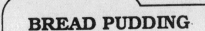

BREAD PUDDING

1/4 cup butter *or* margarine
4 slices bread, cubed
1/2 cup sugar
2 tablespoons lemon juice
1 cup milk
3 eggs
Cinnamon

Microwave butter on HIGH in a 1-quart casserole for about 1 minute;

add bread, sugar and lemon juice; toss to lightly mix. Combine milk and eggs; beat until smooth; pour over bread mixture. Sprinkle with cinnamon. Place casserole in an 8-inch square glass baking dish; add 1 cup warm water to baking dish. Microwave on HIGH, uncovered, for 11–13 minutes, or until center is just about set. Serve with Rum Custard Sauce.

Rum Custard Sauce:
1 1/2 cups milk
1/2 cup light cream
1/3 cup sugar
1/8 teaspoon salt
3 large eggs, lightly beaten
3 tablespoons rum

Combine milk, cream, sugar and salt in a 2-quart glass measure. Place in microwave and cook for 4 minutes on 70 percent power. Stir 1/2 cup milk mixture into eggs; gradually stir eggs into milk mixture and microwave on 50 percent power for 2 1/2 minutes.

Stir, then microwave for 2 1/2 minutes on 30 percent power. Let stand until cooled; stir in rum. Serve over Bread Pudding.

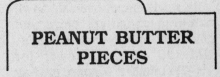

PEANUT BUTTER PIECES

2 sticks butter
1 pound powdered sugar
1 cup graham cracker crumbs
1 cup peanut butter
1 (12 ounce) package chocolate chips

Place butter in large bowl and microwave on HIGH for 2-3 minutes. When butter is melted, add sugar, crumbs, and peanut butter. Mix until smooth; press into 8x8 dish; microwave on HIGH for 2 minutes. Put chocolate chips in large bowl and microwave 50% for 3-4 minutes; stir several times while cooking.

When melted, spread over peanut butter layer; chill. Cut into squares and store in airtight container.

MEXICAN CHOCOLATE CAKE

- 1 package microwave chocolate cake mix with pan
- ⅔ cup water
- ⅓ cup oil
- 1 egg
- 1 teaspoon cinnamon

Topping:

- 1 (6-ounce) package (1 cup) semisweet chocolate chips
- ¼ cup amaretto *or* 2 teaspoons almond extract *and*
- 2 tablespoons water
- ½ cup whipping cream
- 1½ teaspoons confectioners' sugar
- ½ teaspoon vanilla
- ¼ cup sliced almonds

Using solid shortening, grease a 7-inch round pan. In a medium bowl, combine all cake ingredients. Beat with a spoon for about 75 strokes; pour into a prepared pan; microwave on HIGH for 6½ minutes. Cake is done when it pulls away from sides of pan. If cake is not done, add additional time in 30-second intervals. Immediately invert onto serving plate. Cool completely.

In small microwave-safe bowl, combine chocolate chips and amaretto; microwave on MEDIUM (50 percent) power for 1½–2½ minutes; stir once partway through cooking, beating until smooth. Cool 20 minutes; spread on top of cake.

In small bowl, beat whipping cream until soft peaks form. Blend in confectioners' sugar and vanilla; beat until stiff peaks form. Spread over chocolate mixture; top with almonds. Store in refrigerator.

FROZEN DELIGHT

- 2 tablespoons butter *or* margarine

- 1½ cups chocolate cookie crumbs
- ½ cup sliced almonds
- ½ teaspoon cooking oil
- ½ gallon vanilla ice cream
- ¼ cup flaked coconut
- 1 teaspoon almond extract
- ½ cup grated semisweet chocolate (3 ounces)

Microwave butter on HIGH in a 12 x 8-inch dish for 45 seconds. Stir in crumbs until well-mixed; press into the bottom of dish. Microwave on HIGH, uncovered, for 1½–2 minutes; set aside to cool. Combine almonds and oil in a small dish; stir and microwave on HIGH, uncovered, for 2½–3 minutes; stir 3 times. When cool, chop half of the almonds finely; set aside. Microwave the ice cream on HIGH for 45–60 seconds in an uncovered container to soften. Place in mixing bowl; add coconut and extract; then add chocolate and chopped almonds; mix. Spoon into crust; sprinkle with remaining almonds. Cover and freeze until firm.

GOLDEN SPICE MARBLE CAKE
Serves 6

- 1 package microwave yellow cake mix
- ⅔ cup buttermilk
- ⅓ cup oil
- 1 egg
- 1 tablespoon molasses
- ½ teaspoon cinnamon
- ¼ teaspoon nutmeg

Frosting:

- 1 cup confectioners' sugar
- 1 tablespoon margarine *or* butter
- ½ teaspoon lemon juice
- 1–2 tablespoons milk

Use solid shortening; grease a 7-inch round pan. In a medium bowl, combine all cake ingredients; beat with a spoon until well-blended. Pour half of batter (about 1 cup) into second bowl. Stir in molasses, cinnamon and nutmeg. Spoon yellow and

spice batter alternately into prepared pan. Pull knife through batter in wide curves; turn pan and repeat for marble effect.

Microwave on HIGH for 5 minutes. Cake is done when it pulls away from the sides of the pan. If any additional time is necessary, add it in 30-second intervals. Immediately invert onto serving plate. In a small bowl combine confectioners' sugar, margarine and lemon juice; gradually add milk until desired spreading consistency.

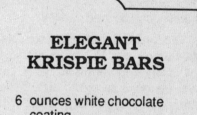

ELEGANT KRISPIE BARS

- 6 ounces white chocolate coating
- 1 cup peanut butter
- 4 cups rice cereal
- 1 cup salted peanuts

Combine coating and peanut butter in a 2-quart bowl and microwave on HIGH for 2½–3 minutes until coating is melted; stir twice. Add cereal and peanuts. Press into 13 x 9-inch baking dish. Refrigerate until set, about 1 hour. Cut into squares.

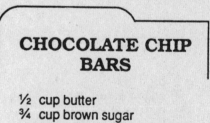

CHOCOLATE CHIP BARS

- ½ cup butter
- ¾ cup brown sugar
- 1 egg
- 1 tablespoon milk
- 1 teaspoon vanilla
- 1¼ cups flour
- ½ teaspoon baking powder
- ⅛ teaspoon salt
- 1 (6-ounce) package chocolate chips, divided
- ½ cup nuts (optional)

Mix all together, using only half of the chips in the batter. The other half goes on top. Using an 8- or 9-inch square dish, microwave on HIGH for 6½ minutes.

PEANUT BUTTER BARS

⅓ cup creamy *or* chunky
   peanut butter
⅓ cup light brown sugar
1 egg
1 teaspoon vanilla
2 tablespoons milk
⅔ cup flour
¼ teaspoon baking soda
¼ cup chopped peanuts
   (optional)
2 milk chocolate bars

Beat peanut butter with sugar, egg, vanilla and milk. Mix flour with baking soda and add to peanut butter mixture. Beat until smooth; add peanuts. Spread in greased 8-inch square dish. Microwave, uncovered, on MEDIUM HIGH (70 percent) for 5½–6 minutes; rotate dish after 3 minutes.

Let stand, uncovered, for 5 minutes. Let cool. Place 2 milk chocolate bars on top while it is standing; swirl for a quick frosting.

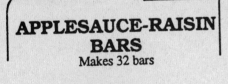

APPLESAUCE-RAISIN BARS
Makes 32 bars

¼ cup margarine
⅔ cup brown sugar, packed
1 egg
1 cup applesauce
1 cup flour
½ teaspoon baking soda
½ teaspoon salt
½ teaspoon ground cinnamon
¼ teaspoon ground nutmeg
⅛ teaspoon ground cloves
½ cup raisins
   Confectioners' sugar

Microwave the margarine on HIGH for 15–30 seconds, or until soft. Blend in brown sugar; beat in egg and applesauce. Stir in remain-

ing ingredients, except raisins and confectioners' sugar; beat until smooth. Stir in raisins. Pour into 12 x 8-inch baking dish greased on bottom only. Microwave on HIGH, uncovered, for 9–10 minutes, or until no longer doughy. Cool. Sprinkle with confectioners' sugar. Cut into bars. The applesauce adds a moist texture to these spicy bars.

MILK CHOCOLATE ALMOND BARS

½ cup butter *or* margarine, softened
½ cup dark brown sugar, firmly packed
1¼ cups flour
¼ teaspoon salt
1 (6-ounce) package milk chocolate morsels
½ cup chopped almonds

Combine butter and sugar until creamy. Sift flour and salt together and blend into butter and sugar mixture. Press evenly into 13 x 9 x 2-inch baking dish. Microwave on HIGH for 4–5 minutes. Rotate the dish after 2 minutes. Sprinkle milk chocolate morsels over top and return to microwave for 1 minute on HIGH. Spread evenly over top; sprinkle with chopped almonds. Cool before cutting.

APRI-ORANGE SAUCE
Makes 2 cups

1/2 cup apricot jam
1 tablespoon cornstarch
1/2 cup orange juice
1/8 teaspoon ground cloves

Combine jam, cornstarch, and orange juice in a 2-cup glass measure; mix well. Microwave on HIGH, uncovered, 2 to 2-1/2 minutes or until mixture boils and thickens; stir once. Stir in cloves.

SWEET POTATO SOUFFLÉ

1 (18-ounce) can sweet potatoes
1/4 cup granulated sugar
1/4 cup dark brown sugar
1/4 cup margarine, melted
2 eggs
3/4 cup evaporated milk
1/2 teaspoon cinnamon
1/2 teaspoon nutmeg
1/4 teaspoon vanilla

Topping:
6 tablespoons margarine, melted
1/2 cup brown sugar
1/2 cup walnuts, chopped
1 cup crushed crackers, Ritz® or Townhouse®

Combine potatoes with next 8 ingredients and mix well. Pour into a 2-quart casserole and microwave on 70% for 13-16 minutes. Rotate dish once, if necessary. Combine topping ingredients and spread over potatoes. Microwave on 70% for 2-4 more minutes.

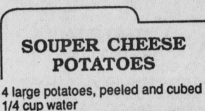

SOUPER CHEESE POTATOES

4 large potatoes, peeled and cubed
1/4 cup water
1/2 can condensed Cheddar cheese soup
1/2 cup sour cream
1/2 cup half-and-half
1 tablespoon snipped chives
1/2 teaspoon garlic salt
1/2 cup (2 ounces) shredded Cheddar cheese
Paprika
1 teaspoon parsley
1/8 teaspoon pepper

Combine potatoes and water in a casserole; cover with lid and microwave on HIGH for 12-14 minutes; stir once. Stir in soup, sour cream, half-and-half, chives, and garlic salt. Microwave on HIGH for 4-5 minutes, uncovered; stir once. Sprinkle with cheese and paprika. Let stand, covered, about 5 minutes or until cheese is melted. Sprinkle with paprika, parsley, and pepper.

PARMESAN POTATO SLICES

1 small onion, chopped
1/2 cup chopped celery
2 tablespoons butter or margarine
3 medium unpeeled potatoes, cleaned
1/2 teaspoon garlic salt
Dash pepper
1/4 cup Parmesan cheese, or to taste
1/4 teaspoon poultry seasoning
1/2 teaspoon dried parsley flakes
Paprika

Combine onion, celery, and butter in an 8-inch square baking dish. Cover with waxed paper. Microwave on HIGH 2-1/2 to 3 minutes or until vegetables are just about tender. Thinly slice potatoes into baking dish; mix lightly. Cover and microwave on HIGH 10-12 minutes or until potatoes are tender; stir once. Add garlic salt, pepper, cheese, seasonings; mix lightly. Sprinkle with paprika. Microwave on HIGH for 1-2 minutes, uncovered.

LIME-THYME POTATOES

1/4 cup melted margarine or butter
1 teaspoon grated lime peel
1 tablespoon lime juice
1 teaspoon dried thyme leaves
3 medium baking potatoes
1/4 cup grated Parmesan cheese
Paprika, salt and pepper

In a pie plate combine butter, thyme leaves, lime peel, and juice. Cut each potato lengthwise into eighths; toss in butter mixture. Arrange skin side down on paper-towel-covered plate; sprinkle with cheese, paprika, salt, and pepper. Microwave on HIGH for 13 minutes, covered with waxed paper; rotate dish halfway through.

SESAME-SPRINKLED BRUSSELS SPROUTS
Serves 4

1 pound brussels sprouts
1 tablespoon water
2 tablespoons butter or margarine
2 teaspoons sesame seed
1 tablespoon soy sauce
1 teaspoon sesame oil
1/8 teaspoon lemon pepper

Combine brussels sprouts and water in a 1-quart casserole; cover; microwave on HIGH for 8-9 minutes or until tender. Drain and set aside. Place butter and sesame seeds in uncovered small glass dish and microwave on HIGH for 3-4 minutes, until toasted; stir twice. Mix in the soy sauce and sesame oil; spoon over the brussels sprouts; sprinkle with lemon pepper. Mix lightly.

PEA PODS ORIENTAL

1 (10-ounce) package frozen pea pods
1 tablespoon oil
1 tablespoon soy sauce

Remove wrapping from box of frozen pea pods. Place box on paper towel in microwave. Microwave on HIGH 3-4 minutes, or until heated through. Place in a bowl; toss lightly with oil and soy sauce. Microwave on HIGH 1-2 more minutes. These are served tender crisp. Do not overcook. Leftovers can be refrigerated and tossed into a salad for another use.

BROCCOLI AND MUSHROOMS

1 pound fresh mushrooms
1 pound fresh broccoli flowerets
1/4 cup hot water
2 cups Italian dressing

In a 3-quart casserole combine broccoli and water; cover and microwave for 1 minute on HIGH. Drain and rinse in cold water. In a bowl or plastic bag combine broccoli, mushrooms, and dressing.

Refrigerate at least 8 hours. If using a bowl stir several times, with a bag just turn bag over several times. Remove vegetables to serving platter with slotted spoon.

CHEESE-STUFFED MUSHROOMS

10 medium large mushrooms
1 tablespoon butter or margarine
1 (3-ounce) package cream cheese
2 tablespoons Parmesan cheese
1/8 teaspoon garlic salt
1/8 teaspoon hot pepper sauce
Paprika

Remove stems from mushrooms by gently twisting them. Place caps, open side up, on microwave-safe plate; set aside. Chop stems; combine stems and butter in a 1-quart casserole. Microwave (HIGH), uncovered, 2-3 minutes or until tender. Add cheeses; mix until softened and creamy. Stir in garlic salt and pepper sauce. Spoon cheese mixture into each cap, mounding mixture. Microwave (HIGH), uncovered, 2-3 minutes or until mushrooms are heated through. Sprinkle with paprika and/or parsley flakes.

PITA CHIPS
Makes 24

1 tablespoon margarine
Dash garlic powder
Dash paprika
1 pocket-bread pita round

Microwave the margarine on HIGH for 30 seconds or until melted. Stir in garlic powder and paprika. Cut pocket bread in half horizontally. Brush inner side with margarine; cut rounds into strips. Place on paper-towel-lined plate. Microwave on HIGH, uncovered, for 1 min. 30 seconds to 1 min. 45 seconds, or until bread is crisp. Serve plain or with favorite dip. (10 calories each)

MICROWAVE TOMATOES

4 large ripe tomatoes
3/4 cup mayonnaise
1/4-1/2 teaspoon curry powder
One-half of a 6-ounce package ranch dressing

Halve the tomatoes and arrange in a circle, cut side up, in a 9-inch pie plate. Mix remaining ingredients and spread over the top of the tomatoes. Microwave for 3-5 minutes on HIGH, turn around halfway through the cooking time. Do not cover. Let stand one minute.

SCALLOPED CORN MICROWAVE

1 (17-ounce) can whole kernel corn
1 (17-ounce) can cream style corn
1/2 cup Ritz Cracker crumbs
1 (5-ounce) can evaporated milk
1 egg, slightly beaten
1/8 teaspoon dry mustard
1 tablespoon dry onion flakes (or 1/4 cup chopped onion, sauted in butter)
1 (2-ounce) jar chopped pimiento
3 tablespoons grated Parmesan cheese
3 tablespoons margarine, cut into small pieces
1 teaspoon paprika

Combine all ingredients, except cheese, butter, and paprika; mix well. Put into a greased 1-1/2 quart casserole. Place cheese on top of casserole and dot with butter. Cover and microwave 10 minutes on Level 8 or until set. Let stand, covered, 3-5 minutes. Sprinkle with paprika before serving.

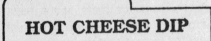

HOT CHEESE DIP

1/4 green pepper (finely chopped)
1/2 bunch green onions (finely chopped)
1-5 ounce jar of sharp Old English cheese

1-8 ounce jar Cheese Whiz
1-7 ounce can minced clams, drained
Garlic powder to taste

Combine all ingredients in a 1-1/2 quart glass casserole dish. Heat uncovered on full power for 2 minutes; stir after one minute. Serve hot with corn chips. This is a very tasty cheese dip!

PUMPKIN SOUP
Serves 5-6

1 can chicken broth
3 cups water
1 tablespoon chicken bouillon or granules
1 small onion, chopped
1/2 cup chopped celery
1/2 cup chopped carrot
1 can (16-ounce) pumpkin
1/3 cup dry white wine (optional)
2 tablespoons butter
1/4 teaspoon thyme
Dash pepper
1/8 teaspoon garlic powder
Sour Cream

Combine chicken broth, water, bouillon, onion, celery, and carrots in 2-quart casserole; cover; microwave 15-30 minutes or until vegetables are tender. Let stand 10 minutes. Transfer vegetable mixture to food processor or blender. Process at medium or until smooth; add pumpkin; process until smooth. Return mixture to casserole; stir in wine, butter, salt, thyme, and garlic powder. Microwave on HIGH, uncovered, for 5-8 minutes, or until heated through, stirring 2 or 3 times. Serve in bowls; top with a spoonful of sour cream.

ICED FRESH TOMATO SOUP

2 tablespoons vegetable oil
6 medium tomatoes, chopped
1/4 cup catsup
1 tablespoon dry dillweed
Dash of Tabasco sauce

1 cup chopped onion
1 (10-ounce) can beef broth
3 cups crushed ice
1 teaspoon salt
1/2 cup heavy cream

Place oil, onion, and tomatoes in 8-cup measure, microwave on HIGH 2-3 minutes to make onion tender. Stir in beef broth and catsup. Microwave on HIGH for 2 minutes, cool slightly, and pour into blender and process until smooth. Return to 8-cup measure; stir in ice and seasonings. Chill until cold. Whip cream, and top each bowl of soup with it.

TACO PORK STRIPS
Serves 4

1 boneless pork chop 1/2 inch thick
2 teaspoons taco breading

Cut pork chop in 1/2-inch thick strips. Coat strips with breading; place in dish; cover with plastic wrap. Microwave on 30% power or MEDIUM LOW or 2 minutes. Turn strips over and rearrange; cover; microwave 2-1/2 minutes on MEDIUM LOW (30%).

Taco Breading:

1/2 cup cornflake crumbs
1-1/2 tablespoons taco seasoning mix

Combine. Makes 1/2 cup for enough for 4 chops.

BACON STICKS
Makes 10

10 thin bread sticks (any flavor)
5 slices of bacon (cut lengthwise)
1/2 cup Parmesan cheese

Dredge one side of bacon strip in cheese. With cheese side out, roll bacon around bread stick diagonally.

Place sticks on microwave dish or paper plate lined with paper towels. Microwave on HIGH 4-1/2 - 6 minutes. When done, roll again in cheese.

ULTIMATE NACHOS
Serves 4

Paper towel
24 large tortilla chips
1 cup shredded Monterey Jack,
   Cheddar or Colby cheese
6-7 tablespoons canned refried
   beans
2 tablespoons chopped onions,
   optional
1 medium tomato, chopped
1-2 cups shredded lettuce
1/4 cup sour cream, optional
1/4 cup sliced black olives
1 tablespoon jalapeño pepper,
   fresh or canned, optional
Taco sauce

Place towel on microwave-safe plate; arrange tortilla chips on the paper towel-lined plate. Spread chips with refried beans; top with shredded cheese and chopped onions. Microwave 2-5 minutes at 50% (medium). Before serving, after cheese has melted, top with shredded lettuce, chopped tomato, olives, jalapeño pepper, taco sauce, and small dollops of sour cream.

OUTRAGEOUS SPINACH DIP

1 (10-ounce) box frozen chopped
   spinach
1 (8-ounce) can water chestnuts,
   finely chopped
1-1/2 cups sour cream
1 cup mayonnaise
1 package dried vegetable soup
   mix
2 green onions, finely chopped
1/4 teaspoon garlic powder
1/2 teaspoon seasoning salt

Remove paper from box of spinach; place box on paper towel in microwave oven. Microwave on HIGH for 6 minutes. In mixing bowl combine remaining ingredients; drain and squeeze spinach before adding to cream mixture. Refrigerate for 2 hours before serving. Serving suggestion: Take a round un-

sliced loaf of pumpernickel bread and cut a circle in the top and remove. Gently pull bread from inside to be later used to dip. When ready to serve, pour dip into bread.

PUMPERNICKEL SURPRISE MUFFINS

1 cup milk
1/3 cup oil
1 egg
2 tablespoons molasses
3/4 cup whole wheat or white flour
1/2 cup rye flour
1/4 cup packed brown sugar
1/4 cup unsweetened cocoa powder
2 teaspoons baking powder
1 teaspoon caraway seeds
1/2 teaspoon salt
1 (3-ounce) package cream cheese
1/2 teaspoon grated orange rind

Beat together milk, oil, egg, and molasses in 2-cup measure. Combine flours, brown sugar, cocoa, baking powder, caraway seeds, and salt in a bowl. Add milk mixture; stir just until moistened. Cut cream cheese into 12 equal cubes; roll grated orange rind in as you roll into a ball. Line the muffin cups with paper liners; spoon a little batter into each cup, filling 1/4 full. Place a cream cheese ball in the center of each muffin. Top with remaining batter; fill 3/4 full. Microwave, uncovered, on HIGH for 2 to 2-1/2 minutes for 6 muffins.

VEGETABLE CORN MUFFINS
Makes 12 muffins
(Microwave - Diabetes Exchange)

1 cup all-purpose white flour
1/2 cup cornmeal
1 tablespoon sugar
1 tablespoon baking powder
1/2 teaspoon salt
3/4 teaspoon Italian seasoning
1/8 teaspoon garlic powder
2 eggs, beaten
1 tablespoon vegetable oil
1/2 cup corn, drained
1/3 cup skim milk

1/3 cup chopped green pepper
1/4 cup finely chopped onion

Combine all ingredients in mixing bowl. Stir just until blended. Line each muffin or custard cup with 2 paper liners. Fill 1/2 full. Microwave on HIGH as directed below or until top springs back when touched, rotating and rearranging after 1/2 the time.

Cooking time:
1 muffin = 1/4 to 3/4 minutes
2 muffins = 1/2 to 2 minutes
4 muffins = 1 to 2-1/2 minutes
6 muffins = 2 to 4-1/2 minutes

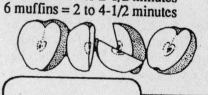

OATMEAL APPLE MUFFINS

1/4 cup water
1/2 cup quick cooking oats
3 tablespoons butter or margarine
2 tablespoons oil
1 egg
1/2 cup packed brown sugar
1/2 cup whole wheat or white flour
1 teaspoon baking powder
1/4 teaspoon salt
1/2 teaspoon cinnamon
1/4 teaspoon nutmeg
3/4 cup chopped apple

Topping:
1 tablespoon butter or margarine
2 tablespoons brown sugar
1 tablespoon flour
1 tablespoon chopped nuts
1/4 teaspoon cinnamon

Microwave water in mixing bowl for 2-3 minutes or until boiling. Stir in oats; let stand 5 minutes. Add butter and oil; stir until butter is melted. Beat in egg and brown sugar; add flour, baking powder, salt, cinnamon, nutmeg; stir until moistened; stir in apple.

Line 12 microwave-safe muffin cups with paper liners; spoon batter into cups, filling 2/3 full. Combine topping ingredients in small bowl; mix with fork until crumbly; spoon mixture evenly onto muffin batter. Microwave on HIGH, uncovered, 2 to 2-1/2 minutes. Repeat with remaining muffins.

FROSTY PUMPKIN PRALINE PIE

Crust:
1/4 cup butter or margarine
1-1/4 cups graham cracker crumbs
2 tablespoons sugar

Praline pieces:
1/4 cup firmly packed brown sugar
1/4 cup sliced or slivered almonds
1 tablespoon butter or margarine
1 teaspoon water

Filling:
1 cup canned pumpkin
1/2 cup firmly packed brown sugar
1/4 cup milk
1 teaspoon cinnamon
1/2 teaspoon nutmeg
1/4 teaspoon ginger
1/4 teaspoon salt
1 pint (2 cups) vanilla ice cream

Topping:
1 cup whipping cream
2 tablespoons sugar
1 teaspoon vanilla

In bowl microwave butter on HIGH 1/2-1 minute or until melted; stir in crumbs and sugar until combined. Press mixture into bottom and up sides of a 9-inch pie plate; microwave uncovered 1-1/2 to 2-1/2 minutes or until heated through. Rotate twice, if necessary. Cool.

In an 8-inch round glass baking dish, combine all ingredients for praline pieces; microwave on HIGH, uncovered, 2-3 minutes or until bubbly and nuts are lightly toasted, stirring several times. Cool; break into pieces.

Combine in glass mixing bowl, all ingredients for filling, except ice cream. Microwave on HIGH for 3-4 minutes, uncovered; stir once. Stir in ice cream; let stand until ice cream can be easily mixed in. Pour into crust. Freeze until firm. Beat cream until thickened; beat in sugar and vanilla. Spread over pie; sprinkle with praline pieces. Freeze until served. You can use crushed gingersnaps for cracker crumbs.

SPECIAL CHOCOLATE PIE

Yield 1-9 inch pie

24 large marshmallows
1/2 cup of half & half
1-6 ounce package of semi-sweet chocolate chips (it must be real chocolate, not the food type)
2 tablespoons creme de cocao
2 tablespoons Kahlua
1 cup whipping cream
1-9 inch chocolate wafer crust;
   (recipe on page 50)

Microwave marshmallows, milk (half & half), and chocolate, in a 3 quart casserole at MEDIUM, 3-4 minutes; stir and cool slightly. Add the creme de cocao and Kahlua to the half & half mixture. Chill 20-30 minutes. Whip the cream until stiff. Fold into chocolate mixture. Pour filling into the chocolate wafer crust and freeze. Remove from freezer 5-10 minutes before serving.

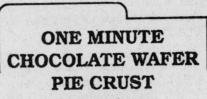

ONE MINUTE CHOCOLATE WAFER PIE CRUST

Makes one pie crust

7 tablespoons butter
1-1/2 cups chocolate wafers crushed crumbs
2 tablespoons walnuts, crushed crumbs.

Microwave butter in a 9 inch glass pie plate at HIGH for 1 minute. Stir in the wafer and walnut crumbs. Press mixture evenly in the pie plate. Chill, pour pie filling into shell and freeze.

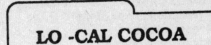

LO-CAL COCOA

1 cup nonfat dry milk powder
2 teaspoons unsweetened cocoa

2 - 4 packets Equal

Combine the dry milk and cocoa. Store at room temp. Makes enough for 4 cups of cocoa. Fill mug with 3/4 cup water. Microwave on **HIGH** for 1 minute or until hot. Stir in 1/4 cup Cocoa mix and 1/2 - 1 packet of Equal.

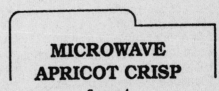

MICROWAVE APRICOT CRISP

Serves 4

1-14 ounce can apricot pie filling
1 tablespoon sugar
2 oranges, grated rind and juice
1/4 cup soft margarine
3/4 cup raw oats
1/3 cup light brown sugar
3 tablespoons flour
4 gingersnaps, crushed

Mix together pie filling, sugar, orange rind, and juice in a shallow, oven-proof dish. Combine margarine, oats, brown sugar, and flour, until crumbly. Spoon evenly over fruit mixture and sprinkle with the crumbs. Place in microwave and cook about 10 minutes or until fruit juices begin to bubble through crisp crust.

Serve warm with whipped cream.

SEASONED SEEDS

1 cup pumpkin seeds
1 tablespoon butter or margarine
1/2 teaspoon Worcestershire sauce
1/4 teaspoon garlic salt
1/4 teaspoon onion salt or seasoned salt

Remove membrane from seeds. If seeds are washed, pat dry. Place in a 9-inch glass pie plate; add remaining ingredients; microwave on HIGH for 8-10 minutes until lightly toasted, stirring 4-5 times. Cooking time will depend on size of seeds and moistness.

CORN MUFFINS

1/2 cup buttermilk
3 tablespoons oil
1 egg
3/4 cup cornmeal
1/2 cup whole wheat or white flour
3 tablespoons sugar
2 tablespoons baking powder
1/2 teaspoon soda
1/2 teaspoon salt
1 (4-ounce) can green chilies
1 cup fresh or canned corn, drained
1/2 teaspoon dried minced onion
1 teaspoon jalapeno peppers
(optional)

Beat together buttermilk, oil, and egg in a 2-cup measure. Place cornmeal, flour, sugar, baking powder, and soda and salt in mixing bowl. Add buttermilk mixture; stir just until moistened. Mix in chilies, corn, minced onions, and jalapeno peppers. Line muffin cups with paper liners; spoon batter into cups, fill 3/4 full. Microwave 6 muffins at a time on HIGH, uncovered, 2 to 2-1/2 minutes.

CARAMEL TOPPED RICE CUSTARD

(Microwave Method)

Combine caramels and 1/4 cup milk in 2-cup glass measure. Cook on HIGH (maximum power) 2 minutes, or until caramels melt, stirring every minute. Pour equal amounts into 6 buttered cups. Spoon 1/3 cup rice into each cup. Blend remaining ingredients; pour evenly into each cup. Place cups in shallow micro-proof dish, containing 1 inch water. Cook at 70% power for 15 minutes, or until almost set, rotating dish 1/4 turn every 5 minutes. Let stand 10 minutes. Loosen custard with knife and invert onto dessert plates. Garnish with chopped nuts or coconut, if desired. Serve warm.

CHOCOLATE AMARETTO MOUSSE

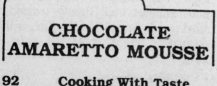

2 ounces cream cheese
2 tablespoons semisweet chocolate pieces
1/2 tablespoon Amaretto liqueur
1/2 cup whipping cream
2 tablespoons sugar

Combine cream cheese and chocolate pieces in 1-cup glass measure. Microwave on HIGH, uncovered, 30-45 seconds or until chocolate is soft. Stir to melt chocolate; blend in liqueur; set aside.

Beat cream and sugar until thick; fold in chocolate. Spoon into individual dishes. Refrigerate until set, about 2 hours. Top with shaved chocolate or chocolate jimmies.

CARAMEL NUT POPCORN CLUSTERS

1 (14-ounce) bag approximately 40 caramel squares
2 tablespoons light cream
2 quarts popped popcorn, lightly salted
1 cup salted, roasted peanuts

Combine caramel squares and cream in small bowl. Microwave 2 minutes, 30 seconds to 3 minutes on MEDIUM HIGH, stirring several times or until caramel is smooth. In large bowl, mix popcorn and peanuts together, adding caramel sauce gradually. Stir until combined. Drop by spoonfuls onto wax paper. Let cool.

LEMONY BARBECUE SAUCE

Makes 1 cup

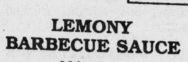

2 tablespoons butter or margarine
1/2 cup chopped onion
1 clove garlic, minced
1/2 cup catsup
1/4 cup lemon juice
2 tablespoons molasses
1 tablespoon Worcestershire sauce
1/4 teaspoon dry mustard
1/4 teaspoon salt
1/4 teaspoon pepper
1/4 teaspoon ground cumin
5 thin slices lemon, seeded and quartered

Place butter in a 1-1/2-quart casserole. Microwave on HIGH for 45 seconds or until melted. Add onion and garlic; cover with lid; microwave on HIGH for 2 minutes. Add remaining ingredients; cover and microwave on HIGH for 3-4 minutes; stir once. Use as a basting sauce for beef, pork, or chicken.

ALMOND VANILLA CUSTARD SAUCE

Makes 1 cup

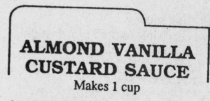

1 egg, beaten
3/4 cup half-and-half
2 tablespoons sugar
1/2 teaspoon vanilla extract
1/4 teaspoon almond extract

Combine all ingredients in a 2-cup measure; mix well. Microwave on MEDIUM (50%) power for 4-7 minutes or until thickened. Stir with whisk after 2 minutes and every minute thereafter. Stir well; cover and chill. Serve over pound cake or fruit.

SWEET AND TANGY BARBECUE SAUCE

Makes 1-1/2 cups

1 cup chopped onion
3 cloves garlic, minced
2 tablespoons oil
1/2 cup brown sugar, packed
1/2 cup red wine vinegar
1/3 cup water
1 (6-ounce) can tomato paste
2 tablespoons soy sauce
1 teaspoon instant beef bouillon
1 teaspoon prepared mustard

Combine onion, garlic, and oil in 1-quart casserole; cover with lid. Microwave on HIGH for 2 to 2-1/2 minutes or until tender. Stir in remaining ingredients. Cover. Microwave on HIGH, 5-6 minutes. Sauce can be covered and refrigerated for up to 2 weeks.

BARBECUED LAMB SHANKS
Serves 4

12 thin lemon slices
4 lamb shanks (about 3-1/2 pounds)
Barbecue sauce
8 paper towel sheets

For each lamb shank, place 2 paper towel sheets, one on top of the other, on the counter. Place three lemon slices diagonally across center of paper towel sheets. Place lamb shank on lemon slices. Fold three corners toward center, covering lamb like an envelope. Roll up over remaining corner. Hold under running water until soaked, but not dripping. Place loose corner down on microwave-safe plate.

Microwave on HIGH for 5 minutes. Rotate plate half turn. Microwave on MEDIUM (50 per cent power) for 5 minutes per pound, rotating plate once. Remove and discard paper towel sheets. Brush lamb shanks with barbecue sauce. Place lamb on hot grill. Grill to desired doneness, 20 to 30 minutes, turning and brushing occasionally with barbecue sauce.

CRAB AND CORN BISQUE
8 servings

2 tablespoons butter or margarine
1 small onion, chopped
1 small red pepper, chopped
1 large celery stalk, chopped
1/4 teaspoon dried thyme leaves
1/8 teaspoon ground red pepper
1 can condensed cream of potato soup, undiluted
2 cups milk
1 (17-ounce) can cream-style corn
1 (12-ounce) package fish and crab blend (surimi)

In 3-quart casserole, melt butter on HIGH one minute; add chopped onion, pepper, celery, thyme and ground red pepper; cover with plastic wrap; turn back one corner to vent. Cook on HIGH for 5 minutes, stirring once. Stir in soup, milk, corn and surimi; cover and vent; microwave on HIGH for 7 minutes or until boiling.

CHEDDAR FISH BUNDLES
Serves 4

1-1/2 cups shredded cheddar cheese
1-1/2 cups fresh bread crumbs
2 tablespoons mayonnaise
2 teaspoons horseradish
1 pound sole fillets
1 tablespoon margarine, melted

Combine 1 cup cheese, crumbs, mayonnaise, and horseradish; mix lightly. Spoon mixture over fish; roll up; secure with wooden toothpicks. Place fish, seam side down, in baking dish, drizzling with margarine. Microwave on HIGH for 5-6 minutes or until fish flakes easily; turn dish after 3 minutes. Sprinkle with remaining cheese; microwave 1-1/2 to 2 minutes or until melted.

QUICK AND LIGHT FISH PLATTER
Serves 1

2 carrots, cut into 2 inch x 1/8 inch strips
1 stalk celery, cut into 1" slices
1 tablespoon water
Parsley flakes
1 tablespoon butter or margarine
4 to 6 ounces defrosted flounder fillets
2 teaspoons lemon juice
Paprika
1 tablespoon sliced green onion
2 tablespoons almonds, toasted

Place carrot strips around edge of a dinner plate; top with celery, water and parsley; dice 1 teaspoon of butter and place on vegetables. Cover with plastic wrap; turn back one edge to vent. Microwave on HIGH for 2 minutes. Uncover; place fish on center of plate. Top with lemon juice, remaining butter, paprika, and onion. Re-cover with plastic wrap; microwave on HIGH for 2 minutes. Let stand 2 minutes. Sprinkle with toasted almonds.

ITALIAN CHICKEN SUPREME

2 medium carrots, cut in thin strips
1 medium zucchini, cut in thin strips
1 medium onion, thinly sliced
2 whole boneless chicken breasts, skinned and cut in half (about 1 pound)
1 teaspoon Italian seasoning
4 pats butter
Salt and pepper

Divide carrots, zucchini, and onion evenly among the 4 paper towels. Place a pat of butter, salt, and pepper over assembled vegetables. Cover vegetables with boneless chicken breast. Sprinkle with Italian seasoning. Fold towel around chicken and vegetables to completely enclose. Moisten under running water. Place paper towel bundles in a round glass baking dish. Microwave on HIGH for 9-10 minutes, or until chicken is cooked. Remove from microwave and let stand 1 minute before serving.

Makes 4 servings of 1 chicken breast and 1/2 cup vegetables each.

For 2 servings: 6 minutes on HIGH
For 1 serving: 3 minutes , 30 seconds on HIGH
Calories per serving: 167

APPLESAUCE BARS

¼ cup margarine
¾ cup brown sugar, packed
¾ cup sweetened apple-sauce
1 cup flour
½ teaspoon baking soda
½ teaspoon cinnamon
⅛ teaspoon nutmeg
⅛ teaspoon cloves
½ cup chopped nuts
¼ cup raisins
2 tablespoons confectioners' sugar

Microwave margarine on HIGH for 30 seconds; blend in brown sugar; beat in applesauce. Stir in flour, soda, cinnamon, nutmeg and cloves. Mix in nuts and raisins. Spread in an 8-inch baking dish, greased on bottom only. Microwave on HIGH for 6–7 minutes, uncovered. Cool and sprinkle with confectioners' sugar.

PUMPKIN CUSTARD
Serves 6

1 (16-ounce) can pumpkin
2 eggs, beaten
1 cup evaporated skimmed milk
1/3 cup packed brown sugar
1/4 cup granulated sugar
1-1/2 teaspoons ground cinnamon
1/2 teaspoon salt
1/4 teaspoon ground ginger
1/4 teaspoon ground nutmeg
Whipped topping

In medium mixing bowl, combine all ingredients, except whipped topping. Blend with whisk. Divide evenly among 6 (6-ounce) custard cups. Arrange in circular pattern in microwave oven. Microwave at 50 percent, MEDIUM, for 18–23 minutes, or until centers are soft-set, rearranging and rotating cups 2 or 3 times. Serve warm or cool. Garnish with dollop of whipped topping.

Sharon M. Crider, Stoughton, Wis.

FIESTA ROLL-UP
Serves 4

1 strip ham, 1-1/2-inches wide and 6 inches long
1/4 cup butter *or* margarine
1/2 cup green pepper, chopped
1 medium onion, chopped
5 eggs, beaten
1/4 cup water
2 tablespoons chopped pimiento

Place ham in an 8 x 8 x 2-inch baking dish. Cover. Microwave on HIGH (100 percent) for 3–4 minutes, or until heated through. Cover with aluminum foil and let stand while cooking eggs and vegetables.

Place butter, green pepper and onion in an 11-3/4 x 7-1/2 x 1-3/4-inch baking dish. Microwave on HIGH (100 percent) for 3–4 minutes, or until vegetables are tender. Stir together eggs and water. Pour over vegetables. Sprinkle with pimiento. Cover with plastic wrap. Microwave on HIGH (100 percent) for 8–10 minutes, or until set, but glossy on top. Turn dish 4 times during cooking. Remove plastic wrap. Loosen bottom and edges of omelette with a rubber spatula. Cover dish with waxed paper. Place cookie sheet over waxed paper. Flip omelette out onto cookie sheet. Place the ham on small end of omelette. Roll ham inside omelette in jelly-roll fashion. Place seam side down on serving dish. Set parsley around edge of dish. Place sliced olives on top of the "egg roll-up." Serve immediately.

Marie Fusaro, Manasquan, N.J.

PEANUT BUTTER BLONDIES
Makes 1 dozen

1/2 cup sifted cake flour (not self-rising)
1/4 teaspoon baking powder
1/8 teaspoon coarse (kosher) salt
1/4 cup (1/2 stick) unsalted butter
1/2 cup creamy peanut butter

1/2 cup firmly packed light brown sugar
2 eggs
1 teaspoon vanilla
1/3 cup unsalted peanuts, coarsely chopped (1-3/4 ounces)

Sift together flour, baking powder and salt onto sheet of waxed paper. Set aside. Place butter and peanut butter in a microwave-safe, 4-cup glass measure. Cover tightly with microwave-safe plastic wrap. Microwave at full power (100 percent) or HIGH for 2 minutes. Carefully pierce plastic wrap with tip of small knife to release steam. Uncover glass measure carefully. Stir in sugar and eggs, 1 at a time. Stir in vanilla, flour mixture and peanuts. Spread mixture in microwave-safe 9-1/2 x 6 x 2-inch dish. Microwave, uncovered, at full power (100 percent) or HIGH for 3–3-1/2 minutes, or until set. Center bottom may be slightly fudgey. If you prefer blondies more done, cook 1 minute longer. Cool on rack before cutting.

Leona Teodori, Warren, Mich.

APPLE CRISP AND BRAN

5 cups sliced baking apples
1 tablespoon water
¼ cup margarine
⅓ cup brown sugar, packed
⅓ cup quick-cooking oats
½ cup oat bran
1 teaspoon vanilla
¼ teaspoon nutmeg
1 teaspoon cinnamon
1 cup non-fat yogurt

Combine apples and water in an 8-inch round baking dish. Set aside. Microwave margarine on HIGH in an uncovered bowl for 20–30 seconds. Blend in brown sugar, mix in rolled oats, bran, cinnamon, nutmeg and vanilla until crumbly. Sprinkle over apples. Microwave on HIGH, uncovered, for 9–10 minutes. Serve warm or cold, topped with non-fat yogurt.

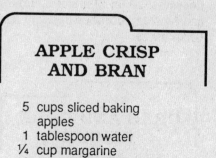

CHICKEN AND DUMPLINGS
Serves 4–6

1 (3-pound) broiler-fryer, cut up
3 small onions, quartered
4 medium carrots, cut in 1-inch
   pieces, then halved
2 stalks celery, diced
4 sprigs parsley
1 (13-3/4-ounce) can chicken broth
2 bay leaves
2 teaspoons salt
1/4 teaspoon thyme
1–2 cloves garlic, cut in half
1/4 teaspoon poultry seasoning
1/8 teaspoon pepper
2 cups water
4 tablespoons cornstarch
1/3 cup water

Dumplings:
1 cup biscuit baking mix
1/3 cup milk
1/4 teaspoon poultry seasoning

Place chicken, vegetables and parsley in 4-quart casserole. Mix together the broth, bay leaves, salt, thyme, garlic, poultry seasoning and pepper. Pour over chicken. Cover and cook on HIGH power for 20–25 minutes, or until vegetables are tender. Remove chicken. Add the 2 cups water; cover and microwave on HIGH power for 5 minutes longer.

Mix cornstarch and water; add to vegetable mixture; blend well. Microwave, uncovered, 5 minutes on HIGH power, or until thickened. Return chicken to casserole.

To make dumplings, mix together biscuit mix, milk and seasoning until moistened. Spoon mixture over casserole by the tablespoon. Microwave, *covered*, on HIGH power for 5–6-1/2 minutes, or until dumplings are done.
Tip: For a low-fat dish, skin the chicken before cooking.
Yvonne Schilling, Wauwatosa, Wis.

GOURMET STUFFED YAMS
Serves 4

4 medium-size yams
¼ cup apple juice *or* cider

½ cup chopped apple (do
   not peel)
¼ cup chopped pecans
¼ teaspoon cinnamon
   Thin apple wedge for
   garnish

Microwave yams on HIGH for 10–13 minutes, or until tender. Cut a thin, horizontal slice from top of each yam with sharp knife. Scoop out pulp, leaving ¼-inch shell. Heat apple juice or cider in microwave for 30 seconds, or until hot. Mash and whip pulp with juice. Stir in apples, nuts and cinnamon. Pile into shells. Garnish with apple wedge to serve.

Hint: For more servings add 2 tablespoons chopped apple, 1 tablespoon chopped pecans, 1 tablespoon juice or cider and a dash of cinnamon for each additional yam.

Delicious with any kind of poultry, roast pork or ham! For the health-conscious cook, there is no salt, butter or sugar in this recipe!
Mary E. Finley, Jonesville, Mich.

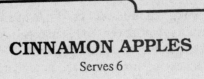

CINNAMON APPLES
Serves 6

6 large apples
3/4 cup raisins
1/2 cup brown sugar
1 tablespoon butter
1 teaspoon ground cinnamon
1/2 teaspoon ground nutmeg
1/2 cup water
1 cup half-and-half

Core apples. Cut a strip of peel around the top of each apple. Place apples in a round, 2-quart microwave casserole or microwave ring mold. Fill apples with raisins. In a 1-quart microwave bowl, place brown sugar, butter, cinnamon, nutmeg and 1/2 cup water. Cover and microwave on HIGH for 1 minute, 30 seconds. Sugar should be melted, and mixture very hot. Pour hot sugar mixture over and around apples. Cover and microwave on HIGH for 12 minutes. Turn dish 1/4 turn every 3 minutes. Apples will be very tender. Put apples

into individual serving dishes. Serve with half-and-half.
June Harding, Royal Oak, Mich.

BAKED APPLES
Serves 4

2 large baking apples, cored and cut
   in half
2 tablespoons margarine
1/2 cup dark corn syrup
Cinnamon
Red hot cinnamon candies

Slice apples in half and core. Set half-apples in a shallow 1-1/2-quart microwave-proof baking dish. Place 1/4 tablespoon margarine in center of each apple half. Spoon 1 tablespoon corn syrup into each half. Sprinkle with cinnamon.

Put 1 or 2 red hot cinnamon candies in center of each apple half (adds color and flavor).

Cover with plastic wrap. Microwave on HIGH for 4 minutes, turning apples and spooning syrup over them after 2 minutes. When cooking time is up, let stand 2 minutes before serving.
Flo Burtnett, Gage, Okla.

HOT HAM SALAD
Single serving

2 slices (1 ounce each) sliced,
   chopped ham, cut into 1/2-inch
   pieces
1/4 cup herb-seasoned croutons
1/4 cup thinly sliced celery
1/4 cup frozen green peas, thawed
1/4 cup mayonnaise
1/4 teaspoon instant minced onion
Dash of pepper
1 tablespoon shredded cheddar
   cheese

Mix all ingredients, except cheese. Spoon lightly into 14-ounce shallow casserole. Sprinkle with cheese. Cover loosely and microwave on MEDIUM-HIGH (70 percent) for 2-1/2–3-1/2 minutes, or until hot and bubbly.
Barbara Nowakowski, North Tonawanda, N.Y.

MICRO-GOOD BEEF STROGANOFF

Serves 2

1 pound round steak, trimmed
4 tablespoons butter
1 (3-ounce) can mushrooms with liquid
1 package dry onion soup mix
1 tablespoon steak sauce
1/4 teaspoon garlic powder
1 cup sour cream

Cut meat diagonally across the grain into thin strips. In 1-1/2-quart casserole dish microwave in butter 3 minutes on HIGH. Add mushrooms and liquid to equal 1 cup; stir in soup mix; heat to boiling. Add steak sauce and garlic powder; cook on MEDIUM 3 minutes; stir in sour cream. Serve on thin or broad egg noodles.

Gwen Campbell, Sterling, Va.

TINY PEAS AND LETTUCE AU VIN

Serves 4

2 (15-ounce) cans tiny peas, drained
8 whole white pearl onions
8 Boston lettuce leaves, coarsely shredded
1/2 teaspoon sugar
1/4 teaspoon salt
3 tablespoons butter
3 tablespoons chicken broth
1 tablespoon cornstarch
2 tablespoons dry white wine

Place first 7 ingredients in a 1-1/2-quart microwave casserole. Cover; cook 8 minutes on HIGH. Combine cornstarch and white wine; stir into casserole gently; cook 2 minutes on HIGH.

Gwen Campbell, Sterling, Va.

TEN-MINUTE MEAT LOAF

Serves 4–6

1 pound ground beef
1 egg
1/2 cup bread crumbs
1/4 cup milk

2 tablespoons onion soup mix
2 tablespoons ketchup
2 tablespoons soy sauce
1/2 cup shredded Swiss cheese

Combine all ingredients and shape in round or oval loaf. Place in microwave-safe dish; cover with waxed paper and microwave on HIGH for 10 minutes, turning dish after 5 minutes of cooking. Drain and cover with foil. Let stand 10 minutes before slicing.

Microwaves vary. Test for doneness.

Marian B. Hamilton, Ypsilanti, Mich.

TANGY MUSTARD CAULIFLOWER

Serves 6–8

1 medium head cauliflower, broken into florets
1/2 cup mayonnaise *or* salad dressing
1/4 teaspoon instant minced onion
1 teaspoon prepared mustard
1/2 cup shredded cheddar cheese

Place cauliflower in 1-1/2-quart casserole with cover. Add 2 tablespoons water. Cook, covered, on HIGH 7–8 minutes, or until just about tender. Combine mayonnaise, onion and mustard, mixing well. Place cooked cauliflower in serving dish. Spread mayonnaise mixture over cauliflower. Sprinkle with cheese. Cook, uncovered, on HIGH for 1 minute to heat topping and melt cheese.

Mary Ann Donlan, Waterloo, Iowa

SIMPLY ELEGANT TOMATOES

Serves 4

4 fully ripe medium tomatoes
1/4 cup chopped onions
1/4 cup chopped green pepper
1/3 cup grated Parmesan cheese
1/2 teaspoon oregano
1/2 teaspoon garlic powder
1/8 teaspoon pepper
1 tablespoon parsley flakes

Wash and core tomatoes; scoop out pulp and put into a bowl. Add remaining ingredients and mix. Place back into tomatoes and microwave on HIGH for 6–7 minutes.

Mrs. Merle Mishler, Hollsopple, Pa.

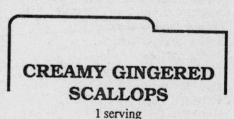

CREAMY GINGERED SCALLOPS

1 serving

1 tablespoon chopped green onion (with tops)
1-1/2 teaspoons margarine
1-1/2 teaspoons flour
1/4 cup half-and-half
1 tablespoon dry white wine
1/4 teaspoon grated gingerroot
1/8 teaspoon salt
3 ounces bay *or* seal scallops, cut into 1/2-inch pieces (about 1/3 cup)
1 (2-1/2-ounce) jar whole mushrooms, drained

Place onion and margarine in 2-cup measure. Microwave, uncovered, on HIGH about 30 seconds, or until margarine is melted. Mix in flour. Stir in half-and-half, wine, gingerroot and salt.

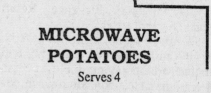

MICROWAVE POTATOES

Serves 4

5 large potatoes, peeled and diced
1/4 cup margarine
1/4 cup minced onion
1/2 teaspoon garlic powder
1/2 teaspoon black pepper
1/4 cup Parmesan cheese

Place all ingredients, except cheese, into a 3-quart microwave-safe dish with lid. Microwave, covered, on HIGH for 10 minutes. Stir; add cheese; stir again. Cover, microwave on HIGH for 10 minutes. Stir again just before serving.

Christine Sweet, Green, N.Y.

PEANUT BUTTER ROCKY ROAD

(6-ounce) package semisweet chocolate chips
(6-ounce) package butterscotch chips
1/2 cup peanut butter
3 cups miniature marshmallows
1/2 cup salted peanuts

Place chocolate chips, butterscotch chips and peanut butter in 2-quart bowl. Microwave, uncovered, on HIGH (100 percent) until softened, 2–2-1/2 minutes. Stir until melted and smooth. Mix in marshmallows and peanuts until evenly coated. Spread in buttered square 8 x 8 x 2-inch baking pan. Refrigerate until firm, at least 1 hour. Cut into squares.

Shari Crider, Stoughton, Wis.

ATLANTIC CITY TAFFY
Makes 1 pound

2 cups dark corn syrup
1/4 cup strong black coffee
2 squares unsweetened baking chocolate
1/4 teaspoon salt
1 tablespoon butter *or* margarine
1 teaspoon vanilla

In a 2-quart glass measure combine first 4 ingredients. Cook on HIGH for 12–18 minutes. Add butter and vanilla; pour into 8-inch square baking dish; cool enough to "pull." Grease hands; pull taffy until elastic and light in color. Cut into pieces; wrap in waxed paper or rainbow-colored cellophane; twist ends to close.

Gwen Campbell Sterling, Va.

FRENCH POTATOES
Serves 4

1-1/2 pounds potatoes, peeled and very thinly sliced

1 medium-size onion, sliced into rings
3 tablespoons butter
Salt
Pepper
6 tablespoons milk
Paprika

Put potato slices to soak in cold water. Put the onion rings in a bowl. Cover with plastic wrap and pierce. Microwave on full power or HIGH for 1 minute. Grease a 5-cup microwave dish with a little of the butter. Layer drained potatoes and onions in dish, starting and finishing with potatoes. Season each layer well with salt and pepper.

Pour milk over potatoes and dot with the rest of the butter. Sprinkle the top with paprika. Cover with plastic wrap and pierce. Microwave on full power or HIGH for 13 minutes, giving the dish 1/2 turn twice during cooking. Allow to stand, covered, for 5 minutes before serving.

Flo Burtnett, Gage, Okla.

PIZZA HAMBURGER PIE
Serves 4

1 pound ground beef
1-1/2 teaspoons garlic salt
Salt and pepper
1-1/2 teaspoons horseradish
1 teaspoon Worcestershire sauce
1-1/2 teaspoons mustard
1 (8-ounce) can tomato sauce
2 teaspoons chopped onion
1/2 teaspoon oregano
1/2 teaspoon red pepper
1 cup mozzarella cheese

Lightly toss beef with garlic salt, salt, pepper, horseradish, Worcestershire sauce and mustard. Press meat against sides and bottom of an 8- or 9-inch pie plate; spread tomato sauce over top surface. Sprinkle with a little onion, oregano, red pepper and cheese. Cook at 70 percent power for 8–10 minutes.

Sheila Symonowicz, Hubbardston, Mass.

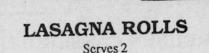

LASAGNA ROLLS
Serves 2

1/2 pound bulk Italian sausage
1/4 cup chopped onion
1 egg, beaten
1/2 cup cream-style cottage cheese
2 tablespoons grated Parmesan cheese
4 lasagna noodles, cooked
1 (8-ounce) can pizza sauce
1 tablespoon water or dry red wine
1/4 cup shredded mozzarella cheese

Crumble sausage into a 1-quart casserole dish. Stir in onion. Microwave, uncovered, on 100 percent power or HIGH for 3–4 minutes, or until sausage is done and the onion is tender. Drain off fat. Stir in the beaten egg, cottage cheese and Parmesan cheese. Spread each lasagna noodle with some of the cheese-meat mixture. Roll each noodle, jelly-roll style. Place seam side down in a small greased baking dish.

Stir together pizza sauce and water or wine. Pour over rolls. Microwave, covered, on 100 percent power or HIGH for 4–5 minutes, or until heated through. Sprinkle mozzarella over rolls. Microwave, uncovered on 100 percent power or HIGH until cheese is melted.

Laura Hicks, Troy, Mont.

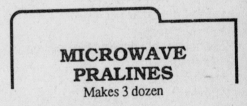

MICROWAVE PRALINES
Makes 3 dozen

3/4 cup Milnot milk
2 cups brown sugar, packed
1/8 teaspoon salt
3 tablespoons butter *or* margarine
1-1/2 cups pecans
1 teaspoon vanilla flavoring

Mix Milnot, sugar, salt and butter in a 2-1/2–3-quart dish or casserole. Microwave on HIGH for 8–10 minutes. Stir and rotate at 3-minute intervals. Allow to cool slightly, add vanilla. Beat until creamy (about 3 minutes). Stir in pecans. Drop from teaspoonfuls onto waxed paper. Allow to cool at room temperature.

Sarah Burkett, Centralia, Ill.

REUBEN CASSEROLE

Serves 6–8

1 (16-ounce) can sauerkraut, un-drained
12 ounces corned beef, canned *or* sliced, crumbled
2 cups Swiss cheese, shredded
1/2 cup light mayonnaise
1/4 cup Thousand Island dressing
2 fresh tomatoes, sliced
2 tablespoons melted butter
1/4 cup pumpernickel *or* rye bread crumbs

Place sauerkraut in 1-1/2-quart baking dish. Top with layer of beef, then cheese. Combine both dressings; spread over cheese. Top with tomato slices; set aside. Combine butter and bread crumbs in small bowl; sprinkle over tomato slices. Microwave at 70 percent power for 12–14 minutes, or bake at 350 degrees for 45 minutes. Let stand 5 minutes before serving.

Mrs. Merle Mishler, Hollsopple, Pa.

ONION AND CHEESE CHICKEN BAKE

Serves 6

6 chicken breast fillets
4 tablespoons butter
1 teaspoon seasoned salt
1 teaspoon pepper
1/2 pound fresh mushrooms, sliced
1 (3-ounce) can french-fried onion rings
1/2 cup grated Monterey Jack cheese

Melt butter in 3-quart baking dish on MEDIUM power for 1 minute, or until melted; add seasonings. Roll chicken in seasoned butter to coat and arrange in dish. Cover with waxed paper; cook on HIGH for 5–6 minutes. Turn chicken over; top with mushrooms. Continue to cook on HIGH for 4 minutes. Sprinkle with onion rings and grated cheese. Cook on HIGH for 2–3 minutes, or until cheese bubbles.

Kim Joslin, Enid, Okla.

WALNUT PENUCHE

1-1/2 cups toasted coarsely chopped walnuts*
2/3 cup butter *or* margarine
1 cup packed light brown sugar
1 (14-ounce) can sweetened con-densed milk
1-1/2 teaspoons vanilla

*To toast walnuts, spread in a single layer in a 9-inch glass pie plate or a microwave pie plate. Stirring every 2 minutes, microwave on HIGH for 6 minutes.

Place butter in a 2-quart glass measure. Microwave on HIGH for 1 minute. Blend in light brown sugar and con-densed milk. Stirring every 2 minutes, microwave on HIGH for 8–9 minutes, or until mixture is a medium-caramel color. Stir in vanilla and beat with a wooden spoon, 2–3 minutes. Fold in walnuts. Pour into a buttered 8-inch square dish. Cool to lukewarm; then refrigerate until set. Cut into squares.

Joy B. Shamway, Freeport, Ill.

HONEY ORANGE CHICKEN

Serves 4

2 boneless, skinless whole chicken breasts
2 tablespoons honey
2 tablespoons cornstarch
1/2 cup orange marmalade
1/2 cup orange juice
1/2 cup whiskey
2 cups hot, cooked rice

Cut chicken into 4 serving pieces. Place in a 2-quart microwave casse-role. In bowl, blend together honey, cornstarch, marmalade, orange juice and whiskey. Pour over chicken. Cover and microwave on HIGH for 12 min-utes. Turn; stir in chicken, and micro-wave for 8 more minutes until chicken is tender. Serve immediately with hot, cooked rice.

June Harding, Royal Oak, Mich.

CHICKEN PIZZA "BURGERS"

Serves 4

1 (12-ounce) package frozen chicken patties
4 hamburger buns, split
1/2 cup pizza sauce (canned)
4 slices (4 ounces) mozzarella cheese

Place chicken patties on microwave bacon rack or paper-towel–lined plate. Microwave on HIGH, uncovered, for 4–5 minutes, or until heated through, rotating plate once. Place bottom halves of buns on microwave-safe serving plate. Spread each with about 1 table-spoon pizza sauce. Top each with a chicken patty and additional 1 table-spoon sauce. Top each with cheese slice and bun tops. Microwave on HIGH, uncovered, for 1–1-1/2 min-utes, or until cheese is melted.

Mrs. A.S. Warren, Charlotte, N.C.

ONE MORE TIME

Serves 6

1 or 2 large onions
1 teaspoon sugar
1 tablespoon butter
3 cups leftover mashed potatoes
2 tablespoons Parmesan cheese
Salt and pepper
6 slices cooked roast beef
1 (17-ounce) can peas, drained
1 (10-1/4-ounce) can beef gravy

Brown onion in dry frying pan. Sprinkle with sugar. Cook on stove, stirring until browned. Add butter. Cook until tender. Remove from heat. Spread half the mashed potatoes in baking dish. Sprinkle surface with Parmesan cheese, salt and pepper. Arrange meat on top of potatoes. Spread onion over meat, then peas, and gravy. Cover with remaining potatoes. Cook, covered, on 80 percent power for 6–8 minutes.

Sheila Symonowicz, Hubbardston, Mass.

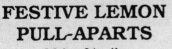

FESTIVE LEMON PULL-APARTS

Makes 24 rolls

1/4 cup butter *or* margarine
1/2 cup chopped nuts
1/3 cup chopped maraschino cherries, patted dry with paper towel
1 (3-1/2-ounce) package instant lemon pudding mix
1 (16-ounce) loaf frozen white bread dough, thawed
1/2 cup flaked coconut

Place butter in 1-cup glass measure and cook on HIGH for 30–40 seconds, or until melted. Spoon half of butter into 8-inch square casserole. Set aside remaining butter. Sprinkle nuts, cherries, and 3 tablespoons pudding mix over butter in baking dish. Cut bread dough into 24 pieces and roll each into a ball. Combine remaining pudding mix and coconut in a shallow dish. Dip each ball into melted butter; then roll in coconut mixture. Place in baking dish. Sprinkle remaining coconut mixture over dough. Cover with plastic wrap. Microwave on WARM (10 percent) for 3 minutes. Let stand 10 minutes. Repeat once or twice, or until dough is doubled in size. Preheat conventional oven to 350 degrees. Remove plastic wrap and bake rolls 15–20 minutes, or until golden brown. Invert onto serving plate and serve warm.

Mrs. A.S. Warren, Charlotte, N.C.

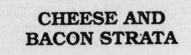

CHEESE AND BACON STRATA

5 slices bread, toasted and buttered
2 cups cheddar cheese, grated
4 eggs
1 1/2 cups half-and-half
1/2 teaspoon salt
1 teaspoon dry mustard
4 slices bacon, cooked and crumbled
1/2 teaspoon paprika
Dash of pepper

Cut toast into 1-inch cubes. Spread toast cubes and cheese in a deep tube pan. Combine eggs, half-and-half, salt and mustard; pour over the bread-cheese layer. Cover and refrigerate at least 4 hours. Sprinkle with bacon, paprika and pepper. Cover with waxed paper and microwave on MEDIUM (50 percent) power for 16-18 minutes; rotate dish if necessary. Let stand 5 minutes before serving.

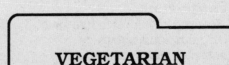

VEGETARIAN ASPARAGUS DELIGHT

Serves 2

1 (16-ounce) can asparagus spears, drained (reserve liquid)
1 (3-ounce) can sliced mushrooms, drained (reserve liquid)
1 (1-1/4-ounce) package cheese sauce mix
1 tablespoon onion flakes
1 hard-cooked egg, chopped
1/4 cup (1 ounce) shredded cheddar cheese
2 tablespoons slivered almonds
Paprika

In 2-cup glass measure, add enough water to reserved liquids to equal 1 cup. Stir in cheese sauce mix and onion. Cook on HIGH 3–3-1/2 minutes, or until thickened; stir occasionally. Add mushrooms, egg and shredded cheese. Arrange asparagus in 9 x 5 x 3-inch loaf dish. Pour on cheese mixture. Sprinkle with almonds and paprika. Cook, covered with waxed paper, at HIGH 4–5 minutes, or until bubbly.

Let stand 5 minutes before serving.

Mrs. Merle Mishler, Hollsopple, Pa.

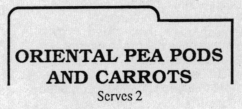

ORIENTAL PEA PODS AND CARROTS

Serves 2

1/4 cup water
1 tablespoon soy sauce
1 teaspoon cornstarch
Dash crushed red pepper
1 medium carrot, thinly sliced
2 teaspoons water
3 ounces frozen pea pods
2 tablespoon broken walnuts
1 teaspoon butter·*or* margarine

Stir together 1/4 cup water, soy sauce, cornstarch and crushed red pepper. Microwave, uncovered, on HIGH (100 percent power) for 1–1-1/2 minutes, or until thick and bubbly, stirring every 30 seconds.

Put carrot in casserole dish. Sprinkle with 2 teaspoons water. Microwave, covered, on HIGH (100 percent power) for 2-1/2 minutes. Drain. Toss together carrot, pea pods and walnuts. Add butter or margarine. Microwave, covered, on HIGH (100 percent power) for about 1-1/2 minutes, or until the vegetables are crisp-tender. Toss with soy sauce mixture.

Laura Hicks, Troy, Mont.

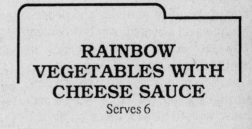

RAINBOW VEGETABLES WITH CHEESE SAUCE

Serves 6

Butter
Paprika
1/2 cup herb-seasoned stuffing mix
1 cup cauliflower
1 cup broccoli florets
1 cup carrots, thinly sliced
Cheese Sauce (recipe follows)

Butter a 10-inch tube pan; sprinkle paprika on bottom; scatter stuffing mix on paprika. Press vegetables gently on top of stuffing mix, alternating vegetables. Cover; microwave 8–10 minutes on HIGH. Invert onto serving dish; drizzle with hot cheese sauce.

Cheese Sauce:
1 (10-1/2-ounce) can cheddar cheese soup
2 tablespoons water

Blend soup and water in a 2-cup measuring cup. Microwave 3 minutes on MEDIUM; stir after 1-1/2 minutes.

Gwen Campbell, Sterling, Va.

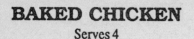

BAKED CHICKEN
Serves 4

2 cups boiling water
1 cup bulgur wheat
1 teaspoon instant chicken bouillon
   granules
1/8 teaspoon pepper
2 tablespoons butter *or* margarine
1/4 cup fine dry seasoned bread
   crumbs
2 tablespoons grated Parmesan
   cheese
1/4 teaspoon garlic powder
1/8 teaspoon paprika
2 whole medium chicken breasts
   (about 1-1/2 pounds total),
   skinned, deboned and halved
   lengthwise

To cook bulgur, in a 1-quart microwave-safe casserole combine water, bulgur, bouillon granules and pepper. Microwave, covered, on 100 percent power or HIGH for 4–5 minutes, or until bulgur is done, stirring once.

In a 1-cup glass measure cook butter, uncovered, on HIGH for 45–60 seconds, or until melted. In a shallow dish combine bread crumbs, cheese, garlic powder and paprika.

Brush the meaty side of each chicken piece with some of the melted butter or margarine; coat the same side with some of the crumb mixture. Place chicken, crumb side up, on a microwave-safe rack in a 12 x 7-1/2 x 2-inch microwave-safe dish. Sprinkle with the remaining butter or margarine.

Cover loosely with waxed paper. Cook on HIGH for 6–7 minutes, or until chicken is tender, giving the dish 1/2 turn once. Serve with bulgur mixture.

Note: If you wish to eat at different times, stir together the crumb mixture in advance and keep it in your refrigerator. Then, you can coat a halved chicken breast and cook it in less than 10 minutes.

Marcella Swigert, Monroe City, Mo.

IMPERIAL CRAB CARIBBEAN
Serves 6

3 (6-1/2 or 7-1/2-ounce) cans
   crabmeat, drained
1/4 cup mayonnaise
1/4 cup sour cream
1/4 cup peanuts, chopped finely
1 teaspoon pimiento, chopped
1/4 teaspoon salt
1/2 teaspoon Worcestershire sauce
2-1/2 drops liquid hot sauce
6 pineapple slices, drained
2/3 cup cornflakes crumbs
1 tablespoon vegetable oil
1/4 cup cornflakes crumbs

In a bowl combine mayonnaise, sour cream, peanuts, pimiento and seasonings. Add to crabmeat; mix lightly.

In a 12 x 7-1/2 x 2-inch lightly buttered microwave dish, place pineapple slices that have been coated on both sides with cornflakes crumbs. Place 1/3 cup crab mixture on top of each pineapple slice. Combine oil and crumbs; sprinkle over top of crab mixture. Microwave on HIGH for 5 minutes.

Gwen Campbell, Sterling, Va.

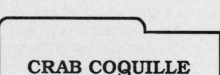

CRAB COQUILLE
1 serving

1-1/2 teaspoons margarine
1 green onion (with top), thinly sliced
1/2 teaspoon cornstarch
1/4 cup half-and-half
1 teaspoon lemon juice
Dash of salt
Dash of white pepper
1/3 cup cooked crabmeat
2 mushrooms, thinly sliced
1 tablespoon dry bread crumbs
2 teaspoons grated Parmesan
   cheese
1-1/2 teaspoons margarine, melted

Place 1-1/2 teaspoons margarine and the onion in 2-cup measure. Microwave, uncovered, on HIGH for 1–2

minutes, or until crisp-tender. Mix in cornstarch. Stir in half-and-half, lemon juice, salt and pepper.

Microwave, uncovered, about 1 minute, stirring after 30 seconds, until thickened. Stir in crabmeat and mushrooms. Spoon into shell-shaped dish or 12-ounce, shallow casserole. Mix bread crumbs, cheese and 1-1/2 teaspoons margarine. Sprinkle over top. Cover loosely and microwave, 1–2 minutes, or until hot.

Barbara Nowakowski, North Tonawanda, N.Y.

TURKEY ALMONDINE
Serves 4–6

1/2 cup slivered almonds
2 teaspoons butter *or* margarine
2 cups (8 ounces) sliced fresh mushrooms
3 green onions, sliced
2 tablespoons butter *or* margarine
1-1/2 tablespoons cornstarch
1 tablespoon instant chicken bouillon
   granules
1 tablespoon soy sauce
1/4 teaspoon garlic powder
1 cup water
2 cups cubed cooked turkey
1 (6-ounce) package frozen pea
   pods, thawed and halved
1 (2-ounce) can chopped pimiento,
   drained
6 baked patty shells

Combine almonds and butter in small glass baking dish. Microwave on HIGH, uncovered, for 2–3 minutes, or until toasted, stirring twice. Set aside. Combine mushrooms, onions and butter in 1-1/2-quart shallow casserole. Microwave on HIGH, uncovered, 3–4 minutes, or until mushrooms are almost tender, stirring once. Stir in cornstarch, bouillon, soy sauce, garlic powder and water. Microwave on HIGH, uncovered, for 2–3 minutes, or until mixture boils and thickens, stirring twice. Stir in turkey, pea pods and pimiento. Cover and microwave on HIGH for 4–5 minutes, or until heated through, stirring once. Spoon into patty shells; top with almonds.

Mrs. A.S. Warren, Charlotte, N.C.

STIR-FRY STEAK TERRIYAKI

Serves 2

1/4 pound round steak
2 tablespoons light soy sauce
1–2 tablespoons lemon juice
1 tablespoon brown sugar
2 teaspoons cornstarch
1/2 cup onion, thinly sliced
1 cup sliced mushrooms
1/2 cup green pepper, chopped
1 garlic clove, minced
1 tablespoon oil

Cut steak into 1/8-inch strips (cuts best when meat is partially frozen). Make a marinade of soy sauce, lemon juice, brown sugar and cornstarch. Add meat to marinade and let stand 15–20 minutes, or longer. In a 9-inch pie plate combine oil, garlic and onion. Microwave on HIGH (100 percent power) for 2 minutes. Move onions to center of pie plate. Remove meat from marinade (save marinade). Arrange meat around onions. Cover tightly; microwave on HIGH for 2 minutes. Stir meat and onions together. Add mushrooms, green peppers, 1/4 teaspoon ginger and marinade sauce and stir. Cover tightly; microwave on HIGH for 2 minutes, stirring once. Serve over rice.
Note: Use slotted spoon when removing meat from marinade sauce.
Karen Blunt, Mason City, Iowa

CURRIED CHICKEN AND APPLES

Serves 4–6

3/4 cup apple juice
1 tablespoon lemon juice
2 tablespoons chopped parsley
1 teaspoon curry powder
1/2 teaspoon salt
1/2 teaspoon paprika
1/8 teaspoon pepper
1-1/2–2 pounds chicken breast, deboned and skinned
2 medium-size Golden Delicious apples, cored and sliced into rings
1 teaspoon cornstarch

Combine apple juice, lemon juice, parsley, curry powder, salt, paprika and pepper. Marinade chicken 1 hour. Remove chicken from marinade; reserve marinade. Microwave chicken on HIGH for 3 minutes; turn 1/4 turn after 2 minutes. Let stand 5 minutes. Slice chicken. Add cornstarch to 1/4 cup marinade. Alternate chicken and apple rings on microwave-proof platter; brush with marinade mixture. Microwave on HIGH for 2 minutes. Brush chicken and apples and turn 1/4 turn. Microwave 1–2 minutes longer. Remove from microwave and let stand 5 minutes. Add remaining marinade to basting mixture in 2-cup measure; microwave on HIGH for about 6 minutes, or until mixture comes to a boil.
Note: Turkey breast can also be used instead of chicken.
Leona Teodori, Warren, Mich.

SWISS SCALLOPED CORN

Serves 6

1 tablespoon butter
1/4 cup unseasoned dry bread crumbs
Dash paprika
3 slices bacon
2 (16-ounce) cans whole-kernel corn, drained
1 cup shredded Swiss cheese
1 (5-1/4-ounce) can evaporated milk
1 egg
1 tablespoon flour
1/2 teaspoon onion powder
1/8 teaspoon pepper

Place butter in small bowl. Microwave at HIGH 45–60 seconds. Stir in crumbs and paprika. Set aside. Arrange bacon on rack. Cover with paper towel. Microwave at HIGH for 3 minutes until bacon is crisp; crumble into a 1-1/2-quart casserole. Stir in corn and Swiss cheese. In small mixing bowl, blend remaining ingredients. Stir into corn mixture. Microwave at MEDIUM for about 12–14 minutes until cheese melts, stirring occasionally. Sprinkle with bread crumb mixture. Microwave at MEDIUM for about 2 minutes until hot.
Mrs. Merle Mishler, Hollsopple, Pa.

RYE AND MUSTARD ENGLISH MUFFIN BREAD

Makes 2 loaves

3-1/2 cups unsifted all-purpose flour, divided
1-1/2 cups unsifted rye flour
2 packages dry yeast
1 tablespoon sugar
2 teaspoons salt
1/4 teaspoon baking soda
1 tablespoon caraway seeds, optional
2 cups milk
1/2 cup water
2 tablespoons Dijon-style mustard
Cornmeal

In a large bowl combine 1-1/2 cups all-purpose flour, rye flour, yeast, sugar, salt, baking soda and caraway seeds.

In a 1-quart measure, microwave milk, water and mustard on HIGH power, using probe if available, until very warm (120–130 degrees). Add to dry ingredients and beat well. Stir in remaining flour to make a stiff batter.

Spoon batter into 2 microwave-proof (8-1/2 x 4-1/2 *or* 9 x 5-inch) loaf pans that have been greased and sprinkled with cornmeal. Sprinkle tops with cornmeal. Cover and let rise in warm place for 45 minutes, or until doubled.

Microwave each loaf individually on HIGH power for 6-1/2 minutes. Surface of loaf will be flat and pale in color. Turn out onto racks to cool. Slice bread and toast as you would for English muffins.
TIP: Use your microwave to proof your bread by microwaving 1 cup water on HIGH power for 6–7 minutes. Place bread loaves in microwave with hot water; close door and let rise. This will help to shorten rising time.
Yvonne Schilling, Wauwatosa, Wis.

SCALLOP MILANGE
Serves 2

1/2 pound scallops
2 stalks celery, cut into 1/2-inch
   pieces
1/2 of a sweet red *or* green pepper,
   cut into 3/4-inch squares
2 teaspoons cornstarch
1/4 teaspoon salt
1/8 teaspoon dried basil, crushed
Dash pepper
2/3 cup milk
1 cup cooked rice
1/2 cup shredded Swiss cheese
1 tablespoon dry white wine

In a 1-1/2-quart dish combine scallops, celery and pepper squares. Microwave, covered, on 100 percent power or HIGH for 4–5 minutes, or until scallops are nearly done, stirring once. Drain and set aside.

In the same dish combine cornstarch, salt, basil and pepper. Stir in milk. Microwave, uncovered, on 100 percent power or HIGH for 1-1/2–2 minutes, or until thick and bubbly, stirring every minute.

Gently stir in rice, cheese, wine, scallops and vegetables. Spoon mixture into 2 (15-ounce) casseroles. Microwave, uncovered, on 100 percent power or HIGH for 1 minute, or until heated thoroughly.

Laura Hicks, Troy, Mont.

SEAFOOD SPLASH
Serves 4

1 (6-ounce) package frozen crabmeat
   and shrimp
2 cups shredded potatoes *or* 12
   ounces frozen hash brown potatoes, thawed
1 tablespoon butter
2 green onions, sliced, including tops
1 (10-3/4-ounce) can condensed
   cream of celery soup
3/4 cup sour cream

1 tablespoon lemon juice
1/4 teaspoon garlic salt
1/2 cup cheddar cheese
Paprika, if desired

Partially thaw frozen crabmeat and shrimp. Combine in 1-1/2-quart glass casserole potatoes, butter and onions. Cover with casserole lid. Microwave on HIGH for 4-1/2–5-1/2 minutes, or until potatoes are almost tender, stirring once. Stir in celery soup, sour cream, lemon juice and garlic salt. Add seafood. Cover and microwave on HIGH for 5 minutes, or until hot. Stir well.

Sprinkle with cheese and sprinkle with paprika, if desired. Microwave, uncovered, on HIGH 2-1/2 minutes.

Angela Biggin, Lyons, Ill.

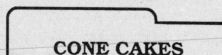

CONE CAKES

Prepare your favorite cake recipe *or* box mix. Using ice-cream cones with flat bottoms, fill each cone with 2 tablespoons of prepared batter. When cooking more than 2 cones at a time, arrange cones in a circle.

Microwave on HIGH (100 percent) until surface springs back when lightly touched. Always check for doneness at minimum suggested time. If cones are not done at the same time, remove the baked cones and continue cooking the remaining cones. Cool, then frost.

Quick Cream Cheese Frosting:
2 (3-ounce) packages cream cheese
1/2 cup butter *or* margarine
4 cups confectioners' sugar
1 teaspoon almond extract

Place cream cheese and butter in a 2-quart casserole. Microwave on LOW (30 percent) for 1-1/2–2 minutes or until softened. Stir in the sugar and almond extract until well-blended. Beat mixture until spreading consistency. Spread on tops of cooled cones. Garnish with nuts and cherries, or as desired.

Marie Fusaro, Manasquan, N.J.

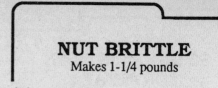

NUT BRITTLE
Makes 1-1/4 pounds

1/4 cup water
1 cup sugar
1/4 cup light corn syrup
1-1/2 cups salted *or* unsalted nuts,
   coarsely chopped
1 tablespoon margarine
1 teaspoon vanilla
1 teaspoon baking soda

Note: I use mixed salted nuts.

Grease large cookie sheet; set aside. In a 2-quart microwave casserole, combine sugar, syrup and 1/4 cup water. Stretch sheet of microwave plastic wrap over 3/4 of top of casserole. Cook on 100 percent power, HIGH, for 10–12 minutes until small amount of candy mixture dropped into very cold water separates into hard, brittle threads. Stir in nuts' cook on HIGH power for 1 minute longer.

Mixture will foam and bubble up. Carefully stir in margarine, vanilla and baking soda. Work quickly. Pour mixture onto greased cookie sheet, spreading rapidly to edges. Pull ends to make brittle fairly thin. Let stand 45 minutes until hard and completely cooled. Break cooled brittle into pieces. Store in air tight container; will keep up to 3 weeks.

Flo Burtnett, Gage, Okla

PEANUTTY CEREAL TREATS

4 tablespoons unsalted butter
1/2 cup peanut butter
3 cups miniature marshmallows
4 cups dry, crunchy cereal
1 cup dry roasted peanuts

Place butter, peanut butter, and marshmallows in an 8-to 12-cup measure. Microwave on HIGH for 2-1/2 to 3-1/2 minutes. Stir until smooth. Stir in cereal and peanuts. Blend well. Press in a 9-inch square pan. Cool.

HOT GERMAN POTATO SALAD

Serves 4–6

4 medium potatoes
6 strips bacon
2 tablespoons flour
1/4 cup sugar
1-1/2 teaspoons salt
1/2 teaspoon celery seed
1/8 teaspoon pepper
1 cup water
1/2 cup vinegar

Wash and pierce potatoes through with fork. Place on paper towel in microwave oven. Microwave on HIGH for 10–12 minutes, turning over and rearranging after 4 minutes or until tender. Remove from oven; cool slightly; peel potatoes and cut in 1/8-inch slices to make about 4 cups.

In 2-quart casserole cut bacon in small pieces. Cover with paper towel. Microwave at HIGH for about 6 minutes, stirring after 3 minutes, until crisp. With slotted spoon remove bacon to paper towels to drain. set aside.

Stir flour, sugar and seasonings into bacon fat until smooth. Microwave on HIGH for 1–2 minutes until bubbly, stirring after 1 minute.

Add water and vinegar to flour mixture. Microwave on HIGH for 4 minutes, or until mixture boils and thickens, stirring after 1 minute. Remove from oven and stir. Add potatoes and bacon; stir gently so potatoes hold their shape. Cover casserole and let stand until ready to serve.

Karen Waldo, Mendota, Ill.

CHICKEN KIEV APPETIZERS

Makes 28 appetizers

2 chicken breasts, boned, skinned, and cut lengthwise

1/4 cup butter *or* margarine in a stick
2 tablespoons chopped parsley
1/2 teaspoon onion salt
Butter *or* margarine, melted
Paprika
Seasoned salt

Pound chicken until 1/4-inch thick. Cut butter lengthwise into 4 sections. Place 1 piece of butter at narrow end of *each* chicken breast. Sprinkle with parsley and onion salt. Fold over sides to cover butter. Roll up in jelly-roll fashion starting at butter end. *Refrigerate for 1-1/2 hours.* Cut into bite-size pieces and secure with toothpicks. Place in a baking dish. Brush with melted butter. Sprinkle with seasoned salt and paprika. Cover with waxed paper.

Microwave on HIGH (100 percent power) for 3–4 minutes. Allow to stand 3 minutes before serving. Arrange on a platter with dates *or* apple slices between each piece of appetizer before serving. Set toothpicks in an attractive holder next to platter and it's ready for guests!

Marie Fusaro, Manasquan, N.J.

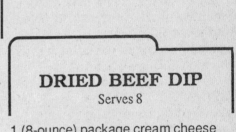

BUTTERFLIED WIENERS

1 pound wieners
1/4 cup honey
1 (20-ounce) bottle of your favorite barbecue sauce

Cut wieners crosswise in 3 pieces. Cut each piece in half lengthwise to make 6 pieces. Slit each piece through ends, leaving 1/4-inch joint in center. Set aside. Mix honey and barbecue sauce in 1-1/2-quart casserole. Cover lightly with plastic wrap or waxed paper. Microwave 1 minute on HIGH. Stir. Add wieners. Cover lightly. Microwave 3 minutes on HIGH, or until ends of wieners curl. Serve with cocktail picks.

Ann Elsie Schmetzer, Madisonville, Ky.

CHOCOLATE CRACKLES

Makes 4 dozen

1/2 cup plus 2 tablespoons Butter Flavor Crisco
6 tablespoons cocoa
1 cup sugar
2 teaspoons baking powder
1/2 teaspoon salt
2 eggs
1 teaspoon vanilla
2 cups flour
1/2 cup chopped nuts
1/2 cup confectioners' sugar in sifter

In medium bowl microwave Butter Flavor Crisco on HIGH power for 45–60 seconds or until melted. Add cocoa; blend. Beat in sugar, baking powder, salt, eggs and vanilla. Stir in flour and nuts. Mix well. Cover and refrigerate until firm. Shape dough into 1-inch balls; roll in confectioners' sugar. Arrange 8 balls, 2 inches apart, in a circle on waxed-paper-lined plate.

Microwave at MEDIUM power for 1-1/2–2 minutes or until cookies are puffed and surface is dry, but cookies should be soft to touch. Cool on waxed paper on countertop. Before serving, sprinkle with confectioners' sugar, if desired.

DRIED BEEF DIP

Serves 8

1 (8-ounce) package cream cheese
2-1/2-ounce package dried beef, finely chopped
2 tablespoons onion, finely chopped
2 tablespoons Worcestershire sauce
3/4 cup sour cream
Dash liquid hot sauce

In a 4-cup glass measuring cup, soften cream cheese on MEDIUM for 2 minutes. Mix other ingredients with cheese; microwave on MEDIUM for 4 minutes; stir halfway through cooking time. Serve with assorted crackers.

Gwen Campbell, Sterling, Va.

MICROWAVE BUN BARS

Makes 60 bars

1 (12-ounce) package (2 cups) semisweet chocolate chips
1 (12-ounce) package (2 cups) butterscotch chips
2 cups peanut butter
2 cups salted peanuts
1 cup margarine *or* butter
1 (3-1/8-ounce) package vanilla *or* milk chocolate pudding and pie filling mix (not instant)
1/2 cup evaporated milk
1 (2-pound) bag (7-1/2 cups) *sifted* confectioners' sugar
1 teaspoon vanilla

Butter 15 x 10-inch jelly roll pan. In medium microwave-safe bowl, combine chocolate chips and butterscotch chips. Microwave on MEDIUM for 6–7 minutes, stirring every 2 minutes. Stir until smooth. Stir in peanut butter; mix well. Spread half of mixture into prepared pan; refrigerate. Stir peanuts into remaining chocolate mixture; set aside.

In large microwave-safe bowl, place margarine. Microwave on HIGH for 15–60 seconds, or until melted. Stir in pudding mix and evaporated milk; blend well. Microwave on HIGH for 45–60 seconds, or until hot. DO NOT boil. Stir in confectioners' sugar and vanilla. Carefully spread over chocolate layer. Refrigerate 30 minutes to set. Drop remaining chocolate-peanut mixture by tablespoonfuls over chilled pudding layer. Carefully spread to cover. Refrigerate until firm; cut into bars. Store in covered container in refrigerator.
Note: I prefer the vanilla pudding but for an extra-chocolaty bar, you can use milk-chocolate pudding instead of vanilla.

Marilyn J. Hoffmann, Oostburg, Wis.

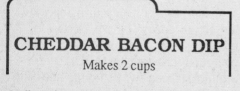

CHEDDAR BACON DIP

Makes 2 cups

6 slices bacon
1 (8-ounce) package cream cheese
1-1/2 cups (6 ounces) shredded sharp cheese
1/4 cup whipping cream
1 teaspoon Worcestershire sauce
1/4 teaspoon dry mustard
1/8 teaspoon onion powder
1/8 teaspoon hot sauce (I use 1 teaspoon)
Parsley

Place bacon on a rack in a 12 x 8 x 2-inch baking dish; cover with paper towels. Microwave on HIGH for 3-1/2–4-1/2 minutes or until done. Crumble bacon and set aside.

Place cream cheese in a 1-quart casserole. Microwave on HIGH for 1 minute, or until melted. Stir in shredded sharp cheese and next 5 ingredients. Microwave at MEDIUM HIGH for 2-1/2 minutes, or until cheese is melted and mixture is heated, stirring once.

Stir in crumbled bacon, reserving 1 tablespoon to sprinkle on top. Garnish with a parsley sprig. Serve with apple wedges on crackers and raw vegetables.
Carolyn Griffin, Macon, Ga.

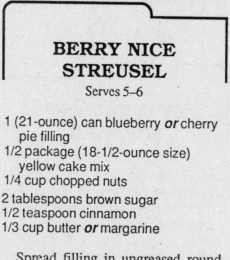

BERRY NICE STREUSEL

Serves 5–6

1 (21-ounce) can blueberry *or* cherry pie filling
1/2 package (18-1/2-ounce size) yellow cake mix
1/4 cup chopped nuts
2 tablespoons brown sugar
1/2 teaspoon cinnamon
1/3 cup butter *or* margarine

Spread filling in ungreased round glass baking dish, 8-inch size. Sprinkle dry cake mix over filling. Mix nuts, sugar and cinnamon in a small dish; sprinkle over cake mix. Microwave butter on HIGH to melt, about 30 seconds. Dribble over mixture in dish. Microwave, uncovered, for 7 minutes on HIGH. Turn dish 1/4 turn. Microwave on HIGH until mixture bubbles and topping is almost firm, 7–9 minutes. Serve warm or cool.

Barbara Penland, Goshen, Ind.

CARAWAY CABBAGE AND KIELBASA

Serves 4–6

4 cups shredded green cabbage
2 cups chopped tart apple
1 small onion, chopped
2 tablespoons white wine *or* water
1 teaspoon instant beef bouillon
1 teaspoon caraway seeds
1 pound cooked kielbasa

Combine cabbage, apple, onion, wine, bouillon and caraway seeds in a deep 2-quart casserole. Cover and cook on HIGH for 12–14 minutes, or until tender-crisp, stirring once. Cut kielbasa into 1-inch pieces; add to cabbage mixture and stir lightly. Cover and cook on HIGH, or until completely heated through.
Mrs. A.S. Warren, Charlotte, N.C.

VEGGIE MUFFIN MELTS

Serves 4–6

1 cup sliced, fresh mushrooms
1-1/2 cups shredded zucchini (1 medium)
2 green onions, sliced
3 tablespoons mayonnaise *or* salad dressing
1/2 teaspoon tarragon leaves
1/8 teaspoon salt
Dash pepper
3 English muffins, split and toasted
1 medium to large tomato
6 slices Monterey Jack cheese

Combine mushrooms, zucchini and onions in 4-cup glass measure. Cook on HIGH for 3–4 minutes, or until almost tender, stirring once; drain well. Mix in mayonnaise, tarragon, salt and pepper. Arrange muffins, cut-side-up, on glass serving plate. Cut tomato into 6 slices; place a slice on each muffin; top with zucchini mixture. Cut cheese into small pieces and place over top, allowing some of the vegetables to show. Cook on HIGH for 1–1-1/2 minutes, or until cheese starts to melt, rotating plate once.
Mrs. A.S. Warren, Charlotte, N.C.

CHERRY CRUNCH
Serves 6–8

1 (9-ounce) package white *or* yellow single-layer cake mix
1/2 cup chopped *or* ground nuts
2 tablespoons brown sugar, packed
2 teaspoons cinnamon
1 (21-ounce) can cherry pie filling
1/4 cup butter *or* margarine, melted

In a bowl combine cake mix, nuts, brown sugar and cinnamon. In an 8-inch glass baking dish, spoon cherry pie filling into bottom. Sprinkle cake mix mixture evenly over pie filling. Drizzle melted butter or margarine over top. Cook on HIGH for 12–14 minutes, or until topping is no longer doughy (rotate dish during cooking if cake does not appear to be rising evenly). Let stand 5 minutes. Serve warm with whipped cream or vanilla ice cream.
Ann Elsie Schmetzer, Madisonville, Ky.

CARAMEL NUT CRUNCH
Makes 8 cups

1/2 cup packed brown sugar
1/2 cup dark corn syrup
1/4 cup butter *or* margarine
1/2 teaspoon salt
6 cups toasted oat cereal
1/2 cup pecan halves
1/2 cup dry roasted peanuts
1/2 cup slivered almonds

Combine sugar, syrup, butter and salt in 2-quart mix-and-pour bowl. Microwave on HIGH, uncovered, 3–4 minutes, or until mixture boils, stirring once. Stir well, then microwave on HIGH for 1-1/2 minutes longer. Combine cereal and nuts in large buttered microwave-safe bowl; pour hot mixture over all and mix until evenly coated. Microwave on HIGH for 6–8 minutes, or until cereal is toasted, stirring *thoroughly* every 2 minutes. Spoon onto

buttered foil. Cool 5–7 minutes, or until it starts to set. Break into pieces; cool completely. Store in covered container.
Mrs. A.S. Warren, Charlotte, N.C.

HOT BANANA SPLIT
Serves 1–2

1 firmly ripe medium banana, peeled
2 tablespoons creamy peanut butter
2 tablespoons milk-chocolate pieces
2 tablespoons miniature marshmallows

Using a table knife, cut banana down the center lengthwise into 2 halves. Place cut side up in shallow, microwave-safe serving dish. Spread cut sides with peanut butter. Gently press chocolate pieces and marshmallows into peanut butter. Microwave on HIGH for 20–30 seconds, or until chocolate and marshmallows begin to melt. Serve with a scoop of ice cream for an extra-special treat.
Note: Recipe may be doubled or tripled, if desired.
Mrs. A.S. Warren, Charlotte, N.C.

MICROWAVE TOFFEE

1/2 cup chopped pecans
1 cup sugar
1/4 cup water
1/2 cup butter
1 teaspoon salt
4 ounces milk-chocolate chips

Sprinkle pecans in a 9-inch circle on a greased cookie sheet and set aside. Rub the inside top 2 inches of a glass mixing bowl with butter and place remaining butter in bowl. Pour sugar directly onto butter (avoid getting on the sides of bowl). Add salt and water, but do not stir. Microwave on HIGH for about 8–10 minutes. Candy is done when it is the color of brown sugar. Pour hot candy over nuts. Top with chocolate, spreading to frost when chocolate melts. Break into pieces when cooled.

Jan Ramsey, Quitaque, Texas

FRUIT CRISP
Serves 6–8

4 cups sliced fruit—apples, peaches, pears, *or* a combination, *or* 2 (16-ounce) cans fruit cocktail, drained
1/2 cup granulated sugar, sprinkled over if fruit is unsweetened
1 (7–8-ounce) package dry blueberry muffin mix *or* other muffin mix
1/4 cup diet margarine
1/4–1/2 cup sliced nuts—almonds, pecans, black walnuts

Place fruit in greased or Pam-sprayed 8-1/2 x 11-inch dish. Sprinkle sugar, if needed. Sprinkle dry muffin mix over fruit. Cut up margarine and dot dry mixture. Sprinkle nuts over top.

Microwave on HIGH for 12–14 minutes. Turn 1/4 turn after 6–8 minutes. Serve warm or cold with ice cream, whipped cream or whipped topping. May also drizzle with chocolate *or* butterscotch sauce.

This is so easy for unexpected guests. The pears with ice cream and chocolate topping are especially good. I've also used raspberries, blueberries and other muffin mix, gooseberries, cherries—really whatever is on hand.
Mrs. J.C. Mantel, Orange City, Iowa

MEXICAN CHEESE PIE
Serves 2

1/2 cup jalapeño peppers, seeded and sliced
1 (10-ounce) package longhorn cheese, grated
4 eggs, slightly beaten
1/8 teaspoon paprika

Line bottom of greased 1/2-quart glass ring mold with peppers. Sprinkle with cheese; mix eggs and paprika; pour over cheese; cover completely. Microwave on HIGH for 6 minutes; turn every 2 minutes; let stand 5 minutes.
Gwen Campbell, Sterling, Va.

SLOPPY JOES
Serves 6–8

1-1/2 pound ground beef
2/3 cup finely chopped onion
1/2 cup diced celery
1/4 cup diced green pepper
1/2 cup ketchup
1 tablespoon Worcestershire sauce
1/2 teaspoon salt
1/8 teaspoon pepper

In 1-1/2-quart casserole crumble beef. Add onion, celery and green pepper. Cover. Microwave on HIGH for 6 minutes, stirring after 3 minutes. Drain meat well.

To cooked meat mixture, add ketchup, Worcestershire sauce, salt and pepper. Cover. Microwave on HIGH for 5–6 minutes, stirring after 3 minutes, until hot. To serve, spoon onto buns.

Karen Waido, Mendota, Ill.

HOT AND HEARTY CASSEROLE
Serves 6

1 (15-ounce) can corned beef hash
1 (16-ounce) can pork and beans
1/4 cup fresh spinach, chopped
1 (16-ounce) can tiny green peas, drained
1 (6-ounce) can tomato-vegetable juice
1 tablespoon ground nutmeg
2 tablespoons butter *or* margarine, melted
1 cup rye bread crumbs
1/3 cup Parmesan cheese, grated
1/4 cup fresh parsley, chopped

In the bottom of a 2-1/2-quart, microwave-safe casserole spread half the hash. Combine next 5 ingredients; spoon half over hash. Layer remaining hash and vegetables; cover with plastic wrap; vent 1 corner. Microwave on HIGH for 12 minutes; rotate dish twice during cooking. Combine butter, rye bread crumbs, cheese and parsley in a glass pie plate. Microwave on HIGH for 2 minutes; sprinkle on top of cooked casserole.

Gwen Campbell, Sterling, Va.

CHILI BURGERS
Serves 4

1 pound ground beef
1 cup chopped celery
1 cup chopped onion
1/2 cup chopped green pepper
1 (10-3/4-ounce) can tomato soup
1/4 cup ketchup
1 tablespoon brown sugar
1-1/8 teaspoon chili powder
1/2 teaspoon dry mustard
1/2 teaspoon salt
1/8 teaspoon cayenne pepper
1/8 teaspoon pepper
1/8 teaspoon garlic powder
1 tablespoon cornstarch
1 (15-ounce) can kidney beans, drained

In 2-quart casserole combine ground beef and vegetables. Cover and microwave on HIGH for 5–6 minutes, stirring once to break up meat. Drain. Stir in rest of ingredients. Cover and microwave on HIGH for 5 minutes. Reduce power to MEDIUM and cook 7–10 minutes until blended. Serve on steak buns.

Patricia Anderson, Fremont, Neb.

HOT FUDGE PUDDING
Serves 8

1 cup flour
1 teaspoon baking powder
1/4 teaspoon salt
3/4 cup sugar
2 tablespoons cocoa
1/2 cup milk
2 tablespoons oil
1 teaspoon vanilla
1 cup brown sugar
1/4 cup cocoa
1-3/4 cups hot water

In a 3-quart casserole combine flour, baking powder, salt, sugar and cocoa. Stir in milk, oil and vanilla. Sprinkle top with brown sugar and 1/4 cup cocoa, mixed together. Heat water in a 2-cup glass measure in microwave until boiling. Pour over batter. Microwave on HIGH for 9–10 minutes, turning 3 times. Spoon into dishes and top with ice cream.

Ruth Meinert, Davis, Ill.

VANILLA PUDDING
Serves 4–6

1/2 cup sugar
2 tablespoons cornstarch
2 tablespoons flour
1/4 teaspoon salt
2 cups milk
2 eggs, beaten
2 tablespoons butter
1 teaspoon vanilla
1 can drained fruit (fruit of your choice)

In 2-quart microwave-safe bowl combine sugar, cornstarch, flour and salt. Stir in milk. Microwave on HIGH for 8 minutes or until thickened; stir every 3 minutes. Stir about 1/2 cup milk mixture into eggs and then add eggs to mixture; stir well. Microwave on HIGH for 2 minutes. Stir in butter and vanilla. Divide drained fruit in serving bowls; pour pudding over top.

Another way, instead of the fruit, fold in 1–2 sliced bananas in pudding.

Elaine Belisle, Red Rock, Ontario, Canada

STUFFED BEEF ROLLS
Serves 1

1/4 pound beef boneless sirloin steak, about 1/2-inch thick
1/2 cup cooked long-grain and wild rice mix
2 teaspoons grated Parmesan cheese
1 green onion (with top), finely chopped
1 tablespoon margarine, melted
1/4 teaspoon browning sauce
1/8 teaspoon salt

Pound beef sirloin to 1/4-inch thickness. Mix rice, cheese and onion; spread over beef. Roll up; secure with string. Mix remaining ingredients; brush over beef roll. Place on rack in rectangular dish, 11 x 7 x 1-1/2 inches.

Cover with waxed paper and microwave on MEDIUM (50 percent) for 4–6 minutes, turning beef roll over after 3 minutes, until beef is done. Remove string.

Barbara Nowakowski, North Tonawanda, N.Y.

Party
FARE

SMOKY CHEESE BALL

1/2 teaspoon Worcestershire sauce
Several drops Liquid Smoke®
1 roll cheese spread (bacon, garlic or sharp cheese flavor)
2 small packages (3 ounces each) cream cheese, softened
1 cup shredded sharp cheddar cheese
1/2 cup chopped fresh parsley
1/2 cup chopped pecans.

Unwrap cheese spread and microwave on "High" for 1 minute in a large casserole. Add cream cheese and microwave again for 1 minute, or until cheeses mix well. Add Liquid Smoke® and Worcestershire sauce and blend well. Stir in shredded cheddar. Chill for about 15 minutes in freezer, or for about 1 hour in refrigerator. Roll mixture into a ball. Roll in parsley, then in chopped pecans to cover ball. Chill for several hours. Serve with crackers.

Monica W. Cox, Cleveland, Miss.

DRIED FRUIT CHEESE BALL

Makes 2 9-ounce cheese balls

1 large package (8 ounces) cream cheese, softened
1 cup (4 ounces) grated sharp cheddar cheese
1 tablespoon honey
6-ounce package dried fruits and raisins, cut up

Beat cheeses and honey together until light and smooth. Stir in 1 cup dried fruit. Wrap tightly. Chill until firm. Divide in half and shape each into

a ball. Garnish with remaining dried fruit. Wrap tightly. Keeps for up to 2 weeks in refrigerator.

CHEESE BALL

1 large package (8 ounces) cream cheese, softened
4-ounce package blue cheese, softened.
1/2 cup shredded cheddar cheese
1 teaspoon Worcestershire sauce
2 teaspoons dry onion-soup mix
Pinch of paprika
Pinch of dried parsley
Crushed salted peanuts

Cream softened cheeses together. Add seasonings and mix well. Roll into a ball, then roll in crushed salted peanuts. Serve with crackers.

Mrs. Ronda Oborne, Packwood, Wash.

HOT BEEF DIP

Makes 2 cups

1 cup (2 1/2-ounce jar) dried beef
1/4 cup chopped onion
1 tablespoon margarine
1 cup milk
1 large package (8 ounces) cream cheese, cubed
1/2 cup sliced mushrooms, drained
1/4 cup grated Parmesan cheese
2 tablespoons chopped parsley

Rinse dried beef in hot water; drain and chop. Cook onion in margarine until tender. Stir in milk and cream cheese; mix until well-blended. Add dried beef and remaining ingredients. Mix well. Serve hot.

Mrs. Agnes Ward, Erie, Penn.

MARSHMALLOW FRUIT DIP

1 large package (8 ounces) cream cheese
13-ounce jar marshmallow creme
1/2 teaspoon ginger
2 tablespoons grated orange rind
Dash of nutmeg
Pineapple juice
Red and green apples

Cream together cream cheese, marshmallow creme, orange rind and spices. Wash, core and slice apples into wedges. Dip wedges in pineapple juice to prevent discoloration. Serve apple wedges with dip.

Mary Kauphusman, Rochester, Minn.

SALMON BALL

1-pound can salmon, drained (2 cups)
1 large package (8 ounces) cream cheese
1 tablespoon lemon juice
2 teaspoons grated onion
1 tablespoon prepared horseradish
1/4 teaspoon salt
1/4 teaspoon paprika
1/2 cup chopped pecans
3 tablespoons chopped parsley

Combine all ingredients except pecans and parsley; blend mixture well. Roll into a ball; roll tightly in plastic wrap; chill for several hours. Roll in combined parsley and pecans. Chill until ready to serve. May be frozen.

CHILI DIP

2 pounds process American cheese, cubed
2 4-ounce cans green chilies, seeded and chopped
1 large tomato, peeled, seeded and chopped
3 tablespoons minced onion
1/2 teaspoon Worcestershire sauce
1/8 teaspoon garlic powder
1/8 teaspoon salt
1/8 teaspoon oregano
1/8 teaspoon pepper

Melt cheese in top of a double boiler over hot (*not* boiling) water, stirring constantly. Combine remaining ingredients in blender container. Process at medium speed until smooth. Add to cheese and cook over low heat, stirring occasionally, for about 15 minutes, or until hot. Serve with corn chips.

Margaret Russo, Winsted, Conn.

SPICY BEEF DIP
Makes 12 party servings

1 pound ground beef
1/2 cup chopped onion
1 clove garlic, minced
8-ounce can tomato sauce
1/4 cup catsup
1 teaspoon sugar
3/4 teaspoon dried oregano
1 large package (8 ounces) cream cheese, softened
1/3 cup grated Parmesan cheese

Cook beef, onion and garlic in a skillet until meat is browned and onion is tender. Drain off fat. Stir in next 4 ingredients. Cover and simmer gently for 10 minutes. Spoon off excess fat. Add cheeses. Heat until cream cheese melts and is well-combined.

It's easy to double this recipe; keep warm in a slow cooker on low heat for easy serving during your party.

Mrs. Marion Frost, Princeton, Wis.

HOT CRAB MEAT DIP

1 large package (8 ounces) cream cheese, softened
7-ounce can crabmeat (drained, flaked, cartilage removed)
Dash of white horseradish
1 tablespoon milk
2 tablespoons chopped onion
1/2 teaspoon salt
1/3 cup sliced almonds

Blend all ingredients together until well-mixed, except almonds. Spoon mixture into greased baking dish; sprinkle almonds on top. Bake in a preheated 375-degree oven for 15-20 minutes. Serve hot with chips, crackers, or raw vegetables.

Margaret Russo, Winsted, Conn.

NACHO DABS
Makes 6 1/2 dozen

8-ounce bag tortilla chips
16-ounce can refried beans
1-2 cups (4-8 ounces) shredded cheddar cheese
5-6 jalapeno peppers, sliced into rings

Preheat oven to 400 degrees.

Set aside 6 1/2 dozen whole tortilla chips, reserving any broken ones for another use. Place chips on cookie sheet and top each with about 1 teaspoon beans, some cheese, and a jalapeno pepper ring.

Bake at 400 degrees for 2-3 minutes, or until cheese melts. Serve at once.

CUCUMBER DIP

1 cucumber
1 small package (3 ounces) cream cheese, softened
1/2 cup chopped nuts
Mayonnaise

Grate cucumber; drain well. Add cream cheese; mix well. Add nuts and enough mayonnaise to moisten mixture. Mix until blended.

VEGETABLE-COFFEE DIP
Makes 1 1/2 cups dip

1 large package (8 ounces) softened cream cheese
3 tablespoons cold brewed coffee
1 tablespoon finely grated carrot
1 tablespoon finely chopped parsley
2 teaspoons finely chopped onion
1/4 teaspoon salt
1/2 teaspoon Worcestershire sauce

Combine cream cheese and coffee until smooth. Stir in remaining ingredients and blend well. Chill. Serve with raw vegetables.

JALAPENO CRACKER SPREAD
Makes about 2 1/2 cups spread

2 small packages (3 ounces each) cream cheese, softened
1/2 pound grated sharp cheddar cheese
7 1/2-ounce can chopped tomatoes with jalapeno peppers
1 tablespoon ground cumin
1 teaspoon garlic powder
1/8 teaspoon hot pepper sauce

Beat cheeses together to blend well. Gradually beat in remaining ingredients to blend well. Chill. Stores in refrigerator up to one week.

CURRY DIP
Makes 1 cup

1 cup mayonnaise
1 tablespoon minced onion
1/2 teaspoon curry powder
Dash of salt

Combine all ingredients. Chill. Sprinkle with extra curry, if desired. Serve with raw vegetables.

CHILI PEPPER DIP

1 can cream of chicken soup
1 can green chilies, chopped
1 cup grated cheddar cheese
2 teaspoons instant minced onion

Combine all ingredients in saucepan; stir over low heat to melt the cheese. Serve with chips.

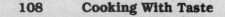

PARTY WEDGE-A-PIZZA

Makes 24

1 1/2 cups corned beef, broken up, or 2 packages corned beef, chopped
6-ounce can tomato paste
1/2 cup shredded cheddar cheese
2 tablespoons minced dehydrated onion or 1/2 cup chopped fresh onion
1 teaspoon leaf oregano
2 eggs
1 can refrigerated crescent dinner rolls
Pasteurized process cheese spread or shredded cheddar cheese

In bowl, combine corned beef, tomato paste, 1/2 cup shredded cheddar cheese, onion, oregano and eggs; mix well. On ungreased baking sheets, separate dough into 8 triangles. Spread each with about 1/3 cup beef mixture. Bake in a preheated 400-degree oven for 20-25 minutes, until edges are golden brown. Cool slightly. Cut each triangle into 3 pieces and garnish with additional cheese. Serve warm or cold.

Mrs. Agnes Ward, Erie, Penn.

YOGURT DIP

Makes 2 cups

2 cups plain yogurt
1 garlic clove, crushed
1 teaspoon dill
1 teaspoon mint
1 teaspoon minced parsley

Combine all ingredients and chill. Serve with chips, etc.

Mrs. Agnes Ward, Erie, Penn.

WHEAT THINS

1 3/4 cups whole-wheat flour
1 1/2 cups white flour
1/3 cup salad oil
3/4 teaspoon salt
1 cup water

Mix flours; add liquids. Knead as little as possible. Make a smooth dough and roll as thin as possible onto ungreased cookie sheet (not more than 1/8 inch thick). Score with a knife to size desired, but do not cut through. Sprinkle lightly with salt or onion salt as desired.

Bake at 350 degrees until crisp and light brown (about 30-35 minutes). Remove from baking sheet and break into crackers.

Mrs. S.R. Burt, Imlay, Nev.

DEVILED CHEESE DELIGHT

5-ounce jar pimiento cheese spread
2 1/2-ounce can deviled ham
2 tablespoons finely snipped parsley
2 tablespoons mayonnaise
1 teaspoon grated onion
3-4 drops hot pepper sauce

In small bowl combine cheese spread, deviled ham, parsley, mayonnaise, onion and hot pepper sauce. Beat with electric mixer until creamy; chill well. Turn into serving dish, garnish with fresh parsley. Serve with crackers, etc.

Mrs. Agnes Ward, Erie, Penn.

CHEESE DIP DELUXE

1 teaspoon granulated beef bouillon
1 tablespoon hot water
1 large package (8 ounces) cream cheese, softened
1/4 cup milk
1 tablespoon instant minced onion
1/4 teaspoon basil leaves

Combine beef bouillon and hot water, stirring to dissolve. Mix with remaining ingredients. Leave for 20 minutes to allow flavors to mingle. Serve with chips, etc.

Variation:

Add an 8-ounce can of minced clams, or 1/2 cup finely chopped shrimp or crabmeat.

Mrs. Agnes Ward, Erie, Penn.

SPINACH-EGG SPREAD

2 packages frozen chopped spinach, thawed and drained well
1/2 cup chopped onion
1/2 cup diced celery
1/2 cup shredded cheddar cheese
1 1/2 cups mayonnaise
2 tablespoons lemon juice
1 1/2 teaspoons horseradish
4 hard-cooked eggs, chopped
1/8 teaspoon salt

Mix drained, thawed spinach with remaining ingredients. Refrigerate until serving time.

Beatrice Mickelson, Cadott, Wis.

RYE CRACKERS

1/4 cup warm (105-115 degrees)
   water
2 packages active dry yeast
1 teaspoon salt
1 teaspoon sugar
1 cup milk
1 1/2 teaspoons crushed caraway
   seed
1 3/4 cups medium rye flour, divided
About 1 1/4 cups all-purpose flour

In medium bowl, combine water, yeast, salt and sugar; leave for about 3 minutes to soften yeast. Add milk, caraway seed, 1 1/2 cups rye flour and 1 cup all-purpose flour. Beat until smooth.

On floured surface, using remaining all-purpose flour, knead dough until smooth and elastic. Cut into 8 equal pieces and shape each into a round bun. Place on a greased cookie sheet, turning to grease tops. Cover and let rise in a warm place until almost doubled (about 30 minutes).

Punch down. Remove to lightly floured cloth, and with remaining 1/4 cup rye flour and stockinette-covered rolling pin, roll out each piece into a 9-inch round. Place each rolled-out round on ungreased cookie sheets, pricking entire surface with a fork.

Bake in a preheated 400-degree oven, two sheets at a time, for 4 minutes. Flip breads over, reverse positions of sheets in oven, and bake 4 minutes more, or until light brown and crisp.
Cool on racks. Store in a dry place for up to 2 months. Serve, broken into pieces, with dips and spreads.

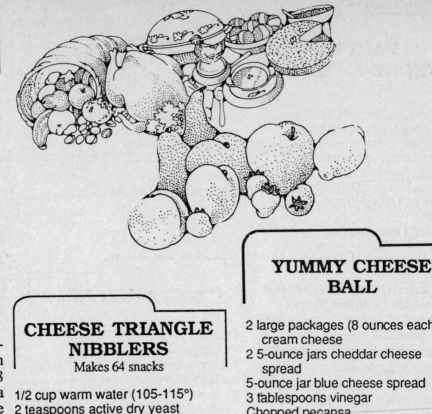

CHEESE TRIANGLE NIBBLERS
Makes 64 snacks

1/2 cup warm water (105-115°)
2 teaspoons active dry yeast
1 teaspoon sugar
1/4 teaspoon cayenne pepper
1/4 teaspoon salt
About 2 cups flour, divided
1/2 cup margarine, softened slightly
1/4 cup grated Parmesan cheese

In medium bowl, combine water, yeast and sugar. Let mixture sit for about 3 minutes. Add cayenne pepper, salt and 1 1/4 cups flour. Beat until well-blended and smooth. Cover; let rise in a warm, draft-free place for about 30 minutes, or until doubled in bulk. Add margarine and Parmesan cheese. Beat until well-blended. Add 1/2 cup flour, beating until smooth.

Turn dough out onto lightly floured surface; divide in half. Roll out each half into a 10-inch square. Prick with fork. With a pastry wheel or a sharp knife, cut 16 2 1/2-inch squares from each square of dough, and cut each of those squares in half diagonally to make triangles.

Place triangles 1/4 inch apart on ungreased cookie sheets. Bake in preheated 425-degree oven for 8-10 minutes, until golden brown. Remove to racks to cool. Store in a tightly covered container in a cool place. Keep up to two weeks. (When ready to serve after storing, freshen for 3-4 minutes in a 350-degree oven.)

YUMMY CHEESE BALL

2 large packages (8 ounces each)
   cream cheese
2 5-ounce jars cheddar cheese
   spread
5-ounce jar blue cheese spread
3 tablespoons vinegar
Chopped pecansa

Mix all together and chill well. Shape into large ball or individual-size balls. Roll in chopped pecans.

Mrs. Florence Satterfield
Greenfield, Ohio

SPINACH BALL

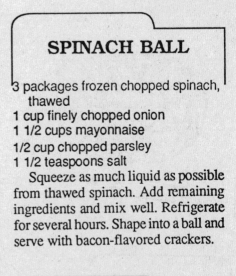

3 packages frozen chopped spinach,
   thawed
1 cup finely chopped onion
1 1/2 cups mayonnaise
1/2 cup chopped parsley
1 1/2 teaspoons salt

Squeeze as much liquid as possible from thawed spinach. Add remaining ingredients and mix well. Refrigerate for several hours. Shape into a ball and serve with bacon-flavored crackers.

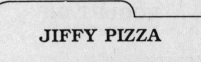

JIFFY PIZZA

For a quick homemade version of Italian pizza, split *English muffins*, spread with *butter, grated cheese,* and *tomato* or *chili sauce*. Toast under the broiler. Delicious and easy!

Helene Levine

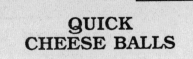

QUICK CHEESE BALLS

2 cups flour
2 cups shredded cheddar cheese
1 cup margarine, softened
Salt and pepper to taste
2 cups crispy rice cereal

Preheat oven to 350 degrees.

Combine all ingredients; mix well. Roll into balls and place on an ungreased baking sheet; flatten slightly. Bake at 350 degrees for 10-12 minutes. These may be frozen after baking; place in the oven for several minutes to crisp before serving.

CHEESE CRISPS

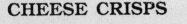

1/2 cup butter
1 roll (3 ounces) sharp cheese
1 cup sifted flour
1/8 teaspoon dry mustard
1 teaspoon Worcestershire sauce
1/2 teaspoon garlic salt
2 drops hot pepper sauce (optional)

Combine and mix all ingredients, working together with fingers to form dough. Shape into 3/4-inch balls; place on ungreased cookie sheets. Bake in preheated 450-degree oven for 10 minutes. Serve hot.

These may be prepared the day before and refrigerated until baking time.

CHOCOLATE POPCORN
Makes about 4 quarts

2 cups sugar
1 cup water
1/2 cup light corn syrup
2 ounces unsweetened chocolate
4 quarts freshly popped corn

Combine sugar, water, corn syrup and chocolate in saucepan. Cook, stirring constantly, until syrup hardens when dropped in cold water. Pour over fresh popcorn and stir to coat well. Shape into balls and store in tightly covered container.

Louise Hicks, Chicago, Ill.

CARAMEL POPCORN I
Makes about 8 quarts

1 cup sugar
1 cup packed brown sugar
4 tablespoons corn syrup
8 tablespoons water
2 cups butter
8 quarts popped popcorn

Combine all ingredients except popcorn in a large saucepan. Cook over medium heat, stirring occasionally, to soft-ball stage on a candy thermometer. Cool until the bubbles subside. Pour over popcorn. Cool and break up. Store in covered containers.

Eileen DeBeukelar, DePere, Wis.

PRETTY PARTY TARTS
Yield: 24

1/3 cup butter
1 cup confectioners' sugar, sifted
1 egg, well beaten
Dash salt
1/3 cup red raspberry jam
1-1/2 tablespoons lemon juice
1/3 cup blanched, chopped almonds
24 small baked party tarts

Cream butter; add confectioners' sugar, egg, salt, jam and lemon juice. Beat together until light and blended. Stir in almonds. Spoon into tart shells. Chill for 1-2 hours; serve.

Agnes Ward, Erie, Pa.

HARVEST MOON POPCORN
Makes about 2 1/2 quarts

1/3 cup melted butter
1 teaspoon dill weed
1 teaspoon Worcestershire sauce
1 teaspoon lemon pepper
1/2 teaspoon onion powder or onion salt
1/2 teaspoon garlic powder or garlic salt
1/4 teaspoon salt
2 quarts popped popcorn
2 cups canned shoestring potatoes

Combine all ingredients except popcorn and potatoes. Put popcorn and potatoes in a large bowl. Pour seasoned butter over all and toss well.

Spread mixture in a 15x10x1-inch pan. Bake in a preheated 350-degree oven for 8-10 minutes, stirring once.

Mary Kauphusman, Rochester, Minn.

SPICED NUTS

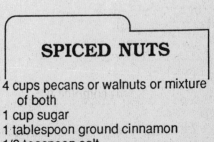

4 cups pecans or walnuts or mixture of both
1 cup sugar
1 tablespoon ground cinnamon
1/2 teaspoon salt
1 egg white
1 tablespoon water

Put nuts in large bowl; set aside. Mix sugar, cinnamon and salt in small bowl. In another bowl, beat egg white and water until almost stiff; add to nuts and stir until nuts are well coated. Add sugar mixture and stir. Grease cookie sheet. Pour nuts in pan; bake in 300 degree oven for 30 minutes, stirring after 15 minutes. When cool, separate nuts; store in tightly-covered container.

Patricia Habiger, Spearville, Kan.

PEANUT BUTTER PARTY MIX
Makes 4 cups

2 tablespoons butter
1/3 cup creamy peanut butter
2 cups Wheat Chex cereal
2 cups Rice Chex cereal
1/4 cup dry roasted peanuts

Melt butter and then add peanut butter; stir until well mixed. Toss cereal and nuts in mixture until coated. Remove from heat.

Spread on ungreased cookie sheet. Bake at 375 degrees for 8 minutes or until golden brown. Drain on paper towels. A very healthful snack!

Vickie Vogt, Kewaskum, Wis.

SUNSHINE SWEET POTATO BALLS

Makes 18-20 balls

1/4 cup butter, melted
1/4 cup milk
2 tablespoons sugar
1/2 teaspoon salt
1/4 teaspoon pepper
4 cups cooked, mashed sweet potatoes
18-20 miniature marshmallows
3 cups coarsely crushed cornflakes

Beat butter, milk, sugar, salt, and pepper into mashed sweet potatoes. Form 2-inch balls with a center of a marshmallow. Roll in cornflakes. Place in greased 9-1/2x12-3/4-inch baking pan. Bake in moderate oven of 375 degrees for 25-35 minutes. May be frozen first, then baked without defrosting for 45 minutes at 375 degrees.

Audrey L. Reynolds, Lumberport, W.V.

POTATO 'N BROCCOLI SUPREME

Serves 8

3 cups hot mashed potatoes (5-6 medium)
1 (3-ounce) package cream cheese, softened
1/4 cup milk
1 egg
2 tablespoons margarine
1 (2.8-ounce) can Durkee French fried onions
2 (10-ounce) packages frozen broccoli spears, cooked and drained
1 cup (4 ounces) shredded American cheese

Whip together first 5 ingredients until smooth. Season to taste with salt and pepper. Fold in 1/2 can onions. Spread potato mixture over bottom and sides of a buttered 8x12-inch baking dish; form a shell. Bake, uncovered, at 350 degrees for 20-25 minutes. Arrange hot broccoli in potato shell. Sprinkle with cheese and remaining onions. Bake, uncovered, 5-10 additional minutes.

Lonetta Natale, Madison, N.J.

BUBBLE AND SQUEAK (CABBAGE AND POTATOES)

3 cups unpeeled potatoes, boiled (approximately 3 large)
4 cups cabbage, chopped, par-boiled, and drained well
1 small onion, chopped
4 slices bacon, cut up and fried

With paring knife chop cooked, unpeeled potatoes. In large skillet, fry cut-up bacon; drain on paper towel. Add onion and sauté until golden brown; add chopped, cooked cabbage and chopped, cooked potatoes. Sprinkle bacon bits over top surface. Allow potatoes to become golden brown on bottom over medium heat, about 20 minutes or less. Invert skillet over large serving plate and serve. Garnish with parsley, if desired.

Donna Holter, West Middlesex, Pa.

SPINACH MASHED POTATOES

6-8 large potatoes
3/4 cup sour cream
1 teaspoon sugar
1 stick butter
2 teaspoons salt
1/4 teaspoon pepper
2 tablespoons chopped dried chives
1/4 teaspoon dill leaves
1 (10-ounce) package spinach (cooked)
1 cup shredded Cheddar cheese

Cook and mash potatoes; add sour cream, sugar, butter, salt, and pepper. Beat with mixer until light and fluffy. Add chives, dill, and drained spinach. Place in casserole and sprinkle with cheese. Bake at 400 degrees for 20 minutes. Delicious!!

Kristy Schemrich, Shreve, Ohio

CRUNCHY-TOP POTATOES

6 tablespoons butter or margarine
3 or 4 large potatoes
3/4 cup crushed cereal flakes (non-sweet)
1 cup shredded Cheddar cheese
1 teaspoon salt
1 teaspoon paprika

Place butter/margarine in casserole and put in oven that is pre-heated to 375 degrees. Peel potatoes and slice into 1/4 inch crosswise slices. Place slices in melted butter, coating well. Mix remaining ingredients; sprinkle over top of sliced potatoes. Bake 30 minutes, or until potatoes are done and tops are crisp

CREAMY CHIVE-STUFFED POTATOES

Serves 8

8 medium baking potatoes
Vegetable oil
1/2 cup butter or margarine, softened
1 (2-ounce) carton frozen chopped chives, thawed
2 tablespoons chopped onion
1 (16-ounce) carton commercial sour cream
1/2 teaspoon salt
1/4 teaspoon pepper
Paprika

Scrub potatoes thoroughly, and rub skins with oil; bake at 400 degrees for 1 hour or until done.

Allow potatoes to cool to touch. Slice skin away from top of each potato. Carefully scoop out pulp, leaving shells intact; mash pulp.

Combine potato pulp, butter, chives, onion, sour cream, salt, and pepper; mix well. Stuff shells with potato mixture; sprinkle with paprika. Wrap in heavy-duty aluminum foil; bake potatoes at 400 degrees for 10 minutes or until heated thoroughly.

Gloria Pedersen, Brandon, Miss.

PIZZA TURNOVERS
Makes 3 dozen

1/3 cup chopped mushrooms
1/4 cup chopped green pepper
1/4 cup chopped onion
2 tablespoons margarine
1 (6-ounce) can tomato paste
1/4 cup water
1 teaspoon oregano leaves
1/2 teaspoon salt
1/4 teaspoon garlic powder
1 cup shredded mozzarella cheese
Pastry for double-crust 9-inch pie

Saute mushrooms, green pepper, and onion in margarine. Stir in tomato paste, water, and seasonings; simmer 15 minutes. Stir in cheese. On lightly floured board, roll pastry to 1/8-inch thickness; cut into 3-1/2-inch rounds. Spoon 1 teaspoon mixture onto center of each round. Fold in half; press edges together with fork. Bake at 450 degrees, 10-15 minutes or until lightly browned.

Diantha Susan Hibbard, Rochester, N.Y.

PUMPKIN MUNCH

8 cups unsalted popped corn
1/2 cup butter
1 (3-ounce) package orange gelatin
1/4 cup light corn syrup
1/4 teaspoon soda

In 4-quart bowl place popped corn. Set aside. In a 1-quart bowl place butter and microwave on HIGH power, 30-60 seconds or until melted. Stir in gelatin and corn syrup. Microwave on HIGH, 2-3 minutes, or until mixture comes to a boil, stirring once. Mix in soda until well blended. Pour over popped corn. Toss to coat evenly. Microwave on HIGH, 4-5 minutes or until mixture is evenly coated, stirring 3-4 times. Turn onto waxed paper. Spread out and allow to cool. Break into small pieces. Store in covered container.

Donna Holter, West Middlesex, Pa.

GHOSTLY CRUNCH

8 cups unsalted popped corn
3 cups pretzel sticks
1 (6-ounce) package cheese-flavored goldfish crackers
4 cups toasted-oat cereal
1/3 cup butter
1/2 teaspoon onion salt
1/4 cup Parmesan cheese

In a 4-quart bowl combine popped corn, pretzels, crackers, and cereal. Set aside. In a 1-cup glass measure, place butter and microwave on HIGH power 45-60 seconds or until melted. Drizzle over popped corn mixture. Sprinkle with onion salt and cheese. Toss to coat. Microwave on HIGH power 3-4 minutes or until mixture is lightly toasted, stirring 2 or 3 times. Cool. Store in tightly covered container, or make *individual ghost* by placing 1/2 cup of mixture on a white paper napkin. Tie with yarn or string forming a head and allow the remainder of the paper to hang free for the body.

This could be used for Halloween, and is a great treat for the kids instead of candy.

Donna Holter, West Middlesex, Pa.

CHEWY DIPS

2/3 cup peanut butter
1/4 cup margarine
2 cups powdered sugar
1/2 teaspoon salt
1 cup chopped nuts
1 cup flaked coconut
12 maraschino cherries, chopped
3-1/2 tablespoons shaved paraffin wax
1 (12-ounce) package chocolate chips

Combine peanut butter, margarine, powdered sugar, salt, nuts, coconut, and cherries; shape mixture into 1-inch balls. Combine paraffin and chocolate chips in double boiler; stir over hot water until melted. Dip balls in chocolate mixture; place on wax paper to cool.

Sharon Crider, Evansville, Wis.

GORP
Makes 6 cups

3 cups fruit-and-nut granola cereal
3/4 cup unsalted peanuts, pecans, or walnuts
1/2 cup semisweet chocolate morsels
1/2 cup raisins
1 cup peanut butter pieces
1 cup toasted coconut

Combine all ingredients; store in airtight container.

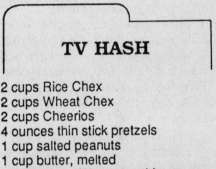

TV HASH

2 cups Rice Chex
2 cups Wheat Chex
2 cups Cheerios
4 ounces thin stick pretzels
1 cup salted peanuts
1 cup butter, melted
1 tablespoon Worcestershire sauce

Mix cereal, pretzels, and peanuts in large roasting pan. Combine butter and Worcestershire; pour over. Cover; bake in 225-degree oven for 1-1/2 hours.

Dorothy E. Snyder, Pine Grove, Pa.

CRACKLY CORN

4 quarts popped corn
1 cup brown sugar
1/2 cup butter
1/2 cup dark corn syrup
1/2 teaspoon salt
1/2 teaspoon vanilla

Put popped corn in large greased pan. Combine sugar, butter, corn syrup, salt, and vanilla. Cook over medium heat, stirring constantly, until mixture boils. Boil 5 minutes. Pour over corn. Stir to coat well. Bake at 250 degrees for 1 hour. Stir every 15 minutes while cooling. Store in tightly covered container.

Mrs. Jay Spyker, Dallastown, Pa.

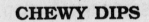

HAPPY PIES

1 cup sugar
2 1/2 cups flour
1 1/2 teaspoons baking soda
3/4 cup dry cocoa
1/2 teaspoon salt
1/2 cup shortening
1 cup milk
1 egg
1 1/2 teaspoons vanilla
Filling:
1 2/3 cups confectioners' sugar
3/4 cup (1 1/2 sticks) margarine
1/2 jar marshmallow creme

Sift together flour, sugars, baking soda, cocoa and salt into a bowl. Add shortening, milk and egg; beat. Add vanilla and mix. Drop by tablespoonsful onto greased cookie sheet. Bake in preheated 425-degree oven for 8 minutes.

Remove and cool.

Combine filling ingredients, beating until smooth. Fill between two cookies, sandwich style.

Lois Smith, Grants Pass, Ore.

GREEN TUNA DIP
Makes 8-10 appetizer servings

2 cans (6 1/2 to 7 ounces each) tuna in oil
8-ounce package farmer cheese, divided
1 cup milk, divided
2 cups fresh parsley, divided
1/4 teaspoon hot pepper sauce
1 teaspoon salt
1/4 cup chopped, dry-roasted mixed nuts
Raw vegetables for dip

Drain tuna and flake with fork. Combine half the farmer cheese with half the milk and 1 cup parsley in blender. Cover and process at high speed until smooth (or beat on high speed of mixer). Add tuna. Repeat process with remaining cheese, milk and parsley. Add to tuna mixture in bowl. Stir in pepper sauce, salt and nuts. Chill. Serve with raw vegetables.

Mrs. Agnes Ward, Erie, Penn.

CRAB DIP

2/3 cup margarine
1 large package (8 ounces) cream cheese, softened
1 pound crabmeat (or 1 can)
Hot pepper sauce and Worcestershire sauce to taste

Melt margarine and cheese together in top of double boiler over boiling water. Cook raw crabmeat and shred finely. Fold into cheese mixture. Season to taste. Serve warm dip with crackers and raw vegetables.

Marjorie W. Baxla, Greenfield, Ohio

COFFEE COCKTAIL DIP
Makes 1 cup

1 cup sour cream
1 tablespoon brewed cold coffee
1 tablespoon catsup
1 tablespoon spicy mustard

Combine all ingredients. Blend and chill. Sprinkle with paprika. Serve with raw vegetables and cold shrimp.

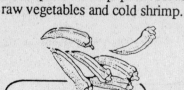

SHOCKING PINK PINTO BEAN DIP
Makes 4-6 servings

1 1/2 cups pinto beans, cooked and mashed
1 large package (8 ounces) cream cheese
6 cooked baby beets, mashed (or a jar of "baby food" beets)
1 tablespoon vinegar
2 tablespoons lemon juice
1/4 teaspoon celery salt
1/2 teaspoon salt
1 small onion, grated
Dash of hot pepper sauce
Horseradish to taste

Blend all ingredients until smooth. Store in refrigerator. Serve with chips and crackers.

Miss M.J. Witham, Fort Wayne, Ind.

TUNA SENSATION

7-ounce can tuna, drained and flaked
1 large package (8 ounces) cream cheese, softened
1/2 cup thick sour cream
1 tablespoon horseradish
1 teaspoon Worcestershire sauce
2 tablespoons minced garlic
1 clove garlic, minced
1 teaspoon crushed chervil
1/2 teaspoon salt
Dash of pepper
1/4 teaspoon Accent®

Blend cream cheese until very soft; add sour cream, horseradish, and Worcestershire sauce; beat until mixture is smooth. Blend in flaked tuna and seasonings. Cover and refrigerate several hours. Remove from refrigerator 30 minutes before serving to soften for dipping.

Mrs. Beverly Brannon, Vidor, Texas

TASTY GUACAMOLE DIP
Makes about 2 cups

2 small avocados, peeled and mashed
1 tablespoon lemon juice
1 medium onion, minced
1 small clove garlic, crushed
1 large tomato, peeled, and finely chopped
1/2 teaspoon salt
1/2 teaspoon seasoned salt
1/2 teaspoon pepper
1/2 teaspoon chili powder

Combine all ingredients; mix well. Cover. Refrigerate several hours.

DILL DIP
Makes 3 cups dip

2 cups sour cream
1 cup mayonnaise
2 heaping tablespoons dill weed
2 tablespoons dehydrated onion
2 teaspoons lemon juice

Mix all ingredients together, combining until smooth. Refrigerate.

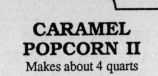

CARAMEL POPCORN II

Makes about 4 quarts

4 quarts freshly popped popcorn
Peanuts (optional)
1 cup firmly packed brown sugar
1/2 cup margarine (1 stick)
1/2 cup corn syrup (light or dark)
1/2 teaspoon salt
1/2 teaspoon vanilla
1/2 teaspoon baking soda

Spread popcorn in large buttered roasting pan.

In heavy saucepan, stir together sugar, syrup, margarine and salt. Cook, stirring constantly, until mixture boils. Continue cooking, without stirring, for 5 more minutes. Remove from heat; stir in vanilla and baking soda. Pour syrup over popcorn, and stir to coat well.

Bake in a preheated 250-degree oven, uncovered, for 1 hour, stirring occasionally.

This recipe can be doubled; it stores well.

Fay Duman, Eugene, Ore.

BEEFY POPCORN

Makes about 3 quarts

1 jar (2 1/2 ounces) dried beef, finely chopped
1/2 cup butter (1 stick)
3 quarts unsalted popped popcorn

Cook dried beef in butter for about 3 minutes. If popcorn is not fresh, heat it in a 250-degree oven. Pour beef and butter over popcorn and toss to mix.

Serve immediately while still hot.

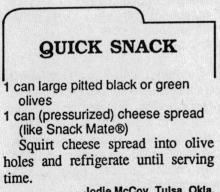

QUICK SNACK

1 can large pitted black or green olives
1 can (pressurized) cheese spread (like Snack Mate®)

Squirt cheese spread into olive holes and refrigerate until serving time.

Jodie McCoy, Tulsa, Okla.

MOST CEREAL SNACK

Makes about 4 cups

1/3 cup margarine, melted
1/2 teaspoon garlic salt
2 teaspoons Worcestershire sauce
2 1/2 cups Kellogg's Most® cereal
1 cup thin pretzel sticks
1/2 cup salted peanuts

Combine melted margarine, garlic salt and Worcestershire sauce in a 13x9-inch pan. Stir in cereal, pretzel sticks and peanuts, stirring gently but thoroughly to coat all pieces. Bake in a 250-degree oven for 40-45 minutes, stirring occasionally. Cool and store in an airtight container.

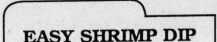

PINK POPCORN BALLS

Makes 10 medium popcorn balls

7 cups popped corn
3 cups miniature marshmallows
2 tablespoons butter
1/4 teaspoon salt
Few drops of red food coloring

Place popped corn in large buttered bowl. In bottom of double boiler, heat about 1 inch of water to boiling. Combine butter, marshmallows and salt in top of double boiler, over hot water. Stir until melted together. Stir in food coloring to desired shade. Pour over popcorn; stir gently to coat.

Grease hands with butter and quickly shape popcorn into 10 medium-size balls.

Mrs. Sharon Crider, Evansville, Wis.

EASY SHRIMP DIP

1 can cream of shrimp soup (frozen)
1 small package (3 ounces) cream cheese, softened
1 teaspoon lemon juice
Dash of garlic powder
Dash of paprika

Thaw frozen soup. Gradually blend soup with other ingredients. Beat until smooth. Chill.

Lois L. Smith, Grants Pass, Ore.

SPICY PUMPKIN SEEDS

Makes 2 cups

1/4 cup oil
1 teaspoon Worcestershire sauce
1/2 teaspoon paprika
1/4 teaspoon cumin
1/4 teaspoon cayenne pepper
2 dashes hot pepper sauce
2 cups hulled pumpkin seeds

Preheat oven to 300 degrees.

Combine all ingredients except seeds in a large skillet. Heat mixture well, stirring to mix. Add seeds and stir to coat well. Spread in a shallow pan and bake at 300 degrees for 10 minutes, or until crisp. Stir occasionally during the baking. Cool.

SAVORY PECANS

Makes 2 cups

2 cups pecan halves
1 tablespoon salad oil
1 tablespoon Worcestershire sauce

Combine oil and Worcestershire sauce. Place pecans in a shallow baking dish and cover with the oil mixture, stirring to coat well. Bake in a slow oven (250 degrees) for about 30 minutes, stirring once or twice. Sprinkle lightly with salt.

Store in tightly covered container.

Marjorie W. Baxla, Greenfield, Ohio

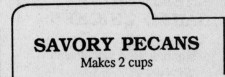

CHIVE CHEESE BALLS

Makes 30 pieces

1 small package (3 ounces) chive-flavored cream cheese
1 package (10-count) refrigerated biscuits

Divide cream cheese into 30 equal pieces. Separate biscuits and cut each into thirds. Wrap a cube of cheese inside each piece of dough, forming a small ball.

Place on lightly greased cookie sheets and bake in a preheated 350-degree oven until lightly browned.

Mrs. M. Piccinni, Ozone Park, N.Y.

BACON-CHILI DIP

4 strips bacon, fried crisp, drained
   and crumbled
1 large package (8 ounces) cream
   cheese, softened
1 cup sour cream
4-ounce can diced green chilies
1/4 teaspoon garlic salt

Beat cheese and sour cream together until smooth and fluffy. Fold in chilies and garlic salt, then bacon. Chill. Serve with crackers, vegetable sticks, or chips.

Jean Baker, Chula Vista, Calif.

HERB-BATTER BAKED CHICKEN

⅔ cup prepared ranch salad
   dressing
1 egg, lightly beaten
1 (3-pound) broiler-fryer
   chicken, cut up
½ cup flour
2 cups cornflake crumbs

Combine salad dressing and egg; set aside. Rinse chicken; pat dry with paper towels. Roll chicken pieces in flour; dip into dressing mixture. Roll in cornflake crumbs. Place chicken on large foil-lined baking pan. Bake at 350 degrees for 50–60 minutes, until tender.

SHRIMP DIP

large package (8 ounces) cream
   cheese, softened
2 tins baby shrimp, drained
3 tablespoons mayonnaise
Salt and pepper
1/4 pound (1 stick) butter, softened
1/8 teaspoon garlic powder
1 tablespoon lemon juice

Beat together lemon juice, cream cheese, mayonnaise, butter and seasonings until smooth. Fold in drained shrimp. Serve with raw vegetables, chips or melba toast.

Mrs. Nan Bomak, Edmonton, Alberta

GRANOLA SNACK

1/2 cup peanut butter (smooth or
   crunchy)
1/4 cup honey
1/4 cup vegetable oil
2 tablespoons firmly packed brown
   sugar
1 package (9 ounces) None-Such
   Condensed Mincemeat®
2 cups quick-cooking oats
1 cup dry-roasted peanuts

Preheat oven to 250 degrees. In a large saucepan, combine peanut butter, honey, oil and sugar; blend well. Break mincemeat into small pieces and add to peanut butter mixture. Boil briskly, stirring constantly, for 1 minute. Remove from heat. Add oats and peanuts and stir well.

Spoon into a 13x9-inch pan. Bake at 250 degrees for 45 minutes, stirring every 15 minutes. Cool; break into chunks. Store in a tightly covered container.

To re-crisp the snack, place desired amount on a cookie sheet and heat at 250 degrees for 10 minutes. Cool.

Agnes Ward, Erie, Penn.

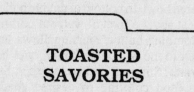

TOASTED SAVORIES

2 egg whites
2 cups unsalted pecans
1 teaspoon salt
1 teaspoon dry mustard
1 teaspoon garlic powder

Cover cookie sheet with foil; grease and set aside.

Beat egg whites until foamy. Drop pecans into egg whites and stir to coat well. Lift with fork or slotted spoon to drain; place on greased foil.

Mix salt, dry mustard and garlic powder. Pour into empty salt shaker. Sprinkle over nuts.

Bake in a 250-degree oven for 25 minutes, or until coating is set. Lift foil to loosen nuts and break them apart. Cool. Store in airtight container or freeze. Keep for 1 week or freeze for no more than 2 weeks.

MICROWAVE CARAMEL CORN

Makes about 4 quarts

1 cup brown sugar
1/4 pound soft margarine
1/4 cup light corn syrup
1/2 teaspoon salt
4 quarts plain popped popcorn (no
   salt or butter added)
1/2 teaspoon baking soda

Combine sugar, margarine, corn syrup and salt in a microwave pan and bring mixture to boil in a microwave oven set on "High." Boil for 3 minutes. Remove from oven and stir in baking soda, mixing well. Pour over popcorn. Mix to coat well.

Pour caramel corn into a large brown grocery bag. Fold the top of the bag down loosely until it will fit in the microwave oven. Cook on the highest setting for 3 minutes; shake sack well every minute during cooking.

Cool the caramel corn on waxed paper. Store in a 5-quart plastic ice-cream pail or in other suitable containers.

J. Kopperud, Forest City, Iowa

PARTY POTATO SALAD

Serves 12-14

1 (2-pound) bag frozen hash-brown
   potatoes
1 can cream of potato soup
1 can cream of celery soup
1/2 cup sour cream
1 cup shredded cheddar cheese
1 (8-ounce) package cream cheese
1/2 green pepper, finely chopped
1/2 cup chopped onion
2 teaspoons salt
1/4 teaspoon pepper
1 teaspoon paprika

Combine soups with softened cream cheese. Add sour cream, green pepper, onion, and seasonings. Put potatoes in a 3-quart shallow baking dish. Pour soup mixture over potatoes and stir. Spread out evenly; sprinkle with cheddar cheese. Bake at 325 degrees for 1-1/2 hours.

Laura Braun, Fond du Lac, Wis.

Pies
FESTIVE

PRINCESS ANN TART

Serves 6–8

Crust:

½ cup flour
1 teaspoon baking powder
2 tablespoons sugar
6 tablespoons butter
2 tablespoons cold water
1 (8-ounce) jar raspberry jam

Combine flour, baking powder and sugar. Work in butter until mixture resembles cornmeal. Add water; stir into stiff dough. Roll out dough on floured surface. Place in a 9-inch pie pan. Spread jam on bottom crust.

Custard:

2 egg yolks
1 cup milk
1 tablespoon sugar
1 teaspoon flour
1 teaspoon vanilla

Combine all ingredients; Beat well; pour over jam in crust. Bake at 350 degrees for 30 minutes.

Meringue:

2 egg whites
4 tablespoons sugar
¼ teaspoon cream of tartar

Beat egg whites and cream of tartar until soft peaks form, adding sugar gradually. Beat until stiff peaks form. Pour over cooked and cooled filling. Bake at 375 degrees until browned.

June Harding, Ferndale, Mich.

PECAN PIE

1 (9-inch) unbaked pie crust
1 cup light corn syrup
1 cup dark brown sugar, packed
3 eggs, slightly beaten
⅓ cup butter, melted
Pinch salt
1 teaspoon vanilla
1 cup chopped *or* halved pecans

Preheat oven to 350 degrees. In large bowl, combine corn syrup, sugar, eggs, butter, salt and vanilla. Mix well. Pour filling into prepared pie crust. Sprinkle with pecans. Bake 45–50 minutes, or until center is set. Toothpick inserted in center will come out clean when pie is done. Cool. Top with whipped cream or ice cream, if desired.

Lynn D. Jones, Gatesville, Texas

HOT FUDGE PIE

1/4 cup cocoa
1/4 cup butter
1 1/4 cups sugar
1/4 cup flour
3 eggs, beaten

Melt butter; add to mixture of dry ingredients. Add eggs, one at a time, mixing well after each addition. Pour into an ungreased 9-inch pie pan. Bake at 300 degrees for 30–40 minutes. Serve warm with ice cream.

Sue Thomas, Casa Grande, Ariz.

EASY COCONUT PIES

1-1/2 cups sugar
3 tablespoons flour
1 stick butter, melted
3 eggs
2 cups milk
2 teaspoons vanilla
1 can shredded coconut
2 unbaked pie shells

In large bowl combine sugar and flour. Add remaining ingredients and stir well. Pour into pie shells and bake at 450 degrees for 10 minutes. Reduce oven temperature to 325 degrees and bake for an additional 25 minutes. Let cool before slicing.

Brenda Peery, Tannersville, Va.

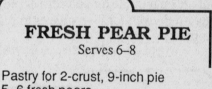

FRESH PEAR PIE

Serves 6–8

Pastry for 2-crust, 9-inch pie
5–6 fresh pears
1/2 cup sugar
2 tablespoons quick-cooking tapioca
1/4 teaspoon cinnamon
1/4 teaspoon ginger
1/4 teaspoon nutmeg
1/8 teaspoon salt
1 tablespoon lemon juice

Line 9-inch pie pan with pastry. Pare, quarter and core pears. Arrange slices in pie shell. In small bowl combine sugar, tapioca, cinnamon, ginger, nutmeg and salt; pour over pear slices; sprinkle with lemon juice. Cover with top crust; seal edges; flute. Bake 40 minutes at 425 degrees.

Leota Baxter, Ingalls, Kan.

APPLE MINCEMEAT PIE
Serves 6–8

1 cup flour
¼ teaspoon salt
3 tablespoons butter
2 tablespoons shortening
3–4 tablespoons milk
4 cups cooking apples, peeled and sliced
2 tablespoons flour
2 cups prepared mincemeat
1 cup dairy sour cream
2 tablespoons confectioners' sugar
1 tablespoon grated orange peel

Combine 1 cup flour and salt. Cut in butter and shortening until mixture resembles small peas. Sprinkle milk over flour mixture, 1 tablespoon at a time, mixing lightly with a fork after each addition. Shape into a ball. On lightly floured surface, flatten dough slightly; roll ⅛ inch thick into a circle, 1 inch larger than diameter of a 9-inch pie plate. Fold under and flute edge. Combine apples and 2 tablespoons flour; turn into crust. Top with mincemeat. Bake at 400 degrees for 35–40 minutes. Blend together sour cream, sugar and orange peel. Place dollops of cream mixture around edge of pie; return to oven for 3–4 minutes to set topping.

Sharon Crider, Stoughton, Wis.

COCONUT DREAM PIE

1/2 gallon vanilla ice cream, softened
1-1/2 cups milk
1 package instant coconut pudding
1 prepared butter-flavored pie crust
Whipped cream (optional)

In a large mixing bowl, combine ice cream, milk, and pudding. Blend well. Pour mixture into pie crust and freeze overnight. Before serving, spoon on whipped cream in desired amounts. Enjoy!

CREAM CHEESE RHUBARB PIE
Serves 8

4 cups rhubarb, cut in 1-inch pieces
1 cup sugar
3 tablespoons cornstarch
1/4 teaspoon salt
1 (9-inch) unbaked pie crust
1 (8-ounce) package cream cheese
2 eggs
1 cup sour cream
1/2 cup sugar
Almonds for garnish

Preheat oven to 425 degrees. In saucepan over medium heat, cook rhubarb, 1 cup sugar, cornstarch, and salt, stirring often, until mixture boils and thickens. Pour into pie crust. Bake 10 minutes; remove from oven.

Meanwhile, in small bowl, with mixer at medium speed, beat cream cheese, eggs, and 1/2 cup sugar until smooth; pour over rhubarb mixture. Turn oven control to 350 degrees. Bake pie 30-35 minutes until set; cool on wire rack; chill.

To serve:

Spread sour cream on top of pie. Garnish with almonds. Just simply delicious!!

Mrs. George Franks, Millerton, Pa.

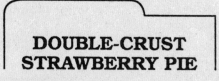

DOUBLE-CRUST STRAWBERRY PIE

1 cup sugar
1 tablespoon cornstarch
1/8 teaspoon salt
3 cups fresh strawberries
1 tablespoon margarine
Crust for 2-crust (9-inch) pie

Mix sugar, cornstarch and salt together; add to the berries and mix gently. Pour into unbaked bottom crust and dot with margarine. Cover with top crust and cut slits in crust for steam to escape. Bake at 400 degrees for 10 minutes; reduce oven to 325 degrees and bake 30 minutes longer.

Jodie McCoy, Tulsa, Okla.

PEANUT BUTTER CREAM CHEESE PIE

2 (3-ounce) packages cream cheese, softened
¾ cup sifted confectioners' sugar
½ cup peanut butter
2 tablespoons milk
1 (9-ounce) carton Cool Whip
1 (8-inch) pie shell, baked Coarsely chopped roasted peanuts

In a small mixer bowl beat cream cheese and sugar together until light and fluffy. Add peanut butter and milk, beating until smooth and creamy. Fold topping gently into peanut butter mixture. Turn into prepared shell and chill 5–6 hours. Garnish with coarsely chopped peanuts.

Shari Crider, Stoughton, Wis.

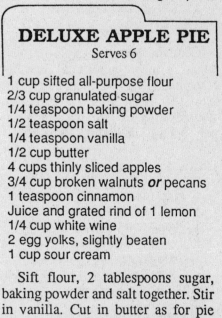

DELUXE APPLE PIE
Serves 6

1 cup sifted all-purpose flour
2/3 cup granulated sugar
1/4 teaspoon baking powder
1/2 teaspoon salt
1/4 teaspoon vanilla
1/2 cup butter
4 cups thinly sliced apples
3/4 cup broken walnuts *or* pecans
1 teaspoon cinnamon
Juice and grated rind of 1 lemon
1/4 cup white wine
2 egg yolks, slightly beaten
1 cup sour cream

Sift flour, 2 tablespoons sugar, baking powder and salt together. Stir in vanilla. Cut in butter as for pie crust. Press mixture in bottom and halfway up sides of a deep-dish (9-inch) pie pan. Combine apples, nuts, 1/2 cup sugar, cinnamon, lemon juice, rind and wine. Pile mixture in prepared crust. Bake at 425 degrees for 10 minutes. Combine egg yolks, remaining sugar and sour cream. Pour over apple mixture. Bake at 350 degrees for 35 minutes. Serve warm or cold.

Trenda Leigh, Richmond, Va.

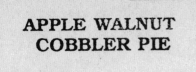

APPLE WALNUT COBBLER PIE

1/2 cup sugar
1/2 teaspoon cinnamon
3/4 cup coarsely chopped walnuts, divided
4 cups thinly sliced, pared apples
1 cup sifted flour
1 cup sugar
1 teaspoon baking powder
1/4 teaspoon salt
1 beaten egg
1/2 cup evaporated milk
1/3 cup butter or margarine, melted

Mix 1/2 cup sugar, cinnamon, and 1/2 cup walnuts. Place apples in bottom of a greased 8-1/4x1-3/4-inch round ovenware cake dish. Sprinkle with cinnamon mixture. Sift together dry ingredients. Combine egg, milk, and butter, add dry ingredients all at once. Mix until smooth. Pour over apples; sprinkle with remaining walnuts. Bake in a slow oven at 325 degrees for about 50 minutes. Cut in wedges; serve with whipped cream or Cool Whip.

Sarah Burkett, Centralia, Ill.

PEANUT TOFFEE PIE WITH OATMEAL CRUST

Crust:
1 cup flour
2 cups quick rolled oats
1/2 cup shortening
1/2 cup cold water
1 teaspoon cinnamon

Combine dry ingredients with shortening, cutting into mixture. Add cold water slowly. Roll out and bake in pie pan for 12 minutes at 450 degrees. Remember to put dry beans in bottom so it will keep it shape.

Filling:
1-1/2 cups brown sugar
3 tablespoons flour
1-1/2 cups milk
2 egg yolks
4 tablespoons peanut butter

1/2 teaspoon vanilla extract
Whipped cream
Nut toffee or Heath bits

Mix sugar and flour in double boiler; add milk slowly. Cook until thickened. Add egg yolks and cook 3 minutes longer. Remove from heat; add peanut butter and flavoring. When cool, pour into baked crust and cover with whipped cream and shaved nut toffee or Heath bits.

PERFECTLY RICH CUSTARD PIE

10 eggs, beaten
1 cup sugar
1/2 teaspoon nutmeg
1 teaspoon vanilla
1 quart scalded milk
1 tablespoon butter

Scald milk and butter. Let cool and then add to egg mixture composed of eggs, sugar, nutmeg and vanilla. Pour mixture into pie crust-lined (deep-dish) 9-inch pie plate. Place in a 450-degree preheated oven. Bake 20 minutes only. Turn heat completely off. Let pie stand in oven for 1 hour.

Lynn Sylvester, Lewiston, Maine

PUMPKIN PECAN PIE
Serves 6-8

4 slightly-beaten eggs
2 cups canned pumpkin
1 cup sugar
1/2 cup dark corn syrup
1 teaspoon vanilla
1/2 teaspoon cinnamon
1/4 teaspoon salt
1 unbaked 9-inch pie shell
1 cup chopped pecans

Preheat oven to 350 degrees. Combine first seven ingredients. Pour into pie shell. Top with pecans. Bake 40 minutes or until set. Cool in pan on wire rack. Serve with whipped cream or ice cream.

Mrs. H. W. Walker, Richmond, Va.

OATMEAL PIE

1/4 cup butter
1/2 cup sugar
1 teaspoon cinnamon
1/4 teaspoon salt
3/4 cup dark corn syrup
1/4 cup honey
3 eggs
1 cup quick oats
1 9-inch unbaked pie shell

Cream sugar and butter. Beat in cinnamon and salt. Add syrup and honey, then eggs, one at a time. Beat until well-blended. Stir in oats. Pour in shell and bake at 350 degrees for about an hour, or until center tests done. During baking, the oatmeal rises and forms a chewy, nutty crust on top of pie.

Helen Weissinger, Levittown, Pa.

STRAWBERRY-BANANA PIE

Crust:
2-1/2 cups graham cracker crumbs
1/2 cup sugar
1-1/2 sticks butter, melted

Filling:
1 (8-ounce) package cream cheese
3/4 cup confectioners' sugar
2 cups chopped walnuts
2 medium-size bananas, sliced
1 quart strawberries, sliced
1 (8-ounce) container Cool Whip

Crust: Mix crumbs, sugar, and butter together and press into 2 deep-dish, 9-inch pie pans. Bake at 325 degrees for 10 minutes.

Filling: Use beater and mix cream cheese and confectioners' sugar together. Divide between the 2 crusts evenly and spread along bottom. Sprinkle on top of the cream chees a layer of chopped walnuts. Next layer sliced bananas and then a layer of sliced strawberries.

Divide Cool Whip and spread evenly over the pies. Top with another layer of walnuts.

June Harding, Ferndale, Mich.

SOUR CREAM APPLE PIE

1 cup sour cream
1 cup sugar
1/2 cup flour
1 egg
2 teaspoons vanilla
8 Granny Smith apples, peeled, cored, and sliced
1 deep-dish pie shell

Topping:

1-1/2 cups walnut pieces
1/2 cup granulated sugar
3/4 cup flour
1 tablespoon cinnamon
1/2 cup brown sugar
1/2 cup butter pieces, chopped

Blend all ingredients, except apples, until smooth. Add apples and pour into pie shell. Bake for 45 minutes at 400 degrees or until apples are tender. Mix together all the topping ingredients. Evenly sprinkle the pie with topping and bake pie 15 minutes longer.

This is a very delicious version of apple pie.

June Harding, Ferndale, Mich.

CREAM CHEESE-PECAN PIE

Serves 8

10-inch unbaked pie-shell
1 egg
1 (8-ounce) package cream cheese, softened
1/3 cup sugar

1 teaspoon vanilla
1-1/4 cups coarsely chopped pecans
3 eggs
1 cup light corn syrup
1/4 teaspoon salt
1 teaspoon vanilla

Beat together cream cheese, sugar, 1 egg, and 1 teaspoon vanilla until smooth; spread over bottom of pie shell. Sprinkle pecans over cheese mixture. Combine 3 eggs, corn syrup, salt, and 1 teaspoon vanilla; pour over pecans. Bake at 375 degrees for 40 minutes. Cool.

Lisa Varner, Baton Rouge, La.

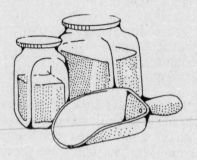

GRAPE JUICE PIE

1 (9-inch) pie shell, baked
3/4 cup sugar
1/2 cup cornstarch
1 1/3 cups grape juice
1 egg, beaten
2 tablespoons butter *or* margarine
2 tablespoons lemon juice

Combine sugar and cornstarch; stir in grape juice. Cook over medium heat, stirring until bubbly and thickened; cool 1 minute. Pour small amount of hot mixture into beaten egg, mixing well. Add rest of mixture, stirring constantly. Add butter and lemon juice; return to heat and boil 1 minute, stirring all the time. Pour into the baked shell. Cool. Serve with whipped cream or Cool Whip.

Marjorie W. Baxla, Greenfield, Ohio

FRESH PEACH PIE

5 cups fresh peaches, sliced
1 unbaked 9-inch pastry shell
1/3 cup butter or margarine, melted
1 cup sugar
1/3 cup all-purpose flour
1 egg
1/2 teaspoon cinnamon

Place peaches in pastry shell. Combine remaining ingredients; pour over peaches. Bake at 350 degrees for 1 hour and 10 minutes.

Sarah M. Burkett, Centralia, Ill.

COMPANY PIE

1 (9-inch) pie shell
1/2 cup seedless raisins
1/2 cup chopped walnuts or pecans
1 teaspoon vinegar
1/2 cup butter or margarine
1/4 cup sugar
2 eggs
1/2 teaspoon cinnamon
1/2 teaspoon nutmeg
1/4 teaspoon salt

Bake in a 9-inch pastry shell. Mix raisins, nuts, and vinegar; let stand. Combine butter, sugar, and eggs; beat until thick. Beat in spices and salt. Stir in raisin mixture. Bake at 400 degrees for 30-35 minutes.
Note: Butter bubbles up through the crust, making it flaky and light.

Karin Shea Fedders, Dameron, Md.

CHOCOLATE CREAM PIE

Serves 6

1 (9-inch) baked pie shell
2-2/3 cups milk
3 eggs, separated
3 squares chocolate, cut in quarters
3/4 cup sugar
1/4 cup cornstarch
1/4 teaspoon salt
1 tablespoon butter or margarine
1 teaspoon vanilla extract

Meringue:
3 egg whites
6 tablespoons sugar
Whipping cream, if desired

Combine 1-2/3 cups of the milk, egg yolks, chocolate, 3/4 cup sugar, cornstarch, salt, and butter or margarine in blender. Cover and blend at high speed for 15-20 seconds. Turn into saucepan. (I use a double boiler.) Add remaining milk and cook over moderate heat until thickened, stirring constantly. Remove from heat and add vanilla extract. Cool slightly. Pour into baked pie shell. Top with meringue made from egg whites and 6 tablespoons sugar. Bake at 325 degrees for 12-15 minutes, until lightly browned. Instead of meringue, you may cover the thoroughly cooled pie with sweetened whipped cream.

Meringue: Whip egg whites until very, very stiff. Add sugar and beat.
Virginia Essig, Bridgman, Mich.

PINEAPPLE PIE

1 (20-ounce) can crushed pineapple, not drained
1 box instant vanilla pudding
1/2 pint sour cream
1 (8-ounce) container Cool Whip

Put pineapple and vanilla pudding mix in bowl and stir. Add sour cream and fold in Cool Whip. Pour into 2 (8-inch) baked pie shells. Refrigerate and chill 3 hours. Delicious and easy!!
Marie Wyszynski, Timberlake, Ohio

CRANBERRY WALNUT PIE

3 eggs
1 cup Karo light corn syrup
2/3 cup sugar
2 tablespoons margarine, melted
1/8 teaspoon salt
1 cup cranberries, chopped
3/4 cup coarsely chopped walnuts
1 tablespoon grated orange rind
1 unbaked (9-inch) pie shell

In medium bowl beat eggs slightly. Stir in next 4 ingredients. Gently stir in cranberries, nuts and rind. Pour into pastry shell. Bake in 350-degree oven for 1 hour, or until knife inserted halfway between center and edge comes out clean. Cool.

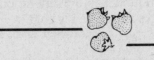

CHILLED FRUIT COCKTAIL PIE

1 baked 9-inch pie shell
1 envelope unflavored gelatin
1/2 cup cold water
3 eggs, separated
1/8 teaspoon salt
1 (6-ounce) can frozen lemonade concentrate
1/2 cup sugar
1 (1-pound) can fruit cocktail, drained

In a double boiler soften gelatin in water; add slightly beaten egg yolks and salt; cook, stirring constantly, until mixture thickens. Remove from heat; stir in frozen lemonade concentrate; stir again until mixture thickens. Beat egg whites to soft-peak stage; add sugar slowly; beat until stiff peaks form. Fold into gelatin mixture; add drained fruit, reserving a small amount to place on individual servings. Chill at least 2 hours in refrigerator.
Gwen Campbell, Sterling, Va.

LIMEADE PIE WITH CHOCOLATE CRUST

1 (6-ounce) can limeade frozen concentrate
1 pint vanilla ice cream, softened
4 cups thawed whipped topping
Green food coloring
1 chocolate cookie crust

Place concentrate in large mixing bowl and beat about 30 seconds. Gradually spoon in ice cream and blend. Fold in whipped topping and 5 drops of food coloring, whipping until smooth. Freeze until mixture will mound. Then spoon into pie crust. Freeze until firm, at least 3-4 hours, and store leftovers in freezer. Can decorate with crumbled cookies or cookie halves, if desired. A lovely, refreshing summer dessert!!
Kathy Thompson, Midland, Ark.

CHOCOLATE SHOO-FLY PIE

9-inch unbaked pie shell
1/4 teaspoon soda
1 1/3 cups boiling water
1 1/2 cups (1-pound can) chocolate-flavored syrup
1 teaspoon vanilla
1 1/3 cups flour
1/2 cup sugar

1/4 teaspoon soda
1/4 teaspoon salt
1/3 cup butter or margarine
Cinnamon

Dissolve 1/4 teaspoon soda in boiling water; stir in chocolate syrup and vanilla; set aside. Combine flour, sugar, 1/4 teaspoon soda and salt; cut in butter to form coarse crumbs. Set aside 1 cup *each* of chocolate mixture and crumbs; gently combine remaining chocolate and crumbs, stirring just until crumbs are moistened. Pour reserved 1 cup chocolate mixture into pie shell. Pour chocolate-crumb mixture evenly over liquid in pie shell. Top with remaining 1 cup crumbs. Sprinkle with cinnamon.
Lisa Varner, Baton Rouge, La.

FLUFFY FROZEN PEANUT BUTTER PIE

Crust:
3/4 cup peanut butter chips, chopped
1 cup vanilla wafer crumbs
5 tablespoons water

Filling:
1-1/4 cups peanut butter chips
3 ounces cream cheese, softened
1/2 cup milk
1/2 cup powdered sugar
2 cups frozen non-dairy whipped topping

To make crust, chop peanut butter chips in blender or food processor, or with nut chopper. In 9-inch pie pan, combine chips and crumbs. Drizzle with melted butter; mix well. Press onto bottom and up sides of pie pan; freeze.

For filling, in top of double boiler over hot water, melt peanut butter chips; cool slightly. Beat cream cheese until smooth; gradually add milk, blending well. Beat in sugar and melted peanut butter chips until smooth; fold in whipped topping.

Spoon into prepared crust. Cover and freeze until firm. Chocolate curls may be used for decoration on pie.

Julie Habiger, Spearville, Kan.

CHOCOLATE CREAM PIE

1/2 cup white sugar
1/2 teaspoon salt
1 tablespoon flour
3 tablespoons cornstarch
3 cups milk
3 squares chocolate
3 egg yolks
1 teaspoon vanilla
1 tablespoon butter or margarine

Combine ingredients in saucepan and boil over medium heat until thick. Pour into baked pie shell. Cool and serve with whipped topping.

Pat Linie, Haure, Mont.

ICE-CREAM PIE
Serves 10

1   (9-inch) gingersnap *or* cookie crust
1½   cups canned pumpkin
½   cup granulated sugar
½   teaspoon cinnamon
¼   teaspoon nutmeg
¼   teaspoon salt
⅛   teaspoon ginger
⅛   teaspoon allspice
1   quart vanilla ice cream, softened
½   cup chopped pecans

In large bowl, combine pumpkin, sugar, cinnamon, nutmeg, salt, ginger and allspice; mix well. Fold pumpkin mixture into softened ice cream; stir in pecans, and spoon into *chilled* pie shell. Sprinkle with additional crumbs of crust mixture. Freeze, uncovered, for 30 minutes, or until set. Cover with plastic wrap or foil; keep frozen until ready to serve. Remove from freezer 10 minutes before serving; cut into wedges and serve icy cold.

Agnes Ward, Erie, Pa.

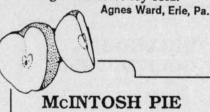

McINTOSH PIE

6 cups McIntosh apples, sliced
5/8 cup white sugar
1/4 cup golden seedless raisins
1 teaspoon cinnamon
1 package (3-1/4 ounce) dry tapioca pudding mix (not instant)
1 tablespoon butter
Crust for two-crust pie, deep dish

Prepare crust for two-crust pie, deep dish. Place apples in layer at bottom of pie crust. Mix together sugar, cinnamon and pudding powder. Toss with raisins, sprinkle half over apples. Place another layer of apples and cover with mix. Dot with butter. Place top crust on pie and bake at 400 degrees for about 15 minutes. Reduce heat to 350 degrees and finish baking 25 minutes.

Pearle Goodwin, South Ryegate, Vt.

MYSTERY PECAN PIE

1 (8-ounce) package cream cheese
1/3 cup sugar
1/4 teaspoon salt
2 teaspoons vanilla, divided
4 eggs
1 (10-inch) pie shell, unbaked
1-1/4 cups chopped pecans
1 cup light corn syrup
1/4 cup sugar

Preheat oven to 375 degrees. Combine the 1/3 cup sugar, salt, cream cheese, 1 teaspoon vanilla, and 1 egg. Mix well. Pour into pie crust. Sprinkle pecans on top. Combine remaining eggs, sugar, vanilla, and syrup. Mix well. Pour over pecans. Bake 35-40 minutes, or until center is firm.

Diantha Susan Hibbard, Rochester, N.Y.

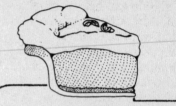

LAYERED PECAN CREAM PIE
Serves 8

1   (10-inch) unbaked pastry shell
1   (8-ounce) package cream cheese, softened
⅓   cup sugar
1   egg
1   teaspoon lemon flavoring
¼   teaspoon salt
1¼   cups chopped pecans
3   eggs
1   cup dark corn syrup
¼   cup sugar
1   teaspoon vanilla

Combine cream cheese, sugar, 1 egg, lemon flavoring and salt; blend until smooth and creamy. Spread in pastry shell; sprinkle with pecans. Combine remaining ingredients; beat until well-blended. Pour over cream cheese mixture and pecans. Preheat oven to 375 degrees. Bake for 35 minutes, or until center is firm to touch.

Erma Jackson, Huntsville, Ala.

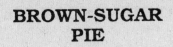

BROWN-SUGAR PIE

1 (9-inch) unbaked pie shell
3 eggs, beaten together
2 cups brown sugar
1/2 cup butter or margarine, soft
1/2 cup rich cream or evaporated milk

Mix cream, sugar, and beaten eggs together. Melt butter or margarine; cool a little and beat into egg mixture. Pour into the unbaked pie shell. Bake in 425-degree oven for 10 minutes, then reduce oven temperature to 350 degrees and bake 30 additional minutes or until pie filling is brown on top and shakes like jelly in the center. Rich, but oh, so good!

Sarah Drury, Brandenburg, Ky.

PEANUT BUTTER ICE CREAM PIE

Serves 8

1 quart vanilla ice cream, slightly softened
1/2 cup chunky peanut butter
1/2 cup crushed unsalted peanuts
1-1/2 tablespoons vanilla
1 (10-inch) graham cracker crust
Whipped cream and maraschino cherries for garnish

Combine ice cream, peanut butter, 1/4 cup peanuts, and vanilla in large bowl; mix well. Turn into crust and sprinkle with remaining peanuts. Freeze. Decorate with cream and cherries.

Kit Rollins, Cedarburg, WI

NO-BAKE PEANUT ICE CREAM PIE

4 cups Corn Chex cereal, crushed to 1 cup
1/4 cup firmly-packed brown sugar
1/3 cup butter or margarine, melted
1/4 cup flaked coconut
1/4 cup light corn syrup
1/4 cup peanut butter
3 tablespoons chopped salted nuts (peanuts)
1 tablespoon chopped peanuts (for topping)
1 quart vanilla ice cream, softened

Preheat oven to 300 degrees. Butter 9-inch pie plate. Combine cereal and sugar; add butter; mix well. Press this mixture evenly on bottom and sides of pie plate. Bake 10 minutes; cool. Combine next 4 ingredients. Mix with ice cream until rippled throughout. Turn into pie shell.

Sprinkle peanuts on top. Freeze 3 hours or until firm. Let stand 10-15 minutes at room temperature, before serving.

Monica Turk, Milwaukee, Wis.

"BREATH OF SPRING" PARFAIT PIE

Graham Cracker Crust:
1-1/2 cups graham cracker crumbs (about 20 crackers)
3 tablespoons sugar
1/3 cup melted butter or margarine

Combine all ingredients. Press mixture firmly and evenly against bottom and sides of pie pan. Bake at 350 degrees for 10 minutes. Cool.

Lime Parfait Pie:
1 (3-ounce) package lime gelatin
1 cup boiling water
1/4 cup frozen lemonade concentrate, thawed
1 pint vanilla ice cream

Dissolve gelatin in boiling water. Add lemonade. Add ice cream and stir until melted and smooth. Chill mixture until it begins to thicken, about 20 minutes. Pour into pie shell. Chill at least 3 hours before cutting.

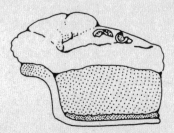

MOCHA SUNDAE PIE

Serves 6-8

Crust:
1-1/4 cups crushed chocolate wafers (about 20)
1 tablespoon sugar
1/4 cup melted butter or margarine

Filling:
1 cup evaporated milk
1 cup miniature marshmallows
1 cup semi-sweet chocolate pieces
Dash salt
1 quart coffee ice cream, softened and divided

Combine wafers, sugar, and butter. Press firmly into 9-inch pie plate. Bake in preheated 300 degree oven for 12-15 minutes. Cool, then chill. Over low heat, stir evaporated milk, marshmallows, chocolate pieces, and salt until melted and thick. Cool. Spoon half the ice cream into crust; drizzle with half the filling (chocolate sauce); spoon on remaining ice cream; drizzle with remaining filling. Freeze at least 4 hours.

Pauline Dean, Uxbridge, MA

MELT AWAY PIE

2 cups (24) crushed cream-filled chocolate cookies
1/4 cup margarine, melted
1/4 cup milk
1 (7-ounce) jar marshmallow creme
Few drops strawberry extract
Few drops red food coloring
2 cups whipping cream, whipped

Combine crumbs and margarine; reserve 1/2 cup for topping. Press remaining crumb mixture onto bottom of 9-inch spring form pan or pie plate. Chill. Gradually add milk to marshmallow creme, mixing until well blended. Add extract and food coloring; fold in whipped cream. Pour into pan; freeze until firm. Sprinkle with remaining crumbs.

A frozen pie that's quick and easy.

Barbara Nowakowski, No. Tonawanda, NY

MACAROON PIE

3 egg whites, beaten stiff
1/2 teaspoon baking powder
1 cup sugar
1 teaspoon vanilla extract
1 dozen graham crackers, rolled
  fine
1/2 cup finely cut dates
1 cup pecans, chopped
Whipped cream for topping

Beat egg whites until frothy, sprinkle baking powder over whites and continue beating until stiff. Gradually beat in sugar; add vanilla. Mix together graham cracker crumbs, dates and pecans; fold into egg white mixture. Spread in 9-or 10-inch unbuttered pie pan. Bake in 300-degree oven for 30 minutes or until set and very lightly browned. When cool, spread with whipped cream.

Mrs. J.L. Marvin, Jacksonville, FL

LEMON CHESS BUTTERMILK PIE

1/4 cup butter or margarine
1 cup sugar
1 tablespoon flour
1 tablespoon corn meal
4 eggs
1/2 cup lemon juice
1 teaspoon lemon peel (optional)
1/2 cup buttermilk

Melt butter; add sugar, flour, and corn meal. Add eggs, one at a time, beating well after each addition. Add lemon juice, lemon peel, and buttermilk. Pour into unbaked 8- or 9-inch pie shell. Bake 45 minutes at 350 degrees or until a knife comes out clean and pie is golden brown.

Mrs. P. B. Brother, Richmond, VA

FROZEN CRYSTAL LEMON PIE

3 eggs, separated
1/2 cup sugar
1/4 cup fresh lemon juice
1 teaspoon lemon zest (rind)

1/2 pint whipping cream, whipped
Crushed vanilla wafers

Beat egg yolks; add sugar, lemon zest, and juice. Cook gently until thickened; cool. Fold whipped cream into custard; fold in stiffly beaten egg whites. Crush enough vanilla wafers to cover the bottom of a freezing tray, pan, or dish. Pour lemon mixture over crumbs; cover top with crumbs. Place in freezer for at least 24 hours.

Remove from freezer 10 minutes before serving; cut into squares or slices.

Gwen Campbell, Sterling, Va.

AMISH LEMON PIE

2 tablespoons margarine, softened
1 cup sugar
3 eggs, separated
3 tablespoons flour
1/2 teaspoon salt
Juice and grated rind of one lemon
1-1/2 cups hot milk
1 (9-inch) unbaked pie shell
Cool Whip or 1/2 pint heavy whipping cream, whipped

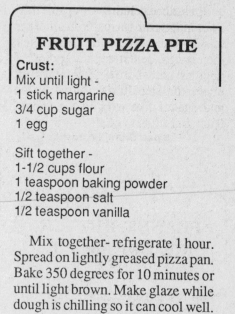

Cream margarine and sugar; add egg yolks, beating well. Add flour, salt, lemon juice, lemon rind, and milk; blend well.

Beat egg whites until stiff; fold into lemon mixture. Pour into pie shell; bake at 350 degrees for 35 minutes. Cool; top with Cool Whip or whipped cream sweetened with 3 tablespoons sifted confectioners' sugar.

This is a very simple pie to make.

Mrs. Albert H. Foley, Lemoyne, Pa.

LEMON CHIFFON PIE

1 (8- or 9-inch) graham cracker
  crumb crust
1 (14-ounce) can Eagle Brand
  sweetened condensed milk
1/2 cup lemon juice
Few drops yellow food coloring
3 egg whites
1/4 teaspoon cream of tartar
Whipped cream or Cool Whip
  topping

Lemon slices, optional

In medium bowl, combine sweetened condensed milk, lemon juice and food coloring; mix well. In a small bowl beat egg whites with cream of tartar until stiff but not dry. Gently fold into condensed milk mixture. Turn into crust. Chill 3 hours or until set. Garnish with whipped cream and lemon slices, if desired. Refrigerate leftovers.

Aldora Hohman, Manassas, Va.

FRUIT PIZZA PIE

Crust:
Mix until light -
1 stick margarine
3/4 cup sugar
1 egg

Sift together -
1-1/2 cups flour
1 teaspoon baking powder
1/2 teaspoon salt
1/2 teaspoon vanilla

Mix together- refrigerate 1 hour. Spread on lightly greased pizza pan. Bake 350 degrees for 10 minutes or until light brown. Make glaze while dough is chilling so it can cool well.

Glaze:
1/2 cup sugar
Dash of salt
2 tablespoon cornstarch
1/2 cup orange juice
2 tablespoons lemon juice
1/4 cup water

Cook until mixture thickens (about 4 minutes). Remove from heat and let cool.

When crust is cool make filling. Mix together 1 - 8 ounce cream cheese and 1 - 8 ounce cool whip. Spread on cool crust.

Fruit:
Place grapes around outer edge, strawberries next to grapes, sliced bananas next row or two, peaches next row, fill in remaining space wiht chunk pineapple. Spoon glaze over fruit. Glaze bananas first to keep from turning dark. (KEEP REFRIGERATED).

Patricia Parsons, Shinnston, W VA

ICE CREAM PARFAIT PIE

1 (3-ounce) package strawberry
  gelatin
1-1/4 cups hot water
1 pint vanilla ice cream
1 cup sliced strawberries
1 pie shell, baked
Whipped cream, optional

Dissolve gelatin in 1-1/4 cups hot water. Spoon in ice cream and stir until melted. Place in refrigerator until thickened. Let it set 15-25 minutes. Fold in strawberries. Turn filling into baked pie shell. Chill until firm, 30-60 minutes. Serve with whipped cream, if desired.

Beulah Schwallie, Cincinnati, Ohio

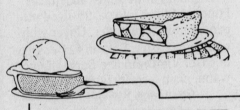

BLACK FOREST PIE

1 (9-inch) unbaked pie shell
3/4 cup sugar
1/3 cup unsweetened cocoa
2 tablespoons flour
1/4 cup margarine
1/3 cup milk
2 eggs, beaten
1 (21-ounce) can cherry pie filling
1 (9-ounce) container frozen whipped
  topping
1 (1-ounce) square unsweetened
  chocolate (coarsely grated)

In saucepan, combine sugar, cocoa, and flour; add margarine and milk. Cook until mixture begins to boil, stirring constantly. Remove from heat. Add small amount of hot mixture to eggs; return mixture to pan. Fold half the can of pie filling into mixture. Pour into crust-lined pan. Bake at 350 degrees for 35-45 minutes or until center is set but still shiny. Cool. Chill one hour. Combine 2 cups topping and grated chocolate; spread over pie. Place remaining pie filling around edge of pie. Cool.

Suzanne Dawson, Cypress, TX

AMISH VANILLA PIE

1/2 cup firmly packed brown sugar
1 tablespoon flour
1/4 cup dark corn syrup
1-1/2 teaspoons vanilla
1 egg, beaten
1 cup water
1 cup flour
1/2 cup firmly packed brown sugar
1/2 teaspoon cream of tartar
1/2 teaspoon baking soda
1/8 teaspoon salt
1/4 cup butter
1 unbaked 9-inch pie shell

Combine first 5 ingredients in 2-quart saucepan. Slowly stir in water. Cook over medium heat until mixture comes to a boil, stirring constantly. Let cool. Combine rest of ingredients (except pie shell) and mix until crumbly. Pour cooled mixture into pie shell and top with crumbs.

Bake at 350 degrees for 40 minutes or until golden brown.

Helen Weissinger, Levittown, Pa.

HAWAIIAN WEDDING PIE

1 (9-inch) baked pie shell
1/2 cup sugar
1/3 cup cornstarch
1-1/2 cups milk
3 beaten egg yolks
1 tablespoon butter or margarine
1-1/2 teaspoons vanilla
1 small can crushed pineapple, well
  drained
1/2-3/4 cup coconut
Whipped cream for topping
Toasted coconut for garnish

Combine sugar, cornstarch, and milk; mix well. Add beaten egg yolks. Cook over medium heat, stirring constantly, until mixture begins to boil and is thickened. Remove from heat. Add butter, vanilla, crushed pineapple, and coconut, thoroughly combining all. Pour mixture into pie shell and chill. When chilled, cover top with whipped cream. Sprinkle with toasted coconut.

Carme Venella, Laurel Springs, NJ

PENNSYLVANIA DUTCH SHOOFLY PIE

2 (8-inch) pastry shells, unbaked
2 cups flour
1 cup sugar
1 teaspoon baking powder
1 stick butter or margarine
1 cup dark molasses
1 teaspoon baking soda
1 cup boiling water
Pinch of salt
1 egg, beaten

Sift together flour, sugar, and baking powder. Cut in butter. In a separate bowl, mix molasses, baking soda, and water. Stir in salt, egg, and 2 cups of the flour-butter mixture. Pour into prepared pie shells and sprinkle with remaining crumbs. Bake at 375 degrees for 45 minutes.

Dorothy Garms, Anaheim, Calif.

4TH OF JULY PIE

1 pint blueberries
20-25 strawberries, hulled
Whipped cream
1 (3-1/4 ounce) package regular
  vanilla pudding mix
2 cups milk
1 (8-ounce) package cream cheese,
  softened
1/2 teaspoon vanilla
1 8-inch graham-cracker pie crust

Combine pudding mix and 2 cups milk in saucepan. Bring to full boil over medium heat, stirring constantly. Remove from heat. Add cream cheese and stir until smooth. Add vanilla. Let mixture cool for 5 minutes, stirring twice. Pour pudding mixture into pie crust. Refrigerate 3 hours or overnight. Place strawberries in circle on outer edge of pie. Place one in center. Place blueberries over remaining pudding.

Serve chilled, with whipped cream on top.

Chris Bryant, Johnson City, Tenn.

FRUIT SALAD PIE

1-1/4 cups water
3/4 cup white sugar
3 tablespoons pineapple juice
3 tablespoons maraschino cherry juice
3 tablespoons cornstarch
1/4 teaspoon red food coloring

Cook above ingredients until thick and then let cool.
Add:
2 large bananas, sliced
1/2 cup drained, crushed pineapple
1 (3-ounce) bottle maraschino cherries, drained and sliced in half

Pour into baked pie shell. Sprinkle with 1/2 cup coconut and 1/2 cup chopped walnuts. Chill; serve topped with whipped cream.
Clare R. Bracelin, Decatur, Ill.

ICE BOX CHERRY PIE

1 can red pie cherries, drained
1 cup nuts
1 can condensed milk
1/4 cup sugar
1 cup whipped cream
Juice of 2 lemons
1 graham cracker pie crust
Cool Whip

Mix milk, lemon juice, and sugar. Add cherries and nuts. Fold in whipped cream. Pour into pie crust. Top with Cool Whip. Refrigerate 4 hours or more before serving.
Monica Turk, Milwaukee, Wis.

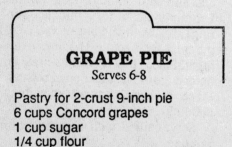

GRAPE PIE
Serves 6-8

Pastry for 2-crust 9-inch pie
6 cups Concord grapes
1 cup sugar
1/4 cup flour
1/4 teaspoon salt

1 teaspoon lemon juice
1 tablespoon butter

Wash and peel grapes, saving skins. Cook pulp in a saucepan with no water; bring to a hard boil. Rub through a strainer or food mill to remove seeds. Mix strained pulp with the reserved skins. Mix flour, sugar, and salt; stir into grapes. Add lemon juice and butter. Pour into pastry-lined 9-inch pie pan. Top with second crust. Slip top crust and seal edges. Bake at 400 degrees for about 40 minutes or until crust is brown and pie is bubbly.
Joy Shamway, Freeport, Il

BUTTERMILK RAISIN PIE

1/4 cup cornstarch
1 cup sugar
1/4 teaspoon salt
2 cups buttermilk
1/2 cup raisins
2 tablespoons lemon juice
2 eggs, separated (use whites for meringue)
1 tablespoon butter

Cool baked 8- or 9-inch pie shell. Mix cornstarch, sugar, salt, and beaten egg yolks in top of double boiler; add buttermilk, raisins, and lemon juice. Cook over direct heat stirring constantly, until mixture boils and thickens. Remove from heat and stir in butter until melted. Cool slightly. Pour into baked pie shell. Beat egg whites until stiff. Gradually add 1/4 cup sugar; spread over pie. Bake at 350 degrees for 12-15 minutes until browned.
Helen Taugher, Nicholson, PA

RAISIN PIE

2 cups raisins (seedless or seeded)
2 cups boiling water
1/3 cup granulated sugar
1/3 cup brown sugar
2 tablespoons cornstarch
1/8 teaspoon salt
2 teaspoons grated lemon rind
1/2 teaspoon grated orange rind
2 tablespoons lemon juice
1 tablespoon orange juice
Pastry for 2-crust (9-inch) pie
2 tablespoons butter or margarine

Add raisins to water; simmer until tender (3-5 minutes). Combine sugars, cornstarch, and salt; stir into hot raisins. Cook slowly, stirring constantly, to full rolling boil; boil 1 minute. Remove from heat.

Blend in fruit rinds and juices. Pour hot filling into pastry-lined pie pan; dot top with butter. Cover with remaining pastry. Bake in 425-degree oven for 30-40 minutes. Serve slightly warm, plain, or with whipped cream.
Grace Lane, Redondo Beach, Calif.

BEST-EVER PUMPKIN PIE
Makes 2 (9-inch) pies

Pastry for 2 1-crust pies
1-1/2 cups sifted brown sugar
1 (No. 2-1/2) can pumpkin
4 eggs
3 tablespoons butter
2 tablespoons molasses
1-1/2 teaspoons cinnamon
3/4 teaspoon ginger
1/2 teaspoon nutmeg
1 teaspoon salt
1-1/2 cups milk

Line pastry in pie plates. Add sugar to the pumpkin. Beat eggs until thick and add with butter, molasses, seasonings, and milk to the pumpkin mixture; stir. Pour pumpkin mixture into pastry-lined pans. Bake at 425 degrees for 10 minutes; reduce heat to 325 degrees and bake 25 more minutes.

Lucy Dowd, Sequim, Wash.

CRANBERRY APPLE PIE

Pastry for 9-inch two-crust pie
1 cup sugar
1/3 cup all-purpose flour
1 teaspoon apple pie spice
4 cups sliced pared tart apples
2 cups Ocean Spray fresh cranberries
2 tablespoons butter or margarine

Preheat oven to 425 degrees. Prepare pastry. In a bowl, stir together sugar, flour, and spice. In pastry-lined pie pan alternate layers of apples, cranberries, and sugar mixture, beginning and ending with sugar mixture. Dot with butter. Cover with top crust. Cut slits in crust; seal and flute edges. Bake 40 to 50 minutes. Cool.

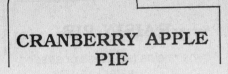

APPLE-BUTTER CINNAMON PIE

Pastry for 9-inch pie, plus strips for lattice
1/2 cup apple butter
2 eggs, beaten lightly
1/2 cup sugar
1-1/2 tablespoons cornstarch
1-1/2 teaspoons cinnamon
1/4 teaspoon mace
2 cups milk

Combine apple butter, eggs, sugar, cornstarch, cinnamon, and mace; mix well. Add milk gradually; blend well. Pour into unbaked pie shell; top with lattice made from 1/2-inch wide strips of crust. Bake 350 degrees for 35 minutes.

Gwen Campbell, Sterling, Va.

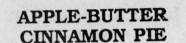

DATE AND NUT PIE

1 unbaked 9-inch pie crust
1/2 cup butter, at room temperature
1 cup light brown sugar
4 eggs
1 teaspoon pure vanilla extract
1 teaspoon cinnamon
1/2 teaspoon nutmeg
3/4 cup whipping cream
1/2 cup chopped dates
1/2 cup raisins
1/2 cup chopped walnuts

Preheat oven to 350 degrees. Cream butter, then cream in the brown sugar, mixing until fluffy. Beat in eggs. Blend in vanilla, cinnamon, nutmeg, and cream, mixing well. Stir in dates, raisins, and nuts. Pour into pie crust. Bake in a preheated oven for about 45 minutes or until the surface is crisp and lightly browned.

This is worth the calories!

Lillian Smith, Montreal Quebec, Canada

APPLESAUCE CHEESE PIE

6 graham crackers, crushed
1 tablespoon butter or margarine, melted
2 cups cottage cheese
2 eggs
1/4 cup sugar
1/4 cup flour
1 tablespoon lemon juice
1 cup thick applesauce

Mix crackers and butter; press into bottom and sides of 8- or 9-inch pie plate. Put cottage cheese through fine sieve; add eggs, one at a time, beating after each. Add sugar, flour, lemon juice, and applesauce. Beat until well blended. Pour into crumb-lined pie plate and bake in preheated 325-degree oven for 1 hour and 10 minutes or until mixture is set and lightly browned.

Kit Rollins, Cedarburg, WI

BLUEBERRY BOTTOM PIE

2 (4-serving) packages vanilla pudding and pie filling
1-1/4 cups milk
1-1/2 cups blueberries, puréed (1 cup)
1/2 teaspoon cinnamon
1 baked 9-inch pie shell, cooled
2 teaspoons grated lemon rind
3-1/2 cups frozen whipped topping (thawed)

Combine 1 package pudding mix, 1/4 cup of the milk, the puréed berries, and cinnamon in saucepan. Cook and stir until mixture comes to a full boil. Pour into crust; chill. Prepare remaining pudding mix with milk, as directed on package for pie. Add 1 teaspoon of the lemon rind; pour into bowl and cover with plastic wrap. Chill 1 hour. Fold in 1 cup of the whipped topping and spoon over blueberry layer. Combine remaining whipped topping and lemon rind. Spoon over filling. Chill in refrigerator, at least 3 hours before serving. Garnish with blueberries, if desired.

Suzanne Dawson, Cypress, Texas

FRUIT COCKTAIL PIE

1 (1 pound, 13 ounces) can fruit cocktail, well drained
32 vanilla wafers
1/2 cup sugar
1 teaspoon vanilla
2 cups sour cream

Preheat oven to 350 degrees. Place fruit cocktail in drainer; stir. Line bottom and sides of 9-inch glass pie plate with vanilla wafers. Add sugar and vanilla to sour cream; stir. Stir fruit cocktail again to be sure it is well drained. Add to sour cream mixture, folding gently. Pour into wafer-lined pie plate. Top with additional vanilla wafer crumbs, if desired. Bake at 350 degrees for 25 minutes, or until middle is set. Cool. Chill thoroughly before serving.

Marsha Miller, Hilliard, Ohio

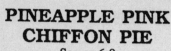

PINEAPPLE PINK CHIFFON PIE

Serves 6-8

Crust:
1 inner seal packet graham crackers (finely crushed, 1-2/3 cups)
1/4 cup sugar
1/2 cup flaked coconut
1/4 cup softened butter

Thoroughly blend crumbs, sugar, coconut, and softened butter. Press firmly against bottom and sides of 9-inch pie plate. Bake in 350-degree oven for 8 minutes; cool.

Filling:
1 (3-ounce) package strawberry-flavored gelatin
1 envelope unflavored gelatin
1-1/2 cups boiling water
1 pint heavy cream
1 (1-pound, 4-1/2-ounce) can crushed pineapple, well-drained

Dissolve both gelatins in boiling water. Chill until syrupy. Whip cream; continue beating, adding gelatin gradually. Fold in pineapple. Pile into crust; chill. Garnish with whipped cream and toasted coconut. Chill until firm.

Theresa Rouleau, Cornwall, Ontario, Canada

CRANBERRY PIE

2 cups whole raw cranberries
1½ cups sugar
½ cup chopped nuts
2 eggs
1 cup flour
½ cup margarine, melted
¼ cup shortening, melted
1 (10-inch) unbaked pie shell

Combine cranberries, ½ cup sugar and nuts; place in pastry-lined pie pan. Beat eggs; add remaining 1 cup sugar, flour, melted margarine and shortening. Pour over cranberry mixture and bake 1 hour at 325 degrees.

Sharon McClatchey, Muskogee, Okla.

BANANA MALLOW PIE

Crust:
2 cups shredded coconut
1/3 cup margarine

Combine coconut and margarine in skillet; cook over low heat, stirring constantly until toasted and golden. Press into 9-inch pie pan to form crust. Chill.

Filling:
1 (3 1/4-ounce) package vanilla pudding and pie filling (*not* instant)
1 3/4 cups cold milk
2 cups miniature marshmallows
3/4 cup whipping cream
2 bananas

Follow directions on pudding package. Cook, then refrigerate until cool. Whip cream. Fold into whipping cream the cooled pudding and miniature marshmallows.

Take crust from refrigerator; slice bananas onto bottom of crust. Pour filling over bananas. Chill 3 hours before serving.

Dixie Goodman, Brooklyn, Mich.

SWEET POTATO PIE

1 (9-inch) unbaked pie shell
3 eggs
2 cups sugar
½ stick margarine
1 small can evaporated milk
1 teaspoon vanilla
1 cup mashed sweet potatoes
½ to 1 cup coconut (optional)

Combine all filling ingredients together; pour into unbaked pie shell. Bake at 350 degrees for approximately 1 hour, or until inserted toothpick comes out clean.

Helen Harlos, Ethel, Miss.

MINCEMEAT PECAN PIE

1 (9-ounce) package condensed mincemeat, broken up
½ cup Karo light **or** dark corn syrup
¼ cup margarine
3 eggs, slightly beaten
½ cup coarsely chopped pecans
1 tablespoon grated orange rind
1 unbaked (9-inch) pastry shell
¼ cup sherry

In medium saucepan stir together first 3 ingredients. Stirring constantly, bring to boil over medium heat. Remove from heat. Gradually stir into eggs. Add pecans and rind. Pour into pastry shell. Bake in 350-degree oven for 40–50 minutes, or until knife inserted near center comes out clean. Pour sherry over filling. Cool.

BANANA RHUBARB PIE

2 (9-inch) pie crusts
1 pound rhubarb, sliced (3 cups)
3 medium-ripe bananas, peeled and sliced (3 cups)
1 cup sugar
1/4 cup orange juice
3 tablespoons flour
1/4 teaspoon salt
1/4 teaspoon cinnamon
1/4 teaspoon nutmeg
1 tablespoon butter or margarine

Combine rhubarb, bananas, sugar, orange juice, flour, salt, cinnamon, and nutmeg; turn into pastry-lined pie plate. Dot with butter. Preheat oven to 450 degrees. Place top crust on filling; cut vents. Bake 15 minutes; reduce oven temperature to 350 degrees and bake for 30 minutes longer, or until pie is brown. Cool completely.

Kit Rollins, Cedarburg, Wis.

IMPOSSIBLE CHERRY PIE

This is the pie that's impossibly easy because it makes its own crust, and it's filled with the harvest-fresh goodness of Thank You brand pie filling.

1 cup milk
2 tablespoons margarine or butter, softened
1/4 teaspoon almond extract
2 eggs
1/2 cup Bisquick baking mix
1/4 cup sugar
1 (21-ounce) can Thank You cherry pie filling
Streusel (recipe follows)

Heat oven to 400 degrees. Grease pie plate, 10x1-1/2-inches. Beat together all ingredients, except pie filling and Streusel, until smooth, 15 seconds in blender on high or 1 minute with hand beater. Pour into plate. Spoon pie filling evenly over top. Bake 25 minutes. Top with Streusel. Bake until Streusel is brown, about 10 minutes longer. Cool; refrigerate any remaining pie.

Streusel:

Cut 2 tablespoons firm margarine or butter into 1/2 cup Bisquick baking mix, 1/2 cup packed brown sugar, and 1/2 teaspoon ground cinnamon until crumbly.

PINEAPPLE ANGEL PIE

1 cup crushed pineapple
1 cup water
1 cup granulated sugar
Pinch salt
2-1/2 tablespoons cornstarch
3 egg whites, stiffly beaten
1 (9-inch) baked pie shell
1 cup cream, whipped
1/2 cup chopped walnuts

1/2 cup coconut
6 maraschino cherries, quartered

Mix together pineapple, water, sugar, salt, and cornstarch. Cook over boiling water in top of double boiler, stirring; cook until thick. Set aside to cool. When cold, fold in stiffly beaten egg whites. Pour into baked pie shell. Cover with whipped cream and sprinkle with nuts, coconut, and maraschino cherries. Chill in refrigerator.

Donna K. Gore, Aztec, N.M.

MISSISSIPPI MUD PIE

3 (1-ounce) squares unsweetened chocolate
1-1/2 cups sifted confectioners' sugar
1/2 cup whipping cream
1/3 cup butter or margarine
3 tablespoons light corn syrup
Dash salt
1 tablespoon vanilla extract
1 (9-inch) graham cracker crust
1 cup chopped pecans, divided
3 cups coffee-flavored ice cream, softened and divided
Sweetened whipped cream

Melt chocolate in a heavy saucepan over low heat; add confectioners' sugar and next 4 ingredients. Cook, stirring constantly, until mixture is smooth. Remove from heat; stir in vanilla and let mixture cool. Spread 1/2 cup chocolate sauce in graham cracker crust; sprinkle with 1/4 cup pecans. Freeze 10 minutes. Remove from freezer and spread 1 cup ice cream over pecans; freeze 20 minutes. Repeat layers twice. Cover pie and freeze at least 8 hours. Drizzle remaining chocolate sauce over pie. Top with whipped cream and sprinkle with remaining pecans.

Edna Askins, Greenville, Texas

HONEY RICE PIE

2-1/2 tablespoons cornstarch
1/2 teaspoon salt
1 cup milk
1/2 cup honey
1 egg, beaten
1 tablespoon butter or margarine
2 teaspoons grated lemon peel
1/4 cup lemon juice
1/2 teaspoon vanilla
2 cups cooked rice

Crust:
3/4 cup saltine crackers
1/2 cup flour
1/4 cup soft butter or margarine
1/3 cup honey
1 teaspoon grated lemon peel
1 (7-ounce) can shredded coconut

Blend cornstarch with salt, milk, and honey. Cook over low heat, stirring constantly until thick. Stir some of the mixture into egg. Blend both mixtures. Add butter and peel. Remove from heat and stir in lemon juice, vanilla, and rice. Cool.

To prepare crust, blend crumbs, flour, and butter. Add honey, lemon peel, and coconut. Press about 3/4 mixture into bottom and sides of 10-inch pie pan. Pour filling into crust. Top with remaining crumb mixture. Bake at 375 degrees for 25 minutes.

Kit Rollins, Cedarburg, Wis.

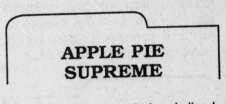

APPLE PIE SUPREME

6–8 large apples, peeled and sliced
1 large can frozen apple juice concentrate
2 tablespoons cornstarch
1 teaspoon cinnamon
1 (9-inch) unbaked pie shell
1 egg white, beaten

Heat juice; add cornstarch. Cook until thick. Add cinnamon and apples. Place in pie shell. Brush top crust with beaten egg white. Bake at 350 degrees for 60 minutes.

Sharon McClatchey, Muskogee, Okla.

MILE-HIGH MINCEMEAT PIE

2 quarts vanilla ice cream
2 cups prepared mincemeat
1/2 cup slivered, toasted almonds
5 egg whites
1/2 teaspoon vanilla
1/2 teaspoon cream of tartar
1/2 cup sugar
10-inch baked pie shell

Let ice cream stand at room temperature to soften slightly. Meanwhile, line a 10-inch pie plate with foil. Combine mincemeat and almonds, mixing well. Into foil-lined plated, spoon ice cream in alternate layers with mincemeat mixture, ending with ice cream. Freeze until ready to use (several hours).

To serve: In large bowl of electric mixer, let egg whites warm to room temperature (for about 1 hour). Mix in vanilla and cream of tartar, and beat mixture at high speed just until frothy. Add sugar, 2 tablespoons at time, beating well after each addition. Continue beating until meringue is shiny and stiff peaks form. Preheat oven to 425 degrees.

Remove foil from bottom of frozen ice cream-mincemeat layer, and place ice cream-mincemeat in baked pie shell. Use metal spatula to spread meringue over the pie, covering the ice cream and edge of crust completely. Make decorative swirls on top of meringue, and place on lowest shelf of oven. Bake 7-8 minutes, or just until meringue is golden brown. Serve immediately. Serves 10.

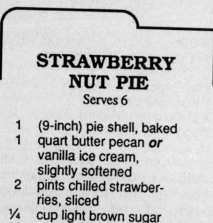

STRAWBERRY NUT PIE
Serves 6

1 (9-inch) pie shell, baked
1 quart butter pecan *or* vanilla ice cream, slightly softened
2 pints chilled strawberries, sliced
¼ cup light brown sugar
⅔ cup finely chopped toasted nuts

Spoon ice cream into baked crust. Mix together strawberries, sugar and toasted nuts; layer over ice cream. Freeze immediately. Remove from freezer to refrigerator 10 minutes before serving time for easier slicing.

Peggy Fowler Revels, Woodruff, S.C.

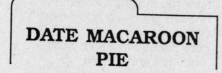

KEY LIME PIE

1 (14-ounce) can sweetened condensed milk
1/2 cup fresh lime juice
3 large egg yolks
1 9-inch baked pastry crust
3 large egg whites
1/4 teaspoon cream of tartar
6 tablespoons sugar

Combine condensed milk and lime juice in medium-size bowl. Blend in egg yolks; turn into cooled crust. Heat oven to 325 degrees. Beat egg whites with cream of tartar in small bowl until soft peaks form. Beat in sugar, 1 tablespoon at a time, until egg whites form stiff, glossy peaks. Spoon over filling; spread to edge of crust to seal. Bake 15 minutes or until golden. Cool on wire rack to room temperature.

Edith Holmes, Brookfield, Mass.

DATE MACAROON PIE

3 egg whites
1/2 cup finely-chopped dates
12 saltines
1 cup white sugar
1/2 teaspoon baking powder
1 teaspoon vanilla
1 teaspoon water

Beat egg whites, water and vanilla together until they form stiff peaks. Crush saltines fine and add remaining ingredients to whites, fold in. Butter 9-inch pie plate and pour mixture into it. Bake in preheated 325 degree oven for 30 minutes. Cut into wedges and serve with whipped cream, garnished with maraschino cherry.

Pearle Goodwin, South Reygate, Vt.

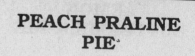

PEACH PRALINE PIE

4 cups fresh peaches, peeled and sliced
1 teaspoon lemon juice
2 tablespoons tapioca
1/4 cup sugar
3/4 cup sugar
1/2 cup flour
4 tablespoons flour
1/2 cup nuts, chopped
1 unbaked pie shell

Mix first 4 ingredients for 10 minutes. Combine next 4 ingredients and sprinkle 1/3 of mixture over bottom of unbaked pie shell. Top with peach mixture, then rest of topping. Bake at 450 degrees for 10 minutes. Reduce heat to 350 degrees and bake 20 minutes more. Serve with ice cream or whipped topping.

Sue Thomas, Casa Grande, Ariz.

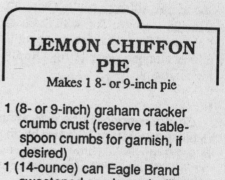

LEMON CHIFFON PIE
Makes 1 8- or 9-inch pie

1 (8- or 9-inch) graham cracker crumb crust (reserve 1 tablespoon crumbs for garnish, if desired)
1 (14-ounce) can Eagle Brand sweetened condensed milk (not evaporated milk)
1/3 cup ReaLemon juice concentrate
Few drops yellow food coloring
3 egg whites
1/4 teaspoon cream of tartar
2 cups whipped topping

In medium bowl, combine sweetened condensed milk, ReaLemon and food coloring; mix well. In small bowl, beat egg whites with cream of tartar until stiff but not dry; gently fold into sweetened condensed milk mixture. Pour into prepared crust. Chill 3 hours, or until set. Top with whipped topping and reserved crumbs before serving. Refrigerate leftovers. A dramatic finish to a company dinner!

Theresa McClarrin, Waynesville, N.C.

LEMON BUTTERMILK PIE

4 eggs
3/4 cup sugar
2 tablespoons flour
1-1/2 cups buttermilk
1/4 cup melted butter or margarine
Grated peel of 1 lemon
3 tablespoons lemon juice
1 teaspoon vanilla
1 (9-inch) pie shell, baked
Cinnamon

Beat eggs and sugar together in large mixer bowl until light and lemon-colored. Beat in flour, buttermilk, butter, lemon peel, juice, and vanilla. Pour into pie shell. Sprinkle lightly with cinnamon.

Bake in preheated oven of 375-degrees for 20-30 minutes, or until knife blade inserted near center comes out clean. Cool on rack, then serve.

Mrs. L. Mayer, Richmond, Va.

JAMAICAN COCONUT PIE

1-1/3 cups Baker's Angel Flake Coconut
1 unbaked (9-inch) pie shell
3 tablespoons butter or margarine
1/2 cup sugar

3 eggs
1 cup dark corn syrup
1/8 teaspoon salt
1 teaspoon cinnamon
1 teaspoon nutmeg
1 teaspoon vanilla
2 tablespoons dark rum

Sprinkle coconut in pie shell. Cream butter; gradually beat in sugar. Add eggs and beat well. Blend in remaining ingredients. Pour over coconut in pie shell. Bake at 350 degrees for 50 minutes, or until slightly puffed on top. Cool to room temperature.

Diantha Susan Hibbard, Rochester, N.Y.

VERY BLUEBERRY PIE

1/4 cup cold water
5 tablespoons flour
Pinch of salt
4 cups fresh or dry-pack frozen blueberries, rinsed and drained
1 cup sugar
1/2 cup water
1 (9-inch) baked pie shell

Make a smooth paste of the water, flour and salt. Boil 1 cup of the blueberries with sugar and water. Add the flour paste and stir until it thickens. Remove from stove and cool. When cool, add the remaining blueberries and put into baked pie shell. Refrigerate. When cold, garnish with sweetened whipped cream or whipped topping.

North American Blueberry Council, Marmora, N.J.

STRAWBERRY-SOUR CREAM PIE

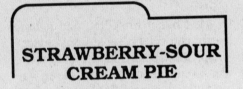

2 cups strawberries, crushed
3 tablespoons sugar
1/2 cup sour cream
1 (8-ounce) container Cool Whip, thawed
1 Easy Crumb Crust (recipe follows)

Mix ingredients in order given. Place in crust and chill 4 hours, or freeze until firm. Garnish with more strawberries.

Easy Crumb Crust:
Use either fine graham cracker, chocolate or vanilla wafer, shortbread or gingersnap crumbs.

1 1/4 cups crumbs
1/4 cup melted margarine

Press on bottom of a 9-inch pie pan; chill 1 hour.
A must when strawberries are in season!

Betty Brennan, Faribault, Minn.

MINCEMEAT APPLE PIE
Makes 9-inch pie

9-inch unbaked pastry shell
2 cooking apples, pared and sliced
6 tablespoons flour
1 (28 ounce) jar ready-to-use mincemeat
1/4 cup firmly-packed light brown sugar
2 teaspoons ground cinnamon
2 tablespoons margarine or butter
1/4 cup chopped nuts

Preheat oven to 425 degrees. Toss apples with 2 tablespoons flour. Arrange in pastry shell. Top with mincemeat. In small bowl, combine remaining flour, sugar and cinnamon. Cut in margarine until crumbly. Mix in nuts. Sprinkle over mincemeat. Bake 10 minutes, reduce oven temperature to 350 degrees and continue baking 25-30 minutes or until browned. Serve warm or cold with vanilla ice cream.

Melba Bellefeuille, Libertyville, Ill.

DISTINCTIVE RHUBARB PIE

3 eggs, separated
1-1/4 cups sugar
1/4 cup soft butter or margarine
3 tablespoons frozen orange juice concentrate
1/4 teaspoon salt
1/4 cup all-purpose flour
2-1/2 cups rhubarb, cut in 2 inch pieces
1/3 cup chopped pecans
1 unbaked 9-inch pie shell

Beat egg whites in a bowl until stiff. Gradually add 1/4 cup sugar, beating well after each addition. Add butter or margarine and orange juice concentrate to egg yolks; beat thoroughly. Add 1 cup sugar, flour, and salt; beat well. Add rhubarb to the yolk mixture; stir well. Gently fold in the beaten egg whites (meringue). Pour into unlined pie shell; sprinkle with pecans.

Bake on bottom rack of oven at 375 degrees for 15 minutes. Reduce heat to 325 degrees; bake 45 to 50 minutes more. Let cool on rack.

Marie Fusaro, Manasquan, N.J.

APPLE-MINCEMEAT PIE

Pastry for 1-crust pie
2 cups prepared mincemeat
2 cups thinly sliced tart apples
1 teaspoon cinnamon or nutmeg
2 tablespoons lemon or lime juice
Grated rind of 1 lemon or lime
1/2 cup flour
1/2 cup brown sugar
1/4 cup butter or margarine, melted

Prepare pie crust. Cover bottom of the crust with mincemeat. Cover the mincemeat with apples. Mix juice, rind and spice and sprinkle mixture over apples. Mix flour, sugar and butter and spread mixture over pie. Bake in a 450-degree oven for 10 minutes; reduce heat to 350 degrees and bake 30-35 minutes more. Serve with cheese wedges, hard sauce, or flavored whipped cream or whipped topping.

CHOCOLATE CHEESECAKE PIE

1　ready-made chocolate pie crust
12　ounces cream cheese, softened
½　cup sugar
2　eggs
2　teaspoons vanilla
　　Dash of salt
½　cup semisweet chocolate chips, melted

Preheat oven to 325 degrees. Beat cream cheese and sugar together until smooth. Add eggs, vanilla and salt. Beat until well-blended. Put crust on baking sheet and pour filling into crust. Drop melted chocolate by teaspoonfuls onto filling. Swirl chocolate into filling with tip of knife. Bake on sheet for 25–30 minutes, or until knife inserted in center comes out clean. Cool and chill about 3 hours.

Suzan L. Wiener, Spring Hill, Fla.

CRANBERRY CHIFFON PIE
Makes 9-inch pie

1 cup cooked cranberries
2/3 cup sugar
4 eggs, separated
1 tablespoon unflavored gelatin
1/2 teaspoon salt
1 tablespoon lemon juice
9-inch baked pie shell
1/2 cup whipping cream, whipped

Place cranberries in saucepan. Add half as much water. Cook until skins pop. Strain through a sieve. Measure 1 cup. Place cranberries, 1/3 cup sugar and egg yolks in top of double boiler. Cook over hot water for 8 minutes or until thickened and smooth, stirring constantly. Soften gelatin in 1/4 cup cold water in large bowl. Pour cranberry mixture over gelatin, mix well. Beat in salt and lemon juice. Beat egg whites until soft peaks form. Add 1/3 cup sugar gradually, beating until stiff. Fold into cranberry mixture. Pour into baked pie shell. Chill until firm. Top each serving with whipped cream.

Melba Bellefeuille, Libertyville, Ill.

CRUSTLESS APPLE PIE

6 apples, pared and sliced
1/8 teaspoon nutmeg
1/2 cup sugar
1 tablespoon butter
1 tablespoon water
1 cup brown sugar
2/3 cup flour
1/2 cup shortening
Hard sauce or whipped cream

Mix nutmeg with 1/2 cup sugar. Put apples in baking dish, sprinkle with sugar and nutmeg mix. Dot with butter. Add water. Mix brown sugar with flour and shortening. Blend mixture to crumb texture. Cover apples in baking dish with crumb mixture. Bake at 325 degrees for 30 minutes or until apples are soft. Serve with hard sauce or whipped cream.

Bea Comas, Portland, Maine

PINTO PIE WITH CORNMEAL CRUST
Serves 6–8

2　cups yellow cornmeal
½　teaspoon salt
3　tablespoons vegetable oil
　　Reserved bean cooking water
2　tablespoons butter
1　onion, chopped
½　cup carrot, chopped
½　cup celery, chopped
1　cup dried pinto beans, cooked and drained (save cooking water)
　　Dash pepper
1　teaspoon chili powder
　　Salt to taste
1　cup shredded sharp cheddar cheese

Mix the first 3 ingredients together along with enough of the reserved bean cooking water to make a batter. Press mixture into the bottom and sides of a greased 9-inch pie plate. Set aside.

Melt butter in skillet; add onion, carrot and celery; sauté until tender-crisp. Stir in beans, pepper, chili powder, ¼ cup reserved bean cooking water and salt to taste. Pour mixture into cornmeal crust. Sprinkle top of pie evenly with cheese. Bake at 350 degrees for 30 minutes, or until cheese begins to brown. Cut in wedges to serve.

TAFFY PIE

2 eggs
2 teaspoons water
1 tablespoon melted butter
2 teaspoons vanilla
1 1/2 cups dark brown sugar
8-inch gingersnap or graham cracker crust

Place ingredients in blender and mix well for a few seconds. Add 1 cup pecans and blend until chopped. Pour mixture into an 8-inch gingersnap or graham cracker crust. Bake at 350 degrees for 30 minutes, or until firm.

Agnes Ward, Erie, Pa.

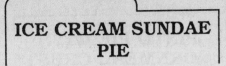

ICE CREAM SUNDAE PIE

1 Ready Crust Chocolate flavored pie crust
1 quart ice cream
1 (12-ounce) jar chocolate fudge topping
Whipped cream
Maraschino cherries
Walnuts

Allow ice cream to soften or stir with spoon until pliable. Spoon into pie crust. Cover and freeze until firm, about 3 hours. Serve pie wedges with fudge topping, whipped cream, and cherries. Add nuts, if desired.

Annie Cmehil, New Castle, IN

CUSTARD PIE

4 slightly beaten eggs
1/2 cup sugar
1/4 teaspoon salt
1/2 teaspoon vanilla
2-1/2 cups scalded milk
9" unbaked pastry shell
Nutmeg or 1/2 cup flaked coconut

Blend eggs, sugar, salt and vanilla. Gradually stir in milk. Pour into pastry shell. Sprinkle lightly with nutmeg or coconut. Bake in moderate oven at 350 degrees for 35 to 40 minutes, or until knife inserted halfway between center and edge comes out clean. Cool on rack, then chill.

Elsie Abeln, Traverse City, MI

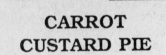

CARROT CUSTARD PIE

1/2 cup sugar
2/3 cup milk
1 teaspoon vanilla
1 tablespoon cornstarch
1-1/2 cups mashed, cooked carrots
1 unbaked 9 inch pie shell
2 eggs, beaten
1 tablespoon lemon juice
1/4 teaspoon cinnamon

Combine sugar and cornstarch. Add eggs, milk, carrots, lemon juice, and vanilla. Mix well; pour into pie shell. Sprinkle with cinnamon. Bake at 375 degrees for 45 minutes or until custard is set. Serve warm or cooled. "Really delicious!"

Agnes Ward, Erie, Pa.

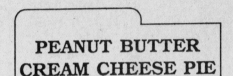

CARAMEL CUSTARD PIE

3 cups milk, scalded
1/3 cup caramelized syrup (below)
4 eggs, well beaten
1/3 cup sugar
1/2 teaspoon salt
1 teaspoon vanilla
Baked 10-inch pie shell

Blend together milk and caramelized syrup. Combine beaten eggs, sugar, salt, and vanilla. Slowly stir egg mixture into milk. Bake in a buttered 10-inch pie plate in a 350 degree oven for 40 minutes, or until a knife inserted in center comes out clean. Cool. Loosen edges of custard carefully with spatula. Shake gently to loosen bottom. Slide custard from pie plate into cooled pie shell.

Caramelized Syrup:
2 cups sugar
1 cup boiling water

Pour sugar into heavy skillet that heats uniformly. Melt over low heat, stirring constantly with wooden spoon to prevent scorching; the lumps will melt away.

When sugar becomes a clear brown syrup, remove from heat. Stir in boiling water slowly so that it does not splatter. Return to low heat, and stir until syrup is smooth again. Cool. (What you don't use can be put into a clean pint jar and stored in refrigerator for several weeks.)

Mrs. S. R. Burt, Imlay, NV

OLD-FASHIONED VANILLA CUSTARD PIE

Serves 6

1 (9 inch) pie shell, unbaked
3 eggs
4 tablespoons granulated sugar
1/8 teaspoon salt
3 cups scalding hot milk
1-1/4 teaspoons vanilla extract
1/4 teaspoon freshly grated nutmeg

Beat eggs until thoroughly mixed and bubbly. Add sugar and salt; mix well. Add 3 tablespoons of the scalding hot milk to egg mixture; mix well. Add egg mixture to the milk; stir in vanilla. Beat gently until all is evenly mixed; pour into unbaked shell. Bake 400 degrees for 12 minutes; reduce heat to 350 degrees and bake 25 minutes or until tested done in middle. Remove from oven; cool; refrigerate at least 2 hours before cutting.

Gwen Campbell, Sterling, Va.

PEANUT BUTTER CREAM CHEESE PIE

Pecan crust:
1-1/2 cups pecans, toasted and finely chopped
1/2 cup sugar
1/4 cup butter
1/4 teaspoon cinnamon
To make crust: Mix together all crust ingredients and press into a 9 inch metal pie pan. Freeze.
Topping:
1/2 cup fudge ice cream topping
Filling:
1 cup whipping cream
1-1/4 cups powdered sugar (divided)
1 tablespoon vanilla
1 (8 ounce) package cream cheese at room temperature
1 cup creamy peanut butter
2 tablespoons butter
To make filling: Beat cream with 1/4 cup powdered sugar and vanilla, until stiff peaks form; set aside. In another bowl, beat remaining 1 cup powdered sugar, cream cheese, peanut butter, and butter until fluffy. Fold in half the whipped cream mixture. Spoon cream cheese mixture into reserved crust. Cover and chill 2 hours. Spread fudge topping on pie, leaving a 1 inch border. Rebeat reserved whipped cream mixture and spoon around border. Chill 1 hour.

Leah Maria Daub, Milwaukee, Wis.

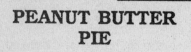

PEANUT BUTTER PIE

1 cup "chunky" peanut butter
1 (8 ounce) package cream cheese
   at room temperature
3/4 cup sugar
2 tablespoons melted butter
1 cup whipping cream, whipped
1 tablespoon vanilla
1 prepared graham cracker crust
1/3 cup melted hot fudge topping

Cream together peanut butter, cream cheese, and sugar. Add butter and vanilla; blend. Fold in whipped cream until well blended. Pour into a graham cracker crust; chill 4-5 hours or until set. Drizzle top with hot fudge topping. Chill anywhere from 30 minutes longer to overnight.

This is very rich! It will serve several, because you only need a tiny slice.   Pam Portillo, Culver City, Calif.

DEER MEAT PIE

1 pound ground venison (2 cups)
1-1/2 teaspoons salt of less
1/2 teaspoon pepper or less
1 cup drained canned tomatos
1/2 cup grated or shredded American
   cheese
1 tablespoon chopped parsley (optional)
1 tablespoon chopped onion or more
1/2 teaspoon dried basil (optional)

Combine ground venison, salt and pepper; spread in 9-inch pie pan, bringing meat up the sides. Cover with drained tomatos. Sprinkle with cheese, parsley, onion and basil. Bake at 375 degrees for 20 to 25 minutes. Pour off fat; cut in wedges and serve hot. Ground beef can be substituted for the venison.
          Mary Ann Altobell, Virginia, MN

MERRY MINCE PIE

1 cup sugar
1/2 teaspoon salt
1/2 teaspoon cinnamon
1/4 teaspoon cloves

1/4 teaspoon ginger
1-1/2 cups finely chopped pared
   apples
1 cup raisins
1/2 cup jellied cranberry sauce
1/3 cup chopped walnuts
1 teaspoon grated orange peel
1/2 teaspoon grated lemon peel
1/4 cup lemon juice
4 tablespoons butter
Pastry for 2-crust pie

Combine sugar, salt, and spices. Add next seven ingredients; mix well. Pour into pastry-lined 9 inch pie plate. Dot with butter. Apply top crust; cut slits, and crimp edges. Bake in 400 degree oven for 35 minutes. Serve warm.

          June Harding, Ferndale, Mich.

APPLESAUCE PECAN PIE

1 unbaked pie shell
2 tablespoons butter
1 cup light brown sugar
1/4 teaspoon cinnamon
3/4 cup dark corn syrup
1/2 cup applesauce
1 cup chopped pecans
3 eggs, beaten

Combine butter, sugar, and cinnamon. Add syrup, applesauce, pecans, and eggs. Blend well. Pour into pie shell. Bake in a 400 degree oven for 15 minutes. Reduce heat to 325 degrees and bake for 25-30 additional minutes. Delicious!

          Mrs. Bruce Fowler, Woodruff, SC

BLACK WALNUT PIE

1 cup black walnut halves
2 eggs, slightly beaten
1 cup dark corn syrup
1 teaspoon vanilla
1 tablespoon melted butter
1 cup white sugar
1/8 teaspoon salt
1 unbaked 9-inch pie shell

Mix ingredients, adding black walnuts last. Pour into unbaked pie shell and bake in conventional oven at 400 degrees for 15 minutes. Reduce temperature to 300 degrees and

bake about 30 minutes more or until a toothpick inserted in the center comes out clean. Serve warm or cold. Enjoy!

          Mary Davis, Cookeville, Tennessee

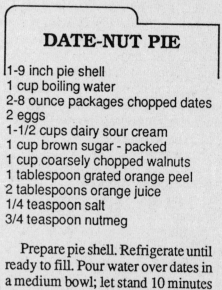

CHOCOLATE CHIP WALNUT PIE

2 eggs
1/2 cup flour
1/2 cup sugar
1/2 cup packed brown sugar
1 cup butter, melted, cooled to room
   temperature
1 (6 ounce) package chocolate
   chips
1 cup chopped walnuts
1 (9 inch) unbaked pie shell

Beat eggs in large bowl until foamy. Beat in flour, granulated and brown sugars until well blended. Blend in melted butter. Fold in chocolate chips and walnuts. Spoon into unbaked pie shell. Bake at 325 degrees for 1 hour or until knife inserted in center comes out clean.

Do not overbake. Serve warm.
          Karen Krugman, Tampa, Fla.

DATE-NUT PIE

1-9 inch pie shell
1 cup boiling water
2-8 ounce packages chopped dates
2 eggs
1-1/2 cups dairy sour cream
1 cup brown sugar - packed
1 cup coarsely chopped walnuts
1 tablespoon grated orange peel
2 tablespoons orange juice
1/4 teaspoon salt
3/4 teaspoon nutmeg

Prepare pie shell. Refrigerate until ready to fill. Pour water over dates in a medium bowl; let stand 10 minutes and drain. In a large bowl with rotary beater, beat eggs until fluffy. Blend in remaining ingredients, except dates. The final step, stir in dates.

Pour into unbaked pie shell. Bake at 375 degrees for 45-50 minutes or until filling is set in center when pie is gently shaken.

          Nancy Johnson, Kenosha, WI

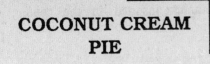

COCONUT CREAM PIE

2 cups milk
1/2 cup granulated sugar
2 tablespoons all-purpose flour
2 tablespoons cornstarch
2 large eggs, separated
1 tablespoon butter
1/2 teaspoon salt
1-1/4 cups shredded coconut
1 teaspoon vanilla

Scald 1-1/2 cups milk in top of a double boiler. Combine sugar, flour, cornstarch, and salt. Stir in remaining 1/2 cup milk and egg yolks. Stir this flour mixture into hot milk; cook until thickened. Remove from heat. Add butter, vanilla, and 3/4 cup coconut. Allow mixture to cool, then pour into baked 9 inch pie shell. Cover with meringue and remaining coconut. Bake at 350 degrees 10-12 minutes, or until meringue browns lightly.

Dorothy E. Snyder, Mifflinburg, PA

CRAZY PIE

1 cup flour
1 teaspoon baking powder
1/2 teaspoon salt
1 tablespoon sugar

Mix well the flour, baking powder, salt and sugar. Blend in:
2/3 cup butter-flavored shortening
3/4 cup water

Beat 2 minutes on medium speed with electric mixer. Pour batter into 9" pie pan. Do not spread. Pour favorite pie filling in center of batter. Do not stir. Bake 45-50 minutes in preheated 425 degree oven.

Lucille Roehr, Hammond, IN

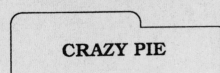

END OF THE LINE PIE

Serves 8

1 (4 ounce package) German Sweet Chocolate

1/4 cup butter
1 (13 ounce can) evaporated milk
1-1/3 cups flaked coconut
3 eggs, slightly beaten
1/2 cup sugar

In saucepan melt chocolate and butter. Gradually add milk and coconut. Combine eggs and sugar, and stir into chocolate mixture. Pour mixture into pie crust. Bake at 400 degrees for 45 minutes. Completely cool before cutting the individual servings.

FOURTH OF JULY PIE

1 (3-ounce) package lemon gelatin
2/3 cup boiling water
2 cups ice cubes
1 (8-ounce) container frozen whipped topping, thawed
1/2 cup sliced fresh strawberries
1/2 cup whole fresh blueberries
1 (9-inch) prepared graham cracker crumb crust

Dissolve gelatin in the boiling water, stirring about 3 minutes. Add ice cubes and stir constantly until gelatin is thickened, about 2 to 3 minutes. Remove any unmelted ice. Using a wire whip, blend in whipped topping and whip until smooth. Fold in strawberries and blueberries. Chill, if necessary, until mixture will mound. Spoon into pie shell. Chill about 2 hours.

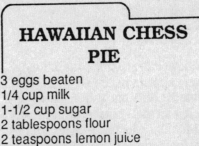

HAWAIIAN CHESS PIE

3 eggs beaten
1/4 cup milk
1-1/2 cup sugar
2 tablespoons flour
2 teaspoons lemon juice
1/4 cup melted margarine
1 - 8 ounce can crushed pineapple, with juice
2/3 cup flaked coconut
1 - 9 inch deep dish unbaked pie shell

Combine eggs, milk, sugar, flour, lemon juice, and margarine. Beat until smooth. Add pineapple and coconut. Pour into pie shell. Bake at 350 degrees for 50-55 minutes or until center of pie is set. Cool and serve. Yummy!

Barbara June Ohde, Atkinson, NE

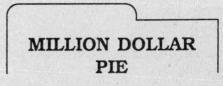

MILLION DOLLAR PIE

1/3 cup lemon juice
1 can sweetened condensed milk
1 (No. 2 can) crushed pineapple, drained
1 (9 ounce) container frozen dessert topping, thawed
1 cup chopped nuts (reserve some for top to garnish)
1 (8 ounce) package cream cheese, softened
1 large (or 2 small) baked pastry or graham cracker shells.

Mix all ingredients together well and pour into pie shells. Sprinkle with reserved nuts and chill. Cut into small wedges.

Laura Scheer, New Haven, Mo.

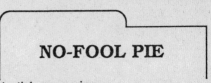

NO-FOOL PIE

1 stick margarine
1 cup self-rising flour
3/4 cup sugar
3/4 cup milk
1 to 1-1/2 cups fruit, drained (blueberries, peaches, cherries, etc.)

Preheat oven to 350 degrees. Melt margarine in deep 8-inch cobbler pan while oven is preheating; set aside. Combine flour, sugar, and one-half of milk; stir until dry ingredients are moistened. Add remaining milk and stir until smooth. Pour batter over melted margarine. DO NOT MIX! Sprinkle drained fruit over top of this mixture. Do not stir to combine. Bake 30-40 minutes, or until lightly browned and center springs back when lightly touched with finger. Serve hot, with or without ice cream.

Larry Luttrell, Marietta, GA

MOM'S CHEESE PIE

Crust:
1 cup sifted flour
1/2 teaspoon baking powder
2 tablespoons sugar
4 tablespoons shortening
1 egg, beaten

Note: Crust dough forms a ball. Do not roll out crust; press into 10-inch lightly greased glass pie plate.

Filling:
1 large and 1 small package cream cheese (11 ounces total)
7 heaping tablespoons sugar
2 heaping tablespoons flour
1 egg
Juice of half a lemon
1 teaspoon vanilla
2 cups milk (regular whole milk is best)

Have cheese, milk, egg and lemon at room temperature; mix together in large bowl. Pour into pie plate. Batter will be watery. Place carefully in oven. Bake in preheated 350 degree oven about 1 hour or until knife inserted in center comes out clean. Sprinkle with cinnamon.

Adele A. Roselli, Longhorne, PA

PINA COLADA TOFU PIE

Tofu makes this a healthy dessert without sugar. Great for people on restricted diets.

1 pie crust (regular or graham cracker)
1 pound tofu cut-up and drained
1-1/2 tablespoons oil
1/3 cup plus 2 tablespoons honey
1-1/2 teaspoons cornstarch
1 teaspoon vanilla
1-1/4 cups drained crushed pineapple
3/4 cups shredded unsweetened coconut

Blend well all ingredients. Bake at 350 degrees for 20-30 minutes. Let cool to set.

Sande Guetthoff, Butler, PA

SAWDUST PIE

1-1/4 cup white or brown sugar
1-1/2 cups chopped pecans
1-1/2 cups vanilla wafers or graham cracker crumbs
1-1/2 cups flaked coconut
1/2 teaspoon cinnamon
1/2 teaspoon nutmeg
7 egg whites, unbeaten
1 unbaked 9-inch pastry shell
1 sliced banana
Whipped cream

Combine the first seven ingredients in a large mixing bowl. Stir until just blended. Pour into pie shell and bake at 375 degrees for 35 minutes or until filling is set.

Presentation: Top each slice with a dollop of whipped cream and a slice of banana. Serve warm or at room temperature.

Edna Lawrence, San Antonio, TX

SHOO-FLY-PIE

Combine the following ingredients to make crumbs:

1/4 cup shortening
1-1/2 cups flour
1 cup brown sugar

Liquid filling:
3/4 teaspoon baking soda
1/8 teaspoon nutmeg
Dash of ginger
Dash of cinnamon
Dash of cloves
1/4 teaspoon salt
3/4 cup molasses
3/4 cup hot water

Mix well the baking soda, nutmeg, ginger, cinnamon, cloves, salt, and molasses. Add hot water. In an unbaked pie shell, place crumbs and liquid in alternate layers, with crumbs being on both bottom and top. Bake 15 minutes at 450 degrees; lower heat to 350 degrees and bake for an additional 20 minutes.

Gracie Miesen, Phoenix, Ariz.

TRANSPARENT PIE

4 egg yolks
3/4 cup sugar
1 stick butter
1 cup evaporated milk
1 teaspoon vanilla
1 partially baked pie shell
8 tablespoons of sugar (additional)

Beat together egg yolks and sugar. Place in medium saucepan over low heat. Melt butter in egg mixture, stirring constantly. Remove from heat as soon as butter melts. Add evaporated milk and vanilla. Pour into crust and bake for 15 minutes at 400 degrees. Then reduce heat and bake until custard is set. Cover pie with meringue made form 4 egg whites and 8 tablespoons sugar. Return to oven to brown meringue. (Watch carefully)

Mary Bowles, Killen, AL

BRAN PIE CRUST SHELLS
Makes two 8" or 9" shells

1/3 cup bran
2 cups sifted flour
1/2 teaspoon salt
2/3 cup shortening
6 tablespoons cold water

Crush bran into fine crumbs; mix with flour and salt. Cut in 1/3 cup of the shortening to the consistency of cornmeal. Cut in remaining shortening to the consistency of peas. Sprinkle cold water over top of mixture, a little at a time. Mixing with a fork until dough is just moist enough to hold together. Turn onto a sheet of waxed paper and shape the dough into a ball. Roll out according to directions.

Marcella Swigert, Monroe City, MO

GARDEN OF EDEN PIE

1 cup Carnation evaporated milk
1 tablespoon lemon juice
1 cup brown sugar
1/4 teaspoon salt
1/4 teaspoon cinnamon
1/8 teaspoon mace
1/2 teaspoon nutmeg
2 cups finely chopped apples
2 cups ground raisins
1 (9-inch) pie pastry shell, unbaked

Mix milk, juice, sugar, salt, and spices. Add fruits; pour into unbaked pie shell and bake in hot oven 450 degrees for 10 minutes to set crust; then reduce temperature to 325 degrees and bake an additional 40 minutes or until filling is set.

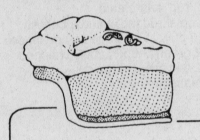

ORANGE COCONUT CHESS PIE

1 stick butter, at room temperature
2 cups sugar
5 eggs
1/2 cup thawed orange juice concentrate
1/3 cup water
1 tablespoon flour
1 tablespoon yellow cornmeal
1/2 cup coconut
2 unbaked 9-inch pie shells

Preheat oven to 350 degrees. Cream butter in large bowl with electric mixer. Gradually add sugar and beat well. Beat in eggs, one at a time. Combine orange juice concentrate and water; blend with butter mixture. Beat in flour and cornmeal. Fold in coconut. Divide mixture evenly between 2 pie crusts. Bake until golden—about 50-60 minutes. Let pie cool before serving.

ORANGESICLE PIE

1 (14-ounce) can Eagle Brand Sweetened Condensed Milk (not evaporated)
4 egg yolks
1/2 cup orange juice
1 tablespoon grated orange rind
1 (6-ounce) package graham cracker crumb crust
1 (3-ounce) package cream cheese, softened
1/3 cup confectioners' sugar
1/4 cup sour cream
1/4 teaspoon vanilla extract

Preheat oven to 325 degrees. In large bowl combine sweetened condensed milk, egg yolks, orange juice, and rind; mix well. Pour into crust. (Mixture will be thin). Bake 35 minutes or until knife inserted near center comes out clean. Meanwhile in small mixer bowl, combine remaining ingredients. Beat until smooth and well blended. Spread evenly on top of pie. Bake 10 additional minutes. Cool; chill thoroughly.

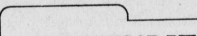

SHAKER SUGAR PIE

1 unbaked 9-inch pie shell
3/4 cup firmly-packed light brown sugar
1/4 cup flour
2 cups half-and-half
1 teaspoon vanilla extract
Few grains ground nutmeg
1/2 cup butter or margarine, softened

Prick pie shell and bake at 450 degrees for 5 minutes. Set aside. Reduce oven temperature to 350 degrees. Mix brown sugar with flour until blended. Spoon over bottom of partially-baked pie shell. Combine half-and-half, extract, and nutmeg; pour over sugar in pie shell. Dot with butter. Bake at 350 degrees for about 55 minutes, or until crust is lightly browned and filling is set.

A most delicious pie.

FRENCH COCONUT PIE

3 eggs, beaten well

Add:
1-1/2 cups sugar
1 stick margarine, melted
Pinch of salt
1 cup Angel Flake coconut
1 tablespoon lemon juice

Pour into unbaked pie shell; bake 1 hour at 325 degrees.

SOUTHERN MOLASSES CRUMB PIE

1 unbaked pie crust

Filling:
1/2 cup molasses
1 egg yolk

Add:
1/2 teaspoon soda dissolved in 3/4 cup boiling water. Mix.

Crumb portion:
3/4 cup flour
2 tablespoons shortening
1/2 teaspoon cinnamon
1/8 teaspoon nutmeg
1/8 teaspoon ginger
1/8 teaspoon cloves
1/2 cup brown sugar, well packed
1/4 teaspoon salt

To make the crumbs combine: flour, sugar, spices, and salt; then work in shortening. Put alternate layers of crumbs and filling into unbaked pie shell. Top with crumbs. Bake in hot oven 450 degrees until edges of crust begin to brown. Reduce heat to 375 degrees and bake until firm (about 20 minutes). Serve plain or with whipped cream.

Potato
DISHES

OVEN-FRIED SWEET POTATOES
Serves 8

6   medium potatoes (3 pounds)
½   cup vegetable oil
    Sugar (optional)

Preheat oven to 450 degrees. Scrub potatoes under cold running water. Peel and cut up into ½-inch pieces. In a bowl coat all pieces evenly with oil and arrange on baking sheet not touching each other as much as possible. Bake about 20 minutes, or until tender, turning once. Sprinkle with sugar (optional).

May be cut into long slices like french fries, if desired.

Edna Askins, Greenville, Texas

APRICOT YAMS
Serves 6–8

6   cooked, pared yams *or* sweet potatoes
1½ cups brown sugar
1½ tablespoons cornstarch
1   teaspoon grated orange peel
¼   teaspoon ground cinnamon
1   cup apricot juice
1   cup canned apricots, drained
3   tablespoons butter *or* margarine
½   cup chopped pecans

Cut yams in half. Arrange in a buttered baking dish. Combine brown sugar, cornstarch, orange peel, cinnamon and apricot juice in a saucepan. Cook and stir until sauce thickens. Stir in apricots, butter and pecans. Pour apricot mixture over yams. Bake at 375 degrees for 25 minutes, or until heated.

Shari Crider, Stoughton, Wis.

PARTY POTATO SALAD
Serves 12-14

1 (2-pound) bag frozen hash-brown potatoes
1 can cream of potato soup
1 can cream of celery soup
1/2 cup sour cream
1 cup shredded cheddar cheese
1 (8-ounce) package cream cheese
1/2 green pepper, finely chopped
1/2 cup chopped onion
2 teaspoons salt
1/4 teaspoon pepper
1 teaspoon paprika

Combine soups with softened cream cheese. Add sour cream, green pepper, onion, and seasonings. Put potatoes in a 3-quart shallow baking dish. Pour soup mixture over potatoes and stir. Spread out evenly; sprinkle with cheddar cheese. Bake at 325 degrees for 1-1/2 hours.

Laura Braun, Fond du Lac, Wis.

POTATO SALAD

6 large potatoes, baked
5 hard-cooked eggs, chopped
3 sticks celery, chopped
1 small onion, minced
1/4 cup French dressing
2 tablespoons mayonnaise
1/2 cup pickle relish

Place potatoes, eggs, celery, and onion in a large bowl and toss lightly. In a separate bowl, combine French dressing, mayonnaise, and pickle relish. Mix together and chill.

QUICK POTATOES

5 large potatoes
1/4 cup melted butter
3/4 cup shredded cheddar cheese
3 tablespoons grated Parmesan cheese

Slice potatoes and place in casserole dish. Pour butter over potatoes. Sprinkle with cheeses. Bake covered for 25 minutes at 475 degrees. Serve hot.

HASH BROWN POTATOES

5 cups cooked potatoes, cubed
1/3 cup butter
1 teaspoon salt
1 teaspoon minced onion

Heat the butter in a skillet and brown potatoes, stirring constantly. Add the remaining ingredients and cook well. Sprinkle parsley on top and serve immediately.

WINTER POTATOES ANNA
Serves 6

6 tablespoons margarine, melted
2 medium white potatoes, peeled and sliced
1 medium sweet potato, peeled and sliced
1 cup winter squash (your choice), peeled and sliced
1 apple, peeled and sliced
1 tablespoon thyme, crushed
Salt and pepper

Slice all vegetables and apple very thin, about ⅛ inch thick. A food processor works well. Cut waxed paper to cover bottom of an 8-inch cast iron skillet or baking dish. Brush the bottom and sides of skillet with margarine. Arrange a layer of one white potato in the bottom of the skillet. Put 1 slice in center and arrange overlapping circles of potatoes around it, from center to sides. Spoon 1 tablespoon of margarine over them; sprinkle with thyme, salt and pepper. Continue layering sweet potatoes, squash, apples and other white potato, seasoning each layer and spooning margarine over it, along with thyme, salt and pepper. Pour any leftover margarine on top.

Bake at 375 degrees for 45 minutes, or until vegetables are crisp and brown around the edges and tender when pierced with a fork. Remove from oven and run a knife around edge to loosen. Put a plate on top of the pan and quickly invert it so the cake unmolds onto platter. Remove waxed paper. To serve, cut into wedges.

Alternate: Use only white potatoes or half white and half sweet potatoes. I never knew how good sweet potatoes and winter squash tasted until I tried this dish.

Leone Keune, Maryland Heights, Mo.

QUICK-FIX POTATO SALAD FOR 20
Serves 20

1 (24-ounce) package frozen hash-brown potatoes with onions and peppers
1-1/2 cups chopped celery
1 (8-ounce) container sour cream dip with chives
2/3 cup mayonnaise or salad dressing
1 tablespoon sugar
1 tablespoon white wine vinegar
1 tablespoon prepared mustard
1/2 teaspoon salt
3 hard-cooked eggs, coarsely chopped

In covered 3- to 4-quart saucepan, cook potatoes with onions and peppers in large amount of boiling water 6-8 minutes, or until potatoes are tender. Drain well. In large bowl, combine cooked potatoes and celery. Set aside.

To make dressing: In small bowl, stir together sour cream dip, mayonnaise or salad dressing, sugar, vinegar, mustard, and salt. Add dressing to potato mixture. Toss gently to coat. Gently fold in chopped eggs. Turn into a 2-1/2-quart moisture-proof container. Cover and chill several hours, or overnight.

SPIRITED POTATO SALAD

3/4 cup mayonnaise
3/4 cup sour cream
1/4 cup beer
6 cups peeled, cubed, cooked potatoes
1/2 cup onions, chopped
3/4 cup celery, chopped
1/2 pound bacon, crisped and crumbled
Salt and pepper to taste

Blend mayonnaise, sour cream, and beer. Toss lightly with potatoes, onion, celery, and bacon. Add salt and pepper to taste. Chill 3 hours and serve cold or heat at 275 degrees for 20 minutes and serve hot.

Joy Shamway, Freeport, Ill.

MASHED POTATO CASSEROLE

8 to 10 medium potatoes, peeled
1 (8-ounce) carton sour cream
1 (8-ounce) package cream cheese
1 stick margarine
2 tablespoons chives
2 teaspoons salt
Paprika

Cook, drain, and mash potatoes. Beat cream cheese until smooth with electric mixer. Add remaining ingredients, except paprika; stir just to combine. Put in buttered 2-quart casserole and refrigerate overnight. Next day, sprinkle with paprika and bake, uncovered, at 350 degrees, just long enough to heat through.

Brenda Peery, Tannersville, Va.

OVEN–FRIED POTATOES
Serves 4

4 large baking potatoes, unpeeled
1/4 cup vegetable oil
1-2 tablespoons Parmesan cheese
1/2 teaspoon salt
1/4 teaspoon garlic powder
1/4 teaspoon paprika
1/8 teaspoon pepper

Wash unpeeled potatoes and cut lengthwise into 4 wedges. Place skin side down in 13x9x2-inch baking dish or pan. Combine remaining ingredients; brush over potatoes. Bake at 375 degrees for 1 hour, brushing with oil/cheese mixture at 15-minute intervals. Turn potatoes over for last 15 minutes. (These are wonderful with any type of roasted meat.)

This change-of-pace way to make potatoes tastes good with just about every meal—from sloppy joes to barbecue-grilled meat, poultry, or fish. They are also a tasty snack. These days, it's nice to have something quick to make for supper!

Marcella Swigert, Monroe City, Mo.

SWEET 'TATER CASSEROLE

Medium sweet pota-
toes, canned *or* fresh
(8–10)
1 (29-ounce) can Bartlett
pear halves
½ cup butter
1 cup maple syrup
½ teaspoon cinnamon
¼ teaspoon nutmeg
(optional)

If potatoes are canned, drain. If fresh, cook in boiling, salted water until tender. Peel; slice as desired. Combine butter, syrup, cinnamon and nutmeg. Arrange potatoes and drained pears in a shallow buttered casserole. Pour syrup mixture over all. Bake at 350 degrees for 35–40 minutes, or until glazed, basting several times with syrup in casserole.

Kit Rollins, Cedarburg, Wis.

POTATO KISSES
Serves 2

3 cups water
⅛ teaspoon plus ¼
teaspoon salt
½ pound potatoes, pared
and cut into 1-inch
cubes
¼ cup shredded Swiss
cheese
1 tablespoon butter *or*
margarine
⅛ teaspoon pepper
1 egg, beaten
2 tablespoons half-and-
half
1½ teaspoons chopped
parsley

Grease a baking sheet and set aside. Bring water and the ⅛ teaspoon salt to a boil over high heat. Add potatoes. Simmer 10–12 minutes, or until potatoes are tender; drain.
Preheat oven to 350 degrees. In medium bowl, mash potatoes. Stir in cheese, butter, the ¼ teaspoon salt and pepper until cheese is melted. Stir in egg, half-and-half and parsley; cool 10 minutes. Fit a pastry bag with a star-shaped tube. Spoon potatoes into bag. Pipe into 6 mounds on baking sheet. Bake 20–25 minutes or until lightly browned.

Gail Jordon, Sturgis, Mich.

SWEET 'N' SOUR POTATO MEDLEY
Serves 6

2 slices bacon
2 cups water
1 tablespoon sugar
3 tablespoons vinegar
1 medium clove garlic, crushed
4–5 drops red pepper sauce
1 can condensed cream of mushroom soup
1 package au gratin potatoes
1 cup thinly sliced carrots
1-1/2 cups frozen green peas
1 cup chopped tomato

Fry bacon until crisp; crumble. Stir water, sugar, vinegar, garlic, pepper sauce and soup into bacon fat in skillet. Stir in potatoes, sauce mix and carrots. Heat to boiling, stirring frequently; reduce heat. Cover and simmer about 25 minutes, or until potatoes are tender, stirring occasionally. Add peas and cook 5 minutes longer. Stir in chopped tomato. Garnish with crumbled bacon.

Laura Hicks, Troy, Mont.

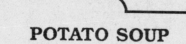

POTATO SOUP

4 cups water
3 baking potatoes
1 small onion, chopped
3 tablespoons margarine
1/2 cup chopped celery
2 cups milk

In a large Dutch oven, boil water; add peeled potatoes that have been sliced and cook until potatoes are tender. Add the remaining ingredients, except milk, and cook about 20 minutes. Add milk to warm and serve.

BRAISED POTATOES

4 medium potatoes, peeled and
quartered lengthwise
3 tablespoons corn oil
1 chicken bouillon cube
1 cup boiling water
Paprika

Fry potatoes in oil until lightly browned on all sides. Dissolve the bouillon cube in boiling water. Pour over potatoes. Cook, covered, over medium heat for 10-15 minutes, or until potatoes are done. (Since only a small amount of liquid is used, take care that the potatoes do not boil dry.) Sprinkle with a little paprika and serve hot. I am sure these will be a family favorite!

Lillian Smith, Montreal, Quebec, Canada

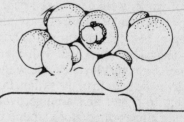

POTATO BOATS
Serves 2

2 large potatoes, boiled
and cooled
2 pieces fried bacon,
crisp and crushed
2 tablespoons sour cream
½ cup shredded cheddar
cheese
1 tablespoon chives

After the potatoes have been boiled and cooled, take a sharp knife and cut a circle in the potato. Then take a spoon and hollow the potato out leaving very little of the meat or potato around the sides of the skin. Place in hot oil and deep-fry until golden brown and slightly crispy. While still very hot, add half of the sour cream and 1 piece of bacon (crushed). Then sprinkle half of the cheddar cheese and half of the chives over the top. Serve warm.

This makes a wonderful appetizer and is also good as a snack.

Shannon Justice, Johnson City, Texas

TWICE-BAKED POTATOES

6 baking potatoes
1/2 teaspoon salt
1/2 teaspoon pepper
3 tablespoons margarine
3 ounces cream cheese
1 egg, beaten
1/3 cup cream

Bake potatoes for 1 hour at 450 degrees. Scoop out potato from skin and mash. In a separate bowl, combine all other ingredients and beat well. Combine the two mixtures and blend until creamy smooth. Fill the potato skins and bake for 25 minutes at 400 degrees. Serve hot.

COMPANY MASHED POTATOES
Serves 6

4 cups hot, seasoned, mashed potatoes
1 cup sour cream
1/3 cup chopped onions
4 ounces sharp cheddar cheese, grated
1/2 teaspoon seasoned salt

Combine all ingredients, except seasoned salt, in greased 1-1/2-quart casserole. Sprinkle with seasoned salt. Bake at 350 degrees for 25 minutes.

Can be made ahead of time and refrigerated.

Helen Weissinger, Levittown, Pa.

RED FLANNEL HASH
Serves 4

1 large or 2 medium-size baking potatoes
1 onion, diced
1 (12-ounce) can corned beef
1 (15-ounce) can diced beets

Thinly peel potatoes, and dice them. Peel and dice onion. Cook them for 10 minutes in enough boiling water to barely cover and in a pan with lid ajar to let onion vapors escape.

Cut the hash into bits. Drain the potato-onion mixture and the can of beets, saving the juices for soup.

Combine all ingredients in a baking dish. Bake at 350 degrees for 25 minutes. Garnish with parsley sprigs, if desired.

SOUR CREAM SCALLOPED POTATOES
Serves 6

1/2 cup chopped onion
2 tablespoons butter, melted
1 cup dairy sour cream
2 eggs, well-beaten
1 teaspoon salt
Dash of pepper
4 cups cooked, sliced new potatoes
1 cup shredded sharp cheddar cheese

Saute onion in butter; combine with sour cream, eggs, salt, and pepper. Place potatoes in buttered 1-quart casserole and pour sour cream sauce over top. Top with shredded cheddar. Bake 20 to 25 minutes at 350 degrees.

Kit Rollins, Cedarburg, Wis.

CREAMED POTATOES

6 large potatoes
1/2 pound butter, melted
1/2 teaspoon salt
1/2 teaspoon pepper
1/2 cup heavy cream
3/4 cup shredded Swiss cheese

Cook potatoes for about 20 minutes in boiling water. Let cool and peel. Break up coarsely, but do not mash. Add butter, salt, and pepper; combine and mix ingredients. Put into baking dish or 9-inch pie plate. Pour heavy cream over potatoes and butter mixture; let stand about 20 minutes. Sprinkle with cheese. Bake 20 minutes in a 175-degree oven or until cheese is melted.

Sheila Symonowicz, Loganville, Pa.

CRAB-STUFFED POTATOES
Serves 4–6

4 baking potatoes
½ cup butter (no substitute)
½ cup light cream
1 teaspoon salt
4 tablespoons grated onion
1 cup sharp cheese, grated
1 (5-ounce) can crabmeat
Tabasco sauce
Pepper to taste

Bake potatoes at 350 degrees for 1½ hours, until tender. Cut in half lengthwise; scoop out potato and whip with remaining ingredients. Refill shells and reheat at 425 degrees for 15 minutes. These freeze nicely.

Pat Habiger, Spearville, Kan.

FESTIVE POTATO WEDGES
Serves 6

2 tablespoons margarine
3 medium potatoes, unpeeled
1 tablespoon Parmesan cheese
1 teaspoon dry salad dressing mix
1 teaspoon parsley flakes
¼ teaspoon salt, optional

Microwave margarine on HIGH in an 8-inch round microwave dish for 30–45 seconds, or until melted.

Scrub potatoes. Cut each in half lengthwise; cut each half into 4 wedges. Coat each potato in margarine, arrange in dish.

Combine Parmesan cheese, dry salad dressing mix, parsley flakes and salt in small dish. Sprinkle evenly over potatoes. Cover with plastic wrap.

Microwave on HIGH for 8–10 minutes, or until potatoes are tender, rotating dish once. (85 calories per serving)

Mrs. John S. Novak, Melrose Park, Ill.

Relishes
& PRESERVES

CORN RELISH

3 dozen ears sweet corn
1/2 pound cabbage
4 onions
1 quart vinegar
2 cups sugar
3 green peppers
1/2 cup salt
3 tablespoons mustard
3 pimientos
1/2 teaspoon pepper

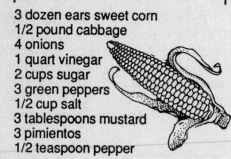

Cut corn from ear and chop cabbage, onions, peppers and pimientos. Mix all ingredients together and boil 1 hour. Pour into sterilized jars and seal.

Suzan L. Wiener, Spring Hill, Fla.

APRICOT RHUBARB JAM

8 cups finely chopped rhubarb
4 cups sugar
1 can apricot pie filling
1 (3-ounce) package orange-flavored gelatin

Combine rhubarb and sugar in a bowl (not metal). Allow to stand overnight. In the morning transfer to a pan; bring to a boil and simmer 10 minutes. Add the apricot pie filling and bring to a boil. Add the gelatin and stir until dissolved. Put in jars; cover and refrigerate or freeze.

TOMATO PEACH CHUTNEY

2 1/2 cups fresh tomatoes (canned may be used)
2 cups chopped peaches
1/2 cup white seedless raisins
1 cup chopped bell pepper
1/2 cup chopped onions
1 cup brown sugar
3/4 cup white sugar (more may be used)
3/4 cup white vinegar
1/2 teaspoon ground ginger
1 teaspoon curry powder

Remove skins from fresh tomatoes and peaches. If using canned, include juice. Combine all ingredients. Cook slowly, about 1 hour, until thickened. Pack boiling hot in sterilized jars and seal tightly. Process in boiling water bath, 5 minutes for half-pints and 10 minutes for pints.

TOMATO PRESERVES

11 cups chopped tomatoes
4 pounds granulated sugar
2 lemons, thinly sliced

Put tomatoes and juice, accumulated while chopping, into pan. Cover with water; add sugar and stir. Let this sit overnight. Drain off moisture and boil rapidly until it spins a thread when dropped from spoon. Add tomatoes and lemons; continue to boil until thick and clear.

FREEZER PICKLES

7 cups sliced, unpeeled cucumbers (1/4 inch thick)
1 cup chopped green bell pepper
1 cup thinly sliced onions
2 tablespoons pickling salt
2 cups sugar
1 cup cider vinegar
1 tablespoon celery seed

Put cucumbers, green pepper and onions in large bowl. Sprinkle 2 tablespoons pickling salt over mixture in bowl and distribute. Set in refrigerator for 2 hours. Drain well. Then mix sugar, vinegar and celery seed. Stir to dissolve sugar. Place cucumbers in freezer containers, tightly packed. Cover with syrup, just enough to cover. Leave 1-inch head space.

Peggy Fowler Revels, Woodruff, S.C.

SPRING COMBINATION MARMALADE

2 pounds strawberries
3 oranges
1 pound fresh pineapple
Grated rind of 1/2 orange
3 1/2 pounds granulated sugar

Wash and stem strawberries. Peel, core and grate fresh pineapple. Dice pulp of orange. Combine pineapple, oranges and grated rind with sugar. Boil 15 minutes. Add strawberries and continue cooking 12 minutes, or until mixture is transparent and thick, approximately 225 degrees. Cool and pour into sterilized jars.

SPICED PRESERVED CANTALOUPE

Makes 4 (1/2-pint) jars

1 tablespoon whole allspice
1 tablespoon chopped crystallized
  ginger
3-1/2 cups sugar
1 cup Karo light corn syrup
1 lemon, thinly sliced and seeded
1/2 cup water
1/2 cup dry white wine
1/4 teaspoon uniodized salt
6 cups cantaloupe, cut in 1-inch
  cubes

Tie allspice and ginger in cheese-cloth bag. In 5-quart saucepan place spice bag, 2 cups sugar and next 5 ingredients. Stirring occasionally, bring to boil over medium-high heat. Add fruit. Stirring occasionally, boil gently for 20 minutes. Remove from heat; place plate on fruit to hold below syrup level. Let stand overnight. Stir in remaining sugar. Stirring occasionally, bring to boil and boil gently for 20 minutes, or until fruit is transparent and syrup is thick. Skim surface; remove spice bag. Immediately pack fruit in clean, hot half-pint jars. Add boiling syrup, covering fruit and leaving 1/4-inch headspace. Wipe top edges with damp towel. Seal according to jar manufacturer's directions. Process in boiling-water bath for 5 minutes.

PEAR RELISH

4 pounds pears, peeled and cored
6 green sweet peppers
6 red sweet peppers
6 onions
1 tablespoon celery seed
1 tablespoon salt
3 cups sugar
3 cups vinegar
1 tablespoon allspice

Grind pears, peppers and onions in food chopper or processor. Add all the ingredients to the vinegar and sugar. Boil 30 minutes. Put in jars and seal.

Diantha Susan Hibbard, Rochester, N.Y.

MIXED VEGETABLE RELISH

Makes 5–6 (1/2-pint) jars

3 cups finely chopped carrots
1-1/2 cups finely chopped onion
3/4 cup finely chopped green
  pepper
3/4 cup finely chopped red pepper
3/4 cup finely chopped cabbage
2 cups cider vinegar
2 cups Karo light corn syrup
1 tablespoon uniodized salt
1-1/2 teaspoons mustard seed
1-1/2 teaspoons celery seed

Place first 5 ingredients in 5-quart saucepan. Cover with boiling water; let stand 5 minutes. Drain well. Return to saucepan; stir in remaining ingredients. Stirring frequently, bring to boil over medium heat. Reduce heat. Stirring occasionally, boil gently 20 minutes, or until mixture thickens. Immediately ladle into clean, hot half-pint jars, leaving 1/4-inch headspace. Wipe top edges with damp towel. Seal according to jar manufacturer's directions. Process in boiling-water bath for 10 minutes.

HOMEMADE PICNIC RELISH

Makes 3 cups

1 1/2 cups onion, chopped
1 cup green pepper, chopped
2 tablespoons salad oil
4 firm tomatoes, peeled and
  chopped
2 tablespoons white vinegar
1/4 teaspoon salt
1/2 teaspoon sugar
1/4 teaspoon dry mustard
1/4 teaspoon pickling spice
1/4 teaspoon pepper

In large skillet, cook and stir onion and green pepper in oil over medium heat until tender. Stir in remaining ingredients; heat to boiling; cool; cover and refrigerate several days.

Gwen Campbell, Sterling, Va.

PEAR LIME PRESERVES

Makes 4 (12-ounce) jars

8 cups pears, peeled, cored and
  chopped
1/2 cup water
1 tablespoon lime juice
1 package powdered pectin
1 tablespoon grated lime peel
1 thinly sliced lime
5-1/2 cups sugar

Prepare home-canning jars and lids according to manufacturer's instructions. Combine pears, water and lime juice in a large saucepan. Simmer, covered, for 10 minutes. Stir in pectin and bring to a full rolling boil, stirring frequently. Add lime peel, lime slices and sugar. Return to a full rolling boil. Boil hard 1 minute, stirring frequently. Carefully ladle into hot jars, leaving 1/4-inch headspace. Adjust caps. Process 15 minutes in a boiling-water bath canner.

COLD-PACKED PICKLES

Prepare sterile quart jars. Wash, and pack into the jars small cucumbers. Add to each quart jar:

1 tablespoon sugar
1 tablespoon salt
1 teaspoon mustard seed
1/2 teaspoon celery seed
2 saccharin tablets (1-grain)
Mixture of: 1 part vinegar and 2
  parts cold water

Seal; place in cold water bath. Heat to very hot, just to a boil. Turn off heat and let stand until cucumbers turn color. Remove from water and let cool, out of a draft. Allow to age 3 weeks before using.

For variety, use sliced cucumbers, onions, and green or red peppers. This combination makes a very pretty mixed pickle.

Alice Dick, Montpelier, Ohio

Salad
BOWL

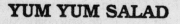

YUM YUM SALAD

1 (3-ounce) package lime gelatin
1 (8-ounce) package cream cheese, softened
1 cup boiling water
1 cup whipping cream *or* 1 package whipped topping mix, prepared
1 small can crushed pineapple
½ cup chopped pecans
Toasted coconut

Place gelatin, hot water and cream cheese in pan and stir over low heat until cheese is blended well into mixture. Remove from heat; add crushed pineapple and pecans. Place in refrigerator until it begins to thicken. Add whipped cream and let set until firm. Sprinkle with toasted coconut before serving.

GREEN AND WHITE VEGGIE SALAD

1 cup salad dressing
½ cup sour cream
1 tablespoon vinegar
1 tablespoon granulated sugar
1 small onion
⅛ teaspoon Worcestershire sauce
Dash hot sauce
Salt and pepper to taste

1 head cauliflower, pulled into florets
1 bunch broccoli, washed and cut up

Place the onion in food processor and process until finely chopped. Add remaining ingredients, except veggies, and process until well-blended. Pour over the broccoli and cauliflower.

CHEESE-LIME SALAD
Serves 10

3 cups boiling water
2 (3-ounce) packages lime-flavored gelatin
1 cup pineapple juice
1 teaspoon vinegar
½ teaspoon salt
2 cups creamed cottage cheese
1 teaspoon onion, finely chopped
1 teaspoon green pepper, finely chopped
½ cup cucumber, coarsely chopped
½ cup celery, coarsely chopped

Pour boiling water on gelatin in bowl; stir until gelatin is dissolved. Stir in pineapple juice, vinegar and salt. Pour 1 cup of the gelatin mixture into an 8-cup mold. Refrigerate until firm.

Refrigerate remaining mixture until slightly thickened, but not set; beat with beater until light and fluffy. Mix in remaining ingredients and pour on gelatin layer in mold. Refrigerate until firm. Unmold on serving plate.

SWEET AND SOUR PINEAPPLE COLESLAW

1 (1 pound, 4½-ounce) can crushed pineapple, drained
3 cups crisp cabbage, shredded
½ cup celery, chopped
¼ cup green pepper, chopped
1 cup miniature marshmallows
½ cup heavy cream
4 tablespoons wine vinegar
¼ teaspoon salt
⅛ teaspoon pepper

Combine first 5 ingredients. Beat cream until stiff; fold in vinegar, salt and pepper. Continue beating until well-blended; mix with salad; chill.

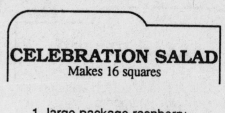

CELEBRATION SALAD
Makes 16 squares

1 large package raspberry gelatin
1 cup boiling water
1 (20-ounce) can pineapple, undrained
1 pint raspberry sherbet
2 cups vanilla ice cream, softened

Prepare gelatin in boiling water. Allow to cool before adding pineapple and sherbet. Fold in ice cream. Place in an 8 x 8-inch glass cake dish. Allow to set.

HARVEST CARROT SALAD
Serves 6–8

3 cups shredded carrots
1 (17-ounce) can apricot halves, drained and chopped
½ cup sliced celery
⅔ cup raisins
¼ cup chopped walnuts, toasted
½ cup salad dressing *or* mayonnaise

Combine all ingredients, tossing well. Cover and refrigerate before serving.

SPINACH SOUFFLÉ SALAD

1 (10-ounce) package frozen, chopped spinach
1 envelope unflavored gelatin
½ cup sugar
¾ teaspoon salt
1 cup cold water
¼ cup lemon juice
⅓ cup mayonnaise *or* salad dressing
1 cup cream-style cottage cheese, drained
¼ cup celery, finely chopped

Cook spinach according to package directions. Press against sides of a sieve to drain very thoroughly. Cool. In small saucepan soften gelatin in ½ cup cold water. Heat and stir until gelatin dissolves. Add sugar, salt, remaining water and lemon juice. Mix well. Place mayonnaise in a small bowl. Gradually stir in gelatin mixture. Chill until mixture begins to set. Beat gelatin mix-ture until fluffy. Fold in spinach, cottage cheese and celery. Turn into a 5-cup mold. Chill 4 hours or overnight.

PASTA AND VEGETABLE SALAD
Makes 5 quarts

1 pound mostaccioli noodles *or* other large pasta
2 tablespoons chicken soup mix
1 or 2 cucumbers, diced
1 large tomato, diced
1 small onion, finely chopped
1 green pepper, finely diced
   Sweet Herb Dressing (recipe follows)

Cook mostaccioli according to package directions, except substitute chicken soup mix for salt; drain and cool. Add cucumbers, tomato, onion and green pepper. Pour enough Sweet Herb Dressing over salad to moisten. Refrigerate several hours.

Sweet Herb Dressing:
Makes 2 cups
1 cup salad oil (or less)
1 cup vinegar
½ cup sugar
1 tablespoon parsley
2 teaspoons seasoning salt
2 teaspoons sweet 'n hot mustard
2 teaspoons minced green onion
1 teaspoon garlic powder
¾ teaspoon black pepper
½ teaspoon celery seed

Combine all ingredients in covered jar; shake well.

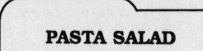

PASTA SALAD

1 pound medium shell macaroni
1/2 pound Provolene cheese
1/4 pound salami
1/2 pound pepperoni
1 can black olives
1 small bottle green olives
1 green pepper
3 stalks celery
1 small onion
1-1/2 teaspoons salt
1 teaspoon pepper
1 teaspoon oregano
3/4 cup oil
1/2 cup cider vinegar
3 tomatoes, chopped

Cook macaroni and drain. Cool. Cut cheese, salami, and pepperoni in bite-size pieces. Slice olives. Dice pepper, celery, and onions. Add salt, pepper, oregano, oil, and vinegar. Combine dressing with other ingredi-ents, except tomatoes; chill overnight. Add tomatoes just before serving.

TOMATO CHEESE SALAD
Serves 8

1½ cups hot condensed tomato soup, undiluted
½ cup cream cheese
1 tablespoon butter
¼ teaspoon salt
1 tablespoon onion juice
1 tablespoon unflavored gelatin
¼ cup cold water
½ cup mayonnaise
½ cup heavy cream *or* evaporated milk
¼ cup stuffed olives, chopped

Heat soup, cheese, butter, salt and onion juice until cheese has softened. Soften gelatin in cold water and dis-solve in hot mixture; cool until mix-ture starts to thicken. Whip cream and add with mayonnaise and stuffed ol-ives. Turn into mold and chill. When firm, unmold on lettuce and garnish with stuffed olives, sliced. Serve with mayonnaise sprinkled with paprika.

ARTICHOKE GRAPEFRUIT SALAD
Serves 4
(Pastel and picture pretty)

- 1 (15-ounce) can artichoke hearts
- ¼ cup salad oil
- 2 tablespoons vinegar
- 1 teaspoon Worcestershire sauce
- ½ teaspoon salt
- ⅛ teaspoon pepper
- 1 tablespoon chopped parsley
  Lettuce, romaine, endive
- 2 pink grapefruit, sectioned

Drain artichoke hearts and cut in halves. Combine oil, vinegar, salt, Worcestershire sauce, pepper and parsley, mixing well. Pour over artichokes in bowl and chill for several hours. Combine greens; add artichoke mixture and grapefruit; toss and serve.

ARTICHOKE RICE SALAD

- 1 package chicken rice combination mix (cooked as directed)
- 3 green onions, chopped
- ½ green pepper, chopped
- 8 to 10 pimiento green olives, chopped
- 2 jars marinated artichoke hearts in oil (dice and reserve liquid)
- ¼ teaspoon curry powder
- ⅓ cup mayonnaise
  Oil from 1 jar artichokes
  Salt and pepper to taste

Mix onion, pepper, olives and artichokes with cooled rice combination mix. In separate bowl, mix mayonnaise, oil and curry powder. Pour this dressing over rice mixture. Add salt and pepper. Mix and refrigerate overnight.

BROCCOLI SALAD

- 1 large bunch broccoli, finely cut (may use frozen)
- 2 cups grated mozzarella cheese
- ½ pound bacon, fried and crumbled
- 1 small red onion, finely cut

Mix together and add dressing (recipe follows).

Dressing:
- 1 cup mayonnaise
- 2 tablespoons vinegar
- ¼ cup sugar

Refrigerate several hours.

LETTUCE STUFFED SALAD

- 1 medium head iceberg lettuce, washed and well-drained
- 1 (1¼-ounce) package blue cheese
- 2 (3-ounce) packages cream cheese
- 2 tablespoons mayonnaise
- 2 tablespoons minced green onion
- 6 sliced pimiento-stuffed olives
- 2 teaspoons sweet relish
  Salt and pepper to taste
- ½ teaspoon Worcestershire sauce
  Dash hot pepper sauce
- 2 slices crisp-fried bacon, well-drained
  Sliced apples for bed

Hollow out the heart of lettuce, leaving a 1½-inch shell. Beat cheeses and mayonnaise together until smooth. Add remaining ingredients and mix well. Fill lettuce shell; wrap well in a clean towel and chill 1–2 hours, or until cheese is firm. Cut into crosswise slices ¾-inch thick. To serve,

layer a platter with sliced apples. Set the sliced lettuce over apples and serve.

BAKED MACARONI SALAD
Serves 4

- 2 pounds macaroni salad
- ½ pound baked **or** boiled ham, diced
- ¼ pound sliced cheddar cheese, cut up
- 1 tablespoon melted margarine
- ¼ cup seasoned bread crumbs

Preheat oven to 350 degrees. In greased 1¼-quart casserole, combine macaroni salad, ham and cheese. In cup combine melted margarine and bread crumbs. Sprinkle over top of macaroni salad. Bake for 20–25 minutes.

SANTA FE SALAD
Serves 4–6

- 1 head iceberg lettuce
- 2 cups cooked pinto beans
- ¼ pound grated longhorn cheese
- 2 tablespoons chopped green chili
- 6½ ounces tortilla chips, crushed
- 4 ounces prepared herb oil and vinegar salad dressing
- 1 avocado, sliced
- 2 tomatoes, cut in wedges
  Ripe pitted olives

Tear crisp lettuce into bite-size pieces. Toss with beans, grated cheese, green chili and tortilla chips. Toss salad lightly with dressing. Garnish with avocado slices, tomato wedges and ripe olives. Serve chilled.

RED AND GREEN HOLIDAY SALAD
Serves 4

- 2 cups torn lettuce leaves, rinsed and patted dry
- 2 cups fresh broccoli florets
- ½ pint cherry tomatoes
- ⅓ cup olive oil
- 2 tablespoons lemon juice
- ¼ teaspoon mustard
- ¼ teaspoon salt
  Pinch of pepper
- ½ cup croutons, seasoned with herbs and cheese

Line salad bowl with lettuce. Arrange broccoli and tomatoes on top. Combine oil, lemon juice, mustard, salt and pepper in a small bowl. Mix well; pour over salad. Sprinkle with croutons.

FRENCH-POTATO AND CUCUMBER SALAD
Serves 6

- 2 pounds medium-size red-skinned potatoes (about 12), cut in quarters
- ¼ cup vegetable oil
- 2 tablespoons red-wine vinegar
- 2 tablespoons coarse-grain prepared mustard
- 1 teaspoon salt
- 1 large cucumber, peeled or not peeled

Cook potatoes in boiling water to cover for 15–20 minutes until fork-tender. Meanwhile, whisk oil, vinegar, mustard and salt in a large serving bowl. Drain potatoes and add while hot to the dressing. Gently stir to coat. When cool, cover and marinate at least 2 hours, turning occasionally. Just before serving, cut cucumber in half lengthwise, then cut crosswise in thin slices. Add to potatoes and toss to mix.

BROCCOLI AND MUSHROOMS ELEGANT SALAD

- 2 bunches (stalks) fresh broccoli
- 1 pound fresh mushrooms
- 1 bottle Zesty Italian dressing

Cut broccoli into flowerets. Add thickly sliced mushrooms. Pour Italian dressing over broccoli and mushrooms. Add tight-fitting cover. Refrigerate several hours or overnight, turning occasionally. This is very good and is really elegant-looking when served in a pretty dish. Perfect for potluck dinners and church suppers. Only you will know how easy it is!

CHICK-PEA AND SPINACH SALAD

- 6 ounces dried chick-peas
- 1 pound fresh spinach
- 6 tablespoons olive oil
- 2 tablespoons wine vinegar
  Salt and pepper
- ½ cup plain yogurt
- 2 tablespoons chopped parsley

Soak chick-peas in cold water overnight. Strain. Put in large saucepan and add about 4 cups fresh water. Bring to a boil; cover; simmer gently for 1½ hours, or until peas are tender but not mushy. Let peas cool in the cooking liquid, then drain.

Wash spinach; discard any coarse or damaged leaves, and pull off all stems. Cut large leaves into pieces; leave small leaves whole. Combine chick-peas and spinach in a salad bowl. Pour in oil and vinegar; add salt and

pepper to taste. Toss ingredients together, but gently, so as not to break up peas. Chill salad until ready to serve. At serving time, arrange the mixture in a shallow bowl and top with yogurt. Sprinkle parsley over all.

BEST PEA SALAD

- 1 (14-ounce) can small-kernel white corn
- 1 can small-size peas
- 1 can French green beans
- 1 cup diced celery
- 1/4 cup fresh onion
- 1 green pepper, chopped
  Sliced olives as desired for taste

Dressing:
- 1 cup sugar
- 3/4 cup white vinegar
- 1/2 cup oil
- 1/2 teaspoon salt
- 1/4 teaspoon pepper

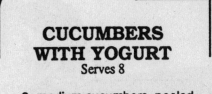

Boil together dressing ingredients for about 3 minutes—then cool.

Put vegetables in bowl. Pour dressing over vegetables and marinate in refrigerator for about 24 hours before serving.

CUCUMBERS WITH YOGURT
Serves 8

- 2 medium cucumbers, peeled, seeded and diced
  Salt
- 1 garlic clove, mashed *or* minced
- 2 cups yogurt
- 2 tablespoons fresh lemon juice
- 1 teaspoon chopped dill
- 2 tablespoons olive oil
- 1 tablespoon chopped fresh mint *or* 1 teaspoon dried mint

Sprinkle cucumbers with salt; let stand 15 minutes and pour off liquid. Mash garlic in bowl with lemon juice; add yogurt, dill and cucumbers; mix well and chill. When serving, sprinkle with oil and mint.

GAZPACHO SALAD MOLD

- 1 envelope unflavored gelatin
- ¼ cup chicken broth
- 1¾ cups tomato juice
- ¼ cup minced green pepper
- ¼ cup chopped celery
- ¼ cup sliced green onion
- ¼ cup chopped cucumber
- 1 tablespoon Worcestershire sauce
- ¾ teaspoon lemon juice
  Dash celery salt
- 2 small tomatoes, chopped
  Lettuce

In small bowl sprinkle gelatin over chicken broth. Soften for 10 minutes. In medium saucepan combine tomato juice, green pepper, celery, green onion, cucumber, Worcestershire sauce, lemon juice and celery salt. Simmer 5 minutes. Remove from heat and stir in gelatin. Stir until dissolved. Set saucepan in cold water and stir until cool. Fold in tomatoes. Pour mixture into a small, shallow rectangular-s̲ _____ Chill covered, for 4 h_____ _____ _____ _____ or r_____ _____ _____ _____ uce _____

BROCCOLI-RAISIN SALAD

- 3 heads broccoli, cut in small pieces
- ½ cup chopped onion
- 4 slices bacon, cooked and crumbled
- ¾ cup raisins

Toss ingredients together.

Dressing:
- 1 cup mayonnaise
- 2 tablespoons sugar
- 2 tablespoons white vinegar

Dressing should be tangy in flavor. Pour over salad. Again, toss lightly.

LEMON-LIME VEGETABLE SALAD
Serves 5–6

- 2 medium carrots, grated
- 1 stalk celery, thinly sliced
- 1 medium green pepper, seeded and finely chopped
- ½ small onion, finely chopped
- 2 tablespoons lemon juice
  Dash paprika
- 1 tablespoon water
- 1 envelope gelatin
- 1½ cups lemon-lime–flavor soda

Prepare vegetables and set aside. In small saucepan, mix lemon juice, paprika and water; heat almost to boiling point. Remove from heat and add gelatin, stirring until thoroughly dissolved. Add soda and stir until well-mixed. Add vegetables and pour into small, rectangular dish. Chill for several hours or overnight until set. Cut into squares and serve. Top with a dollop of mayonnaise, if desired.

BURGUNDY BEET SALAD
Serves 7

- 1 pound cooked beets, skinned and diced
- ½ cup walnuts, finely chopped
- 1 tablespoon prepared horseradish
- ⅓ cup unflavored yogurt
- 1¼ teaspoons mayonnaise
- ¼ cup half-and-half *or* cream
- ⅓ cup orange juice
- ¼ teaspoon salt
- ⅛ teaspoon pepper
- 2 tablespoons parsley, chopped

Place beets and walnuts in a salad or serving bowl; stir in horseradish, yogurt, mayonnaise, half-and-half and orange juice. Mix thoroughly; season with salt and pepper. When serving, sprinkle each serving with the chopped parsley.

CHINESE COLD PLATE
Serves 6

- 4 cups shredded lettuce
- ⅔ cup cooked rice, chilled
- 1 cup frozen peas, thawed
- ¾ cup lean pork, cooked and diced
- ½ cup water chestnuts, sliced
- ¼ cup Miracle Whip salad dressing
- ¼ cup sour cream
- ½ teaspoon celery seed
  Salt to taste

Toss first 5 ingredients together. Combine next 4 ingredients for dressing. Pour over vegetable-meat mixture and toss.

Chill until served. Garnish with pineapple slices and fresh strawberries.

FRESH SPINACH SALAD

- 1 package fresh spinach
- 1 (No. 2) can bean sprouts, rinsed and drained
- 1 (8-ounce) can water chestnuts, drained and sliced
- 4 hardcooked eggs, sliced
- 1 medium onion
- ½ package bacon, fried and crumbled

Dressing:
- ¾ cup sugar
- ¾ cup vinegar
- ¼ cup oil
- ⅓ cup ketchup
- 2 teaspoons salt
- 1 teaspoon Worcestershire sauce

Tear clean, crisp, well-drained spinach leaves in a large bowl. Add other ingredients. Mix dressing ingredients and pour over salad. Toss well and serve immediately.

QUICK MACARONI SALAD
Serves 10

1 box macaroni and cheese dinner
1 can tuna, drained
4 eggs, hard cooked
5 tablespoons mayonnaise
1/4 cup chopped pickles

Cook macaroni and cheese dinner as directed on package. Then add and mix all additional ingredients; refrigerate.

FROZEN SEAFOOD SALAD MOLD
Serves 4–6

2 teaspoons unflavored gelatin
1/3 cup cold water
2 cups flaked cooked seafood (crab, shrimp or lobster)
2/3 cup tomato ketchup
2 tablespoons lemon juice
3 tablespoons vinegar
1 teaspoon prepared horseradish
1/4 teaspoon salt
1/2 cup mayonnaise
  Tomatoes or lettuce

Soften gelatin in cold water and dissolve over hot water. Combine with seafood, ketchup, lemon juice, vinegar, horseradish and salt. Fold in mayonnaise. Freeze in refrigerator tray until firm, about 2 hours. Cut into cubes and arrange on slices of tomatoes or lettuce.

Note: Serve Frozen Seafood Salad in hollowed-out tomatoes or in cucumber boats ... or serve as a loaf on watercress with border of overlapping cucumber and tomato slices.

FROZEN WALDORF SALAD

1/2 cup sugar
1/2 cup pineapple juice
1/8 teaspoon salt
1/4 cup lemon juice
1/2 cup diced celery
1/2 cup crushed pineapple, drained
2 medium apples, diced with skins left on
1/2 cup walnuts or pecans, broken in small pieces
1 cup heavy cream, whipped

Combine sugar, pineapple juice, salt and lemon juice in saucepan. Cook over medium heat, stirring until thick. Let cool. Stir in celery, pineapple, apples and nuts. Fold in whipped cream.

Spoon into an 8-inch square pan or individual molds. Freeze. Garnish with maraschino cherries. Allow salad to be at room temperature for about 20 minutes before serving.

CUCUMBER DELIGHT

1 (3-ounce) package lime gelatin
3/4 cup boiling water
1 package unflavored gelatin
1/4 cup cold water
1 cup salad dressing
1 tablespoon finely minced onion
1 cup cottage cheese
1 cucumber, peeled and chopped
1/8 to 1/4 teaspoon Tabasco sauce
1 clove garlic, minced
1/2 cup slivered almonds
  Green food coloring

Dissolve lime gelatin in boiling water, then unflavored gelatin in cold water. Put salad dressing, onion, cottage cheese, cucumber, Tabasco sauce, garlic and almonds in blender; blend well. Then add lime and unflavored gelatins; blend again. Add green food coloring for a more vivid color. Mold and chill overnight.

This is so creamy and good!

ORANGE CHICKEN SALAD
Serves 2

2 cups cooked, cubed chicken
1 cup sliced celery
1/4 cup chopped walnuts
1 teaspoon grated onion
1/2 teaspoon salt
1/3 cup orange juice
1/4 cup mayonnaise
2 oranges, peeled and sectioned
1/4 cup dry bread crumbs
1/4 cup grated Parmesan cheese

Combine chicken, celery, walnuts, onion, salt, orange juice and mayonnaise in mixing bowl; mix well. Cover and refrigerate for 1 hour. Stir in orange sections. Spoon mixture into casserole; sprinkle with bread crumbs and Parmesan cheese. Bake in a preheated 350-degree oven for 25 minutes, or until mixture is heated through and cheese is lightly browned. Serve with rolls.

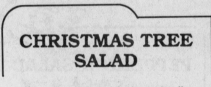

CHRISTMAS TREE SALAD

1 1/2 cups canned fruit cocktail
1 package lime gelatin
2 tablespoons lemon juice
  Whipped cream

Drain fruit cocktail, reserving syrup. Add enough hot water to syrup to make 2 cups liquid. Dissolve gelatin in hot liquid; stir in lemon juice. Cool until slightly thickened; fold in 1 cup fruit cocktail. Set cone-shaped paper cups lined with waxed paper into small glasses. Fill with thickened gelatin mixture. Chill until firm. Unmold onto individual dessert plates, gently pulling off paper. Trim trees with whipped cream festoons piped on with cake decorating tube; decorate base of tree with remaining fruit cocktail.

This is bound to get raves and compliments from your guests!

SANTA'S RED RASPBERRY RING
Serves 8–10

1 (10-ounce) package frozen red raspberries, thawed
2 (3-ounce) packages raspberry-flavored gelatin
2 cups boiling water
1 pint vanilla ice cream
1 (6-ounce) can (¾ cup) frozen pink lemonade concentrate, thawed
¼ cup pecans

Drain raspberries, reserving syrup. Dissolve gelatin in boiling water. Add ice cream by spoonfuls, stirring until melted. Stir in lemonade concentrate and reserved syrup. Chill until partially set. Add raspberries and pecans. Turn into a 6-cup ring mold. Chill until firm.

PEPPERONI SALAD
Serves 6–8

1 medium onion, thinly sliced
8 ounces pepperoni, thinly sliced
¼ cup crumbled bleu cheese
⅔ cup salad oil
⅓ cup cider vinegar
Salt and freshly ground pepper to taste
10 ounces fresh spinach, washed thoroughly, dried and chopped
½ head iceberg lettuce, chopped

One day before serving, separate onion slices into rings and place in large bowl; add pepperoni slices and bleu cheese. Add oil, vinegar, salt and pepper. Toss in the spinach and lettuce. Chill salad overnight in covered bowl.

ORANGE-CREAM SALAD
Serves 10

1 (20-ounce) can pineapple chunks, drained
1 (16-ounce) can peach slices, drained
1 (11-ounce) can mandarin orange sections, drained
3 medium bananas, sliced
2 medium apples, cored and chopped
1 (3-1/3 to 3-3/4 ounce) package vanilla instant pudding mix
1-1/2 cups milk
1/2 of a 6-ounce can (1/3 cup) frozen orange juice concentrate, thawed
3/4 cup dairy sour cream
Lettuce

In a large bowl combine pineapple chunks, peaches, orange sections, bananas, and apples; set aside. In small bowl combine dry pudding mix, milk, and orange juice concentrate. Beat with rotary beater 1 to 2 minutes or until well blended. Beat in sour cream. Fold into fruit mixture. Cover and refrigerate several hours. Serve salad on lettuce leaves.

RASPBERRY-WINE MOLD
Serves 4–6

1 (16-ounce) can raspberries
½ cup red wine
Water
2 (3-ounce) packages raspberry-flavored gelatin

Drain raspberries into 2-cup measure; add ½ cup red wine and water to make 2 cups. Prepare raspberry gelatin, using berry-wine-water mixture. Pour into individual molds. Add raspberries to molds when gelatin has cooled. When firm, invert onto serving plates.

THREE-FRUIT MOLDED SALAD

2 envelopes unflavored gelatin
½ cup grapefruit juice
½ cup sugar syrup*
¼ cup orange juice
1 teaspoon lemon juice
2 cups ginger ale
Pinch of salt
½ cup cherries, drained
1 cup grapefruit sections
1 cup orange sections
Lettuce

In top of double boiler over medium heat, combine gelatin with the grapefruit juice and stir to dissolve the gelatin. Remove from heat. Add sugar syrup, orange and lemon juices, ginger ale and salt. Stir well. Chill until slightly thickened. Add cherries, grapefruit and orange sections. Pour and spoon into a lightly oiled 6-cup mold or 6 individual (1-cup) molds. Chill until firm, about 1–2 hours. Unmold and serve on a bed of lettuce. Top each serving with a dollop of mayonnaise.
*To make sugar syrup, combine ½ cup sugar and ½ cup boiling water.

YOGI BERRY SALAD

1 Red Delicious apple, cored and chopped
1 cup halved, seedless green grapes
1 cup sliced strawberries
½ cup sliced celery
¼ cup raisins
½ cup lemon yogurt
2 tablespoons sunflower seeds
Lettuce

In a bowl, combine apple, grapes, strawberries, celery and raisins. Toss gently. Fold in yogurt. Cover and chill. Just before serving, stir in sunflower seeds. Serve on lettuce leaves.

OLIVE WREATH MOLD

- 1 (20-ounce) can crushed pineapple
- 1 (3-ounce) package lime gelatin
- ¼ teaspoon salt
- ½ cup grated cheddar **or** American cheese
- ½ cup chopped pimientos, drained
- ½ cup chopped celery
- ⅔ cup chopped pecans
- 1 cup whipping cream
  Stuffed green olives

Drain pineapple into saucepan. Reserve pineapple. Heat juice; add gelatin and dissolve thoroughly. Let cool in refrigerator until it starts to thicken. Stir in salt. Add cheese, pimientos, celery, pecans and reserved pineapple. Whip cream and fold into gelatin mixture. Line bottom of a 4-cup mold with sliced green olives. Carefully spoon mixture into mold. Chill until firm. Unmold and serve.

HOLIDAY DELIGHT
Serves 10–12

- 2 large packages lime gelatin
- ½ pint whipping cream, whipped
- 1 small can crushed pineapple, drained
- 1 small jar maraschino cherries, drained and sliced
- 1 cup miniature marshmallows

Prepare gelatin in large bowl according to package directions. Place gelatin bowl on ice. Beat with rotary beater until fluffy and firm. Fold in whipped cream. Combine pineapple, cherries and marshmallows with gelatin. Pour into lightly greased mold. Refrigerate overnight.

24-HOUR SALAD

- 1 can Eagle Brand sweetened condensed milk (not evaporated)
- 1 cup large grapes, seeded and halved
- 1 cup nuts, coarsely broken
- 1 (8-ounce) can crushed pineapple, including juice
- ½ pound small marshmallows
- 1 package Dream Whip (whipped) **or** equal amount of Cool Whip
- ¼ cup vinegar
- 1 teaspoon prepared mustard

Mix milk, vinegar and mustard together, then add all other ingredients. Make the day before, if needed.

CRANBERRY MALLOW SALAD
Serves 10–12

- 2 cups raw cranberries, ground
- 4 cups miniature marshmallows
- ½ cup sugar
- 1 (8-ounce) can crushed pineapple, drained
- ½ cup chopped nuts
- ¼ cup unpared, chopped apple
- 1 cup whipping cream, whipped

Add marshmallows, sugar and pineapple to ground cranberries. Chill overnight. Add apple and nuts. Fold in whipped cream. Chill.

BING CHERRY SALAD

- 1 (3-ounce) package cherry gelatin
- 1 cup boiling water
- 1 large can black bing cherries
- ½ pint sour cream
- ½ cup chopped pecans

Dissolve gelatin in bowl with boiling water. Drain cherry juice and add to water. Refrigerate until gelatin begins to form, about 70 minutes. Beat sour cream into gelatin; add cherries and pecans. Pour mixture into a 9 x 9 x 2-inch square pan and refrigerate until firm.

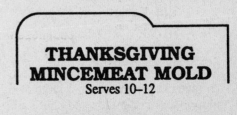

THANKSGIVING MINCEMEAT MOLD
Serves 10–12

- 2 large packages cherry gelatin
- 3½ cups hot water
- ½ cup walnuts, finely chopped
- 2 cups moist mincemeat

Dissolve cherry gelatin in hot water. Pour ¾ cup mixture into 1½-quart mold; chill until firm. Chill remaining gelatin until slightly thickened; fold in nuts and mincemeat. Turn into mold over firm gelatin; chill again until firm; unmold. Garnish with sweetened whipped cream, maraschino cherry halves and mint leaves.

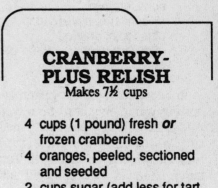

CRANBERRY-PLUS RELISH
Makes 7½ cups

- 4 cups (1 pound) fresh **or** frozen cranberries
- 4 oranges, peeled, sectioned and seeded
- 2 cups sugar (add less for tart taste)
- 1 apple, unpeeled and cut up
- ½ teaspoon almond flavoring
- 1 (8½-ounce) can crushed pineapple, undrained

Chop cranberries in a food processor, then add oranges and chop. Add remaining ingredients; pulse for several seconds to blend. Chill several hours before serving.

FRUIT AND COTTAGE CHEESE MOLD
Serves 4

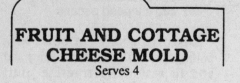

2 teaspoons unflavored gelatin
3 tablespoons canned pineapple juice
2½ cups cottage cheese
Lettuce *or* other greens
Sliced pineapple
Strawberries
French dressing

Soften gelatin in pineapple juice and dissolve over hot water. Stir into cottage cheese. Pour into 1 large or 6 individual oiled molds and chill until firm. Unmold on lettuce or other greens and garnish with sliced pineapple and halved strawberries. Serve with French dressing.

LOW-CALORIE PINEAPPLE SALAD
Serves 8

2 (8-ounce) packages lemon gelatin
2 cups boiling water
1 (1-pound) can grapefruit sections, drained
1 (8-ounce) can crushed pineapple, drained
2 cups (1 pint) plain low-fat yogurt

In bowl, combine the gelatin and boiling water. Stir until dissolved. Add drained fruits; mix until blended. Chill until mixture is syrupy. Add the yogurt and mix well. Turn into a 1½-quart mold and chill until firm.

CONGEALED FRUIT SALAD

2 (3-ounce) packages strawberry gelatin
2 cups boiling water

1 (10-ounce) package frozen strawberries, thawed
2 ripe bananas
1 (8-ounce) can crushed pineapple, not drained
1 cup sour cream

Mix strawberry gelatin with boiling water; add strawberries, mashed bananas and pineapple. Chill until set. Top with sour cream.

CELERY AND ORANGE SALAD
Serves 6

3 medium oranges
2 ribs celery
2 shallots, chopped
4 tablespoons oil
1 tablespoon lemon juice
Salt and pepper
Chopped parsley

Peel oranges, cutting just beneath the pith. Hold the fruit in one hand and cut out each segment, freeing it from its protective membranes as you cut. Cut the celery into 1½-inch julienne strips. Put the shallots, oranges and celery into a bowl; add the remaining ingredients and toss. Allow salad to rest for 1–6 hours before serving.

SALAD BY CANDLELIGHT
Serves 2

2 lettuce leaves
1 banana, cut in half crosswise
2 pineapple rings
1 cherry *or* red grape, cut in half

On two small plates, place lettuce leaves. Place pineapple in center of leaf. Stand ½ banana in hole of each pineapple ring. Attach cherry half on top of each banana to represent a flame. Now doesn't that look like a candle?

ORANGE DELIGHT

2 cups small-curd cottage cheese
2 cups crushed pineapple, drained
2 small *or* 1 large package orange-flavored gelatin
2 cups whipped topping

Fold all ingredients together; chill before serving. For fewer calories, use low-fat cottage cheese, unsweetened pineapple and sugar-free gelatin.

FRUIT WALDORF
Serves 4

2 cups diced apples (small)
1 cup diced pineapple
2 tablespoons (*or* less) honey
½ cup chopped walnuts
½ cup coconut

Combine and mix all ingredients together well. Chill thoroughly before serving on a bed of lettuce.

FRUIT SALAD

1 can fruit cocktail, drained
1 can tidbit pineapple, drained
3 apples
1 orange
2 or 3 bananas
1 bottle maraschino cherries
1 cup miniature marshmallows
1 cup Cool Whip
Sauce (recipe follows)

Sauce for Fruit Salad:
2 tablespoons vinegar
2 eggs
2 tablespoons sugar

Beat eggs. Add sugar and beat well. Add vinegar. Cook mixture in double boiler until thick; cool. Add cooled sauce to salad; fold in Cool Whip.

FRUIT COCKTAIL SALAD

1 (5-5/8 ounce) package vanilla
  flavored Jello instant pudding mix
1-1/3 cups buttermilk
1 (8-ounce) container Cool Whip
1 (30-ounce) can fruit cocktail, well-
  drained
2 cans mandarin oranges, well-
  drained
1 cup miniature rainbow-colored -
  marshmallows (optional)

Blend buttermilk into pudding mix
using medium speed of mixer. When
smooth, blend in Cool Whip. If consistency of mixture seems too thick,
add a little more buttermilk. Fold in
fruit cocktail and mandarin oranges,
reserving half a can of oranges for
garnish. Swirl a design on top of salad
with a tablespoon. Gently arrange
balance of mandarin orange slices in
swirled design on top of salad.

Add colored marshmallows to
mixture before garnishing, if desired.

GOLDEN FRUIT SALAD

2 large Golden Delicious apples,
  diced
2 large Red Delicious apples,
  diced
4 large bananas, sliced
2 (20 ounce) cans pineapple
  chunks, drained (reserve juice)
2 (16 ounce) cans Mandarin
  oranges, drained
Whole green grapes, optional

Mix Together:
1 cup sugar
4 tablespoons corn starch
Reserved pineapple juice
2 tablespoons lemon juice
2/3 cup orange juice

Stir and boil 1 minute. Pour hot
mixture over fruit. Leave uncovered until cool.

SHORTCUT FROZEN SALAD

1 small package *instant* lemon
  pudding
1 pint whipped topping, thawed
1/2 cup mayonnaise
2 tablespoons lemon juice
1 (1-pound) can fruit cocktail,
  drained
1 cup miniature marshmallows
1/4 cup chopped pecans

Prepare pudding according to package directions; blend in whipped topping, mayonnaise, and lemon juice.
Fold in remaining ingredients. Turn
into a 9x5x3-inch loaf pan and freeze
until firm. Slice to serve.

GUM DROP FRUIT SALAD

Serves 8

1 (#2 can) pineapple tidbits
1/4 cup sugar
2 tablespoons flour
1/4 teaspoon salt
3 tablespoons lemon juice
1-1/2 teaspoons vinegar
2 cups seedless grapes, halved
2 cups miniature white marshmallows
2/3 cup gumdrops, halved (do not use
  black drops)
1 (4-ounce) bottle maraschino cherries, drained and halved
1/4 cup chopped pecans
1 cup whipping cream, whipped

Drain pineapple, reserving 1/3 cup
of syrup. Combine sugar, flour, and
salt. Add reserved pineapple syrup,
lemon juice, and vinegar. Cook over
medium heat, stirring constantly until
thick and boiling. Continue cooking 1
minute. Set aside and cool. Combine
pineapple and remaining ingredients,
except the whipped cream. Fold the
cooked dressing into the whipped
cream. Cover and refrigerate for 12-
24 hours.

BANANA BAVARIAN CREAM

1 (6-ounce) package lemon-flavored
  gelatin
2 cups hot water
1/4 teaspoon salt
2/3 cup sugar
1/2 cup heavy cream
5 bananas

Dissolve gelatin in hot water. Add
salt and sugar. Chill until cold and
syrupy. Fold in cream, whipped only
until thick and shiny, but not stiff.
Crush bananas to pulp with fork, and
fold at once into mixture. Chill until
slightly thickened. Turn into mold.
Chill until firm. Unmold. Serve with
Strawberry Sauce. (Recipe below)

Strawberry Sauce:
1/3 cup butter
1 cup powdered sugar
1 egg white
2/3 cup strawberries

Cream butter and sugar, gradually
add crushed strawberries and egg
whites. Beat well.

BUNNY SALAD

Serves 6-8

1 (3-ounce) package orange gelatin
1 cup boiling water
1 cup pineapple juice and water
1 teaspoon grated orange rind
1-1/3 cups crushed pineapple,
  drained
1 cup grated raw carrots

Dissolve gelatin in boiling water.
Add pineapple juice/water mixture
and orange rind. Chill until slightly
thickened. Then fold in pineapple and
carrots. Pour into 6-8 individual round
molds. Chill until firm. Unmold on
crisp lettuce. Add carrot strips to form
ears, a large marshmallow for the
head, and half a marshmallow for the
tail. Serve plain or with mayonnaise,
if desired.

SLICED CUCUMBERS IN SOUR CREAM
Serves 4

2 cups thinly sliced cucumbers
1/4 cup sliced Spanish onions
1/4 cup seasoned vinegar
1/4 cup sour cream

Pour vinegar over cucumbers and onions, let stand 15 minutes. Drain in a strainer and discard liquid. Combine sour cream with cucumbers. Serve icy cold.

CUCUMBER-YOGURT SALAD
Serves 6

5 cups thinly sliced cucumbers (2 large)
3/4 cup thinly sliced red onion (1 small)
1 (8-ounce) carton plain low-fat yogurt
3 tablespoons wine vinegar
1 tablespoon lemon juice
1 tablespoon minced fresh basil
1 clove garlic, crushed
1 teaspoon Dijon mustard
1/8 teaspoon salt
1/8 teaspoon pepper

Combine cucumber and onion in large bowl; cover and chill. Combine yogurt and remaining ingredients in a small bowl; stir to blend. Cover and chill. Pour mixture over vegetables and toss. Serve immediately. (45 calories per serving)

CELERY SLAW
Serves 6

3 cups celery, thinly sliced
1/2 cup carrots, grated
1 apple, unpeeled, cored, and diced
1/2 cup mayonnaise
2 tablespoons sugar
1/2 teaspoon salt

2 tablespoons vinegar
1/2 cup walnuts, coarsely chopped (optional)

Combine celery, carrots, and apples. Thoroughly blend remaining ingredients and fold into celery mixture. If desired, fold in walnuts or sprinkle over top as a garnish. Chill at least 30 minutes before serving in lettuce-lined bowl. Delightfully crunchy!

SWEET-SOUR CABBAGE SLAW
Serves 6-8

3 cups finely-shredded cabbage
1 tablespoon grated onion
1/2 teaspoon celery salt
1 tablespoon sugar
1 tablespoon vinegar
1/4 teaspoon salt
1/8 teaspoon cayenne pepper
1/2 cup heavy cream, whipped or sour cream

Combine cabbage, onion, and celery salt. Blend together sugar, vinegar, salt, pepper, and cream. Pour over cabbage and toss.

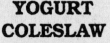

YOGURT COLESLAW
Serves 10-12

1 cup unflavored yogurt
1/4 cup mayonnaise
1/2 teaspoon dry mustard
1 teaspoon seasoned salt
1/2 teaspoon salt
1/2 teaspoon celery salt
1/8 teaspoon pepper
1/4 cup chopped onion
2 tablespoons sugar
8 cups shredded cabbage
1 medium carrot, grated
1/2 cup grated green pepper

Combine yogurt, mayonnaise, dry mustard, seasoned salt, salt, celery salt, pepper, onion, and sugar in a medium bowl. Cover and chill.

Combine cabbage, carrots, and green peppers in large bowl. Pour chilled dressing over vegetables, tossing lightly. Serve immediately.

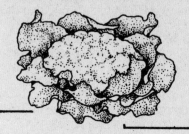

FRUITED COLE SLAW

1 medium head cabbage, shredded
1 medium carrot, grated
1/2 cup crushed pineapple, drained
1 teaspoon salt

Mix salt with cabbage and let stand about half an hour. Squeeze out excess moisture and add carrot and pineapple.

1 cup vinegar
1/2 cup water
1-1/2 cups sugar
1 teaspoon dry mustard
1 teaspoon celery seed

Combine and boil these ingredients 1 minute. Cool. Pour over cabbage, carrot and pineapple mixture; toss to blend. Serve as a chilled salad, if desired. (This slaw can be frozen.)

SPINACH SALAD

2 to 3 packages fresh spinach
1 pound cooked bacon, chopped
1 can water chestnuts, chopped
1 can bean sprouts
2 hard-cooked eggs, chopped

Wash spinach thoroughly and break into bite-size pieces. Add remaining ingredients.
Dressing:
1 cup salad oil (Mazola)
1/4 cup ketchup
1/2 cup vinegar
1/2 cup sugar

Stir dressing into salad and toss well.

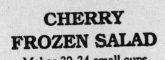

CHERRY FROZEN SALAD

Makes 32-34 small cups

1 (16-ounce) can cherry pie filling
1 large can crushed pineapple, drained
1 can sweetened condensed milk
1 large carton Cool Whip
2 cups miniature marshmallows
1 cup chopped pecans

Mix all together in order given. Spoon into paper cups. Freeze.

This is delicious and can also be used as a dessert.

SPRINGTIME SALAD

Serves 6

1 (1-pound) can grapefruit sections
4 green onions, thinly sliced
1/2 cup sliced radishes
1/2 cup cucumber, sliced or greens of your choice

Drain grapefruit. Wash and dry greens (of your choice) and tear into bite-size pieces. Add grapefruit sections, onions, radishes, and cucumber. Toss and serve with a Roquefort dressing, before serving.

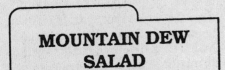

MOUNTAIN DEW SALAD

1 large package lemon gelatin
1-2/3 cups boiling water
1 cup small marshmallows
1 cup Mountain Dew soda
1 (#303 can) crushed pineapple, drain
1 can lemon pudding or pie filling
1 medium container Cool Whip

Mix gelatin in boiling water with marshmallows until dissolved. Add Mountain Dew and drained pineapple. Chill until set. Mix pudding and Cool Whip. Spread on top of gelatin which has set.

SILHOUETTE SALAD

Serves 4

1 envelope Knox unflavored gelatin
1 cup water, divided
1 (10-1/2 ounce) can condensed cream of chicken soup
1 tablespoon lemon juice
1/8 teaspoon pepper
1 (5-ounce) can boned chicken, diced
1/2 cup diced celery
1/4 cup chopped green pepper
2 tablespoons chopped pimiento
2 teaspoons grated onion

Sprinkle gelatin on 1/2 cup water to soften. Place over low heat and stir until gelatin is dissolved. Remove from heat; stir in soup until well-blended. Add other 1/2 cup water, lemon juice, and pepper. Chill until the consistency of unbeaten egg white. Fold in chicken, onion, green pepper, and pimiento. Turn into a 3-cup mold and chill until firm.

PINEAPPLE SALAD

1 (6-ounce) package lemon gelatin
1 cup boiling water
1 can cold Mountain Dew beverage
1 (15-ounce) can pineapple chunks or tidbits, drained and juice reserved
1 package lemon pudding (cooked type)
1 cup whipping cream (whipped) or Cool Whip
1 cup colored mini marshmallows

Dissolve gelatin in boiling water; add Mountain Dew and juice drained from pineapple; chill until it begins to thicken. Cook pudding according to package instructions; cool.

Mix gelatin, lemon pudding, and whipped cream, beating together. Add drained pineapple and marshmallows. Pour into a large bowl and chill.

COTTAGE CHEESE DELIGHT

1 quart cottage cheese
1 can crushed pineapple, drained
1 (6-ounce) box orange gelatin
1 small package miniature marshmallows
1 large container Cool Whip

Mix cottage cheese, pineapple, and gelatin powder together. Blend in marshmallows and Cool Whip; chill before serving.

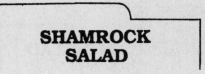

SHAMROCK SALAD

First Layer:
1 (3-ounce) package lime gelatin
1 small can undrained crushed pineapple

Dissolve gelatin in one cup hot water, then cool. Add pineapple. Pour mixture into large mold and chill until set.

Second Layer:
1 (3-ounce) package lemon gelatin
2 (3-ounce) packages cream cheese
10 marshmallows
2 cups whipping cream

Dissolve lemon gelatin in one cup hot water. Mix one package cream cheese with one cup whipping cream. Pour mixture on top of set lime gelatin. Chill until set. Mix remaining cream cheese with one cup whipped cream and the marshmallows cut into small pieces. Turn out mold on lettuce green and top with this mixture. You may decide to serve this creation as a dessert.—Whip 1/2 cup cream; add drained maraschino cherries and drained pineapple slices, arranged, to form an attractive circle on top.

St. Patrick's Day is a special one, not only because it is the beginning of spring, but because of the teasing, elfish nature of this man who makes "everything come up green" on this day. Special foods are your way of contributing to a genial atmosphere for both children and adults. On this day, we are all the same age—Happy St. Patrick's Day!

BANANA YOGURT SALAD

2 large bananas
2 cups yogurt
1/4 cup nuts, chopped
Orange sections
Lettuce

Peel and split bananas; place in serving dishes. Spoon one cup of yogurt onto each banana. Sprinkle with nuts; surround with orange sections and shredded lettuce.

APRICOT SALAD
Serves 10-12

2 (16-ounce) cans apricots in syrup, drained. (Reserve juice)
1 (8-ounce) package cream cheese, diced
1 (3-ounce) package lemon gelatin
1 (3-ounce) package lime gelatin
1 (12-ounce) package Cool Whip

Put both gelatins in large bowl and add 2 cups boiling apricot juice, adding enough water to make 2 cups, if not enough juice. Mix until dissolved. Add diced cream cheese. Mix until smooth. Mash apricots slightly and add to gelatin mixture. Fold Cool Whip into mixture.

Pour into 13x9-inch pan. Chill overnight. May be kept in refrigerator for 2 weeks. Spoon serve, or cut into squares. This is a delicious, refreshing, simple-to-prepare salad.

BLUEBERRY SALAD

2 (3-ounce) packages grape gelatin
2 cups boiling water
1 (No. 2) can undrained crushed pineapple
1 (16-ounce) can blueberry pie filling
1 cup sour cream
1 (8-ounce) package cream cheese
1/2 cup granulated sugar
1 teaspoon vanilla

In a 9x13-inch pan, mix the gelatin and boiling water until dissolved. Add undrained pineapple and blueberry pie filling. Stir and let set in refrigerator. Mix sour cream with the softened cream cheese, sugar, and vanilla. Do not overbeat. Spread on top of the set gelatin mixture. Chill again in refrigerator. This is a great potluck dish. It can be served as salad or dessert.

TASTY APPLE SALAD

1 (20-ounce) can pineapple tidbits, drain and save juice
2 cups miniature marshmallows
1/2 cup sugar
1 tablespoon flour
1 egg, beaten
1-1/2 tablespoons vinegar
1 (8-ounce) container Cool Whip
2 cups chopped apples with skins (Red Delicious)
1-1/2 cups dry roasted peanuts, chopped

Mix pineapple juice, sugar, flour, egg, and vinegar in pan. Cook until thick. Refrigerate overnight. Next day, or 8 hours, mix together apples, nuts, Cool Whip, pineapple, marshmallows and pineapple juice; mix and refrigerate until ready to serve.

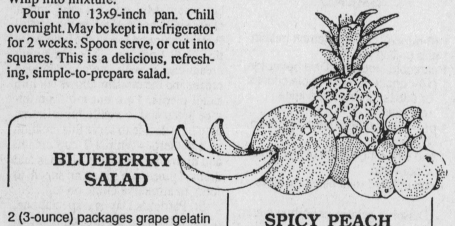

SPICY PEACH SALAD

6 large canned peach halves
1/2 stick whole cinnamon
1 teaspoon whole cloves
1/2 cup white vinegar
1/2 cup sugar

1 (3-ounce) package cream cheese
1/4 cup fresh lime juice
1/4 cup pecans, chopped

Place cinnamon stick and cloves in a small cheesecloth bag; tie firmly; cook with sugar and vinegar for 3 minutes. Remove spice bag; pour over peaches; chill. Fill center of each peach with cream cheese seasoned with lime juice and chopped pecans. To serve: Arrange each peach half on a chilled, crisp lettuce leaf.

PEACH PARTY SALAD
Serves 12

1 (6-ounce) package orange flavored gelatin
2 cups boiling water
1 (15-1/4 ounce) can crushed pineapple, undrained
2 cups canned or fresh sliced peaches, drained
1 egg, beaten
1/4 cup sugar
1-1/2 tablespoons all-purpose flour
1-1/2 tablespoons butter or margarine, softened
1/2 cup whipping cream, whipped
1/2 cup miniature marshmallows
1/2 cup (2 ounces) shredded Cheddar cheese

Dissolve gelatin in boiling water; set aside. Drain pineapple, reserving juice; set pineapple aside. Add enough water to juice to make 1 cup. Add 3/4 cup of juice mixture to gelatin mixture; chill until consistency of unbeaten egg white. Set remaining 1/4 cup of juice mixture aside. Arrange peach slices in a lightly-oiled 12 x 8 x 2 inch dish. Pour gelatin mixture over peaches. Chill until almost firm. Combine egg, sugar, flour, butter, and remaining 1/4 cup juice mixture in a small saucepan. Cook over low heat, stirring constantly until smooth and thickened; cool. Combine pineapple, whipped cream, marshmallows, and cheese; fold in egg mixture. Spread evenly over salad. Cover; chill overnight.

SPINACH-ORANGE TOSS
Serves 6

1 small onion, thinly sliced
Boiling water
6 cups (8 ounces) fresh spinach, torn
1 (11-ounce) can mandarin oranges, drained
1 cup fresh mushrooms, sliced
3 tablespoons salad oil
1 tablespoon lemon juice
1/4 teaspoon salt
Dash pepper
3/4 cup almonds, slivered

Place onions in bowl and cover with boiling water; allow to stand 10 minutes; drain; and dry on paper towels. Place spinach, which has been torn into pieces, in large salad bowl. Add onions, mandarin orange slices, and mushrooms. Toss lightly with hands; cover with plastic wrap and chill thoroughly.

For dressing, place salad oil, lemon juice, salt and pepper in a screw-top jar and shake well. Chill. Before serving, shake again and pour over spinach-orange mixture. Toss lightly until ingredients are coated. Sprinkle almonds over top and serve immediately. This is a very good side dish with Chinese food.

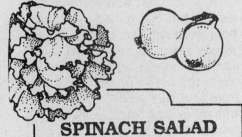

SPINACH SALAD
Serves 6

1/2 pound spinach
1/2 head iceberg lettuce
1 small red onion, thinly sliced and separated into rings
1 slivered hard-cooked egg white (yolk saved for vinaigrette)
Vinaigrette (recipe follows)

Tear spinach and lettuce into bite-size pieces and layer with onion and slivered hard-cooked egg white in a salad bowl. Add vinaigrette and toss well.

Vinaigrette:

In a small bowl mash saved hard-cooked egg yolk; add 1 teaspoon salt, 1/4 teaspoon pepper, 1/4 teaspoon paprika, 1/4 teaspoon dry mustard, 1/4 cup red wine vinegar,

1/2 cup vegetable oil, and 2 tablespoons finely chopped parsley; whisk well.

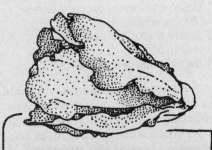

GREEN VEGETABLE SALAD

1 small can English peas, drained
1 can French style green beans, drained
1 can shoe peg corn, drained
1 cup chopped celery
1 cup chopped green pepper
1 cup chopped onion
1 small jar pimientos, chopped

Mix together 1/2 teaspoon salt, 1/2 cup vinegar, 1/2 cup salad oil and 1/3 cup sugar; stir until dissolved. Pour over vegetables; mix well and chill 4-5 hours before serving. Will keep for several days in refrigerator.

FRESH VEGETABLE SALAD

1 bunch broccoli, broken into flowerettes
1 head cauliflower, broken or sliced
1 bunch celery, sliced
1 box mushrooms, sliced
1 box cherry tomatoes, halved
1 can ripe olives, pitted and drained
1 bag radishes, sliced
3 or 4 carrots, sliced

Toss with one large bottle Italian dressing mixed with one package dry Italian dressing mix. Can prepare several hours ahead of time before serving.

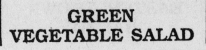

GREEN VEGETABLE SALAD

1 can English peas, drained
1 can French-style green beans, drained
1 can shoe peg corn, drained
1 cup diced celery
1 cup diced green peppers
1 cup chopped green onions or regular onions
1 small can pimientos, diced

Mix together:
1/2 teaspoon salt
1/2 cup sugar
1/2 cup vinegar
1/2 cup salad oil

Stir until sugar is dissolved. Pour over vegetables. Chill overnight. Will keep for several days.

MUSHROOM SALAD
Serves 4

1 tablespoon butter
1/2 pound mushrooms, cleaned and stems trimmed
3 ounces champagne
1 teaspoon clear Karo syrup
2 tablespoons catsup
2 tablespoons raisins
1 teaspoon pine nuts (pignoli)
Coarsely shredded lettuce

Soak raisins in 1 tablespoon of champagne for 5 minutes. Drain well and set aside. Melt butter in a saucepan. Add mushrooms, and gently sauté for 2 minutes over medium heat, stirring constantly. Add the Karo syrup; mix well a few seconds. To this add champagne, catsup, pignoli, and raisins. Simmer only 1 minute. Pour mixture into a bowl and chill thoroughly. When ready to serve, be sure to serve on a bed of shredded lettuce.

EASTER CROWN SALAD

3 (3-ounce) packages cream
 cheese
1/2 teaspoon salt
2 cups grated cucumber, drained
1 cup mayonnaise
1/4 cup minced onion
1/4 cup minced parsley
1 clove garlic
1 tablespoon unflavored gelatin
1/4 cup cold water
1 head lettuce
2 hard-cooked egg yolks, sieved

Mix first 6 ingredients in a bowl
that has been rubbed with garlic.
Soften gelatin in cold water and dissolve over hot water. Cool to lukewarm and combine with cheese mixture. Beat thoroughly and pack into a
deep spring-form pan. Chill until
mixture is firm. Remove from mold
onto a bed of lettuce and sprinkle
sieved egg yolks over top. Garnish
with radish roses, if desired.

BEAN AND TOMATO SALAD

1 (15-1/2 ounce) can garbanzo beans
3 tablespoons vegetable oil
1 tablespoon wine vinegar
Salt and pepper
1 pound tomatoes, peeled and sliced
1 medium-size onion, sliced into thin
 rings
2 teaspoons fresh chopped basil or 1
 teaspoon dried basil

Drain beans; rinse under cold
water. Beat oil and vinegar together;
season with salt and pepper. Add the
beans and mix until well coated,
being careful not to break up the
beans. Arrange tomato and onion
slices in a shallow dish; sprinkle with
basil, salt, and pepper. Spoon beans
on top. Serve chilled.

ZESTY MEXICAN BEAN SALAD

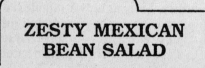

2 medium limes
1/2 of a 12-ounce jar chunky salsa
 (about 3/4 cup)
1/3 cup salad oil
1-1/2 teaspoons chili powder
1 teaspoon salt
1 (16-ounce) can black beans,
 drained
1 (15 to 19-ounce) can red kidney
 beans, drained
1 (15 to 19-ounce) can garbanzo
 beans, drained
2 celery stalks, thinly sliced
1 onion, sliced
1 medium tomato, diced

Squeeze lime juice into bowl; stir
in salsa, oil, chili powder, and salt.
Add beans, celery, onion and tomato.
Toss to mix well. Serve at room temperature or cover and refrigerate, to
serve chilled later. Many ingredients
may be purchased in the Ethnic De-
partment of your food store.

CARROT SALAD
Serves 6

1 pound carrots
1 bunch chives, chopped
1 cup mayonnaise (homemade or
 commercial variety)
2 tablespoons vinegar
Salt and pepper

Peel and finely grate carrots.
Combine chives, mayonnaise, and
vinegar; season with salt and pepper;
blend with a whisk. Pour over carrots
and let stand 15 minutes. Serve.

RAISIN-CARROT SALAD
Serves 8

1 cup seedless raisins
1-1/2 cups shredded carrots
1/2 cup celery, finely chopped
1/2 cup chopped walnuts
Pinch of salt
Dash cayenne
4 tablespoons mayonnaise

Rinse raisins in hot water; drain;
cool and combine with remaining
ingredients. Chill and serve on crisp
lettuce.

CARROT-RAISIN SALAD

1/2 cup shredded carrots
1/2 cup seedless (or seeded) raisins
4 tablespoons lemon juice
1/4 cup mayonnaise
6-12 lettuce leaves or 1-1/2 cups
 shredded cabbage

Shred carrots. Soak raisins in lemon
juice. Combine ingredients; mix with
dressing. Serve in lettuce cups.

PICNIC SALAD BOWL
Serves 6

1 (No. 2) can asparagus tips
Mustard French Dressing (recipe follows)
3 hard-cooked eggs
1/3 cup deviled ham
Hearts of lettuce
2 strips pimiento
6 wedges Swiss cheese

Marinate asparagus in dressing;
chill. Cut eggs lengthwise and remove yolks. Stuff with deviled ham
and mashed egg yolks which have
been moistened with dressing. Toss
lettuce hearts in salad bowl with
dressing. Arrange asparagus tips in
center (held together with pimiento
strips); surround with cheese; border
with stuffed egg halves. May substitute cooked green beans for asparagus
tips.

Mustard French Dressing:
1 cup olive or salad oil
1/4 cup vinegar
1/2 teaspoon salt
Few grains cayenne
1/4 teaspoon white pepper
2 tablespoons chopped parsley
2 teaspoons prepared mustard

Combine; beat or shake thoroughly before using. Makes 1-1/4
cups dressing.

SEAFOOD SALAD
Serves 6-8

1/2 small cabbage (about 1 pound) washed and pulled apart
1 small onion, peeled and sliced
4 tablespoons sweet pickles, finely chopped
1 cup mayonnaise
3 tablespoons sugar
12 fish sticks
12 popcorn shrimp

Combine cabbage, onion, and pickles, and chop until fine, using a hand chopper. Mix mayonnaise and sugar, and add to cabbage salad. Fry fish sticks and shrimp until golden brown; drain on paper towels. Cut six fish sticks and six shrimp into chunks. Mix into cabbage salad. Place in serving bowl. Place remaining fish sticks

---

SKILLET HAM SALAD
Serves 4

1/4 cup chopped green onions
1/4 cup chopped green pepper
2 cups diced cooked ham
1 tablespoon fat
3 cups potatoes, cooked and diced
1/4 teaspoon salt
Dash pepper
1/4 cup mayonnaise
1/2 pound sharp, processed American cheese, diced (1-1/2 cups)

Cook onions, green pepper, and meat in hot fat, stirring occasionally until meat is lightly browned. Add potatoes, salt, pepper, and mayonnaise. Heat, mixing lightly. Stir in cheese; heat just until it begins to melt. Garnish with green onions, if desired.

---

1 can whole cranberry sauce
2 cups cooked diced turkey
1 cup finely diced celery
1/2 cup chopped walnuts
1/4 cup mayonnaise
2 tablespoons lemon juice
Lettuce leaves

Combine all ingredients except lettuce leaves and mix well. Arrange salad on lettuce leaf. Garnish with additional reserved walnut pieces, if desired.

CHUNKY CHICKEN SALAD

1 cup raw carrot, shredded
1/2 cup Miracle Whip, thinned slightly with cream
1 cup chicken, cooked and diced
1/4 cup minced onion
1 cup diced celery
1 tablespoon pickle relish
1 small can shoestring potatoes or 2 cups sesame sticks

Combine vegetables with dressing and relish. Add chicken and potato sticks or sesame sticks just before serving.

SHRIMPLY GREAT MOLD
Serves 8

1-1/2 tablespoons unflavored gelatin
1/4 cup cold water
1 (10-ounce) can tomato soup
1 (8-ounce) package cream cheese, softened
20 salad shrimp, cooked, peeled and coarsely chopped
1 cup mayonnaise
1 small onion, grated
3/4 cup celery, diced finely
1 tablespoon prepared horseradish

Dissolve gelatin in cold water; set aside. In a saucepan, heat soup; add gelatin mixture; stir until dissolved. Add cream cheese; remove from heat; beat until well blended. Add remaining ingredients. Pour into a well-oiled 1-quart mold; chill until firm. Serve portion on a crisp lettuce leaf; garnish with a lemon twist.

SUPER SUPPER SALAD
Makes 6-1/2 cups

1 (8-ounce) package chicken-flavored rice mix
2 (5-ounce) cans Swanson Mixin' Chicken
1-1/2 cups (about 2 medium) diced tomatoes
1/2 cup chopped fresh parsley
1/2 cup chopped green onion
2 tablespoons vinegar
3/4 cup undiluted evaporated milk
1/2 cup mayonnaise
1/2 teaspoon Italian seasoning

Cook rice mix according to package directions. Cool. Mix rice with chicken, tomatoes, parsley, and onion. Stir vinegar into evaporated milk until milk thickens. Add mayonnaise and Italian seasoning. Stir into rice mixture. Chill thoroughly.

CRANBERRY TURKEY SALAD
Serves 4-6

POPCORN SALAD
Serves 6-8

6 cups popped popcorn
1/2 cup green onion, sliced
1 cup celery, diced
3/4 - 1 cup mayonnaise
3/4 cup chopped cooked bacon (reserve some for top)
1 cup grated cheese (reserve some for top)
1/2 cup sliced water chestnuts

In bowl, combine popcorn, sliced onion, diced celery, mayonnaise, bacon, cheese, and water chestnuts. Chill. Top with reserved bacon and grated cheese. Best when used within 3-4 hours.

ARTICHOKE RICE SALAD

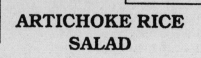

6-ounce package long grain and wild rice mix
14-ounce can artichoke hearts, drained and chopped
2-ounce jar chopped pimentos, drained
3 green onions with tops, chopped
1 cup chopped celery
1/2 cup mayonnaise
1 teaspoon curry powder

Cook rice according to package directions, omitting butter; cool. Add remaining ingredients; mix well. Cover and chill thoroughly.

TASTY MACARONI SALAD

3 cups macaroni
12-ounce can corned beef
2 medium cucumbers, diced
2 medium tomatoes, diced
1 medium carrot, diced
1 cup plus 4 tablespoons mayonnaise
Salt to taste
Celery seed and boiled egg to garnish

Cook macroni; drain. Rinse with hot water. Turn macaroni into mixing bowl. While macaroni is still hot, add corned beef, which has been broken apart and shredded; mix together until corned beef has been thoroughly worked through macaroni. (Macaroni must be hot or corned beef will not mix through properly). Set aside to cool.

Add cucumbers, tomatoes and onion. Add mayonnaise; mix all ingredients together thoroughly. Add salt to taste. Garnish with celery seed and sliced boiled egg.

CHICKEN SALAD

Serves 8-10

4 cups large chunks cooked chicken (white meat)
1 cup drained pineapple chunks
3/4 cup raisins
1 cup mayonnaise
1/4 cup plain, low-fat yogurt
1/2 cup chopped walnuts

In large bowl, mix chicken, pineapple, and raisins. In small bowl, mix mayonnaise and yogurt. Combine the two mixtures and sprinkle walnuts on top. Chill thoroughly before serving.

Could be served in half of pineapple shell, cut lengthwise, for an attractive display.

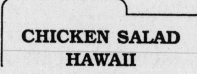

CHICKEN SALAD HAWAII

1 cup cooked, cubed chicken
1/4 cup diced celery
1/4 cup blanched slivered almonds
1/4 cup chunk pineapple
1/2 teaspoon onion juice
1/2 teaspoon salt
Salad greens

Toss all ingredients together except salad greens. Serve over greens.

Dressing:
2 tablespoons finely chopped candied ginger
1/4 cup chopped nuts
1 teaspoon honey
1 cup sour cream

Mix together and serve over chicken salad.

CRABMEAT SALAD

2 cups cooked shell macaroni
1/2 small jar pimiento peppers, cut up
1 tablespoon diced onion
1/2 cup diced celery

3 hard-cooked eggs, diced
2 sweet pickles, diced
1 cup mayonnaise
1 can crabmeat, cut up

Mix all ingredients together in bowl and chill before serving.
Mrs. W. Gergen, Phoenix, AZ

PICNIC TUNA SALAD

2 pounds potatoes
1 cup tuna fish
1-1/2 cups diced celery
1 teaspoon onion juice
1 clove of garlic
1/2 cup French dressing
1/2 cup mayonnaise
2 tablespoons chopped sweet pickle
1 tablespoon minced parsley
1/2 teaspoon salt

Boil potatoes in their skins. When cool, peel and dice into a large bowl that has been rubbed with a cut clove of garlic. Sprinkle with salt. Add onion juice to French dressing; mix lightly, and let stand in refrigerator for 1 hour. Drain fish and flake into tiny pieces. Combine potatoes, tuna, celery, sweet pickle, and mayonnaise. Sprinkle with minced parsley. Serve very cold. The longer this stands, the better the flavor.

Makes a good main supper dish on a hot summer night.

TURKEY CRANBERRY SALAD

Serves 4-6

1 cup cubed cranberry jelly
1 cup diced turkey
1 cup diced celery
3 tablespoons French dressing
Several lettuce cups
1/4 cup walnut meats.

Lightly toss cranberry jelly, turkey, celery, and French dressing. Place in lettuce cups and sprinkle with walnuts.

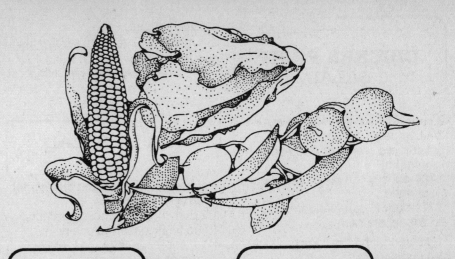

EASY FRUIT SALAD

1 cup seedless grapes
1 (11-ounce) can mandarin oranges (chill and drain)
1 (8-ounce) can pineapple chunks (chill and drain)
1 red apple, sliced
Yogurt Dressing (recipe follows)

Combine grapes, oranges, apple and pineapple. Spoon onto salad greens. Serve with Yogurt Dressing.

Yogurt Dressing:
2/3 cup plain yogurt
1 tablespoon honey
1 tablespoon lemon juice

Mix all ingredients together.
Cheryl Santefort, South Holland, Ill.

GREEN AND GOLD SALAD
Serves 4-5

1 (10 ounce) package frozen green peas
1/2 cup shredded natural cheddar cheese
2 tablespoons chopped onion
2 tablespoons mayonnaise or salad dressing
1-1/2 teaspoons prepared mustard
1/4 teaspoon salt
Crisp salad greens

Rinse peas with small amount of running cold water to separate and remove ice crystals; drain. Mix all ingredients, except salad greens. Serve salad on greens.
Substitution: For frozen green peas use 1 (8-ounce) can green peas, drained.
Marcella Swigert, Monroe City, Mo.

PINEAPPLE CHANTILLY

1-1/2 cups pineapple juice
1 cup water
1/4 cup tapioca
1/2 cup sugar
1 teaspoon salt
2 tablespoons lemon juice
1 (13-1/2-ounce) can crushed pineapple, undrained
1 cup heavy cream, whipped
Maraschino cherries for garnish

In saucepan combine pineapple juice, water, tapioca, sugar, and salt. Bring to boil. Stir constantly over medium heat until tapioca is cooked. Stir in lemon juice and pineapple. Refrigerate 2 hours before serving; fold whipped cream into pineapple mixture. Chill. Garnish with maraschino cherries.
Sharon M. Crider, Evansville, Wis.

SPAGHETTI SALAD

1 pound spaghetti, cooked in unsalted water
1 medium onion
1/2 bottle Italian salad dressing
1 package pepperoni, diced
1 medium green pepper, diced
1 medium tomato, chopped
3–4 stalks celery, thinly sliced

Mix spaghetti, green pepper, onion, tomato, dressing, pepperoni and celery; let sit overnight or at least several hours before serving. Mix well again before serving.
Sandra Russell, Gainesville, Fla.

CHERRY CREAM SALAD
Serves 6

1 (1-pound) can pitted, dark sweet cherries, drained
¾ cup chopped pecans
2 (11-ounce) cans mandarin oranges, drained
1 cup dairy sour cream

Combine ingredients; chill thoroughly. If desired, garnish with additional cherries, oranges and pecan halves.
Sharon Crider, Stoughton, Wis.

LIME SALAD
Serves 6

1 (3-ounce) package lime gelatin
1 cup boiling water
1 cup pineapple juice
2 tablespoons vinegar
1/2 teaspoon salt
3 slices pineapple, diced
1 pimiento, finely cut
1 orange, in sections
1/2 cup finely cut celery

Dissolve gelatin in 1 cup boiling water. Add pineapple juice, vinegar, and salt to gelatin mixture. Mix well and add remaining ingredients. Pour into molds. Serve on curly endive.
Lucy Dowd, Sequim, Wash.

CHICKEN FRUIT SALAD

Serves 6

3 cups cooked, chunked chicken
3/4 cup celery, chopped
3/4 cup red grapes, halved and seeded
1 (20-ounce) can pineapple chunks, drained
1 (11-ounce) can mandarin oranges, drained

1/4 cup chopped pecans
1/4 cup salad oil
1/8 teaspoon salt
Lettuce leaves, as desired

Lightly toss chicken, celery, grapes, pineapple, oranges and 3 tablespoons pecans. Blend in salad oil and salt. Chill.

Serve on lettuce leaves. Garnish with remaining pecans.

Mrs. E. O'Brien, Richmond, Va.

TRIPLE ORANGE SALAD

Serves 10–12

2 cups boiling liquid (water *or* fruit juices)
1 (6-ounce) package orange gelatin
1 pint orange sherbet
2 (11-ounce) cans mandarin orange segments, drained
1 (13¼-ounce) can pineapple chunks, drained
1 cup flaked coconut
1 cup miniature marshmallows
1 cup sour cream *or* ½ cup chilled whipping cream, whipped

Pour boiling liquid on gelatin in bowl; stir until gelatin is dissolved. Add sherbet; stir until melted. Stir in 1 can orange segments. Pour into 6-cup ring mold; refrigerate until firm.

Mix remaining orange segments, pineapple, coconut and marshmallows. Fold in sour cream. Refrigerate

at least 3 hours.

Unmold gelatin onto serving plate and fill center with fruit salad.

Vivian Nikanow, Chicago, Ill.

APPLE SALAD

Serves 10

6 apples, sweet-tart and crisp; peel, core and chop
1/2 cup chopped English walnuts
1 cup finely chopped celery
1 1/2 cups purple grapes, halved and seeds removed
1/4 cup sugar
1 heaping tablespoon Miracle Whip
1/2 pint whipping cream, stiffly whipped

Prepare fruit. Sprinkle with sugar; stir in Miracle Whip. Stir well to cover all the fruit and nuts with a light coating of sugar/dressing mixture. Add stiffly beaten whipped cream. You can do everything, except the cream, ahead of time; refrigerate for a couple of hours, then add the whipped cream just before serving.

Linda Taylor, Gravois Mills, Mo.

FRUIT SALAD SUPREME

Serves 10

1 (16-ounce) can sliced peaches
2 (11-ounce) cans mandarin oranges
1 (16-ounce) can apricots
1 (20-ounce) can chunk pineapple
2 (10-ounce) packages frozen strawberries
1 (3½-ounce) box instant vanilla pudding

Drain peaches, oranges, apricots and pineapple very well. Pat dry on paper toweling. Place fruit in bowl and add 2 packages of thawed strawberries; do not drain. Add box of instant vanilla pudding. Stir together and place in refrigerator overnight.

Shari Crider, Stoughton, Wis.

BEET AND CABBAGE SALAD

Serves 3-4

2 (16-ounce) cans sliced beets, reserve liquid
1 cup mayonnaise
3 tablespoons milk
1 tablespoon vinegar (optional)
1 small head cabbage
1/2 cup reserved beet juice
1 small onion, chopped (optional)

Shred cabbage and place in large bowl. Add sliced beets. In a small bowl, mix together beet juice, milk, and mayonnaise. Add vinegar, if desired.

Add onion (if desired) to cabbage and beets; toss well. Pour dressing over vegetables and toss until well-coated. Prepare and refrigerate at least 1 hour before serving to allow flavors to blend.

Michaeline Duncan, Dudley, N.C.

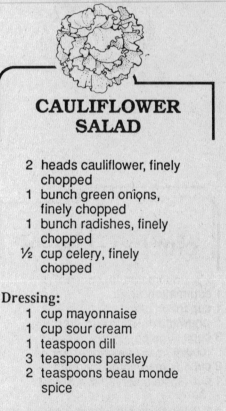

CAULIFLOWER SALAD

2 heads cauliflower, finely chopped
1 bunch green onions, finely chopped
1 bunch radishes, finely chopped
½ cup celery, finely chopped

Dressing:
1 cup mayonnaise
1 cup sour cream
1 teaspoon dill
3 teaspoons parsley
2 teaspoons beau monde spice

Combine dressing ingredients and add to vegetables. Best if refrigerated overnight.

I use my food processor to chop the vegetables.

Laura Hicks, Troy, Mont.

CREAMY CRANBERRY SALAD

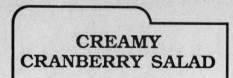

1 (6-ounce) package strawberry gelatin
1 cup hot water
1 (1-pound) can whole cranberry sauce
½ cup diced celery
¼ cup chopped nuts
1 (8-ounce) package cream cheese, softened

Dissolve gelatin in hot water. Cool and chill slightly. Break up cranberry sauce with a fork and add to gelatin with celery and nuts. Fold in cream cheese. Pour into an 8x8x2-inch pan. Refrigerate.

This recipe is easy to make and you can make it any time of year. It is nice to take to a covered-dish supper.

Mrs. Albert Foley, Lemoyne, Pa.

SUMMERTIME CHICKEN SALAD

Serves 8

1 cup mayonnaise
1 cup frozen whipped topping, thawed
3 cups cooked chicken, cut into chunks
2 cups sliced celery
1 cup seedless grapes, cut into halves
1 cup slivered, toasted almonds
1/2 cup pimiento-stuffed olives, sliced
Lettuce cups

Mix together mayonnaise and whipped topping. Mix together the rest of the ingredients, except lettuce cups. Pour mayonnaise and whipped topping over chicken mixture; toss lightly but thoroughly. Refrigerate until serving time. Serve in crisp lettuce cups.

Agnes Ward, Erie, Pa.

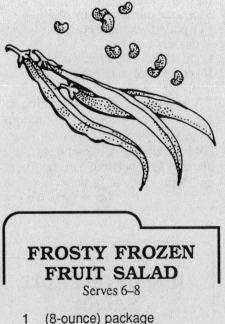

FROSTY FROZEN FRUIT SALAD

Serves 6–8

1 (8-ounce) package cream cheese, softened
1 cup dairy sour cream
¼ cup sugar
1 (17-ounce) can apricot halves, drained and halved
1 (8¾-ounce) can crushed pineapple, drained
1 (16-ounce) can pitted, dark sweet cherries, drained
1¼ cups miniature marshmallows
Crisp lettuce *or* watercress

In large mixer bowl, beat cheese until smooth; blend in sour cream and sugar; stir in fruit and marshmallows. Pour into 6–8 individual molds or into 4½-cup mold. Freeze overnight. Ten minutes before serving, unmold on crisp lettuce leaves or watercress.

Gwen Campbell, Sterling, Va.

HOLIDAY SALAD

Serves 10–12

6 cups raw broccoli
1 head raw cauliflower
⅔ cup cheddar cheese, cut up
3 tablespoons raw onion, cut up
3 tablespoons pimiento
Salt and pepper to taste

Dressing:
½ cup mayonnaise
½ cup plain yogurt
1 teaspoon pepper
1 teaspoon Lawry's seasoned salt

Put all cut-up salad ingredients in bowl. Mix all dressing ingredients together and put on salad; toss well.

Katherine V. Frierson, DeLand, Fla.

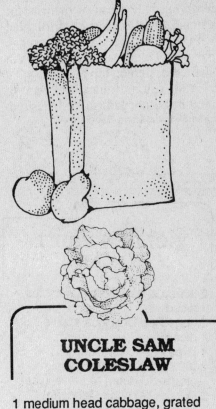

UNCLE SAM COLESLAW

1 medium head cabbage, grated
1 carrot, grated
1 green pepper, diced
3/4 cup vinegar
1 teaspoon mustard seed
1 1/2 cups sugar
1 teaspoon celery seed

Toss the cabbage, carrot, and pepper in a large salad bowl. In a saucepan combine vinegar, mustard seed, sugar and celery seed. Bring mixture to boil for 1 minute and allow to cool. Pour over cabbage mixture and serve chilled.

FRUIT COCKTAIL SALAD

1 (5-5/8 ounce) package vanilla flavored Jello instant pudding mix
1-1/3 cups buttermilk
1 (8-ounce) container Cool Whip
1 (30-ounce) can fruit cocktail, well-drained
2 cans mandarin oranges, well-drained
1 cup miniature rainbow-colored marshmallows (optional)

Blend buttermilk into pudding mix using medium speed of mixer. When smooth, blend in Cool Whip. If consistency of mixture seems too thick, add a little more buttermilk. Fold in fruit cocktail and mandarin oranges, reserving half a can of oranges for garnish. Swirl a design on top of salad with a tablespoon. Gently arrange balance of mandarin orange slices in swirled design on top of salad.

Add colored marshmallows to mixture before garnishing, if desired.

Lalla Fellows, Long Beach, Calif.

GOLDEN FRUIT SALAD

2 large Golden Delicious apples, diced
2 large Red Delicious apples, diced
4 large bananas, sliced
2 (20 ounce) cans pineapple chunks, drained (reserve juice)
2 (16 ounce) cans Mandarin oranges, drained
Whole green grapes, optional

Mix Together:
1 cup sugar
4 tablespoons corn starch
Reserved pineapple juice
2 tablespoons lemon juice
2/3 cup orange juice

Stir and boil 1 minute. Pour hot mixture over fruit. Leave uncovered until cool.

Pat Stump, Dunnell, MN

SHORTCUT FROZEN SALAD

1 small package *instant* lemon pudding
1 pint whipped topping, thawed
1/2 cup mayonnaise
2 tablespoons lemon juice
1 (1-pound) can fruit cocktail, drained
1 cup miniature marshmallows
1/4 cup chopped pecans

Prepare pudding according to package directions; blend in whipped topping, mayonnaise, and lemon juice. Fold in remaining ingredients. Turn into a 9x5x3-inch loaf pan and freeze until firm. Slice to serve.

Agnes Ward, Erie, Pa.

GUM DROP FRUIT SALAD

Serves 8

1 (#2 can) pineapple tidbits
1/4 cup sugar
2 tablespoons flour
1/4 teaspoon salt
3 tablespoons lemon juice
1-1/2 teaspoons vinegar
2 cups seedless grapes, halved
2 cups miniature white marshmallows
2/3 cup gumdrops, halved (do not use black drops)
1 (4-ounce) bottle maraschino cherries, drained and halved
1/4 cup chopped pecans
1 cup whipping cream, whipped

Drain pineapple, reserving 1/3 cup of syrup. Combine sugar, flour, and salt. Add reserved pineapple syrup, lemon juice, and vinegar. Cook over medium heat, stirring constantly until thick and boiling. Continue cooking 1 minute. Set aside and cool. Combine pineapple and remaining ingredients, except the whipped cream. Fold the cooked dressing into the whipped cream. Cover and refrigerate for 12-24 hours.

Carmen J. Bickert, Dubuque, IA

BANANA BAVARIAN CREAM

1 (6-ounce) package lemon-flavored gelatin
2 cups hot water
1/4 teaspoon salt
2/3 cup sugar
1/2 cup heavy cream
5 bananas

Dissolve gelatin in hot water. Add salt and sugar. Chill until cold and syrupy. Fold in cream, whipped only until thick and shiny, but not stiff. Crush bananas to pulp with fork, and fold at once into mixture. Chill until slightly thickened. Turn into mold. Chill until firm. Unmold. Serve with Strawberry Sauce. (Recipe below)

Strawberry Sauce:
1/3 cup butter
1 cup powdered sugar
1 egg white
2/3 cup strawberries

Cream butter and sugar, gradually add crushed strawberries and egg whites. Beat well.

Lucille Roehr, Hammond, Ind.

BUNNY SALAD

Serves 6-8

1 (3-ounce) package orange gelatin
1 cup boiling water
1 cup pineapple juice and water
1 teaspoon grated orange rind
1-1/3 cups crushed pineapple, drained
1 cup grated raw carrots

Dissolve gelatin in boiling water. Add pineapple juice/water mixture and orange rind. Chill until slightly thickened. Then fold in pineapple and carrots. Pour into 6-8 individual round molds. Chill until firm. Unmold on crisp lettuce. Add carrot strips to form ears, a large marshmallow for the head, and half a marshmallow for the tail. Serve plain or with mayonnaise, if desired.

Marcella Swigert, Monroe City, Mo.

ORANGE SHERBERT GELATIN SALAD

Serves 8

2-3 ounce packages orange gelatin
1 cup boiling water
1 pint orange sherbert
1 can mandarin oranges, drained
1 cup heavy cream, whipped

Dissolve gelatin in boiling water; add sherbert, and mix well. When partially set, add mandarin oranges and fold in whipped cream. Pour into square pan or individual molds.

Margaret Hamfeldt, Louisville, KY

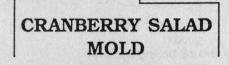

CRANBERRY SALAD MOLD

1 (3 ounce) package lemon gelatin
2 cups boiling water
1-1/4 cups sugar

Dissolve and set aside to cool, but not to set.

Add:
1 small can crushed pineapple
1 cup diced celery
1 orange, cut up
1 tablespoon grated orange peel
2 cups diced apples
3 cups ground cranberries

Pour into gelatin mold; refrigerate until ready to serve. Unmold on green lettuce leaves. Stores well, and may easily be made in advance.

Fay Duman, Eugene, Ore.

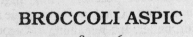

BROCCOLI ASPIC

Serves 6

1 envelope unflavored gelatin
1 can condensed consomme
Salt & pepper to taste
3/4 cup mayonnaise
3 hard-cooked eggs, sliced
Juice of 1-1/2 lemons
2 cups cooked broccoli flowerets

Soften gelatin in 1/4 cup cold consommé. Add to the rest of the consommé and heat. Stir until dissolved; add salt and pepper, if needed. Let thicken until consistency of raw egg whites. Fold in mayonnaise, sliced eggs, broccoli and lemon juice. Pour into individual molds and chill until firm.

Agnes Ward, Erie, PA

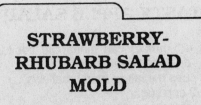

STRAWBERRY-RHUBARB SALAD MOLD

3 (3-ounce) packages strawberry gelatin
3 cups hot water
2 packages frozen rhubarb
1 quart sliced fresh strawberries
Watercress or other salad greens
1 fresh whole strawberry
Chantilly Mayonnaise (recipe follows)

Dissolve 3 packages gelatin in 3 cups hot water. Drop in 2 packages of frozen rhubarb. Stir to separate the rhubarb. When jelly begins to set, add the strawberries. Pour into individual wet molds and chill until set. Unmold on watercress. Garnish each mold with whole strawberry. Serve with Chantilly Mayonnaise.

BUTTERMILK SALAD

1 (6 ounce) package apricot gelatin
1 (20 ounce) can crushed pineapple, undrained
2 cups buttermilk
1 (8 or 9 ounce) container Cool Whip

Bring pineapple to a boil in saucepan. Stir dry gelatin into pineapple and mix until dissolved. Chill until partially set. Stir in buttermilk. Chill again until partly set. Fold in Cool Whip. Refrigerate until firm.

Ruby Beheber, Ransom, IL

HOLIDAY STRAWBERRY GELATIN

1 large (6 ounce) package strawberry gelatin
2 bananas, sliced
1 can crushed pineapple with juice
1/2 cup chopped nuts
1 large package sour cream
2 packages frozen strawberries with juice

Dissolve gelatin in 1 cup boiling water; add pineapple, bananas, strawberries, and nuts. Let jell in refrigerator for about 1 hour. Pour one half mixture into 9x12 inch pan. Let jell in refrigerator about 10-15 minutes; spread sour cream on top. Pour remaining gelatin as top layer.

Refrigerate until serving; may want to garnish for the holidays.

Donna Holter, West Middlesex, Pa.

SPARKLE SALAD

1 (3 ounce) package lime gelatin
1 cup miniature marshmallows
1 cup 7-UP, heated to boiling
3/4 cup finely chopped cabbage
1/2 cup finely chopped carrots
1 cup crushed pineapple, well drained
1/2 cup chopped pecans
1 cup mayonnaise
1 cup whipped cream

Dissolve gelatin and marshmallows in 7-UP. Chill until slightly thickened. Add cabbage, carrots, pineapple, nuts, and mayonnaise. Fold in whipped cream.

Note: For convenience, use blender for cabbage and carrots.

Mrs. Charles Sharp, Newton, Kan.

BANANA YOGURT SALAD

2 large bananas
2 cups yogurt
1/4 cup nuts, chopped
Orange sections
Lettuce

Peel and split bananas; place in serving dishes. Spoon one cup of yogurt onto each banana. Sprinkle with nuts; surround with orange sections and shredded lettuce.

Suzan L. Wiener, Spring Hill, Fla.

APRICOT SALAD
Serves 10-12

2 (16-ounce) cans apricots in syrup, drained. (Reserve juice)
1 (8-ounce) package cream cheese, diced
1 (3-ounce) package lemon gelatin
1 (3-ounce) package lime gelatin
1 (12-ounce) package Cool Whip

Put both gelatins in large bowl and add 2 cups boiling apricot juice, adding enough water to make 2 cups, if not enough juice. Mix until dissolved. Add diced cream cheese. Mix until smooth. Mash apricots slightly and add to gelatin mixture. Fold Cool Whip into mixture.

Pour into 13x9-inch pan. Chill overnight. May be kept in refrigerator for 2 weeks. Spoon serve, or cut into squares. This is a delicious, refreshing, simple-to-prepare salad.

Irene Adney, Eureka Springs, Ark.

BLUEBERRY SALAD

2 (3-ounce) packages grape gelatin
2 cups boiling water
1 (No. 2) can undrained crushed pineapple
1 (16-ounce) can blueberry pie filling
1 cup sour cream
1 (8-ounce) package cream cheese
1/2 cup granulated sugar
1 teaspoon vanilla

In a 9x13-inch pan, mix the gelatin and boiling water until dissolved. Add undrained pineapple and blueberry pie filling. Stir and let set in refrigerator. Mix sour cream with the softened cream cheese, sugar, and vanilla. Do not overbeat. Spread on top of the set gelatin mixture. Chill again in refrigerator. This is a great potluck dish. It can be served as salad or dessert.

Edna Mae Seelos, Niles, Ill.

TASTY APPLE SALAD

1 (20-ounce) can pineapple tidbits, drain and save juice
2 cups miniature marshmallows
1/2 cup sugar
1 tablespoon flour
1 egg, beaten
1-1/2 tablespoons vinegar
1 (8-ounce) container Cool Whip
2 cups chopped apples with skins (Red Delicious)
1-1/2 cups dry roasted peanuts, chopped

Mix pineapple juice, sugar, flour, egg, and vinegar in pan. Cook until thick. Refrigerate overnight. Next day, or 8 hours, mix together apples, nuts, Cool Whip, pineapple, marshmallows and pineapple juice; mix and refrigerate until ready to serve.

Barbara L. Henwood, Glenview, IL

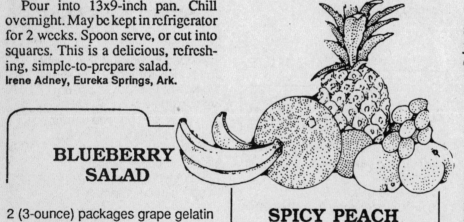

SPICY PEACH SALAD

6 large canned peach halves
1/2 stick whole cinnamon
1 teaspoon whole cloves
1/2 cup white vinegar
1/2 cup sugar

1 (3-ounce) package cream cheese
1/4 cup fresh lime juice
1/4 cup pecans, chopped

Place cinnamon stick and cloves in a small cheesecloth bag; tie firmly; cook with sugar and vinegar for 3 minutes. Remove spice bag; pour over peaches; chill. Fill center of each peach with cream cheese seasoned with lime juice and chopped pecans. To serve: Arrange each peach half on a chilled, crisp lettuce leaf.

Gwen Campbell, Sterling, Va.

PEACH PARTY SALAD
Serves 12

1 (6-ounce) package orange flavored gelatin
2 cups boiling water
1 (15-1/4 ounce) can crushed pineapple, undrained
2 cups canned or fresh sliced peaches, drained
1 egg, beaten
1/4 cup sugar
1-1/2 tablespoons all-purpose flour
1-1/2 tablespoons butter or margarine, softened
1/2 cup whipping cream, whipped
1/2 cup miniature marshmallows
1/2 cup (2 ounces) shredded Cheddar cheese

Dissolve gelatin in boiling water; set aside. Drain pineapple, reserving juice; set pineapple aside. Add enough water to juice to make 1 cup. Add 3/4 cup of juice mixture to gelatin mixture; chill until consistency of unbeaten egg white. Set remaining 1/4 cup of juice mixture aside. Arrange peach slices in a lightly-oiled 12 x 8 x 2 inch dish. Pour gelatin mixture over peaches. Chill until almost firm. Combine egg, sugar, flour, butter, and remaining 1/4 cup juice mixture in a small saucepan. Cook over low heat, stirring constantly until smooth and thickened; cool. Combine pineapple, whipped cream, marshmallows, and cheese; fold in egg mixture. Spread evenly over salad. Cover; chill overnight.

Peggy Fowler Revels, Woodruff, SC

SPECIAL FRUIT SALAD

1 (3 ounce) box non- instant vanilla pudding
1 (3 ounce) box non-instant tapioca pudding
1 heaping tablespoon frozen orange juice concentrate
3 (11 ounce) cans mandarin oranges
3 (15 ounce) cans pineapple tidbits
3 large bananas, sliced

Drain one can of oranges and pineapple. Use the juice and add enough water to make 3 cups of liquid. Cook puddings and orange juice with the liquid until thickened. Cool slightly and add to drained fruit.

Kristy Schemrich, Shreve, Ohio

CIDER WALDORF SALAD
Serves 12

2 envelopes Knox unflavored gelatin
2-1/2 cups cold apple cider or apple juice
1 cup apple cider or juice, heated to boiling
2 tablespoons lemon juice
1-1/4 cups chopped apple
1/2 cup diced celery
1/2 cup raisins
1/2 cup coarsely chopped walnuts

In large bowl, sprinkle unflavored gelatin over 1/2 cup cold cider; let stand 1 minute. Add hot cider and stir until gelatin is completely dissolved. Stir in remaining cold cider and lemon juice. Chill, stirring occasionally, until mixture is consistency of unbeaten egg whites. Fold in remaining ingredients. Turn into 6-1/2 cup mold or bowl; chill until firm.

Sue Hibbard, Rochester, N.Y.

FROZEN WALDORF SALAD
Serves 9-12

1 (8 ounce) can crushed pineapple
2 eggs, slightly beaten
1/2 cup sugar
1/4 cup lemon juice
1/8 teaspoon salt
2 cups unpeeled apples, diced
1 cup celery, diced
1/2 cup pecans, chopped
1/2 cup whipping cream

Drain juice from pineapple into sauce pan. Add slightly beaten eggs, sugar, lemon juice, and salt. Cook over low heat, stirring constantly, until thickened. Cool slightly. Add pineapple, apples, celery, and pecans. Mix to blend.

Whip cream. Fold into pineapple mixture. Pour into an 8-inch square dish. Freeze overnight. Before serving, place in refrigerator for about 3 hours.

Margaret Hamfeldt, Louisville, Ky.

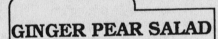

GINGER PEAR SALAD
Serves 4-5

1 (10-1/2 -ounce) can condensed consomme
1/4 teaspoon ground ginger
Dash cinnamon
1 (3-ounce) package lemon-flavored gelatin
3/4 cup cold water
6 walnut halves
1 (1-pound) can pear halves, drained and diced
1/2 cup thinly sliced celery
1/3 cup coarsely chopped walnuts
Crisp salad greens
Sour cream

Combine consomme, ginger, and cinnamon. Bring to a boil. Add gelatin and stir until dissolved. Add water. Chill until slightly thickened. Pour a small amount into a 1-quart mold. Arrange walnut halves and several pieces of pear on gelatin. Stir remaining pears, celery, and walnuts into remaining gelatin. Spoon into

mold. Chill until firm, about 3 hours. Unmold. Serve on crisp salad greens. Garnish with sour cream.

MANDARIN ORANGE SALAD

60 Ritz crackers, crushed
1/4 pound butter, melted
1/4 cup sugar
1 (6 ounce) can unsweetened frozen orange juice, thawed
1 can Eagle Brand Sweetened Condenced Milk
1 (8 ounce) container Cool Whip
2 small cans Mandarin oranges, drained

Crush crackers finely and add melted butter and sugar to them. Press mixture firmly into 9x13x2 inch baking dish. Reserve some of crumb mixture for garnish.

Blend thawed orange juice and milk. Stir in Cool Whip and oranges. Fold in. Do not beat. Pour mixture over crumb crust. Top with reserved crumbs.

Refrigerate or freeze until serving.

This is delicious, refreshing, and appetizing.

Patty White, Indianapolis, IN

GREEN BEAN SALAD

1 can (16 ounce) French-style sliced green beans
1 green onion
1/3 cup white vinegar
1/4 cup sugar
1/8 teaspoon garlic salt
4 tablespoons water
2 tablespoons oil

Drain beans well. Transfer to medium bowl. Use scissors to snip in green onion. Set aside.

In pint pitcher, measure vinegar. Add sugar and garlic salt; mix well. Add water and oil; beat with whisk or fork. Pour over beans; toss with fork to mix. Cover; refrigerate overnight for flavors to blend. Serve cold.

BROCCOLI-RAISIN SALAD

3 heads broccoli, cut in small pieces
½ cup chopped onion
4 slices bacon, cooked and crumbled
¾ cup raisins

Toss ingredients together.

Dressing:
1 cup mayonnaise
2 tablespoons sugar
2 tablespoons white vinegar

Dressing should be tangy in flavor. Pour over salad. Again, toss lightly.

BANANA PEANUT BUTTER SALAD

6 bananas
⅓ cup peanut butter
4 red apples, diced, unpeeled
⅓ cup chopped nuts
½ teaspoon salt
¼ cup lemon juice
Mayonnaise
Lettuce leaves

Cut bananas lengthwise. Spread with peanut butter. Place on lettuce. Toss together the apples, nuts, salt and lemon juice. Sprinkle over bananas, accompanied by mayonnaise.

RICH-N-COOL SALAD

1 large package lemon gelatin
1 large container Cool Whip
1 (8-ounce) package cream cheese

Make gelatin according to directions on package. Soften cream cheese. Just before gelatin sets, add Cool Whip and cream cheese. Beat with hand mixer until smooth. Chill and serve.

SCRUMPTIOUS SALAD MOLD

1 (30-ounce) can fruit cocktail, drained
1 (9-ounce) carton whipped topping
1 (1-pound) container cottage cheese
1 (3-ounce) package gelatin, any flavor
½ cup chopped nuts

Drain fruit cocktail. Fold together whipped topping, cottage cheese and dry gelatin. Fold in fruit cocktail and nuts.

This is a delicious salad—no effort to make.

VEGETABLE-BULGUR SALAD
Serves 2

⅓ cup bulgur wheat
1 cup hot water
1 teaspoon vegetable oil
¼ cup chopped sweet red pepper
¼ cup chopped zucchini
¾ cup vegetable juice cocktail
1 teaspoon lemon juice
¼ teaspoon dried basil leaves, crushed
  Lettuce leaves (optional)
2 tablespoons chopped green onion for garnish

In 2-cup measure, stir together bulgur and hot water. Let stand 5 minutes; drain. Meanwhile, in 6-inch skillet over medium heat, in hot oil, cook red pepper and zucchini until tender-crisp, stirring often. Stir in vegetable juice, lemon juice, basil and drained bulgur. Heat to boiling; reduce heat to low. Cover, simmer 15 minutes, or until liquid is absorbed, stirring occasionally. Serve warm or chilled. To serve chilled: Cover, refrigerate until serving time, at least 2 hours. Spoon into lettuce-lined salad bowl. Garnish with green onion. (150 calories per serving)

This Midwestern-style salad makes a great carry-along for brown-bag lunches or picnics.

SEAFOOD SALAD
Serves 4

2 envelopes low-calorie, lemon-flavored gelatin
1 teaspoon salt
2 cups hot water
2 teaspoons vinegar
1 cup flaked tuna, crabmeat, salmon or diced shrimp
⅓ cup finely chopped celery
2 tablespoons chopped green pepper
2 teaspoons finely chopped onion

Dissolve gelatin and salt in hot water. Add vinegar and chill until slightly thickened, then add seafood, celery, green pepper and onion. Pour into individual molds. Chill until firm. Unmold and garnish with crisp greens. (75 calories per serving with tuna, 50 calories with crab or shrimp.)

CUCUMBER & ONION SALAD
Serves 3

¼ cup vinegar
2 tablespoons water
¼ teaspoon salt
¼ teaspoon liquid no-calorie sweetener
  Paprika
  Pepper
1 cucumber, thinly sliced
1 onion, thinly sliced
1 teaspoon chopped mint or parsley, if desired

Combine vinegar, water, salt, sweetener, paprika and pepper in bowl; add cucumber and onion. Chill in refrigerator to blend flavors. Garnish with mint or parsley. (12½ calories per serving)

MARINATED ZUCCHINI SALAD
Serves 12

2 medium-size zucchini, halved lengthwise and sliced
1 pint cherry tomatoes
½ bunch broccoli, cut in florets
½ medium-size head cauliflower, cut in florets
4 large ribs celery, sliced diagonally
4 large carrots, cut in strips
1 (8-ounce) jar pickled baby corn, drained
1 cup olive oil
½ cup white wine vinegar
½ cup water
1 teaspoon sugar
1 teaspoon dried thyme
1 teaspoon marjoram
1 teaspoon basil
2 teaspoons salt
1 teaspoon pepper
1 small clove garlic, peeled
1 bay leaf

Place vegetables in large bowl. Mix remaining ingredients; pour over vegetables; refrigerate several hours, tossing occasionally. Before serving, drain vegetables; discard garlic and bay leaf.

Leona Teodori, Warren, Mich.

PERFECTION SALAD

2 (3-ounce) packages lemon gelatin
2 cups finely chopped celery
12 chopped sweet pickles
4 tablespoons vinegar
4 finely chopped pimientos
1 teaspoon salt
2 cups finely chopped cabbage

Prepare gelatin according to directions. Add vinegar; refrigerate until partially set. Add remaining ingredients and refrigerate several hours.

Julie Habiger, Manhattan, Kan.

TANGY FRUIT SALAD
Serves 6-8

Fruit Salad Dressing:
1/2 cup sugar
2 tablespoons cornstarch
3/4 cup pineapple juice
Juice of 1 lemon
Juice of 1 orange
Grated rind of orange

In small saucepan, mix together sugar and cornstarch. Add the remaining ingredients and cook until thickened. Boil about 1 minute. Cool.

Salad:
2 red apples, cut into wedges
2 green apples, cut into wedges
1/2 cup green seedless grapes
1/2 cup red seedless grapes
1 (11-ounce) can mandarin oranges, drained
1 (16-ounce) can peach slices, drained
1 (16-ounce) can pineapple chunks, drained

In a glass bowl, mix together the apples, grapes, oranges, peaches, and pineapple chunks. When the dressing has cooled, pour over the fruit and mix well. Refrigerate several hours before serving.

Sharon Jones, Indianapolis, Ind.

BROCCOLI AND MUSHROOMS ELEGANT SALAD

2 bunches (stalks) fresh broccoli
1 pound fresh mushrooms
1 bottle Zesty Italian dressing

Cut broccoli into flowerets. Add thickly sliced mushrooms. Pour Italian dressing over broccoli and mushrooms. Add tight-fitting cover. Refrigerate several hours or overnight, turning occasionally. This is very good and is really elegant-looking when served in a pretty dish. Perfect for potluck dinners and church suppers. Only you will know how easy it is!

Brenda Peery, Tannersville, ,Va.

CREAM CHEESE AND CUCUMBER MOUSSE

2 envelopes unflavored gelatin
2 1/2 tablespoons white wine vinegar
1/3 of a long English cucumber, unpeeled
12 ounces cream cheese
Salt and pepper to taste
6 egg whites

Sprinkle gelatin over the vinegar in a small saucepan. Dice cucumber and liquify in a blender or grate by hand. Soften cream cheese with a fork; add cucumber, and mix together well. Place softened gelatin over low heat and stir constantly until gelatin dissolves, about 3–5 minutes. Remove from heat and add to the cream cheese. Whip egg whites until fluffy and fold into mixture. Add salt and pepper. To garnish, place very thin cucumber slices in the bottom of a large mold or 6 individual ones; then pour in a small amount of additional dissolved gelatin and allow to set before pouring in the mixture. Chill 3–4 hours before unmolding. This is a very pretty and refreshing salad.

Lillian Smith, Montreal, Canada

RHUBARB RASPBERRY SALAD

3 cups cut-up rhubarb pieces
1 cup water
1 (3-ounce) package raspberry-flavored gelatin
1 cup sugar
1 cup diced celery
1 cup chopped nuts

Cook rhubarb in the water about 10 minutes, until rhubarb is tender. Add gelatin and sugar; stir until dissolved. Cool until syrupy. Add celery and nuts. Chill until firm. (Do not try to mold this salad, because it does not get that firm).

24-HOUR SALAD
Serves 8–10

1 (17-ounce) can pitted sweet
  cherries, drained
2 (13-ounce) cans pineapple tidbits,
  drained (reserve 2 tablespoons
  syrup)
2 (11-ounce) cans mandarin oranges, drained
1 cup miniature marshmallows
Old-Fashioned Fruit Dressing
  (recipe follows)

Prepare dressing. Combine fruits
and marshmallows. Pour dressing over
ingredients and toss. Cover and chill
12–24 hours.

Old-Fashioned Fruit Dressing:
2 eggs, beaten
2 tablespoons lemon juice
1 tablespoon butter
2 tablespoons sugar
2 tablespoons reserved pineapple
  juice
Dash of salt
2 cups Cool Whip, thawed

Combine all ingredients, except
Cool Whip, in small saucepan. Heat
just to boiling, stirring constantly.
Remove from heat and cool. In a
chilled bowl with Cool Whip in it,
fold in the cooled egg mixture.

Sharon Lucas, Johnstown, Pa.

PINEAPPLE CARROT SALAD
Serves 6

1 large package lemon or orange
  gelatin
1 cup pineapple juice
1 cup boiling water
1 cup crushed pineapple
1-1/2 cups grated raw carrots
1/2 cup nuts (optional)

Dissolve gelatin in boiling water
and add pineapple juice. Chill. When
this begins to thicken, add other ingredients. Pour mixture into mold and
chill until set. Unmold on a plate of
lettuce and serve with mayonnaise.

Jean Hugh, Pittsburgh, Pa.

MANDARIN LETTUCE SALAD
Serves 6

1/4 cup sliced almonds
1/2 head lettuce
1 (11-ounce) can mandarin oranges
2 green onions, thinly sliced
2 tablespoons **plus** 1 teaspoon
  sugar
1 cup chopped celery

Cook almonds and sugar over low
heat until sugar is dissolved, stirring
constantly. When almonds are coated
remove from heat. Cool and break
apart. Keep at room temperature. Place
lettuce, which is broken into bite-size
pieces, celery and onions in a bowl.
Pour the following dressing over this
just before serving and toss. When
serving individually or in a large bowl,
sprinkle the caramelized almonds over
top.

Dressing:
1/4 cup vegetable oil
2 tablespoons sugar
2 teaspoons vinegar
1 tablespoon snipped parsley

This recipe has been used for a
number of benefit dinners as the salad.
It has received many compliments
from those who enjoyed it.

Sister Mary Kenneth Hemann, Dubuque, Iowa

BANANA YOGURT SALAD

2 large bananas
2 cups yogurt
¼ cup nuts, chopped
  Orange sections
  Lettuce

Peel and split bananas; place in
serving dishes. Spoon 1 cup yogurt
onto each banana. Sprinkle with nuts
and surround with orange sections
and shredded lettuce.

Suzan L. Wiener, Spring Hill, Fla.

CALICO COLE-SLAW FOR 10

1 cup mayonnaise
1 cup sour cream
1/3 cup sugar
3 tablespoons oil (preferably olive)
2 tablespoons lemon juice
1 tablespoon Old Bay Seasoning
1 teaspoon Dijon mustard
1/2 teaspoon dried basil, crumbled
Dash of hot pepper sauce
Salt and pepper
1 head cabbage, thinly sliced
1 onion, diced
1/2 apple, peeled and chopped
1 carrot, chopped

Combine first 9 ingredients in bowl.
Season with salt and pepper. Let dressing stand 15 minutes. Meanwhile, mix
remaining ingredients together in
bowl. Mix in enough dressing to season to taste. Cover and refrigerate 1 to
8 hours. Stir. Serve chilled.

MY FAVORITE CUCUMBER SALAD

3 medium cucumbers
1/4 teaspoon salt
1 teaspoon sugar
4 tablespoons sour cream *or*
  mayonnaise
3 tablespoons chopped green
  onions
1 teaspoon lemon juice
2 tablespoons vinegar
1/2 teaspoon dry mustard
1 tablespoon minced parsley

Peel cucumbers and thinly slice.
Spread cucumbers over bottom of a
colander and sprinkle salt and sugar
on top. Let them drain for 30 minutes;
press gently to remove excess liquid,
then chill. Blend sour cream or mayonnaise, onions, lemon juice, vinegar
and dry mustard together. Add salt to
taste. Toss dressing with cucumbers.
Sprinkle parsley on top and serve
chilled.

Lucille Roehr, Hammond, Ind.

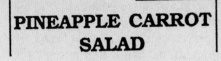

PINEAPPLE CARROT SALAD

1 (#2 can) crushed pineapple, drained
1/4 teaspoon salt
1 cup finely-grated carrots
1 (3 ounce) package lemon gelatin
1/2 cup sugar
2 tablespoons lemon juice
1 cup whipping cream

Add enough water to pineapple syrup to make 1-1/2 cups liquid. Heat to boiling. Remove and stir in gelatin; stir until dissolved. Add sugar, salt, and lemon juice. Chill until slightly thickened. Add pineapple and carrots. Whip cream; fold into gelatin mixture. Pour into mold or bowl; chill until firm. Unmold onto lettuce leaves. This is an attractive holiday salad.

Viola C. Prinsen, Cedarburg, Wis.

WISCONSIN CRANBERRY SALAD
Serves 8

1 cup ground fresh cranberries
1 cup ground MacIntosh apples or other tart apples
1 cup sugar

Combine in a bowl. Cover and chill 24 hours. Next day add:
1 cup mini-marshmallows
1/2 cup finely-chopped, toasted pecans
1 cup whipped cream or Cool Whip

Mix and chill. Serve cold. This is a very refreshing salad, tangy, light in texture, and full of crunch—a super side dish!

Mrs. Larry Morris, Bradenton, Fla.

STRAWBERRY NUT SALAD

2 (3 ounce) packages strawberry jello
1 cup boiling water
2 (10 ounce) packages frozen strawberries, thawed and undrained
2 mashed bananas
1 can (1 pound-4 ounce) crushed pineapple, drained
1 cup pecan pieces
2 cartons (8 ounce) sour cream

Dissolve jello in boiling water. Add strawberries with juice, drained pineapple, bananas, and nuts. Put 1/2 of mixture in rectangular glass dish; refrigerate until firm. When congealed, spread sour cream over top of this layer. Pour balance of jello mixture over sour cream. Refrigerate until firm. To serve: cut into squares; arrange on lettuce.

Agnes Ward, Erie, PA

TAFFY APPLE SALAD
Serves 8-10

1 large can pineapple chunks, in natural juice (reserve juice)
2 cups miniature marshmallows
1 (8 ounce) container Cool Whip
2 red apples, pared
2 green apples, pared
1-1/2 cups chopped pecans or walnuts
1 tablespoon flour
1 egg, beaten
1-1/2 tablespoons vinegar
1/2 cup sugar

First day:
Mix drained pineapple chunks with marshmallows. Refrigerate overnight in covered dish. Cook pineapple juice with flour, sugar, beaten egg, and vinegar until thick. Refrigerate overnight.

Second Day:
Combine Cool Whip with cooked dressing. Add rest of ingredients and refrigerate until served.

TRANSCONTINENTAL TOSS
Serves 10

1 cup peach slices
1 cup pear slices
1 cup pineapple chunks
1 cup green seedless grapes
2 cups strawberries
1 (11 ounce can) mandarin oranges
Combine fruits in bowl.

Dressing:
1 small can evaporated milk
1 (7 ounce jar) marshmallow creme
2 tablespoons orange juice

Toss fruit lightly with dressing before serving.

MYSTERY SALAD

1 can cherry pie filling
1 can crushed pineapple (drained)
1 can mandarin oranges (drained)
1 cup mini marshmallows
1 can Eagle Brand sweetened condensed milk
1-8 ounce container of whipped topping
1/4 cup walnuts coarsely chopped

Mix all ingredients together. Pour into large bowl or in a large pan. Put more nuts on top if desired. Cover and refrigerate until served.

Donna Coakley, Parrottsville, TN

FRUIT COCKTAIL SALAD

1 (5-5/8 ounce) package vanilla flavored Jell-O instant pudding mix
1-1/3 cups buttermilk
1 (8 ounce) container Cool Whip
1 (30 ounce) can fruit cocktail, well-drained
2 cans mandarin oranges, well-drained
1 cup miniature rainbow-colored marshmallows (optional)

Blend buttermilk into pudding mix using medium speed of mixer. When smooth, blend in Cool Whip. If consistency of mixture seems too thick, add a little more buttermilk.

Fold in fruit cocktail and mandarin oranges, reserving half a can of oranges for garnish. Swirl a design on top of salad with a tablespoon. Gently arrange balance of mandarin orange slices in the swirled design on top of the salad.

Add colored marshmallows to mixture before garnishing, if desired.

Lalla Fellows, Long Beach, CA

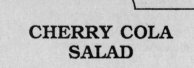

CHERRY COLA SALAD

1 (3 ounce) package (dark) cherry
  gelatin
1 cup hot water
1 bottle (16-ounce) cola
3/4 teaspoon lemon juice
4 ounces cream cheese (cut into
  small cubes)
1/2 cup chopped nuts
1 can dark sweet cherries (drained
  and cut)

Put gelatin into hot water and stir
until dissolved. When it cools, add
cola and refrigerate until gelatin begins to harden. Add cherries, nuts,
and cream cheese. Pour into gelatin
mold and chill.

Karin Shea Fedders, Dameron, Md.

DREAM SALAD

1 small box lime gelatin
1 (8-ounce) package cream cheese,
  softened
1/8 teaspoon salt
1/2 cup mayonnaise
1 cup chopped celery
1/2 cup finely chopped nuts
1 (8-ounce) can crushed pineapple,
  drained
1 cup whipped cream
1/2 pound mini marshmallows
1 cup cottage cheese
1-3/4 cups boiling water

Dissolve gelatin in boiling water.
Beat cream cheese, salt, and mayonnaise until light and fluffy. Add gelatin, celery, nuts, whipped cream,
marshmallows, cottage cheese, and
pineapple. Put in 9 x 13 inch pan with
a cover; chill.

Betty Brennan, Faribault, MN

CHERRY SALAD

Serves 15

2 (6-ounce) packages cherry gelatin
2 cups hot water
1 cup cold water
1 can cherry pie filling

1 (8-ounce) package cream cheese
1 cup crushed pineapple, drained
Cool Whip

Dissolve gelatin in hot water; add
cold water and pie filling. Pour into
13x9-inch pan. When completely set,
cover with the following topping:
Whip together 1 large package cream
cheese and 1 cup crushed pineapple,
drained; spread on gelatin. A container of Cool Whip (whipped topping) may be folded into the whipped
cream cheese layer and spread over
the gelatin.

Marguerite Garvey, Boone, Iowa

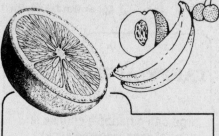

APRICOT GELATIN MOLD

2 (6-ounce) packages apricot
  gelatin
3 cups boiling water
1 (9-ounce) container frozen
  whipped topping, thawed
2 cups cold water
2 bananas, sliced
1/2 cup pecans or walnuts
1 (13-1/4-ounce) can pineapple
  tidbits, drained

Dissolve gelatin in boiling water.
Add whipped topping and let dissolve. Mix well. Add cold water.
Refrigerate until thickened. Blend in
sliced bananas, nuts, and pineapple
tidbits. Chill overnight. Must be prepared a day ahead.

Leota Baxter, Ingalls, Kan.

GOLDEN GLOW SALAD

1 cup boiling water
1 package lemon gelatin
1 cup pineapple juice
1 cup diced pineapple
1 tablespoon lemon juice
1/3 cup chopped nuts
1/2 teaspoon salt
1 cup grated carrots

Canned pineapple and juice *must*
be used. Dissolve gelatin in boiling
water; add juice and salt. When
slightly thickened, add pineapple,
carrots, nuts, and lemon juice. Turn
into mold and chill until firm. Unmold on bed of shredded lettuce.

Mrs. Larry Morris, Cedar Hills, TX

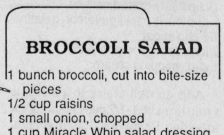

BROCCOLI SALAD

1 bunch broccoli, cut into bite-size
  pieces
1/2 cup raisins
1 small onion, chopped
1 cup Miracle Whip salad dressing
1/4 cup sugar
2 tablespoons vinegar
12 slices bacon, fried, and crumbled

Mix sugar and vinegar with salad
dressing. Pour over broccoli, raisins,
onion, and bacon. Mix well, set in
refrigerator a couple hours to cool and
blend flavors.

Mrs. Tom McNiel, Constantine, Mich.

CARROT-DATE SLAW

Serves 4

1/2 cup commercial sour cream
1/4 cup milk
1 tablespoon lemon juice
1 teaspoon sugar
1/4 teaspoon salt
3 cups shredded carrots
1/2 cup chopped dates

Combine all ingredients; stir well.
Chill thoroughly.

Mrs. Bruce Fowler, Woodruff, S.C

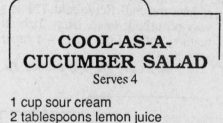

COOL-AS-A-CUCUMBER SALAD

Serves 4

1 cup sour cream
2 tablespoons lemon juice
1/4 teaspoon dried dill weed
2 medium cucumbers pared and
  sliced

Combine first 3 ingredients, stirring well. Add cucumbers and coat
gently. Chill at least 2 hours before
serving.

AMSTERDAM SPINACH SALAD

Serves 4

3 cups fresh spinach, cut into bite-size pieces
5 slices crisp bacon, crumbled
1 medium carrot, shredded
1 tablespoon minced onion
1/4 cup bottled Italian dressing
1/8 teaspoon dry mustard.
Dash of pepper

Combine spinach, bacon, carrots and onion in medium bowl. Heat Italian dressing with mustard and pepper in a small saucepan; pour over spinach and toss.

Sue Hibbard, Rochester, NY

CHINESE CABBAGE SALAD

Serves 6-8

1 large head Chinese cabbage, chopped
2 small purple onions, sliced in rings
1 (8 ounce) carton sour cream
1/2 cup chopped onion
2 tablespoons vinegar
2 tablespoons celery seed
1/2 teaspoon salt
1/4 teaspoon pepper

Combine chopped cabbage and onion rings. Set aside.

Combine sour cream, chopped onion, vinegar, celery seed, salt, and pepper. Stir well. Mix into cabbage and onion rings. Chill well before serving.

Lily Jo Drake, Satellite Beach, FL

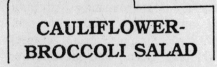

CAULIFLOWER-BROCCOLI SALAD

1 head cauliflower
2 stalks broccoli
1/4 cup sliced green onions
1 pound bacon, cooked and crumbled
6 ounces Cheddar cheese, cubed
6 ounces Mozzarella cheese, cubed

2 tablespoons vinegar
2 cups mayonnaise
1/4 cup sugar
1/2 teaspoon salt

Cut up the cauliflower and broccoli into very small pieces. Add to diced cheeses and onion. Mix mayonnaise, sugar, salt, and vinegar together; stir into vegetables. Add bacon last.

This is an excellent salad and can be made ahead and kept for a day or two in the refrigerator.

Sharon Sisson, Longview, Wash.

MARINATED CARROTS

Serves 8

1 bunch large carrots
2 cloves garlic, sliced
1/2 teaspoon salt
1/2 teaspoon pepper
1/4 cup olive oil
2 tablespoons wine vinegar
1 teaspoon oregano

Scrape carrots and cut into thick slices. Boil carrots in water 10 minutes, or until tender, taking care not to overcook. Drain well and place in bowl with garlic, salt, pepper, oil, vinegar, and oregano. Stir; mix well. Let stand in marinade 12 hours before serving.

Helen V. Robiolio, Union City, N.J.

ELEGANT WHITE SALAD

2 envelopes plain gelatin
1/2 cup cold pineapple juice
1-1/2 cups hot pineapple juice
1/2 cup sugar
Juice of 1 lemon
1 teaspoon almond extract
1 cup half and half cream
1 cup heavy cream, whipped

Dissolve gelatin in cold pineapple juice. When dissolved, add hot juice, sugar and lemon juice. Let cool. Then add half and half; refrigerate. (Mixture looks curdled at this point.) When partly set, add extract and whipped cream. Pour into ring mold.

When ready to serve, unmold on large serving plate. Surround with pineapple chunks, mandarin oranges or any fruit combination. Place fruit in the center, too.

Mrs. Martha Mehloff, Eureka, SD

SPRING SPINACH SALAD

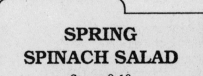

Serves 8-10

1 pound fresh spinach
1 medium sliced cucumber
1/4 cup diced celery
8 sliced radishes
1/4 cup sliced green onions
1/2 cup French dressing
2 tomatoes, quartered

Rub bowl with cut clove of garlic; remove garlic. Add spinach. (Use small spinach leaves whole; shred larger leaves.) Arrange other vegetables over spinach. (Score cucumber with fork before slicing.)

Pour on dressing. Garnish with tomato quarters. Also, if desired, cut one tomato into a "flower" and fill center with sieved hard-cooked egg yolk.

Amelia M. Brown, Pittsburgh, PA

GARDEN FRESH CUCUMBERS

Makes 3 cups

1/4 cup vinegar
1 tablespoon lemon juice
1 teaspoon celery seeds
2 tablespoons sugar
3/4 teaspoon salt
1/8 teaspoon pepper
2 tablespoons chopped onion
3 cups sliced peeled cucumbers

Combine vinegar, lemon juice, celery seeds, sugar, salt, pepper, and onion. Pour over cucumbers. Chill.

Sharon M. Crider, Evansville, WI

PEANUT CRUNCH SALAD

Serves 12-15

4 cups shredded cabbage
1 cup finely chopped celery
1/2 cup sour cream
1/2 cup mayonnaise
1 teaspoon salt
1/4 cup chopped green onion
1/4 cup chopped green pepper
1/2 cup chopped cucumber
1 tablespoon butter
1/2 cup coarsely chopped dry roasted peanuts
2 tablespoons grated Parmesan cheese

Toss cabbage and celery together; chill. Combine sour cream, mayonnaise, salt, onion, green pepper and cucumber in small bowl; chill.

Just before serving, melt butter in small skillet. Add peanuts; heat until lightly browned and immediately stir in cheese.

Toss chilled vegetables with dressing. Sprinkle peanut mixture on top of salad and serve.

Sue Hibbard, Rochester, NY

SUPER DELICIOUS STRAWBERRY GELATIN SALAD

Serves 8

1-1/3 cups coarsely ground pretzels
3/4 stick margarine
4 ounces cream cheese
1/2 cup sugar
1/2 cup whipped cream
1 cup pineapple juice
1 package (3 ounce package) strawberry jello
1 (10 ounce package) frozen strawberries

Combine pretzels and margarine. Press into 8 x 8 x 2 inch pan. Bake at 400 degrees for 10 minutes. Cream sugar and cream cheese; fold in whipped cream. Pour over pretzel crust and refrigerate. Dissolve jello in hot pineapple juice; add partially thawed strawberries. When mixture starts to set, pour over other layers. Refrigerate until firm.

Lucille Roehr, Hammond, IN

BUTTERMINT SALAD

2 (13 ounce) cans crushed pineapple, undrained
1 package dry lime gelatin
1 (10 ounce) package miniature marshmallows
1 (7 ounce) package soft buttermints; crushed
1 (9 ounce) container Cool Whip

Mix pineapple, gelatin, and marshmallows in large bowl. Cover and refrigerate overnight. Add mints and Cool Whip in morning and serve one of three ways:

1) Pour into a 9 x 13 inch pan and freeze. Cut into squares and serve on lettuce leaves.

2) Pour into large bowl and refrigerate. Serve chilled. Salad will be soft.

3) Pour into individual aluminum foil muffin tins and freeze. Serve when solid.

Kathy Ericksen, Rockwell City, IA

GARDEN GATE SALAD

1/2 teaspoon grated onion
1/2 teaspoon vinegar
1/4 teaspoon paprika
1/2 teaspoon salt
1/2 cup mayonnaise or salad dressing
2 cups cubed cooked potatoes
1/2 cup diced celery
1/2 cup diced cucumbers
1/4 cup sliced radishes
1/4 cup chopped green peppers
Lettuce
Watercress

Mix onion, vinegar, paprika, salt and mayonnaise or salad dressing. Combine with potato, celery, cucumber, radishes, and green pepper. Chill and serve on lettuce and watercress. This is a very simple salad that is tasty and most attractive.

Lillian Smith, Montreal, QUE

MOLDED CHERRY SALAD

Serves 6

1 package apple gelatin
1 cup boiling water
1 cup cherry juice
1 tablespoon lemon juice
1-1/2 cups pitted white cherries
1 (3 ounce) package cream cheese
1 tablespoon mayonnaise
Lettuce leaves

Dissolve apple gelatin in boiling water; add cherry juice and lemon juice. Pour one-third of the mixture into bottom of a mold. Chill. Fill pitted cherries with cream cheese which has been whipped with mayonnaise; arrange on gelatin. Pour slightly thickened gelatin around the cherries and allow to set. When completely chilled and set, unmold and serve on lettuce leaves. Serve with additional mayonnaise, if desired.

Betty Slavin, Omaha, Neb.

VELVET SALAD

1 (3 ounce) package lemon gelatin
2 cups boiling water
1 pound marshmallows
1 medium can crushed pineapple, drained
1 (3 ounce) package cream cheese
1 cup whipping cream
1 cup mayonnaise
1 (3 ounce) package cherry gelatin
2 cups hot water

Dissolve lemon gelatin in boiling water. Add marshmallows; stir until dissolved. Mix together drained, crushed pineapple, cream cheese, whipping cream, and mayonnaise. Combine with lemon gelatin mixture. Chill. Dissolve cherry gelatin in hot water. Cool, then pour over lemon gelatin mixture.

This is a colorful and refreshing salad for the Christmas holidays.

Cathy Cecava, Lincoln, Neb.

MIXED SALAD
Serves 6

⅓ cup olive *or* vegetable oil
2 tablespoons fresh lemon juice
2 tablespoons white wine vinegar
1 small clove garlic, minced
¼ teaspoon salt
¼ teaspoon basil, crushed
⅛ teaspoon white pepper
½ head romaine lettuce
½ head Boston lettuce
1 cucumber, sliced
¼ cup shredded carrot
2 tablespoons sliced scallion

In small bowl, combine oil, lemon juice, vinegar, garlic, salt, basil and pepper. Cover and chill at least 1 hour.

At serving time, wash lettuce leaves and tear into bite-size pieces; place in a large bowl. Add cucumber, carrot and scallion. Pour dressing over salad and toss to coat evenly.

Mary Dale, Cincinnati, Ohio

LUNCHEON SALAD

1 cup sliced fresh mushrooms
1 cup chopped cooked shrimp
1 teaspoon tarragon leaves
1/2 cup Italian dressing
3 ripe avocados, chilled
Red leaf or romaine lettuce

Combine all ingredients, except avocados and lettuce. Chill for 1 hour in refrigerator. Arrange lettuce leaves on individual salad plates. Peel and halve avocados. Place an avocado half on each salad plate and fill with marinated combination. Garnish with whole cherry tomatoes and radish roses, if desired. This is a great salad for company in the summertime!

Suzan L. Wiener, Spring Hill, Fla.

PEPPERONI SALAD
Serves 6–8

1 medium onion, thinly sliced
8 ounces pepperoni, thinly sliced
¼ cup crumbled bleu cheese
⅔ cup salad oil
⅓ cup cider vinegar
Salt and freshly ground pepper to taste
10 ounces fresh spinach, washed thoroughly, dried and chopped
½ head iceberg lettuce, chopped

One day before serving, separate onion slices into rings and place in large bowl; add pepperoni slices and bleu cheese. Add oil, vinegar, salt and pepper. Toss in the spinach and lettuce. Chill salad overnight in covered bowl.

Agnes Ward, Erie, Pa.

TART APPLE SALAD
Serves 10

6 apples, sweet-tart and crisp
½ cup chopped English walnuts
1 cup finely chopped celery
1½ cups purple grapes, halved and seeds removed
¼ cup sugar
1 heaping tablespoon Miracle Whip
½ pint whipping cream, whipped

Prepare the fruit and celery. Combine fruit, nuts and celery. Sprinkle with sugar; stir in Miracle Whip. Stir well to cover all the fruit, nuts and celery with a light coating of the sugar/dressing mixture. Add stiffly beaten whipped cream. You can do everything except the cream ahead of time, and refrigerate for a couple of hours. Add whipped cream just before serving. Be sure to refrigerate immediately in a covered container.

Linda Taylor, Gravois Mills, Mo.

FROZEN PEA SALAD

1 (10–12-ounce) package frozen peas
1 (4-ounce) package Hidden Valley Original Ranch salad dressing
1 cup buttermilk
1 (8-ounce) carton sour cream
1 small onion, chopped
1 small head lettuce, cut in bite-size pieces
4 hard-cooked eggs, diced
8 to 10 strips bacon, fried and drained

Thaw peas; drain on paper towels. In a small bowl put dry dressing mix, buttermilk and sour cream; whip this mixture until creamy and smooth. Add onion, salt and pepper to taste. In a large bowl combine lettuce, diced eggs, drained bacon and drained peas. Add dressing mixture and toss lightly until salad ingredients are coated. Refrigerate until chilled; serve.

Rose Mary Dietz, Hoisington, Kan.

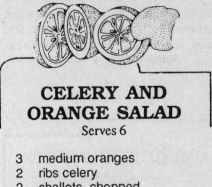

CELERY AND ORANGE SALAD
Serves 6

3 medium oranges
2 ribs celery
2 shallots, chopped
4 tablespoons oil
1 tablespoon lemon juice
Salt and pepper
Chopped parsley

Peel oranges, cutting just beneath the pith. Hold the fruit in one hand and cut out each segment, freeing it from its protective membranes as you cut. Cut the celery into 1½-inch julienne strips. Put the shallots, oranges and celery into a bowl; add the remaining ingredients and toss. Allow salad to rest for 1–6 hours before serving.

Marcella Swigert, Monroe City, Mo.

CHICK-PEA AND SPINACH SALAD

6 ounces dried chick-peas
1 pound fresh spinach
6 tablespoons olive oil
2 tablespoons wine vinegar
Salt and pepper
½ cup plain yogurt
2 tablespoons chopped parsley

Soak chick-peas in cold water overnight. Strain. Put in large saucepan and add about 4 cups fresh water. Bring to a boil; cover; simmer gently for 1½ hours, or until peas are tender but not mushy. Let peas cool in the cooking liquid, then drain.

Wash spinach; discard any coarse or damaged leaves, and pull off all stems. Cut large leaves into pieces; leave small leaves whole. Combine chick-peas and spinach in a salad bowl. Pour in oil and vinegar; add salt and pepper to taste. Toss ingredients together, but gently, so as not to break up peas. Chill salad until ready to serve. At serving time, arrange the mixture in a shallow bowl and top with yogurt. Sprinkle parsley over all.

Marcella Swigert, Monroe City, Mo.

ZUCCHINI–APPLE SLAW
Serves 6

4 cups coarsely shredded zucchini
1/4 cup green onions, thinly sliced on the diagonal
2–3 medium-size red or green tart apples (unskinned)
1/2 cup mayonnaise
3 tablespoons cider vinegar
1 tablespoon sugar
1 teaspoon poppy seeds
Salt and pepper to taste

In a large bowl combine zucchini and onions. Core apples and cut into 1/4- to 1/2-inch chunks. Add apples to zucchini mixture. Combine may-

onnaise, vinegar, sugar and poppy seeds until well-blended. Pour dressing over salad and mix lightly until well-coated. Season with salt and pepper to taste. Cover and refrigerate for 2–4 hours. Use a slotted spoon to transfer to serving bowl or individual plates.

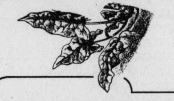

GREEN BEANS AND BACON SALAD
Serves 6

6 slices bacon, coarsely chopped
1-1/2 pounds fresh beans, trimmed and cooked crisp-tender, drained
or
2 (9-ounce) packages frozen whole green beans, thawed
1 medium yellow, red, or green bell pepper, coarsely chopped
3 tablespoons olive oil
1/4 teaspoon pepper

Cook bacon in skillet over medium heat until crisp, stirring at least twice. Remove bacon with a slotted spoon; transfer to paper towel to drain. Pour all but 1 tablespoon drippings from skillet. Add all remaining ingredients, except bacon. Cook about 3 minutes, stirring constantly until beans are heated through. Transfer to a large bowl. Stir in bacon. Cool completely. Cover and refrigerate overnight. Can be prepared at least 2 days before serving. Serve at room temperature. This salad is great with fried chicken!

Leota Baxter, Ingalls, Kan.

FIVE-CUP FRUIT SALAD

1 cup flaked coconut
1 cup mandarin oranges
1 cup miniature marshmallows
1 cup pineapple bits, well-drained
1 cup commercial sour cream

Toss fruit, coconut and marshmallows with sour cream. Chill and serve.

Dovie Lucy, McLoud, Okla.

GOURMET FRUIT MOLD

1 (3-ounce) package raspberry gelatin
1-1/4 cups Dr. Pepper beverage, boiling
1 (10-ounce) package frozen raspberries
3/4 cup canned crushed pineapple, drained
1 large banana, sliced
1/4 cup chopped pecans

Dissolve gelatin in boiling Dr. Pepper. Add partially thawed raspberries. Stir until berries are separated. Chill until mixture is thickened. Fold in remaining ingredients. Pour into molds. Chill until firm; unmold. Garnish with salad greens. Serve with Sour Cream Fruit Dressing (recipe follows).

Sour Cream Fruit Dressing:
Combine 1 cup sour cream with 1-1/2 cups miniature marshmallows, 1 tablespoon sugar, and 2-1/2 tablespoons lemon juice. Chill several hours. Stir well before serving.

Mrs. Bruce Fowler, Woodruff, S.C.

ORIENTAL SLAW
Serves 6

1 small to medium head of Ñappa or Chinese cabbage, washed and crisped (reserve 6 outer leaves)
1 cup pineapple tidbits, drained (fresh, if possible)
1 large tart apple, diced and unskinned
1 cup plain low-fat yogurt
1/4 cup mayonnaise
Juice of 1 lemon
1 tablespoon honey (more, if desired)

Cut cabbage crosswise into thin 1/8- to 1/4-inch slices. Combine with pineapple and apples. Mix yogurt, mayonnaise, lemon juice and honey; pour over cabbage mixture. Chill. When ready to serve, place whole cabbage leaf on plate, mound slaw on top and serve.

Salad DRESSINGS

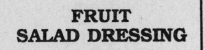

FRUIT SALAD DRESSING

1/4 cup Karo light corn syrup
1/2 cup sour cream
1/2 cup mayonnaise

Mix sour cream with mayonnaise until smooth. Add Karo syrup and blend well. Spoon over a salad of assorted fresh fruits or canned fruits.

FRENCH DRESSING
Makes 2 cups

1 cup vegetable oil
½ cup sugar
½ cup ketchup
¼ cup vinegar
¼ cup chopped onion
1 teaspoon celery seed
½ teaspoon salt

Combine all ingredients in an electric blender; process until smooth. Cover and chill thoroughly.

FABULOUS ROQUEFORT DRESSING
Makes 1 quart

1 (3-ounce) package Roquefort cheese
2 cups mayonnaise
3 teaspoons chives *or* green onion, finely chopped

1 teaspoon black pepper
1 teaspoon garlic powder
½ teaspoon Worcestershire sauce
1 cup sour cream
½ cup buttermilk

Blend all ingredients, mixing in sour cream and buttermilk last. Chill. If dressing is too thick, thin with additional buttermilk at serving time. We use this recipe as a dip with corn chips and potato chips, as well as salad dressing.

MASON JAR DRESSING

1 can condensed tomato soup
3/4 cup herb salad vinegar
1 teaspoon salt
1/2 teaspoon paprika
1/2 teaspoon pepper
1 teaspoon onion juice
1 tablespoon mustard
1-1/2 cups oil, (salad or olive)
1/2 cup sugar

Combine dry ingredients separately. Combine liquid ingredients separately. Moisten dry ingredients with a little of the liquid, then pour all together into a quart fruit jar and *shake*.

Worcestershire sauce or a little liquid from dill pickles may be added for additional zest.

Always shake well before using.

SUPER SALAD SEASONING MIX

2 cups Parmesan cheese
2 teaspoons salt
1/2 cup sesame seeds
1/2 teaspoon garlic salt
3 tablespoons celery seed
1 tablespoon instant minced onion
2 tablespoons parsley
1/2 teaspoon dill seeds
1/8 cup poppy seeds
2 teaspoons paprika
1/2 teaspoon freshly grated black pepper

Mix all ingredients together well. Use as a sprinkle on salads, baked potatoes, buttered French bread, and rolls. Also good as a garnish for potato and egg salads.

FAMOUS FRUIT-SALAD DRESSING
Makes 2 cups

1 cup sweet cream
½ cup brown sugar
¼ cup vinegar
½ cup granulated sugar
Salt to taste

Beat cream until slightly thickened; add remaining ingredients and mix well. Refrigerate overnight to thicken. Delicious on spinach salad, too!

ONION SALAD DRESSING

Makes 1 cup

1/2 cup finely chopped onion
1/4 cup cider vinegar
1/4 cup sugar
1/2 teaspoon salt
1/2 teaspoon dry mustard
1/4 teaspoon celery seed
1/2 cup oil

Combine all ingredients, except oil, in blender; mix well, stopping as necessary to scrape down sides of container. With blender running, gradually pour in oil, blending until dressing is creamy. Transfer to container with tight-fitting lid and refrigerate before using. Whisk or shake, if dressing separates on standing.

ITALIAN DRESSING MIX POWDER

(One envelope of commercial dressing mix equals this entire recipe)

2 teaspoons onion powder
1 tablespoon white sugar or sugar substitute
1/8 teaspoon black pepper
1/8 teaspoon powdered allspice
1 teaspoon dry minced onions
1 teaspoon dry celery flakes
1/8 teaspoon crushed marjoram leaves
1/4 teaspoon dry oregano, crushed
1 clove garlic peeled, sliced fine or 2 teaspoons bottled minced garlic
1/8 teaspoon paprika
2 squares of soda crackers (1-1/2" x 1-1/2")

Mix all ingredients in blender. Keep covered. Will keep up to 3 months.

To Use: Combine all the above with 1/2 cup vinegar, 2/3 cup cold water and 1/3 cup corn oil. Mix well. Keeps in refrigerator up to 1 month. Shake well before using. Makes 1-1/2 cup prepared dressing.

TANGY LOUIS DRESSING

Makes 4 cups

2 cups mayonnaise
1-1/2 cups chili sauce
1/3 cup minced celery
1/3 cup minced sour pickles
2 tablespoons lemon juice
1 tablespoon Worcestershire sauce
1 teaspoon prepared horseradish

Combine all ingredients, stirring well; chill. Store covered, in refrigerator. Serve over seafood, ham, or salad greens.

NOTE: This recipe may be halved very successfully for smaller quantity.

DILLED YOGURT DRESSING

1 cup non-fat plain yogurt
2 tablespoons vinegar
1/2 small onion
1/2 teaspoon dill seeds
1/4 teaspoon dry mustard
1/4 to 1/2 teaspoon fresh garlic

Combine all the ingredients in blender until smooth. Great topping for salads, vegetables, or dip for crackers or chips.

LOW CALORIE SALAD DRESSING

Makes 1-1/2 cups

1/2 cup cottage cheese
1/2 cup low fat milk
1 teaspoon salt
1 teaspoon paprika
2 tablespoons lemon juice
1 sliver garlic
1/2 green pepper, cut into strips
4 radishes
2 green onions, coarsely cut

Put all ingredients into blender container. Cover; blend on high speed for 10 seconds or until vegetables are finely chopped. Refrigerate dressing for proper storage.

CREAMY LOW-CAL DRESSING

2 cups of dressing

1/2 cup skim milk
2 tablespoons lemon juice
1 tablespoon vegetable oil
1-1/2 cup low-fat cottage cheese (12 ounce)
1 small onion, chopped
1 cloves garlic, crushed
1/2 teaspoon salt
1/4 teaspoon pepper
1/4 teaspoon paprika

Place all ingredients in blender container in order listed above. Cover and blend on medium speed until smooth, about 1 minute. Cover and refrigerate.

CHILI FLAVORED DRESSING

1/2 teaspoon chili powder
1 tablespoon wine vinegar
2 tablespoons orange juice
3 tablespoons mashed green chilies
1-1/4 cups mayonnaise

Blend chili powder with wine vinegar and orange juice. Then add green chilies and stir into mayonnaise.

VINAIGRETTE DRESSING

Makes 1-1/2 cups

1 cup oil and vinegar dressing
2 tablespoons chopped parsley
1/4 cup finely chopped pickle
2 teaspoons chopped onion
2 teaspoons capers (optional)

Blend above ingredients thoroughly.

CREAMY SALAD DRESSING

Makes 1 pint

1/4 cup sugar
3/4 teaspoon dry mustard
1/2 teaspoon salt
2 tablespoons flour
2 egg yolks or 1 whole egg
1/2 cup vinegar
1/3 cup hot water
1/2 cup cream, whipped

Mix dry ingredients in saucepan. Add beaten egg; stir to blend well. Add vinegar and hot water. Cook on low heat; stir until mixture is thickened. Remove from heat; cool. Fold in whipped cream. Store in covered jar; refrigerate.

THOUSAND ISLAND DRESSING

3 large dill pickles
3 medium onions
3 large green peppers, seeded
1 small can pimientos
5 hard-cooked eggs
1 quart mayonnaise
1 bottle chili sauce

Grind ingredients together and drain well. Clean grinder and grind 5 hard-cooked eggs. Combine all ingredients with 1 quart mayonnaise and one bottle chili sauce. Store in refrigerator until ready to serve.

RANCH SALAD DRESSING

Makes 2-1/4 cups

2 cups plain lowfat yogurt
1/4 cup mayonnaise
1/2 teaspoon garlic powder
1/4 teaspoon monosodium glutamate
1 teaspoon dried minced onion
1/4 teaspoon pepper
1/4 teaspoon paprika
1/2 teaspoon onion powder
1 teaspoon dried parsley flakes
1/4 teaspoon dried dill weed
1/2 teaspoon celery salt

Mix all ingredients together. Refrigerate for 1 hour to blend flavors. Use as dip for raw vegetables or salad dressing.

POPPY SEED SALAD DRESSING

1 small onion, grated
1-1/2 cups sugar
2/3 cup cider vinegar
2 teaspoons dry mustard
1-1/2 teaspoons salt
2 tablespoons poppy seeds
2 cups oil

Blend first six ingredients. With blender still running, pour in oil in a slow but steady stream. Continue to blend until thick and creamy.

An old, but delicious family favorite.

TARRAGON DRESSING

Makes 3/4 cup

1/2 cup vegetable oil
1/4 cup cider vinegar
1-1/2 teaspoons sugar
1 teaspoon tarragon
1/2 teaspoon salt
1/4 teaspoon freshly ground black pepper
Dash liquid hot pepper sauce

Whisk together oil, vinegar, sugar, tarragon, salt, pepper, and hot sauce, until slightly creamy.
Note: Dressing can be made in advance. Shake or whisk before serving.

GARLIC DRESSING

3 cups Miracle Whip
1-1/2 cups salad oil 1/2 cup vinegar (scant) white or wine
2-1/2 tablespoons sugar
1-1/2 teaspoons salt
1-1/2 teaspoons Accent
1 or more cloves garlic
1/3 cup onion
Parsley

Mix all together in blender. Store in covered container in refrigerator. Add blue cheese, if desired. Shake well before serving.

LOW-CAL DRESSING

Makes 1/2 cup

1/2 cup skim milk
1 teaspoon onion juice
1 tablespoon lemon juice
1 tablespoon minced parsley
1 tablespoon minced pimiento

Combine milk with lemon juice and flavoring agents; shake thoroughly in a small jar with tightly fitting lid. More or less lemon juice may be used according to taste.
Use at once; serve immediately. Great dressing for all types of salads.

TRUE RUSSIAN DRESSING

Makes 3 cups

2 cups mayonnaise
2/3 cup chili sauce
2/3 cup chopped dill pickles
1/2 teaspoon seasoned salt
1 tablespoon minced onion
2 tablespoons sugar

Blend all ingredients in a bowl and chill.

CREAMY BLUE CHEESE DRESSING

Makes 2 cups

6 ounces crumbled blue cheese
1 cup real mayonnaise
3/4 cup buttermilk
1/4 teaspoon onion powder
1/4 teaspoon garlic powder

Combine all ingredients; mix until well blended and creamy. Serve over tossed green salad.

Sandwich
TASTIES

BARBECUED BEEF

6 pounds boneless chuck (*or* pork), cut in pieces
2 stalks celery, chopped
2 medium onions, chopped
1 green pepper, chopped
1 medium bottle ketchup
3 tablespoons barbecue sauce
3 tablespoons vinegar
1 tablespoon Tabasco sauce
1 tablespoon chili powder
1 tablespoon salt
1 teaspoon pepper

Cut meat into pieces and place in large oven roaster. Place remainder of ingredients in large mixing bowl and stir well. Pour over meat and cook in a slow oven (250 degrees) for 6 or more hours. When meat is tender, shred with 2 forks. Serve on hamburger buns.

This is a great dish to prepare on busy weekends!

Phyliss D. Dixon, Fairbanks, Alaska

ENGLISH MUFFIN SNACKWICHES

1 can chopped ripe olives
1/2 cup chopped green onions
1-1/2 cups grated cheddar cheese
1/2 cup mayonnaise
1/2 teaspoon curry powder
1/2 teaspoon chili powder
6 split English muffins

Mix all ingredients and spread on muffins. Broil until bubbly. Quarter and serve. Variations: May add shrimp, crab, or tuna to the spread.

Sue Thomas, Case Grande, Ariz.

BEEF MUSHROOM PASTIES
Serves 8

1 loaf frozen bread dough
1 pound lean ground beef
1 can condensed cream of mushroom soup
1 (4-ounce) can sliced mushrooms, drained
2 tablespoons dried, chopped onion
2 tablespoons Worcestershire sauce

Thaw dough until pliable. Cook beef until well-browned; drain grease. Add soup, mushrooms, onion and Worcestershire sauce to beef.

Cut loaf of bread dough crosswise, into 8 slices. Using a little flour on board and rolling pin, pat and roll dough pieces out to 5-inch circles. Place filling in centers of dough circles. Pull all dough edges up to the center and pinch tightly to seal filling inside. Place buns, smooth sides up, on greased baking sheet. Using a sharp knife, make a large cut on top of each bun for steam to escape. Bake at 375 degrees for 35 minutes, or until well-browned.

Good hot or cold. A picnic treat.

Mrs. W.T. Gore, Aztec, N.M.

OPEN-FACED EGG AND CHEESE SANDWICHES
Makes 6 sandwiches

1 tablespoon butter
2 tablespoons onions
2 tablespoons green pepper, finely chopped
6 eggs, beaten
1/3 cup milk
1/4 teaspoon salt
1/8 teaspoon pepper
6 English muffin halves, toasted
1 tablespoon butter
6 1-ounce slices American cheese

Melt 1 tablespoon butter in frying pan; saute onion and green pepper, stirring often, until tender. Combine eggs, milk, salt and pepper. Pour over onion and green pepper in frying pan and cook over low heat, stirring often to let uncooked portion of eggs flow beneath cooked portion. Continue cooking until eggs are set but still moist.

Divide eggs into six portions. Spread toasted muffin halves with remaining tablespoon of butter, and top muffin halves with egg mixture and a slice of cheese. Broil until cheese melts and is lightly browned (about 5 minutes).

Charlotte Adams, Detroit, Mich.

PIZZA BUNS
Serves 8–12

1 pound lean ground beef
2 onions, chopped
1/2 pound grated cheddar cheese
1 can tomato soup, undiluted
1 teaspoon oregano
1 teaspoon minced garlic
1/4 cup oil
English muffins
Mozzarella cheese

Brown ground beef, onions and garlic; add rest of ingredients, except mozzarella cheese. Spread mixture on split English muffins and sprinkle grated mozzarella over top. Broil until brown.

Quick and easy, plus kids love these!

Jodie McCoy, Tulsa, Okla.

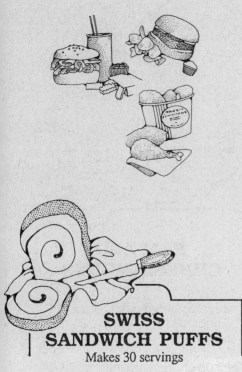

SWISS SANDWICH PUFFS
Makes 30 servings

1/2 cup mayonnaise
1/4 cup chopped onion
2 tablespoons snipped parsley
30 slices tiny cocktail rye
7-8 slices Swiss cheese

Combine mayonnaise, onion and parsley. Spread on bread slices, and top each with one-quarter of a slice of Swiss cheese. Broil for 2-3 minutes, watching carefully to avoid burning cheese.

TEXAS/TACO

1 (9-ounce) can bean dip (Frito Lay's)
1/2 cup sour cream
1/2 cup taco sauce
1/2 cup chopped green onions
1/2 cup sliced black olives
1/2 cup chopped tomatoes
1/2 cup browned ground beef
1/2 cup browned sausage
2 cups shredded mozzarella cheese
2 cups cheddar cheese
Meijer Nacho Chips

Spread bean dip over large pizza pan, first covered with foil. Add sour cream, taco sauce, onions, olives, tomatoes, ground beef and sausage. Top with mozzarella and cheddar cheese. Serve cold or place in 425-degree oven, or until cheese melts. Delicious served with nacho chips.

Sally Doran, Saginaw, Mich.

PINEAPPLE-CHEESE SANDWICH SPREAD
Makes 3/4 cup

1 (3-ounce) package cream cheese, softened
1/2 cup crushed pineapple, drained
1/4 cup finely chopped pecans

Beat cream cheese until light and fluffy; stir in pineapple and pecans. Mix well; spread on sandwich bread.

Edna Askins, Greenville, Texas

HAM SALAD
Makes 3 cups

2 cups ground ham
2 hard-boiled eggs, chopped
½ cup chopped celery
2 tablespoons or more pickle relish *or* chopped sweet pickles
Mayonnaise

Grind ham coarsely in a meat grinder. Add chopped eggs. Add remaining ingredients and moisten with mayonnaise. Serve in sandwiches, as a salad on lettuce leaves, or stuff in fresh, hollowed-out tomatoes.

TUNA BURGERS
Serves 6

6 hamburger buns
1 (6-1/2-ounce) can tuna, drained and flaked
1/2 cup finely chopped celery
2 tablespoons minced onion
4 (3/4-ounce) slices processed American cheese, diced
1/2 cup mayonnaise or salad dressing

Combine all ingredients, except buns. Toss gently to coat. Spoon about 1/3 cup on bottom half of each hamburger bun; cover with bun tops. Wrap each sandwich in aluminum foil. Bake at 350 degrees for 18–20 minutes.

Mrs. Bruce Fowler, Woodruff, S.C.

BARBECUED FRANKS
Serves 6

3 tablespoons salad oil
1 medium onion, chopped
1 teaspoon dry mustard
1 teaspoon paprika
1 tablespoon sugar
Salt
Pepper
1/2 cup water
1/2 cup ketchup
1/4 cup vinegar
1 tablespoon Worcestershire sauce
Drop of Tabasco sauce
12 wieners or franks

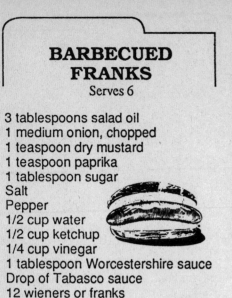

Simmer onion in salad oil until golden. Add all remaining ingredients, except the wieners; simmer for 15 minutes. Split wieners; place cut side down in shallow baking dish. Pour barbecue sauce over wieners. Bake in preheated oven at 350 degrees for 30 minutes, basting several times.

Leota Baxter, Ingalls, Kan.

FRENCH TOASTED TUNA SANDWICHES

9 1/4-ounce can tuna, drained and flaked
1/4 cup finely chopped celery
1/4 cup finely chopped onion
1/4 cup sweet pickle relish

1/4 cup mayonnaise
12 slices dry bread
2 beaten eggs
1/3 cup milk
1/2 teaspoon vanilla
2 tablespoons oil

Combine tuna, celery, onion, relish, and mayonnaise. Spread tuna mixture on six slices of bread; top with remaining slices.

Combine eggs, milk and vanilla. Dip sandwiches into egg mixture to coat each side. Brown in hot oil in a hot skillet or on griddle, about 3 minutes on each side.

Charlotte Adams, Detroit, Mich.

SLOPPY JOES
Serves 6

1 pound ground beef
1 (8-ounce) can tomato sauce
1/2 onion, chopped
1/4 cup ketchup
1 tablespoon vinegar
1 tablespoon sugar
1-1/2 teaspoons Worcestershire sauce
1/2 green pepper (use whole, not chopped)

Brown hamburger; drain off fat. Mix remaining ingredients and simmer until hot. Remove green pepper. Put in Crockpot to keep warm. Spoon on hamburger buns.

Betty Slavin, Omaha, Neb.

CONEY ISLAND HOT DOGS
Serves 10

1 package onion soup mix
1 cup hot water
1/2 pound ground beef
2 tablespoons shortening
1 teaspoon chili powder
3/4 cup catsup
1 pound cooked hot dogs or franks
Hot dog buns

Soak onion soup mix in hot water for about 15 minutes. Strain out onion pieces and save liquid. Brown onion pieces and ground beef in shortening in large skillet. Add seasonings, catsup, and liquid drained from onions. Simmer together about 30 minutes. Serve on hot dogs in buns.

Sharon M. Crider, Evansville, Wisc.

HAM AND CHEESEWICHES

1 can refrigerated quick crescent dinner rolls
4 slices ham
4 slices cheese
Ketchup or prepared mustard

Separate dough into 4 rectangles. Place slice of ham and 1/2 slice of cheese at one end of each. Spread with ketchup or mustard, if desired. Fold over. Bring edges of dough together to cover filling; fork edges to seal. Top with another 1/2 slice of cheese. Bake at 375 degrees for 10–13 minutes. Serve hot.

Shari Crider, Stoughton, Wis.

Sauces
& TOPPINGS

MOCK WHIPPED CREAM
Makes 2 cups

1/2 cup skim milk
1/2 cup nonfat dry milk powder
1/8 teaspoon cream of tartar
4 teaspoons lemon juice
2 teaspoons sugar (optional)
1/2 teaspoon vanilla extract (optional)

Put the skim milk in a small metal bowl; set in the freezer, and let stand just until ice crystals begin to form — about 15 minutes. Remove from the freezer and add the dry milk powder and cream of tartar. With a hand electric mixer, whip the mixture at high speed until foamy. Beat in 1 teaspoon of the lemon juice and continue beating until the mixture begins to thicken. Beat in another teaspoon of the lemon juice and, if desired, the sugar, and continue beating until the mixture peaks softly. Add the remaining 2 teaspoons lemon juice and continue whipping to stiff peaks. Fold in the vanilla extract, if desired, and serve immediately as a dessert topping.
Sally Joy, Tulsa, Okla.

HONEY BUTTER

Mix equal amounts of *soft butter* and *honey* until smooth. Add the grated *rind of 1 lemon*. Store in refrigerator in a tightly covered dish. Keeps for 4-6 weeks. Good on pancakes.
Lillian Smith, Montreal, Quebec

YOGURT-DILL SAUCE
Serves 6

1-1/2 cups non-fat, plain yogurt
2-1/2 teaspoons low-sodium dijon mustard

Combine all ingredients and mix well. Chill. Serve with cold poached salmon or fresh vegetable crudite. Note: This sauce may be served warm over fish or poultry, be careful not to heat it too quickly or the sauce will "break" (separate into water and yogurt). It heats best on a low setting in the microwave oven or over a double boiler, with constant stirring. (25 calories per serving)

SATIN FRUIT SAUCE

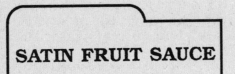

1 (3-1/2-ounce) package vanilla pudding (not instant)
1-1/4 cups water
2 tablespoons lemon juice
1 (10-ounce) package frozen strawberries, peaches, or raspberries
1 tablespoon butter

Pour pudding mix in saucepan; blend in water. Add frozen fruit, breaking apart with fork. Cook over medium heat until mixture comes to a boil and is thickened. Remove from heat. Stir in lemon juice and butter. Serve over cake or ice cream, either warmed or chilled.
Brenda Peery, Tannersville, Va.

MOCK "TWINKIE" FILLING

1 cup milk
1 cup sugar
1/2 cup Crisco
1 teaspoon vanilla
5 tablespoons flour
1/2 teaspoon salt
1/2 cup butter

Mix flour with milk; boil until thick then cool. After mixture has cooled, beat until fluffy (10-15 minutes). Add rest of ingredients, beating well, as you add them individually, one at a time. Spread the filling between layers of cake. Delicious!!
Note: The longer the milk and flour mixture is beaten, the fluffier the finished filling will be.
Susie Caldwell, Lima, Ohio

CHIVE-CHEESE SAUCE

1 (3-ounce) package chive cream cheese
1/4 cup mayonnaise
1/4 cup milk

Mash cheese in saucepan; stir in mayonnaise and milk. Heat over low heat, stirring until cheese is melted and sauce is smooth.

Plain cream cheese may be used instead of chive cream cheese; then add desired amount of green onions (plus some tops in 1/2-inch slices).
Serve on baked potatoes.
Edna Askins, Greenville. Texas

ZESTY MUSTARD SAUCE
Makes 1¼ cups

4 teaspoons butter
1 teaspoon instant chicken bouillon
2 tablespoons flour
2 tablespoons coarsely ground, Dijon-style prepared mustard
1 cup skim milk
3 tablespoons low-fat lemon yogurt
½ teaspoon Worcestershire sauce
¼ teaspoon sugar

Place butter and instant bouillon in a 4-cup glass measuring cup. Microwave on HIGH (100 percent) for 30–40 seconds. Stir in flour and mustard until smooth. Gradually stir in milk. Microwave on HIGH for 5–6 minutes until thick and bubbly. Stir every minute. Stir in yogurt, Worcestershire sauce and sugar. Serve warm over steamed fresh vegetables. (18 calories per serving)

Mabel Phillips, Dallas, Texas

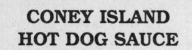

CONEY ISLAND HOT DOG SAUCE

3 medium onions, chopped
2-1/2 pounds hamburger
1-1/2 teaspoons oregano
1-1/2 teaspoons cumin
2 tablespoons paprika

2 tablespoons chili powder
1-1/2 teaspoons celery salt
1-1/2 teaspoons garlic salt
1 tablespoon salt
1/2 teaspoon cinnamon

Chop onions and boil in enough water to cover; boil until completely cooked. Add spices. Break up hamburger into small pieces and put into onion mixture. Cook about 1 hour, stirring occasionally.

This is also great on hamburgers, as well as hot dogs!

Mrs. W.T. Gore, Aztec, N.M.

TOMATO MUSHROOM SAUCE

1 tablespoon olive oil
1 cup chopped onions
2 cups chopped celery
1 clove minced garlic
10 ounces sliced, fresh mushrooms
1 (6-ounce) can tomato paste
1 (32-ounce) can tomatoes

1 bay leaf
3 tablespoons snipped, fresh parsley
Pepper to taste
1/2-3/4 pound pasta
1/2 cup grated Parmesan cheese

Sauté onions, celery, and garlic in olive oil until tender. Add mushrooms and sauté lightly. Add tomato paste, tomatoes, bay leaf, parsley, and pepper; simmer for 30 minutes. Remove bay leaf. Top with Parmesan cheese.

Cheryl Santefort, South Holland, Ill.

CREAMY HOT SAUCE
Makes 1/2 cup

1/3 cup Heinz 57 Sauce
3 tablespoons dairy sour cream
1/2-3/4 teaspoon hot pepper sauce

Combine ingredients. Use as a dipping sauce for bite-size cooked chicken pieces, french fries, or tortilla chips.

Sharon Jones, Indianapolis, Ind.

WILDLY SCRUMPTIOUS BLACKBERRY SAUCE

1-1/2 cups sugar
1/3 cup cornstarch
4 cups fresh *or* frozen blackberries
1-1/2 tablespoons margarine
1 tablespoon fresh lemon juice
1 cup water

Combine all ingredients and cook over low heat. Stir with wire whip until consistency is smooth. Add more water, if desired.

MOCK CHOCOLATE SYRUP

4 cups brown sugar
2 cups cocoa
1/2 cup light corn syrup
4 cups granulated sugar
4 cups water
1/4 cup vanilla

Mix first 4 ingredients in a large pan. Add 2 cups of the water and mix well. Add remaining water. Bring to a rolling boil. Do be sure to watch this closely — it will very likely boil over. Boil for 5 minutes. Add vanilla. Pour into sterilized jars and seal. Will keep for about 8 months. Wonderful on ice cream, but you can use it to make hot cocoa or chocolate milk and much cheaper than those cans your children are always pestering you to buy!

Phyliss Dixon, Fairbanks, Alaska

SUZIE'S SWEET MUSTARD

5 tablespoons dry English mustard
10 tablespoons confectioners' sugar
Cider vinegar

Mix enough vinegar with the mustard and sugar to make a smooth paste. Stir until the sugar is completely dissolved.

Delicious on ham, cold cuts, and cheeses.

Agnes Ward, Erie, Pa.

CRANBERRY-MARMALADE SAUCE
Makes 3 cups

1 (14-ounce) can whole cranberry sauce
1 (8-ounce) jar 3-fruit marmalade (orange, lemon and grapefruit)

In a small mixing bowl, combine cranberry sauce and 3-fruit marmalade until well-blended. Cover and chill in the refrigerator before serving.

BARBECUE SAUCE

1/3 cup vinegar
1/4 cup ketchup
2 tablespoons salad oil
2 tablespoons soy sauce
1 tablespoon Worcestershire sauce
1 teaspoon mustard
1 teaspoon salt

Mix all ingredients together and allow mixture to come to a boil. This is a basic barbecue sauce to be used with all types of meats.

Jean Hugh, Pittsburgh, Pa.

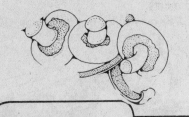

BARBECUE SAUCE

1/4 cup soy sauce
1/2 cup soybean sauce
1/2 teaspoon garlic salt
2 teaspoons sugar
1 teaspoon lemon juice
2 tablespoons cooking sherry
Dash of salt and pepper

Mix all ingredients together. Pour over 2 or 3 pieces of chicken. Refrigerate chicken in a covered dish for a few hours. Cook chicken on the barbecue grill.

M. Piccinni, Ozone Park, N.Y.

BARBECUE SAUCE

1 cup ketchup
1 chopped onion
1/2 clove garlic, finely cut
2 teaspoons chopped green chili peppers
1/2 small bay leaf
1/4 teaspoon pepper
1/3 cup lime juice
1/2 teaspoon salt
1/2 cup water
1 teaspoon dry mustard

Combine all ingredients in a 2-quart saucepan. Cover and heat to boiling; reduce heat and simmer for 40 minutes. Strain, forcing pulp through into the sauce.

MUSHROOM SAUCE

Makes 1-1/2 cups

1/2 pound fresh mushrooms, sliced
3 tablespoons melted margarine, divided
1 tablespoon all-purpose flour
3/4 cup half-and-half
1 teaspoon soy sauce

Sauté mushrooms in 2 tablespoons margarine; set aside. Combine flour and remaining margarine; place over low heat, stirring until smooth. Gradually add half-and-half; cook, stirring constantly, until smooth and thickened. Stir in soy sauce and mushrooms. Serve hot with toast or steak.

Barbara Beauregard-Smith, Northfield, S.A., Australia

MUSHROOM SAUCE

Makes 2-1/2 to 3 cups sauce

1/2 pound mushrooms, washed and thinly sliced
1 teaspoon chopped onion
1/2 teaspoon chopped parsley
6 tablespoons butter
4-5 tablespoons flour
1 cup stock or bouillon
1/4 cup sour cream
Salt to taste
1/2 teaspoon lemon juice
Butter for sautéing

Melt butter (about 2 tablespoons) and sauté onion and parsley. Add mushrooms and allow to cook for about 5 minutes. In another pan melt remaining butter; blend in flour, mixing well. Gradually add the stock and mix thoroughly. Blend in sour cream; then add salt. Pour sour cream-stock mixture into pan with mushrooms, stirring constantly, and allow to simmer gently for 15 minutes. Remove from heat and add lemon juice.

Agnes Ward, Erie, Pa.

LOW-CALORIE HOLLANDAISE SAUCE

Makes 1-1/2 cups

1 cup skim milk
2 tablespoons lemon juice
Dash red pepper
3 drops imitation butter flavoring
4 egg yolks
1/4 teaspoon salt
1-1/2 teaspoons cornstarch

Heat milk in saucepan until bubbles form around edge. Combine egg yolks, salt, red pepper, lemon juice, flavoring, and cornstarch in electric blender; cover and swirl until smooth. Slowly, add hot milk to mixture with blender on medium speed. Pour mixture into the saucepan in which milk was heated. Heat over medium heat until it reaches boiling, stirring often. Serve over Eggs Benedict or hot cooked vegetables of your choice. (45 calories per tablespoon)

Ruby Pate Bodkin, Jacksonville, Fla.

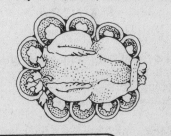

HERB AND HONEY SAUCE FOR CHICKEN

3/4 cup onion, finely chopped
1 clove garlic, minced
1/4 cup salad oil (or olive oil)
1/2 cup wine vinegar
2 tablespoons Worcestershire sauce
1 teaspoon dry mustard
1 teaspoon salt
1/4 teaspoon rosemary
1 (12-ounce) can pear nectar
1/4 cup honey
1 teaspoon prepared horseradish
1/2 teaspoon thyme
1/4 teaspoon pepper

Cook onions and garlic in hot oil until tender, but not brown. Add all remaining ingredients. Simmer uncovered for 5 minutes. Let cool, then pour over chicken and let it marinate for 3 hours minimum. When broiling chicken, use as a basting sauce. Heat leftover sauce and serve separately with chicken.

Sue Thomas, Casa Grande, Ariz.

CRAN-RASPBERRY CHOCOLATE SAUCE

7 ounces semi sweet chocolate
1 cup whipping cream
1/4 cup cran-raspberry juice concentrate, thawed, undiluted

In double boiler over medium heat, combine chocolate, whipping cream, and cran-raspberry juice concentrate until well blended and heated through. Serve hot or warm.

INSTANT HOT FUDGE SAUCE
Makes 1-1/2 cups

2 (4-ounce) bars semi sweet chocolate
3 tablespoons cream
1 to 4 tablespoons water

Melt chocolate bars over boiling water. Stir in cream, a tablespoon at a time. Stir until smooth and glossy. Remove from heat. Thin to desired consistency with 1 to 4 tablespoons water.

LEMON SAUCE
Makes 3/4 cup

Grated peel and juice of 1/2 lemon (about 1-1/2 tablespoons juice)
1 tablespoon butter
1/4 cup sugar
1 tablespoon flour
1/2 cup boiling water

Grate peel and squeeze lemon; set aside. In a small saucepan melt butter over low heat. In a custard cup thoroughly combine sugar and flour; add to melted butter. Over low heat whisk in water until smooth; stir in lemon

juice and peel. Stir over low heat until boiling; set aside to cool. Serve slightly warm. Keeps several days in refrigerator.

Dorothy E. Cornell, Elkton, Md.

PINE-COT SAUCE
Makes 2 cups

1 cup dried apricots
3/4 cup water
1/2 cup sugar
1 (8-1/2-ounce) can crushed pineapple, undrained

Place apricots and water in heavy saucepan and cook, covered, over very low heat until fruit is pulpy and falls apart when stirred. Add sugar and stir until dissolved. Add crushed pineapple with juice and bring mixture to a boil. Remove from heat. Chill. Stores well in refrigerator.

PEACH PRESERVES
Makes 6-1/2 pints

3-1/2 cups sugar
2 cups water
5 cups sliced, peeled, hard-ripe peaches
1/2 teaspoon ginger

Combine sugar and water; cook until sugar dissolves. Add peaches and cook rapidly until fruit becomes clear. Stir occasionally. Cover and let stand 12-18 hours in a cool place. Drain fruit and pack into hot jars, leaving 1/4-inch head space. Adjust caps. Process half-pints or pints, 20 minutes at 180-185 degree hot water bath.

Joy Shamway, Freeport, IL

PEAR CONSERVE

8 cups pears, sliced thin
6 cups sugar
1 small can crushed pineapple
1-1/2 cups chopped nuts
1/2 cup cherries (canned or bottled)

Peel pears and slice thin, measuring after preparation. Combine with sugar and let stand overnight. Add pineapple and simmer until pears are soft. If syrup is not as heavy as desired, remove fruit; boil down to desired consistency or add a little pectin, perhaps a teaspoon if preferred, to thicken quickly.

Add cherries and nuts to mixture. Bring to a rolling boil and put into sterilized canning jars. Seal with rings and lids that have been sterilized.

Good on breads, muffins, poultry, and meats.

Deborah Hooker, San Bernardino, CA

BLUEBERRY-PEACH CONSERVE

1 medium-size navel orange
1 lemon
2-1/2 pounds firm ripe peaches, peeled and sliced
1 pint fresh blueberries
1/3 cup granulated sugar
1/2 cup grape juice
1 tablespoon plus 1 teaspoon Sweet 'N Low® granulated sugar substitute

Peel orange and lemon; finely chop rind. Remove pits from pulp and chop pulp. Place fruit, their juices and rind in large pot. Add peaches and blueberries; sprinkle with sugar and let stand 30 minutes. Add grape juice and Sweet 'N Low. Over medium heat, bring to a boil; boil, stirring frequently, 35 to 45 minutes or until fruit is thick and translucent.

Spoon into hot sterilized jars, allowing 1/4 inch headspace (or follow jar manufacturer's instructions if different). Wipe rims with clean cloth dipped in hot water. Close according to jar manufacturer's instructions and process in boiling-water bath 15 minutes. Makes four 8-ounce jars.

Calories: 15 per tablespoon

CHIMICHURRI (ARGENTINE PARSLEY SAUCE)

Makes 1 cup

1/4 cup red wine vinegar
1/3 cup olive oil
1/2 cup minced onion
1/4 cup minced parsley
1 large clove garlic, minced
1 teaspoon oregano
1 teaspoon pepper
Cayenne to taste
Salt to taste

Combine all ingredients in a bowl. Let stand at room temperature, cover, for 2 hours. Serve sauce over broiled meats, steaks, sausages, etc. This is very delicious!
Agnes Ward, Erie, Pa.

CELERY GARLIC SAUCE FOR BROILED FISH

1 cup butter or margarine
1/3 cup finely chopped celery
2 tablespoons finely chopped onion
2 cloves garlic, crushed
3 tablespoons finely chopped parsley
Salt and Pepper

Melt butter in saucepan. Sauté celery, onion, and garlic until tender and onion is transparent. Add remaining ingredients; simmer 10-15 minutes. Brush fish with half of sauce. Broil. Turn fish. Brush with other half of sauce. Fish is done when it flakes easily with a fork.
Kit Rollins, Cedarburg, Wis.

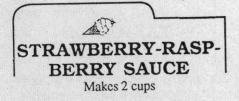

STRAWBERRY-RASPBERRY SAUCE

Makes 2 cups

2 cups fresh strawberries, hulled
1 (10-ounce) package frozen raspberries, thawed and drained

Combine strawberries and raspberries and purée.

BUTTERSCOTCH MARSHMALLOW SAUCE

Makes 2 cups

1 cup firmly packed light brown sugar
2 tablespoons light corn syrup
2 tablespoons unsalted butter
1/2 cup heavy cream
1/4 teaspoon salt
1 teaspoon vanilla
1 cup miniature marshmallows

In heavy saucepan combine brown sugar, corn syrup, butter, cream and salt. Bring mixture to a boil, stirring until sugar is dissolved and boil, undisturbed, until it registers 235 degrees on a candy thermometer. Stir in vanilla and let mixture cool for 10 minutes. Stir in the marshmallows and serve sauce warm over vanilla or chocolate ice cream. Sauce keeps, covered, in refrigerator up to 1 week. Reheat sauce before serving.

CHERRY SAUCE

1-1/2 pounds fresh sweet cherries, stems and pits removed
1/2 cup white grape juice
1 tablespoon lemon juice
1 whole cinnamon stick
1 teaspoon Sweet 'N Low granulated sugar substitute

In medium-size saucepan over medium heat, combine all ingredients; cook, stirring frequently, 35 to 40 minutes or until slightly thickened. Cool and pack in freezer containers or sterilized jelly jars. Seal and cool completely; freeze. Makes two 8-ounce freezer containers or jars.

Serve over ice milk, fresh fruit, angel food cake or sponge cake.

Calories: 75 per 1/4 cup.

PRALINE SAUCE

1 cup firmly packed dark brown sugar
1/2 cup chopped pecans
3 tablespoons boiling water
2 teaspoons butter
Ice cream (flavor of your choice)

Combine sugar, nuts, boiling water, and butter in small saucepan and bring to a rolling boil. Remove from heat and cool. Cover and refrigerate.

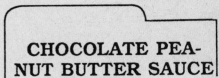

CHOCOLATE PEANUT BUTTER SAUCE

Makes 3/4 cup

1/2 cup water
1/3 cup sugar
1 (1-ounce) square unsweetened chocolate
1 tablespoon light corn syrup
1/8 teaspoon salt
1/4 cup smooth or chunky peanut butter
1/4 teaspoon vanilla
Vanilla ice cream

Combine water, sugar, chocolate, corn syrup, and salt in medium saucepan. Bring to a boil over medium heat, stirring constantly until sugar dissolves and chocolate melts. Reduce heat to low and simmer 3 minutes. Remove from heat and whisk in peanut butter and vanilla. Serve warm over vanilla ice cream.

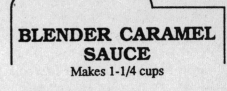

BLENDER CARAMEL SAUCE

Makes 1-1/4 cups

3/4 cup brown sugar
2 tablespoons soft butter or margarine
1/4 teaspoon salt
1/2 cup hot evaporated milk

Put all ingredients into blender container. Cover and process at *mix* until sugar is dissolved.

PANCAKE SYRUP

2 cups sugar
3-1/3 cups Grandma's molasses
3 cups water
2 tablespoons cornstarch

Combine all ingredients together in saucepan. Bring to a boil and cook for about 2 minutes, or until slightly thickened. Inexpensive to make; ready-made syrup costs much more!!

Bernice Magnant, New Bedford, MA

MANGO-PEACH CHUTNEY

1-1/2 cups cider vinegar (5% acetic acid)
1/2 cup water
1/2 cup brown sugar, packed to measure
3 tablespoons Sweet 'N Low granulated sugar substitute, or to taste
2-1/2 pounds peaches, peeled, pitted and diced (about 5 cups)
3 mangoes (about 2-1/2 pounds), peeled and cubed (about 3-1/2 cups)
1/2 cup golden raisins
1 tablespoon lime juice
1-1/2 teaspoons ground cinnamon
1-1/2 teaspoons grated lime rind
1-1/2 teaspoons dry mustard powder
1 teaspoon salt
1/2 teaspoon ground ginger
1/4 teaspoon garlic powder

In large heavy saucepan over high heat, bring vinegar, water, brown sugar and Sweet 'N Low to a boil. Reduce heat to low; add remaining ingredients and cook, stirring, 1 to 1-1/4 hours or until mixture is thick and has texture of preserves. Taste for sweetness; add more Sweet 'N Low, if desired.

Spoon into hot sterilized jars, allowing 1/4 inch headspace (or follow jar manufacturer's instructions if different). Wipe rims with clean cloth dipped in hot water. Close according to jar manufacturer's instructions and process in boiling-water bath 20 minutes. Make 3 pints or 6 half pints.

Calories: 20 per tablespoon

SPICED PLUM SPREAD

3-1/2 pounds ripe red plums, pitted and quartered
1/2 cup unsweetened apple juice
1/4 cup honey
2 tablespoons plus 2 teaspoons Sweet 'N Low granulated sugar substitute
1 teaspoon bottled lemon juice
2 whole cinnamon sticks
8 whole cloves

In medium-size saucepan over medium heat, combine all ingredients. Cook, stirring frequently, 40 to 45 minutes or until thickened. Remove cinnamon sticks and cloves. Spoon into hot sterilized jars, allowing 1/4 inch headspace (or follow jar manufacturer's instructions if different). Wipe rims with clean cloth dipped in hot water. Close according to jar manufacturer's instructions and process in boiling-water bath 15 minutes. Makes three 8-ounce jars.

Calories: 30 per tablespoon

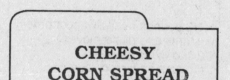

CHEESY CORN SPREAD

(Makes 3-1/2 cups)

1 (12-ounce) package (3 cups) shredded sharp Cheddar cheese
1/2 cup dairy sour cream
1/2 cup mayonnaise or salad dressing
1/4 cup finely chopped onion
1/2 teaspoon salt
1 (12-ounce) can "Green Giant Mexicorn," drained (golden sweet corn with sweet peppers)

Bring cheese to room temperature. In large bowl, crumble cheese with fork or blend with mixer to form small bits. Mix in remaining ingredients, except corn, until well blended. Stir in corn. Cover; chill several hours or overnight. Can be stored in refrigerator up to 1 week. Serve with raw vegetables or crackers.

Agnes Ward, Erie, Pa.

CHEESE & HERB BUTTER

1/4 cup butter
1/4 teaspoon basil
1/4 teaspoon oregano
1/4 teaspoon marjoram
1/4 teaspoon thyme
Dash of Worcestershire sauce
Dash of Tabasco sauce
1 tablespoon grated Parmesan cheese

Melt butter; remove from heat and stir in remaining ingredients. Serve sauce with meat and vegetables, fish, or bread.

Stella Trulove, Somerville, Texas

ONION AND HERB BUTTER

1/4 cup butter
1 teaspoon onion powder
1 teaspoon basil
1 teaspoon chervil
1/2 teaspoon oregano

Melt butter; add onion powder. Remove from heat and stir in remaining herbs.

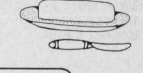

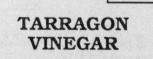

TARRAGON VINEGAR

2 cups white, cider or wine vinegar
1 teaspoon crushed dried tarragon

Bring vinegar to a boil. Add tarragon. Pour into heat-safe container, close tightly. No need to refrigerate. Let stand a few days and strain before using.

Agnes Buxton, Oklahoma City, Okla.

SWEET MUSTARD

1/4 cup mustard seed
6 tablespoons dry mustard
1 tablespoon turmeric
1-1/4 cups boiling water
1/2 cup dry white wine
1/4 cup vinegar
1 tablespoon peanut oil
1/4 cup sugar
1/2 cup finely chopped onion
2 teaspoons finely minced garlic
1/4 teaspoon allspice
1/4 teaspoon cinnamon
1/4 teaspoon ground cloves
3 tablespoons cornstarch

Combine mustard seeds, mustard, turmeric, and water in a small bowl. Let stand one hour. Meanwhile, combine vinegar, wine, oil, sugar, onion, garlic, allspice, cinnamon, and cloves in a saucepan. Bring to a boil and simmer five minutes. Pour mixture into a blender with cornstarch and blend for two minutes. Spoon and scrape the mixture back into a double boiler and cook for five minutes or until thick, stirring constantly.

HOT HONEY MUSTARD

3/4 cup cider vinegar
3/4 cup dry mustard
1/2 cup honey
2 eggs

Combine mustard and vinegar in small bowl. Blend well; cover and let stand overnight. Next day combine the mustard mixture, honey, and eggs in a small saucepan. Cook over low heat, stirring constantly, until thickened, about seven minutes. Cool. Refrigerate, covered, up to several weeks. This is great brushed on ham steak, just before broiling, or spoon thickly over brie that has had the rind removed. Sprinkle with almonds and heat at 400 degrees until the cheese is soft. Serve with French bread..

ALL-PURPOSE HERB BLEND
Makes 1/4 cup

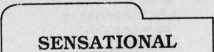

1 tablespoon onion powder
1 teaspoon black pepper
1 tablespoon dried oregano
1 tablespoon parsley flakes
1-1/2 teaspoons tarragon
1-1/2 teaspoons basil

Blend all ingredients well. Store in tightly covered jar. Serve with poultry, meats, roasts, salads and vegetables.

SENSATIONAL SEASONING

1 (26-ounce) box of salt
1-1/2 ounce ground black pepper
2 ounces pure garlic powder
1 ounce chili powder
1 ounce MSG (or Accent)
2 ounces ground red pepper

Combine above ingredients and mix well. Store in airtight container. Use the seasoning as you would salt. Great on eggs, hamburger, and vegetables.

Sharon McClatchey, Muskogee, Okla

MUSHROOM GRAVY
(Low fat and low salt)

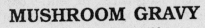

3 tablespoons arrowroot (thickener)
1 large chopped onion
1 pound sliced mushrooms
4 cups water
1 package no-oil salad dressing mix (preferably one with garlic and cheese)
2 tablespoons low-sodium soy sauce

Make a paste by stirring some of the cold water into the thickener until a creamy consistency is reached. Sauté onion in water in a non-stick pan and add the mushrooms. Stir until browned or beginning to cook. Cover with remaining water; add the salad dressing mix and soy sauce. When very hot, stir in the thickener. Continue to stir until smooth. Allow to

boil lightly. Remove from heat and cover.

Susan L. Wiener, Spring Hill, FL

CALICO RELISH
Makes 2-1/2 quarts

2 cups sliced cauliflower flowerets
2 carrots, cut into julienne strips
1 green pepper, cut into strips
10-12 green beans
1 zucchini, sliced
1 small jar stuffed olives
3/4 cup wine vinegar
1/4 cup olive oil
1 tablespoon sugar
1 teaspoon salt
1/2 teaspoon oregano
1/4 teaspoon pepper
1/4 cup water
Cherry tomatoes (optional)

In large pan, combine all ingredients except tomatoes. Bring to a boil and simmer covered, 5 minutes. Cool and let marinate at least 24 hours. Store in refrigerator. Cherry tomatoes may be added just before serving.

Marcella Swigert, Monroe City, MO

UNCOOKED RELISH

1 pint sweet red peppers, chopped
1 pint sweet green peppers, chopped
1 quart cabbage, chopped
1 pint white onions, chopped
2 teaspoons celery seed
4 cups sugar
1 quart cider vinegar
1 or 2 hot peppers (optional)
5 tablespoons salt

Put each vegetable through food chopper, using coarse blade. If vegetables are covered with liquid, drain off and discard liquid. Measure each vegetable after chopping. Mix vegetables with salt and let stand overnight. Next morning, drain off and discard all liquid. Add spices, sugar, and vinegar to drained vegetables and mix well. Pack into sterilized jars and seal at once. This relish is very good on hot dogs or hamburgers.

Helen Taugher, Nicholson, PA

Soups & STEWS

HOT LEEK SOUP

4 thick leeks, washed and trimmed
4 medium-size potatoes
2 tablespoons butter
4 cups stock (chicken *or* veal)
Yolk of 1 egg
2 cups coffee cream
⅛ teaspoon nutmeg
Salt and pepper to taste
1 tablespoon chopped chives, for garnish

Slice cleaned leeks, crosswise, and sauté in butter. Thinly slice the potatoes; add to leeks and cook together. (Do not let potatoes fry.) Cover with the stock and cook, covered, until both are soft. Drain and sieve; then combine with hot stock for purée. Beat egg yolk lightly and gradually combine with some of the stock; then add to rest of soup. Check for seasonings. Add nutmeg; pour in the cream and heat, but do not boil. Garnish with chives and serve.

OLD-FASHIONED BEEF STEW

2–3 tablespoons shortening
2 pounds stewing beef (cut in 1½-inch cubes)
1 large onion, sliced
½ teaspoon garlic powder
4 cups boiling water

1 tablespoon salt
1 tablespoon lemon juice
1 teaspoon sugar
1 teaspoon Worcestershire sauce
½ teaspoon pepper
½ teaspoon paprika
1–2 bay leaves
¼ teaspoon allspice
Carrots and potatoes, cut in cubes *or* bite-size pieces

Heat shortening in large pot or Dutch oven. Brown stewing beef for about 20 minutes. Add onion and garlic along with all remaining ingredients, except for carrots and potatoes. Cover and simmer for about 1½–2 hours. Add carrots and potatoes; cook until tender. Thicken with a mixture of flour and water.

Variation: Try adding a small can of sliced mushrooms and desired amount of egg noodles, instead of carrots and potatoes, for terrific beef and noodles. Do not forget to discard the bay leaves before serving.

WASHDAY SOUP
Serves 6–8

2 cups dried beans, any kind
½ cup dried split peas
2 tablespoons rice (not instant)
2 tablespoons barley
2 quarts cold water
2 large ribs celery, sliced
2 medium onions, peeled and sliced
2 medium potatoes, peeled and cubed
1 cup diced turnip

2 cups canned tomatoes, undrained
1 teaspoon salt
¼ teaspoon pepper
1 ham bone (with some meat left on it)

Cover beans, peas, rice and barley with cold water and let stand overnight. Bring to a boil, in the same water. Add vegetables, salt and pepper. Simmer about 1 hour. Add ham bone and simmer for another hour. If water cooks away, add a bit more from time to time. Remove ham bone; pick off bits of meat and add to soup.

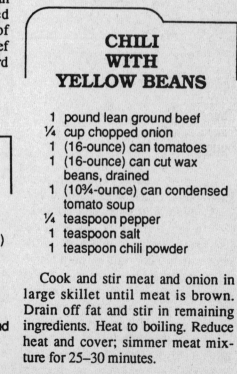

CHILI WITH YELLOW BEANS

1 pound lean ground beef
¼ cup chopped onion
1 (16-ounce) can tomatoes
1 (16-ounce) can cut wax beans, drained
1 (10¾-ounce) can condensed tomato soup
¼ teaspoon pepper
1 teaspoon salt
1 teaspoon chili powder

Cook and stir meat and onion in large skillet until meat is brown. Drain off fat and stir in remaining ingredients. Heat to boiling. Reduce heat and cover; simmer meat mixture for 25–30 minutes.

DEER (VENISON) CAMP CHILI

1 pound dried pinto beans
2 teaspoons ground cumin
2 pounds venison, cut into ¼-inch cubes
1½ teaspoons salt
2 cloves of garlic, chopped
4 large onions, chopped
2 tablespoons chili powder
1 (28-ounce) can crushed tomatoes
1 (28-ounce) can peeled tomatoes

Wash beans and place in a pot with salt and water to cover well. Bring to a boil. Remove from heat and soak for about 1 hour. Add more water, if necessary, just to cover the beans; simmer while preparing rest of chili, for about 1 hour. In a large, heavy iron pot, brown the salted venison cubes with 3 or 4 tablespoons of bacon fat or oil. Add garlic, onions and spices. Cook, covered, until onions and garlic are soft. Add both cans of tomatoes and heat until simmering. Then add beans, including bean juice. (Two cans of cooked pinto beans may be substituted.) Bring to a slow boil then lower heat and simmer for 3–4 hours. It is better if served reheated the next day.

Ladle into serving bowls and sprinkle with chopped raw onions or coarsely shredded sharp cheddar cheese. Serve with crusty fresh-baked bread or hot corn bread and butter.

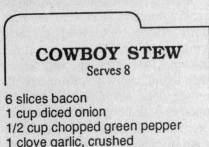

COWBOY STEW
Serves 8

6 slices bacon
1 cup diced onion
1/2 cup chopped green pepper
1 clove garlic, crushed
1-1/2 pounds ground beef
2 (1-pound, 13-ounce) cans tomatoes
1 teaspoon salt

1/4 teaspoon pepper
1 tablespoon chili powder
1 (12-ounce) can whole-kernel corn, drained
1 (1-pound) can red kidney beans, drained
2 cups cubed potatoes, cooked
2 cups sliced carrots, cooked

Cook bacon until crisp; drain on paper towels; crumble and reserve. Sauté onion, green pepper, and garlic in bacon drippings until tender.

Add ground beef; cook until well-browned, breaking up with fork as it cooks. Add tomatoes, salt, pepper, and chili powder. Cover; simmer 30 minutes. Add vegetables; simmer 15 minutes. Sprinkle with bacon.

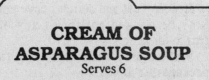

CREAM OF ASPARAGUS SOUP
Serves 6

4 tablespoons butter, divided
2 tablespoons all-purpose flour
1 bunch (10 ounces) fresh asparagus*
1 small onion, finely chopped
1 quart chicken stock *or* broth
½ cup heavy cream, warmed
Salt and pepper

Melt 2 tablespoons butter in small saucepan; stir in flour. Cook 3 minutes over low heat, stirring constantly. Cool. Wash and cut asparagus into ½-inch pieces, reserving ¼ cup tips for garnish. Sauté onion in remaining 2 tablespoons butter in large saucepan until tender. Stir in asparagus; cover. Cook for 3 minutes. Stir in stock/broth; heat to simmering. Stir in small amount of asparagus/stock mixture into butter/flour mixture until smooth; return blended mixture to saucepan, stirring until smooth. Simmer, covered, until asparagus is tender, about 20 minutes. Remove from heat; cool slightly. Purée in small amounts in container of electric blender; return to saucepan. Blend cream into soup. Taste; add salt and pepper, if needed. Steam asparagus tips in microwave, or on stove until tender-crisp. Spoon

soup into individual bowls; garnish with tips.

*You may substitute about 2 cups of broccoli or cauliflower for asparagus.

BLUE NORTHER' CHILI
Serves 8–10

¼ cup olive oil
1 large onion, chopped
1 tablespoon chopped parsley
2 (8-ounce) cans tomato paste
1 (15-ounce) can tomato sauce
1 (1½-ounce) can chili powder
Dash of pepper
2 cloves garlic, minced
4 stalks of celery with leaves, chopped
2 pounds ground beef, cubed *or* ground coarsely
5–6 cups water
1¼ teaspoons salt
1 cup cooked red beans (optional)

Heat olive oil in a 5-quart Dutch oven. Add garlic, onion, celery and parsley; sauté just until tender, about 5 minutes. Add ground beef, and brown, stirring occasionally. Drain off pan drippings, reserving 3 tablespoons. Add reserved pan drippings to meat mixture. Stir in tomato paste, tomato sauce, water, chili powder, salt and pepper. Bring to a boil; reduce heat and simmer for 1 hour. Add red beans during last 15 minutes, if desired.

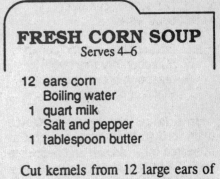

FRESH CORN SOUP
Serves 4–6

12 ears corn
Boiling water
1 quart milk
Salt and pepper
1 tablespoon butter

Cut kernels from 12 large ears of fresh corn and cover them with boiling water. Simmer for 30 minutes, then slowly stir in a quart of milk. Season with salt, pepper and butter.

CHILI CON CARNE IN A HURRY
Makes 3 cups

- ¼ pound ground beef
- ½ cup chopped onion
- 1 medium clove garlic, minced
  Generous dash ground cumin seed
- 1 (16-ounce) can pork and beans
- ½ cup tomatoes and green chilies

In saucepan, brown beef and cook onion with garlic and cumin until tender (use shortening if necessary). Stir to separate meat. Add remaining ingredients. Bring to boil; reduce heat. Simmer 10 minutes; stir occasionally.

CHILI
Serves 4–6

- 2½ pounds beef brisket, cut in 1-inch cubes
- 1 pound lean ground pork
- 1 large onion, finely chopped
- 2 tablespoons oil
  Salt and pepper to taste
- 2–3 cloves garlic, minced
- 2 tablespoons diced green chilies
- 1 (8-ounce) can tomato sauce
- 1 beef bouillon cube
- 1 (12-ounce) can beer
- 1¼ cups water
- 4–6 tablespoons chili powder
- 2½ tablespoons ground cumin
- ⅛ teaspoon dry mustard
- ⅛ teaspoon brown sugar
  Pinch of oregano

In a large iron kettle or Dutch oven, brown beef, pork and onions in heated oil. Add salt and pepper to taste. Add remaining ingredients. Stir well. Cover and simmer 3–4 hours, until meat is tender and chili is thick and bubbly. Stir occasionally.

GIBLET SPINACH SOUP WITH DUMPLINGS
Serves 4–6

- Giblets from 4 chickens
- 1 (10-ounce) package spinach
- 1 medium onion, chopped
- 4 garlic cloves, minced
- 2 bay leaves, crumbled
- 4 cups water
  Salt and pepper to taste
- 2 eggs
- 1 (2½-ounce) envelope matzo ball mix

Clean giblets; put in heavy soup pot with onion, garlic, bay leaves, and water, salt and pepper. Bring to a boil.

Reduce heat and simmer covered. May be cooked earlier in day or frozen for later.

Make matzo balls according to package directions.

Clean spinach and break leaves into smaller pieces. Add to pot. Cook for 5 minutes, or until giblets are tender.

Put matzo balls in pot and cook according to package directions.

Note: Precooked rice and additional water may be added to feed more.

HOME-STYLE STEW
Serves 4

- 1 pound white turkey meat, cut in cubes
- 1 (8-ounce) can peas with liquid
- 1 cup sliced carrots
- 1 chopped onion
- ½ cup chopped celery
- 1 can cream of chicken soup
  Salt and pepper to taste
- 1 raw potato, peeled and sliced
- ¼ teaspoon sage
- 1 (12-ounce) jar brown gravy

Place raw turkey meat in greased 2-quart casserole. Combine all other ingredients and pour over meat. Cover and bake for 5–6 hours at 275 degrees.

CHEF TOM'S PEANUT VEGETABLE SOUP
Serves 8–10

- ¼ cup butter
- ½ cup julienne carrots
- ½ cup julienne zucchini
- ½ cup julienne red *or* green pepper
- ½ cup shredded red cabbage
- ½ cup chopped onion
- 3 tablespoons flour
- 5 cups chicken broth
- 1 cup creamy peanut butter
- 1 cup light cream
  Salt and pepper to taste

In a large saucepan or Dutch oven melt butter. Add carrots, zucchini, red pepper, cabbage and onion; sauté 3 minutes. Add flour and stir until smooth. Gradually stir in chicken broth; bring to a boil. Stir in peanut butter; reduce heat and simmer 15 minutes.

Remove from heat. Stir in cream, salt and pepper. Garnish with chopped peanuts.

CARROT SOUP
Makes 11 cups

- 1/4 cup butter or margarine
- 1 large onion, chopped (about 1 cup)
- 4 large carrots, chopped (about 4 cups)
- 1 tablespoon sugar
- 4 cups liquid and braising vegetables from ham
- 2 cups water
  Pepper to taste
  Garnish; sprigs of fresh or dried thyme

In large pot melt butter; add onion; cook 5 minutes over medium heat until translucent. Add carrots; sprinkle with sugar; cook and stir 1 minute. Add braising vegetables, their liquid, and water. Bring to boil; reduce heat; cover, and simmer 40 minutes or until carrots are very tender. Skim off any surface fat. Purée soup in blender or force vegetables through food mill. Season with pepper. Sprinkle with thyme leaves for garnish.

CHEESY CHICKEN CHOWDER
Serves 8

8 tablespoons butter
2 cups carrots, shredded
½ cup onion, chopped
½ cup flour
3 cups chicken broth
4 cups milk
2 cups diced cooked chicken
1 cup corn, fresh *or* frozen
1 teaspoon Worcestershire sauce
8 ounces cheddar cheese, shredded
2 tablespoons white wine (optional)
1 teaspoon salt
½ teaspoon pepper

Melt butter in a skillet. Add carrots and onion; sauté until tender. Blend in flour. Add broth and milk. Cook and stir until thick and smooth. Add remaining ingredients and stir until cheese is melted.

FISH CHOWDER

1 pound fish fillets
¹/₂ cup chopped onion
2 tablespoons shortening, melted
2 cups cubed potatoes
1 cup boiling water
³/₄ teaspoon salt
Pepper to taste
2 cups milk
1 (8³/₄-ounce) can creamed corn

Cut fish into 1-inch squares. Sauté onions in melted shortening until soft. Add potatoes, water, salt, pepper and fish. Cover and simmer for 15 minutes, or until potatoes are tender. Add milk and corn; serve immediately.

MINESTRONE (THICK ITALIAN SOUP)

1 cup dried great northern beans
Salt and pepper to taste
1 small head cabbage, coarsely cut
2 medium potatoes, diced (optional)
2 medium onions, finely cut
3 ribs celery, diced
2–3 (6-inch) zucchini, sliced
3 cups chicken broth *or* bouillon
4 carrots, peeled and sliced
6 cups tomatoes, fresh *or* canned
1 clove garlic
1 cup broken thin spaghetti *or* macaroni

Wash beans; parboil in water to cover; drain. Add chicken broth and 2 quarts water. Use a large 8-quart kettle; add salt and pepper. Cook slowly for 1 hour. In the meantime, prepare vegetables; add potatoes, carrots, garlic and onions. Cook for ½ hour. Then add zucchini, cabbage, celery and tomatoes; cook 20 minutes; add spaghetti; cook 15 minutes longer. Serve in bowl; top with grated cheese.

BEEF CHOWDER
Serves 8-10

1-1/2 pounds ground beef
1/2 cup chopped celery
1/2 cup chopped onions
1/3 cup chopped green pepper
2 (10-1/2 ounce) cans condensed cream of celery soup
2 (16-ounce) cans tomatoes, cut up
1 (17-ounce) can whole kernel corn
1/4 cup snipped parsley

Cook beef, celery, onions, and green pepper until meat is browned; drain. Add remaining ingredients and 1/2 teaspoon salt. Simmer, covered, for 20 minutes. Stir often. Add salt to taste.

BROCCOLI CHOWDER

2 pounds fresh broccoli, coarsely chopped
2 (12½-ounce) cans chicken broth
3 cups milk
1 cup cooked, chopped ham
2 teaspoons salt (optional)
¼ teaspoon pepper

Cook broccoli in broth until tender. Add remaining ingredients and bring just to a boil.

Stir in:
1 cup light cream
½ pound grated *or* cubed Swiss cheese

Add to chowder and heat through, but *do not boil* as cheese will curdle. This broccoli chowder is a favorite at our house. It is easy to fix, and very filling. It's delicious with warm French bread and a fresh fruit salad.

CHILLY DAY BEEF HOT POT

1-1/2 pounds ground beef
3-1/2 tablespoons steak sauce
1 egg
1 (46-ounce) can vegetable-tomato juice
2 envelopes dry onion soup mix
1 (15-ounce) can red kidney beans, undrained
1 (14-ounce) can pinto beans, undrained
1 can mixed vegetables
1 cup fresh parsley, chopped

Mix ground beef with steak sauce and egg; shape into 1-inch meatballs. Heat vegetable-tomato juice to boiling. Stir in onion soup mix; cover; simmer 10 minutes. Place meatballs in simmering soup; cover; simmer 15 minutes. Stir in kidney beans, pinto beans, and mixed vegetables.

To garnish, sprinkle chopped parsley over individual servings of soup.

CHINESE HOT-AND-SOUR SOUP
Serves 5

- ½ pound boneless pork loin
- ½ teaspoon cornstarch
- ½ teaspoon soy sauce
- 4 cups chicken broth
- 3 tablespoons white vinegar
- 1 tablespoon soy sauce
- 1 can bamboo shoots
- 1 can sliced mushrooms *or* 1 cup fresh mushrooms
- 2 tablespoons cornstarch
- 2 tablespoons cold water
- ¼ teaspoon pepper
- 2 eggs, slightly beaten
- 2 whole green onions, chopped with tops
- 2 teaspoons red pepper sauce (to taste)
- ½ teaspoon sesame oil

Trim fat from pork and shred. Toss pork with ½ teaspoon cornstarch and ½ teaspoon soy sauce. Cover; refrigerate for 15 minutes.

Heat chicken broth, vinegar and soy sauce in 3-quart saucepan. Stir in bamboo shoots, mushrooms and pork. Heat to boiling; reduce heat. Cover and simmer 5 minutes. Mix 2 tablespoons cornstarch, water and pepper. Stir into soup. Add eggs, stirring with fork until egg forms shreds. Stir in green onions, pepper sauce and sesame oil.

QUICKIE CORN CHOWDER

- 1/4 cup butter
- 1 large onion, diced
- 1 large can cream-style corn
- 2 (7-ounce) cans tuna fish
- 3 cups milk
- 1 teaspoon seasoned salt
- 1/2 teaspoon salt
- 1/4 teaspoon pepper

Melt butter; sauté onions until lightly browned. Add remaining ingredients. Heat and serve.

Serve this with crusty rolls and a salad for a quick, nutritious meal.

WHITE BEAN SOUP
Serves 4

- 2 tablespoons margarine
- ⅓ cup diced celery
- ⅓ cup diced carrots
- ⅓ cup diced onion
  Dash minced, dry garlic
- 1 (16-ounce) can white kidney beans
  Dash dried thyme
- ⅛ teaspoon pepper
- 2 cups water
- 1 packet Pillsbury chicken gravy mix
- 1½ cups diced, smoked ham

Cook celery, onion, carrots and garlic seasoning in margarine in saucepan over medium-low heat for 5 minutes.

Add remaining ingredients; bring to a boil over medium-high heat. Reduce heat; cover and simmer for 20 minutes. Pour ½ cup of soup into blender and purée smooth. Return to pan and simmer 5 minutes longer.

SAVORY TOMATO-SPINACH SOUP
Serves 4

- 1 pound lean beef, cut into 1-inch cubes
- 4 cups beef bouillon
- ¼ teaspoon salt
- 4 potatoes, cubed
- 3 green onions, sliced
- 1½ pounds fresh spinach, washed and coarsely chopped
- 4 tomatoes, peeled and cut into wedges
- ¼ teaspoon nutmeg

Combine beef, bouillon, salt, potatoes and onions; cover; cook 20 minutes. Add spinach and tomatoes; cook 5 minutes. To serve: Sprinkle each serving lightly with nutmeg.

MICROWAVE COCK-A-LEEKIE SOUP
Serves 4

Tastes like it has simmered all day—but is ready in an hour.

- 4 cups chicken stock
- 2 leeks
- 2 carrots
- 4 chicken thigh/drumstick combinations, skinned
- 1 teaspoon white pepper

Trim the roots off the leeks and cut leeks into 2-inch pieces. Peel carrots and slice diagonally into thin slices. Put chicken stock, leeks, carrots, chicken and white pepper into a 3-quart microwave-proof casserole; cover (venting the cover if you have to use plastic wrap) and cook at MEDIUM (50 percent power) setting for 50 minutes to an hour (depending on the size of the thighs), stirring occasionally. Serve, accompanied with hot, crusty buttered bread.

GRANDMA'S BEEF RIVEL SOUP
Serves 4

- 1 pound rib boiling beef *or* chuck roast, cut in chunks
- 1 medium onion, finely chopped
- 2 quarts cold water
- 2 teaspoons salt
- ½ teaspoon pepper
- 1 large egg
- ¼ cup (or more) flour

Slowly boil beef with water, onion, salt and pepper until tender. Mix flour and egg with your fingers until in small chunks, called rivels. Add to broth and cook for 5 minutes. Serve in soup bowls with crackers or croutons. Beef could be cooked in Crockpot for convenience.

MEXICAN ABONDIGAS SOUP
Serves 8

5 cups water
1 onion, chopped
1 (7-ounce) can chili salsa
1 can stewed tomatoes
1 teaspoon coriander
1 pound lean ground beef
1/2 teaspoon garlic powder
1/4 teaspoon oregano
Salt and pepper to taste

Cook onion in salted water for 10 minutes. Add 2/3 can chili salsa. Add tomatoes and coriander; simmer for 30 minutes. Mix remaining ingredients into ground beef and form into small balls. Add meatballs to broth and bring to boil. Simmer 30 minutes.

When the Irish fled their country and its famines, we were glad they brought this taste to our shores.

SLOW-COOKER BEAN WITH BACON SOUP

1½ cups dry Northern
     beans
1   pound bacon
     Salt and pepper to taste
     Carrot shavings
     Parsley
     Water

Put beans in slow-cooker. Fill with water to about 2 inches from top. Add remaining ingredients and stir. Cook on high for about 9 hours (time will vary for different slow-cookers). Ingredients can be put in slow-cooker and kept in refrigerator overnight, so all you do in the morning is take it out and plug it in.

CAULIFLOWER SOUP
Serves 4–6

1 large cauliflower
2 onions, finely diced
1 clove garlic, finely minced
2 cups vegetable stock
3 tablespoons flour
2 cups milk
  Chopped parsley

Cook cauliflower, onion and garlic in vegetable stock until very tender. Add flour dissolved in milk and stir soup until it comes to a boil. Simmer for 20 minutes. Sprinkle with parsley when served.

VEGETABLE BEEF SOUP
Serves 6

1 pound ground beef
1-1/2 cups cold water
1 medium onion, chopped
3 medium carrots, diced
3 medium potatoes, cubed
2 cups tomatoes or tomato juice
1/3 cup uncooked noodles
Salt and pepper to taste

Simmer beef and water 15 minutes. Add remaining ingredients. Simmer until vegetables are tender.

YANKEE CHOWDER
Serves 6

1 can condensed cream
   of mushroom soup
3 soup cans water
1 can condensed turkey
   noodle soup
1 can condensed vegetarian vegetable soup

Stir mushroom soup until smooth in a large saucepan; gradually stir in water. Add remaining soups. Heat thoroughly, stirring often. (115 calories per serving)

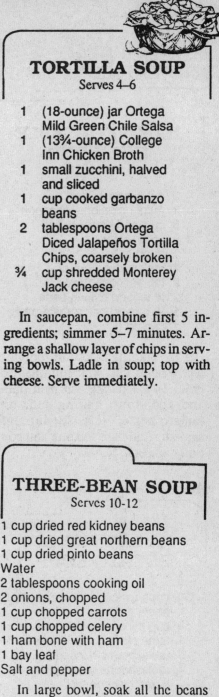

TORTILLA SOUP
Serves 4–6

1 (18-ounce) jar Ortega
   Mild Green Chile Salsa
1 (13¾-ounce) College
   Inn Chicken Broth
1 small zucchini, halved
   and sliced
1 cup cooked garbanzo
   beans
2 tablespoons Ortega
   Diced Jalapeños Tortilla
   Chips, coarsely broken
¾ cup shredded Monterey
   Jack cheese

In saucepan, combine first 5 ingredients; simmer 5–7 minutes. Arrange a shallow layer of chips in serving bowls. Ladle in soup; top with cheese. Serve immediately.

THREE-BEAN SOUP
Serves 10-12

1 cup dried red kidney beans
1 cup dried great northern beans
1 cup dried pinto beans
Water
2 tablespoons cooking oil
2 onions, chopped
1 cup chopped carrots
1 cup chopped celery
1 ham bone with ham
1 bay leaf
Salt and pepper

In large bowl, soak all the beans together in 6 cups water overnight. The next day, drain and rinse. In 5-quart Dutch oven, heat oil. Add onions, carrots, and celery; cook for a few minutes. Add 7 cups water; drain soaked beans; add with ham bone and bay leaf. Cover and bring to boil over high heat. Reduce heat to low, and simmer gently for 1-1/2 hours or until beans are tender. Remove ham bone to bowl; cool until easy to handle. Cut ham off bone; discard bone. Cut ham into bite-size pieces; return to soup. Heat through. Add salt and pepper to taste.

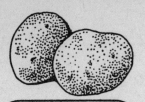

HAM-VEGETABLE CHOWDER
Serves 10–12

- 2 cups ham, cubed
- 2 medium onions, chopped
- 5 cups potatoes, cubed
- 1½ cups water
- 1 quart milk
- 2 tablespoons butter
- 2 tablespoons flour
- ¼ teaspoon baking soda
- 1 (6-ounce) can tomato paste
- 1 cup corn

Combine ham, onion, potatoes and water. Cook until soft, then add milk. In a separate pan melt butter and add flour, baking soda and tomato paste. Heat, stirring until smooth. Add ham mixture and corn; bring to a boil. Serve.

A LAWYER'S POTATO SOUP

- 1½ cups minced leeks, including some green
- ¼ cup minced onion
- 1 large clove garlic, minced
- 3 tablespoons minced carrots
- 4 tablespoons butter or rendered chicken fat
- 4 cups chicken stock
- 1½ cups diced potatoes
- 1½ cups heavy cream
- Salt
- White pepper
- Beau monde seasoning

Sauté leeks, onion, garlic and carrots in butter or fat until leeks are soft. Do not brown. Add stock and potatoes. Cover and bring to a boil. Simmer until potatoes are tender. Pour into blender and purée. Add cream. Return to stove; reheat, but do not boil. Season to taste with

salt, pepper and beau monde. If soup is too thick, thin with more stock or half-and-half.

One tasty bowl equals a full meal. The secret of success is in the beau monde seasoning and in taking the time to purée.

FRESH TOMATO SOUP
Serves 6

- 12 fresh tomatoes, peeled (or 1 large can)
- 1 quart boiling water
- 1 onion
- 1 carrot
- ½ turnip
- 1 stalk celery
- Salt and pepper to taste
- 1 tablespoon sugar
- 1 cup milk
- 1 tablespoon butter
- 2 tablespoons flour

Dice all vegetables very fine. Put into water and simmer for 1 hour. Season with salt, pepper and 1 tablespoon sugar. Add milk. Thicken with flour which has been mixed in ⅓ cup water. Add butter and season to taste. Simmer for 5 more minutes.

FISH CHOWDER
Serves 2

- 1 teaspoon butter
- 1/4 cup finely diced onion
- 1/2 pound lean white fish
- 1 teaspoon minced parsley
- 1 bouillon cube
- 3/4 cup milk
- Salt and pepper

Place butter in small saucepan. Add onion and let cook about minute. Cut fish in 1-inch cubes and add to onion. Add 3/4 cup water, parsley, and bouillon cube. Bring to boil. Let simmer, covered, over low heat, until fish is done, about 5 minutes. Add milk and season to taste with salt and pepper. Heat thoroughly.

DIFFERENT TOMATO SOUP
Serves 6

- 1 pint canned tomatoes (crushed fine with potato masher, or strained tomatoes may be used)
- 1 medium-sized potato, peeled and grated
- 2 tablespoons butter
- 1/2 cup water
- 1 medium-sized onion, grated
- 1/8 teaspoon soda
- 3-4 cups milk
- Salt and pepper to taste

Mix together the tomatoes, grated potato, butter, and water. Cook and stir over medium heat about 5 minutes, until butter melts, and potato begins to thicken the tomatoes. Add salt and pepper to taste. Stir in the soda, which prevents curdling; add the milk. Add the grated onion. Stir over low heat and cook to desired temperature. Preparation time: 45 minutes.

HEARTY ALPHABET SOUP

- ½ to 1 pound stew meat or round steak
- 1 (1-pound) can stewed tomatoes
- 1 (8-ounce) can tomato sauce
- 1 cup water
- 1 package onion soup mix
- 1 (16-ounce) package frozen mixed vegetables
- 1 cup uncooked alphabet macaroni

Cut beef into cubes. Combine meat, stewed tomatoes, sauce, water and soup mix. Cover and cook in Crockpot on low for 6–8 hours. Turn to high; add vegetables and macaroni. Cover; cook on HIGH 30 minutes, or until vegetables are done.

GOLDEN PUMPKIN SOUP

Serves 4-6

1 cup onion, chopped
1/2 cup celery, chopped
2 tablespoons butter or margarine
2 cups chicken broth
1-1/2 cups mushrooms, sliced
1/2 cup rice, uncooked
1/4 teaspoon salt
1/4 teaspoon curry powder
1/4 teaspoon tarragon
1 (16 ounce) can pumpkin
2 tablespoons margarine
Salt and pepper to taste

Sauté celery and onion in margarine, while potatoes are cooking. Mash potatoes and add all ingredients. Add more milk, if a thinner soup is desired. Bring to a boil and remove from heat. This is a delicious and rich-tasting soup made with evaporated milk. Try it, you'll like it!!

CREAM OF BROCCOLI SOUP

Makes 2 quarts

2 teaspoons chopped onion
3 teaspoons butter or margarine
3 teaspoons flour
1-1/2 teaspoons salt
3 cups milk
3 cups chicken broth
3 chicken bouillon cubes dissolved in 3 cups boiling water
1 (10 ounce) package frozen chopped broccoli, slightly thawed
2 cups carrots, sliced
Pepper

In large saucepan, sauté onion and butter until tender. With a whisk, stir in flour and salt. Gradually add milk, chicken broth, and bouillon cubes, stirring constantly; bring to a boil. Add broccoli and carrots. Cook over low heat (do not boil), stirring occasionally, about 25 minutes until carrots are tender. Add pepper to taste. Serve hot.

EASY CREAM OF BROCCOLI SOUP

Makes 8 cups

2 (10 ounce) packages frozen chopped broccoli
2 cans cream of mushroom soup
2-2/3 cups milk
3 tablespoons butter
1/2 teaspoon tarragon
Dash pepper

Cook broccoli; drain well. Add remaining ingredients and simmer over low heat until thoroughly heated.

CREAMY CARROT SOUP

2 tablespoons butter
1/4 cup chopped onion
1 rib celery, chopped
2 cups carrots, pared and sliced
2 cups chicken broth
1 cup milk or half-&-half
1 teaspoon salt
1/4 teaspoon nutmeg
1/8 teaspoon pepper

Melt butter; add onion and celery; cook until tender. Add carrots; cook 5 minutes. Add broth and bring to boil. Cover; cook over medium heat for 20 minutes until carrots are tender. Puree in blender. Add milk, salt, nutmeg, and pepper. Simmer 5-10 minutes, but do not boil.

CREAM OF MUSHROOM SOUP

Serves 4-6

1 cup (1/4 pound) mushrooms
2 tablespoons chopped onion (1 medium)
2 tablespoons butter
2 tablespoons all-purpose flour
2 cups chicken stock or beef broth
1/2 cup light cream
1/4 teaspoon salt

1/4 teaspoon ground nutmeg
1/8 teaspoon white pepper

Slice mushrooms through cap and stem; cook with 2 tablespoons onion in butter for 5 minutes. Blend in flour; add broth. Cook; stir until slightly thickened. Cool slightly; add cream and seasonings. Heat through; serve at once.

ITALIAN RICE AND PEA SOUP

1/3 cup olive oil
1 slice bacon, chopped
1 slice ham, chopped
1 small onion, chopped
1 tablespoon parsley, minced
1 package frozen peas
1 quart soup stock or water
1/2 cup uncooked rice
Salt and pepper
3 tablespoons grated Parmesan cheese

Sauté onion, bacon, ham and parsley in oil until light brown. Add peas; cook 5 minutes, stirring frequently. Add liquid and bring to a boil. Add washed rice, seasonings, and cheese; cook over medium heat until rice crushes easily between fingers. Serve very hot.

NOODLE EGG DROP SOUP

Serves 4

2 cans (10-3/4 ounce each) chicken broth
4 cups water
1-1/2 cups fine egg noodles, uncooked
2 eggs, beaten
2 tablespoons chopped parsley
2 tablespoons butter

Bring chicken broth and water to boil; gradually add noodles, stirring occasionally; cook 8 minutes. Reduce heat to low, stir in eggs. Simmer 3 minutes longer. Remove from heat; stir in parsley and butter.

CORNED BEEF CHOWDER

Serves 5

3 cups milk
1 can cream of potato soup
1 (10 ounce) package frozen
   Brussels sprouts, thawed
1 can corned beef, broken up

In a large saucepan, blend 1-1/3 cups milk and soup. Cut up Brussels sprouts and add to soup. Bring to boil. Reduce heat; simmer 15 minutes. Add remaining milk and beef. Heat through.

POTATO HAM CHOWDER

Serves 6

4 potatoes
2 tablespoons margarine
1/2 cup diced onions
2 cups water
1 teaspoon salt
1/8 teaspoon pepper
4 tablespoons flour
1/3 cup water
2 cups milk
1 (12 ounce) can whole kernel corn
2 cups diced cooked ham

Peel and dice potatoes. In large saucepan, melt margarine. Add onion, and cook until tender. Add potatoes, 2 cups water, and seasonings. Cover; simmer until potatoes are done. Make a paste of flour and 1/3 cup water; add to potato mixture. Add milk and cook until slightly thickened. Stir in corn and ham. Heat thoroughly, but do not boil.

MAINE CORN CHOWDER

Makes 9 cups

5 slices bacon
2 medium onions, sliced
3 cups diced, pared potatoes
2 cups water
1 teaspoon salt
1/2 teaspoon pepper
1 (1-pound, 1-ounce) can cream-
   style corn
2 cups milk

Cook bacon in Dutch oven until crisp. Drain on paper towels. Set aside. Sauté onion in bacon drippings until soft. Add potatoes, water, salt, and pepper. Bring to a boil. Reduce heat; cover and simmer about 15 minutes until potatoes are tender. Add corn and milk. Heat thoroughly. When serving, garnish with crumbled bacon.

CHILI

1 pound chunk beef
1-1/2 pounds ground beef
1 pound pork, cut into 1/4-inch
   cubes
1 large onion
1 can beer
Chili powder to taste
1 teaspoon salt
Sugar to sweeten
1 tablespoon oregano
1 (16 ounce) can kidney beans
1 (16 ounce) can butter beans
1 (16 ounce) can garbanzo beans
1 (No. 2-1/2) can tomatoes
1 (15 ounce) can tomato sauce
1 (6 ounce) can tomato paste
1 (16 ounce) can mushrooms
   (optional)
1 (16 ounce) can northern beans
1 cup beef broth made from bouillon
Garlic powder to taste
Add more tomato juice, as needed

Brown beef, pork, and onion; place in large kettle. Add all the rest of ingredients. If very thick, add water and tomato juice; simmer several hours until flavors are blended and meat is tender.

LUMBERJACK CHILI

2 pounds ground beef
1 large onion, diced
1/2 green pepper, diced
4 stalks celery, diced
1 large can tomato juice
1 can whole tomatoes
2 cans red kidney beans
2 tablespoons chili powder
1 teaspoon garlic powder
1 teaspoon celery salt
1 teaspoon Italian seasoning
1/2 teaspoon pepper

Brown beef and drain well. Sauté onion, green pepper, and celery. Combine all in large saucepot with remaining ingredients. Simmer for about 1 hour. Freezes well, and is very good reheated.

CHI CHI CHILI

1-1/2 pounds chopped meat or
   ground chuck
1-1/2 cups onion, cut up
1-1/2 celery, chopped
2 cloves garlic
2 teaspoons salt
1 teaspoon sage
2 tablespoons chili powder
1 tablespoon paprika
1 teaspoon thyme
1 bay leaf
2 cans kidney beans or chili beans (if
   you like it hotter)
1 large can tomatos
1 small can tomato paste

Brown meat, onion, garlic and celery. Add remaining ingredients and simmer 1 to 2 hours.

TOMATO SOUP ALA HERBS
Serves 8

An attractive, hearty soup using herbs to make it appear more elegant.

1 medium onion, chopped
1 clove garlic, minced
2 tablespoons butter or margarine
4 cups water
2 pounds ripe tomatoes, peeled and chopped
2 carrots, thinly sliced
4 red potatoes, unpeeled, and cubed
2 stalks celery, chopped
1 chicken bouillon cube
1/2 teaspoon fresh or 1/4 teaspoon dried of the following herbs: thyme, basil, and rosemary
Salt and pepper to taste

In large kettle or Dutch oven, sauté onion and garlic in margarine or butter. Stir in water, tomatoes, carrots, potatoes, celery, bouillon cube and spices. Bring to boil; reduce heat and simmer, covered, about 45 minutes or until vegetables are well-done.

BOUNTIFUL BEAN SOUP
Serves 6

1 pound dry navy beans
2 quarts cold water
1 meaty ham bone
1 bay leaf
1/2 teaspoon salt
6 whole black peppercorns
Vinegar to taste

Rinse 1 pound beans. Add 2 quarts cold water. Bring to a boil and simmer 2 minutes. Remove from heat. Cover; let stand 1 hour. Do not drain. Add remaining ingredients. Cover; simmer 3 hours. Remove ham bone. Mash beans slightly, using potato masher. Cut ham off bone. Add ham to soup. Cook 30 minutes more. Season to taste. This is a wonderful nutritious soup; prepare in a slow cooker or slow pot.

CREAMY RUTABAGA SOUP
Serves 6

3 cups cubed rutabaga
2 chicken bouillon cubes dissolved in 1-1/2 cups boiling water
1 small onion, chopped
2 tablespoons margarine
1/4 teaspoon celery salt
1/2 teaspoon salt
Dash of pepper
1 teaspoon sugar
1-1/2 cups milk
1 cup light cream
Nutmeg

Sauté onion in margarine; add rutabaga, bouillon cubes, and water. Cook until very soft. Press through sieve (or use blender). Add remaining ingredients, except cream and nutmeg. Add cream; heat through but do not boil. Serve hot, sprinkled with nutmeg, bacon bits, or toasted croutons.

CREAMY PIMIENTO SOUP
Serves 7

2 tablespoons butter or margarine
3 tablespoons flour
1/4 teaspoon salt
1/8 teaspoon pepper
1 teaspoon onion, grated
3 cups milk
4 cups chicken broth
3/4 cup pimientos
Chopped parsley, for garnish

In a saucepan melt butter; add flour, seasonings, and onion. Place milk, broth, and pimientos into food processor; pulse 5 times; add to flour/butter mixture. Cook, stirring constantly, until thickened. Sprinkle chopped parsley on individual servings.

CREAM OF PEANUT SOUP
Serves 6

1/2 cup butter or margarine, melted
1 cup celery, thinly sliced
1 medium onion, minced
2 tablespoons flour
2 quarts chicken broth
1 cup creamy peanut butter
1 cup light cream or evaporated milk
1/4 cup fresh snipped parsley
1/4 cup coarsely chopped peanuts

In 3- or 4-quart saucepan, melt butter. Add celery and onion. Cook until lightly browned, stirring constantly. Stir in flour. Blend well. Gradually stir in chicken broth. Bring to a boil. Stir in peanut butter. Simmer 15 minutes. Just before serving, reheat over very low heat. Stir in cream. Garnish with snipped parsley and chopped peanuts.

SOME LIKE IT HOT VICHYSSOISE

1/4 cup butter
1 large onion, sliced (1 cup)
8 small Idaho® potatoes, pared, halved
3 medium carrots, sliced
1 quart water
1 tsp ground ginger
3/4 tsp salt
1/8 tsp pepper
2 cups milk
1 tbsp soy sauce
2 tbsps chopped scallion

In large saucepot or heavy kettle melt butter; saute onion until tender. Add potatoes, carrots, water, ginger, salt and pepper. Bring to a boil. Reduce heat. Simmer 30 minutes or until vegetables are tender. Remove 4 potato halves; dice and set aside. Puree remaining vegetables and cooking liquid in blender or food processor. Return to saucepot. Stir in milk, soy sauce and cubed potatoes; heat. Sprinkle soup with scallions before serving.

SPONGE SOUP
Serves 16-20

12 eggs
1-1/2 pounds ground beef
14 tablespoons flour (heaping)
14 tablespoons grated Parmesan
   cheese (heaping)
1 tablespoon salt
1 tablespoon baking powder

Beat eggs until frothy. Then mix in the ground beef, flour, grated Parmesan cheese, salt, and baking powder. Knead ingredients together. Spread in a 9x12-inch cake pan, and bake 25-30 minutes at 350 degrees. Remove from oven, let cool, and cut into 1/2-inch cubes. Place the cubes in a beef broth and reheat. The mixture also can be made ahead and frozen until the day before serving.

END-OF-THE-GARDEN SOUP

1-1/2 pounds beef soup meat
3 quarts water
1-1/2 cups green beans
1-1/2 cups potatoes
2 cups carrots
1 cup turnips
1 cup sweet corn
1 onion
1 clove garlic
Salt and pepper to taste

Wash all vegetables and chop. Combine vegetables, meat, and water; boil slowly for about 4 hours. Serve with crackers.

Very good for those cool fall evenings.

SHERRIED WILD RICE SOUP
Serves 4

2 (10-ounce) packages frozen
   white and wild rice combination
2 tablespoons butter or margarine
1 tablespoon onion, minced

1 tablespoon celery, minced
1 tablespoon carrot, minced
1/4 cup flour
4 cups chicken broth
1 cup light cream
3 tablespoons dry sherry
2 tablespoons chives, minced

Prepare rice according to package directions. In a saucepan, melt butter; sauté vegetables until tender. Blend in flour; cook 2 minutes; blend well. Stir in the prepared rice; simmer 5 minutes. Blend in cream, broth, and sherry. To serve, garnish each individual serving with minced chives.

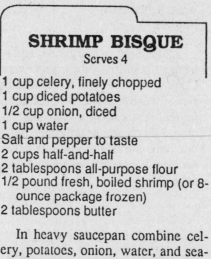

SHRIMP BISQUE
Serves 4

1 cup celery, finely chopped
1 cup diced potatoes
1/2 cup onion, diced
1 cup water
Salt and pepper to taste
2 cups half-and-half
2 tablespoons all-purpose flour
1/2 pound fresh, boiled shrimp (or 8-ounce package frozen)
2 tablespoons butter

In heavy saucepan combine celery, potatoes, onion, water, and seasonings. Bring to boil; reduce heat and simmer, covered, until potatoes are done, about 15 minutes.

Blend half-and-half and flour together; stir into potato mixture. Add shrimp and butter. Cook, stirring constantly, until thickened.

Chowders are well known in the northeast part of our country because of the origination. This inviting dish takes its name from the French word, chaudiére, a large kettle used by French settlers to cook soups and stews. These settlers often contributed part of their daily catch to a community kettle, adding potatoes and corn.

BASQUE BREAD SOUP
Serves 4

2 large cloves garlic, lightly crushed
1/4 cup olive oil
4 cups water
2/3 cup fine stale bread crumbs, toasted
1 teaspoon salt
2 eggs, slightly beaten
Salt and pepper to taste

In a small heavy skillet, sauté garlic in oil over moderately high heat until golden brown. Remove and discard the garlic; keep oil warm. In a saucepan, bring water to a boil and stir in the toasted bread crumbs, oil, and salt. Remove the pan from the heat; whisk in the eggs. Season with salt and pepper. Ladle into heated bowls.

ROCKY MOUNTAIN SOUP
Serves 8

3 cups water
1-1/4 cups dried pinto beans
3 slices bacon, chopped
2 cloves garlic, minced
1/2 cup chopped onion
1 (1-pound) can tomatoes, cut up
2/3 cup uncooked brown rice
1 teaspoon salt
1/2 teaspoon paprika
1/4 teaspoon pepper

Rinse beans. In a large kettle or Dutch oven, combine beans and 3 cups water. Bring to boiling. Reduce heat; simmer 2 minutes. Let stand one hour. Drain. Add 5-1/2 cups fresh water to beans. Simmer, covered, 1 hour. While beans are simmering, cook bacon until almost crisp. Add onion and garlic. Cook until vegetables are tender, but not brown, stirring occasionally. Stir bacon mixture, tomatoes, rice, salt, pepper, and paprika into bean mixture. Bring to boiling. Cover and simmer for 45 minutes to 1 hour or until rice and beans are tender. Stir occasionally.

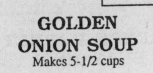

GOLDEN ONION SOUP
Makes 5-1/2 cups

2 cups finely chopped onion
1/4 cup butter
2 cups water
1-1/2 cups (10-3/4 ounce can) cream of chicken soup
2 slightly beaten eggs
1 teaspoon salt
1/4 teaspoon nutmeg
1-2/3 cups undiluted Carnation evaporated milk

Sauté onion in butter until tender. Add water. Bring to boil; reduce heat and boil gently for 20 minutes, stirring occasionally. Combine chicken soup, eggs, salt, and nutmeg in small bowl. Add to onion mixture. Cook over medium heat, stirring continually, until mixture comes to a boil and thickens. Stir in milk. Heat to serving temperature.

HEARTY LENTIL SOUP

1 cup lentils
Small chopped onion
1/2 can tomato sauce
Salt and pepper to taste
1 cup cooked elbow macaroni
1 package frozen cauliflower
2 tablespoons olive oil
3 cups water
1 teaspoon sugar
Grated cheese

Brown onion in oil. Add remaining ingredients, except macaroni; cook until cauliflower is tender. Add cooked macaroni. Before serving, sprinkle with grated cheese.

MEATY SPLIT PEA SOUP
Serves 8

1 pound lean ground pork
1-pound package dry split peas
2 medium potatoes, peeled, chopped

3/4 cup onion, chopped
1/2 cup chopped celery
2 teaspoons seasoned salt
1/2 teaspoon garlic powder
1/4 teaspoon pepper
6 cups water

Brown ground pork in skillet, stirring until crumbly; drain. Combine with remaining ingredients in Crockpot. Cook, covered, on low for 10 to 12 hours; stir before serving.

GREAT GRANDMA'S OLD-FASHIONED SOUP

Veal shank, broken in two
Beef marrow bone
5 diced carrots
2 diced onions
5 diced potatoes
1 diced green pepper
2 or more stalks cut up celery
1 medium can tomatoes
1/8 teaspoon summer savory
1/8 teaspoon salt
Pepper to taste

Cover veal and marrow bone with cold water; cook for several hours until meat is nearly done. Add vegetables and seasonings. Cook until meat and vegetables are tender. If a more hearty soup is wanted, macaroni, noodles or a tablespoon of barley may be added.

POTATO SOUP

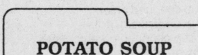

6 cups potatoes
1 onion, chopped
1 small can evaporated milk
2 cups milk or half and half
2 stalks chopped celery
2 cups cream
Toasted bread cubes, for garnish

Sauté onion and celery in butter; add broth, mushrooms, rice, and seasonings. Cover; simmer 25 minutes or until rice is cooked. Stir in pumpkin; cook 5 minutes more. Stir in cream; heat thoroughly. Garnish with toasted bread cubes.

POTATO SOUP WITH RIVELS

2 pounds white potatoes, peeled and cubed
1-1/2 quarts water or chicken broth
2 stalks celery, diced
Parsley to taste
1/8 teaspoon pepper
2 eggs
1/2 cup flour

Boil potatoes in chicken broth with celery, parsley; salt and pepper to taste.

Rivels:
Beat the eggs and flour together with a fork. Drizzle the mixture from a spoon into the cooked potato soup. Boil for about 10 minutes.

When my mother, who is now 84 years old, was a young girl of about 9 years, she used to visit her father's sister. Her father was a Pennsylvania Dutch descendent and lived in the back hills of central Pennsylvania. Her favorite dish made by this aunt was potato soup with what she called rivels.

POTATO BROCCOLI CHEESE SOUP

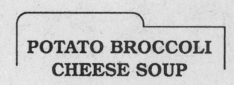

4 or 5 baking potatoes with skins, cut into bite-sized pieces
1 large or 2 small onions, cut into small pieces
2 bunches broccoli flowerets, chopped into bite-size pieces
3 carrots, cut into small pieces
1-1/4 sticks butter
3 tablespoons arrowroot
1 pint milk, plus some
Grated cheese

Cook all vegetables together in water and a little milk. Add arrowroot to 1/4 stick melted butter; stir with fork. Add 1 stick butter; melt. Add milk and grated cheese; stir and heat thoroughly.

CAULIFLOWER-HAM CHOWDER

2 cups diced potatoes
3/4 cup diced celery
1 (13-3/4-ounce) can chicken broth
1/4 cup water
2 tablespoons butter
1/8 teaspoon white pepper
2 cups sliced cauliflower
1/2 cup diced onions
1 cup cream
1-1/2 cups milk
3 tablespoons cornstarch
2 cups diced cooked ham

In large saucepan cook cauliflower, potatoes, onions, and celery covered in chicken broth until almost tender (about 10 minutes). *Do not drain*. Add butter to melt. In mixing bowl, gradually stir in milk and cream. Blend water, cornstarch, and pepper; stir into milk mixture. Pour over vegetables. Cook and stir until thickened and bubbly. Stir in ham. Simmer over low heat for 10 minutes. Season to taste. Garnish with parsley.

CHEESE VEGETABLE CHOWDER

Serves 8-10

2 cups chopped cabbage
1 cup celery slices
1 cup thin carrot slices
1 (16-ounce) can cream-style corn
1 teaspoon salt
1/4 teaspoon thyme
2-1/2 cups (10 ounces) shredded American process cheese
1 cup onion slices
1 cup peas
1/2 cup (1 stick) butter
3 cups milk, reconstituted
1/8 teaspoon pepper

Sauté cabbage, onion, celery, peas, and carrots in butter in saucepan 8-10 minutes, stirring frequently. Add corn, milk, and seasonings; heat over low heat for 15 minutes, stirring occasionally. Add cheese; stir until melted. Makes approximately 2 quarts.

FRENCH MARKET BEAN SOUP

1-1/2 cups mixed beans
2 or 3 smoked ham hocks
1 pound smoked sausage, thinly sliced
1 large onion, chopped
Juice of 1 lemon
1 (16-ounce) can tomatoes
2 cloves garlic, chopped
1 (4-ounce) can green chilies, chopped
1 (8-ounce) can tomato sauce
Salt and pepper to taste

Rinse and drain beans; cover with water; soak overnight. Cook in same water with ham hocks and onion until tender, about 3 hours. Remove meat from bones and return meat to mixture. Add remaining ingredients. Simmer 30-60 minutes. Soup should be thick, but add small amount of water, if desired.

CLAM CHOWDER

Serves 6-8

1 cup potatoes, diced
1 small onion, diced
1 tablespoon butter
2 tablespoons flour
3 cups whole milk
Pinch of pepper
1/2 teaspoon salt, or to taste
1 (8-ounce) can minced clams

Simmer potatoes and onion together in small amount of water until tender. Melt butter in small pan, then blend in flour making a smooth paste. Drain juice from clams and blend into butter and flour mixture. Add to cooked potatoes and onions; stir in milk and clams. Heat to serving temperature, *but do not boil*. Season to taste and serve.

ITALIAN BEAN SOUP

Serves 8

1 cup dry navy beans
1 teaspoon salt
1 (8-ounce) can tomato sauce
1 cup chopped onion
1 cup chopped carrots
1/2 cup chopped green pepper
2 cloves garlic, minced
2 beef bouillon cubes
1-1/2 teaspoon each crushed dried basil and oregano, or 3 teaspoons Italian seasoning mix
1/2 cup macaroni

Rinse beans; add 8 cups water. Soak overnight. Do not drain. Stir in 1 teaspoon salt and remaining ingredients, except macaroni. Cover and simmer 1-1/2 hours. Stir in macaroni and cook, uncovered, until macaroni is done, about 15 minutes.

Our neighbors to the south certainly knew how to cure any ills with this savory broth.

CABBAGE AND TOMATO SOUP

Serves 8-10

1 small head of cabbage
2 cans tomato soup
1 (16-ounce) can tomatoes, cut into quarters
1 large onion, sliced thin
2 tablespoons freshly-squeezed lemon juice
1/2 cup firmly-packed brown sugar
1/2 pound chuck steak, cubed
1/2 cup ground gingersnaps

Place cabbage in stock pot. Cover with hot water. Simmer over medium-low heat for 30 minutes; stirring occasionally. Add remaining ingredients. Simmer uncovered 1-1/2 hours, stirring occasionally.

FAMILY FARE CHICKEN VEGETABLE SOUP

1 cup potatoes, cut into small squares (diced)
4 cups chicken stock or broth
1 teaspoon salt
1/8 teaspoon pepper
1 cup onions, thinly sliced
1 cup carrots, diced
1 cup celery, chopped
1 cup fresh green beans, cut in 2-inch pieces
2 cups cooked chicken, diced
1 cup zucchini, sliced

In saucepan over medium heat, bring potatoes to boiling point in enough salted water to cover. Cook potatoes 5 minutes; drain and set aside. In large saucepan, heat stock to boiling. Season with salt and pepper. Add onion, carrots, and celery; simmer 5 minutes. Stir in green beans and chicken; heat soup to boiling. Add zucchini and potatoes; simmer 1 minute longer.

CREAMY ASPARAGUS SOUP
Serves 4

1 (10-ounce) package frozen asparagus
1/2 cup chicken broth
2 egg yolks
1/4 cup whole milk
1/2 teaspoon salt
1/4 teaspoon pepper
2 drops Worcestershire sauce
Parsley for garnish
Paprika for garnish

In large pan, combine asparagus and chicken broth; heat to simmer and cook, covered, for 8 minutes. Cool. Put in blender or food processor, and blend until smooth. Add egg yolks and blend well. Return asparagus mixture to pan; stir in milk, salt, and pepper; add Worcestershire sauce. Heat well, but do not boil. Top with parsley and paprika.

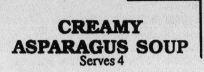

TACO SOUP
(teenage favorite)
Makes 3-1/2 quarts

1 pound lean ground beef
2-1/2 quarts chicken stock
1 (2-1/2-ounce) package taco seasoning mix
1/2 teaspoon cumin
1/2 teaspoon salt
1/4 teaspoon pepper
2 cups green onions, thinly sliced
2 cups tomatoes, chopped
1 (18-ounce) can pitted black olives, drained and sliced
1 (14-ounce) package corn chips
4 cups iceberg lettuce, shredded
2 cups cheddar cheese, shredded

In medium-size skillet, brown ground beef. Drain well and set aside. In large skillet, combine the chicken stock, taco seasoning mix, cumin, salt, pepper, and ground beef. Bring to a boil. Reduce heat and simmer covered for 10 minutes. Add green onions, tomatoes, and black olives. Simmer another 10 minutes. Ladle into bowls; top with chips, lettuce, and cheese.

COCK-A-LEEKIE SOUP
Serves 4
(dates back to the 14th century)

1 dozen leeks
1 ounce butter
2 stalks celery, chopped
1 carrot, chopped
1-1/2 quarts chicken broth
1 cup cooked chicken, diced
Salt and pepper to taste
1 egg yolk

Wash and trim leeks. Cut into 1/2-inch-long pieces. Discard roots and tops. Fry in butter with celery and carrot. When brown, add 1 quart broth and chicken. Cover and simmer for 2 hours. Salt, pepper, and stir in egg yolk which has been blended with remaining broth. Heat thoroughly.

CREAMY TOMATO SOUP
Serves 4

1 diced potato
2 diced carrots
2 diced celery stalks
1 medium onion, chopped
2 bay leaves
1-1/2 teaspoons dried basil
3/4 teaspoon oregano
1/4 teaspoon chili powder
1/4 teaspoon pepper
1-1/2 cups stock

Place all ingredients in saucepan. Bring to a boil; reduce heat; and simmer, covered, for 10 minutes or until tender.
Then stir in:
1 (16-ounce) can undrained tomatoes
2 tablespoons tomato paste
1/3 cup tiny pasta, cooked

Simmer 5 minutes more; remove from heat and stir in 1 cup low-fat yogurt. Serve immediately.

VEGETABLE BEEF SOUP
Serves 8

1 pound ground beef
1 large can tomatoes, whole
1 can tomato soup
1 small onion, chopped
2 cups water
1 can lima beans, drained
1 can whole-kernel corn, undrained
1 cup sliced carrots
1 cup potatoes, cut up
1 cup diced celery
1/4 teaspoon salt
1/4 teaspoon pepper

Combine beef, tomatoes, soup, and onion in cooker. Add water, beans, and vegetables. Add salt, pepper, and other spices of preference. Stir well. Cook at lowest setting, 4 to 6 hours.

CHICKEN SOUP

1 large chicken, cut up
2 eggs
Juice of 2 lemons
2 teaspoons salt
8 cups water

Boil chicken* and salt in water about 2 hours. Remove chicken from broth; skin and debone; dice.

Beat eggs until light. Slowly add lemon juice; add 1 cup warm broth very slowly. Add to remaining broth with diced chicken and continue to heat through.

*For a different taste add finely chopped carrots, celery, and onion to the chicken when originally cooking.

A wonderfully-flavored and hearty soup such as this one needs only warm bread with butter, a tossed salad, and a dessert to make a filling meal.

Soups date back to prehistoric man when he combined bones, meat, water, and hot rocks in animal skin bags to produce a tasty brew. In ancient Roman cookbooks, the first known printed cookbooks contained recipes for soup. Both Queen Elizabeth I and Queen Victoria drank a cup of mutton broth to begin each day. The first soup "restorative" (later to be known as restaurant, and serve other foods) was established in Paris in 1750.

George Washington deserves credit for increasing the popularity of soup in our country. He requested that his personal cook, with few provisions, create a warm meal for his troops at Valley Forge. But it was our European ancestors who brought with them their favorite soups, and over the years, these soups have been adapted and blended to use local ingredients to suit a variety of tastes.

1 (16-ounce) can stewed tomatoes
1 (10-1/2 ounce) can condensed beef broth
1 soup-can water
1 teaspoon chili powder
1/2 teaspoon salt
1/2 teaspoon Worcestershire sauce
1 cup cooked peas

Brown meat in large, heavy Dutch oven or kettle. Drain off fat. Add onion and celery; cook until vegetables are done. Stir in tomatoes, beef broth, water, chili powder, salt, and Worcestershire sauce. Cover and cook until all is tender, about 15 minutes. Stir in peas; heat through.

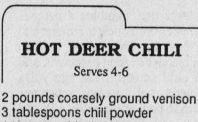

HOT DEER CHILI
Serves 4-6

2 pounds coarsely ground venison
3 tablespoons chili powder
1 teaspoon black pepper
1 medium onion, chopped
1 bell pepper, chopped
1/2 teaspoon chopped jalapeño pepper
1 small can tomatoes (already seasoned with peppers, or regular tomatoes if others are unavailable)
1 (20-ounce) can tomato juice
1/2 teaspoon garlic salt
1/4 teaspoon salt
1 tablespoon oil
1/2 cup water

Sauté onion, bell pepper, and jalapeño pepper in oil in large skillet or pan until onion is clear; add meat and cook until meat loses its redness; add chili powder and black pepper. Mix well and cook 2 minutes, then allow it to set for 3 minutes. Add tomatoes, tomato juice, and salts. Heat to boiling, then simmer for 1 to 1-1/2 hours. Add water, as needed.

Note: You may use beef instead of venison.

2 tablespoons cooking oil
2 cups chopped onions
2 cloves garlic, minced
1 (1-pound) can tomatoes, cut up
1 beef bouillon cube
2 tablespoons chili powder
1-1/2 teaspoons salt
1 teaspoon dried oregano leaves
1 teaspoon ground cumin
2 (15-ounce) cans pinto or kidney beans

Brown meat in hot oil in Dutch oven. Add onion, garlic, tomatoes, bouillon cube, chili powder, salt, oregano, and cumin. Cover and simmer 1-3/4 hours. Add undrained beans; simmer 15 minutes.

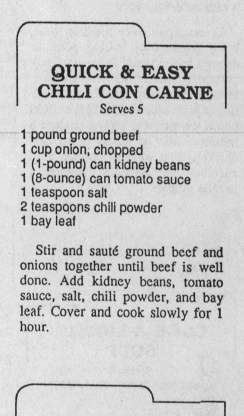

QUICK & EASY CHILI CON CARNE
Serves 5

1 pound ground beef
1 cup onion, chopped
1 (1-pound) can kidney beans
1 (8-ounce) can tomato sauce
1 teaspoon salt
2 teaspoons chili powder
1 bay leaf

Stir and sauté ground beef and onions together until beef is well done. Add kidney beans, tomato sauce, salt, chili powder, and bay leaf. Cover and cook slowly for 1 hour.

BEEF STEW WITH DUMPLINGS
Serves 6

2 (24-ounce) cans beef stew
1 cup water
2 cups Basic Campers' Mix
1 cup milk

Combine canned stew and water. Bring to a boil. Combine Basic Campers' Mix and milk. Spoon onto hot stew. Cook, uncovered, over low coals for 10 minutes; cover and cook 10 minutes longer.

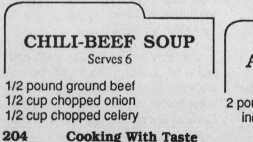

CHILI-BEEF SOUP
Serves 6

1/2 pound ground beef
1/2 cup chopped onion
1/2 cup chopped celery

AMERICAN CHILI
Serves 8

2 pounds stewing beef, cut in 1/2-inch cubes

HEARTY POLISH STEW

1/4 cup butter or margarine, divided
1 pound stewing beef, cut in 1-inch cubes
1 large onion, chopped (1 cup)
1 medium apple, cored, unpeeled, chopped (1 cup)
1 clove garlic, minced
1 pound sauerkraut, drained, rinsed well
1 can (14 1/2 oz) tomatoes, drained, chopped
1 1/2 cups beef broth
7 small Idaho® potatoes, unpared, cut in chunks
1/2 pound Polish sausage (Kielbasa), cut in 3/4 inch slices
3/4 tsp caraway seeds
1/4 tsp pepper

In a Dutch oven or large, heavy kettle melt 2 tbsps butter; brown meat quickly over high heat. Reduce heat to medium. Add remaining 2 tbsps butter; cook onion, apple and garlic until tender. Stir in sauerkraut and tomatoes. Gradually stir in broth, scraping up bits from bottom of pan. Add potatoes, sausage, caraway seeds and pepper. Cover. Simmer 1 hour 10 minutes or until meat is tender.

OYSTER STEW

Serves 4

1 quart milk
1/4 cup butter
1 teaspoon Worcestershire sauce
1 teaspoon salt
2 tablespoons flour mixed with 2 tablespoons water
1 pint oysters (with liquid)
Cayenne pepper

Put all ingredients, except oysters and cayenne pepper in a kettle. Cover; cook and stir well. Add oysters. Cook on low, until oysters curl. Sprinkle with cayenne pepper; serve hot with crackers.

COUNTRY FISH STEW

Serves 3

1 pound frozen fillets of perch, haddock, or other choice
2 teaspoons cooking oil
2 teaspoons cornstarch
1/4 cup cold water
1-1/2 teaspoons instant minced onion or 2 tablespoons fresh grated
1/2 teaspoon salt
1/4 teaspoon black pepper
1/4 teaspoon ground nutmeg
1 cup half-and-half
1 (8-1/2 ounce) can whole kernel corn, undrained
Chopped parsley for garnish

Thaw fish if frozen; cut into 1-inch pieces. In 3-quart saucepan, heat oil. Dissolve cornstarch in cold water; add seasonings. Stir into heated oil. Gradually add half-and-half, stirring constantly. Add fish and corn. Cook over medium heat, stirring often, for 8-10 minutes, or until fish flakes easily when tested with a fork. Garnish with chopped parsley.

FISH CHOWDER

1-1/2 pounds cod or haddock
2 cups diced potatoes
1 cup diced carrots
1 quart water
1/2 pound salt pork, diced
1 onion, chopped
2 tablespoons flour
1 pint milk
Salt and pepper

Cut fish into small pieces; remove bones and skin. Cook fish, potatoes, and carrots in water for 15 minutes. Fry the salt pork until crisp; remove from drippings; cook onion in drippings for a few minutes. Add flour and stir until well blended. Add milk.

Stir this mixture into fish and vegetables with the seasonings, and simmer 10 minutes longer, stirring frequently.

CORN CHOWDER

Serves 5

1/2 pound bacon
1 medium onion, chopped
2 medium potatoes, peeled and chopped
2 cups half-and-half
1 (17-ounce) can cream style corn
1/2 teaspoon salt
Pepper
1/2 cup milk

Fry bacon in a heavy Dutch oven until crisp; remove, reserving 2 tablespoons drippings in Dutch oven. Crumble bacon; set aside.

In reserved drippings, sauté onion until tender; add potatoes and water. Cover and simmer 15-20 minutes or until potatoes are tender. Stir in half-and-half and milk, corn and seasonings. Cook over medium heat, stirring frequently, until thoroughly heated.

Sprinkle each bowl with bacon.

CORN CHOWDER

Serves 4-6

1 tablespoon butter
3 slices bacon
1 large onion, chopped
4 large potatoes, peeled and diced
3 cups milk
1 cup creamed corn, fresh or canned
2 cups corn kernels
1 teaspoon salt
1 teaspoon finely chopped parsley

Heat butter in a large heavy pan. Add bacon and onion; cook until tender. Add potatoes and cook over medium heat for 5 minutes. Stir in 2 cups milk. Bring just to a boil. Cover and simmer until potatoes are tender. Gently stir in the creamed corn, whole kernels, and remaining milk. Heat through; season and sprinkle with parsley. Serve with croutons and sliced cooked sausage.

CABBAGE BEEF SOUP

1-1/2 pounds stewing beef, chopped
1 teaspoon salt
1/2 teaspoon pepper
2 bay leaves
1 cup chopped celery
1/2 cup chopped onion
4-5 medium carrots, sliced
1 cup chopped cabbage
Pinch of oregano
1 (#2 can) Italian style tomatoes
1 tablespoon Worcestershire sauce
1 beef bouillon cube

Place meat in 3 quart kettle; cover with cold water. Add salt, pepper, and bay leaves. Bring to boil; then turn heat to low. Add celery, onion, carrots, and cabbage. Simmer 2-1/2 hours or until meat is tender. Remove bay leaves. Cut meat into small pieces; return to kettle. Add oregano, tomatoes, Worcestershire sauce, and bouillon cube. Simmer 30 minutes. Serve.

MEATBALL SOUP ITALIANO

Serves 6

6 cups tomato juice
1.5 ounce package spaghetti-sauce mix, Italian style
1 small onion, diced
1 cup uncooked small-shell or elbow macaroni cooked according to package instructions
3/4 cup diced green pepper
3/4 cup diced celery
4-ounce can mushrooms, diced
Meatballs, browned (recipe below)
1 tablespoon vegetable oil
Grated Parmesan or Romano cheese

In large, kettle, mix tomato juice and spaghetti-sauce mix; place over medium heat. While juice is heating, brown meatballs in vegetable oil in heavy frying pan over medium heat. Add to juice mixture. Using same frying pan, sauté vegetables until onion is transparent, about 15 minutes. Add to juice mixture; simmer 30 minutes stirring occasionally. Add cooked macaroni; bring to simmer. Serve in bowls with a teaspoon of grated cheese sprinkle on top.

Variation: Replace macaroni with 15-ounce can ravioli or its equivalent of fresh of frozen ravioli or tortellini cooked according to package instructions.

A green salad with an Italian dressing, garlic toast or hard-crust Italian bread and a dessert will make a good meal for a hungry group.

Meatballs:
Makes 16

1/2 pound lean hamburger
2 teaspoons dried minced onion
2 tablespoons seasoned bread crumbs
1 tablespoon grated Parmesan or Romano cheese
1/2 teaspoon Italian herb seasoning
1 egg, slightly beaten
Salt and pepper to taste

Mix together well and form into 3/4 to 1-inch meatballs. (Note: Recipe can be doubled.) After browning, meatballs can be simmered about 30 minutes in your favorite spaghetti sauce and served over spaghetti or other pasta.

DUMPLINGS WITH DILL GRAVY

75 to 100 years old

Dumplings:
1 cup flour
2 teaspoons baking powder
1/4 cup milk
2 eggs
4 slices toast, buttered, cut into fine squares
1 large canning kettle
Water

Mix in order given. Mold into 2 large dumplings. Let stand few minutes before boiling. Make sure kettle full of water is boiling before adding dumplings. Boil 30 - 35 minutes, covered (don't take cover off until done). Remove with slotted spoon onto platter. With heavy thread, cut into slices.

Dill Gravy:
2 tablespoons butter
2 tablespoons flour
1/4 teaspoon salt
Dash pepper
1/2 to 3/4 cup beef broth or 1 beef bouillon cube
1 tablespoon fresh dill, finely chopped   (or more to taste)
1/2 cup sour cream

Melt butter in skillet over low heat. Add flour, salt and pepper; mix until flour is lightly browned. Remove skillet from heat, gradually add beef broth or bouillon cube and dill. Return to stove; bring to boil, stirring constantly. Cook 1 - 2 minutes longer. Remove from heat. Add sour cream stirring constantly.

CABBAGE PATCH STEW

1 medium head cabbage, sliced and cooked until tender
1-1/2 pounds ground beef
2 tablespoons oil
2 medium onions, sliced thin
1/2 cup diced celery
16-ounce can red kidney beans, drained
2 cups tomatoes
6 ounce can tomato paste
Salt, pepper and chili powder to taste
2 cups grated cheese

Brown beef in hot oil; add onion and celery; cook until transparent. Add beans, tomatoes and rest of ingredients; simmer for 15 minutes. In a greased larger casserole, place layer of cabbage, layer of meat mixture; repeat. Top with 2 cups grated cheese. Bake at 350 degrees for 45 minutes.

QUICK POTATO SOUP

1 medium potato, peeled and cubed
1 medium onion, peeled and chopped
2 cups milk
1 teaspoon chicken flavor bouillon granules, or one cube
1 tablespoon sugar
1 cup dried potato flakes
Pinch white pepper
2 slices bacon, diced
1/4 cup smoked ham or diced, boiled ham
2 quarts of water (more or less)

In saucepan, fry bacon until partially cooked, *not* crisp. Drain off most fat; add chopped onions. Cook until transparent. Add water, ham, chicken flavor bouillon, to hot bacon. Simmer until all is tender, about 15 minutes. Add sugar, pepper, and half of dried potato flakes, stirring well until all is mixed. Simmer an additional 10 minutes. Add rest of potato flakes, stirring well, then all milk. Simmer another short time until soup is well thickened. Add diced potato; cook until soft.

Note: If a thinner soup is wanted, add additional milk. Skim milk powder, or canned milk works well, as long as it is added slowly and never boiled, only simmered.

If a brighter soup is wanted, add cubed red pepper, or a few canned or frozen sweet peas at the same time as the potato flakes. When checking for taste, a bit of salt can be added, but as the ham, bacon, and chicken bouillon are cooked, salt may not be needed.

POTATO SOUP

Serves 4-6

2 (10-1/2 ounce) cans of chicken consommé
1 soup can water
2 cups diced potatoes
2 scallions, chopped

1 soup can milk
1 teaspoon Worcestershire sauce
1/2 cup sour cream

Combine consommé, water, potatoes, and scallions in a large saucepan; bring to a boil. Reduce heat; simmer until potatoes are tender, about 12 minutes. Blend smooth in a blender; return to saucepan. Stir in milk and Worcestershire sauce; heat. Stir in sour cream. Can be eaten hot or well chilled.

IRISH CREAM OF POTATO SOUP

Serves 6

4 stalks celery and leaves
2 medium onions
1 medium carrot
1-1/2 cups water
2 chicken bouillon cubes
1-1/2 cups cooked, mashed potatoes
1 tablespoon butter
2 cups half-and-half

Chop celery, onions and carrot; add water and simmer 30 minutes. Strain through sieve (large tea strainer will work). Stir bouillon cubes into strained vegetable-water. While hot, pour over potatoes, stirring until dissolved. Rub through strainer to make sure no lumps remain. Add butter and half-and-half; heat. Sprinkle paprika and parsley flakes on top.

If you have never tried bisques, you do not know what you have missed. The definition of a bisque is a thick, rich creamy soup with shellfish as its base. Bisques always have been popular in the southern states, most of which border a waterway, But today, all regions enjoy their own variety of this thick soup. We will wager that the official definition does not match the taste of this hearty soup which is served both as a first course at dinner or as lunch, all by itself.

EASY POTATO-CHEESE SOUP

Serves 6

1 package au gratin potatoes
1 (#303) can chicken broth
3 cups water
1/4 cup carrots, finely diced
1/4 cup celery, finely diced
1 small can Pet milk
Chopped parsley

Combine contents of potato package, including cheese sauce mix, broth, water, carrots, and celery in a 3-1/2 quart saucepan. Bring to a boil, stirring occasionally. Reduce heat and simmer, covered, for 15 minutes or until potatoes are tender. Remove from heat; add milk. Garnish with parsley.

HAMBURGER SOUP

1 pound hamburger
1 cup chopped onion
1 cup celery
1 cup diced potatoes
1 quart tomatoes
2 large carrots, grated medium
1 tablespoon salt
1 bay leaf
1/4 teaspoon basil
1/4 teaspoon thyme
1/4 teaspoon fresh ground pepper
2 tablespoons beef bouillon
6 cups water
2 small cans whole kernel corn
1 small can yellow wax beans
1 cup frozen peas

Fry hamburger with onion until done. Add everything else except corn, beans, and peas. Simmer 30 minutes. Add last 3 ingredients and simmer another 5 minutes. A really great "hurry up" meal, tastes like it took hours to prepare.

CREAM OF CARROT SOUP

Serves 4 to 6

1 bunch of carrots
1 small onion
Sprig of parsley
1/4 cup of rice
2 tablespoons butter or drippings
1-1/2 teaspoons. salt
Few grains of cayenne
2 cups water
2 cups scalded milk
2 tablespoons flour

Chop enough carrots to make 2 cups; cook in water until tender. Press through sieve, saving cooking water. Cook rice in milk in double boiler. Cook onion in butter or fat; add flour and seasonings. Mix carrots with rice and milk, add butter or drippings, flour and water in which carrots were cooked.Bring to boiling point; serve. If too thick, thin with milk.

CREAMED ZUCCHINI SOUP

Serves 6-8

Here is a great way to use wonderful zucchini. We are always looking for new serving ideas.

2 cups grated zucchini
2 cups water
1 tablespoon dried minced onion
2 chicken bouillon cubes
Grated pepper
1 teaspoon garlic powder
1 teaspoon dillweed
1/2 teaspoon nutmeg
1(13-ounce) evaporated milk
1/2 cup water
2 tablespoons cornstarch

In a 2-quart casserole combine zucchini, water, onion, bouillon cubes, pepper, garlic powder, dillweed, and nutmeg. Microwave for 8 minutes on HIGH. Puree in blender. Pour back into bowl.

In a small dish combine the cornstarch with the 1/2 cup water; mix well. Pour into the puree, add the can of milk, and microwave the entire mixture until thick, for 5-8 minutes on HIGH. Refrigerate to cool. Serve as a cold soup with garnish of paprika and parsley.

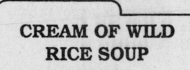

CREAM OF WILD RICE SOUP

Serves 4

1/2 cup wild rice
10-3/4 ounce can condensed chicken broth
1 cup water
1/4 cup chopped onion
1 small bay leaf
1/2 teaspoon dried basil, crushed
4-ounce can sliced mushrooms, drained
1/4 cup fresh parsley, snipped or 1/8 cup dried
2 cups of light cream or milk
1 tablespoon flour
1/4 cup shredded carrot

Rinse rice. In 3-quart saucepan, combine rice, water, broth, onion, carrot, bay leaf and basil; cover, simmer 45 minutes. Remove bay leaf. Add mushrooms and parsley. Stir cream (or milk) into flour; add to soup. Cook and stir until mixture thickens. Cook and stir 1 minute more. Season to taste with pepper.

CREAM OF SPINACH SOUP

Serves 8

2 tablespoons butter
1 leek, chopped, or 6 to 8 green onions, cut in 1-inch pieces
1 clove garlic, cut in half
1 can (13-3/4 ounce) chicken broth
2 packages (10-ozs. each) fresh spinach, cleaned
1 medium potato, shredded
3 cups milk
1 teaspoon salt
1/8 teaspoon nutmeg
Pepper

Dairy sour cream (optional)

In a 5-quart dutch oven, melt butter over medium heat; sauté leek and garlic until tender, but not browned. Add 1/2 cup of chicken broth, spinach and potato. Simmer, covered, over medium heat, stirring occasionally, about 15 minutes. In bowl of food processor, place chopping blade; add spinach mixture. Process just until blended. Carefully return spinach mixture to Dutch oven. Add remaining chicken broth, milk, salt and nutmeg; stir until blended. Cook, covered, over medium heat for 15 minutes or until hot. Season with salt and pepper as desired. Garnish with dollop of sour cream.

ORIENTAL CHICKEN NOODLE SOUP

Serves 6

6 chicken thighs, (about 1-1/2 pounds)
6 cups water
1 cup frozen green peas
2 medium eggs
2 (3 ounce) packages dried ramen or Oriental noodles for soup
Soy sauce or salt

In 5-quart Dutch oven, heat chicken thighs and water to boiling. Cover; simmer chicken over low heat until fork-tender, about 20 minutes. Transfer chicken to bowl; cool until easy to handle. Skim off and discard all fat from surface of broth. Remove and discard skin and bones from chicken. Tear chicken into pieces. Add peas to broth; cook for 1 minute. In cup, beat eggs lightly, just to break yolks. Drizzle eggs into soup. Add noodles and seasoning packets. Cook just until noodles soften. Stir in chicken. Add soy sauce or salt to taste.

BEEF STEW

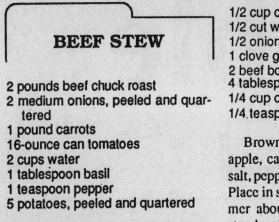

2 pounds beef chuck roast
2 medium onions, peeled and quartered
1 pound carrots
16-ounce can tomatoes
2 cups water
1 tablespoon basil
1 teaspoon pepper
5 potatoes, peeled and quartered

Cube beef; sauté in small amount of fat; slice onions and sauté in fat. Place beef, onions, carrots, tomatoes, basil, pepper and water into large covered pot. Bring to boil; simmer 2 hours. Add potatoes the last 45 minutes.

GREEN PEPPER STEW

Economy dish, serves 4

1 onion, chopped
4 tablespoons shortening
2 cups water
2 green peppers, chopped
2 tomatoes, chopped
1 teaspoon salt
1/2 teaspoon black pepper
4 medium sized potatoes, diced
2 tablespoons flour

Brown onion in shortening. Add water, peppers, tomatoes, salt and pepper. Cook for 20 minutes. Add potatoes and cook until potatoes are soft but not mushy. Mix flour with small amount of water. Add just enough to vegetables to thicken.

GERMAN BROWN STEW AND NOODLES

50 years old

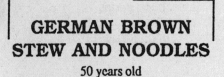

1-1/2 pounds stew beef, cube
2 tablespoons Crisco
1 large apple, pared and shredded

1/2 cup carrots, shredded
1/2 cut water
1/2 onion, sliced
1 clove garlic, minced
2 beef bouillon cubes
4 tablespoons cornstarch
1/4 cup cold water
1/4 teaspoon Kitchen Bouquet

Brown meat in Crisco; drain. Add apple, carrots, onion, 1/2 cup water, salt, pepper, garlic and bouillon cube. Place in saucepan; bring to boil; simmer about 2 hours. Combine cornstarch with 1/4 cup cold water and Kitchen Bouquet; add to meat mixture. Stir until thick and serve over hot noodles.

SEAFARER'S TOMATO CLAM CHOWDER

Makes 10 cups

3 slices bacon, chopped
1 onion, chopped
2 ribs celery, chopped
1 clove garlic, minced
2 cups tomato juice
2-1/2 cups potatoes, diced
1 (28 ounce) can whole tomatoes, undrained and cut
1/4 teaspoon salt
1/2 teaspoon dried whole thyme
1 (8 ounce) bottle clam juice
2 (6-1/2 ounce) cans minced clams, undrained
4 tablespoons cornstarch

In a Dutch oven, cook bacon until lightly browned. Add onion, celery, and garlic; sauté until tender. Add tomato juice and next 5 ingredients. Cover; cook 25 minutes or until potatoes are tender. Drain clams; reserve liquid. Mix cornstarch and clam liquid; stir until smooth. Carefully stir clams and cornstarch mixture into vegetables. Gently boil about 2 minutes, stirring constantly, until slightly thickened.

CHASE THE CHILLS WINTER CHOWDER

1 pound dried lima beans
1 large onion, chopped
2 large ribs celery, chopped
1/4 cup butter
1/4 cup flour
1 teaspoon salt
Pepper to taste
3 cups heavy cream
16-ounce can Italian plum tomatoes
16-ounce can corn
1/4 pound sharp Cheddar cheese, grated

Rinse dried lima beans and soak in 6 cups water for 6 hours or overnight. Drain and cook beans for about 1 hour in large pot with 6 cups fresh water. In large saucepan, sauté onion and celery in butter until slightly tender. Thoroughly blend in flour, salt and pepper. Add cream and bring to a gentle boil. Add beans and their liquid; add remaining ingredients. Bring again to a boil; adjust seasonings before serving.

SMOKY CORN CHOWDER

Serves 6

1/2 cup chopped onion
1/4 cup margarine or butter
1/4 cup all-purpose flour
1 teaspoon salt
1/8 teaspoon pepper
4 cups milk
1 (17 ounce) can whole kernel corn, drained
1 (12 ounce) package fully-cooked smoked sausage links, sliced
1 (8-1/2 ounce) can Lima beans, drained

In saucepan cook onion in margarine or butter until tender, but not brown. Blend in flour, salt, and pepper. Add the milk all at once; cook and stir until thickened and bubbly. Stir in corn, sausage, and Lima beans. Simmer 10 minutes.

Vegetable DELIGHTS

SPINACH SQUARES
Makes 7 dozen

2 (10-ounce) packages frozen, chopped spinach
3 tablespoons margarine
1 small onion, chopped
¼ pound fresh mushrooms, sliced
4 eggs
¼ cup fine dry bread crumbs
1 can cream of mushroom soup
¼ cup Parmesan cheese
⅛ teaspoon *each,* pepper, basil and oregano leaves

Put spinach in strainer and rinse under hot water to thaw. Press out water. Melt butter; add onion and mushrooms. Cook until onion is limp. In bowl beat eggs, then stir in bread crumbs, soup, 2 tablespoons cheese, pepper, basil, oregano leaves, spinach and onion-mushroom mixture. Blend well. Put into a well-greased, 9-inch square pan. Sprinkle with remaining cheese. Bake, uncovered, at 325 degrees for 35 minutes. Cool slightly.Cover, then refrigerate. Cut into 1-inch squares.
Laura Hicks, Troy, Mont.

BAKED-COATED VEGETABLES
Serves 8

1 (10-ounce) package frozen broccoli
2 cups zucchini, sliced

2 tablespoons oil
2 tablespoons water
1 envelope Shake 'n Bake Seasoning and Coating Mixture Original Recipe for Chicken

Thaw frozen vegetables under cold running water just enough to separate. Moisten vegetables with mixture of oil and water; shake off excess. Empty seasoning and coating mixture into plastic shaker bag. Shake vegetables, a few at a time, in the bag until evenly coated. Place in ungreased, shallow baking pan. Bake at 400 degrees for 15 minutes.
Teresa Bridge, Lima, Ohio

OLD SETTLERS BAKED BEANS

1/2 pound bacon
1/2 pound hamburger
1/2 cup chopped onion
1/2 cup bell peppers
3/4 cup (scant) brown sugar
1/4 cup ketchup
1/4 cup barbecue sauce
2 tablespoons mustard
1/2 teaspoon pepper
1/2 teaspoon chili powder
1 teaspoon salt
1 can kidney beans
1 can butter beans
1 (31-ounce) can pork and beans

Fry bacon and drain. Brown onions and pepper with hamburger. Add remaining ingredients along with bacon, and mix. Bake for 1 hour at 350 degrees. This can be prepared ahead and kept refrigerated or frozen.
Marie Walder, Beeville, Texas

MUSHROOM RICE PILAF
Serves 8

1/2 cup onion, minced
1/2 cup celery
1/4 cup butter
1-1/2 cups uncooked regular long-grain rice
1 (6-ounce) can mushroom buttons, drained
1 teaspoon salt (optional)
1/2 teaspoon crumbled thyme
3-1/2 cups chicken broth

Cook onion and celery in butter until tender; add rice and cook until golden. Add mushrooms, salt and thyme. Stir in chicken broth. Bring to boil; reduce heat and simmer, covered, for 20 minutes. At this point spoon into greased 2-quart baking dish. Bake at 325 degrees for 30 minutes.
M. Monson, Castle Rock, Wash.

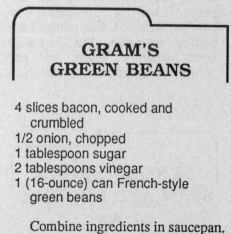

GRAM'S GREEN BEANS

4 slices bacon, cooked and crumbled
1/2 onion, chopped
1 tablespoon sugar
2 tablespoons vinegar
1 (16-ounce) can French-style green beans

Combine ingredients in saucepan. Cook on medium heat until heated through.
Helen Weissinger, Levittown, Pa.

CRUMB-TOPPED TOMATOES

1/2 cup butter
1 medium onion, chopped
2 cups chopped fresh or canned
  tomatoes
1 teaspoon salt
1 tablespoon sugar
1/2 teaspoon black pepper
2 cups unflavored bread crumbs

Preheat oven to 375 degrees. In skillet melt 2 tablespoons of the butter; add onion. Cook until clear, but not brown. In bowl mix onion, tomatoes, salt, sugar and pepper. Butter a medium-size baking dish. Place a layer of tomatoes. Mix and layer bread crumbs. Repeat, alternating layers and ending with crumbs. Dot top surface with remaining butter. Bake 40 minutes until bubbly and browned on top.

Sharon McClatchey, Muskogee, Okla.

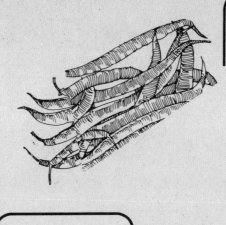

GREEN BEAN PUFF

2 (10-ounce) packages frozen
  French-style green beans
1/4 cup diced celery
3/4 cup mayonnaise
1 teaspoon prepared mustard
1/4 teaspoon salt
1 teaspoon vinegar
1/4 cup milk
1 egg white, stiffly beaten
1/4 teaspoon paprika

Cook and drain beans. Combine hot beans and celery in a 5-cup casserole. Blend mayonnaise, mustard, salt, vinegar and milk. Fold egg white into mixture. Pile lightly on top of beans. Sprinkle with paprika. Bake at 400 degrees for 15 minutes, or until sauce puffs and browns.

Kit Rollins, Cedarburg, Wis.

ARTICHOKE SQUARES

2 jars marinated artichoke hearts
1 medium onion, chopped
1 clove of garlic, chopped
1-1/2 pounds cheddar cheese,
  grated
4 eggs, well-beaten
1/2 teaspoon salt
Pepper to taste
1/2 teaspoon oregano
Dash of Tabasco sauce
1/4 cup bread crumbs

Drain artichokes, reserving oil from one jar. Chop artichokes into small pieces. Sauté artichokes, onion, and garlic in reserved oil until tender. Combine eggs, cheese, seasonings, and artichoke mixture. Pour into 9x13-inch baking dish. Top with bread crumbs. Bake at 350 degrees for about 30 minutes or until knife inserted in center comes out clean. Cut into squares; arrange on serving tray. Serve hot.

Marcella Swigert, Monroe City, Mo.

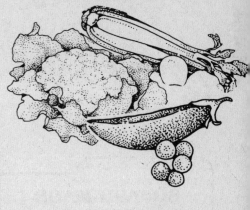

HERBED SPINACH
Serves 4

2 tablespoons melted butter
1 (10-ounce) package frozen
  spinach, thawed
3 shredded lettuce leaves
1 teaspoon sugar
1/2 teaspoon chopped parsley
1/4 teaspoon salt
1/8 teaspoon pepper

In a saucepan, add spinach to butter. Cover; cook slowly for 2 minutes. Add remaining ingredients. Recover; cook slowly for 15 minutes until spinach is tender.

CORN AND CREAM CHEESE CASSEROLE
Serves 4

1 large can whole-kernel
   corn, undrained
1 (3-ounce) package
   cream cheese with
   chives
   Butter, as desired

Cook corn until all juice is gone. Stir in butter; add cream cheese. Heat, stirring constantly until cheese is melted.

Edna Askins, Greenville, Texas

BAKED RICE AND MUSHROOMS

1 can onion soup
1 can chicken broth
1 (4-ounce) can mushrooms
1 stick butter
1-1/2 cups regular rice (no Minute
  Rice)

Mix all the above ingredients together and bake at 350 degrees for 1 hour.

Brenda Peery, Tannerville, Va.

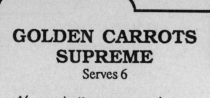

GOLDEN CARROTS SUPREME
Serves 6

¼ cup butter *or* margarine
¾ cup chicken broth *or* bouillon
2 teaspoons salt
⅛ teaspoon pepper
2 teaspoons sugar
5 cups carrots, diagonally sliced (¼ inch)
2 teaspoons lemon juice
¼ cup chopped parsley

Add butter or margarine to boiling chicken broth. Stir in salt, pepper, sugar and carrots. Simmer, covered, until carrots are tender-crisp, about 10 minutes. Stir in lemon juice and parsley.

Marie Franks, Millerton, Pa.

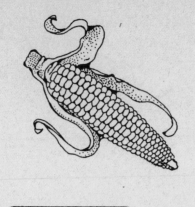

CORN FROM THE ISLANDS

A Hawaiian recipe that is an excellent way to prepare corn on the cob that is a little past its prime.

2 cups milk
2 cups water
1 tablespoon butter
2 tablespoons sugar
6 ears corn, cleaned and rinsed

In a large saucepan, combine milk and water. Add butter and sugar. Stir. Bring just to a boil; add corn and return to almost boiling. Cover and simmer 3–5 minutes. Serve with salt and butter.

Marsha Miller, Hilliard, Ohio

SUMMER GARDEN RICE
Serves 4—6

1 tablespoon vegetable or olive oil
2 onions, chopped
1 zucchini, sliced into rings
1/2 cup yellow corn
1/2 cup white corn
1 green pepper, diced
2 garden-fresh tomatoes, chopped
2 radishes, thinly sliced
2 cups cooked rice

Salt and pepper to taste
1 teaspoon fresh dill

In a saucepan combine all ingredients, except rice and dill; sauté until tender. Add cooked rice; sprinkle dill over individual servings. Can be served hot or cold.

Gwen Campbell, Sterling, Va.

SQUASH-MADE-CHEESY

3 or 4 summer squash
1 onion, chopped
1 can mushroom soup
1/2 small box Velveeta cheese, cubed
1/2 stick butter, melted
Saltine crackers, crumbled

Slice and boil squash until tender; drain. Add onion, cheese and soup. Pour into buttered casserole. Cover top with cracker crumbs and drizzle butter over all. Bake at 350 degrees for 30 minutes.

Brenda Peery, Tannersville, Va.

CORN PUDDING

2 cups corn
1/2 cup milk
1 tablespoon butter
1/2 teaspoon baking powder
1/8 teaspoon pepper
2 eggs, separated
1 tablespoon flour
1/2 teaspoon salt

Mix baking powder with flour; stir milk, egg yolks, and flour into corn. Add seasoning. Add egg whites, beaten stiff. Pour into greased baking dish and dot with butter. Bake 30 minutes in a 325-degree oven. Serve at once.

Suzan L. Wiener, Spring Hill, Fla.

WINTER SQUASH

2 cups squash, cooked
1 cup sugar
1 cup milk
3 eggs
¾ stick margarine
1 teaspoon coconut extract
4 tablespoons coconut
Ritz crackers

Place all ingredients, except crackers, in blender; blend well. Pour into a casserole dish; set in a shallow pan of water. Bake at 350 degrees for 45 minutes. Top with crushed Ritz crackers and brown.

Villa Zicafoose, Humansville, Mo.

CARROT SOUFFLE
Serves 4

2 cups sliced carrots
   Water, unsalted
1/4 cup butter
1 medium onion, chopped
3 tablespoons flour
1 cup milk
1 teaspoon salt
3 eggs, separated

Cook carrots in a small amount of water (just barely enough to cover) until fork-tender. Drain, if necessary. Set aside to cool slightly.

Melt butter in a 10-inch skillet; add onion and sauté until onion is tender. Stir in flour and cook for several minutes, stirring with fork, until flour browns.

Meanwhile, put milk in blender and add cooked carrots. Whirl until carrots are finely grated. Add milk-carrot mixture all at once to the onion-flour mixture. Cook, stirring frequently, until mixture is bubbly and thickened. Remove from heat and stir in salt. Cool slightly.

Beat egg whites until stiff peaks form. Beat egg yolks until thick and lemon-colored. Stir yolks into carrot mixture. Fold in egg whites. Pour into a greased 1½-quart casserole and bake at 350 degrees for 25–30 minutes, or until soufflé is puffed and golden.

SAUCY ONIONS
Serves 6

6 medium onions, peeled and
   washed
1/3 cup strained honey
1/4 cup water
3 tablespoons butter

Arrange onions in single layer in baking dish. Mix honey and water together; pour over onions. Dot with butter; cover. Bake at 400 degrees for 1 hour.

Diantha Susan Hibbard, Rochester, N.Y.

SOUTH–OF–THE– BORDER STUFFED LETTUCE
Serves 6

1 large head iceberg lettuce
1 teaspoon unflavored gelatin
2 teaspoons cold water
4 ounces cream cheese
1 packet dry onion soup mix
1 tablespoon vegetable oil
1/4 teaspoon salt
1 tablespoon chili sauce
1 tablespoon fresh lemon juice
1 cup red kidney beans
1/2 cup corn chips, crushed

Remove core from lettuce; rinse with cold water. Hollow out center; turn upside down; drain thoroughly. Add gelatin to cold water; dissolve over hot water. In mixer bowl, mix together cream cheese, onion soup mix, oil, salt, chili sauce, lemon juice, and dissolved gelatin. Fold in beans and half the corn chips; pack into the hollow of the lettuce. Cover; refrigerate 1-1/2 hours.

Cut into slices to serve; garnish with remaining chips.

Gwen Campbell, Sterling, Va.

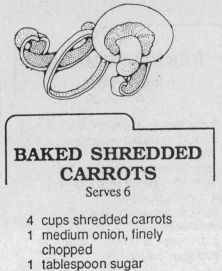

BAKED SHREDDED CARROTS
Serves 6

4 cups shredded carrots
1 medium onion, finely
   chopped
1 tablespoon sugar
1/4 teaspoon salt
2 tablespoons butter

Lightly toss together the carrots, onion, sugar and salt until well-combined. Spread evenly in a shallow 1-quart casserole and dot with butter. Bake, covered, at 325 degrees for 1 hour.

SEASONED BRUSSELS SPROUTS
Serves 6

2 (10-ounce) packages frozen
   brussels sprouts *or* cut broccoli
1 or 2 chicken bouillon cubes
2 (10 1/2-ounce) cans condensed
   cream of celery soup
1/2 cup grated sharp cheese
Pimiento strips

Cook brussels sprouts with bouillon cubes and water until just tender. Heat soup to boiling; pour over sprouts. Garnish with cheese and pimiento. Serve at once.

Ida Bloedow, Madison, Wis.

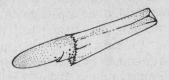

BROCCOLI PARMESAN
Serves 8

2-1/2 pounds broccoli, cut into
   flowerets
1 small onion, minced
6 tablespoons butter
4 tablespoons flour
2 cups milk
1/2 teaspoon salt
1/8 teaspoon pepper
1/2 teaspoon dry mustard
1 egg yolk, beaten
1 cup Parmesan cheese
1/4 cup dry bread crumbs *or*
   1/4 cup cracker crumbs

Cook broccoli until crisp-tender. Sauté onion in 4 tablespoons butter. Stir in flour and stir until smooth. Slowly add milk. Cook until thick and bubbly. Add salt, pepper, dry mustard, egg yolk, and cheese. Pour half of the sauce into a 9x11-inch pan. Place broccoli in pan with stems in center. Pour remaining sauce over broccoli. Brown 1/4 cup bread or cracker crumbs in 2 tablespoons butter and sprinkle down center. Bake at 400 degrees for 20 minutes.

Ida Bloedow, Madison, Wis.

SCALLOPED ASPARAGUS

Serves 4-6

4 cups fresh asparagus, cut into 1-
    inch pieces
1-1/2 cups milk
2 tablespoons flour
1 teaspoon salt
1/2 teaspoon pepper
1/2 cup grated American cheese
1 cup bread crumbs
2 tablespoons butter

Preheat oven to 325 degrees. Cook asparagus in a little water until tender, then transfer to a buttered baking dish. Combine milk, flour, salt, and pepper together. Add to the asparagus. Add the remaining cheese and half the remaining bread crumbs; stir again. Dot with butter; sprinkle remaining bread crumbs on top. Bake 30 minutes, or until brown on top.

SPINACH RING

Serves 6

1 (10-ounce) package frozen
    spinach
2 eggs, beaten
1-1/2 cups dairy sour cream
2 tablespoons flour
2 tablespoons grated Parmesan
    cheese
1/2 teaspoon salt
1/8 teaspoon onion powder
1/8 teaspoon pepper
6 hard-cooked eggs, chopped

Remove outer wrapper from package of spinach. Place unopened carton in dish in microwave and cook 5 minutes on HIGH. Turn out into strainer and drain well, pressing out excess moisture with back of spoon. Set aside. Combine all remaining ingredients, except hard-cooked eggs; blend well. Stir in reserved spinach. Fold in chopped eggs. Pour into well-greased 1-quart ring mold. Cook on 50 percent or 30 percent power, 20-30 minutes, or until knife inserted halfway between center and outer edge

comes out clean. Let stand, uncovered, 10 minutes. Unmold onto serving platter. Use a reduced-power setting for best results.

Suzan L. Wiener, Spring Hill, Fla.

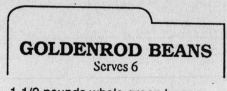

GOLDENROD BEANS

Serves 6

1-1/2 pounds whole green beans
1-1/2 tablespoons butter or marga-
    rine
2 tablespoons flour
1/2 teaspoon salt
1/8 teaspoon pepper
3/4 cup evaporated milk
3 hard-cooked eggs, separated
3/4 cup mayonnaise

Cook beans in boiling, salted water until tender. Save 1/2 cup of the liquid. Melt butter. Blend in flour, salt, and pepper. Add bean stock and cook until thickened, stirring constantly. Add milk and chopped egg whites. Heat thoroughly. Remove from heat and add mayonnaise. Drain beans. Cover with sauce and sprinkle with sieved egg yolks.

BAKED SUMMER SQUASH

Serves 16–20

1/2 cup butter *or* margarine, melted
1 (6-ounce) package herbed stuffing
    mix
2 pounds summer squash *or*
    zucchini, sliced (not too thin)
1/4 cup chopped onion
1 cup carrots, shredded
Salt to taste
1 can cream of chicken soup
1 cup sour cream

Pour melted butter or margarine over stuffing mix; toss well. Cook squash and onion together in small amount of water for 5 minutes; mix in carrots. Drain. Season with salt. Combine soup and sour cream; mix with vegetables. Line 9 x 13-inch casserole dish with 1/2 of the stuffing mixture. Add vegetable mixture.

Cover with remaining stuffing mixture. Bake at 350 degrees for 25 minutes, or until brown.

Good "make-ahead" recipe.

Marty Grant, Marquette, Mich.

BAKED LIMA BEANS IN TOMATO SAUCE

1 (1-pound) package dried lima
    beans
9 slices bacon
2 (8-ounce) cans tomato sauce
1 cup chopped onion
1/4 cup light brown sugar, firmly
    packed
2 teaspoons mustard
2 teaspoons Worcestershire sauce
1/2 teaspoon oregano

Cook beans until just tender. Drain, reserving 1/2 cup liquid. Cut bacon into 1/2-inch pieces. Sauté lightly. Add onion and sauté until it is tender and bacon is browned. Combine all ingredients and mix until well-blended. Turn into 2-1/2-quart shallow baking dish. Bake at 350 degrees for 45 minutes.

Betty Ireton, Kingston, Ohio.

CABBAGE AU GRATIN

1/2 large head cabbage, chopped
3/4 cup grated cheese
Paprika
Salt
2 cups medium white sauce
1/2 cup cracker crumbs
3 tablespoons melted butter

Put a layer of chopped cabbage into a buttered baking dish; sprinkle with grated cheese, paprika, and salt. Cover with a layer of medium white sauce. Repeat the layers until all ingredients have been used.

Cover with cracker crumbs mixed with melted butter. Bake in moderately hot oven at 350 degrees, until bubbling hot and evenly browned.

Betty Slavin, Omaha, Neb.

GOLDEN CROWN CARROT SOUFFLE
Serves 7

5 carrots, cooked and mashed
1 cup milk
1 onion (whole)
1 whole clove inserted into onion
1 bay leaf
1/2 cup butter or margarine
3 tablespoons flour
3 egg yolks, slightly beaten
1/4 teaspoon salt
1/4 teaspoon pepper
1/8 teaspoon paprika
1/8 teaspoon nutmeg
1/8 teaspoon marjoram
3 tablespoons Parmesan cheese, grated
3 egg whites, beaten

Cook carrots; drain; place in buttered 2-quart soufflé mold or round dish. Heat milk with onion and clove; add bay leaf. Simmer 8 minutes; strain; set aside. In a saucepan melt butter; add flour; slowly add strained milk mixture; cook until smooth and thick. Remove from heat; blend in egg yolks slowly; add salt, pepper, spices, and cheese. Beat egg whites until stiff; fold into sauce mixture. Pour over carrots; bake at 350 degrees, until golden crown is well-puffed and firm.

Gwen Campbell, Sterling, Va.

ASPARAGUS– PEANUT BAKE
Serves 4-6

4 cups fresh asparagus, cut in 1-inch pieces
1 (10-3/4-ounce) can cream of mushroom soup
1/2 cup peanuts, crushed
1 cup grated cheddar cheese
Salt and pepper to taste
1/2 stick butter or margarine

Cook asparagus in small amount of water until tender-crisp. Arrange layers of asparagus, soup, peanuts, and cheese in a greased casserole; season with salt and pepper. Dot with butter. Bake at 350 degrees for 30 minutes, or until heated through and bubbly.

CURRIED ASPARAGUS SALAD
Serves 4

1 pound hot steamed asparagus, drained
1/2 cup French dressing
8 lettuce leaves, washed and crisped
1 pimiento, drained and cut into 1/4-inch strips

Curry Dressing:
1/2 cup mayonnaise
1 tablespoon sour cream
1/2 teaspoon curry powder
1/2 teaspoon lemon juice

Marinate asparagus in French dressing for 3 to 4 hours in the refrigerator, turning occasionally. Shortly before serving, mix Curry Dressing. Drain asparagus (reserve French dressing for other salads later) and arrange on lettuce. Top with Curry Dressing. Garnish with pimiento.

FRESH SPINACH AND LETTUCE PIE
Serves 5

1 pound spinach, chopped (or 1 package frozen spinach, thawed)
1 cup onions, finely chopped
1/2 cup green onions, finely chopped
1 cup fresh lettuce, chopped
1 cup fresh parsley, chopped
2 tablespoons flour
1 teaspoon salt
1/4 teaspoon pepper
1/4 teaspoon nutmeg
1/2 cup walnuts, chopped
8 eggs, well-beaten
4 tablespoons butter or margarine

Wash spinach; drain well. Mix together next 10 ingredients. Melt butter in an 11-inch pie plate; pour vegetable mixture into it. Bake at 325 degrees for 1 hour, or until top is golden and crisp. Can be served hot or chilled.

Gwen Campbell, Sterling, Va.

ASPARAGUS– CHEESE PIE
Serves 6

1 (9-inch) pastry shell
6 slices bacon
1 medium-size onion, thinly sliced
1 cup shredded Swiss cheese
2 tablespoons grated Parmesan cheese
2 cups heavy cream
4 eggs, well-beaten
1 teaspoon salt
1/4 teaspoon grated nutmeg
6 stalks asparagus, partly cooked

Bake pastry shell in 350-degree oven for 5 minutes. Sauté bacon until crisp; drain off fat, leaving about 1 tablespoon. Sauté onion in remaining fat until transparent. Combine bacon, onion, and cheeses; place in pastry. Mix cream, eggs, salt, and nutmeg; pour into pie shell. Arrange asparagus in a wagon wheel design on top of pie. Bake for 35-40 minutes in a 375-degree oven, or until golden.

ELEGANT EGGPLANT
Serves 12

3 large eggplants
1/2 pound spicy bulk sausage
3 green onions, chopped
1 cup celery, chopped
1 (6 1/4-ounce) package corn bread stuffing mix
1/2 teaspoon black pepper flakes
1/2 teaspoon salt
2 cups grated cheddar cheese

Peel and dice eggplants; cook in salted water until tender. Drain well and set aside. Sauté sausage in skillet until well-done; remove to paper towels; set aside. Sauté green onions and celery in skillet until transparent; set aside. Prepare stuffing mix according to package instructions. Combine eggplant, sausage, onion/celery mixture, salt, pepper and stuffing mix. Transfer to shallow baking dish. Top with cheese; broil until cheese is melted. Serve hot.

Marcella Swigert, Monroe City, Mo.

RICE PILAF
Serves 8

4 cups chicken broth
2 cups long-grain rice, uncooked
2 tablespoons butter *or* margarine
1 teaspoon salt, optional
¼ teaspoon thyme *or* marjoram
2 tablespoons chopped parsley

In large saucepan heat broth to boiling. Add rice, butter or margarine and salt, if desired, and thyme or marjoram. Return to boiling. Cover; reduce heat and simmer 20 minutes until rice is tender and broth is absorbed. This recipe can be made ahead up to this point. Cover and keep at room temperature for up to 3 hours. To reheat, place covered pan over low heat. Toss with fork after 10 minutes. When hot, garnish with parsley.

M. Manson, Castle Rock, Wash.

CELERY SUPREME
Serves 4-6

4 cups celery, cut in 1-inch lengths
1 (10-ounce) can condensed cream of chicken soup
5 ounces water chestnuts, sliced
1/4 cup chopped pimiento
Buttered bread crumbs

Cook celery in salted water until tender-crisp. Drain and put into a greased 1-1/2-quart casserole.

Mix the soup, water chestnuts, and pimiento together and spoon over top. Melt a small amount of butter in a saucepan and stir in bread crumbs to coat. Spread over top of casserole.

Bake, uncovered, in 350-degree oven for 30 minutes or until celery is tender.

Millicent Corbeene, St. John's, New Foundland., Canada

SIX-LAYER BAKE
Serves 4-6

2 cups sliced potatoes

2 cups chopped celery
2 cups sliced carrots
1 cup sliced onions
2 cups ground beef
2 cups canned tomatoes
2 teaspoons salt
1/4 teaspoon pepper

In a greased casserole make a layer of each ingredient in the order given. Season each layer. Bake for 2 hours at 350 degrees.

Dorothy E. Snyder, Pine Grove, Pa.

STUFFED ZUCCHINI CURRY
Serves 2

1 large zucchini
1 apple, peeled and finely chopped
1/4 cup mozzarella cheese, grated
1/4 cup bread crumbs
1 egg, beaten
1/2 teaspoon curry powder
1/4 teaspoon ginger
3 tablespoons golden raisins

Cut zucchini down the middle, lengthwise. Scoop out pulp; leave 1/2 inch of shell. Place pulp in a bowl; drain off excess water. Add remaining ingredients; place in zucchini shells. Place stuffed zucchini in an ovenproof baking dish; add just enough water to cover the bottom of the dish. Bake at 350 degrees for 20 minutes, or until the zucchini is tender.

Gwen Campbell, Sterling, Va.

MARVELOUS MARINATED MUSHROOMS

3 pounds fresh button mushrooms
1 (½-ounce) package garlic salad dressing mix
1½ cups oil
½ cup lemon juice
Salt and pepper to taste
2 tablespoons Accent
2 tablespoons parsley flakes
2 tablespoons garlic powder (optional)

Wash and cap mushrooms. Cover in salt water and boil 1 minute. Drain. Prepare marinade from rest of ingredients. Pour over caps and chill at least 24 hours. Drain and serve cold.

Diantha Susan Hibbard, Rochester, N.Y.

COPPER PENNIES
Serves 16

2 pounds carrots, peeled and sliced
1 cup diced green pepper
1 cup chopped onions
1 cup tomato soup
1 tablespoon Worcestershire sauce
1 cup sugar
3/4 cup vinegar
1/2 cup salad oil
1 teaspoon dry or prepared mustard
Salt and pepper to taste

Cook carrots until tender; drain. Add green pepper and onions. Combine remaining ingredients; pour over carrot mixture. Mix well. Refrigerate until ready to use. This will keep well for 2 weeks in the refrigerator.

Lorraine Michalski, West Seneca, N.Y.

OVEN-COOKED ASPARAGUS
Serves 6

3 tablespoons melted butter
3 tablespoons flour
1 cup milk
3/4 teaspoon salt
1/4 teaspoon pepper
1-2/3 cups finely chopped, cooked asparagus
2 eggs, beaten

In a pot combine butter and flour thoroughly. Add the milk gradually. Cook, stirring constantly, until thick and smooth. Add salt, pepper, and asparagus. Fold eggs into mixture. Spoon mixture into greased custard cups. Set in a pan of hot water. Bake at 375 degrees for 15 minutes.

VEGETABLE PIZZA

1 package crescent dinner rolls
1 (8-ounce) package cream cheese
1 (8-ounce) container plain yogurt
1/2 package Hidden Valley ranch
    dressing
3/4 cup shredded cheddar cheese
3/4 cup carrots, very finely chopped
3/4 cup tomatoes, very finely
    chopped
3/4 cup onions, very finely chopped
3/4 cup broccoli, very finely
    chopped
3/4 cup cauliflower, very finely
    chopped
3/4 cup celery, very finely chopped

Cover bottom of cookie sheet with crescent rolls. Press in the separations. Bake at 350 degrees until light brown. Cool. Mix yogurt, cream cheese and flavoring until smooth and spread over crust. Cover with vegetable toppings and cheddar cheese.

Kristy Schemrich, Shreve, Ohio

ZUCCHINI–CORN PUDDING
Serves 8

1-1/2 pounds zucchini, thinly sliced
1 medium onion, thinly sliced
1 green pepper, minced
1 clove garlic, minced
1/4 teaspoon rosemary
1/4 cup salad oil
1 (No. 2) can cream-style corn
3/4 cup grated cheese
3 eggs, well-beaten
Salt and pepper to taste

Cook zucchini in boiling, salted water until tender. Drain; squeeze out all liquid. Sauté onion, green pepper, garlic, and rosemary in oil until tender. Add zucchini, corn, cheese, eggs, salt, and pepper. Mix; turn into greased 2-quart casserole. Bake 45 minutes at 350 degrees, or until firm.

June Harding, Ferndale, Mich.

GLAZED ACORN SQUASH
Serves 12

3 acorn squash
1/4 cup margarine
1/4 cup firmly packed brown sugar
2 tablespoons maple-flavored syrup
1/2 cup coarsely chopped walnuts

Heat oven to 350 degrees. Cut squash in half lengthwise; remove seeds. Cut squash halves, crosswise, into 1-inch-thick pieces. Arrange in 13 x 9-inch (3-quart) baking dish; cover. Bake at 350 degrees for 35–40 minutes, or until nearly tender. In small saucepan, melt margarine. Stir in brown sugar, syrup and walnuts; cook over medium heat until sugar dissolves. Spoon over squash and continue baking an additional 10–15 minutes, or until squash in tender. Baste occasionally. (140 calories per serving)

Mrs. Sherwin Dick, Inman, Neb.

FILLED BEET BASKETS
Serves 6

6 medium-size beets, cooked
1 cup beet greens (tops), cooked
    and chopped
1 hard-cooked egg, chopped
1 slice bacon, cooked crisp and
    crumbled
1 tablespoon onion, chopped
1/4 teaspoon salt
1/4 teaspoon pepper
1 tablespoon butter or margarine,
    melted
Parsley

Scoop out centers of cooked beets to form baskets. Chop centers, green tops and egg. Add crumbled bacon, onion, salt, pepper and butter. Heap mixture carefully into beet baskets; garnish with parsley. Can be served on crisp lettuce, as a side dish, or placed around edge of platter with any baked meat, chicken or turkey.

Gwen Campbell, Sterling, Va.

SQUASH BAKE
Serves 6

1 pound yellow squash, finely sliced
1/2 cup almonds, chopped
2–3 white onions, finely sliced
Salt and pepper to taste
1 stick butter
1 cup bread crumbs, toasted
1 egg, beaten
6 tablespoons cream

Cook squash and onions in saucepan with butter over medium heat until mixture is soft. Remove pan from heat and add egg, cream and almonds. Mix well; add salt and pepper. Place in a 1-1/2-quart casserole and top with bread crumbs. Bake at 350 degrees for 30 minutes, or until bubbly.

June Harding, Ferndale, Mich.

LEMON-GLAZED CARROTS
Serves 6

1-1/2 pounds small carrots, peeled
1/2 teaspoon salt
1/2 cup boiling water
1/3 cup brown sugar
2 tablespoons butter
1 teaspoon grated lemon peel
1 tablespoon lemon juice

Cook carrots, covered, in salted water until tender for about 20 minutes; drain. Combine remaining ingredients; heat and pour over carrots.

Melba Bellefeinlle, Libertyville, Ill.

CARROTS IN CUMIN BUTTER
Serves 4

3 cups sliced carrots
    Salted, boiling water
1 tablespoon butter
½ teaspoon ground cumin

Cook carrots in salted, boiling water just until tender. Drain well. Add butter and cumin; stir until butter is melted and cumin is evenly distributed.

MUSHROOM SUPREME

1 (12 ounce) can whole mushrooms
2 beef bouillon cubes
1/2 cup hot water
4 tablespoons butter
2 tablespoons flour
1/2 cup light cream
Pinch of salt and pepper
1/2 cup bread crumbs
1/2 to 1 cup Parmesan cheese.

Saute mushrooms in butter gently for two minutes. Dissolve beef cubes in hot water. Melt butter and blend with flour in another saucepan. Add cream, salt, pepper, beef broth, and mushrooms to butter and flour mixture. Pour into buttered casserole. Top with cheese and bread crumbs, mixed together. Bake for 30 minutes at 350 degrees.

Great for mushroom lovers.

Helen MacFarlane, Monaca, PA

ASPARAGUS-TOMATO STIR FRY
Serves 4

1 pound fresh asparagus
1 tablespoon cold water
1 teaspoon cornstarch
2 teaspoons soy sauce
1/4 teaspoon salt
1 tablespoon cooking oil
4 green onions, bias sliced
   in 1-inch lengths
1-1/2 cup sliced fresh mushrooms
2 small tomatoes, cut in thin wedges
Hot cooked rice

Snap off and discard woody base of asparagus. Bias slice the asparagus crosswise into 1-1/2 inch lengths and set aside. If asparagus spears are not slender and young, cut up pieces, cook uncovered in small amount of boiling salted water about 5 minutes; drain well. (Celery, green beans, broccoli, etc., may be used in place of asparagus.) In small bowl, blend water into cornstarch. Stir in soy sauce and salt; set aside. Stir-fry asparagus and green onions in hot oil 4 minutes. Use a long-handled spoon to turn and lift the food with a folding

motion. Add mushrooms; stir-fry 1 minute more. Stir the soy mixture again. Push vegetables up the sides of the wok; add soy mixture to center of wok. Let mixture bubble slightly, then stir into vegetables. Cook and stir till mixture is thickened and bubbly. Add tomatoes and heat through. Serve at once with cooked rice.

COMPANY ASPARAGUS
Serves 4-6

14-1/2 - ounce can green asparagus
10-1/2 - ounce can Cheddar cheese
   soup
2 hard-boiled eggs, chopped
1/2 cup toasted slivered almonds
1 cup buttered bread crumbs, divided

Combine asparagus, soup, eggs, almonds and 1/2 cup bread crumbs in buttered 1-quart casserole dish. Spread 1/2 cup bread crumbs over mixture. Bake uncovered at 375 degrees for 20 minutes.

Mrs. E. O'Brien, Richmond, VA

ASPARAGUS WITH YOGURT DRESSING
Serves 4

1 pound fresh asparagus
1/2 cup plain yogurt
1 small clove garlic, crushed
1 tablespoon chopped parsley
1/4 teaspoon salt
1 small head Boston or Bibb lettuce
1 hard-cooked egg yolk; sieved

Snap off tough ends of asparagus. Remove scales with knife or peeler. Cook asparagus in boiling water about 10 minutes or until crisp-tender. Drain. Cool and place in refrigerator to chill. Combine yogurt with garlic, parsley, and salt; stir well. Chill. Place asparagus on bed of lettuce; top with yogurt dressing and sprinkle with egg yolk.

Peggy Fowler Revels, Woodruff, SC

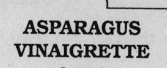

ASPARAGUS VINAIGRETTE
Serves 4

1 pound fresh asparagus (or 1 pound
   fresh whole green beans)
1 head fresh cauliflower (or 1 package
   frozen cauliflower)
1 can (7 ounce) artichoke hearts
Vinaigrette Dressing (below)

Cook asparagus or beans and cauliflower. Drain artichokes. Pour 1/4 cup Vinaigrette Dressing over each vegetable. Chill at least 1 hour. Arrange the three vegetables artistically on individual serving plates or on one large platter. Garnish with cherry tomatoes or parsley.

ASPARAGUS LOAF

1 carton half & half
1 sleeve package soda crackers,
   crumbled
3 eggs, beaten
2 tablespoons butter
2 cans green asparagus spears, cut
Pinch of salt

Mix all ingredients together. Pour into buttered casserole. Bake at 350 degrees for 1 hour.

Ann Fischer, Clarksville, Ind.

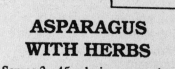

ASPARAGUS WITH HERBS
Serves 3 - 45 calories per serving

1-1/4 cups asparagus
1 tablespoon diet margarine
1/2 teaspoon salt
1/4 cup water
2 tablespoons chives, chopped
1/8 teaspoon seasoned salt
1/16 teaspoon pepper

Separate asparagus. Place margarine, salt, water, and chives in skillet; cover tightly. Bring to boil, add asparagus and cover again. Gently boil until asparagus is tender. Sprinkle with seasoned salt and pepper.

GREEN BEAN AND BACON COMBO
Serves 4

1 (9-ounce) package frozen cut green beans
4 slices bacon, cut into small pieces
2 slices bread, cut into 1/2-inch cubes
1/3 cup condensed cream of mushroom soup

Cook green beans following directions on package; drain. Put bacon into a 1-1/2-quart glass baking dish. Cover with a paper towel. Cook in microwave oven for about 2-1/2 minutes on HIGH, or until browned. Remove bacon from dish. Add bread cubes to bacon fat in dish; mix well. Cook, uncovered, in microwave oven for 2 minutes on HIGH; stir once. Mix bacon with the beans in casserole; spoon undiluted soup over beans and top with bread cubes. Cover with waxed paper. Heat in microwave oven to serving temperature, 3–4 minutes on HIGH.

Sharon Lemasters, Morgantown, W.V.

CHEESY CRUMB TOMATOES
Serves 4

4 tomatoes
1/3 cup dry bread crumbs
2 tablespoons butter
2 tablespoons grated Parmesan cheese
1/2 teaspoon salt
Dash pepper

Cut tomatoes in half crosswise; arrange cut side up on microwave-safe plate. Set aside. In small bowl, combine bread crumbs and butter; microwave on HIGH, uncovered, for 3–4 minutes, or until golden brown, stirring frequently. Stir in cheese and seasonings. Sprinkle crumb mixture over each tomato half. Microwave on HIGH, uncovered, for 3–4 minutes, or until hot.

Jen Lien, Stoughton, Wis.

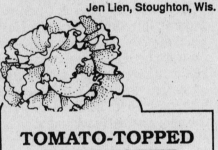

SPINACH–ONION QUICHE
Serves 6

2 cups finely chopped sweet onions
1/4 cup butter
1 (10-ounce) package frozen chopped spinach
3/4 cup grated Swiss cheese
3 eggs
1 cup milk
1 teaspoon salt

1/8 teaspoon pepper
Dash nutmeg
1 unbaked 9-inch pie shell

Sauté onions slowly in butter. Cook spinach according to package directions. Drain thoroughly. Combine onion, spinach, and Swiss cheese. Beat eggs. Blend in milk and seasonings. Combine with spinach mixture. Bake pie shell. Pour in egg-vegetable mixture. Bake in 375 degree-oven, 35-40 minutes, or until knife inserted in center comes out clean.

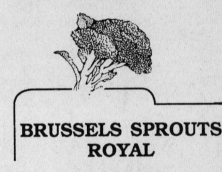

CUCUMBER COMBO

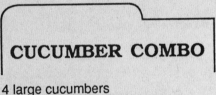

4 large cucumbers
1/4 teaspoon salt
1/8 teaspoon pepper
1/4 teaspoon nutmeg
1-1/2 teaspoons onion, grated
1 teaspoon fresh lemon juice
1 tablespoon water
1/2 cup soft bread crumbs
1 tablespoon butter or margarine

Wash and score 4 large cucumbers; do not peel. Remove seeds; cut into 1/2-inch cubes. In a generously buttered ovenproof casserole, layer cucumber cubes; mix with the next 6 ingredients. Scatter 1/2 cup soft bread crumbs over all; dot with 1 tablespoon butter. Repeat layers until casserole is full; end with bread crumbs; cover. Bake at 350 degrees for 40 minutes. Uncover; bake 15 minutes longer, or until top is nicely browned.

Gwen Campbell, Sterling, Va.

TOMATO-TOPPED CAULIFLOWER
Serves 4

1 1/2–2-pound head cauliflower
Water
Salt

Sauce:
1 onion, chopped
3 tablespoons butter *or* margarine
1 clove garlic, minced
1/4 teaspoon dried basil
1/4 teaspoon dried thyme
1/2 teaspoon dried oregano
1 (16-ounce) can tomato sauce
1 cup cheddar cheese, grated
1/2 cup Parmesan cheese, grated

Place cauliflower in large pot with water and salt; simmer 15 minutes. In a saucepan, melt butter; add onion, garlic, herbs and tomato sauce; cook until thickened. Place cauliflower on warmed serving dish; pour hot sauce over top; sprinkle with cheeses.

Gwen Campbell, Sterling, Va.

BRUSSELS SPROUTS ROYAL

2 (10-ounce) packages brussels sprouts, halved
1 (5-ounce) can water chestnuts, drained (save liquid)

½ cup snip parsley
1 teaspoon sugar
½ cup margarine

Add sufficient water to liquid to make 1 cup. Pour sugar and parsley into saucepan with liquid. Bring to boil; add brussels sprouts. Simmer, covered, for 8–10 minutes. Drain. Add margarine and diced water chestnuts. Add pearl onions and soft buttered bread crumbs, if desired. No one will ever dare say they do not care for brussels sprouts.

HAM, EGG, AND VEGETABLE BAKE
Serves 6

2 medium potatoes, peeled, cooked, and thinly sliced
1/4 cup cooked, minced ham
3 hard-cooked eggs, sliced
1 small head cauliflower, cooked and liquid reserved
1 tablespoon flour
1 tablespoon butter
Salt and pepper to taste
1/4 cup grated cheese

Grease a baking pan. Spread a layer of potato slices over bottom. Sprinkle with minced ham. Spread egg slices over ham. Cover with crumbled cauliflower and one more layer of potatoes. In a small saucepan soften the butter and stir in flour. Mix cauliflower liquid and skim milk to make one cup. Add gradually, stirring constantly. Cook over low heat until sauce thickens slightly. Season to taste and pour over mixture in baking pan. Sprinkle with grated cheese and bake in 350–degree oven for 30 minutes. (145 calories per serving)

Judy Codenys, LaGrange, Texas

SUMMER VEGETABLE MEDLEY
Serves 6

2-3 medium zucchini, washed and coin-sliced
1 cup fresh mushrooms, washed and sliced
1/4 cup chopped onion
1/4 cup chopped green pepper
3 tablespoons butter or margarine
2 tomatoes, coarsely chopped
2 tablespoons grated Parmesan cheese
1/4 teaspoon garlic powder
Salt and pepper to taste

Combine zucchini, mushrooms, onion, green pepper and butter in 1-1/2–quart glass/ceramic casserole. Cover and microwave 8-9 minutes, or until vegetables are tender–crisp, stirring once during cooking. Add toma-toes, cheese, and seasonings. Cover and microwave 2-3 minutes or until heated through.

Mrs. Olen Begly, West Salem, Ohio

CRUSTY BREAD GRATIN OF VEGETABLES
Serves 8

1 tablespoon vegetable oil
1 tablespoon olive oil
1 onion, chopped
1/2 teaspoon garlic, minced
1 pound zucchini, cut into 1/2-inch slices
2 cups cauliflower florets
3 medium-size fresh tomatoes
1 (28-ounce) can crushed tomatoes
1/4 teaspoon salt
1/4 teaspoon pepper
1/2 cup Fontina cheese, shredded
4 slices French bread, halved and buttered

Heat oils in skillet; saute onion and garlic until tender. Add zucchini and cauliflower; saute 5 minutes. Add fresh and crushed tomatoes, salt, and pepper. Cook covered, until vegetables are tender. Pour vegetable mixture into oven baking dish; place halves of buttered French bread along edge of pan; cut side down, buttered side in. Sprinkle cheese on top of vegetable mixture; return to 350-degree oven for 5 minutes to melt cheese.

Gwen Campbell, Sterling, VA

GREEN VEGGIE BAKE
Serves 6-8

2 tablespoons butter or margarine
1/2 cup chopped onion
1 teaspoon salt
1/4 teaspoon pepper
4 ounces sour cream
1 to 1-1/2 tablespoons cornstarch
1 cup broccoli
1 cup green beans
1 cup peas
1 cup American or cheddar cheese, grated
2 tablespoons butter or margarine, melted

1 cup Ritz (salad) crackers

Cook onion in 2 tablespoons butter until tender. Add cornstarch, salt, pepper, and sour cream; mix well. Stir in green vegetables. Put in casserole dish, top with grated cheese. Combine remaining 2 tablespoons butter and cracker crumbs; place on top of cheese. Bake at 350 degrees for 30 minutes. This recipe was created for those "timid" green–vegetable eaters. Also great for leftovers.

Beth Zellars, Franklin, Ind.

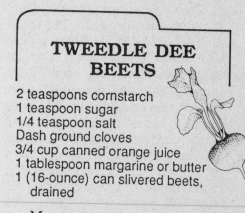

TWEEDLE DEE BEETS

2 teaspoons cornstarch
1 teaspoon sugar
1/4 teaspoon salt
Dash ground cloves
3/4 cup canned orange juice
1 tablespoon margarine or butter
1 (16-ounce) can slivered beets, drained

Measure cornstarch, sugar, salt, and cloves into a medium size saucepan. Stir in orange juice. Add margarine and heat to boiling, stirring constantly to keep sauce smooth. Add beets to sauce. Heat slowly 5 minutes.

Roberta Neely, Riviera, Texas

SAVORY BEETS
2 servings

1 tablespoon butter or margarine
2 teaspoons cider vinegar
1/4 teaspoon salt
1/4 cup sugar
1/8 teaspoon dry mustard
Few drops Worcestershire sauce
3 or 4 mediun beets, cooked and skinned

In a small saucepan, melt butter. Add vinegar, salt, sugar, dry mustard and Worcestershire sauce. Set over low heat; mix well with rubber spatula. Slice in beets; toss to mix; cook until beets are heated through.

The remaining beets can be chilled whole and sliced when used. This is a flavorful way to serve precooked beets.

HARVARD CARROTS

Serves 6-8

2 pounds carrots, scraped
1/2 cup sugar
1-1/2 tablespoons cornstarch
1/4 cup vinegar
1/4 cup water
1/4 cup butter or margarine

Cut carrots into 1/2-inch crosswise slices and cook, covered, in a large saucepan with a small amount of boiling salted water for 15 minutes or until tender; drain. Combine sugar and cornstarch in a small saucepan; add vinegar and water. Cook over medium heat, stirring constantly until thickened. Add sauce and butter to carrots. Cook over low heat until butter melts and carrots are thoroughly heated.

Agnes Ward, Erie, PA

COPPER PENNIES

Serves 12-15

1 pound carrots
1 can tomato soup
1 cup sugar (or sugar substitute)
1/2 cup oil
1/2 cup vinegar
1 onion, chopped
1 green pepper, chopped

Slice and cook carrots. To cooked carrots, add onion and pepper. Add remaining ingredients. Allow flavors to blend several hours before serving. This relish will keep several weeks in refrigerator.

Elizabeth Dunn, Harrisonville, NJ

DILLED BABY CARROTS

Serves 6

3/4 cup white wine vinegar
1/4 cup water
1/4 cup honey
1/2 teaspoon dried whole dillweed
1/2 teaspoon mixed pickling spices

1 teaspoon salt
1/2 pound baby carrots, scraped
Sprigs of fresh dill (optional)

Combine first 6 ingredients in large saucepan; bring to a boil. Add carrots; cover; reduce heat and simmer 10-12 minutes or until crisp and tender. Remove from heat, and pour mixture into plastic container; set container in bowl of ice water to cool quickly. Chill, Serve with slotted spoon. Garnish with sprigs of dill, if desired.

Marcella Swigert, Monroe City, Mo.

CARROT RING SOUFFLE

Serves 8

12 medium carrots, cooked and mashed
1/2 to 2 tablespoons prepared horseradish
1/2 cup mayonnaise
2 tablespoons finely minced onion
3 eggs, well beaten
1/2 teaspoon salt

Mix all ingredients together. Pour into lightly oiled ring mold. Place mold in pan of hot water; bake at 350 degrees for 40 minutes. Turn out onto serving platter; fill center with cooked frozen peas or broccoli. Serve immediately.

Marcella Swigert, Monroe City, Mo.

ROLY-POLY CARROT MARBLES

Makes 35 balls

3 ounces cream cheese, softened
1 cup shredded Cheddar cheese
1 teaspoon honey
1 cup finely shredded carrots
3/4 cup finely chopped dry roasted peanuts

Combine the first 3 ingredients and blend. Stir in carrots. Chill 1 hour. Shape into balls using 1-1/2 teaspoons mixture for each marble. Chill until firm after rolling each marble in the chopped nuts.

RICE PILAF WITH FRESH MUSHROOMS

Serves 8

4 tablespoons butter or margarine
1 large onion, chopped
1 cup sliced mushrooms
1-1/2 cups regular long grain rice
3-1/4 cups water
1 envelope (3/4 ounce) au jus gravy mix
1/2 teaspoon salt
1/2 teaspoon oregano leaves

Melt butter in a 2 quart dutch oven. Cook onion, mushrooms, and rice in butter 4-5 minutes. Stir until rice is golden brown. Add remaining ingredients. Stir to dissolve gravy mix. Cover and bake in 350 degree oven 40 minutes or until all liquid is absorbed.
NOTE: Can be cooked, covered on top of stove over medium heat for 45 minutes. Also can be frozen in "boilable plastic bags" and reheated.

Mrs. Kit Rollins, Cedarburg, WI

MUSHROOM FRITTERS

Makes 12

1 cup packaged biscuit mix
1 cup chopped fresh mushrooms
2 tablespoons sliced green onions
1 tablespoon chopped pimiento
1/4 teaspoon salt
1/4 teaspoon celery seed
1 beaten egg yolk
1/4 cup dairy sour cream
1 egg white
Cooking oil for deep fat frying

In mixing bowl combine biscuit mix, mushrooms, onion, pimiento, salt, and celery seed. Mix together egg yolk and sour cream; stir into dry ingredients just until moistened. Beat egg white to stiff peaks; gently fold into mushroom mixture.

In heavy saucepan or deep fat fryer heat oil to 375 degrees. Drop batter by tablespoons into hot oil. Fry about 2 minutes or until golden brown, turning once. Drain on rack; serve hot.

Judy Fisk, Aberdeen, Wash.

CUCUMBERS SUPREME

2 medium cucumbers
1 large onion, sliced and separated into rings
1 cup Seven Seas Buttermilk Recipe Dressing
Green–onion tops for color

Peel and slice cucumbers. Peel, slice, and separate onions into rings. Mix and add Seven Seas Dressing. Garnish with green onion tops. Cucumbers could not be any tastier!! Also a very quick side dish to add to any meal.

Mrs. C. O. Shepardson, Apple Valley, Calif.

CABBAGE AU GRATIN

1-1/2 pounds cabbage
2 tablespoons butter
6 tablespoons flour
2 cups milk
1/4 pound grated cheese

Cut up cabbage and cook in salted water until tender. Make a white sauce with the butter, flour, and milk. Fill a greased baking dish with alternate layers of cabbage and white sauce. Cover top with cheese; bake in 350 degree oven for 20 minutes.

Joy Shamway, Freeport, IL

CRUNCHY CABBAGE

Serves 6-8

8 cups thinly sliced green cabbage
Boiling water
1 (10-3/4 ounce) can cream of celery soup
1/2 cup mayonnaise
1/2 cup milk
1/2 teaspoon salt
2 cups corn flakes
2 tablespoons butter or margarine, melted
1/2 pound shredded Cheddar cheese

Cook cabbage in boiling water 3-4 minutes. Drain. Combine next four ingredients in saucepan. Heat, just until hot. Toss corn flakes in the bottom of a 1-1/2 quart casserole, reserving some for top. Alternate layers of cabbage and sauce, ending with sauce layer. Top with remaining corn flakes and cheese. Bake at 375 degrees for 15 minutes. Serve hot.

Lori Gerich, Hayward, Wis.

FRENCH SKILLET CABBAGE

4-6 cups shredded cabbage
1 green pepper, shredded
2 large onions, sliced (not chopped)
2 cups diced-sliced celery
2 tomatoes, chopped
6-8 slices bacon
1/4-1/3 cup bacon drippings

Fry bacon; remove from skillet and crumble; reserve drippings. Combine all vegetables in large skillet with bacon drippings. Cover; cook over medium heat for 7-10 minutes or until vegetables are still crisp-cooked. Add bacon just before serving. Do not substitute for bacon or the drippings.

Alice Dick, Montpelier, Ohio

MARINATED CARROTS

Serves 8

1 bag large carrots
2 cloves garlic, sliced
1/2 teaspoon salt
1/2 teaspoon pepper
1/4 cup olive oil
2 tablespoons wine vinegar
1 teaspoon oregano

Scrape carrots; cut into thick slices. Boil in water 10 minutes, or until tender, taking care not to overcook. Drain well; place in bowl with garlic, salt, pepper, oil, vinegar, and oregano. Stir; mix well. Let stand in marinade twelve hours before serving.

Helen Robiolo, Union City, NJ

GLAZED CARROTS

Serves 6

2 cups sliced carrots
1 cup undiluted frozen orange juice
1/2 cup sugar
2 tablespoons cornstarch
Dash of nutmeg

Cook and drain carrots. Mix remaining ingredients; cook until thick. Pour sauce over carrots and let stand a short time. Serve hot.

Juanita Cecil, Mooresville, Ind.

FREEZE AHEAD GOLDEN GLAZED CARROTS

1-1/2 pounds baby carrots or 1-1/2 pounds carrots, cut into strips
2 tablespoons all-purpose flour
1/4 cup light brown sugar
1/2 teaspoon salt
1/4 teaspoon thyme
1 tablespoon cider vinegar
1 tablespoon lemon juice
1/2 cup orange juice
Grated peel of one orange
2 tablespoons butter

Put carrots in saucepan. Pour boiling water over them and boil exactly 5 minutes. Drain thoroughly. Blend together flour, sugar, salt, and thyme. Add vinegar, juices, and orange rind. Bring to a boil while stirring, and continue stirring until creamy. Add butter and cook for 5 minutes over very low heat. Line a casserole with foil, leaving enough around the edges to cover. Add the blanched carrots to foil-lined casserole; pour sauce over them. Freeze uncovered. When frozen, cover completely with the foil. Remove package from casserole and put back into freezer. To serve, unwrap carrots, put back into same casserole. Bake, covered in a 350-degree oven for 40 minutes. Uncover for the last 15 minutes of baking. This is a very nice way to use the first baby carrots from the garden, and then when you serve them it brings back the "taste of summer."

Lillian Smith, Montreal, Que, Canada

10-MINUTE PECAN SQUASH
Serves 4-6

2 (12-ounce) packages frozen cooked squash
2 tablespoons butter
4 teaspoons instant breakfast drink (Tang)
1 teaspoon salt, if desired
Dash of pepper
6 tablespoons chopped pecans

Combine squash, butter, instant breakfast drink, salt, and pepper; cook as directed on package. Stir in pecans.
Karin Shea Fedders, Dameron, Md.

STUFFED PATTY-PAN SQUASH

4 patty-pan squash
4 slices bacon, cooked crisp
1/2 cup onion, chopped
3/4 cup bread crumbs
1/2 cup milk

Cook squash in boiling salted water for 15 minutes. Drain and cool. From the stem end cut a small slice; scoop out center, leaving 1/2-inch rim. Chop the squash which has been removed very finely. Sprinkle the squash cups lightly with salt. Sauté onion in bacon drippings; add crumbs, milk, and reserved squash. Fill cups; sprinkle crisp bacon on top. Place in flat casserole; bake at 350 degrees for 35 minutes.
Gwen Campbell, Sterling, Va.

SCALLOPED EGGPLANT
Serves 6

2 cups cooked eggplant
1/2 cup coarse cracker crumbs
4 tablespoons onion, minced
3 ounces cheese, grated
1 egg, beaten
1/2 cup milk
2 tablespoons margarine or butter

Peel eggplant and cut in 1-inch cubes. Cook in boiling salted water until tender, 8 minutes. Drain. Put eggplant, half of cracker crumbs, onion, and cheese in layers in buttered casserole. Combine egg and milk; pour over other ingredients. Dot with margarine and sprinkle with remaining cracker crumbs. Bake at 350 degrees for 30 minutes.
Suzan L. Wiener, Spring Hill, Fla.

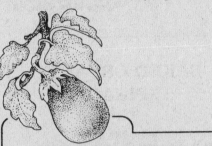

FRENCH FRIED EGGPLANT

1 medium eggplant, peeled and sliced into 1/2 x 2-inch strips
1 cup pancake flour
1 egg
1/4 cup water
1/2 cup Parmesan cheese, grated
Salt
Vegetable oil

Beat egg and water together. Dip eggplant strips into egg mixture; then roll in pancake flour. Drop into hot oil and cook until golden brown, about 2 - 3 minutes. Drain on paper toweling and sprinkle lightly with salt and Parmesan cheese. Serve hot!!
Margean Gilger, Akron, OH

SAUCY ASPARAGUS

2 cans drained asparagus
1 cup cream of mushroom soup
1 can broken pieces mushrooms
1/4 pound squared American cheese
1-1/4 cups bread crumbs
1/2 stick butter

Grease a long flat casserole dish with butter. Place drained asparagus over bottom. Add cream of mushroom soup. Then add mushroom pieces and juice. Cover with Ameri-

can cheese squares. Put bread crumbs over cheese and thinly sliced butter over top. Bake 25 minutes in 350 degree oven or until it bubbles up through and crumbs are browned. Can use 2 chopped hard cooked eggs, if desired, for garnish.
Virginia Beachler, Logansport, Ind.

SAVORY SUCCOTASH
Serves 6-8

1 (1-pound) can (2 cups) French style green beans, drained
1 (1-pound) can (2 cups) whole kernel corn, drained
1/2 cup mayonnaise or salad dressing
1/2 cup shredded sharp cheese
1/2 cup chopped green pepper
1/2 cup chopped celery
2 tablespoons chopped onions
1 cup soft bread crumbs
2 tablespoons butter or margarine, melted

Combine first 7 ingredients; place in 9x9 inch casserole or 10x6x1-1/2 inch baking dish. Combine crumbs and butter; sprinkle over top. Bake in moderate oven 350 degrees for 30 minutes or until crumbs are toasted.
Helen Taugher, Nicholson, Pa.

VEGETABLE BAKE

1 can Veg-All, drained
1/2 cup chopped celery
1/2 cup chopped onion
1/2 cup sliced water chestnuts
1 cup mayonnaise
1 cup celery soup
1 cup shredded cheese
1/2 stick margarine
20 Ritz crackers

Mix together all ingredients except margarine and crackers in a 2-quart casserole. Bake for 45 minutes at 300 degrees. Melt margarine. Mix with crushed Ritz crackers. Sprinkle over the top. Bake 15 additional minutes.

This is truly a super vegetable casserole, a crowd pleaser for church potluck suppers and one which carries and travels well.
Mary Lou Allaman, Kirkwood, Ill.

BAKED GREEN BEANS IN TARRAGON CREAM

1-1/2 pounds green beans
1 tablespoon butter
1/2 teaspoon tarragon leaves
1/2 cup heavy cream
1/4 teaspoon salt
1/4 cup seasoned bread crumbs

Prepare green beans; cook in salted water about 12 minutes. Drain; arrange in shallow baking dish. Dot with butter. Mix 1/4 teaspoon tarragon leaves with heavy cream. Pour tarragon/cream mixture over all; sprinkle with seasoned bread crumbs. Bake in 350 degree oven until golden brown, about 12 minutes.

Mrs. Gwen Campbell, Sterling, VA

GLORIFIED BEANS
Serves 6

1-1/2 pounds ground beef
1-1/2 cups chopped onions
1 tablespoon dried mixed peppers
1-1/4 teaspoons salt
2 tablespoons brown sugar
1 tablespoon chili powder
1 - 12 ounce can tomato paste
1 cup water
1 can pork and beans in tomato sauce
1 can green limas
1 can red kidney beans

Brown ground beef. Combine with rest of ingredients. Bake in 350 degree oven for 1 hour.

Jeanie Blass, Richmond, VA

MOLASSES BAKED BEANS
Serves 8

1 (10-ounce) package frozen lima beans, thawed
1 (15-ounce) can kidney beans, drained
1 (15-ounce) can pinto beans, drained

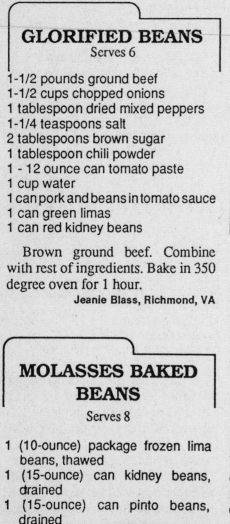

1 (15-ounce) can baked beans, undrained
6 slices crispy fried bacon, crumbled
1/2 cup chopped onion
1/2 cup dark molasses
1/4 cup light brown sugar, packed
2 teaspoons dry mustard

Mix all ingredients in 2-1/2-quart casserole. Bake, uncovered, at 350 degrees for 1 hour, stirring occasionally.

Agnes Ward, Erie, PA

BAKED CREAMED SPINACH
Serves 6

1 cup heavy cream
3/4 cup grated Parmesan cheese
3 cups cooked, chopped spinach
1/2 teaspoon salt
Pepper
Nutmeg

Whip cream until stiff. Fold in 1/2 cup grated cheese. Then fold mixture into spinach and blend well. Season with salt; sprinkle pepper and nutmeg to taste. Put into buttered ovenproof pie plate. Sprinkle 1/4 cup grated cheese on top. Bake in 375 degree oven until slightly browned.

Mrs. Robert Combs, Fair Play, MO

SPECIAL SPINACH SQUARES
Serves 4

1 (10-ounce) package frozen chopped spinach
2 eggs
8 ounces sour cream
1 tablespoon onion, grated
1/2 cup Parmesan cheese, grated
1 tablespoon flour
2 tablespoons margarine
1/2 - 1 teaspoon salt
1/8 teaspoon pepper

Cook spinach as directed on package; drain well. Beat eggs; add to spinach. Blend in other ingredients. Place into greased 9 x 9-inch square dish. Bake, uncovered, at 350 degrees for 25-30 minutes. Cool slightly and cut into squares.

Mrs. George Franks, Millerton, Pa.

SPINACH LOAF
Serves 8-10

2 cups cooked spinach
1 cup soft bread crumbs
1 medium onion, minced
1/2 cup walnuts, chopped
1 teaspoon salt
1/8 teaspoon paprika
2 eggs, beaten
1/8 teaspoon pepper
1 tablespoon butter, melted
Milk or stock

Chop spinach; add crumbs, onions, nuts, seasonings and beaten eggs. Add enough milk or stock to form into a loaf. Place in a greased loaf pan and bake 30 minutes in a 375 degree oven.

Agnes Ward, Erie, PA

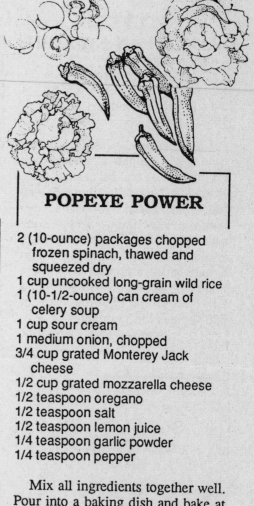

POPEYE POWER

2 (10-ounce) packages chopped frozen spinach, thawed and squeezed dry
1 cup uncooked long-grain wild rice
1 (10-1/2-ounce) can cream of celery soup
1 cup sour cream
1 medium onion, chopped
3/4 cup grated Monterey Jack cheese
1/2 cup grated mozzarella cheese
1/2 teaspoon oregano
1/2 teaspoon salt
1/2 teaspoon lemon juice
1/4 teaspoon garlic powder
1/4 teaspoon pepper

Mix all ingredients together well. Pour into a baking dish and bake at 350 degrees for 30-35 minutes or until it starts to bubble and browns around the outer edges.

Laura Hicks, Newport, Wash.

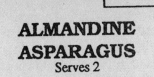

ALMANDINE ASPARAGUS
Serves 2

8 asparagus spears, shaved, cooked halfway and well drained
2-1/2 tablespoons mayonnaise
2-1/4 tablespoons sweet relish
2 pieces of fillet of sole (about 1/2 - 3/4 pounds of sole) wipe dry
1/2 tablespoon chili sauce
1/2 teaspoon margarine
2 tablespoons slivered almonds, toasted

Preheat oven to 350 degrees. In a lightly buttered baking dish lay the asparagus down gently. Mix the mayonnaise and relish; spoon over the asparagus. Place the fish fillets on top over the asparagus. Spoon the 1/2 tablespoon chili sauce over all and top with almonds. Dot with margarine. Bake for 35 minutes or until the fish flakes easily with a fork.

Marie Fusaro, Manasquan, NJ

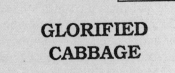

GLORIFIED CABBAGE

1 small head cabbage, shredded
1 large onion, finely chopped
1 green pepper, finely chopped
1/4 cup green onion, chopped
2 ribs celery, sliced 1/8 inch think
2 tablespoons margarine
2 tablespoons vegetable oil
2 cloves garlic, minced
1/2 cup whipping cream
1 cup fresh bread crumbs (optional)
1-1/2 cups Cheddar cheese, shredded
2 tablespoons parsley, minced
1 teaspoon salt
1/2 teaspoon black pepper

Heat butter and oil in large saucepan; add onions, green pepper and celery; saute 5 minutes over low heat. Add cabbage and garlic; cook covered over low heat for 10 minutes or until cabbage is tender; stir in cream. Mix crumbs with 1/2 the cheese and the parsley; set aside. Add remaining cheese to cabbage mixture; stir in salt

and pepper. Turn into 1-1/2 quart buttered, shallow casserole. Top with crumbs-cheese mixture. Bake at 350 degrees for 20 minutes or until crumbs are golden and crisp.

Ella Evanicky, Fayetteville, TX

CREAMED CABBAGE VEGETABLE DISH FROM 1891
Serves 4

1 medium head cabbage
1 gill (1/2 cup) cream
1 ounce butter (walnut size)
Salt and pepper to taste
1 cup water

Slice cabbage as for slaw. Cook in 1 cup water until tender; drain. Return to saucepan. Add cream and salt and pepper. Simmer two to three minutes.
NOTE: Milk may be used by adding a little more butter.

Lou Henri Baker, Killbuck, OH

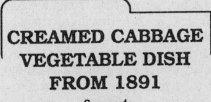

BAKED CREAM CABBAGE
Serves 6

1 medium head cabbage
1/2 cup boiling salted water
3 tablespoons flour
1/2 teaspoon salt
1-1/2 cups milk
1/4 cup bread crumbs
2 tablespoons butter

Shred cabbage very fine and cook 9 minutes in boiling, salted water. Remove cabbage; drain well. Place in buttered 1-1/2-quart casserole. Melt butter in saucepan; stir in flour and salt until smooth. Add milk gradually, continuing to stir until mixture thickens. Pour this sauce over cabbage and sprinkle breadcrumbs over top. Bake at 325 degrees for about 15 minutes or until crumbs are browned.

Karin Shea Fedders, Dameron, MD

ZUCCHINI FRITTERS
Makes 2 dozen

2 large zucchini squash
3 eggs
1/2 teaspoon salt
1/4 teaspoon pepper
1/2 teaspoon sugar
1 teaspoon dried dillweed or 1 tablespoon fresh dill
2 cloves garlic (finely diced)
5 tablespoons flour
1 onion (diced)
Salad oil and margarine

Wash zucchini, do not peel. Dice coarsely; cover with water. Add 1 teaspoon salt and bring to boil for eight minutes. Drain in colander (about 15 minutes). While draining zucchini, heat salad oil and saute onion until soft. Beat eggs; add next 7 ingredients. Stir in drained, mashed zucchini. Mix until well blended, adding sauteed onions.

Drop batter by tablespoon into skillet in which you have 2 tablespoons salad oil and 1 tablespoon margarine. Fry zucchini fritters, a few at a time, until light brown on both sides, turning once.

Place on platter with paper towel to absorb, adding more oil and margarine to skillet as needed and add more batter.

Serve plain or topped with dollop of sour cream or plain yogurt.

Carme Venella, Laurel Springs, NJ

ZUCCHINI SURPRISE
Serves 4
60 calories per serving

1 pound zucchini, sliced
8-ounce can mandarin oranges, drained
1/4 teaspoon nutmeg
Sprinkle cinnamon
1/4 cup pecans, chopped

Steam zucchini slices until tender. Add orange slices, nutmeg and cinnamon. Sprinkle with pecans; serve.

Marie Fusaro, Manasquan, NJ

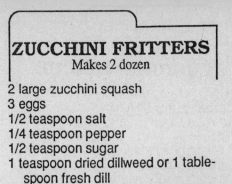

ZUCCHINI QUICHE

1 cup corn muffin mix
3 cups sliced small zucchini squash
1 medium onion, chopped
1/2 cup Parmesan cheese, grated
1/3 cup cooking oil
4 eggs, well beaten
Salt and pepper to taste
1 cup rich cream or half-and-half

Mix all ingredients together. Pour into a buttered 10" pie plate or quiche dish. Bake 45 minutes at 350 degrees. Can be frozen and baked when needed. If preferred, slice tomato or green pepper rings to place on top.

Nice served with relish plate of fresh vegetables and melon or other raw fruit for a luncheon.

Marjorie W. Baxla, Greenfield, OH

ZUCCHINI ROUNDS

1/3 cup commercial biscuit mix
1/4 cup grated Parmesan cheese
Salt and pepper to taste
2 eggs, slightly beaten
2 cups shredded, unpared zucchini
2 tablespoons butter or margarine, softened

In a bowl combine biscuit mix, cheese, salt, and pepper. Stir in eggs just until mixture is moistened; fold in zucchini. For each round, drop 2 tablespoons mixture in soft butter or margarine. Fry 2-3 minutes on each side until brown.

This is an excellent summer luncheon dish or for a brunch.

Alice McNamara, Eucha, OK

ZUCCHINI APPLESAUCE

Makes 2 cups

2 medium zucchini, peeled and diced
2 apples, peeled, cored, and diced
1/4 cup sugar
2 whole cloves
1/8 teaspoon nutmeg
1/2 teaspoon salt
1 tablespoon lemon juice

1/4 teaspoon cinnamon
1/2 teaspoon vanilla extract
Water

In a large saucepan, bring to a boil the zucchini, apples, sugar, cloves, nutmeg, salt, and 1/2 cup water. Reduce heat, cover, and simmer for 20 minutes; stir occasionally. Remove cover; continue cooking until all liquid has evaporated. Discard the cloves, then mash until smooth. Stir in the lemon juice and cinnamon. Cover and refrigerate until ready to use.

Marie Fusaro, Manasquan, NJ

SQUASH PILLOWS

1 yeast cake
1/2 cup lukewarm water
2/3 cup shortening
1 teaspoon salt
1/2 cup sugar
1 cup mashed cooked squash
1 teaspoon grated lemon rind
1/8 teaspoon mace
1 cup scalded milk
2 eggs
6 to 8 cups sifted flour

Mash squash. Add sugar, shortening, salt, lemon rind, mace and eggs. Blend well. Dissolve yeast in water. Add yeast mixture to milk and add to the first mixture. Add sifted flour to make a stiff dough. Mix well. Cover and let rise in a warm place until doubled in bulk. Shape into rolls; place in greased pans. Let rise in warm place until double in bulk. Bake at 325 degrees for 25 minutes.

Mrs. Kit Rollins, Cedarburg, WI

STUFFED ACORN SQUASH

Serves 8-12

Water
4-6 acorn squash, halved crosswise and seeded
1 or 2 (6 ounce) boxes chicken-flavor stuffing mix, prepared according to package directions
Parsley sprigs (garnish)

Preheat oven to 350 degrees. Pour water into 1 large or 2 smaller baking pans to measure 1 inch deep. Arrange acorn squash in water with cut sides up, cutting a thin slice off ends so halves will stand upright. Bake, covered, for 45 minutes or until flesh is tender when pierced with fork. Fill each squash cavity with about 1/3 cup hot stuffing and garnish with parsley.

HOLIDAY STUFFED WINTER SQUASH

Serves 6

3 small acorn or butternut squash
3 green onions, chopped
1 tablespoon oil
1 cup finely-diced celery
1 bunch fresh spinach, coarsely chopped
3/4 cup whole wheat bread crumbs
1/4 teaspoon salt
1/4 cup almonds, finely ground
1 tablespoon butter

Halve and clean the squash. Bake in a 350 degree oven, for 35-40 minutes, or until tender. Sauté onions in oil until soft. Add diced celery. Cover and simmer on medium heat until just tender. Add spinach; stir to wilt. Combine bread crumbs with salt and ground almonds. Stuff the squashes with spinach; sprinkle crumb mixture on top. Dot with butter and return to oven for 10-15 minutes.

Gwen Campbell, Sterling, Va.

DEBBIE'S YUMMY BAKED BEANS

4 cans pork and beans, drained
1/2 cup minced onion
1/2 pound diced bacon
3/4 cup grape jelly
3/4 cup enchilada sauce

Fry onion and bacon; drain. Add jelly and enchilada sauce; mix well. Add beans; pour into casserole dish and bake, uncovered at 350 degrees for 1 hour. Serve hot.

Debbie Vlahovic, Mesa, AZ

MINTED CAULIFLOWER

Serves 2

1 teaspoon vegetable oil
2 cups cauliflower florets, blanched
1/4 teaspoon mint flakes crushed
1/8 teaspoon salt
1/8 teaspoon pepper
2-3 teaspoons lemon juice

In 8-inch skillet, heat oil. Add cauliflower, mint, salt, and pepper; saute until cauliflower is tender-crisp, about 5 minutes. Sprinkle with lemon juice and saute for 2 minutes longer.

Mrs. Robert T. Shaffer, Middleburg, PA

BROCCOLI-CHEESE SQUARES

3 tablespoons butter, softened
2 (10 ounce) packages frozen chopped broccoli
3 large eggs
1 cup milk
1 cup flour
1 tablespoon baking powder
1 teaspoon salt
4 cups mild shredded Cheddar cheese
2 tablespoons finely chopped onion
Seasoned salt

Grease 13x9-inch dish with the butter. Steam broccoli until partly cooked, about 3 minutes; cool and press dry. Beat eggs and milk until frothy. Thoroughly mix flour, baking powder, and salt; stir into egg mixture; mix well. Fold in broccoli, cheese, and onion. Spoon into baking dish; spread evenly. Sprinkle with seasoned salt. Bake in 350 degree oven for 35 minutes.

Pauline Dean, Uxbridge, Mass.

BROCCOLI SUPREME

Serves 12-14

2 (10-ounce) packages frozen chopped broccoli, cooked and drained. Place in 2-quart casserole and add:

1 cup mayonnaise (not salad dressing)
1 small onion, chopped
1 can cream of mushroom soup
1 can cream of chicken soup
2 cups grated Cheddar cheese
2 eggs, beaten slightly

Cover and bake at 350 degrees for 1 hour.

Mrs. Hobert Howell, Waco, Texas

BROCCOLI PUFF

Serves 6

1 (10-ounce) package frozen broccoli
1 can condensed cream of mushroom soup
2 ounces sharp American cheese, grated
1/4 cup milk
1/4 cup mayonnaise or salad dressing
1 beaten egg
1/4 cup fine dry bread crumbs
1 tablespoon butter or margarine

Cook broccoli as directed, omitting salt; drain thoroughly. Place cuts into a 10 x 6 x 1-1/2-inch baking dish. Stir soup and grated cheese together. Gradually add milk, mayonnaise, and beaten egg to soup mixture; stir until blended. Pour over broccoli. Combine bread crumbs and melted margarine; sprinkle evenly over soup mixture. Bake in moderate oven of 350 degrees for 45 minutes until crumbs are lightly browned.

Peggy Fowler Revels, Woodruff, SC

BROCCOLI RING

Serves 10-12

3 eggs
2 tablespoons flour
1 cup half and half
1-1/2 cups chopped and cooked broccoli
1/2 cup chopped onion
3 tablespoons chopped sweet red pepper
1 teaspoon salt
1/8 teaspoon pepper
1/8 teaspoon paprika
Dash of nutmeg

Preheat oven to 350 degrees. Beat eggs slightly. Make a paste with flour and a small amount of water. Put all ingredients in bowl and mix. Add mixture to a greased 1 quart ring mold. Place mold in a pan of hot water and bake at 350 degrees, for 45 minutes or until firm. Turn mold out on plate and garnish with parsley and cherry tomatos; center of the ring may be filled with drained corn (mixed with butter) or any vegetable desired. Pimentos may be substituted for red pepper.

Betty Perkins, Hot Springs, AR

LO-CAL GINGER CARROTS

Serves 2, 48 calories per serving

3 medium carrots, cut in 3 x 1-1/4" strips
1 teaspoon reduced calorie margarine
1 teaspoon brown sugar
1/8 teaspoon ground ginger

Cook carrots in a small amount of boiling water until crisp and tender. Drain and set aside. Melt margarine in a saucepan. Stir in sugar and ginger. Cook over low heat, stirring constantly until sugar melts. Add carrots, cook stirring gently, until carrots are well coated and hot.

Agnes Ward, Erie, PA

DELICIOUS DILLED CARROTS

Fresh carrots, peeled and sliced into strips
Dill weed, to taste
Sugar to taste
1 stick butter
1/2" water in pan bottom

Place water in pan. Add butter and heat to melt. Add remaining ingredients. Bring to a boil. Cover and lower heat. Simmer until tender.

Cynthia Kannenberg, Brown Deer, WI

SCALLOPED CARROTS

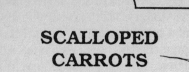

5 cups raw carrots, sliced or diced
1 onion, sliced
1/2 cup butter
1/2 pound Velveeta cheese
12 Ritz crackers

Cook carrots until done; drain. Sauté onion in butter. In baking dish, layer carrots and cheese. Pour onions and butter over top. Break up Ritz crackers and sprinkle over top. Bake at 350 degrees for 30-40 minutes.

Evelyn Eckhart, Alexandria, Minn.

GREEN BEAN AND CARROT COMBO
Serves 6-8

1 pound can green beans, drained
1 pound can sliced carrots, drained
1/2 teaspoon sugar
1/4 teaspoon salt
1/4 teaspoon onion powder
1 can cream of celery soup
1/4 cup milk

Combine all ingredients; mix well. Place in greased casserole and bake for 25-30 minutes at 350 degrees.

Sharon Crider, Evansville, Wis.

GLAZED CARROTS WITH BACON 'N ONION
Serves 4

1 pound carrots, scraped and sliced diagonally
3 slices bacon
1 small onion, chopped
3 tablespoons brown sugar
1/8 teaspoon pepper

Cook carrots, covered, in small amount of boiling water for 15 minutes or until crisp tender; drain. Cook bacon in skillet until crisp; crumble. Reserve 1 tablespoon drippings in skillet. Sauté onion in drippings. Add

brown sugar, pepper, and carrots. Cook until heated; sprinkle with crumbled bacon.

Edna Askins, Greenville, Texas

COLORFUL CARROT RING
Serves 4

1/2 cup soft bread crumbs
3 eggs
1 small onion
1/4 cup parsley
1 tablespoon butter or margarine, melted
1/4 teaspoon cinnamon
1/4 teaspoon salt
1/8 teaspoon pepper
2-1/2 cups carrots, cooked
1 tablespoon brown sugar or maple syrup

Place all ingredients in food processor; process 1 minute or until carrots are cut very fine. Turn into an 8-inch ring mold; set in a shallow pan of water; bake at 375 degrees for 30 minutes or until set and firm. Unmold on serving plate; fill center with tiny peas.

Gwen Campbell, Sterling, Va.

POTATOES AND MUSHROOMS

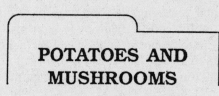

8-10 small, new potatoes
1/4 cup butter, melted
2 tablespoons green onions or chives, chopped
1/2 pound mushrooms, chopped
1 cup meat stock
2 egg yolks
1 teaspoon lemon juice
Salt and pepper

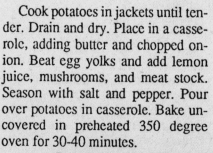

Cook potatoes in jackets until tender. Drain and dry. Place in a casserole, adding butter and chopped onion. Beat egg yolks and add lemon juice, mushrooms, and meat stock. Season with salt and pepper. Pour over potatoes in casserole. Bake uncovered in preheated 350 degree oven for 30-40 minutes.

Betty Perkins, Hot Springs, AR

SWISS POTATOES

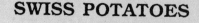

1-1/2 cups large baking potatoes, thinly sliced
1 teaspoon salt
1 teaspoon minced dried onion
2 eggs, beaten
1-1/2 cups milk, scalded
1/4 pound Swiss cheese, grated

Mix together all above ingredients, saving some grated cheese to sprinkle on top. Place into medium-sized, lightly-buttered casserole. Sprinkle top with reserved cheese. Place in preheated 350 degree oven and bake for 1 hour.

Recipe can be doubled easily.

Agnes Ward, Erie, Pa.

POTATO CELERY SUPREME
Serves 4

4-6 medium potatoes, cut into small pieces
Salt and pepper to taste
1/3 stick margarine
1 can cream of celery soup
1/2 cup water

Put cut potatoes into greased casserole; add salt and pepper, margarine, soup, and water. Stir lightly. Bake covered in a 350 degree oven for 1-1/2 hours.

Edna Askins, Greenville, Texas

COUNTRY-FRIED POTATOES

2 tablespoons butter or margarine
2 tablespoons bacon drippings (or shortening)
6 cooked, pared, thickly sliced potatoes
1 medium onion, chopped
Salt and pepper to taste

Melt butter and drippings or shortening in heavy skillet. Add sliced potatoes and chopped onions to hot skillet. Season with salt and pepper. Cook over low fire until bottom crust is brown; turn, and brown other side.

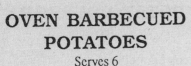

OVEN BARBECUED POTATOES

Serves 6

2 cups (8 ounces) Cheddar cheese, grated and divided
1 (10-3/4 ounce) can cream of mushroom soup
1/3 cup milk
1/4 cup barbecue sauce
1/4 teaspoon salt
1/4 teaspoon oregano
1/8 teaspoon pepper
4 medium potatoes, unpeeled and thinly sliced
1/2 teaspoon paprika

In large bowl combine 1-1/2 cups cheese, soup, milk, barbecue sauce, oregano, salt and pepper; blend thoroughly. Add potato slices; toss until well coated. Spoon mixture into a greased 9-inch square pan; cover with foil and bake at 350 degrees for 45 minutes. Remove foil; bake about 30 minutes longer or until tender. Remove from oven. Sprinkle remaining cheese and paprika on top. Let stand 5-10 minutes before serving.

Agnes Ward, Erie, PA

POTATO-CHEESE LOGS

2 medium potatoes, diced
2 tablespoons cream
2 tablespoons butter
1 egg, beaten lightly
1/2 teaspoon salt
1/8 teaspoon pepper
Dash cayenne pepper
1 clove garlic, crushed
3 tablespoons Parmesan or Romano cheese, grated
1 tablespoon parsley, minced
1/2 cup fine bread crumbs or cornflake crumbs

Boil potatoes until soft; drain and mash with cream and butter and whip until fluffy. Beat in egg, salt, pepper, cayenne, and garlic. Fold in cheese and parsley. Wet hands and shape into rolls, 2 inches long by 1 inch in diameter. *Roll in crumbs. Bake at 400 degrees for 15-20 minutes.
*To freeze, place on baking sheet immediately after rolling in crumbs and before baking. Place in freezer until firm; then pack in container and return to freezer. When needed, place frozen logs on lightly greased baking sheet and bake uncovered for 30 minutes at 400 degrees, turning once.

Eleanor V. Craycraft, Santa Monica, Calif.

BAKED CREAMED POTATOES

2 tablespoons butter or margarine
2 tablespoons flour
1 teaspoon salt
1/8 teaspoon white pepper
1-1/2 cups milk
1/2 teaspoon celery salt
1/4 cup chopped parsley
3-1/2 cups diced cooked potatoes (4 to 5 medium potatoes)
1 cup soft bread crumbs
2 tablespoons butter or margarine, melted

Preheat oven to 375 degrees. Butter a 1-1/2-quart casserole. Melt 2 tablespoons butter in a large saucepan. Sprinkle in flour, salt, and pepper; let it bubble up. Remove from heat and add milk all at once and stir to blend. Return to heat and stir until boiling, thickened, and smooth. Remove from heat and stir in celery salt, parsley, and potatoes. Pour into prepared casserole.

Combine bread crumbs and melted butter; sprinkle over all. Bake at 375 degrees for about 20 minutes or until hot and well-browned. These can be prepared ahead and then heated.

Lillian Smith, Montreal, Quebec, Canada

POTATOES RIO GRANDE

Serves 4

1-1/3 pounds (4 mid-size) potatoes, cut into 3/4 inch cubes
2 teaspoons vegetable oil
1 medium green (or red) bell pepper, seeded and cut into strips
1 (4-ounce) can diced green chiles
1 large clove garlic, pressed
1 (16-ounce) can stewed tomatoes
1/4 teaspoon pepper
Salt to taste
1/2 cup shredded Cheddar cheese
2 tablespoons chopped parsley
Continued on next page

Cook potatoes, covered, in 2-3 inches boiling water in 3-quart saucepan until not quite tender (about 12 minutes). Meanwhile, heat oil in large skillet. Add green pepper; toss over high heat, 5 minutes. Add chiles and garlic; cook and stir, 2 minutes. Stir in tomatoes and pepper. Cook to reduce liquid by half. Drain potatoes; add to skillet. Gently cook; stir to heat through. Stir in salt. Sprinkle cheese over potato mixture; cover to melt cheese. Sprinkle with parsley.

Judie Betz, Lomita, CA

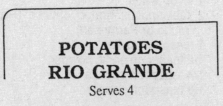

SCALLOPED POTATOES AND GREEN TOMATO BAKE

8 medium-size unpeeled potatoes, thinly sliced
3 large green tomatoes, thinly sliced
1 medium-size onion, diced
1 cup flour
1 pound Cheddar cheese, grated
1/4 pound bacon, browned and crumbled
Salt and pepper to taste
1/2 cup milk

Butter a large baking dish. Put a layer of potatoes on the bottom. Cover with a layer of green tomatoes. Sprinkle on a little bit of onion, flour, Cheddar cheese, bacon, salt, and pepper. Continue layering until dish is full; end with layer of cheese. Pour milk over the top; bake at 350 degrees for 1 hour or until potatoes are cooked and bubbling brown on top.

Gwen Campbell, Sterling, VA

CHEESE POTATO CRISPS

3 tablespoons melted margarine
4-5 medium potatoes
Salt to taste
1-1/2 cups shredded American
  cheese
2 cups crushed crisp-rice cereal
Paprika

Brush melted margarine over bottom of jelly roll pan. Cut potatoes in lengthwise slices, about 1/4 inch thick. Arrange slices in single layer, turning once to coat both sides with margarine. Sprinkle potatoes with salt, then with cheese. Top with crushed cereal. Sprinkle with paprika. Bake at 375 degrees for about 20 minutes. Delicious!!

Cheryl Santefort, Thornton, Ill.

CHEESE DIP FOR BAKED POTATOES

1 (8-ounce) package cream cheese
4 tablespoons milk
1 tablespoon minced onions
1 teaspoon salt
1/4 teaspoon garlic powder

Soften cream cheese to room temperature. Mix all ingredients together. If too thick, add more milk. Serve over baked potatoes in place of sour cream.

Melanie Knoll, Marshalltown, Iowa

SLOW POT POTATOES

Serves 4 - 6

1/4 pound bacon, chopped
2 onions, thinly sliced
4 potatoes, thinly sliced
1/2 pound Cheddar cheese, thinly
  sliced
Salt and pepper
Margarine

Line your slow pot with aluminum foil and leave enough to cover potatoes before cooking. Put half of of the bacon, onions, potatoes and cheese in layers in slow cooker. Season with salt and pepper; dot with margarine. Repeat layers. Again put salt and pepper and dot with margarine. Cover with foil. Place cover on slow pot; cook on low overnight (10 to 12 hours) or cook on high for 3 to 4 hours.

Mrs. Jodie McCoy, Tulsa, OK

CRUMB-COATED BAKED POTATOES

Serves 3-6

6 new red potatoes
1/4 cup butter or margarine
1/2 cup herb-seasoned bread
  crumbs
1 teaspoon garlic salt
1/8 teaspoon pepper
1/4 teaspoon chopped chives
1/8 teaspoon paprika

Scrub potatoes; leave on skin. Melt butter in an 8 x 8 x 2-inch baking pan; roll potatoes in butter, then in bread crumbs to coat. Sprinkle with seasonings; place in baking pan. Bake, uncovered, 45 minutes or until potatoes are fork tender.

Gwen Campbell, Sterling, Va.

OVEN FRIED POTATOES

Cut 4 potatoes (unpeeled) in wedges and place in shallow baking dish. Mix together and pour over potatoes:

1/4 cup cooking oil
1/4 cup water
2 tablespoons grated cheese (Romano or Parmesan)
1 teaspoon salt
1/2 teaspoon garlic powder
1/4 teaspoon paprika
1/8 teaspoon pepper

Bake at 375 degrees uncovered for 45 minutes. Baste occasionally.

Betty Cieri, Endicott, NY

POTATO SUPREME

Serves 6

1 cup sour cream
2 cups cottage cheese
2 teaspoons salt
2 tablespoons grated onion
1 clove garlic, minced
6 medium-sized potatoes, cooked
  and diced
1/2 cup shredded American cheese
Dash paprika

In a bowl, thoroughly mix sour cream, cottage cheese, salt, onion, and garlic. Gently fold in potatoes. Pour into buttered 1-1/2 quart casserole. Sprinkle evenly with cheese and lightly with paprika. Bake at 350 degrees until heated through and lightly browned, 40-45 minutes.

Mrs. E. O'Brien, Richmond, Va.

POTATOES WITH A ZIP

6 large baking potatoes
1 cup shredded sharp Cheddar
  cheese
1/2 cup tomato juice
1/3 cup sour cream
Paprika
Butter or margarine
Salt and pepper

Preheat oven to 375 degrees. Scrub potatoes and rub with butter or shortening. Prick several times with a fork. Bake 1 hour 15 minutes, or until tender. Increase oven temperature to 400 degrees. Slice each potato in half; scoop out inside, leaving a thin shell.

In large mixer bowl, mash potatoes; gradually beat in cheese, tomato juice, and sour cream. Fill potato shells with potato mixture. Garnish with paprika. Bake 15-20 minutes or until tops are lightly browned. Serve with butter. Refrigerate any leftovers. Can be prepared ahead and frozen. If frozen, bake at 350 degrees for 35 minutes.

Diantha Susan Hibbard, Rochester, N.Y.

FRIED GREEN TOMATOES

6 green tomatoes
3 tablespoons flour
1-1/4 teaspoons salt
Pepper to taste
4 tablespoons bacon fat
1 cup evaporated milk
1-1/4 teaspoons sugar

Wash tomatoes, but do not peel. Cut in half crosswise. Mix flour, salt, sugar, and pepper. Roll tomatoes, one at a time, in flour mixture. Brown on both sides in hot bacon fat. Remove to serving dish and keep warm. Add evaporated milk to same frying pan. Boil slowly, stirring constantly until thickened (about 2 minutes). Pour over tomatoes before serving.

Joy Shamway, Freeport, Ill.

BROCCOLI-TOMATO LOAF

2 cups broccoli, cooked
2 eggs
1 cup canned tomatoes
1 cup onion
1/2 cup celery
3 tablespoons butter or margarine
1/4 teaspoon salt
1/8 teaspoon pepper
1/4 teaspoon sugar
1 cup coarse cracker crumbs
Quick Cheese Sauce (recipe follows)

In a food processor or blender, chop and mix first 9 ingredients; stir in crumbs. Bake in a greased loaf pan at 350 degrees for 40 minutes. Serve with Quick Cheese Sauce.

Quick Cheese Sauce:

1/3 cup milk
1 cup Cheddar cheese, cubed
2 tablespoons flour
1/8 teaspoon salt
1/2 teaspoon Worcestershire sauce

In a saucepan over low heat, blend all ingredients until hot, thickened, and cheese has thoroughly melted.
Gwen Campbell, Sterling, Va.

GOLDEN MERINGUE TOMATOES

4 large tomatoes
2-1/2 tablespoons butter, softened
4 eggs, separated
Salt and pepper to taste
1/3 cup grated Romano cheese
2 tablespoons chopped parsley or chives

Stand tomatoes upright; cut a slice from the top of each tomato. Scoop out pulp; finely chop and mix with softened butter, egg yolks, salt, and pepper. Add half the cheese and half the herbs. Put the mixture into tomato shells. Place tomatoes in an ovenproof dish; cook 12 minutes in 350 degree oven. Beat egg whites until stiff; fold in remaining cheese and herbs. Remove tomatoes from oven; top each with the meringue. Bake also at 350 degrees for about 6 minutes, or until meringue is set, puffed, and golden.

Mrs. Gwen Campbell, Sterling, VA

GARDEN SALAD STUFFED TOMATOES

6 firm red tomatoes
1/2 teaspoon salt
1/8 teaspoon pepper
1/4 cup peas, cooked
1/4 cup lima beans, cooked
1/4 cup carrots, raw julienne strips
1/4 cup asparagus tips
1/4 cup zucchini, grated
2 hard-cooked eggs, chopped

Cut a slice from the stem end of each tomato; scoop out pulp; set aside; discard seeds. Sprinkle shells with salt and pepper; invert on rack to drain for 15 minutes. Combine all vegetables and tomato pulp with enough mayonnaise to form a firm mixture; fill tomato shells. Top each shell with chopped hard-cooked eggs.

Gwen Campbell, Sterling, VA

FRIED TOMATOES
Serves 4

6 or 8 firm (or green) tomatoes
1 egg
1 tablespoon water
Fine bread or cereal crumbs
Salt and pepper to taste

Wash the tomatoes; remove the stem end, and slice into 1/2-inch slices. Beat the egg slightly; mix water in; dip tomato slices in this mixture and then roll in crumbs seasoned with salt and pepper. Set aside.

Heat oil in heavy skillet and place tomato slices in hot oil. Brown on one side; turn carefully, and then reduce heat so tomatoes can cook thoroughly before browning.

Lift from skillet onto heated platter and serve immediately.

If you are from the country (or wish you were), and aren't counting calories, you'll pour hot, creamy gravy over the top.

TOMATO-CUCUMBER MARINADE
Serves 6

2 medium tomatoes, sliced
2 cups cucumber, peeled and thinly-sliced
1/2 medium onion, thinly-sliced and separated into rings
1/2 cup salad oil
1/4 cup white wine vinegar
1 teaspoon salt
1 teaspoon basil
1 teaspoon tarragon
1/8 teaspoon pepper
Shredded lettuce

Alternate layers of tomato, cucumber, and onion in shallow glass dish. Combine other ingredients except lettuce; beat well with electric mixer. Pour over layered vegetables; chill covered, for 5-6 hours. Drain, reserving marinade. Arrange marinated vegetables on shredded lettuce. Pass reserved marinade for individual servings of dressing.

Diantha Hibbard, Rochester, NY

Cooking With Taste ....INDEX

INDEX

INDEX

  # INDEX

INDEX